Hellenic Studies 73

THE ART OF READING

Recent Titles in the Hellenic Studies Series

http://chs.harvard.edu/chs/publications

THE ART OF READING
FROM HOMER TO PAUL CELAN

Jean Bollack

Translated by
Catherine Porter and Susan Tarrow
with Bruce King

Edited by Christoph Koenig, Leonard Muellner,
Gregory Nagy, and Sheldon Pollock

CENTER FOR HELLENIC STUDIES
Trustees for Harvard University
Washington, D.C.
Distributed by Harvard University Press
Cambridge, Massachusetts, and London, England
2016

The Art of Reading: From Homer to Paul Celan
  by Jean Bollack

Copyright © 2016 Center for Hellenic Studies, Trustees for Harvard University
All Rights Reserved.

Published by Center for Hellenic Studies, Trustees for Harvard University,
  Washington, D.C.

Distributed by Harvard University Press, Cambridge, Massachusetts, and
  London, England

Production: Kristin Murphy Romano

Cover design: Joni Godlove

*Ouvrage publié avec le concours du Ministère français chargé de la Culture-Centre national
  du livre.*

This work has been published with the assistance of the French Ministry of Culture—
  Centre national du livre.

Library of Congress Cataloging-in-Publication Data

Names: Bollack, Jean, author. | Porter, Catherine, 1941- translator. |
  Tarrow, Susan, 1939- translator.
Title: The art of reading : from Homer to Paul Celan / by Jean Bollack ;
  translated by Catherine Porter and Susan Tarrow.
Other titles: Hellenic studies ; 73.
Description: Washington, D.C. : Center for Hellenic Studies, 2016. | Series:
  Hellenic studies ; 73
Identifiers: LCCN 2016032374 | ISBN 9780674660199 (alk. paper)
Subjects: LCSH: Classical literature--History and criticism. | Classical
  philology.
Classification: LCC PA3003 .B65 2016 | DDC 809--dc23
LC record available at https://lccn.loc.gov/2016032374

Table of Contents

Table of Contents

Translators' Preface
Catherine Porter and Susan Tarrow

THE CHALLENGES OF TRANSLATING Jean Bollack's work are well known to his fellow classicists. His work, published primarily in French, has also appeared in German, either in the author's own text or in translation, but very little was available in English when we agreed to take on this collection. Each of us had translated one of Bollack's essays for publication in the past, so we were somewhat prepared for the difficulties presented by his work. Still, the scope of the collection took us far from our own spheres of academic training and experience. As specialists in twentieth-century French studies, we found ourselves doing extensive background reading in order to come to grips with Bollack's dense texts and their scholarly contexts.

Few scholars can rival the breadth of Jean Bollack's learning—from Homer to Celan, with Empedocles, Sophocles, Parmenides, Heraclitus, Freud, Benjamin, Kafka, Mallarmé, Hölderlin and Szondi in between. Bollack clearly assumed that his readers would understand Greek, Latin, German, Italian, and English as well as French. While between us we could handle all but the Greek (and only a little of the Latin), we are profoundly indebted to Bruce King, who not only found translations for the Greek and Latin citations, but explained many of the minutiae of classical philology of which we were unaware. Bruce edited the entire volume with an eagle eye for stylistic infelicities as well as for factual errors, and he performed an additional critical service by insisting on clarification at points where our renderings of Bollack's prose were overly elliptical or otherwise inadequate. At such points, we were privileged to be able to turn to the author's widow, Mayotte Bollack, a learned scholar in her own right, whose responses were unfailingly generous and astute. Our collaboration with Mme Bollack was exceptionally gratifying: she read, and re-read, each essay, offering insights and suggestions that have significantly improved our work.

Of necessity, we have made a number of adjustments to meet the needs of a new audience. Jean Bollack's French texts addressed a particular scholarly readership—multilingual, erudite, well versed in the classics and/or in modern European literature. Our goal has been to make the English version of his essays accessible and appealing to a broader, less specialized audience. To this end, and with Mayotte Bollack's endorsement, we have incorporated certain clarifications in the text itself, and we have added translators' notes where it seemed appropriate to offer additional information on individuals, events, intertextual allusions, or other background material. Wherever possible, we have cited published English translations of quoted texts; where none was available, the translations are our own or Bruce King's.

The Center for Hellenic Studies has offered steady encouragement and support throughout this three-year endeavor. Director of Publications Leonard Muellner has been unfailing in his attention to our needs, providing timely answers to our urgent questions. And Bruce King, as a seasoned CHS editor, made sure that all the notes and bibliographical information conformed to the Center's sometimes idiosyncratic formatting guidelines. Our own collaboration as co-translators has been seamless; we passed the essays back and forth so many times that we can scarcely recall who produced the first draft in a given instance. We hope the collaborative efforts embodied in this volume will lead to a broader appreciation of Jean Bollack's contributions to literary scholarship and promote increased interaction between classical philology and the other academic fields that are reflected in his work.

Catherine Porter
Susan Tarrow

Foreword
Gregory Nagy

Introduction[1]

Jean Bollack was born in Strasbourg on the 15th of March, 1923, and he died in Paris on the 4th of December, 2012. For a brief biography, I refer to the article "In Memoriam: Jean Bollack,"[2] written by André Laks and translated by Leonard Muellner, published in *Kleos*, the news bulletin of the Center for Hellenic Studies. An online bibliography has been published by a French team.[3]

In what follows, I preview the text of Bollack's *The Art of Reading: From Homer to Paul Celan*, translated into English by Catherine Porter and Susan Tarrow.

Chapter 1. "Learning to Read"

§1A. In this chapter, we see my friend Jean Bollack as an elderly man looking back at a youthful phase of his formation as a Classicist. Here he is, twenty years old, studying at the University of Basel in Switzerland, where he finds "sanctuary," as he says, during the terrible years of World War II. Earlier, he studied at a German-speaking Protestant Gymnasium in Basel, complementing the French-speaking background of his Alsatian French-Jewish family.

§1B. Our thoughts turn to a nostalgic photograph taken in June 2009 by Jean Bollack's granddaughter, Judith Deschamps. This photograph, with the kind permission of the Bollack family, graces the cover of Bollack's English-language

---

[1]   This Foreword was first published online in six parts at *Classical Inquiries* (http://nrs.harvard .edu/urn-3:hul.eresource:Classical_Inquiries), a rapid-publication project of the Center for Hellenic Studies. Readers will find that each paragraph begins with a reference number and letter keyed to the various chapters of this book (e.g. paragraphs numbered §1A, §1B, and so on refer to Bollack's essay in Chapter 1 of this book). This numbering system, which matches the numbering of paragraphs in the online version, will allow the reader to navigate smoothly between the printed and the online versions.

[2]   See: http://kleos.chs.harvard.edu/?p=2146.

[3]   See: http://www.jeanbollack.fr.

book *The Art of Reading: from Homer to Paul Celan*—as well as the cover of the posting in *Classical Inquiries* for 2016.03.10. We see pictured here the old man revisiting Basel and gazing in the direction of the city's famed Kunstmuseum, which is only a few hundred meters away from the old Humanistisches Gymnasium at the Münsterplatz. Friedrich Nietzsche had once taught in that building, then called Pädagogium, or the Burg. When Bollack writes in "Learning to Read" that the city of Basel in Switzerland was where he "survived" during World War II, he means it literally. He found in Switzerland a place of refuge from the anti-Semitic horrors that were ongoing throughout Germany.

§1C. In particular, the University of Basel was for young Bollack a place of refuge metaphorically, since the form of German education that still survived back then in that stronghold of learning had by then been "lost" in Germany, as Bollack himself ruefully observes in "Learning to Read." His observation centers on the idea of *German philology*, as he describes it, and such philology, he says, continued to "retain its appeal" for him throughout his life. It was by practicing this kind of philology that Bollack first learned, he says, that the need to *establish the text* is as essential as the need to *establish the meaning of the text*. For Bollack, the *reading* of a text is a *reactualizing* of the text. But he adds that, as a young student, he had not yet learned to observe, as he did later, the "breaks" in texts, which "allow for a freedom of reading."

§1D. Reminiscing about the young Bollack in the essay "Learning to Read," the old Bollack says "we" as often as he says "I." The rhetoric of this interchangeability is most effective. It is as if Bollack were speaking for a whole generation of Classicists, not only for himself. My favorite moment in the whole essay is when he says: "We were feeling our way, and we made progress empirically and intuitively."

§1E. This kind of approach, for Bollack, is German philology at its best. And, from the start, philology is for him "the science of philology," competing with the "natural sciences."

§1F. Bollack admires in particular the application of philology to Homeric poetry. For him, Homeric criticism is ideally a "virtuoso activity." That said, he adds that he had sided, from the very start, with the "Unitarians" in their approach to Homer, not with the "Analysts."

§1G. All the same, the professor at Universität Basel who receives the most praise from Bollack was more of an "Analyst" than a "Unitarian" in Homeric studies. He was Peter Von der Mühll, a Swiss German philologist who published in 1952 a critical commentary (*Kritisches Hypomnema*) on the Homeric *Iliad*. In class, as Bollack reminisces, Von der Mühll would often admit to not fully understanding what a text really means. That was a far cry, Bollack adds wryly, from what he was to experience later on as a student in Paris.

§1H. The transition from Basel to Paris happens abruptly in "Learning to Read." Skipping from one breath to the next, Bollack says it all at once: "I had always thought that, as soon as it became feasible, I would continue my studies in Paris, and I lost no time moving there after the Liberation." The intellectual scene in post-Liberation Paris is then described vividly but somewhat elliptically. The reader will experience some difficulties, I predict, in sorting out what happened when, but the landmarks in Bollack's eventual academic interests already loom large. In fact, some of these landmarks are already foreshadowed in the Basel narrative.

§1I. The towering figure of Empedocles emerges early on. From the start, Bollack links the fragments of texts attributed to this pre-Socratic thinker with the "indirect tradition, which had given us these fragments." At this point, Bollack begins to explore the importance of what is commonly called the *doxography* relating to thinkers like Empedocles,"...paving the way for an intellectual historiography."

§1J. In the postwar years, Bollack says, experts who studied pre-Socratic thinkers like Empedocles and Parmenides "thought that they could lead readers into direct communication with an archaic way of thinking, and make them understand the heroic language of an origin, beyond any scientific methods, or even in opposition to them." Bollack continues: what really "shielded" him from such an "unscientific" trend in pre-Socratic studies was his decision to work "on ancient interpretations of fragments and on the *opinions* of philosophers— doxography." In the wording I have just quoted, he finally gives his own working definition of *doxography* after having already led up to the concept at an earlier point (as I comment at §1I).

§1K. Bollack makes it clear, already at this early stage of his intellectual autobiography, that he had to learn by himself a methodology for analyzing the thinking of philosophers in terms of the attested doxography. And he refers to his self-taught methodology in shorthand as *hermeneutics*. Back then, in Bollack's student days, "the principles of hermeneutics were neither considered nor taught." This term *hermeneutics*, so vitally important for Bollack throughout his life, will recur many times and in many ways in *The Art of Reading*.

§1L. For the writer of this foreword, Bollack's words hit home in a personal way when he says: "In most cases, readers, whatever their level of interest, latched on to a text constituted by others, pre-formed, as it were, by a scientific method that was rejected as unverifiable, so that they were no longer able to overcome their dependence or even to recognize it." Here my old self in the present is prompted to think back to a remote time in my own personal past when my young self was reading for the first time the texts of the Homeric *Iliad* and *Odyssey*. In my initial quest to find and to analyze the formulaic system that had shaped the diction as recorded in the Homeric textual tradition, I had not yet understood the importance of first making sure to understand the history of that textual tradition. As Bollack puts it (and as I note in §1C), the need to *establish the text* is as essential as the need to *establish the meaning of the text*.

§1M. Bollack's self-taught hermeneutics had a rocky start in postwar Paris, and the reception in the world of German philology as he learned it was not necessarily all that fertile either. Looking back at it all, Bollack could not really identify with either the French or the German worlds of Classics. Here is how he says it, in his own oblique way, speaking first of the French milieu and then of the German: "At the time, one could quickly take the measure of this academic world to which I falsely ascribed a structure that it may have aspired to but had not yet acquired (and perhaps never did). I built up a quite artificial continuity with my earlier years in academe, rebelling against one reality in favor of another. Including among the things I lacked the posture of distanciation that I had adopted earlier, I tried to make that negation operate as a positive factor; I used as a point of reference an absent system with which I had not really identified either. I do not think this double dissociation bothered me. It taught me to see differences, to tolerate them, to resist and reject taboos."

§1N. And here we come to a third and most decisive phase in Bollack's intellectual life: he finds a new home in an academic circle that he himself founded, at the University of Lille. Again I quote from his own oblique wording: "Official doctrine maintained that science was not good for students. In Lille, I tried as hard as I could to organize a somewhat marginal research space alongside the formal education system. With Heinz Wismann, we got the students together in the attics and basements of the university, so to speak, and I continued this practice with Philippe Rousseau, then with Pierre Judet de La Combe and André Laks." (For more on the "Lille" circle and on the research center at Lille, see Judet de La Combe and Wismann 2009 in my Bibliography.)

Chapter 2. "Reading the Philologists"

§2A. Bollack continues where he left off in "Learning to Read." We return to what he calls *philologische Wissenschaft*, "philological science." This science, we are now told, is not necessarily German, but it certainly is not French, either. It is rather the science that Bollack has taught himself. And the essential word is once again hermeneutics. And now we begin to see that the ideal form of hermeneutics is for Bollack a totalizing and perhaps unattainable form of philology: to understand the text in terms of arguments about the text, we must "compare all prior arguments."

§2B. In many ways, this essay "Reading the Philologists" is a prelude to the agenda pursued in the essay that follows this one, "Odysseus among the Philologists." There we will return to the most prestigious of all philological quests, which he has already described (see §1F) as the "virtuoso activity" of studying Homer.

§2C. To understand philology, you have to look at the "social environment" of the philologists themselves—usually associated with their "national origin." A challenging case in point is that ultimate German philologist Ulrich von Wilamowitz-Moellendorff—and his philological reception in France.

§2D. Bollack here introduces—only fleetingly, for the time being—two shining examples of his own philology, centering on the *Oedipus Tyrannus* of Sophocles and on the poetry of Paul Celan.

Chapter 3. "Odysseus among the Philologists"

§3A. Partly because of its social prestige, as Bollack argues, the field of classical philology "has never produced a theory of meaning." Small wonder, then, as he further argues, that there is no theory of meaning to be found in the prestigious subfield of Homeric philology. This subfield, like the overall field, may claim to be a "science," but it lacks the "epistemological grounding" that would and should have long ago "scaled down its pretensions." The debates that persist in the absence of such grounding keep things in the air, so that the Homeric Question for Homerists needs to remain always a question.

§3B. The one big question for Homerists in the nineteenth and twentieth centuries focused on the genesis of Homeric poetry, and those experts who styled themselves as "analysts" tended to hold sway. As Bollack notes, "the Analysts were well ensconced at the top of the university hierarchy," especially in Germany. Ironically and at times even sarcastically, Bollack traces the "successes" of Analysts like Ulrich von Wilamowitz-Moellendorff in dissecting supposedly earlier and later editions, as it were, of the text that we know as the Homeric *Odyssey*. By contrast, those who styled themselves as "Unitarians" were often "on the fringe, considered mere aesthetes." What the Unitarians were thinking was not "science."

§3C. Having found fault with classicists who seek to explain Homer by looking for the genesis of Homeric poetry, Bollack still has some words of praise for models of oral poetics as developed by Milman Parry and Albert Lord in their studies of Homeric poetry, describing their methodology as "new and certainly more accurate" than that of the Analysts. But even in this case, Bollack claims, those who follow Parry and Lord are still looking for the genesis of Homeric poetry. He complains that the publications of "such theorists or proponents of oral poetry as G. S. Kirk" do not take us much further beyond the results achieved by the Analysts. Bollack pursues this complaint by arguing with a book by Kirk (1962), though it could be objected that this book is a far cry from the methodology developed by Parry and Lord.

§3D. Invoking his own hermeneutics, Bollack steers clear of both the Analysts and the Unitarians as he defines them, taking as a case in point the mythological construct of Scylla and Charybdis as signaled at the beginning of *Odyssey* 12. As Bollack argues, Scylla and Charybdis cannot be assimilated into a single strait: they are two consecutive straits. When philologists place Scylla and Charybdis into one strait, "the whole relationship between a world that is rising and a chasm that plunges downward is eliminated." Bollack goes on to say: "error consists in producing a meaning that the text deflects." He strives to save the traveler Odysseus from such errors.

Chapter 4. "Reflections on the Practice of Philology"

§4A. Facing the challenges of philology as a "science," Bollack returns to his concept of hermeneutics as he developed it from the start. How do we get at the truth of what an author says in a text when the transmission of that text has taken us so far away from the original historical context? How do we disentangle what is said by authors from what the successive editors and interpreters of these authors conjecture is being said? Invoking the names of three great humanists who worked on projects of emending the texts of three great authors, Bollack observes: "most readers are unaware that they are reading Marullus in Lucretius, Usener in Epicurus, Diels in Heraclitus." Although he admires each one of these humanists for their masterful conjectures in the project of emending the text, Bollack still worries: "the text," he says, "defends itself poorly."

§4B. To get at the truth behind the textual transmission of any author, Bollack demands of himself a thorough investigation of every historical factor that went into that transmission. Bollack's hermeneutics are demanding to the point of approaching impossible standards. But there is hope: the success of his hermeneutics depends on a continuation into the future. In fact, his near-absolutism in his hermeneutic requirements requires an infinite future.

Chapter 5. "Reading Myths"

§5. The intellectual rigor of Jean Bollack's approach to the text leads him into debates with contemporaries in France who were developing explanatory models centering on the very nature of myth in ancient Greek civilization. In this essay,

Bollack trains his sights on two French studies on Greek myth, one of which is a book by Jean-Pierre Vernant (1962; fifth edition 1992) and the other, an article by Marcel Detienne (1988). Both these studies approach myth as a phenomenon that transcends any instantiation in the form of a text, whereas Bollack by contrast insists on the primacy of the text—and of the author who originally produced the given text within its own historical context. In the case of this essay, Bollack focuses on two of his favorite authors, Hesiod and Anaximander.

Chapter 6. "Purifications"

§6A. Pursuing his insistence on the primacy of the text in studying any myth that is mediated by a given text as produced by a given author, Bollack focuses here on the text known as the *Katharmoi* or *Purifications* by the so-called pre-Socratic thinker Empedocles of Akragas (modern Agrigento) in Sicily, who was a near-contemporary of classical tragedians like Sophocles. Reading this essay, we could easily be led to believe that Empedocles is Bollack's all-time favorite Greek author. And what makes the *Purifications* of Empedocles so special? It is the nature of this text as a myth, which Bollack sees as something actually invented by Empedocles. As Bollack puts it, the *Purifications* is a piece of poetry that literally "invents a myth," and he describes this myth as "a new story that purports to replace all the other stories that have ever been told, from Homer and Hesiod to the contemporary productions of Athenian tragedy."

§6B. For Bollack, Empedocles is a social reformer who produced the text of the *Purifications* as a manifesto for political action on a universal scale. As we read in the *Lives of Eminent Philosophers* by Diogenes Laertius (second or third century CE), Empedocles renounced political deals that would have served the interests of the aristocracy in his city, though he sought the active support of like-minded elite thinkers in seeking a social order that transcended the *polis* or "city-state."

§6C. This essay of Bollack explores also the complementarity of the *Purifications* with another of Empedocles' celebrated poems, the *Peri phuseōs*—a title sometimes known as *On Nature* but better rendered as *The Origins*. Bollack here engages in some lively debates with Walter Burkert (1962, 1972) and with Marcel Detienne (1963, 1970) in the context of comparisons between the thinking of Empedocles and the thinking of his predecessor, Pythagoras.

Chapter 7. "An Anthropological Fiction"

§7A. Bilingual and bicultural as he was in German and French, Jean Bollack preferred to read Sigmund Freud in the original German. The work of Freud that English-speakers know as *Moses and Monotheism* and that Bollack knew by its original title, *Der Mann Moses und die monotheistische Religion* (1939), is the focus of this essay concerning a case of "anthropological fiction"—which for Freud was at the same time a case of psychoanalytical history. That case was the role of Moses as reflected in the Hebrew Bible. This role, in terms of an insight elaborated by Freud, was a kind of reaction to the role of an Egyptian pharaoh named Amenhotep IV (for the Greeks, Amenophis IV), who ruled in the eighteenth Dynasty, in the late fourteenth century BCE, and who in one single decisive moment of world history was given the new name Akhenaten, expressing a monotheistic devotion to a solar god named Aten. Such a historical moment, Freud argued, led to a monotheistic role for Moses as well—a role reconstructed by way of a psychoanalytical insight into a story. At first, as Bollack retells Freud's telling of the reconstructed story, the Egyptian idea of monotheism "gained ground on its own"; but then "it was picked up by a man who was not a king." That man was Moses, who, according to Freud, "behaved as if he were the pharaoh himself."

§7B. The essay, graced as it is with interspersed renderings of Freud's elegant German prose in Bollack's correspondingly elegant French, shows that the Freudian "fiction" about Moses will remain merely that, a "fiction"—unless we can somehow find a way to reconstruct historically an Egyptian origin for Moses. Such a reconstruction has now been made possible, as Bollack points out, by the pioneering argumentation of the Egyptologist Jan Assmann in his book *Moses the Egyptian* (1997). Drawing on the testimony of sources like the Egyptian historian Manetho, who lived in the third century BCE, Assmann argues persuasively for traces of Egyptian cultural patterning in Mosaic ideology.

§7C. But where exactly is the "anthropology" in the "fiction" developed by Freud in telling the "psychoanalytical" story of Moses the monotheist? As Bollack shows, Freud was influenced by "Cambridge School" anthropologists like Sir James Frazer. For example, in positing an ideological construct concerning the murder of Moses by his own people, Freud refers to Frazer's *The Dying God* (1911) as a source for comparative research on lore about primal killings of leaders.

§7D. The essay draws to a close with some startling observations about the agenda of the book *Moses and Monotheism* as Freud's own special way of confronting anti-Semitism as he saw it.

Chapter 8. "Reading Drama"

§8A. For a casual observer, the dating established for Epicurus, whose lifetime extended from the late fourth century BCE into the early third, seems to put this philosopher into a historical time frame that arrives too late—as if the dating were some kind of careless mistake. Perhaps surprisingly, the era of Epicurus postdates the glory days of classical Greek drama, which of course goes back to the second half of the fifth century. I say "surprisingly" because, when we read Jean Bollack in the act of reading drama, our first impression is that his readings are based on Epicurean thinking—as if the life and times of Epicurus came before and not after the golden age of tragic playwrights like Sophocles and Euripides. For Bollack, there is something strikingly foundational about Epicurus that helps us understand the essence of classical drama. When Bollack is reading drama, Epicurus is for him particularly good to think with, since this philosopher had discovered "a lost freedom that was almost archaic and highly utopian," while the likes of Sophocles and Euripides "felt a similar desire for intellectual sovereignty."

§8B. This essay was originally composed when Jean Bollack and his wife Mayotte experienced the actual staging, in theater, of translations that the two of them had made together of three classical tragedies from the original Greek into French. First there was the *Oedipus Tyrannus* of Sophocles (1985), then the *Iphigeneia in Aulis* of Euripides (1990), and then the *Andromache*, again by Euripides (1994). What this pair of translators experienced, in seeing the texts of the tragedies being turned into performance—or, better, being turned back into performance—was that same sense of "intellectual sovereignty" that thinkers like Epicurus had been seeking in their own special ways.

§8C. Bollack concedes that the success of the theatrical experiences he describes depended in each case on fidelity to the text—a fidelity made possible by the director of the tragedy that was being performed on stage. For the *Oedipus Tyrannus*, it was Alain Milianti (La Salamandre, Lille, and Théâtre de l'Odéon, Paris); for the *Iphigeneia in Aulis*, it was Ariane Mnouchkine (Théâtre du Soleil); and for the *Andromache*, it was Jacques Lassalle (Athens, Avignon Festival). If the director manages to remain faithful to the exactness of the translation, Bollack argues, what is achieved is a recreated reality that is "trans-historical." In other words, "the very timelessness of theatrical performance annihilates historical distance."

Chapter 9. "An Act of Cultural Restoration: The Status Accorded to the Classical Tragedians by the Decree of Lycurgus"

§9A. In the third quarter of the fourth century BCE, the statesman Lycurgus initiated reforms in the performance traditions of State Theater in the city-state of Athens, legislating an official "State Script" for the tragedies of three poets and three poets only: Aeschylus, Sophocles, and Euripides. I first used the term "State Script" in a book listed in the Bibliography here as Nagy 1996 (pp. 174–175), in a context where I was citing the essay that I am introducing here, Bollack 1994. In this essay, Bollack interprets in some detail a brief text that provides the only evidence we have for the existence of the legislation to which he refers as the Decree of Lycurgus.

§9B. The ancient text that tells about this Decree comes from *The Lives of the Ten Orators*, attributed to Plutarch—though there is no proof of authorship. I quote here not only the relevant passage but also a passage that precedes it. The two passages together take up the space of one small paragraph:

εἰσήνεγκε δὲ καὶ νόμους, τὸν μὲν περὶ τῶν κωμῳδῶν, ἀγῶνα τοῖς Χύτροις ἐπιτελεῖν ἐφάμιλλον ἐν τῷ θεάτρῳ καὶ τὸν νικήσαντα εἰς ἄστυ καταλέγεσθαι, πρότερον οὐκ ἐξόν, ἀναλαμβάνων τὸν ἀγῶνα ἐκλελοιπότα· τὸν δέ, ὡς χαλκᾶς εἰκόνας ἀναθεῖναι τῶν ποιητῶν, Αἰσχύλου Σοφοκλέους Εὐριπίδου, τὰς τραγῳδίας αὐτῶν ἐν κοινῷ γραψαμένους φυλάττειν καὶ τὸν τῆς πόλεως γραμματέα παραναγινώσκειν τοῖς ὑποκρινομένοις· οὐκ ἐξεῖναι γὰρ αὐτὰς ὑποκρίνεσθαι.

He [= Lycurgus] introduced various pieces of legislation. One of them concerned the performers of comedies. He instituted a competition [in comedy] for the festival of the Khutroi. It [the competition] was held in the Theater, and the winner was to be enrolled among those who have freedom of the city, whereas previously it [= such enrollment] was not possible. He [= Lycurgus] was reinstituting the competition after it had lapsed. Another [piece of legislation that he instituted] was to set up bronze statues of the poets Aeschylus, Sophocles, and Euripides and to transcribe their tragedies and keep them under control in common possession, and that the recorder [*grammateus*] of the city was to read them as a model [*paranagignōskein*] to those acting [the tragedies], since, otherwise, it was not possible to act them [= the tragedies].

"Plutarch" *Lives of the Ten Orators* 841f

§9C. The translation that I just gave here is my own. The interpretations, as reflected in this translation, are for the most part in agreement with the interpretations reflected in the translation given in Bollack's essay as recast at Chapter 9 in the present book, though there are a few slight differences. In my translation,

I interpret ἐν κοινῷ γραψαμένους φυλάττειν as meaning 'to transcribe and keep under control in common possession', where I link ἐν κοινῷ 'in common possession' directly with φυλάττειν 'to keep' and not with γραψαμένους 'to transcribe and ...'. The expression ἐν κοινῷ 'in common possession' is the opposite of ἰδίᾳ 'in private possession' (such an opposition between 'in common possession' and 'in private possession' is overt in, for example, Demosthenes, *Against Leptines* 24). So, the texts of the tragedies have now become a matter of public record, and that is why they become the responsibility of the public recorder: in interpreting τὸν τῆς πόλεως γραμματέα as 'the recorder of the city', I follow Bollack, who compares Thucydides 7.10. Accordingly, I interpret παραναγινώσκειν to mean 'read as a model', comparing the use of this same word in Aeschines, *On the False Embassy* (135), where the orator calls on his audience to listen to a reading ἐκ τῶν δημοσίων γραμμάτων 'from the public texts'. And why do the actors who acted the tragedies have to listen to such a public reading by the public recorder? The compressed wording of the original Greek gives this answer: οὐκ ἐξεῖναι γὰρ αὐτὰς ὑποκρίνεσθαι 'since, otherwise, it was not possible to act them [= the tragedies]'. (For the usage of γάρ in the sense of 'since, otherwise', see Denniston 1954:62–63.) In other words, as I understand it, the actors otherwise would not have been permitted to act those tragedies. I see a parallel in the expression that we encountered earlier in the Greek of the same paragraph, πρότερον οὐκ ἐξόν, meaning 'whereas previously it [=enrollment] was not possible', where the wording that I translate as 'was not possible' is to be understood in the sense of 'was not permitted'.

§9D. Bollack in his essay also entertains and then rejects an alternative interpretation, according to which the texts of the tragedians had already become so corrupted in the era of Lycurgus that it was no longer possible for them to be performed unless the actors consulted the State Script. In terms of this alternative interpretation, the translation 'it was not possible' is not to be understood as 'it was not permitted'. But this alternative interpretation, as I already noted, is in the end rejected. For Bollack, any attempt to distinguish the text of the original composition from the text meant for performance results in the creation of a false dichotomy. The text was always meant for performance:

> The texts of past performances of fifth-century Greek tragedy were collected by the city as the true basis of its political existence; the past had a central presence thanks to the text and its public preservation, even as regular performances updated the past, in the framework of a theatrical restoration of a political (or cultural) nature.

Chapter 10. "From Philology to Theater: The Construction of Meaning and Sophocles' *Antigone*"

§10A. The *Antigone* of Sophocles becomes a starting point here for a debate that juxtaposes Bollack's hermeneutics with the approaches of near-contemporaries like Jacques Lacan (1986). Bollack has picked a worthy opponent, and he starts with a fitting subject for debate: it has to do with the meaning of *atē* in the *Antigone*. This word, which in tragedy can refer both to personal ruin as an effect and to the cause of such ruin, brings out in both Lacan and Bollack a set of different interpretations that say perhaps more about them than about Sophocles himself. Bollack is clearly interested more in the effects of *atē*, not about its causes, whereas he thinks that Lacan's analysis of the causes "is entirely predetermined by the cultural, intellectual, and philosophical history of the nineteenth century."

§10B. The debate extends further. In this essay, Bollack is more explicit than elsewhere about the genealogy of his own hermeneutics. He singles out Friedrich Schleiermacher (1768–1834) as a primary source of intellectual impetus, adding that the decidedly "literary" hermeneutics of this thinker tended to get occluded in the French intellectual scene of Bollack's own era by a rival "philosophical" hermeneutics derived primarily from Martin Heidegger (1889–1976) as mediated by Hans-Georg Gadamer (1900–2002) in his book *Wahrheit und Methode* (1960)—or, to put it more accurately, in the French version, *Vérité et méthode* (1976; complete edition 1996). As Bollack implies, the reception of Heidegger in France was thus not just one step removed from Heidegger, by way of Gadamer: for many, it was two steps removed, since few francophone intellectuals were able to understand German well enough to make do without the French Gadamer.

§10C. It is with his philological insights that Bollack seeks to appreciate the theatrical effectiveness of the *Antigone*. He analyzes this drama as a masterpiece of craftsmanship in wording and even in syntax, so that the myth of Antigone can be viewed as a creation made possible by that craftsmanship, not by the process of mythmaking in and of itself. It should be added, however, that the *Seven Against Thebes* of Aeschylus already shows a myth of Antigone in the making.

Chapter 11. "Accursed from Birth"

§11A. Unlike the myth of Antigone, which is in the process of being created in the drama of Sophocles (and already in a drama of Aeschylus, the *Seven Against Thebes*), the myth of Oedipus in the drama *Oedipus Tyrannus* by Sophocles is already a fully-formed myth that makes the drama possible in the first place.

Such is Bollack's argument in this essay. And, in the course of making his argument, he undertakes a particularly keen and incisive analysis of the drama in terms of its plot.

§11B. The plot here is all a matter of time: "the past is illuminated by what it has produced." So it is pointless to ask whether Oedipus is guilty of killing his father and having sex with his mother: rather, his guilt emerges in the course of time—in the time it takes to proceed from the beginning to the end of the drama: "with Oedipus, the power that has been building up since the beginning turns against itself, taking the shape of brilliant success to achieve its own destruction." This drama, "in which the catastrophe becomes clear in the course of a single day," produces what Bollack calls "a homologous past." And, as the drama progresses, "it makes that past comprehensible."

§11C. The pollution that drives the plot of the *Oedipus Tyrannus*, according to Bollack, is not only the incest or the parricide: it is the regicide. Never mind the witticism, uttered sometime at the expense of the French, that they never really got over their own regicide. The insight of our francophone thinker here cuts even deeper. The regicide in the *Oedipus Tyrannus* is the curse of sterility:

> The lack of descendants is part of the curse. Laius, an infanticide, has to expose his own son, anticipating the parricide: he has killed his own paternal self. When Oedipus commits murder, he echoes his father's action. Thus the execration of the king's assassin is proclaimed in absentia, the accused having been eliminated by his victim.

Chapter 12. "Two Phases of Recognition in Sophocles' *Electra*"

§12A. Electra hates her mother but has always loved her father. So she refuses to be her mother's daughter, defying a primary convention of symbolic filiation, which is that the daughter is to the mother as the son is to the father. As a character who desires to be the avenger of Agamemnon her father, killed by Clytemnestra her mother, Electra becomes the rival of Orestes as the son of Agamemnon, whose primary function it should be to take over the role of the avenger. In the drama of Sophocles named after Electra, the daughter of Agamemnon together with his son participate in a recognition scene where their roles are sorted out (lines 1232–1287). But Bollack argues that this sorting out of roles is at Electra's expense, in that her character as an avenger is nullified in the process. And the nullification is accentuated by the fact that the form of this recognition scene is not recitation, as we might have expected, but song. That is to say, the two actors who are assigned the roles of Electra and Orestes are performing their lines here (to repeat, 1232–1287) in a song that has rhythm and melody. This song, then, as a form, is in sharp contrast with the alternative form that we know as recitative, the form of which is a meter that is not sung. That alternative form would be the iambic trimeter.

§12B. There is more to be said about this remarkable recognition scene in the *Electra* of Sophocles. As Bollack shows, the interaction between the sister and the brother is metatheatrical. In the process of bringing about a change in the role and even in the character of Electra, Orestes is behaving— or, better, acting—like a director of a drama (a 1994 book by Batchelder has elaborated on such an exercise in metatheater). Also, although the rhythm and the melody of the singing performed by the two actors in this recognition scene creates the sense of a higher register of emotion by contrast with the recited iambic trimeters that are ordinarily performed by actors, the mood of this scene is emotionally uneven, since the character of Orestes, by contrast with Electra, sings lines that tend to be less emotional in content and closer to iambic trimeter in form, as if he were speaking while she was singing.

§12C. The sung form of this recognition scene in the *Electra* of Sophocles can be described as a "duet" of sorts. And Bollack understands that such "duets" are attested also in the dramas of Euripides. But can we infer, then, that the *Electra* of Sophocles was composed after the *Electra* of Euripides? Bollack declines to engage in such speculation, preferring an explanation that leaves room for the possibility that the form of these "duets" comes from a tradition that was already well-known to the audiences of Sophocles and Euripides.

Chapter 13. "Reading the Cosmogonies"

§13A. For Bollack, who adheres methodologically to the text of any particular author as the primary empirical given, even if that text is mediated by doxographical traditions that intervene, the vast diversity of content that we find in texts of cosmogonies originating from thinkers like Parmenides (6th and 5th centuries BCE) and Heraclitus (6th and 5th) and Democritus (5th and 4th), leads to a generalizing inference: all philosophers, each and every one of them, can make their own cosmogonies.

§13B. An anthropological understanding of cosmogonies, by contrast, would lead to a different though comparably generalizing inference: as a social institution, a cosmogony articulates the cosmos or social order of the society that it represents, and this is done by way of picturing the cosmos or natural order of things *as if it were the same thing as the social order*. Such a cosmogony, however, would be older than the newer and now personalized cosmogonies of the philosophers, who have for the most part freed themselves from ideological dependence on their societies. So the cosmogonies of the philosophers became independent of the older and more traditional cosmogonies that represented social order in the city-states.

§13C. Bollack adds that the personalized cosmogonies of the philosophers could vary in content from "a closed, unique world," like that of Parmenides, to a "world open to the limitless," like that of the atomists in general.

Chapter 14. "Empedocles: A Single Project, Two Theologies"

§14A. Here in Chapter 14 Bollack returns to what he signaled already in Chapter 6, namely, the complementarity of the *Purifications* of Empedocles with another celebrated poem of this thinker, the *Peri phuseōs* (*The Origins*). In his reading, Bollack shows that the two poems, although they originate from a single authorial mind, convey two different systems of thinking, two theologies, as it were, and that the distinctness of the two systems is actually highlighted in a context where one poem, *The Origins*, refers to the other poem, the *Purifications*.

§14B. Whereas *The Origins*, in Bollack's formulation, is an esoteric text, the *Purifications* is exoteric. Thus, by means of "a verbal re-composition," the discourse of Empedocles passes from "the construction of a world in the text" to "an intentionally cultural or political application." And "there is nature on the one hand, human history on the other."

Chapter 15. "The Parmenidean Cosmology of Parmenides"

§15A. This essay continues where Bollack left off at Chapter 13. Here in Chapter 15, he concentrates again on the cosmic vision of Parmenides. But, this time, the perspective widens to include cosmology alongside cosmogony. And the cosmology of Parmenides, Bollack complains, is based on an ontology that philosophers today tend to neglect. Here Bollack also ventures a more general opinion about what he sees as a widespread pattern of neglect. Such neglect, he argues, stems from an attitude that he detects in the work of many interpreters who have published their views about the cosmology of Parmenides and about the relevant doxography. He summarizes in this way that attitude: "what is not understood by the interpreter is presumed not to have been understood by the author." To signal his deep conviction that Parmenides understood perfectly well the cosmology that he was describing, Bollack calls this cosmology "Parmenidean."

§15B. There is, however, a major problem in coming to terms with the cosmology of Parmenides: the author's fragments and the relevant doxography are in fact difficult to understand. In seeking to achieve a holistic understanding of the cosmology, Bollack applies his *hermeneutics*, as already described in Chapter 1, to a systematic reassessment of both the fragments and the doxography. In the process, Bollack defends the testimony of Aetius (28 A 37 D-K) as "a solid, detailed, and structured summary," which "allows us to rediscover and retrace with precision the phases in the constitution of the world, with the ultimate outcome being a complete theoretical elucidation." He adds that the relevant fragments of Parmenides concerning matter, as cited by Simplicius, can be "clarified" in the context of a doxographic fragment from Theophrastus (46 A D-K). By way of these and other such clarifications, what Bollack describes as "the lost achievement" of Parmenides in formulating his cosmology can be reconstructed and thus brought back to life.

Chapter 16. "Expressing Differences"

§16A. After his frontal assault in Chapter 15 on interpreters who blame their failure to understand an author on the author, Bollack steps back for a moment to reflect, offering a brief manifesto here in Chapter 16 on the *hermeneutics* that he applies to the likes of Parmenides. If the methodology of his hermeneutics is to be valued as a critical tool, it must be *historical* in its orientation.

§16B. Accordingly, Bollack takes exception to a mode of research that concentrates on the argument of the moment and loses sight of the bigger picture, as it were. What results, he insists, is gross reductionism. Giving examples, he comments sarcastically, "Antigone is the family, Creon the State, Heraclitus the river." He follows up with another sarcastic comment, which will lead into the essay following this one: "Heraclitus said almost nothing of what he has been made to say from Plato on: nothing about fire or flow."

Chapter 17. "The Heraclitean *Logos*"

§17A. The thinking of Heraclitus (6th/5th century), as Bollack argues, "does not focus on the presence of Being," in the sense of Heidegger's idea of Being, "but on the universe of meaning," and that meaning is a function of language, of the *logos*. That is why, Bollack continues, we should not try to look for an overarching system of thought in the aphorisms of Heraclitus: "Heraclitus did not have his own system." Further, "the unity of his approach did not lie in any positive content but rather in his critical analysis of cosmological theories, nourished by assertions that were current in the learned circles of his day."

§17B. Heraclitus, says Bollack, "speaks of a reference provided by language; he never tires of talking about situations that show how the people around him miss the point of analysis and fail to grasp the structure of the language that they use and that impinges on their behavior."

Chapter 18. "Reading A Reference"

§18A. The author revisits here briefly his work on Empedocles, whose thinking has already been foregrounded in this book on multiple occasions (§1I-J, §6, §14). Bollack notes that his own work on the *Purifications* and *The Origins* of Empedocles has refuted some old interpretations of the thinking of Empedocles—interpretations to which Freud had once upon a time referred in shaping his theories about "the death principle."

§18B. Reading this old reference made by Freud to old interpretations of Empedocles leads Bollack to reflect on other such references, this time relating to the *Oedipus Tyrannus* and the *Antigone* of Sophocles. In the case of the second of these two tragedies, the author who makes the reference is not Freud but Lacan, and here Bollack returns to a relevant debate that he started to develop in another essay (§10A).

Chapter 19. "The Scientistic Model: Freud and Empedocles"

§19A. We are not yet done with Empedocles—or with Freud on Empedocles. Bollack will now take a closer look at references made by Freud to the thinking of Empedocles. In particular, he will now focus on that ancient Greek philosopher's vision of *Philia* or "Love" and *Neikos* or "Strife." In this context, Bollack will have to confront—just as Freud had to confront—"a theory of universal animation," described as "a pan-psychism that strongly influenced positivist or scientistic descriptions of pre-Socratic thought at the beginning of the century."

§19B. Bollack here has the advantage of hindsight, since the perspective of phenomenology eventually led to "a more ontological position." Still, his critique of Freud here is illuminating. At one point, he makes this striking observation: "by firmly linking the death impulse to life, Freud has in a sense drawn closer to Empedocles, for whom Strife was inseparable from the creative movements of life."

Chapter 20. "Benjamin Reading Kafka"

§20A. Before attempting to read this essay, readers should be advised to brace themselves. To form an idea of the depths and the complexities to be confronted—not even to mention the sheer length of time it takes to read the chapter, which can most easily be grasped from the start by contemplating the total number of footnotes (181)—I list here the main characters that figure in the drama of Bollack's argumentation. First we have Franz Kafka (1883–1924) and Walter Benjamin (1892–1940) themselves, who are already marked as the protagonists in the title of the essay. But then we also have the literary executor and *ex post facto* premier reader of Kafka, Max Brod (1884–1968). And we have as well a number of other eminent readers, especially Gershom Sholem (1897–1982), Theodor Adorno (1903–1969), Max Horkheimer (1895–1973), Bertolt Brecht (1898–1956), Ernst Bloch (1885–1977), Hannah Arendt (1906–1975). And these are only the main characters in what I just called the drama of Bollack's argumentation. There are also some important secondary characters who occasionally rotate into the foreground, and they are too numerous to mention here. The one exception, however, who must not only be mentioned but also spotlighted, is a figure who enters the drama only toward the end of Bollack's essay—and then stays there. He is Paul Celan (1920–1970).

§20B. Mention of Celan in this essay takes place at a point where the reader has already read nearly 20,000 words of argumentation. Only about 8,000 words remain to be read in the essay. But the entrance of Celan in Chapter 20 here signals the essence of Bollack's argumentation

§20C. It all goes back to an essay of Benjamin on Kafka, originally published in 1935 and designated simply as "Essay" in the englishing of Bollack's own essay. As Bollack notes, Celan at one point actually refers directly to the original German text of the Essay, listed as Benjamin 1935 in my Bibliography below. The direct reference is to be found in Celan's Büchner Prize speech, "Der Meridian" ("The Meridian"), delivered at Darmstadt in 1960. But there is more to it, much more. As Bollack shows, Celan creates in his own poetry a readerly response not only to Kafka but even to the reception of Kafka by Benjamin. We see here a kind of poeticized reception of a reception of Kafka, crafted deliberately as an alternative to the theorized reception that plays out in the essay of Benjamin on Kafka. Bollack in his own essay on Kafka says ironically about the theorized reception: "Kafka was unable to prevent readers from speaking about things he was not speaking about." In the end, Bollack senses that Celan is the best mediator for the real *logos* of Kafka. It is as if Kafka would have approved of the mediation.

§20D. Why is the reception of Kafka by Celan so all-important for Bollack in his own essay? It is mostly because the poetry of Celan responds to Kafka in a way that solves the problems created by Benjamin in his readings of Kafka—in inter-action with rival readings as criticized by Bollack in the first 20,000-odd words of his complex essay. What comes into play in Bollack's proposed solution is a matter of *hermeneutics*, that is, the kind of methodology that he himself developed in his approach to such ancient thinkers as Heraclitus. Here we see an implicit return to Bollack's essay on the Heraclitean *logos*, as republished in Chapter 17 of his *Art of Reading*. As Bollack argues there, the thinking of Heraclitus focuses on *meaning* as a function of *language*, that is, of the *logos*. Similarly, the work of Kafka is for Bollack "fully situated in language, by language, and in language."

§20E. Whereas Bollack's comparison of Heraclitus with Kafka is only implicit in this essay, there are works that make the comparison explicit. I have one particular work in mind as I say this: it is a book by David Schur (1998), entitled *Heraclitus and Kafka*. I am betting that Bollack, if he had seen this book, would have approved.

§20F. From time to time in this essay, but not all that frequently, he inter-prets Kafka directly—instead of indirectly through intermediaries, as when he resists or embraces respectively the mediations of the likes of Benjamin or Celan. My favorite example of a direct interpretation is when Bollack comments on a short story of Kafka's entitled "Silence of the Sirens" (1931). As Bollack sees it, the reason why the Sirens do not sing is because they have understood the desire of Odysseus to hear them, not only the stratagem that he has invented to hear them. The Sirens of Kafka do not sing, but Odysseus "*believes* he hears them."

Chapter 21. "Reading the Codes"

§21A. Chapter 21 can serve as a transition. It contains fewer than 500 words, in the wake of the 28,000-odd words of Chapter 20. We have heard already from Paul Celan, who signals modernity, and we will hear more as we read the chap-ters that follow this one. But first, Bollack will stop and take stock before moving further away from the ancient world and taking big steps toward modernity in general. A specific case in point, for the moment, is Saint-John Perse (1887–1975).

§21B. At this point of transition in the book, Bollack needs to make sure that his readers keep in mind something quite basic about his approach to texts both ancient and modern. There is no point, he says, in trying to seek a universal meaning for any text to be studied. Rather, in terms of Bollack's hermeneutics, it suffices to view the text as something that is both *historical* and *trans-historical*. Here is how he puts it: "I have been led to recognize the unity of a global literary phenomenon, the existence of a field that is historical and trans-historical without being eternal, in which every sentence has always been taken up again or has awaited its repetition." For his hermeneutics, it is an absolutist imperative to study each and every instance in the reception of a text—even if the completeness of such a study needs to be deferred beyond a lifetime or even beyond an eternity of study. The meaning of the text may not be eternal, but the study of the meaning needs to be so. There can be no final word about the meaning of the word. Instead, there is only an eternal decoding: "the hermeneutics of texts decodes what has always been coded, in some sense."

Chapter 22. "A Sonnet, A Poetics—Mallarmé: 'Le Vierge, Le Vivace...'"

§22A. In the course of his decisive transition from the ancient to the modern world in Chapter 21, Bollack had already compared the modernist poetics of two figures. One of these two was Paul Celan, whose poetic creations were highlighted also in Chapter 20. But Bollack in Chapter 21 mentioned only in passing the other of the two figures whose poetics he was comparing there, and I in turn did not mention him at all in the part of my foreword that dealt with that chapter. Here in Chapter 22, I make up for that temporary elision. The figure in question is a modernist poet from an earlier era, Stéphane Mallarmé (1842–1898). In Chapter 22, Bollack engages more fully with Mallarmé's poetics, and I take this opportunity to signal the value of this engagement. The primary text that Bollack has chosen from among the poetic creations of Mallarmé is "Le vierge, le vivace et le bel aujourd'hui," which is the second in a tetrad of poems entitled "Plusieurs sonnets" in the 1899 Deman edition. Bollack's translators have chosen for the English translation of Mallarmé here the version crafted by the late Barbara Johnson. This exquisite English version of the French text enhances all the more for me the pleasure of introducing the chapter, since the translator was a dear friend.

§22B. In keeping with his own hermeneutics, Bollack sums up the importance of Mallarmé's poem this way: "the sonnet is a poem about poetry, even about the particular poem that is in the process of being written." In making this argument, Bollack takes the opportunity to disagree with a host of received opinions about the sonnet, emphasizing his own methodological insistence on the importance of the wording as an index of the process that is poetry. Acknowledging the occasional contentiousness of his critiques, he observes: "I am prepared to except, in part or in full, the studies (and there are surely some with which I am not familiar) to which the critiques formulated do not apply." Among those critiques, I submit, is the exegesis by Barbara Johnson, with whose work on the same sonnet Bollack seems to have been unfamiliar.

Chapter 23. "Between Hölderlin and Celan"

§23A. For Bollack, friendships cannot get in the way of fierce polemics. Clearly, Bollack was good friends with André du Bouchet (1924–2001), a poet acclaimed for his creativity with words. A public intellectual, du Bouchet was one of the founders of the prestigious journal *Éphémère*, which published in its first volume, appearing in 1966, a French-language version of Celan's "The Meridian" ("Le Méridien"). Among the many poetic experiments of du Bouchet were his translations, from the original German into French, of poems by Friedrich Hölderlin (1770–1843). He also tried his hand at translating poems composed in German by Paul Celan, often seeking and receiving advice on this or that turn of phrase from his friend Bollack, whose *Sprachgefühl* for the German language—especially for Celan's linguistic idiosyncrasies—he evidently respected. And here is where the trouble begins: it is all about the reception of Hölderlin by Celan as interpreted by du Bouchet, whose interpretations were vigorously resisted by Bollack.

§23B. The year is 1986, and Bollack is attending a session of the Hölderlin Society in Tübingen. One of the speakers is du Bouchet, who recounts a remark he heard once spoken *viva voce* by Celan himself. The remark went back to 1970, sixteen years earlier, on the occasion of a bicentennial commemoration of Hölderlin's birth. And this was just a short time before the death of Celan by suicide in the same year. Bollack goes on to quote the remark of Celan, introducing the exact words proleptically by first describing the astonished reaction of du Bouchet to what he heard: "He would never have expected to hear his friend, whom he so much admired, declare out of the blue: 'There is something rotten in Hölderlin's poetry.'"

§23C. As the story unfolds, we see that du Bouchet struggles to develop an explanatory model for this remark of Celan about Hölderlin. And Bollack undertakes a demolition of this model, applying his own hermeneutics to show that the essence of Celan's remark is already encoded in a poem of his entitled "Tübingen, Jänner" ("Tübingen, January"). This poem, as Bollack shows, refers not only to the poetry of Hölderlin but also to the pernicious appropriation of Hölderlin by Nazi ideologues. Celan's symbol for such an appropriation is an allusion in this same poem to the Wannsee Conference, "where in early 1942 the Nazis decided on the extermination of the Jews."

§23D. The blind spots of French *literati* in interpreting Celan's poetry can be traced back, Bollack finds, to their over-reliance on the thinking of Heidegger, whose hermeneutics he has already attacked in an earlier essay, as mentioned in §10B of this foreword. In the present essay, Bollack sharpens his attack by targeting Heidegger's influence as an interpreter of Hölderlin for the French intelligentsia.

§23E. In this connection, Bollack highlights Celan's poem "Todtnauberg," translated into English as "The Mountain of Death," which centers on the poet's visit in 1967 to the chalet (*Hütte*) of Heidegger himself in the Black Forest. What Bollack says here about this remarkable poem can serve as a preview for what else he will say about it in his final chapter.

Chapter 24. "Grasping Hermeneutics"

§24A. Peter Szondi ... Hardly a word about him in the twenty-three chapters of Bollack that precede this one ... And no word at all so far from me in this Foreword ... But now we get to see the vital importance of Szondi for the *hermeneutics* of Bollack.

§24B. Peter Szondi (1929–1971) and Bollack were long-time friends, and, after Szondi committed suicide in 1971 (so, not long after the suicide of Paul Celan in 1970), Bollack was asked to edit a posthumous publication of his friend's *Nachlass* (Szondi 1974–1975). What Bollack included in this publication was the script, as it were, for an influential course that Szondi had taught, *Introduction to Literary Hermeneutics*, and Bollack's present essay comes from an Afterword that he composed for a French-language version of the *Introduction* (Szondi 1989). This course, as Bollack emphasizes, showed clearly the evolution of Szondi's own interest in "a non-theological hermeneutics, proper to literature, starting in the eighteenth century." What follows this essay, Chapter 25, will delve into the story of that evolution.

Chapter 25. "A Future in the Past: Peter Szondi's Material Hermeneutics"

§25A. Peter Szondi, in redefining what Bollack calls the "science" of literary study, resisted the intellectual influence of Heidegger—especially with reference to the mediation of Heidegger by way of Gadamer and his hermeneutics. Bollack's own general resistance to this same influence is explored already in Chapter 10 (as signaled at §10B of my Foreword). Then in Chapter 23 (as signaled in my §23D) the resistance becomes more specific as Bollack starts to counter Heidegger's role as interpreter of Hölderlin for the French intelligentsia. Here in Chapter 25 the resistance becomes even more specific as Bollack joins forces with Szondi. Bollack mentions here in passing his own rejection of Heidegger as interpreter not only of Hölderlin but also of Georg Trakl (1887–1914) and Rainer Maria Rilke (1875–1926). The intensity of Bollack's criticism here of Heidegger can be explained at least in part by what we read already in Chapter 1—even as an adolescent, as Bollack professes there—"I was imbued with Rilke."

§25B. Addressing directly the literary or "material" hermeneutics of Szondi, Bollack sets up as a foil the philosophical hermeneutics of Gadamer. Comparing the two interpretive systems, Bollack describes Gadamer's hermeneutics as a kind of pseudo-theology. On the overall work of Szondi as philologist and literary critic, I take this opportunity to recommend the incisive analysis of Koenig 2015.

Chapter 26. "Reading the Signifier"

§26A. Here Bollack takes up once again his longtime search to find meaning in the poetry of Paul Celan. This time, the point of departure is the *Cratylus* of Plato, viewed as an idiosyncratic exercise in decoding. Bollack senses that such an exercise leads to understanding, little by little, "a network of truth." And here is where Bollack's study of Celan converges with what he described earlier as the literary hermeneutics of Szondi. Bollack now reminisces about his past efforts in defending Szondi as an interpreter of Celan, seeing beyond—far beyond—the charges of "biographism" that had been leveled against the poet. Szondi in his own right had defended himself against such charges directed at him by none other than Gadamer, arguing that the literary critic must attempt a reconstruction of the context of any code that needs to be decoded.

§26B. Bollack sees Szondi's argument as a key to decoding the poetry of Celan, which is constructed by way of "initially enigmatic words" that come from "a personal encounter with the world." A shining example for Bollack is a poem of Celan entitled "The Mountain of Death," which as we have already noted in §23E centers on the visit of the poet in 1967 to Heidegger's chalet in the Black Forest.

Chapter 27. "The Mountain of Death: The Meaning of Celan's Meeting with Heidegger"

§27A. Now we get to see why Bollack would have wanted to invoke the *Cratylus* of Plato in the previous essay that leads into this last essay of the volume. Much like the word-plays of Plato's Socrates, the "initially enigmatic" turns of phrase in the poem by Celan as featured already in the title of the essay, "Mountain of Death," come from "a personal encounter with the world." The wording of Celan in this poem is enigmatic and at the same time utterly revealing, once the meaning is decoded.

§27B. It all comes down to a primal meeting between the poet Celan and the philosopher Heidegger in the dark forest that is the Black Forest. As Bollack says, "now a poet has come to introduce the philosopher to his own forest and, more than that, to impose on him the truth of a place by remaking it *de profundis*." And what is perceptible, he adds, "vanishes before the truth of words."

Bibliography

Assmann, J. 1978. *Moses the Egyptian: The Memory of Egypt in Western Monotheism.* Cambridge MA.

Batchelder, A. G. 1994. *The Seal of Orestes: Self-Reference and Authority in Sophocles' Electra.* Lanham MD.

Benjamin, W. 1934. "Franz Kafka: Eine Würdigung." *Jüdische Rundschau* 39, nos. 102/103 and 104 (December). Reprinted in Benjamin 1978, 2, part 2:409–438, and notes, 2, part 3:1153–1276.

———. 1978. *Gesammelte Schriften* (ed. R. Tiedemann and H. Schweppenhäuser). 5 volumes. Frankfurt.

Bollack, J. 1990. "La cosmologie parménidéenne en Parménide." *Herméneutique et ontologie. Hommage à Pierre Aubenque* (ed. R. Brague and J. Courtine) 19–53. Paris.

———. 1994. "Une action de restauration culturelle: La place accordée aux tragiques par le décret de Lycurgue." *Mélanges Pierre Lévêque* (eds. M.-M. Mactoux and E. Geny) vol. 8, *Religion, anthropologie et société.* Annales littéraires de l'Université de Besançon, vol. 499:13–24. Paris.

———. 1995. "Né damné." In: Bollack, J. 1995. *La naissance d'Œdipe: traduction et commentaires d'Œdipe roi* 217–237. Paris.

———. 1996. "Durchgänge." *Zeitenwechsel. Germanistische Literaturwissenschaft vor und nach 1945* (ed. W. Barner and C. Koenig) 387–403. Frankfurt. This text is an earlier version of Bollack 1997a.

———. 1997. *La Grèce de personne: les mots sous le mythe.* Paris.

———. 1997a. "Apprendre à lire." In: Bollack 1997:9–21.

———. 1997b. "Lire les philologues." In: Bollack 1997:25–28.

———. 1997c. "Ulysse chez les philologues." In: Bollack 1997:29–59.

———. 1997d. "Réflexions sur la pratique." In: Bollack 1997:93–103.

———. 1997e. "Lire le mythe." In: Bollack 1997:131–136.

———. 1997f. "Lire le théâtre." In: Bollack 1997:309–311.

———. 1997g. "Lire les cosmogonies." In: Bollack 1997:181–182.

———. 1997h. "Dire les différences. " In: Bollack 1997:263.

———. 1997i. "Réflexions sur les interprétations du logos héraclitéen." In: Bollack 1997:288–308.

———. 1997j. "Lire une référence." In: Bollack 1997:106.

———. 1997k. "Le modèle scientiste, Empédocle et Freud." In: Bollack 1997:107–114.

————. 1997l. "Lire les codes." In: Bollack 1997:221–222.

————. 1997m. "Dire les herméneutiques." In: Bollack 1997:115–116.

————. 1997n. "Un futur dans le passé. L'herméneutique matérielle de Peter Szondi." In: Bollack 1997:117–127.

————. 1997o. "Lire le signifiant." In: Bollack 1997:337–339.

————. 1997p. "Le mont de la mort: le sens d'une rencontre entre Celan et Heidegger." In: Bollack 1997:349–376

————. 2001. "De la philologie au théâtre. La construction du sens de l'*Antigone* de Sophocle," *Études théâtrales* 21: "Tragédie grecque. Défi de la scène contemporaine" 103–110. Paris.

————. 2003. "Dieu sur terre." In: *Empédocle. Les purifications. Un projet de paix universelle* (ed. J. Bollack) 9–28. Paris.

————. 2005. "Empedocles: A Single Project, Two Theologies." Translated from the French by C. Porter. *The Empedoclean Kosmos: Structure, Process, and the Question of Cyclicity*. Proceedings of the Symposium Philosophiae Antiquae Tertium Myconense, July 6th-July 13th, 2003, Institute for Philosophical Research (ed. A. L. Pierris), 2005) 45–72. Patras.

————. 2008. "Un sonnet, une poétique—Mallarmé: 'Le vierge, le vivace...'." *Mémoire et oubli dans le lyrisme européen: Hommage à John E. Jackson* (ed. D. Weisner and P. Labarthe) 581–594. Paris.

————. 2010. "Benjamin devant Kafka." *Walter Benjamin, le critique européen* (ed. H. Wismann and P. Lavelle) 213–277. Lille.

————. 2011. "Entre Hölderlin et Celan." *Europe: revue littéraire mensuelle* 986–987:193–207.

————. 2012a. "Une fiction anthropologique." *Savoirs et clinique. Revue de psychanalyse* 15:177–193.

————. 2012b. "Les deux temps de la reconnaissance dans l'*Electre* de Sophocle." *Lexis* 30:268–274.

Burkert, W. 1962. Weisheit und Wissenschaft: Studien zu Pythagoras, Philolaos und Platon. Nürnberg.

————. 1972. *Lore and Science in Ancient Pythagoreanism.* Translated by E. L. Minar, Jr. from Burkert 1962. Cambridge MA.

Denniston, J. D. 1954. *The Greek Particles.* 2nd ed. revised by K. J. Dover. Oxford.

Detienne, M. 1963. *La notion de daïmon dans le pythagorisme ancien: de la pensée religieuse à la pensée philosophique.* Paris.

————. 1970. "La cuisine de Pythagore." *Archives des sciences sociales des religions* 29:141–162.

————. 1988. "La double écriture de la mythologie entre le *Timée* et le *Critias.*" *Métamorphoses du mythe en Grèce antique* (ed. C. Calame) 17–33. Geneva.

Frazer, J. G. 1911. *The Golden Bough: A Study in Magic and Religion* Part III. *The Dying God.* London. This is the version cited in Freud 1939.

Freud, S. 1939. *Der Mann Moses und die monotheistische Religion* (The Man Moses and Monotheistic Religion), in *Gesammelte Werke*, vol. 15 (1950) 101–246. London. = *Moses and Monotheism.* Translated by J. Strachey. *Standard English Edition of the Complete Psychological Works of Sigmund Freud*, vol. 23 (ed. J. Strachey, 1953–1966) 3–137. London.

Johnson, B. 1985. "*Les Fleurs du mal armé:* Some Reflections on Intertextuality." *Lyric Poetry: Beyond New Criticism* (ed. C. Hošek and P. Parker) 264–280. Ithaca, NY.

Judet de La Combe, P., and Wismann, H., eds. 2009. "Liminaire." *La lecture insistante: autour de Jean Bollack.* Colloque de Cerisy (July 11–18), 19–32. Paris.

Kirk, G. S. 1962. *The Songs of Homer.* Cambridge.

Koenig, Ch. 2015. "Philological Understanding: Ethics, Method and Style in the Work of Peter Szondi." *Textual Understanding and Historical Experience: On Peter Szondi* (ed. S. Zepp) 71–88. Paderborn.

Lacan J. 1986. *L'éthique de la psychanalyse, 1959-1960.* Séminaire 7. Paris.

———. 1992. *The Ethics of Psychoanalysis, 1959-1960.* Seminar, Book 7. Translated by D. Porter from Lacan 1986. New York.

Nagy, G. 1996. *Poetry as Performance: Homer and Beyond.* Cambridge. http://nrs.harvard.edu/urn-3:hul.ebook:CHS_Nagy.Poetry_as_Performance.1996

Schur, D. 1998. *Heraclitus and Kafka.* Harvard Studies in Comparative Literature 44. Cambridge MA.

Szondi, P. 1974–1975. *Studienausgabe der Vorlesungen* (ed. J. Bollack). Frankfurt.

———. 1989. *Introduction à l'herméneutique littéraire* (tr. M. Bollack, afterword by J. Bollack). Paris.

Vernant, J.-P. 1962. *Les origines de la pensée grecque.* 5th ed. 1992. Paris.

1

Learning to Read[†]

WHEN I STARTED OUT, I found it hard to distinguish writing projects from re-elaborations of subject matter, and I failed to pay sufficient attention to the breaks, large or very small, that produce the meaning of a text. I gradually came to understand that these breaks allow for freedom in the act of reading, without establishing the potentialities of language as a principle, and without minimizing either the specificity of an innovation or the space opened up by distance.

The act of reading requires reactualizing a text as such while attributing to it all the characteristics of a unitary composition. I first confined myself to making sense of textual networks, concerned with demonstrating their coherence. I examined texts from the inside, in their very structure; the texts themselves were to provide the reader with the means for understanding them. I did not apply myself as passionately then as I have done since to discovering their connectedness and intertextuality, nor did I pursue the transformations that traditions undergo, be they literary, religious, or philosophical, when their territory becomes circumscribed and when they have not been artificially reconstructed from a new pedagogical or dogmatic standpoint.

I had the good fortune to begin my higher education in Basel, where I spent the dark days of World War II. I survived thanks to the circumstances that had offered me refuge in that city. A great university tradition survived there in its own way, protected and free, as if in a sanctuary. Germany's most serious unrealized utopian aspects remained alive in Basel, though Germany itself had lost them.[1] As beginners, we struggled, without any tutoring, to follow courses in Greek philology that were designed to initiate us into all areas of specialization, and kept us at the beginning level for quite a while; for as the courses advanced,

---

[†] Originally published as "Apprendre à lire," in: Jean Bollack, *La Grèce de personne: les mots sous le mythe* (Paris, 1997), pp. 9–21.
[1] I described the general setting of the town and its university, as I knew it during the war years, in a paper delivered at a conference on the problem of continuity after 1945: "Durchgänge" ("Passages"), Bollack 1996.

the mass of material increased so much that it was impossible to digest and assimilate it all. And yet that kind of philology retained its appeal for me; I found it superior to certain of the philosophical discourses I had heard on the topic. The literal aspect of the original text held pride of place, ahead of all the cultural phenomena that accompanied it. I learned in Basel that establishing the text is just as problematic as establishing its meaning.

The opinions of the major philologists were put before us; each of these scholars had contributed to the advancement of knowledge. However, the consensual debates put before us were artificial, despite their obvious pedagogical usefulness. The fundamental questions were never raised. But at least we understood that the subject matter was difficult; that the current state of understanding of the works had already required an immense effort and remained unfinished; and that apart from the subject itself, we had to deal with the boundless layers of interpretation that had been deposited over it. Discouragement did not blunt the appeal of the endeavor: the two were closely connected.

Before taking an outstanding course on the *Agamemnon* of Aeschylus, we had to have read, often in Latin, the major commentaries of the nineteenth and twentieth centuries published in the wake of Gottfried Hermann, one of the most acclaimed scholars in academic criticism; that of Eduard Fraenkel, who had emigrated to Oxford, had not yet been published, but Peter Von der Mühll, who taught Greek at Basel, had pursued a research project of comparable scope, though it too remained unpublished. Humanists were taking renewed interest in the drama so admired by Humboldt and Goethe. But partly owing to ignorance and a misunderstanding of the qualities of literary art, the studies undertaken by these scholars, however skillful, transformed the endeavor into an extremely complex project that was intended to allow philology to compete with the natural sciences but that in practice excluded all the participants.

Apart from the *Kritisches Hypomnema*, a critical commentary on the *Iliad* published in 1952, none of the immense work that Von der Mühll put into preparing his classes led to publication; indeed, it never went beyond the confines of his classroom, so only a very small number benefited from it. For a Basel patrician steeped in the Protestant aristocratic mindset, the activity was sufficient unto itself; he was speaking for this small circle. The great professor displayed and used his erudition in class, but he denied himself the possibility of reaching a larger audience: he remained doubly inaccessible, assured of his own excellence yet renouncing public ambition in any form except professorial practice. Exercises in interpretation were supposed to be paradigmatic; the task was to transmit the practice of historical (or historicizing) philology, but also to go beyond its ethical meaning and demonstrate a scientific practice. With its age-old roots, philology was professed from the heights of the rostrum, and it developed endlessly, constantly updated with new hypotheses, informed by the most recent "critical note."

Meaning was the object of technical skills, and it was revealed at the end of a philological explication. The humanistic tradition surrounding the texts was gradually becoming more scientific than erudite. Historicism was not the problem—it would have been necessary to demonstrate, as Nietzsche advocated, the values that had been lost—as much as the practice of science; we would have liked to master it and to have both historical and aesthetic criteria at our disposal; we would have liked to be able to reach firm conclusions. We were feeling our way, and we made progress empirically and intuitively. The principles of hermeneutics were neither considered nor taught. The practice went without saying; its logic remained for us to discover. Attuning it to the real needs of reading was to make the science of philology the object of scientific study; that is, to write this book [*La Grèce de personne*].

For a twenty-year-old student, the dazzling virtuosity of arguments about the relative age of certain episodes in the *Iliad* seemed like a great feat or a moment of delirium. Taken together, these arguments provided an additional way of reading. Aristophanes of Byzantium, Aristarchus, Karl Lachmann, Erich Bethe, and all the modern Homer scholars contributed their own methods for evaluating criteria of taste, expectations, and prejudices. I quite naturally aligned myself in the opposing camp, that of the Unitarians, who affirmed the unity of the epic at all costs. I contested the scientific approach so as to resist its dizzying temptations, so as to remain in a position to play the game according to my own lights. We trained ourselves at least to uncover problems, and above all to doubt and contradict.

In the university seminars I frequented in Basel, and especially the one taught by Von der Mühll, the conditions for shared research came together. Scholarly techniques were transmitted implicitly through discussion; the meaning of the texts remained to be discovered. We assumed the texts were opaque, and this was confirmed, despite their fate in the classroom; they remained open to the work of elucidation. We would sometimes spend a quarter of an hour, often without speaking for several minutes, on one sentence that the professor said in all seriousness that he did not understand; he would point out the difficulties, accept suggestions, stimulate our thinking. Seminars in Paris had nothing in common with this exercise except the name. There, a general admission of ignorance is rarely the point of departure for a discussion. Of course such a beginning was inadequate; we rarely got as far as analyzing the preliminaries. But at least I had a glimpse of the principle of interpretation.

Speculative exercises were less widespread than they had been earlier. It was difficult to excel at conjecture, and hard to compete with scholars made illustrious by their supposedly irrefutable findings. In Basel and elsewhere, the analysis of Homeric poetry was a virtuoso activity. It seemed less arbitrary, and better able to transmit the feeling of literary quality. Indeed, scholars were certain they possessed the criteria for expertise. In this field, as in others, we thought we could return to the values of a mythic origin and a superior humanity; we rediscovered the heroic age and did our utmost to revive it. In fact, "decadence" was an ancient phenomenon; it was thought to bear witness to the ravages of the intellect and to humanity's separation from nature.

From the start, I systematically took the side of the poets and all writers, choosing to read the original text for powerful expression and unusual features; I understood that these were not self-evident, and I may even have exulted in the fact that literal reading was difficult, for it meant that I could resolve enigmas as yet unraveled. Over the years, mystery itself came to present itself as a form, and enigmas became less enigmatic. I learned that coded writings followed a clear principle, and thus allowed an initiation into the art of reading. Transferences from contemporary poetry, which was of great importance in my life, to philology led me to the classical authors. Less accessible, shielded by an armor of formal difficulties, these authors would provide much greater satisfaction once they were extracted from their envelope. I had to overcome some obstacles—but these increased and extended the pleasure of enlightenment that I had enjoyed with fewer hindrances when reading contemporary writers. The role played by poetry journals during the war is well known. Before that period, like everyone else at the time, I had been imbued with Rilke. His *Rodin* had been my entry into literature, a "first book," different from the others; I read it when I was about fourteen. I then read—and reread—all I could find of his work, before I reached the end of this rite of passage in the 1930s and discovered that there were other less accessible authors who wrote differently and whose modernity made different demands on the reader. (My meeting during that same period with Wilhelm Stein, an art historian in Bern, introduced me to the art of looking, which he applied brilliantly for hours at a time to reading a painting.) I am especially indebted to Albert Béguin, who later became editor of the review *Esprit* and who held the chair in French Literature in Basel in those years, for it was he who introduced me to the world of contemporary literature. He knew this world intimately, and he knew how to kindle a love for it in others; not only Georges Bernanos, one of his guiding stars, but also André Breton and all the Surrealists, René Crevel and Robert Desnos, as well as recently published authors such as André Frénaud and Pierre Emmanuel.

Convinced by this dual apprenticeship that correcting and revising texts applied only to those that we did not accept into the canon or that we did not understand, I took my place on the side of tradition, but in a quite different sense than that of those who defended humanistic values. I saw the abstruse aspect of tradition, a half-known matter that had to be brought into existence. There was no way to avoid working through prior scholarship. We had to embrace science, not only to be capable of using it ourselves, but also to appreciate its weaknesses. Tradition had to be protected from its own glorification.

A seminar on Empedocles initiated me into the methods of complex—analytical and inventive—readings of fragmentary texts, and no doubt instilled in me the desire to try to reconstitute their lost totality, but it also opened up the secret worlds of the indirect tradition, which has given us these fragments. I discovered that knowledge, like understanding, had a history, and I never lost sight of this fact. Understanding the context of a quotation, detecting the traces of a translation, separating readings and distinguishing points of view, using doxographical summaries that condense episodes—all this work was already leading me to a systematic analysis of the constitution of knowledge, paving the way for an intellectual historiography. One of my first paper topics was on the origins of doxography in Plato and his predecessors. The study of mediation was to come into its own later on.

This interest unquestionably strengthened for me the coherence of sets of texts. My long discussions with Kostas Axelos led the two of us to confront different points of view, to outline precarious totalities. In the spirit of the times, I harmonized my work with the ontological conjectures inspired by the pre-Socratic philosophers and on which I was necessarily dependent, one way or another; but I engaged more directly with the counterweight of formal analysis made necessary by the splintering effects of unrestrained positivist scholarship. Without really defending a purpose or a historical position, the concern with composition at least rehabilitated an object that had lost its shape.

I had reached a crossroads, a turning point that strikes me now as decisive. An enormous and dizzying amount of knowledge about literary works had been amassed: this knowledge was necessary, of course, but in a different form, as a prerequisite for understanding the works. The temptation to dispense with any intermediary was strong. We thought we could do without all the intervening scholarship and approach texts closely by more direct means. In most cases, readers, whatever their level of interest, latched on to a text constituted by others, pre-formed, as it were, by a scientific method that was rejected as unverifiable, so that they were no longer able to overcome their dependence or even to recognize it. They often interpreted a mere artifact. Conclusions were drawn and disseminated, leaving no room for further inquiry.

The philological approach, which led to the sources of knowledge in a different way than was commonly thought, took on a special meaning in the philosophical context of the postwar years, when the pre-Socratic thinkers,

Parmenides even more than Empedocles, enjoyed enormous prestige. Nietzsche's *The Birth of Tragedy* was a spiritual guide. As we know, constellations change places in the skies of canonical values. Scholars of that era thought that they could lead readers into direct communication with an archaic way of thinking, and make them understand the heroic language of an origin, beyond any scientific methods, or even in opposition to them. Work on ancient interpretations of fragments and on the *opinions* of philosophers—doxography—shielded me from this trend, but the syntactic problems involved in analyzing the texts prevented me from indulging in verbal iconolatry. Grammar and linguistics revealed their power. Even though the art of putting words together continued to fascinate me, I was able to view the words from a distance, having learned to find and defend the literality of the original text against unsubstantiated claims. In philology, nothing is certain, nothing can be taken for granted. Still, philologists felt the urgent need to set these disparate and broken elements into an appropriate framework that could be conceived as a totality, even if that framework proved artificial.

This is how the Empedoclean construction developed, the cosmological system that lent itself most readily to being set up with the information gleaned from doxography. Ontological positions were applied to a design; they were inscribed within a structure of the world. When homology between a speculation and a representation is difficult to establish, it is because the initial point of view was different, more reflexive than deductive, more analytical than demonstrative. The discovery of the absence of cosmology in Heraclitus was thus the result, no less positive, of the failure of a long research project. It led me inevitably to a radical modification of the interpretation of aphorisms. And when I went back to the famous "fragment" of Anaximander, right at the beginning of philosophical speculation on the *arkhē* (beginning), I was convinced that Anaximander, already so close to the "dawn," was making a statement about the conditions of possibility of assertions made by others before him. In a place, in an environment, that was not that of a solitary thinker, the raw material had a form; it was "made" before it was reconstructed. An authorial intervention took on meaning: it was rooted in a particular cultural situation, and a particular choice was already branching off from the dominant point of view.

I had always thought that, as soon as it became feasible, I would continue my studies in Paris, and I lost no time moving there after the Liberation. The Sorbonne had nothing like the working conditions or the open-mindedness I had found in Basel. The university had withdrawn into itself, despite the strong personalities on the faculty: these scholars were fully aware and independent thinkers, but they found it hard to adapt to the situation, more or less everywhere. The best strategy was to act as if this were not the case. In the École pratique des hautes études, we had to look for courses that were good, sometimes very good, if not very profitable by the accepted standards; they were sometimes outside the curriculum and therefore poorly attended. At the time, one could quickly take the measure of this academic world to which I falsely ascribed a structure that it may have aspired to but had not yet acquired (and perhaps never did). I built up a quite artificial continuity with my earlier years in academe, rebelling against one reality in favor of another. Since, among other things, I lacked the posture of distanciation that I had adopted earlier, I tried to make that negation operate as a positive factor; I used as a point of reference an absent system with which I had not really identified either. I do not think this double dissociation bothered me. It taught me to see differences, to tolerate them, to resist and reject taboos. I had excellent professors in history and philosophy. In the field of Greek studies, I was very drawn to the history of the language, mainly because linguistics, quite advanced in France at all levels, was also the most scientifically oriented of literary subjects, with the fewest constraints, and because I had recognized how useful it could be for the critique of traditions.

Louis Robert's course on epigraphy at Hautes Études, which included students from the École Normale who were candidates for the French School in Athens, helped me a great deal in reading inscriptions; I also participated, through books, in the voyages of all the Waddingtons[2] in Asia Minor, an area that science and discovery seemed to be taking away from aesthetes and reserving for themselves.

Louis Robert (like Hans Georg Pflaum, from Germany, whom I got to know in Robert's classroom) was interested in students and their training, and he answered our questions honestly. Father Festugière, in Religious Studies, whom I knew well, preferred to read to us from the text of the book he was writing. Both of them were engaged in an unbelievably relentless race against the clock to get through the material for the books they were preparing. The linguist Pierre Chantraine took me under his wing. I had been referred to him by Von der Mühll when I arrived in Paris with my letters of recommendation. The two men had Homer in common. The great Jacob Wackernagel, whom Chantraine compared to his mentor Antoine Meillet, had taught in Basel. Chantraine was the leading Greek scholar in France; because of his exposure to the international scene, he knew the limits of the French system but saw no way to reform it. He was sensitive to the difficulties that a student unfamiliar with its customs must face.

---

[2]   [Translator's note (hereafter TN): George Waddington (1793–1869) was an English clergyman and great traveler; he stands for the amateur scholars of the period who began to explore lands that they had previously known only through books.]

I took an excellent course on Terence offered to advanced students by Jean Bayet, an impressive figure at the postwar Sorbonne, imperious yet approachable; it gave me a clear idea of what academic rhetoric could encompass. At the other extreme, there were only two or three of us to enjoy the unforgettable smile and wisdom of Alexandre Koyré, as he translated Spinoza's *Ethics* with his own expressions, brilliant in their clarity, playfulness, and simple intelligence. In another, livelier wing of the Palais de Nénot,[3] I took the courses that Henri-Irénée Marrou offered to a crowded classroom full of ancient history students, in which he developed what would become a classic text, his *Histoire de l'éducation dans l'Antiquité.* Etienne Gilson, who had returned from Canada for his classes at the Collège de France, gave me another example of elevated and scholarly oratory in his course on Duns Scotus. He pursued his arguments in richly cadenced periodic sentences, before an audience that was then mostly ecclesiastical, and usually hit his mark, though not always. Just as with Koyré, there were not many traditional students in Gilson's classes. The worlds were compartmentalized. I chose these four professors for their excellence and their generosity. I could meet them in the hallways, or elsewhere—Gilson would meet students at the Vrin bookshop, near a woodstove fed with unsold remainders. Sometimes professors invited me to their homes. I think they felt as frustrated as I did, swept along by the winds of an intellectual void that no one could do anything to counter. One day Marrou told me: "When in Rome, do as the Romans do"; I had not learned that yet.

From 1956 to 1959, I was at the Free University of Berlin, where, thanks to the recommendation of Karl Reinhardt, professors Uvo Hölscher and Kurt von Fritz had invited me to teach. I conducted seminars on Parmenides, Empedocles, and Plato's *Timaeus,* applying the techniques of open discussion of texts that I had learned in Basel. I realized that this practice was no more than a fiction in Germany, despite all the attempts to restore it after the years of celebrating massacres. It needed to be reinvented, and it required a personal, almost private commitment. Heinz Wismann, a participant in my seminar, followed me to Lille, in France, where I was teaching. We did a great deal of work, going over texts and systems of thought at the same time. We questioned all critical apparatuses. The analysis of error was most productive, methodologically, in the refutation of the idea, propagated by prevailing opinion, that there were two cycles in Empedocles. Our free-wheeling critiques were often taken to be "up-to-date" research, and this was indeed the case, because we were rejecting an opaque and authoritarian past. According to those who defended that past, we took tradition too seriously.

---

[3] Henri-Paul Nénot (1853–1934) was the architect of the Nouvelle Sorbonne (competition of 1882).

Our shared work habits and a suggestion by Pierre Bourdieu led to regular "Saturdays" in our apartment on the rue de Bourgogne in Paris, where, in the company of Pindar and Heraclitus, students from the École Normale Supérieure (chosen by Jean Lallot) joined us and others for discussions. There was a hint of conspiracy in the air in this 1960's milieu. Around a table, the face of things changed; there was no room for lectures, and few assertions stood up to examination. Moreover, philology as such led to exclusion from the fold. There was no institutional framework for this orientation: its technical aspects made it special, but it was too free and personal to be specialized.

A total lack of response from the scientific community—a largely fictitious community, in fact—has the effect of censorship. Exclusion is at once real and unreal; the lack of response actually hinges on a lack of expectations and of appropriate preparation. It has implications for the whole system of recruitment and training of teachers in secondary and higher education. Confronted with these obstacles, one is almost obliged to defend one's way of thinking by creating other forms of exchange. Scholars are led to regroup in circles with common intellectual and scientific interests. This means a different, more limited kind of community. It may appear esoteric, but it tends to make itself known and welcomes publicity; it acquires the means to develop—in private, by substitution, in a common effort—a more legitimate public opinion.

Official doctrine maintained that science was not good for students. In Lille, I tried as hard as I could to organize a somewhat marginal research space alongside the formal education system. With Heinz Wismann, we got the students together in the attics and basements of the university, so to speak, and I continued this practice with Philippe Rousseau, then with Pierre Judet de La Combe and André Laks. By creating new ways of working, we believed we could transform minds. The closed system current at the time had been shattered, but the struggle did not end after 1968; ephemeral agreements masked divergent aims. All the same, new curricula have been introduced, and they have led to the creation of a research center in Lille that strives to live up to its ambition.[4]

Works Cited

Bollack, J. 1996. "Durchgänge." In *Zeitenwechsel. Germanistische Literaturwissenschaft vor und nach 1945*, ed. W. Barner and C. Koenig, 387–403. Frankfurt.

Judet de La Combe, P., and H. Wismann, eds. 2009. "Liminaire." *La lecture insistante: autour de Jean Bollack*. Colloque de Cerisy (July 11-18), 19–32. Paris.

[4] For information on this research center, see Judet de La Combe and Wismann 2009.

2

Reading the Philologists[†]

BY OPTING FOR *PHILOLOGISCHE WISSENSCHAFT*, "philological science," with texts at the center, and not for *Altertumswissenschaft*, or "archaeological science," within the field of criticism—in a sense, against criticism and against a form of "essayism,"[1] as a way of acquiring the means for understanding—I was referring to a practice. At the same time I discovered unresolved problems, as well as good solutions that had been proposed by philologists and then rejected. So my analysis incorporated the study of obstacles that were not mere errors or inadequacies; the point was less to explore the substance of biases than to find the spots where obstructions had been erected. Blockages were closely linked to the way the scientific method was practiced; they revealed what was unscientific about the method. These extrinsic elements were thus linked to the object, but not limited to it; they also touched on its role in an independent and pre-constituted order of representation, so much so that I considered it useful, indeed imperative, to incorporate into my own approach the critic's social environment in its specific aspects: these were usually associated with national origin but sometimes more universal in nature. (A colloquium held in Lille in 1977 was devoted to this topic: "Philology and National Cultural Traditions.")

This was Pierre Bourdieu's central thesis: that censoring mechanisms were linked not only to the specific posture of the interpreter, and thus to an identifiable prejudice, but just as much to the interpreter's function, which determines a practice and, like a matrix, produces a chain of reaction and commentaries. This can be confirmed by going from the study of one culture to another, as I did in the body of work I began in "M. de W.-M. en France": this was some fifty years after the scholar's death, at that crucial point in time when one can

---

[†] Originally published as "Lire les philologues," in: Jean Bollack, *La Grèce de personne: les mots sous le mythe* (Paris, 1997), pp. 25–28.
[1] [TN: In French, the *essai* is a literary or philosophical form in which the author tries to move beyond university scholarship to reach a broader public. "*Essayisme*" indicates an excessive use of the *essai*, which is considered a substitute for a documented analysis. Thanks to Mayotte Bollack for this clarification.]

begin to talk about such things.[2] Next door, in France, scholars had declared an interest in adopting or adapting this scientific method (and had been doing so for a hundred and fifty years), but they never succeeded, because they could not or would not sacrifice the traditional methods that occupied the same space in the field.

Philology as I prefer to understand it, including the comprehension of a work's historical content, had not (and still has not) gained a foothold, because it also forms a closed universe, focused on the search for meaning. It constructs its own horizon, which allows us to read. But it was equally important to show that this science, when it was not rejected as non-science, was still limited by a host of inadequate opinions; it was important to show, moreover, that these restrictions would surely not have been shared by other, better-informed and more open-minded people who had been excluded either by their own choices or by the constraints of academic institutions. The conflict was intense. My essay "Odysseus among the Philologists"[3] tries to highlight a double aberration of ideas in the hermeneutic appearance of the work of the great masters, and, outside the field, in secondary and substitute constructions. Narratology and structural anthropology provided some keys to reading without really adding anything new.

Looked at this way, philology creates its own history, by dint of delving into its inherent alienation. It tries to find itself through cathartic exercises and uncovers the conditions of an internal liberation, at a time when it is subject to outside threats from the standpoint of a dogmatic pluralism and by a radical challenge to choices made by earlier generations. The discipline has a tedious side. It is not of great interest unless one finds the compensatory pleasure of discovery, unless the search for precise meanings, so often lost, is at its center and makes it a matter of contemporary concern. Discovering the forms alienation takes among philologists—their tendency to pursue archaeological, paleological, political, psychological, or other avenues of investigation—makes it possible to reveal and set aside the prejudices that color their readings. However, the meaning, even after part of the obstruction is removed, is not self-evident; only by looking for meaning do we become aware of the obstacles.

My commentary on *Oedipus Rex* (*Oedipe roi*, 1990) led me to the realization that the two approaches are interdependent. One goes straight to the text, and the immediacy that one maintains, undeterred by prior commentaries, nevertheless depends on the analysis of the earlier intermediaries, whether they have produced accurate readings or not. But those mediations need to be taken

---

[2] See Bollack 1997:60–92, on Ulrich von Wilamowitz-Moellendorff (1848–1931).

[3] See below, Chap. 3; first published as "Ulysse chez les philologues" in *Actes de la recherche en sciences sociales* 1 (1975): 9–35; reprinted in Bollack 1997:29–59.

further. The whole range of solutions adopted in the past presents an unquestionable advantage for anyone wanting to legitimize the choice that is to be made. In a way, it is all or nothing, since only a well-founded proposition can be defended and discussed; comparing all prior arguments eliminates arbitrariness while keeping subjectivity in check. The rational and demonstrative criterion for one's choice has to be put forward. Its motive is at once literary and technical.

I used the same method in analyzing the poems of the contemporary poet Paul Celan, whose work has been the object of thousands of scholarly studies all over the world for several decades. Different critical stances are evident here too, with all their biases. I was able to defend a semantic system against an obstinate refusal (which can be analyzed) to accept it. Its "reception" looks like a failure to listen, a rejection. One may wonder what positive progress this battle allowed me to make; my comprehension of the poems improved thanks to the passage of time, but surely also thanks to the struggle itself. In any case, comparing different readings involves the study of theoretical positions, be they implicit or openly stated, and necessarily contributes, at this level, to a deeper understanding of the prerequisites of a universally unknown poetic diction. Would we discover its laws if we did not uphold their specificity and their difference?

Recognition of the results acquired and the concomitant influence exerted on the direction of research are always dependent on pre-constituted intellectual boundaries that, whether they be ontological or analytical, cannot be discounted as long as they are current and take the place of other approaches. Progress requires provisional recourse to specific forms of logic, shielded from any activism or forced contextual adaptations; an in-depth study leads to renewed studies; one accepted correction leads to a second, which calls the first into question. If we start all over again, it is because we are engaging in discussion.

Works Cited

Bollack, J. 1990. *L'Œdipe roi de Sophocle: le texte et ses interprétations*. Lille.
———. 1997. *La Grèce de personne*. Paris.

3

Odysseus among the Philologists[†]

The Controversy

An Outdated Practice

CLASSICAL PHILOLOGY, the dominant discipline in higher education until the early twentieth century, has an ambiguous status; a definition of that status could explain why the field has never produced a theory of meaning, although it has produced numerous methodological works on which the other literary disciplines are based. On the one hand, it evolved into a formidable and illustrious science during the nineteenth century, on the same footing in principle as all the others: thus it relinquished its prerogatives while still defending them by invoking the sacrosanct and prestigious nature of its subject matter. On the other hand, the means at its disposal within academies and universities, even if these were used only to organize subdivisions and auxiliary branches, were granted by virtue of its role within the pedagogical systems of the various countries involved. Yet scientific results were not taken into consideration at this level. Even in the past, the texts for which classical philology was responsible had long borne the imprint of the purposes they were intended to serve, purposes always different from those of the original texts, precisely where those texts had had the most profound influence on systems of thought. This ambiguous status—science and guardianship—prevented philology from questioning the values that it invoked and that were the basis for its influence; this alone explains why it instinctively declined to develop a theory of works or a technique of reading, or to define the nature of the texts under its aegis. Research of that sort would have been incompatible with the stability it represented. And yet, some reflection on the conditions of their practice might have led philologists to conduct a historical review of the uses made of the texts,

[†] Originally published as "Ulysse chez les philologues," in: Jean Bollack, *La Grèce de personne: les mots sous le mythe* (Paris, 1997), pp. 29–59.

uses that created the subject matter of the field. Having failed to engage in such reflection, they have deprived themselves of the epistemological grounding that would have justified the field's ambitions and scaled down its pretentions.

The philologists contrast one interpretation with another; they accumulate points of contention *ad infinitum* through marginal notations and corrections, as if controversy—which they mock, as Montaigne did, but still engage in—were integral to the nature of commentary. But these debates, while necessary to the survival of the practice, would be supplanted if the origins of the proposed translations and of the causes of error were studied; such study would show that, if scholars have not reached a conclusion, it is because, for reasons linked to the way their culture is organized, the very framing of the questions has made it impossible to draw conclusions.

An analytic, rather than descriptive, history of interpretation, which might reconnect opinions with the factors on which they were based, is particularly valuable if it analyzes the process of constituting an illusory science; and, in the specific case of Homeric criticism, it can show how the various approaches, originally intended to clear up difficulties, in fact transformed those difficulties into means appropriate to the organization of a discipline that has prevailed for over a century and still sustains debate. This situation arose because the approach in question had managed to design a virtually autonomous academic and academically profitable system of questions and answers that do not actually refer to the subject; Homer is the case in point. This doxography is necessary to the practice because it isolates the critical points that Homeric analysis, the philological method *par excellence*, exploits; it views them as flaws in the work, whereas the process of reading, in its very flow, blends and assimilates them. Above all, however, only a comprehensive view of the whole series of interpretations and the historical factors that underlie them, even if we are simply looking at errors, can allow us to move beyond doxography. The best way of avoiding the professional game of controversy is to categorize all opinions and to reconstitute, through them, the representational system that is still in use, except when the text is called upon to support an ideology or to implement a theory, aesthetic or otherwise. In the latter case, the material in question is marked by the tradition developed by earlier interpretations, so much so that it is the tradition that makes use of the users. The philologist critic has as his material, on the one hand, the text or the potentiality of a meaning, and, on the other, all the ways the text has been used—that is to say, the history and culture of each interpreter; thus it is necessary to determine whether or not one is speaking in the interpreter's name when one means to speak in the name of the text.

The scholars' disdain for theories—which they teach even though they view them as mere devices or distractions compared to facts, such as archaeological remains or "established" meanings—explains why philologists have never included the history of errors in a systematic deliberation on which their science could have been based. The absence of a theory of their own corresponds to their scorn for the theories of others. The principle for analyzing the Homeric poems, which constituted one of the achievements of the philological method, was rarely discussed by the authors who applied it, and no doubt it would not have been imposed as a practice if it had not produced facts that could be reinterpreted indefinitely. The errors that these facts implied were never discussed, because they lacked believers and advocates. Now, facts established by error cannot be acknowledged in the system in which they lurk without a re-examination of the principles that constituted them; in the same way, one cannot go beyond the accepted meanings without analyzing the tradition those meanings have produced.

The Homeric Question

Philologists have been even more preoccupied with the genesis of Greek epic than with the birth of tragedy; for more than a century, the question of genesis has been at the center of a debate in which what was at issue was certainly not Homer himself, but rather the material attributed to him. The successive positions adopted by philologists are more evident here than elsewhere; they control and encompass hypotheses and theoretical formulations down to the smallest detail, so that readers are authorized to equate a particular hypothesis with a particular theoretical position, thus bypassing the laborious and thankless task of contending with the numerous variants of a given hypothesis. Thus there will never be any question, in the present essay, of criticizing errors or even revealing them as such.

The debate can best be examined starting at the moment when a modern problematic arose, stemming from the Romantic era: it is known as "the Homeric question." Ever since Friedrich August Wolf's 1795 *Prolegomena ad Homerum*,[1] which sought to systematize certain ideas outlined by earlier scholars (d'Aubignac, Vico, and others), the question of the genesis of the Homeric songs has remained on the table. The Romantics had been searching the epic for a Homer more naïve than Homer, more primitive and closer to the gods, while the historians, despite all their hard work, succeeded only in constructing some "earlier states" of the epic, which explained the version that had been transmitted as the end point of an evolution. However, the theory of autonomous songs, given credence by Karl Lachmann's *Betrachtungen über Homers*

---

[1]   Wolf 1985.

Ilias (Reflections on Homer's *Iliad*, 1837), a theory more applicable to the *Iliad* than to the *Odyssey*, to be sure, was still attached to the dream of a primitive popular poetry that had so fascinated the Romantics. But as critical observations became richer and hypotheses were reinforced, history triumphed over myth. In a recent stage, one that survives in contemporary works, the historical perspective, which ought to have made it possible to write an early history of the Greeks based on reconstituted legends, has also been abandoned in favor of an analysis that claims to be the most exact possible description of the subject. Historical precision in such works as Peter Von der Mühll's *Kritisches Hypomnema zur Ilias* (Critical Commentary on the *Iliad*)[2] no longer seeks independent justification beyond itself.

As for the *Odyssey*, certain parts of which I propose to consider here, scientific research, in the sense in which nineteenth-century historicists understood the term, led to University of Berlin professor Adolf Kirchhoff's 1859 study *Die Homerische Odyssee und ihre Entstehung* (The Homeric *Odyssey* and its Origins; expanded in 1879). Kirchhoff's undertaking, which aimed to single out a primitive *Return* (or *Nostos*) in the Homeric poem, was considered the unquestionable basis for later work. Ulrich von Wilamowitz-Moellendorff, in the preface to his *Homerische Untersuchungen* (Homeric Analyses, 1884),[3] declared: "I refer most frequently not to the extant text of the poem, but to Kirchhoff's *Odyssey*" (p. 3); and Eduard Schwartz, in the preface to his 1924 *Odyssey*, remarked that he considered "the method first used by Kirchhoff, and then improved by Wilamowitz, to be the only way to resolve the problems posed by the *Odyssey*" (p. 5). Finally, Peter Von der Mühll reminds us, in his article on the *Odyssey* in the *Real-encyclopädie* (1938), that research "should still and should always start anew from Kirchhoff" and "nowadays from Wilamowitz and above all from Schwartz." Schwartz was considered an absolute pinnacle, "without peer" in the world of criticism.[4]

The nine Wanderings of Odysseus, presented in groups of three, are found in Books 9, 10 and 12. They are arranged in such a way that two brief narratives precede a long one:

> Book 9: Cicones, Lotus-Eaters, *Cyclops*
>
> Book 10: Aeolus, Laestrygonians, *Circe*
>
> Book 12: Sirens, Charybdis and Scylla, *Cattle of the Sun*

---

[2] Von der Mühll 1952.

[3] The title pays homage to the Old Testament studies undertaken by Julius Wellhausen, one of Wilamowitz's colleagues in Greifswald.

[4] Von der Mühll 1940.

The descent into the Underworld, which is closely linked to the Circe episode, is recounted in Book 11.

At a stage when it no longer seemed possible to find any trace of a "collective soul" in the autonomous songs, Kirchhoff separated this group into two cycles, composed by two different authors. Amazingly, the separation was immediately greeted as a great feat of philological science, which was then at its most influential. This speculative thesis was attractive for its extreme simplicity, following the biological model of a body that develops and absorbs other bodies. The earlier poem, *The Return of Odysseus*, with the Calypso episode, the wreck of the raft, and the Phaeacians' welcome, was preserved in the extant *Odyssey*. As in the text we read today, Odysseus tells the Phaeacians what has befallen him since his departure from Troy. But the narratives that we expect to find in the Adventures were not all included; only the three episodes of Book 9 remained (Cicones, Lotus-Eaters, and Cyclops), along with a shortened version of the descent into the Underworld. The original kernel had germinated and produced a series of expansions. The ancient poem was not included in its entirety in Book 9 itself; Kirchhoff construed the ending of that book as the result of an adaptation. In order to "organize" the poem that we call the *Odyssey*, a poet, the writer, the "*diaskeustēs*,"[5] had drawn on another cycle, *The Adventures of Odysseus*, which provided him with the second series of stories, from Aeolia to the sacred oxen of Helios (Books 10 and 12), as well as most of the description of Odysseus with the Phaeacians.

Kirchhoff thought he had two proofs of this division of the poem into layers; according to him, the wrath of Poseidon, which struck after the blinding of the Cyclops, formed the kernel of the epic of the Return, since the god is the hero's implacable enemy. The other "wrath," that of Helios in response to the sacrifice of his cattle, is superfluous. Secondly, Kirchhoff detected traces of a shift from the third to the first person of the verb in the simple fact that Odysseus speaks of events he has not witnessed himself. These indications affected the second cycle, Books 10 and 12, which the organizer had introduced afterwards.

In the absence of such criteria, Kirchhoff attached the story of the Cyclops to the oldest layer on the basis of its quality. Unlike inferiority, excellence did not need to be demonstrated, it was instantly recognizable: "the poetic quality of the description of the Cyclops adventure is equal to the other parts of the ancient Return" (characterized in the same way and needing no explanation); "If there is anyone who cannot feel this difference [between the first and second

---

5 [TN: A *diascévaste* was a critic who edited and corrected texts. The term was applied in particular to Greek critics from Alexandria who worked on Homer, organizing the Songs, checking the authenticity of certain lines, and making corrections.]

series of Adventures], then I can do nothing for him; he must judge as best he can."[6] Such was the tone of academic discourse in those days.

Some years later, Wilamowitz proposed a different structure, which retained the division of the Adventures but shifted the moment of their linkage, and thus the origin of the poem, further back in time; the writer of our *Odyssey* was modifying a text that had already been modified. In fact, Wilamowitz imagined an "earlier *Odyssey*," comprising a certain number of constitutive elements such as the epic of Calypso and a descent into the Underworld; it featured a longer poem that included Books 10 and 12, that is, the second cycle of Adventures that Kirchhoff had isolated. The "editor" who had already compiled the "Ancient *Odyssey*" gathered these scattered parts into a whole. The split motifs and the doublets, considered imperfections, could be explained by the fact that he had to use the same theme more than once. In the Calypso epic, the wreck of the raft led Odysseus to Ithaca; in the poem used by Wilamowitz, Odysseus succeeds in reaching the Phaeacians after the shipwreck. By situating the Calypso episode between the shipwreck and the arrival on the island of the Phaeacians, the "editor" had created confusions that interfered with the reading of the *Odyssey*, as the scholarly readers of the time saw it.

Among the elements that Wilamowitz attributed to the earliest version of the descent into the Underworld, he retained the wrath of Poseidon, the cause of Odysseus' tribulations. He concluded that the blinding of the Cyclops, the origin of the curse, formed part of the same textual unit. He endorsed Kirchhoff's opinion that the beginning of the Wanderings (Book 9) had been composed in the first person, while the adaptation of the other stories (Books 10 and 12) had led to a transposition to direct discourse. Thus the obvious links between the first and second parts of the Wanderings, as well as those between the stories of Calypso and Circe, were not ascribed to authorial intent but to a perfunctory work of adaptation. In fact, they were interpreted as borrowings. From then on, every connection confirmed the hypothesis of a secondary fusion, where traces of the operation had remained visible.

Wilamowitz—who was at the beginning of his career—remained loyal to the principles of Kirchhoff's analysis, but he burrowed further down into the thick of successive historical layers; so successful was he that it became possible to date time periods or situate places thanks to different fragments of poems. The benefits were immense. After Kirchhoff and Wilamowitz, other reconstructions of the poem's genesis were proposed, but the separation into two cycles remained the prevailing dogma.[7] The approach to reading taught by the philologists thus

---

[6] Kirchhoff 1859:216.
[7] See for example Merkelbach 1951:175–176, on Kirchhoff's analysis, and Kirk 1962:234, on the subject of oral poetry.

consisted in spotting the double usages and discussing the contradictions as a way of positing the existence of earlier versions of the text.

Analyzing the Analysis

Analytic criticism (or Separatist criticism, according to some orthodox French scholars) became firmly established after Lachmann presented his "Reflections on Homer's *Iliad*" at the Berlin Academy in 1837 and 1841. This form of criticism developed throughout the expansionist period of classical philology—the expansion no doubt sustained by the sense that philology was in competition with the other sciences. Analytic criticism spread across several countries thanks to the prestige enjoyed by German science, and in the field of Homeric studies it was only supplanted as a scientific theory of the genesis of poems by work on oral poetry. To be sure, the Unitarian thesis had been regularly defended for a century or so in the ebb and flow of protest movements. But the feats of Analysis seemed like great achievements and enjoyed scientific prestige. The Unitarians were reduced to defending themselves with commentaries that smacked of a conventional and sometimes puerile aesthetics. Justifying the text at the same level of interpretation as their adversaries, they deprived themselves of the opportunity to dispute the principles of analytic criticism. Unity could only be defended by another "science." And for the moment, science, one and indivisible, was in the hands of the Separatists. Their opponents were often on the fringe, considered mere aesthetes; some were high-school teachers.[8] The Analysts were well ensconced at the top of the university hierarchy.

The writings of the Analysts proved so difficult that the average reader found them inaccessible, and this acted as a selective principle. It is arduous enough to follow an argument that is based on textual fragmentation. Add to that a critical apparatus indicating attributions, allusions, footnotes, implicit references, and it all showed contempt for literary and non-specialist writing. The theories of earlier scholars and colleagues in the field were presumed to be well known, invoked as self-evident, and relentlessly corrected. Reading the work of an Analyst is a test for the initiated.

In setting themselves apart from ordinary readers, the Analysts abandoned exegesis. Indeed, their operations could not be based on an obscure text needing clarification. Critical explication of a text of any kind was relegated to an inferior level, the realm of teachers. In contrast to Aeschylus, Homer was considered an author without affectation, since he had always been proclaimed a naïve

---

[8] In England, Andrew Lang, a fierce defender of unity, was a man of letters, and in France many men of the cloth, such as Georges-Michel Bertrin (1851–1924) and Victor Terret (1856–?), supported the cause; cf. n. 28 below.

genius. It was easier to construct vast hypotheses than to acknowledge the real difficulties posed by exegesis. But above all, if philology was to retain its stature, it had to be differentiated from an activity that was considered unoriginal, appropriate only for students. Analysis was a science: not a science of the text, but a science that used the text to constitute itself as science. Basing their power on the place society accorded to the humanities in the training of elites, and on the importance assigned to the preparation of schoolteachers, the philologists were all the more powerful because they built their scientific prestige on a subject matter that was never discussed in response to the pedagogical needs of their audience, nor in terms of the usefulness of their knowledge. Science lay elsewhere; it had different goals.

All this led to a paradoxical situation: the leading scholars, conscious of this dualism and of the pedagogical inefficacy of Analysis, belittled the naïve understanding of the classics that had nevertheless been the prerequisite of their own academic power and the basis for their work. Left to the Unitarians and the public at large, aesthetic appreciation characterized what was not science.

The scientific method, cold and relentless, is a necessary evil for "modern man." But the aesthetic sense remains a first cause, which must be used with skill since it offers the wherewithal to support the cult. A certain linguistic violence—the use of a curt anti-rhetorical language—characterizes university society at the highest levels, especially in Germany, and sometimes in England: it is a language of the concrete, of efficacy, through which this group believes it has access to the reality of the affairs and actions from which the University as such is cut off. (In France, the style has remained more pompous and hollow, less aristocratic, because the differentiation between scientific and aesthetic discourse was not produced in the same way.) Like a mask over a brutal and destructive reality, the sense of beauty has the sole function of compensating for a necessary evil and of making the inevitable acceptable—for Homer, division and disparagement. This form of discourse—heir to the rhetoric of the humanists, carefully preserved in France—and even Romantic glorification are occasionally used by a scholarly enterprise that rejects them. Academism is not taken seriously enough for it to get drawn into the game, always remaining prudently allusive, failing to assert itself, and protecting itself by referring to facts.

Thus science, which is addressed to universal reason, occupies the position of an esoteric activity, reserved for the rare initiates. In contrast, meaning, which is hidden and speaks only to visionaries, is in the public domain, with the result that the in-depth exegesis that would have gone beyond pedagogical practice, and that continues to thrive in certain circles, is dismissed as sheer fantasy or theological raving.

The Spoils of Historical Reading

Analytic criticism could be augmented by other sciences because its work with texts led to the discovery of vanished civilizations in their successive stages and their mutual relationships, and because it sought to rely on historical material. It had already taken over the methods of textual criticism by making even accidental defects into something rich in historical meanings. These accidents served the Analysts' aims so well that the repetition of such a fortuitous event might well cause readers to doubt that it had actually occurred. Their criticism became confused with comparisons of documents; as a result, literary history was flooded with factitious works. This historical type of exercise, which produced facts that were then related to other external facts, provided material for much university research, for many published books and endless controversies. Interpretation, confirmed by the text, would unquestionably be less rich, less expansive, and finally less "profitable."

Some Analytic specialists have declared the division of the Adventures to be an established fact: they include such scholars as Von der Mühll (1940 [1938]) and Merkelbach (1951), as well as those more interested in folklore, Karl Meuli (1975 [1921]) and Denys Page (1955),[9] along with such theorists or proponents of oral poetry as G. S. Kirk (1962). By retaining earlier arguments, the Analysts emphasized the difference between the more realistic style of the first cycle of the Wanderings, and the more fantastical style of the second, where metamorphoses, evil spells, and magic tricks are more numerous; they also stressed the differences in locale, the western Mediterranean for the first part, the East for the second: "when Odysseus left the island of Aeolus he was in the Far West of the world; quite suddenly (and without warning to the audience) he finds himself in the Far East."[10] If, on leaving Troy, Odysseus passes through Thrace, land of the Cicones, if he is hurled beyond Cape Malea, south of the Peloponnese, toward the west, toward the coasts of Africa or of southern Italy, where the home of the Cyclops is reputed to be, we cannot understand how, if he were heading for Ithaca, he should be transported to the domain of Circe, in the land of the rising Sun. This inconsistency could only be justified by an interpolation linking the eastern part of the Wanderings to an external source. This source was the epic of the Argonauts' expedition, of which there is no trace in the literature, an epic linked to the Milesian colonization of the shores of the Black Sea (between 700

---

[9] Meuli 1975, 2:593–676. The influence of this doctoral dissertation, which developed a point raised by Kirchhoff, can be explained by the impact of the proof produced by topographical and literary evidence as to the source of the second cycle of the Adventures; see also Page 1955.

[10] Page 1955:2.

and 550 BCE?).[11] Indeed, the east was Jason's domain. Deep internal analysis of the poem led scholars to posit multiple authors, and then to establish a map of the sources, so that all the leaps and vagaries of the imagination, considered typical of Homer, could be attached to actual geographical locations. It was in fact possible to retrace a heroic itinerary in one of the sources, even if the trajectory had been interrupted in the *Odyssey*. The motifs of the legend of the Argonauts, which were more or less well known from later texts, had the advantage of being linked to names of actual people and places. Jason's story provided a useful framework for developing the idea of an objective genre like the epic. Circe is sister to Aietes, king of Colchis, a country that can be pinpointed on a map and the destination of the expedition. She is also a sorceress like Medea, King Aietes' daughter. The wrath of Helios was understood as a familial trait, because Aietes is Helios' son. The Laestrygones were identified as the Dolions of Cyzicus, in the Propontis (Sea of Marmara), since the fountain named Artakia, where the scouts sent by Odysseus meet the king's daughter (*Odyssey* 10.105–106), can be found in Cyzicus, on the road to Colchis. Once the fiction of this phantom poem of the *Argonauts* had been established as the source of all the Wanderings, from Aeolia[12] to the sacred cattle of Helios, other connections could be determined and discussed: that the ship Argos sailed past the Sirens with Orpheus on board to protect the heroes, and that Phineus, combining the roles assigned to Tiresias and Circe in the *Odyssey*, pointed out the route they should take. The replicated elements were considered richer and more realistic: Orpheus, overcoming the lure of the Sirens through his song, afforded a much more beautiful and more ancient evocation than that of Odysseus, who resists by having his crew tie him to the mast;[13] the spell could have been broken by Orpheus, a member of the expedition, competing with the sea monsters.

An Artificial Construction; the Example of the Planctae

The Planctae,[14] at the beginning of *Odyssey* 12, appeared to provide proof of a borrowing—and of a division of the poem—that served as a starting point for all that followed. The explication of this text clearly reveals how the reading material was concocted.

---

[11] See the authors cited by Merkelbach 1951:201n1 (Wilamowitz, Friedländer, Kranz).

[12] Depending on the author, the crucial element, the floating island of Aeolia, does or does not belong to the second series of Adventures.

[13] But according to other critics, Homer surpasses his model in the episode of the Sirens (Merkelbach 1955:207, following Meuli).

[14] [TN: *Planctae* has been translated in various ways: for example, as "Rovers" in Lattimore's translation (1965) and as "Clashing Rocks" (Lindsay 1965).]

Odysseus is presented with two routes to follow: Circe's description of them will help him choose, but he must make up his own mind (lines 57–58). Once past the Sirens, he will find "overhanging rocks" that the gods, in their language, call "Planctae." On one side, among the reefs, there is a smooth rock beyond which no bird flies, where at times even one of the doves bringing ambrosia to Zeus may disappear. Each time, Zeus replaces the dove. On the other side, no boat skirting the rock can avoid shipwreck, whether it is swallowed up by the waves or engulfed in flames. Only the ship Argo has managed to pass safely on her return from Colchis, thanks to Hera, who protected Jason (lines 59–72).

The two routes, the passage of Scylla and that of Charybdis, are in a single strait; Odysseus must pass one after the other, and he has to decide which to pass first; however, commentators have spread them out geographically, as if there were two separate itineraries. No doubt the idea of a single strait, with a dividing line down the middle, did not come to mind immediately. Since no one saw that Scylla and Charybdis formed the outward and return journeys on the same route, or that the smooth rock and the rough chasm offered the choice implied by the advice Circe gives Odysseus to opt for Scylla (lines 106–110), where no one would hesitate for a moment between death and the lesser evil, the interpreters created a second term—the Planctae—in a heroic dilemma that Odysseus was to confront with his virile powers. Should he not have to make a choice, as befits a hero? Very different routes, each one demanding precise navigational instructions, better fulfilled the conditions of a choice. However, Circe not only knows both routes, but she also knows which one Odysseus will choose: "I will no longer tell you in detail which way / of the two your course must lie, but you yourself must consider / this in your own mind. I will tell you the two ways of it."[15] Odysseus will not choose, he will agree to it of his own accord, since he will accept the prescribed course. The power of the deity remains absolute; that of Odysseus too, since he is free to refuse, although only at the cost of his life.

The generic term "overhanging rocks" does not necessarily capture the real antithesis between Scylla and Charybdis. Victor Bérard,[16] for example, distinguishes between the "rocks" and the "reefs," and attributes the two terms to different sites, contrasting the two "reefs" of the Strait of Messina to the rock formations between the islands of Lipari and Vulcano:

> For small ships departing from Monte Circeo on the Lazio coast and heading toward some port in the southern seas, there are two possible routes: one to the east of Sicily via Messina, the other to the west via

---

[15]   *Odyssey* 12.56–58. All references to and citations from the *Odyssey* are from the Lattimore edition.
[16]   Bérard 1924, 2:2.

Trapani. The eastern route passes Charybdis; the western one passes through a "gate" where even today sailors describe, in their *Nautical Instructions* (no. 731, p. 132), "two remarkable rocks: the northern one, the *Pietra Lunga*, 47 meters high, is a volcanic jumble, at the base of which is a large opening that allows small craft to go through it; the other rock, the *Pietra Menalta*, is much lower and is usually covered with large seagulls that are prized by the local inhabitants." The rocks guard the strait between Lipari and the fiery island of Vulcano.[17]

At the outset the two rocks have a name in the language of the gods. But what term corresponds to it in the language of humans? In the Circe episode, humans do not have a name for the plant that the gods call *mōlu* because they are unacquainted with the plant. But the term "Planctae" is a translation of Scylla and Charybdis.[18] Now, the difference in names allowed some scholars to designate two distinct geographic locations.[19] Since Homer mentions here that the ship Argo succeeded in navigating the passage of the Planctae, there seems to be a clear allusion to a different expedition, to another itinerary with different stages. In Pindar (*Pythian Odes* 4.207–211), the Argo's passage resulted in the rocks becoming fixed, rocks that had at first been roving (or "Planctae"), and that by clashing together had always crushed the boats. That is why Homer was thought to have invented another dangerous passage, namely, Scylla and Charybdis ("a gateway to the next world, borrowed from another sailor's tale," according to Meuli[20]). It seems that no one ever accepted the possibility that Jason had been able to pass Charybdis before Odysseus.

However, focusing on the Planctae sometimes led to insurmountable difficulties of comprehension, and the persistence of the error shows how powerful this preconceived idea was. It spread very approximate translations through generations of students (especially in lines 59, 62, 66, and 73). If the two routes—with the birds on one side and the Argo on the other—are part of a distinct itinerary, that of the Planctae, then the smooth rock does not refer to Scylla and the seething vapors are not Charybdis; it must be the case that, after mentioning the Planctae, Homer continues to speak of the other route. The text says, in

---

[17] Bérard 1924, 2:115.

[18] Von der Mühll (1953, col. 729) believes that *Planctae* is the divine "translation" of the name for the Symplegades ("which clash together"); other scholars think that the Planctae have nothing to do with the Symplegades, which lie near the Bosphorus, or with Jason; see Bollack 1976:173.

[19] On the contrary, the double name should lead us to ask why the gods speak differently from humans here, and why, if the etymology of the name is "roving," they should say that the Planctae "rove."

[20] Meuli 1975:89. But if the Planctae were no longer dangerous, why does Circe not advise Odysseus to take this route?

effect, that these "roving" rocks are "two reefs." In the rest of the story, when Odysseus, following Circe's instructions, sails on his way, the interpreters fail to understand why there is no further mention of the Planctae, nor even of the need to avoid them—and this omission is blamed on the poet's ineptitude. Other contradictions have been resolved by the usual means of correction or a skillful translation. The Planctae are mentioned again at the end of the episode (lines 260–261): "when we had fled away from the Rocks, and dreaded Charybdis and Scylla," says Odysseus. The word "Rocks" is replaced by the word "reefs,"[21] or, more commonly, a composite figure is constructed whereby Odysseus flees both the Rocks (the Planctae) and Scylla and Charybdis. At the end of the poem, when the Wanderings are recapitulated, Odysseus is said to have passed by the Planctae and Scylla and Charybdis. Scholars consider this passage to be an interpolation; either the line is written in a slipshod way (evoking the Planctae *and* Scylla and Charybdis) or else, if the words can be taken at face value, the annotator has made a mistake. Bérard writes:

> Ever since ancient times, since Aristotle it seems, in the absence of word for word explanations of the Homeric text, no one knew where to find these Planctae Rocks, which I call by the French name of a similar rock formation in the Anglo-Norman islands [*Pierres du Pinacle*]. In our version of the *Odyssey* we have a strange contradiction here: it is in lines 309–344 inserted into Book xxiii, which some Alexandrian commentators were already reading in their editions, but which others condemned. In line 327, Odysseus is said to have sailed to the Planctae Rocks, as well as to Charybdis and Scylla. So the Planctae ended up being confused with the latter pair.[22]

The commentators did not go back to reconsider what was accepted as an established fact.

The incident of the Planctae shows that an entity and a place can be endowed with a name, shorn of its referents and its links. Even if this entity has been deemed pointless, it is nevertheless retained:

> At this point, the poet mentions the ship Argo, and in so doing, cites his source. It is true that, after the ship's passage, the terror prompted by the strait has abated, and the poet seems to have been aware of this, even though Circe speaks of it as if the Planctae represented a dire peril. The poet lets Circe describe the Planctae, but in what follows he has no

---

[21] Bérard 1924, 2:122.

[22] Bérard 1924, 2:113–114, ad 12.61; Bérard does not construct 13.327 in the same way as 12.260; otherwise he would have had to identify the Planctae with Scylla and Charybdis.

role for them, creating instead a new obstacle for Odysseus: Charybdis and Scylla. Logically, he could have omitted the Symplegades–Planctae, but he seems to have wanted at least to mention this famous story of the Argonauts.[23]

This was how the work of the artist was represented.

Detail, which is of interest only to philologists, the experts, enters the construction built up by the lines of descent and everything that depends on them; here, the Planctae retain only their philological function; they are no longer a sign, as they were when, in the text, they maintained links with other parts of the narrative. The example demonstrates that the enormous work of two centuries of philology has often only minimally improved our understanding of Homer's text. From antiquity on, the Planctae have been Rovers. The error predates the analysis. So Homeric science has deprived readers even of what they could have understood on their own, by subjecting these passages to a scholarly transformation. The text was difficult, but once problems were erased they could never be resolved. From this interpretive void have arisen both constructions that tended to increase the interest of the text by external means and errors that obscured and deformed it.

Despite scholarly differences of opinion, this other route is solidly anchored in Homer's text today, an absurd stump, a vestige of a lost epic, or something like an incidental fact; and what has disappeared is the remarkable transfer of the action into a different action.

The representation of another way to pass between the clashing rocks made it impossible to appreciate the antithesis of the text, which distinguishes the heavenly route (with Zeus's doves) on the outward journey from the earthly route (with the Argo's crew) on the return journey. In the same way, when Charybdis and Scylla are assimilated into a single strait (one that Homer was thought to have invented, so that he could refashion the Planctae as two originally distinct sea monsters), the whole relationship between a world that is rising and a chasm that plunges downward is eliminated. There is a correspondence between the tribute paid by the birds and the tribute paid by Odysseus, between the return of the ship Argo and the solitary return of the hero of the *Odyssey*; within the Planctae themselves we find aspects of both Zeus and Hera, and the relation between these motifs leads to the discovery of the first terms of a meaning. Assigning the Planctae to the Jason legend is obviously the most economical

---

[23] Merkelbach 1951:205. Readings of this sort are very common. Lindsay (1965:8) writes: "In referring to the fact that the Argo's tale is everywhere known, I take [Homer] to be tactfully saying: I know that I have borrowed this whole complex of dangerous passages from that tale, so I ward off criticism by a side-admission." The tact no doubt lies with the critic rather than with Homer.

way of ironing out the difficulty. The restitution implied, for example, by the replacement of Zeus's nourishing birds makes no sense if one confuses the two routes, so as to make the crushing of the last dove, observed by Jason, a signal that the strait is open. Homer says that the birds are continually replaced. Thus it was necessary to accept the fact that he did a poor job of recounting the legend he was supposed to be repeating.[24]

Reaction to Analysis

The Sense of Unity

Analysis expanded rapidly and became a science in Germany. The favorable conditions in the university that had produced far less controversial work—for example, in the domain of verbal criticism and the differentiation of sources— had allowed Analysis to take shape, with all its discoveries and its blindness. Its reception in other countries, in France in particular,[25] reveals the existence of distinct trends; but these reactions all indicate how hard it is to integrate a method that has been developed elsewhere into one's own pedagogical system. Indeed, France had neither the institutions nor the tools needed to construct the sophisticated system that Analysis demanded.

In 1917, while the war was raging, Victor Bérard lamented the lack of organization in the French scientific community, and the victories that it had let slip by:

> In the days of Louis XIV, scholarly practices differed from those of the Scaligers, Casaubons and Turnèbes[26] and other fashions prevailed: the example or influence of the Jesuits had profound consequences for our national educational system, and had a long-term impact on our intellectual production. The Jesuits were concerned above all with literature, with fine speeches and pretty verses; for them, Antiquity represented merely the most useful subject matter for translation either into Latin verse or into "prayers" and French tragedies. From Louis XIV to Napoleon III, from the Revocation [of the Edict of Nantes] to the War of 1870, France left the responsibility for learning to a few

---

[24] It is impossible to include here the elements of an interpretation that has to take all the Adventures into account; I offered the outlines of such an interpretation during the course of several seminars in Lille and at the École Normale Supérieure (1971–1972).

[25] On the difficulties of adaptation in England, see Myres 1958, Chap. 9, on Wilamowitz.

[26] [TN: Joseph Justus Scaliger (1540–1609), a French Protestant scholar; Isaac Casaubon (1559–1614), a Huguenot born in Geneva; Adrien Turnèbe (1512–1565), a French poet and humanist. All were renowned classical scholars and were in contact with one another.]

"Benedictines," "specialists," "bookworms," whom they readily mocked ... For every Villoison that France produced, Germany immediately let loose some Wolf,[27] who, armed with all the resources of an organized scientific community, manufactured the "marketable" product.[28]

The French university system did not have the same power as Germany's; though the latter's power was not originally based on science, it had nevertheless created the conditions for scientific development. What Bérard failed to see was that France's weakness was the result of a state of mind of which he was the perfect example, and which continued to affect academic practices under the influence of his peers. The material situation was even less favorable after 1918.[29]

The opposition between pedagogical purpose and scientific practice did not surface in France; in the field of letters, science was represented by only a few isolated individuals whose prestige and ability to devote themselves to their work rested solely on their literary qualities. Since only one of the terms existed (that is, the training and the exercises that were supposed to develop literary prowess), conflict ensued when new methods of working, perfected over two generations in Germany, were imposed on a system that was incapable of integrating them without abandoning its own values. Reactions were not directed solely against Analysis as such, with its excesses and faults, but also against what it implied.[30]

---

[27] [TN: Jean-Baptiste Gaspard d'Ansse de Villoison (1750 or 1753–1805), a classical scholar; Friedrich August Wolf (1759–1824), a German philologist and critic. With the support of Frederick the Great, Wolf founded the science of philology at the University of Halle. See the Introduction to Wolf 1985 (1795), esp. 5–15, by Grafton, Most, and Zetzel for a particularly lucid brief account of early scholarship on the Homeric text.]

[28] Bérard 1917:283. In this belligerent pamphlet, Bérard asserted that German scholars took advantage of their own critical apparatus to steal from France the discoveries her own brilliant scholars had made.

[29] On the relationship between the rhetorical tradition of teaching and the inadequate conditions and tools of the trade, see Bourdieu and Passeron 1970:151–157.

[30] "For some time now, Europe has been in the grip of a spirit of skepticism. People looked back on the past, not as its heirs but as its adversaries. There was a tendency to take pleasure in contradicting it. As usual, Religion was the first victim. Many people, no doubt otherwise faithful to preconceived ideas, would have liked to contain the movement within the confines of religious matters. But one does not unleash a tempest without consequences. The spirit of criticism, hostile to authorized opinions, passed from the realm of Faith into that of literature, at the same time as it was making a dangerous incursion into questions of social order. The philological school in Germany signaled a sharp reaction against literary tradition. By calling into question the authenticity of several Platonic dialogues, other bold spirits went even further and even removed some of Cicero's works from his bibliography. Wolf went further than anyone in trying to use science to strip Homer of the two poems that have made him the most famous and revered name in all of literature" (Bertrin 1897:20–21).

As a historical science that disassembled the most sacrosanct texts, such as the Bible or Homer, in order to construct periods of history on the basis of a literary document, Analysis triumphed over its dissenters in Germany through the sheer force of its apparatus and the bulk of its production, rather than through debate. But the objections raised to Analysis in France were in fact—as can be seen through this symbolic case—an expression of the difficulties involved in adapting disciplines that were much less controversial, such as historical grammar, comparative grammar or textual criticism, to traditional teaching methods.[31] In conversations or lectures, the words "German" or "Germanic" often referred to science, whether positively or negatively; similarly, Analysis referred to German science in general.

Unitarianism was the natural position for an educational system that was based on the authority of the text (and not on that of the interpreter). It asserted its objection to Analysis in order to prove that Homer could be read without "science." It was not as if anyone, in establishing the text as it stood, had tried to examine it in depth. An initial line of defense consisted of turning to tradition and to the usual practices of scholastic explication. Later on, other scholars tried to demonstrate that Analysis could be considered a heresy.

It is true that Analysis unfairly adopts the forceful speech of the natural sciences, but the resistance mounted by those defending the rhetorical use of texts reveals their motives: by invoking the rights of the imagination and of emotion, they challenge all criticism, be it aesthetic or historical.

False Progress

Twenty years after the Franco-Prussian war of 1870, assimilation between the two intellectual communities had progressed to the point where, at least formally, it might lend itself to getting beyond the divide. Victor Bérard ventured without incident onto our Latin seas, relying on decades of explorers' narratives, but despite all appearances, his was a much less risky initiative than that of a professor and academician such as Alfred Croiset.[32]

---

[31] Even today, candidates for the *agrégation* in letters or grammar, who might aspire to a post in higher education, are not required to know how the text they are explicating is constituted, or even how its authenticity was established. They have not learned to read a critical apparatus.

[32] Aimé Puech (1924:93), in his obituary of Croiset: "Alfred Croiset's essential originality as a professor comes from the clear-sightedness with which he immediately recognized what higher education in France needed in the way of reforms and innovation, especially in the areas of ancient languages and literatures; from the time he entered the Sorbonne, he never forgot or misjudged the sound and useful aspects of the outdated concept of higher education that needed correction and expansion. In all this he remained true to the moderation that ruled his actions, wherever they were directed. He understood what was incomplete and what was still valid in the humanism of the preceding generation. He declared that, during the first two thirds of the

Bérard's work on Homer, the most extensive body of such work in France, is the result of a refusal to accept the divide, or rather of a quest to move beyond it. Everything in his work stems from this quest, and especially his modernism, which reveals a deeper attachment to cultural tradition than even Croiset's academicism. Bérard does not accept the terms of Analysis. Though he delights in pitting his adversaries against one another, as if the choice of method in philology were a matter of fashion, he never went beyond their premises or discussed their objections; but just as the Unitarians call everything that fails to fit into the textual unit an "interpolation," Bérard posits a primitive state so profoundly altered by the most ancient tradition that he feels free to take it apart without even reconstituting it. Prudence prevented him from venturing into the maze of philological constructions; rather than analyzing the science, he instead practiced it with a certain lack of rigor.[33]

Instead of historicizing the text by deriving a prehistory from its stratifications, Bérard starts out with a fact of extra-literary history, the maritime routes of the Phoenicians, and attaches the text to it. In so doing, he deploys all the charms of a simplistic archaeology, in the tradition of noble voyagers of yore, taking his reader around a familiar, tamed Mediterranean where it is hard to decide which is the more touching, the archaic survival of ancient practices in underdeveloped countries or the emotions aroused by the identification and occupation of specific locales.[34] The site and the photograph guide the reading and overshadow it: "All in all, this Odyssean description of the entrance to the

---

nineteenth century, the Germans had pulled ahead of us, and that to overtake them we had first of all to catch up, by making use of what they could teach us. But his aim was always to overtake them once we had matched them. I never heard him speak of his mentors with a severity that might verge on ingratitude, and I saw that he always maintained deliberate independence in regard to Germanic scholarship. If we read the preface to [Croiset's] *Histoire de la littérature grecque*, we shall see ... how, having determined with impartiality, but without allowing himself to be misled, the position taken by the Germans, he described the totally French work that he had decided to undertake with his brother, and [we shall see] whether it is possible to have at once more freedom of spirit and more intelligent loyalty to our national tradition."

[33] "It is a collection," Bérard writes of the epic, "of theatrical plays or dramas, of episodes, acts or scenes, that contain a great many serious conflicts; to reconcile and juxtapose them, scholars had to make additions, or make poorly executed cuts and patches whose traces are still visible; with these additions and splices, a whole series of flaws come to light ... the language and style are almost always of poor quality; imprecise terms obscure the thought; the haphazard assembly of lines or borrowed hemistiches jolts the pace of the narrative; the extravagance of detail and the vulgarity of the whole sometimes verge on brutality and even coarseness" (1931:185–186). The violence of these opinions is worthy of Wilamowitz.

[34] The relation between Bérard's (scholarly) commentaries and the themes addressed in his political writings, during the period of colonial imperialism, is obvious. The disputes among the great powers about trading posts, islands, or straits are prefigured in his *Odyssée d'Homère* (1931). According to his son Armand Bérard, in the biography that serves as a preface to his new edition of *Les navigations d'Ulysse*, "[H]is interest ... continued to be twofold, and would remain so all his

strait features only three or four inaccuracies. One is very serious, the other two or three minor, and all arise from the same source as the errors or inventions that we have already encountered in other landscapes in the tales."[35]

Thus Bérard remains all the more a prisoner of the traditional image of the poet and of poetry, in that he is dealing with literature, and uses scholarship only to compensate for the obvious flimsiness of his work. Even this scholarship is reworked, lightened, enlivened in an artificial way; the author knows how to manipulate erudition as well as anyone, without being bound by it as others are. His Homer is adapted to the tastes of a public he wants to surprise and entertain, teaching his readers that the epic is a drama, a theatrical and verbal staging; the poet is above all a sailor and his knowledge is derived from the Phoenicians, and so on. The *Odyssey* bears witness to a refined civilization very much like ours, almost Christian and French (Athena Polias, for example, is disguised as Notre-Dame-de-la-Ville[36]). In fact, accessibility is established as dogma. Homer's text is as clear as one of Voltaire's tales, at least when it has not been corrupted by an interpolator. Bérard's adaptation of Homer's text to the current fashion betrays the same timidity that in a different way marked Homer's assimilation within the university, immortalizing the scientific developments of the day in academic prose.

Geographic Readings

The lack of interest in the text itself was compensated for by the wealth of scholarly work produced. Since Analysis invited other analyses, the reconstitution of voyages based on elements in the poem, corrected *ad infinitum*, provided more fluid and malleable material for discussion than the text itself, and expanded the field of philology toward the historical and geographical sciences.

The Wanderings proceed among specific landmarks, which are few and far between. Like the characters,[37] space is depicted with a minimum of intellectual vision, as more real than in nature, in a precise, simplified, and elementary way. On leaving Troy, Odysseus visits the Cicones of Thrace, and then, when he is swept south, beyond Cape Malea in Greece, geographers tell themselves he has reached Africa, where they then place the Lotus-Eaters. Another detail: Circe's

---

life. He studied in parallel the politics of the contemporary and ancient worlds, colonizations and commercial practices from thirty centuries ago" (A. Bérard 1971:xi).

[35] Bérard 1929, 4:401, on the subject of the Sirens.

[36] Bérard 1931:111.

[37] As Kakridis (1971:14) remarks, "the poet's great creative power, which enables him to fashion his characters true to life, naturally induces the scholar ... to emancipate the heroic characters from within their poetic framework" so that concrete situations and individual reactions are reconstructed. In the same way, the very rudimentary nature of the topography of the *Odyssey* has encouraged scholars to fill in the gaps.

island is very far to the east. There may be a few other bits of information, about the land of the Laestrygonians and the entrance to the underworld. Apart from that, readers have only the direction of the winds behind the ship and the length of time between stops to give them their bearings, and sometimes even these clues are deliberately omitted. This omission has encouraged innumerable attempts to fix the sites and give the Wanderings a tangible basis in time and space. Indeed, throughout history many readers have enthused about the fantastic nature of the Wanderings, or have insisted on the unlikelihood of identifying a specific location. But in the absence of a theory of narrative, this kind of reading was more frivolous, and Analysis more precise, when it peeled away the layers of the composition. The attempt to assign specific places to the Wanderings must have seemed truly scientific in its turn, but less demanding.

The fantastic, on its own, would belong to the sort of tale that fits into the genre of universal folklore, but according to Bérard the poet uses fantastic elements in a realistic way. So Bérard can recognize in Scylla and Charybdis the theme of the Gate to the next world without using it to enhance his interpretation, and thus can write: "The channel is originally one of those marvelous gates of myth ... , but the poet no longer recognizes its significance, so the question is where the poet wants it to be in reality."[38]

Stripped of its proper purpose, the narrative can nevertheless be salvaged and used to establish a geography. Concrete information is culled from the myth—the configuration of a promontory or a port, a place name with its subsequent positioning; this is linked to authorial intent, while the rest is viewed as material the poet inherited. Bérard goes even further: he believes that the whole tale transposes details that are geographically accurate, so the role of interpretation is to eliminate the myth and to translate the elements into descriptive terms. He considers the difficulties arising from this approach as mere imprecisions, and ascribes them to Homer's lack of knowledge.

Other critics, like Wilamowitz, believed that the descriptions revealed traces of a primitive localization, earlier than the one preferred by the singer, and no longer associated with the narrative but rather with a fixed literary tradition. Thus Thrinacia, the island of the sacred cattle, would be placed in the Peloponnese region, and Scylla and Charybdis would refer to the strait between Cythera and Cape Malea. On this basis, starting from the original localization (which would be compatible with the source of an Oriental poem), once the western land of the Cyclops had been separated from the rest, in the interplay of re-readings the sites could be grouped between East and West, so as to be aligned with three phases of ancient history: the concentration in the Aegean

---

[38] In Finsler 1908, 1:22.

Sea (where the Oriental poem originated), the expansion to the shores of the Black Sea (the poem itself), and the colonization of the west (the land of the Cyclops in Book 9).

In France, Victor Bérard, who did not believe in Analysis or in the Unitarian theory of the poem and who wanted to "give the Poet his due,"[39] did not seek the reflection of an age in this literary stratification ("when the French align themselves with current tastes, it is always with prudence and their customary reticence"[40]); but, with a resolve that amply made up for this reticence, he worked on identifying the places in the poem. His twelve books take the reader across the Mediterranean, like a Baedeker or a Guide Bleu of maritime routes, portraying charming and colorful Italian landscapes with a wealth of detail; Bérard tacks onto the *Odyssey* a topography that lacks any textual support, making his edition of the poem a mere pretext for an archaeological stroll. The Greek colonies in Italy had already appropriated Odyssean names for their capes and islands. In Bérard's opinion, Homer—that is, the "Homeric poems" (including the Alcinous narratives, which can be divided up but not "analyzed")—is so ancient that anomalies can be eliminated as illegitimate, as insertions or interpolations made during the long life of the poem, and the text must also be clear enough so that neither semantic research nor complexity of thought can be attributed to it:

> The clarity of Homer's work is threatened by certain attributes—circumlocution, "profundity," prolixity, abstraction, and above all ambiguity; clarity can never allow the smallest contradiction, apparent or real, in its terms or concepts, nor any kind of implausibility ... including factual implausibility and inappropriate subject matter. Its clarity is so extreme that neither words nor sentences nor substance nor form should, from the Ancients' point of view, ever raise the slightest difficulty, or "aporia," for even the most demanding reader.[41]

No reflection can be allowed to slip between the object and its exact description. This fidelity is all the more rigorous in that the poet does not describe landscapes that he has seen (which, somewhat surprisingly, had not led anyone to doubt the quality of his account). The author of the Alcinous narratives adapts the story of a journey on the western sea, or "Nautical Instructions," and perhaps even Phoenician legends. The world is divided into a civilized part, the well-known East, and a barbarous side, the West: "Hence the importance of

---

[39] Bérard 1931:51.
[40] Bérard 1931:52.
[41] Bérard 1931:104.

Ithaca on the edge of the two worlds in that era, and the renown, in the Achaean legend, of that poor little rock whose very name has disappeared from classical history."[42]

For Bérard, the fantastic and the mythic belong to barbarism. Thus he has no trouble situating the house of Dawn or Circe's dwelling place in the West; he has distinguished a barbarous country, its sites and their contours orientalized by Phoenician travelers, and a Greek order of lines and diction: "This poem is the work of a Hellene; the model bears the hallmark of a Semitic craftsman."[43] The East does not disgust Bérard. His systematic concretization is not based on any source, any description, any exploration that he could have consulted. The descriptions can fit any place, if it is the *landscape* one is looking for.

Albert Thibaudet called Bérard himself a geographer-poet.

What Homer's geographic imagination had done for the Phoenician journey, Bérard's geographic imagination, guided by the meaning of the sites and the science of (Greco-Semitic) doublets, was to do for the *Odyssey*, but in the other direction: that is, by finding the Phoenician journey in the poem, and then by associating that journey and the odyssey in an eternal Mediterranean—after the ancient Mediterranean, then the Venetian, the Greek, or the English versions, came the Mediterranean of which the *Odyssey* remains the unchanged poem, thanks to the enduring nature of its marine setting, the transparency and the soundness of its geography.[44]

The reconstruction of Homeric geography followed two trends: one, obligingly describing the sites and routes, remains within the confines of the Mediterranean, in the Roman world. According to Bérard, Odysseus travels from Thrace (the Cicones) to Tunisia (the Lotus-Eaters), to meet up with the Cyclops in Campania; he then passes by the Aeolian Islands in the Tyrrhenian Sea to Cape Bonifacio in Corsica (the Laestrygonians). He is carried towards Monte Circeo before ending up in the Strait of Messina (Scylla and Charybdis) in Sicily (the island of the sacred cattle), and then through the Straits of Gibraltar (Calypso), to return to Ithaca via Corfu (the Phaeacians).[45] In scholarly books, the voyage is

---

[42] Bérard 1931:263.

[43] Bérard 1929, 4:482.

[44] Cited in Bérard 1929, 4:17.

[45] This itinerary takes no account of the structural elements of the myth. Thus it is agreed that Odysseus, having arrived within sight of Ithaca, is driven back far from the island of Aeolia, but the fact that this island, the island of the winds, is floating is not a factor. The return via Charybdis is not related to the departure point, Circe. There are many equally fundamental objections to be made.

illustrated with photographs.[46] In an itinerary modified by Roger Dion,[47] Circe is dislodged from her promontory in Campania and, with a good deal of supporting evidence, relocated in Malaga, a site supposed to correspond to the description of the island in the *Odyssey*; thus Odysseus can reach the kingdom of the dead after a day's journey (125 km), on the other shore of the Oceanos, identified by the current of the waters that flow from the Atlantic into the Mediterranean.[48] Others, such as Louis Moulinier,[49] prefer Cyrenaica to Corfu for the Phaeacians. In order to explain the oriental topography of the Circe episode, imagination had to play a role in the map's construction, which included, in a provisional split, everything that could not be located in the Mediterranean, the journey to Circe's domain and whatever was associated with it. This concession was intended solely to make a place for the house of Aurora that Bérard had overlooked. Reference to the real is repeated like a *credo*:

> As much as possible, the poet likens legendary countries to ones that were real to him and still are to us, and that were frequented by seafarers.[50]

> The poet of the Wanderings of Odysseus made it a rule to describe only those itineraries that could be carried out by real ships on real seas.[51]

> The reason for the great Odyssean journeys across the western Mediterranean will elude us as long as people persist in making Homer's Circe live on the Italian promontory that bears her name instead of in Malaga. Raising the question ... opens up research that soon yields one of the keys to the "Wanderings of Odysseus" and reveals its value as a historical document of exceptional importance. The poem appears to be the only text through which we can grasp the trace of a colonization or at least of a Hellenic presence on the Ibero-African borders from the time that the great Greek colonies of southern Italy and Sicily were established on less far-flung shores ... . Let us not refuse the title of historian to the first of these Hellenic poets.[52]

---

[46] "The bones piled up in a prehistoric cave that looks out onto this coast at sea level on Cape Palinuro, near to the ancient Molpa, named after another Siren [in another legend], are perhaps the origin of the 'pile of boneheaps' mentioned in xii, line 45." These are the terms in which the scholarly editors René Langumier, Jean Bérard, and Henri Goube (1952:276) present the problematic connection between the Sirens and the human skins and bones strewn on the ground around them.

[47] Roger Dion (1896–1981), professor of French historical geography at the Collège de France.

[48] Dion 1971:479–533.

[49] Moulinier 1958.

[50] Moulinier 1958:122.

[51] Dion 1971:494.

[52] Dion 1971:532–533.

Bérard had laid down a firm rule: "verisimilitude always retains its rightful place in an Odyssean tale."

The stylistic device of allegory (to which Dion reduces the house of Dawn[53]) or symbol, applied to these tales, has only one function—to retain their realistic impact. The language of allegory or symbol is presumed to be used only under desperate circumstances:

> Sometimes we do not recognize the geographic reality represented by a supernatural being. So we speak of symbolism ... But it might be said that the poet is a primitive. Let us acknowledge once again that when we are dealing with an author who is otherwise so concerned with ordinary geographical truth ... we should presume that it is his way of expressing greater realities glimpsed through the prism of perceptible appearances. Is this not in fact a supreme realism? [54]

If the Planctae, along with the whole epic of the Argonauts, have been moved from the Bosphorus further west, it is because "when the Ionian cities of the Aegean, leaders of colonial enterprises with far distant goals ... turned their ambitions towards the West where once they had been focused on the East, their sailors wanted Jason to accompany them on the western seas as well."[55] Dion endorses the claim, regarding the transformation of the legend in Apollonius of Rhodes, that "a patriotic mystique has more than once traced physically unfeasible activities for the heroes of mythology."[56]

The tendency toward establishing realistic sites is not represented as vigorously or as exclusively in other countries, at least among university scholars of the same rank.[57] Another trend, more steeped in Analysis[58] and less attached

---

[53] Dion 1971:494.

[54] Moulinier 1958:122–123.

[55] Dion 1971:499.

[56] Dion 1971:509.

[57] Given the numerous reconstitutions and albums of the journey, these research projects obviously fulfilled a need. Let us take just three examples in different cultural fields. In 1963, in London, an ex-naval officer published the account of his journeys in the Mediterranean in search of the meaning of the lines he carried with him (Bradford 1964). At about the same time (1961–1964), the four volumes of *Géographie de l'Odyssée* were published in Brussels; their author, Auguste Rousseau-Liessens, tries to prove that all the Wanderings took place in the Adriatic. More recently, two German brothers, Hans-Helmut and Armin Wolf, hark back to the failure of past efforts, and propose to start off from the directions indicated in the text in order to project the resulting geometric figure on the Mediterranean, checking on the distances *a posteriori* (1968). Thus they discovered a new center, the island of Malta (Aeolia), and a new Phaeacia in Calabria, where they believed that archaeological digs would produce for the *Odyssey* what Schliemann had brought to the *Iliad*.

[58] Resorting to realism also served the interest of Analysis. If the description of Ithaca does not correspond to the real Ithaca, it is because one of the poets, in this case the good one, did not

to the Mediterranean, maintains the distinction between East and West, and thereby promotes a certain confusion between historical precision and myth. Scholars of this persuasion have no difficulty in assigning a site in the West to the Lotus-Eaters, the Cyclops and Aeolia, nor in situating places like Cyzicus in the East, but since they were not dealing with the enclosed universe of the Mediterranean, they did not hesitate to extend the mythical borders of the world to the shores of the Black Sea, citing the ignorance of the Ancients.[59] This geography, less influenced by organized tour routes in the Mediterranean, was based on certain textual indications, or else on the explanation of a set of data. These data are often integrated into the system of sources

It has often been pointed out that this geographical research is fragile and inconsistent, but production has continued nevertheless. The work was fruitful, and that alone was sufficient reason to continue. It is useless to point out the erroneous details, whether Circe lives in Malaga or Campania, or even to criticize the legitimacy of this research, if error itself is not elevated to the status of a subject to be studied, as a means to uncovering its deeper interest and to understanding that meaningless results have not meant that geographical research itself is meaningless.

If reading does not benefit from the comparison of methods, from "Germanic" Analysis to amateur archaeology, it is because this kind of work, despite the diversity that inspires so many volumes, is based on a consensus[60] as to the way the text and its meaning are taken into consideration, or not. Bérard and Wilamowitz do not disagree about the significance and the documentary value of the *Odyssey*. The poem is used as a basis for pseudo-historical constructs exactly insofar as it is considered as clear content, as an object, severed from the subject who produced it and severed from its reader. The text is examined for facts or for what can be transformed into facts: the doves tell the story of Jason's voyage. No doubt, for philologists, the creation of a work is always modeled on a form of philological study, the collation of readings and sources—a method that, when applied to a given work, is established as a principle for production.

It was a matter of attaching facts drawn from the text to events, so as to give these events a historical dimension. But by bringing in an external principle of explication based on fortuitous and changing data, the historians in question lost any access to a historical perspective, and failed to consider the conditions under which they themselves were exploiting the text. Using Homer for their own purposes, and treating its meaning as already known in advance, they were

---

know the island. And why did he not know it? Because he was from Asia Minor (Von der Mühll 1952, col. 719–20).

[59] Moulinier (1958) took the same liberty in the Mediterranean framework of the French tradition.

[60] The Unitarians do not distance themselves from it either.

not in a position to equip themselves with a theory of the text, nor to secure the conditions under which understanding can emerge from the very difficulties of reading. Fixing the historical location of a work forces the reader to go through the subjectivity of the author, and thus to accentuate the anomalies, as so many means for perceiving the distinctive feature of a gaze. The idea of a narrative as the reproduction of a ready-made history, transmissible and translatable, or as a means of describing something external to the text, prevents readers from seeing that the narration includes signs that make it enigmatic and that are, in a way, detached from it. The *Wanderings of Odysseus*, like other ancient texts, have a depth that has been proven by a tradition of exegesis. Their esoteric nature, the fact that the story cannot be read without demanding reflection on its meaning, precludes any arbitrariness in the interpretation of signs. The elements of the narration maintain a rigorously determined relationship with the interpretive elements within it, so that the meaning remains open only as long as the totality of the relationships, in every episode, has not been explained.

The existence of an exegetic network, of which repetitions, for example, are a part, allowed a blinkered criticism to perceive signs that were incomprehensible on the narrative level as anomalies. Indirectly, the possibility of Analysis vouches for the existence of an accompanying exegesis that replicates the text with a form of allegory that does not replace one text with another but reads the same text differently. Accepting this principle would lead to the definition of a practice that, by carefully distinguishing between the content and the way it is used, as revealed by the text, would retain the specific nature of the reading. We must persuade ourselves that the text disappoints the expectation that the naïve narration encourages. Error consists in producing a meaning that the text deflects. The project is not linked to tradition by a form of dependency, but by the fact that it obliges readers to posit a state of affairs that is different from the one it describes. The object of expectations thus cannot be that of modern critics, who reduce the tale to a primitive form, even as they declare it to be full of urbanity and style: we must reconstitute the expectation that arose from the disappointment of the initial expectation. This means accepting the perceived difficulties while at the same time learning to see the hidden problems.

The insertion of a legend such as the tale of the Argonauts can be considered an intellectual phenomenon, like an element of language. If the Planctae that the ship Argo passes are Scylla and Charybdis, the question arises why, and for what purpose, the solitary passage of Odysseus clinging to the wreck is absorbed into one accomplished by the heroes of all of Greece. The problem of the unity of the poem can only be posed in these terms: unity originates in the necessary relationship among the individual episodes; it is established as the result of the successive interpretations suggested by the text.

The "New Look" of Analysis

The research on what is called "oral poetry" begun by Milman Parry and Albert Lord has made no contributions to the topic of the *Odyssey's* composition beyond those already made by Analysis. Yet the two men consider, in a new and certainly more accurate way than before, not the genesis of Homer's poem—which they do not examine, even though they think they have done so—but the genesis of the monumental compositions favored, long before Homer, by the practice of oral poetry.

They have demonstrated the importance of metrical schemas and formulaic models and actions ("formulaic patterns"). Albin Lesky, in his article "Homeros" for the great encyclopedia of the sciences of antiquity, wrote in 1968:

> The breakthrough between the two world wars of the conviction that the essence, and in large part the evolution, of Homeric poetry must be understood in terms of certain characteristic traits of its language and prosody, is an event whose importance, for Homeric research, can be compared to the initial impetus that Friedrich August Wolf gave to Analysis.

The idea, however, is older than Analysis, which served as a way station.[61] For Friedrich Schlegel, Homer was merely a name, the name of epic poetry (*Histoire de la poésie épique chez les Grecs*, 1798).[62] Kirchhoff's idea of a plurality of authors resurfaces; it presents the theory of a collective voice in a more plausible fashion, even before any investigations could be made in the field.

According to research carried out in Serbia, where Parry[63] and then Lord heard bards inspired by an epic tradition that was still alive forty years ago, very long poems could be memorized and recited thanks to a traditional store of formulas and ready-made lines. The Greek singers are different from the rhapsodes, who would later confine themselves to reciting songs without any

---

[61] The idea goes back to late antiquity.

[62] See also Lord 1960:147: "[Homer] is not an outsider approaching the tradition with only a superficial grasp of it ... He is not a split personality with half of his understanding and technique in the tradition and the other half in a parnassus of literate methods. No, he is not even immersed in the tradition. He *is* the tradition; he is one of the integral parts of that complex."

[63] In two articles published in 1930 and 1932, Milman Parry showed the traditional nature of certain formulaic systems comprising a noun and its epithet, and how certain prosodic irregularities were caused by the use of these formulas; he then took a big step forward, declaring that, based on his study of Turkish, Yugoslav, Russian, and Kara-Khirgiz poetry, Homeric poetry was oral ("Studies in the Epic Technique of Oral Verse-Making. I. Homer and the Homeric Style" and "Studies in the Epic Technique of Oral Verse Making. II. The Homeric Language as the Language of Oral Poetry," both reprinted in Parry 1971:266–364). Hoekstra (1969:11–12) points out that this statement marks "a considerable extension of his previous definition of the formula."

changes,[64] while the Greek bards used the possibilities of expression in their repertoire to improvise, harmonizing formulas, modifying thematic units or combining them in a different way. The single poet of the *Odyssey* and the *Iliad* is great in this respect, both for his memory and for his improvisational genius. His art, which we attribute to him because it is his work that has been preserved, does not differ essentially from that of the poets of a forgotten age, who composed oral poetry for listeners. Indeed, the diffusion of writing coincided with a "monumental" creation that brought the traditional work to its apogee. Kirk believes that the form given to the inherited material by the "main composer" arrested the flow of the text's development owing to its imposing character, just before it was fixed by writing and independently of that phenomenon. Others think that composers, working according to the rules of oral poetry, exploited the discovery of writing to dictate their poems; in any case, it is the sequence of production, with the help of chance, that gave birth to the poem.

Confining Homer to the lineage of the singers and insisting on the mechanisms of oral production made it possible to give a general explanation of anomalies and to pin them once and for all to the specific characteristics of a genre.[65] The defenders of oral poetry accept the schema of the Analysts, the division of the poem, and its composition by additions and splices. Kirk thinks that the adventures of Books 10 and 12, from the Laestrygonians to Thrinacia, were inserted between the arrival on Aeolia and the story of Calypso, and that the descent into the Underworld in Book 11 is another addition within the insertion. All the examples Kirk gives in the chapter "Structural Anomalies in the *Odyssey*"[66] are drawn unaltered from the Analysts' repertoire. The inconsistencies brought to light by Analysis can be attributed, in this perspective, to the "complexity of the material used by each main composer and to their inevitable difficulties in assembling different elements of their repertoire into unified epics of huge length and scope."[67] The scholarly tradition of recent generations is never re-examined. The theory of unity is opposed in its most formal arguments, and the study of correspondences and symmetries is dismissed

---

[64] For the rhapsodes, the epic tradition is not a repertoire from which to draw material for improvisation, but is in principle a canonical text, established by writing and *ne varietur*, not to be changed. Hence the distinction critics could make between the creative and lively "insertions" of the "main composer" and the destructive "interpolations" of the rhapsodists.

[65] "[M]ainly because certain anomalies which appear both in composition ... and in diction ... are of such a nature that they are best explained on the assumption of oral creation" (Hoekstra 1969:18n2).

[66] Kirk 1962:234–235.

[67] Kirk 1962:251.

as over-interpretation.[68] Moreover, to prove the oral nature of the poem, the authors readily accept the objections to the text that Analysis had accumulated.

Instead of going along with the Analysts and representing the poet as an ancient genius whose poem was damaged by succeeding versions—as if primitive poetry, symbolized by Homer, had been lost in his work and needed to be recovered—Kirk's "oral poetry" rehabilitated, in the final stage, the editor and master craftsman. Tradition would lead to a Homer, and this Homer would never stray from tradition. But in the absence of a search for the distinctive traits of this character, by multiplying Homer ad infinitum in his past, Kirk places him back in an unknowable earlier time, since the constitutive act of the Homeric poem is not grasped.

This attempt to differentiate, by scale or scope rather than quality, the culmination of oral poetry from earlier phases of its evolution, and the fortuitous nature of the relationship between the final phase and immediate transcription, show that writing is perceived as belonging to the nature of the poem, and that the fabrication of these vast assemblages is situated in the natural evolution of oral poetry for reasons other than those that would account for the composition of the poem. The simple fact of being written down is not enough to differentiate one oral work from others in the same form and used for the same purposes. Written down, recorded, the song will retain oral form through the transcription, however subtle the splices might be. The *Iliad* and the *Odyssey* were conceived by and for writing, which was perhaps just beginning to spread, and writing itself did not appear miraculously to help in its own preservation; the style was adapted to the means at hand. Homer gives the appearance of a song to what he writes, just as he presents singers in his narratives. Just as the facts of civilization that he describes belong in part to another age and in part to his own times, the features of oral poetry are stylized and give no involuntary hints as to their genesis; they are used consciously, or diverted to serve different literary purposes. Thus they can be accepted and interpreted, while conversely we are unable to explain the techniques of written poetry (literal repetitions of a certain length) in improvisation and song.[69] If the device of iteration and the use of formulas and rhythmic patterns were originally designed for the role that the defenders of oral poetry have assigned to them, as traditional elements of a scene or stereotypical situation and as means of memorization, these practices,

---

[68] See Kirk 1962:262–263, for an argument against structural interpretations that undermine themselves by their formalism.

[69] In keeping with comments made about the bards, the theory of oral poetry is based on the idea that the driving principle of sung composition is improvisation, and that this movement replenishes the traditional elements. Hoekstra accepts this distinction, and proposes that literal repetitions be considered as interpolations, or that oral poetry be enriched by a rhapsodic technique of recitation.

which become evident through reuse, to the great delight of linguists, take on structuring and relational aims that they might not have had at the outset.[70]

No doubt it is more accurate to situate the birth of Homeric poems in one of the guilds in which the craft of composing, of singing—or of dictating—was learned and transmitted, than to attribute to Homer the work habits of a nineteenth-century scholar; but, by an identification of the same type, oral poetry— at least to explain its establishment in written form—has recourse to a feat worthy of an ethnologist. "Perhaps we shall never have a certain solution to the riddle of the writing down of the Homeric poems," writes Lord.[71] Impossible indeed that an oral poet could have wanted to be known under this guise, nor could his colleagues ever have considered changing their habits. Someone outside the tradition must have made the decision to write down the great epics. Lord suggests that this benefactor, jealous of the famous books of certain other peoples, wanted to bestow on Greece a durable treasure, or simply to reproduce the epic form seen elsewhere, thus displacing a problem of aesthetics in time and from one form of empiricism to another.[72] The act of recording ranks with the act of writing, since to it we owe the *Iliad* and the *Odyssey*.

Works Cited

Bérard, A. 1971. Preface to V. Bérard, *Les navigations d'Ulysse,* vol. 1, vii–xviii. Paris.

Bérard, V. 1917. *Un mensonge de la science allemande.* Paris.

———, ed. and trans. 1924. *Odyssée, poésie homérique.* 3 vols. Paris.

———. 1929. *Les navigations d'Ulysse.* 4 vols. Paris. Repr. 1971.

———. 1931. *L'Odyssée d'Homère.* Paris.

Bertrin, G.-M. 1897. *La question homérique.* Paris.

Bollack, J. 1976. "Note sur l'épisode des Planctes." *Actes de la recherche en sciences sociales.* 2:173–176.

Bourdieu, P., and J.-C. Passeron. 1970. *La reproduction: éléments pour une théorie du système d'enseignement.* Paris.

Bradford, E. 1964. *Ulysses Found.* New York.

---

[70] Lord (1960:130–131) believes that the oral technique can be defined by the number of formulas, as if, with the appearance of writing, a whole cultural and expressive tradition could be abandoned. The markers of oral expression do not signify that the poetry was not written.

[71] Lord 1960:156.

[72] Lord 1962:195: "There is a tendency for scribes ... to neglect to write down actually as dictated passages which they recognize as repetitions of passages previously dictated. They assume that the repetition will be word for word, and hence they note down simply that at a given point certain lines are to be repeated. It is worth consideration that some of the repeated passages in the Homeric poems may have been set down in this way." But this dictated text belongs to a mixed period, between the oral and the written; Lord calls this dictated text "oral."

Dion, R. 1971. "Où situer la demeure de Circé?" *Bulletin de l'Association Guillaume-Budé*, suppl. 30:479–533.

Finsler, G. 1908. *Homer*. 2 vols. Leipzig.

Hoekstra, A. 1969. *Homeric Modifications of Formulaic Prototypes*. Amsterdam.

Kakridis, J. T. 1971. *Homer Revisited*. Lund.

Kirchhoff, A. 1879. *Die homerische Odyssee und ihre Entstehung*. Berlin. Orig. pub. 1859.

Kirk, G. S. 1962. *The Songs of Homer*. Cambridge.

Langumier, R., Bérard, J., and H. Goube, eds. 1952. *Odyssée: Chants I, V–VIII, IX–XII, XIV, XXI–XXIII*. Paris.

Lattimore, R., trans. 1965. *The Odyssey of Homer*. New York.

Lesky, A. 1968. "Homeros." *Real-Encyclopädie der classischen Altertumswissenschaft*. Stuttgart.

Lindsay, J. 1965. *The Clashing Rocks: A Study of Early Greek Religion and Culture and the Origins of Drama*. London.

Lord, A. B. 1960. *The Singer of Tales*. Cambridge, MA.

———. 1962. "Homer and Other Epic Poetry." In *A Companion to Homer*, ed. A. J. Wace and F. B. Stubbings, 179-214. London.

Merkelbach, R. 1951. *Untersuchungen zur Odyssee*. Munich.

Meuli, K. 1975. *Odyssee und Argonautika: Untersuchungen zur griechischen Sagengeschichte und zum Epos*. In *Gesammelte Schriften*, ed. T. Gelzer, 2:593–676. Berlin. Orig. pub. 1921.

Moulinier, L. 1958. *Quelques hypothèses relatives à la géographie d'Homère dans l'Odyssée*. Aix-en-Provence.

Myres, J. L. 1958. *Homer and His Critics*. London.

Page, D. L. 1955. *The Homeric Odyssey*. Oxford.

Parry, M. 1971. *The Making of Homeric Verse: The Collected Papers of Milman Parry*, ed. A. Parry. Oxford.

Puech, A. 1924. *Annuaire de l'École normale supérieure*. Paris.

Rousseau-Liessens, A. 1961–1964. *Géographie de l'Odyssée*. 4 vols. Brussels.

Von der Mühll, P. 1940. "Odyssee." *Real-Encyclopädie der classischen Altertumswissenschaft* 7:697–698.

———. 1952. *Kritisches Hypomnema zur Ilias*. Basel.

Wilamowitz-Moellendorff, U. von. 1884. *Homerische Untersuchungen*. Berlin.

Wolf, F. A. 1985. *Prolegomena to Homer*. Ed. and trans. A. Grafton, G. W. Most, and J. E. G. Zetzel. Princeton. Orig. pub. 1795.

Wolf, H.-H., and A. Wolf. 1968. *Der Weg des Odysseus*. Tübingen.

4

Reflections on the Practice of Philology[†]

I

To EDIT A PAGE OF AESCHYLUS OR PLATO, to separate these authors' sentences or their lines of verse—to understand, in a word—is to discover that, to a considerable degree, the composition obtained by a lengthy and coherent tradition, but also by modern science, heir to that tradition, is different from the text that has been preserved, sometimes only in an interrupted fashion within the critical apparatus at the bottom of the pages, but also on the upper part of the pages, in the lines of a standard reading. To go back to even a single well-known sentence is often to reconstruct it according to a different grammar. This doubling of the text at the literal level requires an explanation. It cannot be the product of error, since every analysis stems from precise conditions that justify it, nor can it result from a taste for contradiction. Still, the phenomenon invites us to meditate on the frontiers of hermeticism and the very possibilities of communication.

Several books on classical authors, books that are also editions of these authors' works, have led me to reflect on the reason for the difficulties inherent in the practice of philology. To establish and translate canonical texts was to encounter, from paragraph to paragraph, the protean personality of the interpreter, fettered by authority, and to observe academic ways of proceeding. Most readers are unaware that they are reading Marullus in Lucretius, Usener in Epicurus, Diels in Heraclitus. The text defends itself poorly. It is weak in the face of conjecture. For there were all sorts of good reasons to impose corrections, reasons that are still prevalent today, because biases are a constant and because tradition has the merit of existing and has the force of established fact.

Examples in which description is distorted in an analogous way could be found in abundance among the most widely-read authors. And yet all the

[†] Originally published as "Réflexions sur la pratique," in: Jean Bollack, *La Grèce de personne: les mots sous le mythe* (Paris, 1997), pp. 93–103.

flourishes of free, "creative" reading are poorer than the program that would be imposed by the systematic establishment of the unrecognized dimension in question. Elements that are proper to a text, instead of being analyzed as signs, are characterized as accidental, interpreted as instances of discord or incoherence. The integration of such terms shows on the contrary that the logic of the text is precisely not the logic that has caused these elements to be viewed as discordant. A given sentence no doubt conceals both truth and error, and the creative force it possesses would presumably be able even to trace the route of phantom navigators across the sea. The Ancients (for example, Diogenes Laertius) said that there was a Heraclitus for fools, and probably a Homer as well. Certain interpretations settle for dissociating what the genesis of the work had melded together, or else they reassemble what the genesis of the work had taken apart.[1]

It would be easy—and unfair—to scoff at the efforts expended in the ever so cumbersome apparatus of philological demonstration. Immediate access to the text is demanded insistently. And yet it is impossible to build an interpretation based on the raw material without going through the history of interpretations. Not that the centuries have supplied progressively more accurate approximations on the path toward truth, nor that it is profitable a priori to draw the components of a new mixture from the multiple elements encountered; but, beyond the fact that the justification of the material—that is, of the text retained—cannot be achieved unless one recognizes and refutes the reasons for which it has been altered, the material itself is constituted only to the extent that one interpretation imposes itself as opposed to others (the hermeneutic circle also applies to the discovery of the text over time). No reading of any sort can become clear in the absence of other readings. A correct reading asserts itself only when it is confronted, on its own, with all possible readings.

Even if this heuristic aspect did not exist, a demonstration would not be convincing if it did not win out through refutation. It would appear, owing solely to the fact of its difference, to be more esoteric than the text explained. We know that it does not suffice to argue in order to convince. We know that, in a culture that has always been based on the explication of texts, the greatest share of the commentary produced has no justification but the smooth functioning of the institution—wherever that institution may be—and the perpetuation of the exercise. The quantity, the mass of publications, then forms an insurmountable obstacle, and the decline in real interest has not led to a decrease in production.

Moreover, technique, in the discipline of philology as in others, has a tendency to become automatic with respect to its object. The texts then enter

---

[1]   See Chap. 3, "Odysseus among the Philologists."

into the patrimony of literary culture, which is an established and capitalizable value. The division of labor, problematic in this domain and difficult to reconcile with the distinction between technicians and users, nevertheless takes its legitimacy from the virtual number of workers. A good many technicians, and among the most productive, like to say that they understand nothing, not only about the "ultimate signified" but about meaning of any sort; working blind, they fabricate the material that others, the technicians of meaning, receive from them, fully prepared. This divorce casts suspicion on all the histories of philosophy and on most of the chapters in the history of the sciences. The unfounded constructions in these histories, suspended over uncertain material, weigh in turn on interpretations, that is, on the text in question.

In Empedocles there is a theory, fully developed but wholly consigned to oblivion, according to which the sun that we see is produced in the vault of heaven by the reflection of light on the earth. Not only does this theory explain the fragments of sentences that remain to us, but it is richer than a simple opinion on a point of science would be. It allows us to see the positions of all the bodies in the universe, which are always in relation with the theory.[2] Similarly, the system of blue eyes and black eyes is in its own right the complete, encoded expression of a theory of vision.[3] Now, these two components, discovered in the thickness of a doxographic summary, are almost irremediably lacking in histories of astronomy or optics, because their place in a given constellation did not allow them to enter easily into a linear history of scientific progress, and this progress is necessarily the guiding thread of virtually all particular histories.

The division of labor is probably inevitable in practice, but it is unacceptable in theory, and it is maintained only by self-interest.[4] If the history of philology is to destroy this recourse to partial legitimacies, it can no longer be a history of humanists and learned scholars,[5] or even a history of the perfecting of techniques, but rather must become an analysis in reverse, one that would go back through time to situate interpretations, or more precisely their historical determinations. Not that one would thereby arrive at the meaning of a given text or even of a particular word, and here is the heart of the conflict: it lies in the difference that separates the object that is being pursued in an interminable doxography from the object that properly belongs to the science of discourse. At least in this way, philology, being a mirror of non-comprehension, becomes an invaluable way of studying societies. And one might want to show, in the years

---

2 See Bollack 1992, 2, frag. 322–339, and the commentary in Bollack 1992, 2:263–277.
3 Bollack 1992, 2, frag. 420, §8, and 437–438, and the commentary in Bollack 1992, 2:335–338.
4 On the division of the philological domain, see my preface to Bollack 1975:ix–xliii, and especially p. xxiv.
5 See the history of the humanists in Sandys 1967, Gudemann 1967, and Pfeiffer 1976.

to come, that what the history of philology and interpretations brings to light applies just as much to contemporary cultural systems. Even today, translations are still permeated by national traditions.

II

At the end of the nineteenth century, the Germanic philological-historical method found itself, in the face of its object, in a state of radical contradiction. Reflection on the constitution of knowledge—in other words, traditional hermeneutics—was reduced to its simplest expression, to the point of being merely an appendix to "formal" philology, which was conceived for its part according to the model of the philology of the real (*Realphilologie*).[6] Philology, destined at that time chiefly to smooth over and correct, took pride in its role as censor rather than bemoaning censorship as a thankless task: "It is the role of formal philosophy to follow the expression of the thought, which is sometimes deficient, and to a certain extent to monitor the creative work."[7] The analyst of the written expression steps in as psychologist and therapist at the end of the process of exploring meaning.

That the fundamental science we know as exegesis should be degraded in this way, to the point of holding itself back and censoring itself as it censors the text, in order to devote itself exclusively to the hothouse of correction or suppression, signifies that philology is riven by an internal contradiction. Censorship, paradoxically, defends values that it does not consider its own. Setting itself up as a science, and as such—in order to gain recognition as such— viewing all its objects as equivalent, it ultimately treats authors in a mercenary fashion, since it leaves to the vague and deplored field of aesthetics the responsibility for protecting their reputations. It masks absence of judgment by the amplitude of its scientific apparatus. Subsequently, literary theory has come to occupy the space, without including the conditions under which meaning is produced. The gulf has been deepened. Material difficulty is taken to be more serious than intellectual difficulty. "If Euripides' poems were not corrupted," Wilamowitz writes in his "Introduction to Greek Tragedy," "Hermann would not publish them."[8]

Philological censorship is in power wherever it is charged with a pedagogical mission, but it uses its weapons far from the pedagogical context in order to bring about a rapid increase in the material of knowledge—and the frenetic rhythm of fabrication is not the smallest failing in the activity favored by the

---

[6] On this notion, see Gercke 1910, in the chapter titled "Methodik," 35.
[7] Gercke 1910:35.
[8] "Einleitung in die griechische Tragödie," in Wilamowitz-Moellendorff 1959, 1:239.

philological-historical method. On this basis, classical antiquity no longer has any *raison d'être*, even if philology scrupulously carries out its mission, which is to be at the service of classical antiquity.

The contradiction has been manifested both in individual critics, capable of holding two different discourses depending on whether they are representing the science of philology from an academic platform or praising the values that allowed them to practice that science,[9] and also in the war waged between official science and the inner circles that, in reaction, celebrated the offices of aestheticism. On the Homeric question, for example, the quarrel between the Analysts and the Unitarians is situated almost entirely in this necessary tension between dignitaries and marginal figures. The former are invested with the authority of the academy; the latter are justified by faith. Thus scholars have never been able to get beyond the antinomy through peaceful examination, through a scientifically-based Unitarianism.

The perfecting of tools during the nineteenth century—the inventory and classification of manuscripts, the history of texts, and paleography—offered the support of material accidents as a way of dealing with incomprehension. Thus lacunae and interpolations flourished from a certain point on: at a given moment, between 1850 and 1860, the editions produced by Bernays, Lachmann, Munro, and Brieger broke Lucretius apart by more lacunae than had ever been recognized before, to the point that one of these editors expressed his own amazement at the richness of his harvest. One can take all the so-called interpolations of a tragedy of Aeschylus, as I have done with Pierre Judet de La Combe for the *Agamemnon*, for example, in order to show that all of them have been produced by a sometimes traditional difficulty in comprehension which, for various reasons, had never found another solution.[10] The contemporary tendency to give up, ready to condemn the earlier excesses, changes nothing, because it does not see the link between these interpolations and the practice that consists in resolving difficulties of meaning by invoking accident. In order to be brought back to life, the lost "meaning" waits to be integrated into any explanatory system whatsoever.

Although the appeal to systems of representation and to mental and psychological structures supplies interpretations and, above all, grids, such studies have little to do with real knowledge of the works themselves. It is true that their authors are searching for an illuminating and all-embracing herme-neutic meaning, but the light that is borrowed directly from social reality—generational conflict, *polis*, *genos*, and so on—makes this reality a purely abstract

[9] See Chap. 3, "Odysseus among the Philologists."
[10] See Bollack 1981 and 1982.

matter, too quickly enlarged to the dimensions of a culture or an epoch, and it makes the play or poem a mirror of the schema retained, which is imposed in all cases, *ipso facto*. Yet the very self-evidence of the example is suspect. Because they fail to take an interest at the same time in the unique meaning of the work, the essayists of the structuralist schools do not really use the traditional tools of textual criticism and thus do not succeed in critiquing the inherited meanings.

To be sure, particularity of expression has been recognized since Wilamowitz's day as a proper historical form, and it has been related not only to systems of representation but also to types of teaching and to rhetorical habits.

Reference to the humanist norm has been abandoned among the formalists in favor of specific modes of expression, surely under the influence of ethnology and anthropology. The alienation of the author's viewpoint is perceptible in these writings. Beyond the fact that, in the case of writers such as Pindar,[11] one might ask whether the author is explained by the manual or the manual by the author, this normalization to the second degree precludes, in a schematic assimilation, a deep understanding of the properly esoteric dimension and of the level of "allegory." Only certain simplifications—biographical references, for example—are sacrificed in relation to all that was previously being done in more psychological critiques.

III

The constitution of a horizon of representations is no doubt indispensable, but it must be achieved along different pathways. Wedded from the outset to the idea of an alterity of material and the possibility of historical objectivization, not so much practicing the naturalization of the foreign as postulating its existence, historians project contemporary biases, if only by applying models from all over the place. There is nothing more historically determinable than the introduction of explanatory schemas considered *a priori* as historically applicable.

August Boeckh, in his *Encyklopädie und Methodologie der philologischen Wissenschaft* (Encyclopedia and Methodology of the Science of Philology, the product of a course Boeckh taught regularly at the University of Berlin between 1809 and 1865),[12] defined philology as a historical science. He made it a universal discipline, alternating with philosophy, like Castor with Pollux, but at the same time his view of it encompassed the historical aspect that also characterized every science. Although remote, the object, for him, concerned the interpreter directly, and it was thus on the basis of what he knew that the interpreter was

---

[11] See Bundy 1962.
[12] Boeckh 1886.

led to judge ("foreign ideas are not yet ideas for me," he wrote[13]). The universal philologist, the concept of which he was creating, someone capable of knowing everything since all the objects of history are known through him, introduces distance only in judgment, which is no longer historical when it has appropriated the foreign. Boeckh invites the philologist to tear himself away from his condition and rise above the thing integrated so as to have it in front of him in its atemporal objectivity. It is a matter of knowing what one knows, which has already been known by another. The judgment brought to bear on the critical act operates the appropriation, so that the doubled object is no longer the one that the foreign author had known but belongs to the knowing subject. Historical distance is abolished not only by the concept of a universal history, but also by the agency of judgment that appreciates or invalidates.

Boeckh's hermeneutics—and Boeckh moreover was one of the founders of the science of history—thus reconciled the necessity of investigation and critique, on the one hand, and the obligation to maintain privileged values, values that concern us, on the other; in spite of everything, it closely resembled the hermeneutics codified by Friedrich Ast.[14] Boeckh situated himself in the lineage of Schelling's philosophy of identity, without however believing it possible to purge objects of their historical contingency in order to grasp the movements of the unifying spirit. Other theorists of the eighteenth century and of German idealism had, on the contrary, like Hölderlin, by virtue of the paradigmatic nature of antiquity, ended up espousing the absolute alterity that made it possible for modernity to be recognized.

Ast's theory, which affirms the possibility of identification, nevertheless makes distance a problem, whereas the later philologists, renouncing appropriation, renounce the possibility of knowing the remote object and end up assimilating it.

IV

Determined by his own position in history and in society, the interpreter, an artisan of his material, occupies with respect to his object a place that, in the case of the works of antiquity, is situated at such a great distance that variations between years give him scarcely any sort of handhold. Such distance cannot count, it is absolute. In reality, if the only thing one knows is the unknown, it is this very tension from which one must profit. Moreover, there is just as much

[13] Boeckh 1886:20.
[14] Ast 1808.

distance between Heraclitus and his contemporaries, or between Epicurus and his, so that foreignness in time is accompanied by difference in synchrony.

To objectivize, one would have to agree to take the thing studied as a fixed entity, to take life as fact, to take a play as an opaque event, to take a thought as a body. Now, what one grasps cannot be, in the instantaneous act of grasping, merely a movement in search of itself, merely the inflection in a sentence. It is not the common, known meaning that one is seeking, but the unknown, the unsaid that is revealing itself, combined with the letter of the text. Here is the specific object of philology, the one it shares with no other science.

Because it was seeking literal meaning, philology, in its positivist and chiefly documentary period, renounced allegory, the *sensus spiritualis* that it took to be gratuitous and superfluous; as a result, it did not reach the *sensus litteralis* to which prudence had led it to cling. This is because the relation between the two is not arbitrary, as philologists had believed. Allegory is not only the transfer of a meaning into a different body of thought, as when the Stoics take up Homer anew or the Church Fathers go back to the Old Testament. The "allegory" that transforms fixed discourse by putting it differently (*allēgorein*) belongs to speech. A sentence is not exhausted in what it says. There remains another sentence that is read in another author or in another part of the work; every sentence contradicts another sentence.

Hence, the preliminary necessity of extensive reading, and in the case of the lacuna-ridden information proper to antiquity, the necessity of complementary imaginative readings that decipher the reconstituted texts. The example of Heraclitus is particularly striking because, once the principle of implicit correction was discovered, Heinz Wismann and I were able, in *Héraclite ou la séparation*, to establish that, in their quasi-totality, the adages, no matter how brief, refuted an affirmation, refuted even the negation of an affirmation. In many cases, the two previous stages are not attested, and yet they can be extrapolated.[15]

With other authors, the allegorical practice does not refer to formulas brought forward by a book culture; it has to do with the internal components of the discourse and constitutes the thickness of the speech. This stratification has nothing to do with the use that is made today of the notion of levels of signification, which implies differentiated levels of consciousness. The virtual meaning, as all these complicated compositional embeddings show, is not to be confused with the resurgence of a repressed feeling. The phenomenon is linked rather to a mode of writing that Servius' biography of Virgil brings to light: the poet dictated a large number of verses to a slave every day; he then reduced the

---

[15]   Bollack and Wismann 1995.

number to a single one. The "allegory," in this case, would be all the suppressed verses, which turn up elsewhere in other parts of the work.

Here I am no doubt describing, under the single term allegory, a phenomenon that has diverse applications, and no doubt when other studies have been completed it will be possible to try to establish their typology in relation to the ancient theories of *obscuritas*. There is a closed form in which the relationship among the elements is imposed as the matter to be deciphered, and there is an open form in which autonomous structures interpenetrate. The first corresponds to the philosophy of Being, the other to atomism. The one is obscure from the start and becomes clearer as one reads, the other is clear in appearance and becomes complicated as one reflects. And yet the richer the extraction of these deep meanings, the more it is taken to be subjective. Philology ought to have criteria capable of distinguishing between a fantasy that is taken to be a scientific interpretation and a close reading of the text that, because it astonishes, is taken to be a personal reading.

The literal meaning decides. When reading has finally been able to opt for a text, this literal meaning is not an "interpretation" on the part of the interpreter. The philologist is bound by the interpretation that is the text. This literal meaning is not just any term that could be shifted around like a pawn and set into relation with others in a formal game, for the good reason that this game is one that the author himself has already played. The "allegory" has produced the grammatical construction. The arrangement of words is as it is because it is determined by other arrangements that the position taken by the author includes.

The issue, then, is not that a sentence, bound by these internal links, refers to a single signified. But it is not conceivable that polysemy should escape the project, because the project includes and maintains it. All the variants of interpretive desire that are not positioned along the axis constituted by the project—a project that is historically locatable, even though it is situated only by interpretation—exceed the strict limits of philology and hermeneutics. The work is inexhaustible, but only on its own terms, according to its own autonomy. From Empedocles' poem Aristotle certainly managed to draw answers that the poet had not provided. But Aristotle was right to add at once that, if someone had pointed out to him what he was doing, he would not have denied it.[16] Polyvalence has this avowal as its limit. It is undoubtedly difficult—but difficulty is what we are dealing with here—to trace the line of demarcation that separates the elements that the author uses fully from those that work for him. The teleology of the project encompasses them all equally.

---

[16] Aristotle *Metaphysics* 1.10, 993a23.

Thus ambiguity must not be posited as a principle of composition, and the authors who make that mistake, in the case of Heraclitus or of authors of tragedies, miss the meaning revealed by the device they are studying. This device presupposes a thetic act before it is enriched by the very counter-meaning with which the author has charged it.

The readings that follow the work and transform it, annulling its particularities in a process of assimilation or using it as a point of departure, are new projects for the commentator. The stages of this afterlife (*Wirkungsgeschichte*) are of interest to the interpreter of the primal work only to the extent that they obscure its comprehension.

What is proper to the work, its difference, is another criterion. Among all the improbable meanings, one imposes itself (*probatur*), one that is even more unexpected. The limit, the criterion, would be, here, the entire set of meanings, provided that a given arrangement could be absolutely differentiated in its particular quality. Parallel passages can never confirm an interpretation, far from it; repetition in different contexts cannot be a restatement:

> Even if—and this is doubtful in itself [as Peter Szondi writes in his analysis of a poem by Paul Celan]—one could claim that one or several expressions in the two places are identical, and that the interpretation taken as certain in one of the passages seems to clarify the meaning of the use of the same word in the line one is seeking to understand, this line becomes clear without being understood, since it is what it is only in this particular use and at first rightly withstands comprehension.[17]

If agreement with other homologous sections supplies the means for deciding, it is on condition that one knows at every moment that the agreement is composed of distinct and unheard-of properties that decide in their turn. The constitution of coherence comes about in a circular movement that may never come to an end. Finally, experimentation has the upper hand. As it strives to reproduce the movement of the work in the literal reading, it can try out all possible meanings. The only thing that would bring it to a halt would be the hermeneutic effectiveness of the meanings uncovered. The right explanation is richer than wrong ones.

---

[17] "Lecture de *Strette*," in Szondi 1998:165.

Works Cited

Ast, F. 1808. *Grundlinien der Grammatik, Hermeneutik und Kritik.* Landshut. In French as "Élements de grammaire, d'herméneutique et de critique," in *Critique et herméneutique dans le premier romantisme allemand*, ed. and trans. D. Thouard, 287–314.Villeneuve-d'Ascq, 1996.

Boeckh, A. 1966. *Encyklopädie und Methodologie der philologischen Wissenschaften.* Ed. E. Bratuschek. Darmstadt. Orig. pub. 1886.

Bollack, J. 1975. *La pensée du plaisir. Épicure: textes moraux, commentaires.* Paris.

———. 1981. *L'Agamemnon d'Éschyle: le texte et ses interprétations.* 3 vols. Paris.

———. 1992. *Empédocle.* 3 vols. Paris. Orig. pub. 1965, 1969.

Bollack, J., and H. Wismann. 1995. *Héraclite ou la séparation.* Paris. Orig. pub. 1972.

Bundy, E. L. 1962. *Studia pindarica.* Berkeley.

Gercke, A., ed. 1910. *Einleitung in die Altertumswissenschaft.* Leipzig.

Gudemann, A. 1967. *Grundriss der Geschichte der klassischen Philologie.* Darmstadt. Orig. pub 1907.

Pfeiffer, R. 1976. *History of Classical Scholarship: From 1300 to 1850.* Oxford.

Sandys, J. E. 1967. *A History of Classical Scholarship.* New York. Orig. pub. 1908.

Szondi, P. 1981. *Poésie et poétique de la modernité.* Ed. M. Bollack. Lille.

Wilamowitz-Moellendorff, U. von. 1959. *Euripides Herakles.* 3 vols. Darmstadt. Orig. pub. 1889.

5

Reading Myths[†]

RESEARCH ON THE CYCLE OF BECOMING had to be linked with cosmology. Speculation on ordered movement and the birth of time occupied a central place. The refutation of the thesis that there were two parallel and opposite cycles in Empedocles, under the headings of Love and Hatred (or Strife), was a decisive preliminary condition for the reconstitution of Empedocles' system. And the origin of the arts and of civilization was grafted onto that of the reproduction of living beings. The thematics included a zoogony, a paleontology, and above all a natural, biological, and social anthropology. This narrative of origins is found in an organized and fragmentary form in almost all the poets and philosophers of antiquity. We can observe the construction of the remythified and rethought history that is being substituted for the ancient myths of mythology. Following my own work on Empedocles, I set out to demarcate the corpus of this history, in the seminars I was directing and in the work I was preparing on the subject. Certain books had appeared that tended to establish complex and often fictitious filiations among these speculative narratives and to identify the common structures that were being perpetuated.[1] These were the remote precursors of philosophies of history.

Here again, it was necessary to learn how to read, and how to understand the organization of the elements used when these elements are not treated in themselves, as is the case in Epicurus and Lucretius, on the basis of data that had been sufficiently analyzed to be exempt from conjecture. This is not how Aristotle proceeded. In the present book [*La Grèce de personne*], where "myths" that interrogate myth are concerned, he is opposed to Plato, with whom, on this topic, he is so closely linked. I have addressed this theme more recently in relation to the historical speculation of Theophrastus, in the study I devoted to the philologist Jacob Bernays (1996), *Un homme d'un autre monde* (A Man from

[†]   Originally published as "Lire le mythe," in: Jean Bollack, *La Grèce de personne: les mots sous le mythe* (Paris, 1997), pp. 131–136.
[1]   See, among others, Spörri 1959, Lämmli 1962, and Cole 1967.

Another World). We can in turn interrogate the reduction to the biological paradigm that Aristotle adopts, and conclude that he diminishes in his own way, through accidental catastrophes, the impact of the subject matter addressed, by granting the smallest role possible to an evolution that of course he could not entirely deny, and thus the largest possible role to an eternity co-present with becoming, which supplied the cognitive model for his study. The use of this model is a necessity whenever we envisage myth in literary texts. The autonomy of these narrative and compositional spaces,[2] open to reflection, largely separated from belief and ritual, has since led me to work toward the same end on the lyrical portions of tragedies.

It is only by going very far back in time that the relation with ritual can be usefully considered, at a different anthropological level, before the conclusion of a systematic body of knowledge, in the problematic and provisional zone of an authentic literary prehistory. At least the question cannot be raised directly for "nuclear" elements—material that is unchanging, untransformed and untransformable material. The problem of this differentiation between the mythical tradition and its intra-literary itinerary has been raised several times in my work.

The insertion of a text into a context remains linked to the modalities of a continuing process of transformation. The distance between text and context grows deeper and deeper. Marcel Detienne tries to resolve the problem in his own way, by a synthesis, distinguishing between two manifestations of myth. For the overall structure of thought he refers to Lévi-Strauss; it would be rather a network of references that, in the course of the construction he sets up, allows him to read the whole set of texts as a summation, in their modes of relation, he says, "in unitary fashion."

In a methodical synchrony Detienne goes beyond the schema of a mythical body of thought that remains dependent on an archaic society, a schema defended on several occasions moreover in Jean-Pierre Vernant's work. Within the confines of a Hellenic ethnic group, Detienne projects the idea of a single myth that would be diversified indefinitely in the testimonies that historians consult and interpret. The pre-rational mode of thought, which for Ernst Cassirer is linked with the presence of objects, is concretized by Detienne in the representations that can be identified within a mobile, matricial mass. Detienne then has to introduce cultural traditions, in a different form, as a supplement; these are the mythical continuities of knowledge, which allow him to assign a place to narrative structures in what can only be called a strategy.[3] The myth is lost in

---

[2]   See the study of the composition of the Hecate episode in Bollack 1997:175–179.
[3]   Among other studies by Detienne on this theme, see Detienne 1988.

its own totalization; it turns up doubled in its narrative realizations and in the linking of histories. The analyst thus has a conceptual support at his disposal, with the antitheses and antagonisms of power among the gods, all the interrelationships of an inherited system to which the histories of "myth-knowledge" then refer in a second phase, even as they operate within that system. Detienne appears to offer a status to the composed texts, whether oral or written; but this is only an illusion, since the contents with which we deal, productions or creations, are predetermined in this case by a substitute meaning inherent in the mythical tradition proper that, at the outset, is extrapolated from it.

Thus it was that, in 1962, at a point when I was beginning to direct a group working on archaic texts, those of Hesiod or Anaximander, Jean-Pierre Vernant was radically calling into question the presuppositions of the enterprise, in *Les origines de la pensée grecque.*[4] If dialogue was difficult, indeed almost impossible, it was because he was maintaining, in a new form, an ancient and undoubtedly arbitrary split between *muthos* and *logos*, which precluded searching for the reasoning, or the organizing principle, in written myths, and precluded understanding how reasoning had been separated from that framework and had been given new references. At the same time, the myth of Oriental sovereignty provided him with the explanatory principle for the *Theogony*, and the latter corresponded to a given social system, whereas Ionian thought presupposed a different system. When Hesiod was writing, the hour of *isonomia* (equality of political rights) had not yet come. Hesiod "lacked" the possibility "of representing to himself a universe subject to the rule of law,"[5] as Anaximander would do. The affirmation of an autocratic power exercised its empire; our reading sought in Hesiod a nuanced reflection on the limits of power.

In a symmetrical way, the principle of the *agora* and the equality of rights did not directly supply a key, as I saw it, to the reading of the fragment from Anaximander. My idea of mediation was quite different. I thought that the form given to the organization of the divine in the dynamism of the *Theogony* remained to be understood in relation to the project of the work that I was identifying at the same time. No matter what transformations of earlier or foreign narratives may have been used to contribute to the elaboration of the work, the text did not primordially document an already determined body of thought reflecting a state of society. I was seeking history, in the full sense of the term, in a form. By means of a double mediation, the utterances reinterpreted social realities as well as earlier explanatory systems.[6]

[4]   Vernant 1962.
[5]   See Vernant 1962:96–114, "Cosmogonies et mythes de souveraineté." Vernant later partially modified this viewpoint (see the preface to the 5th edition [1992]).
[6]   For recent studies, see those collected in Blaise et al. 1996.

The problem struck me with new intensity when, in my work on the tragic poets, I undertook to carry out a rigorous dissociation between the mythical tradition and its translated version, which are already two different things. The re-fabrication had been accomplished according to a point of view, and thus according to an intellectual or aesthetic aim. The meaning that was being discovered was not inscribed in the reality of the myth, which undoubtedly had its own meaning. We do not grasp directly this basis in the past that we can reconstruct. In this sense, Hesiod does not belong directly to the mythical universe either; he uses traditions as freely as he reworks and invents them.

As for the myths to which Homer refers and to which the tragic poets return, drawing upon a stock of epics that we no longer know, it is clear that, taken as a whole, they formed a coherent and connected set into which the poets, in their guilds, were initiated. The material was of a referential nature, familiar because it was constantly being taken up again, but at the same time it formed the underpinnings of rearrangements, acts of re-signification that changed the stories into objects made enigmatic and in need of decoding. The transformation that the material underwent as it was reused would not have been possible if this material had not presented itself as a corpus, and if the figures of the myths had not retained consistent features in the process.

One can try to go further back, straying a bit in the meanderings of a reconstituted tradition, and imagine the condition under which this corpus, so fundamentally precursory, with its Helens and its Clytemnestras, was born. Would it not be necessary once again, for such a remote era, for a prehistory of all literatures, to imagine an operation comparable to the one we are trying out on the texts, and tell ourselves, while methodically separating the stages, that a body of specialists, masters of an art whose principles narratologists have tried to reformulate in their wake, must have given the stories their form and—already—their meaning, and must have created a transmissible mythical tradition out of whole cloth? Semantic productions are as ancient as that.

Works Cited

Blaise, F., P. Judet de la Combe, and P. Rousseau, eds. 1996. *Le métier du mythe: lectures d'Hésiode.* Cahiers de philologie 17. Villeneuve-d'Ascq.

Bollack, J. 1996. *Jacob Bernays, un homme d'un autre monde.* Repr. with corrections, 1998, as *Jacob Bernays, un homme entre deux mondes.* Lille.

———. 1997. *La Grèce de personne.* Paris.

Cole, T. 1967. *Democritus and the Sources of Greek Anthropology.* Cleveland.

Detienne, M. 1988. "La double écriture de la mythologie entre le *Timée* et le *Critias.*" In *Métamorphoses du mythe en Grèce antique,* ed. C. Calame, 17–33. Geneva.

Lämmli, F. 1962. *Vom Chaos zum Kosmos: Zur Geschichte einer Idee.* 2 vols. Basel.

Spörri, W. 1959. *Späthellenistische Berichte über Welt, Kultur und Götter.* Basel.

Vernant, J.-P. 1962. *Les origines de la pensée grecque.* Paris.

6

Purifications[†]

God on Earth

A Subversive Action

PURIFICATIONS (*KATHARMOI*) marks a complete break with the cultural tradition, one that could equally well be called literary or religious. The poem[1] invents a myth, a new story that purports to replace all the other stories that have ever been told, from Homer and Hesiod to the contemporary productions of Athenian tragedy. Empedocles' invention, designed to demystify, consists in reworking the mythological themes, making changes that go beyond banishing a god or dismembering his body. The process of reinterpreting written texts comes to the forefront with this poem; so too with the Orphic poets, who are too often invoked for their beliefs in the afterlife by scholars who neglect their work of composition and exegesis of words otherwise taken at face value—work that connects this world to the next and provides access to salvation. Verbal enigmas in Empedocles are not used for their own sake as exotic exercises, no matter how salutary. That stage has been surpassed, as it were. The writing is controlled, brought to the radiance of poetic speech, and, through its aesthetic appeal, made communicable and public. The Panhellenic aim of this text, which, with its techniques of substitution, rivals Homer, can be understood as a desire for cultural growth. The work of interpretation around a table, among learned friends, is raised to the level of a religious and political message. *Purifications* is presented as a manifesto and a project for the universal reform of societies.

[†] Originally published as the preface to: Jean Bollack, ed., *Empédocle. Les purifications. Un projet de paix universelle* (Paris, 2003), pp. 9–28. Selected fragments appear in Greek and in English translation at the end of this chapter.
[1] "Empedocles," in Diels and Kranz 1951 (hereafter D-K). In this chapter, all fragment numbers from Empedocles refer to the Diels-Kranz edition.

In the few lines that remain to us, tension is expressed between the subject matter of the exegesis, based on rereading and meditating upon books (to be precise: *all* books), and the voice of a political program that is undoubtedly revolutionary. If there is not, properly speaking, a "religion of the book" in Greece, it is no less true that there is a bookish culture, all the more influential in that it does not justify any specific practice directly; in addition there is a powerful interpretive tradition, which stimulates all the liberties taken by the author.

The form, the tone, and the content of this work emanate from a particular social dynamic: the "friends," a group of fairly highly placed people, reject power as it is exercised, along with the passions that it unleashes, in order to intervene more directly in favor of the masses and their needs. These are not simply "friends": they are "kin" (*philoi*), to the extent that they know the principles of the universal affinity that connects them. The mediation of a counterpower, engaged in an egalitarian action (in a democratic sense, but above all anti-tyrannical), appears clearly through the information gathered in the section devoted to Empedocles' political activity, as a statesman, in Diogenes Laertius' *Lives of Eminent Philosophers* (second or third century CE); Empedocles, who could have been a king or a tyrant, rejected power and adopted the popular party.[2] The city-state does not count: it is only the site of a struggle for power in which violence is unleashed.

To renounce is to take a position. The work of improving sanitary conditions or protecting against epidemics circumscribes, as medicine does, a domain of truth. The primacy granted to knowledge within the group is translated in political terms outside the group. The rejection of power in favor of ascetic rules that are more intellectual than warlike is based on a foundational countermyth. The text of *Purifications* legitimizes a double movement: the withdrawal to the autonomy of a citadel of knowledge, and the project of universal expansion on the basis of a new extraterritorial truth. Diogenes (8.66) recalls the recital of *Purifications* at the Olympic Games.[3] This was a Panhellenic intervention with vast repercussions.

It falls to political history to study the conditions under which an important segment of the ruling class freed itself from its position of political ascendancy and turned toward a cultural legitimation belonging to another order. At the same time, on the level of religious sociology, one can wonder how this group

---

[2] Diogenes Laertius "Life of Empedocles," in *Lives of Eminent Philosophers*, vol. 2, trans. R. D. Hicks (Cambridge, MA, 1931), 8.63–8.66.

[3] [TN: "At the time when he visited Olympia he demanded an excessive deference, so that never was anyone so talked about in gatherings of friends as Empedocles" (Diogenes Laertius "Life of Empedocles" 8.66).]

imposed upon itself the ascetic discipline and way of life from which the charismatic figure of Empedocles emerged like a character in a play.

In Empedocles more than in any of the other pre-Socratic philosophers, the social aspiration to freedom is felt in every word. All the pre-Socratics are inclined toward the transmission of what is known. Knowledge alone is not sufficient; its capacity to analyze has to be converted and allowed to manifest its own power freely. Empedocles' historical reality, which scholars are trying to constitute (the poet was a citizen of Agrigento, a large city in Sicily, in the mid-fifth century BCE), helps us see the signification of a work that declares its dependencies and integrates them into a stance of total independence. It is the specific import of a rupture that has to be pinned down; the rupture is unique. Nothing of the cultural universe with which Empedocles and the Greeks of his time were familiar is maintained in its original signification. We must presuppose that the entire horizon was known to Empedocles, but at the same time this horizon remains unknown to us, as long as we have not measured the angle of its transformation.

Nothing is taken up again without being recast; none of the doctrines that are evoked in the fragments can in any way be invoked positively in order to decipher the texts: neither Hesiod's (according to Günther Zuntz [1971]) nor the Pythagorean doctrine (as Marcel Detienne [1963] tried to reconstitute it). Empedocles is a Pythagorean, but after his own fashion, differently. According to the Sicilian historian Timaeus, who was dealing with the cities of Locris and Croton, Empedocles was accused, as Plato was later on, of an illegitimate appropriation of intellectual property belonging to the Pythagorean School (*logoklopia*)—of plagiarism, in short, and he was excluded for that reason. Two lines from *Purifications* (frag. 129) are cited in support of doctrinal filiation, but Timaeus envisages another possibility at the same time: "Timaeus in the ninth book of his *Histories* says ... that Empedocles himself mentions Pythagoras ... Others say that it is to Parmenides that he is here referring."[4] We are, then, in the realm of interpretation, and we are dealing with identifications after the fact. Of all the tendencies to which Empedocles has been attached (despite any evidence of eclecticism on his part), Pythagoras and Parmenides are by far the most important. The tradition retains the differences. Plotinus (*Enneads* 4.8.1) refers to the interpretations of initiates—Empedocleans—and compares Empedocles' revelations to those of Pythagoras, claiming that "Empedocles—where he says that it is law for faulty souls to descend to this sphere ... reveals neither more nor less than Pythagoras and his school seem to me to convey on this as on many other

---

[4] Diogenes Laertius "Life of Empedocles" 8.54.

matters."[5] That there has been hesitation between Pythagoras and Parmenides is instructive. Empedocles' poetry is anti-Parmenidean in its construction and its tonality by dint of its repoetization. The way the poem is presented—its style—is anti-Pythagorean.

Empedocles operates on beliefs; he knows that everything rests on them, and that philosophical speculation, which has been liberated, was built on the basis of beliefs. This speculation can impose the authority of its conceptual truth only if the consequences to be drawn from an effective supremacy of thought are envisaged. For those who limit themselves to that sovereignty alone and view it as reigning in the order of the living, there are no other sovereignties, there are no longer any gods. Philosophy may seek to occupy the place of religion in society and make religion understandable, but in vain; the beliefs installed at the heart of every stronghold have neither been reformed nor suppressed. As they are constitutive of the order of city-states, they can only be given a new expression. The most just and the best adapted beliefs will be the loftiest and most abstract, the most in conformity with what has been acquired through reflection. If we consider the welfare of humankind first and foremost, philosophical knowledge requires a retranslation. Hence the redefinition of the divine in the light of Being, which forms the content of the second part of *Purifications*. Ontological difference is abolished, as it were, when the radiance of Being finds itself invested in the forms taken by human destiny. Difference is reincarnated in god-men. Transcendence is condemned to immanence. The necessity for a break in its plenitude and its perfection can be imposed on transcendence, precisely owing to its unitary character. Concentration tends to be achieved and thus manifested. Unity is therefore pushed toward its own shattering, to ensure the life in which it is found. This is the law of an opening reserved in a distinctive way to the divine, including a distancing from the self in view of a return to the self.

At the center, there will always be the struggle against violence in the world. Disorder cannot be originary. Good is primary if it is the reason for life. The entrance of the divine into the human can thus be achieved only by a relaxing of concentration. Violence can be overcome only inasmuch as it is a negation of a former state. Destruction still belongs to the unity destroyed. The most tenacious thinking will discover that negation has not emerged out of nothing, but that, dialectically, it proceeds from a dynamism inherent to being, from a need for separation and then reconstitution of self through the regulation of the

---

5   Plotinus, *The Enneads*, trans. Stephen MacKenna, 3rd ed., rev. (London, 1962), 8th Tractate, 4.1, 357.

forces that have been liberated. Life is, indeed, the will to be. The consequence drawn from this is that one must trust in evil, if it is an emanation of good. The operation is purely intellectual, and it is visibly presented as a construction, as if it emanated from a discussion that had concluded as follows: there exists a truth that leads to making war on war; this is because war is originally the negation of peace. In a poem, one can give birth to a new myth that, marvelously, tells the truth. It will be a different theogony, in which good engenders evil through a primal murder. Violence allows the divine to diversify. Here we have a veritable utopia, responding as always to some despair, a utopia in which one places one's faith decisively, clinging to the idea that violence is contained, that excess is not winning out, whatever tragedy may say.

As a result, there is nothing left of the traditional religion of the Greeks: neither Homer's version nor Hesiod's. Nothing is left but religion itself. No anthropomorphism is thinkable, no god with a human face that one can picture, neither Zeus nor any other, and while it has been remarked that Apollo is privileged, this is because his verbal and oracular faculties lend themselves best to reconcentration and spiritual transfiguration ("You shall make yourselves no images, no signs substituting for the truth; the ineffable has no images."). In the golden age, when creatures simply loved one another, the primary salient feature was that there was no war, no Iliadic terror, and thus no preoccupation with power or rivalry. No dynasty, no war of succession, neither against the father, Kronos, nor against Poseidon, the brother and rival, master of the earth. Nothing but love. With Empedocles, there is no longer any room for the gods of the city-state. They lie beneath the text, buried in words, in what people have done with them. If the god is a man, he is god with man, in him and for him: god-man on earth, leaving man a chance to be or to become that god who has always occupied his dreams and his thought. Thus everything has to be done again, everything spelled out anew, if one wants to speak the truth; everything has to be called back into question. Empedocles offers an analysis of moral standards, a study of religious practice, and a reflection on the relation between the domain of order and the domain of the irrational, domains that confront one another in Greek mythology. This aspect, whether we call it critical, analytical, or reflexive, gradually comes to the fore and remains primordial; it is somewhat lessened by the dependencies that are attributed to it when it is re-immersed in its own traditions. Nothing of what has been believed and practiced in rituals can claim to be divine, nor can it accede to divinity if it does make such a claim. The Other is in nature; it is seen in living beings. The separation from altars and temples is absolute.

The Two Poems: Nature and Religion

Nineteenth-century editors, when they saw Empedocles as a learned philosopher and the precursor of modern science, removed from the cosmological framework that was reconstituted in the poem on nature, the *peri phuseōs* (which I have titled *The Origins*[6]), everything that belonged to another order. These editors had ready access to a quite secure line of demarcation that allowed them to collect the fragments of a second group, the *Katharmoi*, or *Purifications*. The difference between the two groups, *Origins* and *Purifications*, became more and more visible (as it had not been before), and it posed a problem: some scholars went so far as to suppose a conversion, and, depending on the individual, had Empedocles abandon or rejoin a religion. Empedocles' viewpoint was confused with the content attributed to the object—the reconstituted texts—by scholars. Ever since, instead of accepting the duality and problematizing the relation—which is nevertheless quite perceptible in the vocabulary—between the developments of two distinct literary and philosophical projects, scholars have returned, to varying degrees, to the lack of distinction characteristic of the very earliest collections, as if unity could be found in the mix, whereas it obviously resides in the meaning given to complementary transpositions.

The relation between the two poems, between the genesis of the world bringing to light the variety of living beings in *Origins* and the demythifying myth of the incarnation of the gods in *Purifications*, becomes clear if we define with precision the major outlines of a political aim. Owing to their positivist representations, the nineteenth-century scholars who created the basis for our investigation had come up against the irreconcilable character of the two undertakings, each an object in its own field, one scientific, enlightened, and empirical, the other religious, sectarian, or obscurantist, with all the nuances that such an irreducible antagonism could include and tolerate. During the last few decades, however, the problem has been set aside by a curious but characteristic tendency to suppress the duality of the propositions, by refusing to dissociate and choose between them. This was a large-scale attack on the hermeneutics and the critical traditions of the science of philology. All classifications, whether they had already been accepted or not, were suspended. So they remained to be discovered. It was convenient but deceptive to refer to elements that did not fit well together, to conclude that "the irreconcilable" had never been reconciled, and to decide to leave everything as it was, unchanged.

---

[6] [TN: In translation, this poem is often titled *On Nature*. For the best scholarly editions in English, with excellent translations, see B. Inwood, *The Poem of Empedocles* (Toronto, 2001), and M. R. Wright, *Empedocles: The Extant Fragments* (London, 1995).]

Daimonology was reintroduced into the heart of the portion that had been attributed to science. A dose of sorcery was injected in *Origins*. The impasse was absolute. What should have been acknowledged was precisely the difference between the two works; it was indeed the distinct logic of each that made it possible to grasp the unity that the two formed together, in their connection and their interrelation. Neither one is directly explained in the framework of the other. There was simply a correspondence between them, and each work can be explained in relation to the other. In the modern history of interpretation, over the last two centuries, there are, in fact, some rather inexplicable divergences among the interpreters, who were disarmed before the coherence of two forms of logic; these divergences ended up taking scholars back to the starting point and canceling out assured discoveries. The impasses were exploited naively. Scholarship had simply gone backwards.

Going back and forth, defending contrary theses regarding the two poems or the different cycles of cosmic becoming, Love and then Strife, or Strife and then Love, or one of these alone instead of half of one and half of the other, creates the impression of an eternal and, as it were, predestined beginning all over again. Scholars present the history of the problem without defining the selection criteria, and almost without taking sides, as if there were an objective science with its own logic and its own coherence that could, although contradictory, be substituted for that of the system being studied; the consensus that is established rests on a factitious exhaustiveness. On this basis one can play the game indefinitely. It is the opposite of a carefully argued questioning of the results, some of which hold up while others are obsolete.

"Physics" is linked to the birth of the world, and in a sense this genesis comes first. In *Purifications*, the world exists with its "gods," the same as in *Origins* (frags. 63, 12); it does not have to be formed. It was a real aberration to make the narrative of *Purifications* coincide with the cycle of supposed physical alternations between Love and Strife. Their cosmic supremacies are intermingled in a single unitary logic.

The poems have their own temporality. They bring it into being; it is deployed in them and is abolished there. There is succession and anteriority in matter; genesis comes before the world, but that does not rule out presupposing an anteriority of a different type. In the order of composition, *Purifications* came first, sketching out a political goal and an unsurpassable outcome. In the Strasbourg papyrus,[7] where we find a variant of fragment 139, it does seem as though we are dealing with an explicit reference, in *Origins*, to *Purifications*;

---

[7] The Strasbourg papyrus (P.Strasb.gr 1665–66) was published in 1991 by A. Martin and O. Primavesi (*L'Empédocle de Strasbourg* [Berlin and New York]).

elsewhere, too, following the epic model, lines have been taken up again and modified. One can read these passages in the papyrus as signifying adaptations of a key passage, in a new context. There is a homology to be established between the episodes of the birth of death, better known now in *Origins*, and the irruption of violence through murder.[8] The work dialogues with itself in the framework of a hierarchy. The iterations studied in *Origins* highlight a concordance between the two poems. The first-person plural, the "we" found in the papyrus, might very well be understood as a reference to the group of friends, reproducing the situation defined by the rule of community life, although it is not possible to deduce from this that "daimones" are implicated in the passage in the papyrus that comes from *Origins*. The correspondences are real, but this does not allow anything to be simply assimilated. The sense attributed to the relationship remains a determining factor.

In *Purifications*, there is no god Sphairos; that god exists only in relation to the cosmos, to its mode of destruction. The "gods" of *Origins* are not touched by him. He translates a homology between the world to come and the world that has become. Strife, Neikos, given this name in fragment 115, is not the antagonist in the cosmogonic struggle, even if the concept of antagonism, no less purely negative, remains the same. Destruction demands to be strictly isolated. The daimon plays that card; he integrates evil, which was unknown to him, into his role; he represents the divine in its fall. The two principles, good and evil, meet and rub shoulders in him. While the idyll of fragment 128 offers a fine reproduction of the peaceful scene of a Golden Age, it does not directly evoke the reign of Love, of Philia, even when it is Philia that rules, in this state of the world. One may say that the world existed, with light and stars, and that it knew a different state prior to our own; such a world existed in the plurality of possible worlds; before the primal murder, creatures lived in peace without fighting over anything.

The true presence of the divine among men is due to a rupture in the world, to the irruption of violence. Murder led to this—murder multiplied in a mass, a multitude of substitutes separated from unity, adapting to a truth made worldly, humanized. Men thus gained access to the divine, benefiting from an entry into the logic of its destruction. "Empedocles' philosophy" is developed around this dialectic, which makes the loss of a unitary state the condition for surpassing mere humanity, a process involving individuals and no longer the whole. From the human standpoint, evil becomes the condition of a good that can only be located in consciousness, which has emerged from innocence. Paradise is no

---

[8] See frag. 115, p. 84.

more. The good had simply been a given; a lost origin, it becomes the remote endpoint of an aspiration. Reparation, bringing purpose to moral life, has yet to be achieved. History cannot be directly combined with the cosmic cycle of *Origins*; it supplies no elements for the reconstitution of that cycle. It is in harmony with the cycle, but it applies to something else. The duality of perspectives has to be fully accepted. Thought is unified, but it is developing; the domains differ in every respect. It was not a mistake to oppose a natural order to reforms of a social, political, and religious order, subjecting human behavior to respect for the living.

The New Myth

The new "myth" purifies; it is based on the rupture that affects the divine as such, the organizing principle in the absolute difference of its celestial unity, which, contradictorily, makes itself visible, but in the most abstract and most immaterial manner imaginable. Its form, if one is required, will be revealed by the inaccessible radiance of the ether, or the concentration of light. This form will be alienated in the obscurity of bloodshed. The murder, which can be carried out only by a god, institutes the initial act of a contrary life. If there exists a strictly identical moment in the development of the two poems, it is that of the rupture itself, which puts an end to the state of stability outside of time, drags it away from eternity, to bring into being the order of things created by the law of Necessity (frag. 115). It is the fatality of the event of the rupture that leads at once to the reconstitution of the state that has been destroyed, the necessity that the One be divided and reproduced in innumerable living beings. Good undergoes the trial that it imposes on itself, obliged to deny itself the better to find itself again: it triumphs in the end over self-negation and its letting-go. Here we have the Muses of Sicily, according to Plato's *Sophist* (242C–E), as opposed to the Ionian Muses of Heraclitus. The other succeeds the same, in a second phase, then the same succeeds the other, which is not the same thing; it succeeds itself. The other presents itself as a negative reproduction. Unlike the model, one can reconnect with it by overcoming evil.

The daimon, in his exile, can call himself the "vassal of Strife" (frag. 115.13), knowing that he has alienated himself so as to restore order to chaos. The evil that oppresses men proceeds from the bloody act through which the gods gave up their power in favor of a rebellion, giving birth to individual consciousness through the intervention of "someone," a *tis*, which is at first only that, an entity that separates itself. Following this self-sacrifice, committed by the gods at one point in the world, the separation between beings is immediately installed everywhere. Order was unitary; division will be just as universal. The rupture of any singularity whatsoever leads the whole into plurality. "The one" is not just one daimon but a multitude of daimones. Their name is legion: the entire explosion of the divine spreads into the wound. Duality rests on the strictest antithesis and on mutual exclusion. Organized speech, even if it is the expression of anger or indignation, stems from a power that overcomes death.

An attempt at an approximate reconstitution of the whole has as its framework the diffusion of the divine, coinciding with the separation of beings. Happiness preexists; it is lost. The divine is cut off from itself, so as to widen the gap and have it recognized; so as to engender, finally, the desire for a return that rejoins physical life. This is the very fault, the transgression that the gods have produced among themselves by making themselves one with men; they have given men the gift of cohabitation with the divine. Redemption for the fault implies the presence of the divine on earth. Evil has been done. The summary of *Purifications* that Porphyry gives in his introduction to *On Abstinence* (1.1.2) connects the cathartic lamentation to a better life.[9] This is not a line of text, as had been thought, but a concentration of the whole. The ritual tears, accentuated in every form, have the task of helping to overcome the mortal condition.

In the order of human destinies, this act is primal. There remains only to purify oneself by purifying the daimon who has defiled himself and inhabits us like a delegate from some elsewhere—we have to adapt to him, to his duality. *Purifications* puts words to this work of asceticism, which leads to a simple exit from the world, a disappearance. The only salvation, if there is one, lies in the contribution to reestablishing the divine, as long as it lasts. The superhuman forces that are drawn from the exercises of purification can, during the lifetime of the saviors, be placed at the service of other, less fortunate men. Complementary political action, the struggle against violence from all sources, takes over.

Crossing the limits of the human condition remains tied to the exploration of an unknown domain and to the growth of the resources of knowledge. Transmigrations follow a certain logic. The conception of metasomatosis (or metempsychosis) probably takes local forms everywhere. At the end of his "Life of Empedocles," Diogenes Laertius, summarizing the doctrine, writes that "the soul ... assumes all the various forms of animals and plants."[10] There are partial migrations of daimones, beyond human limits in certain incarnations. It does not seem as though, for Empedocles, the nature of the reincarnations is determined by the faults committed during one's life, as in Plato's eschatological myths. There is no fault and no punishment other than the murder and the fall

---

[9] Porphyry, *On Abstinence from Killing Animals*, trans. G. Clark (Ithaca, NY, 2000).
[10] "Life of Empedocles," 8.77.

to earth that is reproduced at each birth. Procreation (more than the sex act) becomes problematic for this reason. Life extends beyond its human limits to a larger life, led by the daimon, if one can cling to him and follow him in his peregrinations. The "I" who says "I have been this or that—laurel or lion" is speaking of the daimon in himself. The migrations are those of a double free of the constraints that other daimones, having become masters and decision-makers, have assigned him. The daimones circulate. The logic of the chain of existences is charged with a collective positivity, even if destinies are differentiated each time according to the quality of the daimones, divided between natural good and borrowed evil. Are the daimones not the ones who decide and who have the last word? It is through them that one becomes, or is, a god.

Metempsychosis is attributed to Empedocles by his ancient commentators. Origen deems it mythical. Christians have their mortification in its place. Moderns question the extent of the process and its systematic character, most often concluding that the application of the principle was partial. A double legitimation may be found in thinking about metempsychosis. On the one hand, the integration of animal natures foreign to man is a powerful factor in the combat consisting in non-violence. The incursion into that reign is substituted for a factitious primitive understanding that has been lost. On the other hand, knowledge in the order of the living can be strengthened in this form, less mythical than it seems, of methodical investigations of behaviors and morphologies that differ from our own. We shall know what we do not absorb.

Non-violence, which is expressed in the rejection of blood sacrifices, is the leading principle. Withdrawal is a mode of life, and, through the conversion of the forces that command the radical respect of animal life, it is in harmony with the extension of consciousness. One loses one's strength by devouring beasts, even cooked flesh. But one appropriates the energy of animals with the help of a daimonic knowledge that extends to the living on a broad scale.

Daimones Male and Female

Daimonology is not a fixed body of knowledge, however it may have been used in later theories; since Plato, these theories have very often been syncretic. The way Empedocles conceives of daimonology is wholly original, bound up with the poet's inventiveness, something that is legible although difficult to decipher, given the state of the extant documents. It suffices to note that a daimon, a fallen god, in his cohabitation with the body of a man, is distinguished from the soul in all its aspects, whether the soul is construed as breath, blood, or vital principle. The soul is part of the body; the daimon is not. Daimones are of a different nature, noetic and immaterial just like the gods of the ether, losing themselves in their own brilliance. We have to accept this highly paradoxical presence of pure philosophical transcendence, transferred into the sphere of the religious imaginary, before we approach the readings produced by Plato, Xenocrates, Plutarch, and many others. Empedocles rethought the concepts of gods, daimones, and divinity. We have to free these concepts from associations that are foreign to them, and retain, from the texts in which they are applied, the elements that make it possible to construct the system that gives them meaning.

In his book on ancient Pythagoreanism, Walter Burkert (1972) sees "a veritable maze of conflicting tendencies" without structured doctrines.[11] Like Marcel Detienne, Burkert fails to consider the possibility that logic, without being entirely idiosyncratic, may be particular and personal. In the logic of ancient Pythagoreanism he identifies a "mythical tradition persisting along with newly developing concepts of the world, the tradition of mystery cults, ethical demands and a growing recognition of natural law." According to the author, it is a catch-all: "It is only too easy for the modern scholar, from the vantage point of his own rationalistic and systematic activities, to suppose that at the beginning there was a unified, carefully worked out and firmly defined theory" (ibid.). Methodical syncretism projected onto the object is a trap in which the coherence of a construction is lost. It is this very skepticism that ought to have been rethought.

Nonetheless, Burkert's book raises some very pertinent questions,[12] given below along with some possible answers:

Is there a soul in each being, even in plants, and do "daimones" designate a destiny reserved for certain privileged human beings? One may say that the soul, as diversified as need be, is part of all beings, and that all humans—but at the outset humans only—have a daimon double, who is allied with the body on which he lands by chance.

Does the word "soul," *psukhē*, correspond to a precise representation? Empedocles does not use the term in a sense that is directly related to our vision of things. Daimones are wholly distinct from corporeal souls, from material nature. This distinction and this dualism need to be introduced.

The introduction of dualism also allows us to answer the question about the nature of the souls involved in migrations. In Empedocles, is there a new, even revolutionary, conception of the unity of vital movements and consciousness, or is there a more mysterious and meta-empirical "self"? The question is moot if

---

[11] Burkert 1972:135.
[12] Burkert 1972:133–135.

we consider that in essence a share in divinity is associated with human natures: this explains the choice of the word "daimon" in an idiomatic sense specific to the system.

Do reincarnations occur immediately following death, or must we introduce a transitory station that reserves a function to Hades? And, concomitantly, is the soul inhaled by an organism that is being born in the cycle of becoming, or must we bring into play a tribunal that rules on the destiny of souls? The extant texts allow us to conclude (contrary to the opinion of certain scholars) that there is no Hell and no Rhadamanthus; only the world exists, already an obscure place in which men live and die without noticing any changes of scenery.

We still need to ask whether we are dealing with a circular chain of perpetual reincarnations or whether a definitive deliverance or damnation corresponds to the initial fall: the Champs Elysées or Tartarus? It is time to get rid of the mythological traditions, or at least to give priority to their transformation. The received representations are rejected. The gods have wagered on separating themselves from themselves by mixing with men through a crime that must be taken into account. The rest is nothing but an infinitely long work of reparation and a series of cathartic tasks that allow certain men to be virtual gods on earth at the conclusion of their incarnations, and to await a return to the fold, which no longer has a mythological dimension, unless the forms of visualization characteristic of philosophical speculation are included under this term. If the gods are absolutely transcendent, they have no places that would limit their power; they are nowhere in the world. If there is a "hearth," it can be only a point that they choose as a center where they gather, at the same "table" (frag. 147). The forms of their representation are determined by their nature. Nothing distinguishes the immortal beings from one another. But their abstraction is configured.

Internal and Citational Testimony

In the first part of the poem, the narrator recounted, in his own name and as an example, the adventure of his birth and the daimon's incarnation in his body. He needed to tell the story of that cohabitation and follow the peregrinations of his *alter ego*, the god who became man through blood, and was initiated into the evils that oppress men even while remaining the god that he is, in order to become a god again, purified, in the end.

The doxographer Aetius (1.7.28 = 31 A 32), seeing *Purifications* as a psychological presentation, says that Empedocles calls divine souls daimones and calls pure beings—those "who take purely their own part"—divine. Theophrastus, in his "Opinions,"[13] was unequivocal. He knew that there were souls, and souls. The definition of the divine includes, on the side of the daimones, the common form, god-men, and, on the other side, the exception, men-gods.

Referring to the lines from Aeschylus (*Suppliants*, 214), "pure Apollo, god exiled from heaven," Plutarch makes an allusion that he clears up only in part, by saying "'let my lips,' in the words of Herodotus, 'be sealed.'"[14] As for Empedocles (in frag. 115, which Plutarch cites), it is not he (who puts himself in the foreground), but, on the basis of his example, it is all of us who are out of our element here below: we are foreigners and exiles. Empedocles addresses men in order to tell them that it is not a blend of blood or breath that has provided us with the essence and the principle of the soul; it is the body that is formed of that matter, since the body is born of the earth (as shown in *Origins*) and is mortal; like the soul, the daimon has come here from elsewhere. Empedocles calls birth a voyage, using the tenderest of terms (a "distancing").

> But it is truest is to say that the soul is an exile and a wanderer, driven forth by divine decrees and laws; and then, as on an island buffeted by the seas, "like an oyster in its shell," as Plato says [*Phaedrus* 250c], because it does not remember or recall ... [w]hat honour and what high felicity [Empedocles frag. 119] it has left, ... leaving ... Heaven and the Moon for earth and life on earth.[15]

For Empedocles, it was rather the heavens that the soul leaves (Plutarch, a Platonist, confused the horizons). As for the life that one leads on earth, it is made uncomfortable by this distancing and suffers from it, even if the distance crossed is short; human life is like that of a wretched plant left to dry out. In this Platonizing context, Empedocles is defended by virtue of his originality against later enrichments and legitimizations. The daimon lives out his exile, consents to act against his multiple nature in order to complete his mission. He is the other in us—or with us—who suffers from all the elsewheres of existence, insofar as he has not recovered his own place elsewhere, according to the desire inscribed in the wheel depicted in the second part of fragment 115 (lines 9–12). What does this mean? Does the desire institute the struggle, or the end of the return?

---

[13] [TN: The reference is to *Theophrastou phusikōn doxōn Bibliōn II*, as reconstituted by Diels, on the basis of the ancient commentators, in *Doxographi Graeci* (Berlin, 1879), 475–495.]

[14] Plutarch, *On Exile*, in *Moralia*, vol. 7, trans. P. H. De Lacy and B. Einarson (Cambridge, MA), 607C.

[15] Plutarch, *On Exile*, 607D–E.

The great scandal for Plutarch, in *The Obsolescence of Oracles*, is the death of the gods: the fact that they are immortal and survive and yet die with the bodies they inhabit and leave behind, retaining in their figures the marks of cohabitation. As we read in Plutarch:

> That it is not the gods who are in charge of the oracles, since the gods ought properly to be freed of earthly concerns; but that it is the [daimones], ministers of the gods, who have them in charge, seems to me not a bad postulate; but to take, practically by the handful, from the verses of Empedocles sins, rash crimes, and heaven-sent wanderings, and to impose them upon the demigods, and to assume that their final fate is death, just as with men, I regard as rather too audacious and uncivilized.[16]

If there has been an interpretation of Empedocles that attributed death to the daimones, thrust into mortality, this is because the initiation to evil that they underwent logically occupied a large place. This accounts for the confusion denounced by Plutarch, and it brings to light the paradox of the cohabitation between mortals and immortals. In *Purifications*, Empedocles' daimones are not a separate category of beings known in the divine order, distinct from the gods and endowed only with a long life span instead of eternity; they are gods like the others, who have fallen far from their place.

The region of the powers of evil, where the fallen god is led (frag. 121), evokes a decisive phase in the preparation and initiation of the daimon. It is not only his terrestrial exile. We have to keep in mind that the essence of the daimon is divine; that is his basis, his initial nature. In order to adapt to the bodies of the divided world, he takes contrary forces into himself, undergoing the baptism of evil.

These daimones are surrounded by daimon colleagues who take care of them, govern their affairs, and follow them in their travels throughout the world of the living. Here we have, transferred, something like a group of *philoi*, citizens of another world living among us—angels, fairies, the marvelous folk of tales

Porphyry, in *On the Cave of the Nymphs*[17] (cf. frag. 120), indeed says that there are daimones who are not incarnated in living beings. He calls them "powers that escort souls," that is, the other daimones. We learn that these powers used to intervene to explain what they were doing.

---

[16] Plutarch, *The Obsolescence of Oracles*, in *Moralia*, vol. 5, trans. F. C. Babbitt (Cambridge, 1936), 418E.

[17] *On the Cave of the Nymphs*, trans. Thomas Taylor, intro. Kathleen Raine (Grand Rapids, MI, 1991), section 8; cf. frag. 120.

According to Porphyry, again[18] (see frag. 126), the principle that presides over the distribution of "souls" among bodies, a principle that can be viewed as "destiny" (*heimarmenē*) or as "nature" (*phusis*), is declared by Empedocles to be a female daimon. This principle is charged with clothing each soul with a body.

The distribution of destinies by the daimones, who are manipulators of life, corresponds to a new or true birth, presided over by the Moirai, and above all by Lachesis (who is profiled in the verb *lelakhasi*, frag. 115.5). The idea of distribution is related to that of a function, implied in the "fates" (*klēroi*) that the daimones ultimately manage to leave behind.

Some are more purified than others. Let us agree that the psychopomps, soul escorts, work things out so as to incarnate the more purified souls in the body of a sage. They then become "great intellectuals," healers and saviors, real gods.

In Plutarch's *On the Sign of Socrates*, the daimon is detached from the soul, which is tied to the body. The part that escapes corruption is usually called "intelligence" (*nous*), and it is presumed to be lodged inside, as an image is believed to be lodged inside a mirror. However, "those who conceive the matter rightly call it a daemon, as being external" (591E). The voice heard by Timarchus, one of the interlocutors in the treatise, establishes a correspondence between celestial visibility and the nature of the soul: fires extinguished during their absorption into the body, lighted up upon the arrival of the dead souls; but there is a third category that is seen to move: these are "the daimones of men 'said to possess understanding'" (591F)—applying it to Empedocles, we might well call them "purified and rid of evil." In Plutarch, it is a matter of recognizing the link that every daimon maintains with the bodily complex of the soul. In any case, the distinction is made visible. Nostalgia—the desire to return—is inscribed in the daimones' nature. Men can count on the daimones, and this helps the latter become redivinized while being purified.

The second citation from fragment 115 (lines 9–12, cited in Plutarch, *Isis and Osiris*) defines the daimones according to Empedocles, in a doxography that includes Homer, Hesiod, and Plato. Empedocles' daimones pay for their fault, for the murder that they have disseminated: this is the descent, under the sign of Strife. The inverse path, the climb back up, is shown here just as clearly: they remain in this accursed cycle "until, when they have thus been chastened and purified, they recover the place and position to which they belong in accord

---

[18] Stobaeus *Eclogae* 1.49.60, p. 446.7–11, in *Ioannis Stobaei Anthologium*, ed. C. Wachsmuth and O. Hense, 5 vols. (Berlin, 1958; orig. ed. 1884–1912).

with Nature."[19] They are neither good nor bad, but both at once, impure entities that purify themselves. This is where their originality lies.

A History of Man

What is the history of humanity? One cannot rule out the possibility that *Purifications* contains a non-mythic or anti-mythic history of humanity and a certain philosophy of history. The world first, then the men who inhabit it, existed before there was anything like a "religion." Religion intervened at a certain point. What is the philosophy of this history that can be retraced? Man lived in peace with the other creatures—if this is the primitive state that is to be reconstituted. Originally, a pure, non-conflictual goodness (*philophrosunē*) occupied the place of justice (*dikaiosunē*, with the same suffix *sunē*); this was before the murder.

Man was not conceived in violence. However, he became man socially by escaping the carnage unleashed by the murder. If the daimones were the ones who saved him and protected him from the beasts, one can conclude that, at this initial stage, they were incarnated only in men's bodies; it was to this encounter that the daimones' intervention was destined. There were men, and the gods associated themselves with them.

Having left behind the war of all against all, men were able to institute the symbolic act of sacrifice to appease the gods. It was a matter of satisfying them in order to survive. This was already a form of "purification," but not the right one, and it was challenged by Empedocles. Blood engendered the bloodshed in the rite (see Heraclitus, frag. 5: "they vainly [try to] purify themselves ...")[20]; it was necessary to follow the contrary path with the greatest possible determination, and choose non-blood. This was the thesis, divine rather than religious, and the underlying principle.

The logic of this thesis can be reconstructed. It is not so much that men free themselves by denouncing the Hesiodic sacrificial pact (*Theogony* 535–616; *Works and Days* 42–105), as Detienne (1970), along with others, has suggested, and that they reject the difference sanctioned by the rite. Philosophical reflection

---

[19] Plutarch, *Isis and Osiris*, in *Moralia*, vol. 5, 361C. [TN: Here is the citation in context: "Empedocles says also that the demigods must pay the penalty for the sins that they commit and the duties that they neglect:
Might of the Heavens chases them forth to the realm of the Ocean;
Ocean spews them out on the soil of the Earth, and Earth drives them
Straight to the rays of the tireless Sun, who consigns them to Heaven's
Whirlings; thus one from another receives them, but ever with loathing;
until, when they have thus been chastened and purified, they recover the place and position to which they belong in accord with Nature."]

[20] Heraclitus, *Fragments*, trans. T. M. Robinson (Toronto, 1987), p. 13.

did not follow this logic: Pythagoras did not, nor did Empedocles. The gods were conceived and men with them. Even savages can be divinized, men-gods at the other pole. A new cult is proposed in place of the other, the latter being viewed as the "animal" pole by Empedocles, in any case. The initial de-animalization, provoked by daimonization, is still going on.

The forcible entry of violence, projected into the exemplary narrative of sacrifice, did not imply simply an extension to all beings, but the primary effect, in the order of the living, was allelophagia, a universalized cannibalism that pitted men against animals, as well as against themselves (see frag. 130). It was a second point of departure, another origin; the first may be regretted, the second lamented. Men had to fight to rid themselves of the animal component, aided by their daimones, who were becoming human. In this, in the universal consequence of the primal murder, all men are complicit with the crime that made them truly men. The two poles that have been established in the history of the world, the divine and its sacrificial negation—a sacrifice offered to men—open a path to reestablishment. This would have to be deduced from the very logic of the global construction, but one finds a double testimony to it in the fragments, direct testimony with the mutual devouring and indirect with the evocation of the peace that had reigned earlier. One did not kill (1), then there was the murder that changed everything (2); to escape the logic, there must be no more killing (3).

Works Cited

Burkert, W. 1972. *Lore and Science in Ancient Pythagoreanism*. Trans. E. L. Minar, Jr. Cambridge, MA. Orig. pub. *Weisheit und Wissenschaft: Studien zu Pythagoras, Philolaos und Platon*, Nuremberg, 1962.

Detienne, M. 1963. *La notion de daïmon dans le pythagorisme ancien: de la pensée religieuse à la pensée philosophique*. Paris.

———. 1970. "La cuisine de Pythagore." *Archives des sciences sociales des religions* 29:141–162.

Diels, H., and W. Kranz, eds. 1951. *Die Fragmente der Vorsokratiker*, 6th ed. Berlin, 1951.

Zuntz, G. 1971. *Persephone: Three Essays on Religion and Thought in Magna Graecia*. Oxford.

Fragments

[TN: The fragments discussed in this essay are provided here in Brad Inwood's translation (in *The Poem of Empedocles*, revised edition, Toronto, 2001; © University of Toronto Press, reprinted with permission of the publishers). Readers will note that Jean Bollack's readings often reflect alternative interpretations, justifications for which appear in his commentary.]

Fragment 112

ὦ φίλοι, οἳ μέγα ἄστυ κατὰ ξανθοῦ Ἀκράγαντος
ναίετ' ἀν' ἄκρα πόλεος, ἀγαθῶν μελεδήμονες ἔργων,
<ξείνων αἰδοῖοι λιμένες κακότητος ἄπειροι,>
χαίρετ'· ἐγὼ δ' ὑμῖν θεὸς ἄμβροτος, οὐκέτι θνητός
5   πωλεῦμαι μετὰ πᾶσι τετιμένος, ὥσπερ ἔοικα,
ταινίαις τε περίστεπτος στέφεσίν τε θαλείοις·
πᾶσι δ' ἄμ' εὖτ' ἂν ἵκωμαι ἐς ἄστεα τηλεθάοντα,
ἀνδράσιν ἠδὲ γυναιξί, σεβίζομαι· οἱ δ' ἄμ' ἕπονται
μυρίοι ἐξερέοντες, ὅπη πρὸς κέρδος ἀταρπός,
10 οἱ μὲν μαντοσυνέων κεχρημένοι, οἱ δ' ἐπὶ νούσων
παντοίων ἐπύθοντο κλύειν εὐηκέα βάξιν,
δηρὸν δὴ χαλεπῇσι πεπαρμένοι <ἀμφ' ὀδύνῃσιν>.

O friends, who dwell in the great city of the yellow Acragas,
up in the high parts of the city, concerned with good deeds,
<respectful harbours for strangers, untried by evil,>
hail! I, in your eyes a deathless god, no longer mortal,
5   go among all, honoured, just as I seem:
wreathed with ribbons and festive garlands.
As soon as I arrive in flourishing cities I am revered
by all, men and women. And they follow at once,
in their ten thousands, asking where is the path to gain,
10 some in need of divinations, others in all sorts of diseases
sought to hear a healing oracle,
having been pierced <about by harsh pains> for too long a time.

Fragment 115

ἔστιν ἀνάγκης χρῆμα, θεῶν ψήφισμα παλαιόν,
ἀίδιον, πλατέεσσι κατεσφρηγισμένον ὅρκοις·
εὖτέ τις ἀμπλακίῃσι φόνῳ φίλα γυῖα μιήνῃ
†ὃς καὶ† ἐπίορκον ἁμαρτήσας ἐπομώσει
5 δαίμονες οἵτε μακραίωνος λελάχασι βίοιο,
τρίς μιν μυρίας ὥρας ἀπὸ μακάρων ἀλάλησθαι,
φυόμενον παντοῖα διὰ χρόνου εἴδεα θνητῶν
ἀργαλέας βιότοιο μεταλλάσσοντα κελεύθους.
αἰθέριον μὲν γάρ σφε μένος πόντονδε διώκει,
10 πόντος δ' ἐς χθονὸς οὖδας ἀπέπτυσε, γαῖα δ' ἐς αὐγάς
ἠελίου φαέθοντος, ὁ δ' αἰθέρος ἔμβαλε δίνῃς·
ἄλλος δ' ἐξ ἄλλου δέχεται, στυγέουσι δὲ πάντες.
τῶν καὶ ἐγὼ νῦν εἰμι, φυγὰς θεόθεν καὶ ἀλήτης,
νείκεϊ μαινομένῳ πίσυνος.

There is an oracle of necessity, and ancient decree of the gods,
eternal, sealed with broad oaths:
whenever one, in his sins, stains his dear limbs with blood
... [the text is corrupt here] by misdeed swears falsely,
5 [of] he daimons [that is] who have won long-lasting life,
he wanders for thrice then thousand seasons away from the
    blessed ones
growing to be all sorts of forms of mortal things through time,
interchanging the hard paths of life.
For the strenth of aither pursues him into the sea,
10 and the sea spits [him] onto the surface of the earth and earth
    into the beams
of the blazing sun, and throws him into the eddies of the air;
and one after another receives [him], but all hate [him].
I too am now one of these, an exile from the gods and a wanderer,
trusting in mad strife.

Fragment 119

ἐξ οἵης τιμῆς τε καὶ ὅσσου μήκεος ὄλβου

from what honour and how great a height of bliss

Fragment 120

ἠλύθομεν τόδ᾽ ὑπ᾽ ἄντρον ὑπόστεγον

we came down into this roofed-in cave

Fragment 121*

..............................ἀτερπέα χῶρον
ἔνθα Φόνος τε κότος τε καὶ ἄλλων ἔθνεα κηρῶν,

....

Ἄτης ἀν λειμῶνα κατὰ σκότος ἠλάσκουσιν.
αὐχμηραί τε νόσοι καὶ σήψιες ἔργα τε ῥευστά

...............................an unpleasant place
where there are blood and wrath and tribes of other banes
....

they wander in darkness in the meadow of Atè.
and parching diseases and rots and deeds of flux [?]

*Note: Inwood splits this into two separate fragments.

Fragment 122

ἔνθ᾽ ἦσαν Χθονίη τε καὶ Ἡλιόπη τανάωπις,
Δῆρίς θ᾽ αἱματόεσσα καὶ Ἀρμονίη θεμερῶπις,
Καλλιστώ τ᾽ Αἰσχρή τε, Θόωσά τε Δηναίη τε,
Νημερτής τ᾽ ἐρόεσσα μελάγκουρός τ᾽ Ἀσάφεια

where there were Earth and Sun far-seeing
and bloody Battle and Harmony of solemn aspect
and Beauty and Ugliness and Speed and Delay
and lovely Truth and dark-haired obscurity

Fragment 123

Φυσώ τε Φθιμένη τε, καὶ Εὐναίη καὶ Ἔγερσις,
Κινώ τ᾽ Ἀστεμφής τε, πολυστέφανός τε Μεγιστώ,
κἀΦορίη Σωπή τε καὶ Ὀμφαίη.

and Birth and Waning and Repose and Waking
and Movement and Stability and much-crowned Greatness
and Barrenness and Silence and Prophecy.

Fragment 128

> οὐδέ τις ἦν κείνοισιν Ἄρης θεὸς οὐδὲ Κυδοιμός
> οὐδὲ Ζεὺς βασιλεὺς οὐδὲ Κρόνος οὐδὲ Ποσειδῶν,
> ἀλλὰ Κύπρις βασίλεια ....
> ....
> τὴν οἵ γ᾽ εὐσεβέεσσιν ἀγάλμασιν ἱλάσκοντο
> 5 γραπτοῖς τε ζώοισι μύροισί τε δαιδαλεόδμοις
> σμύρνης τ᾽ ἀκρήτου θυσίαις λιβάνου τε θυώδους,
> ξουθῶν τε σπονδὰς μελίτων ῥίπτοντες ἐς οὖδας,
> ....
> ταύρων δ᾽ ἀκρήτοισι φόνοις οὐ δεύετο βωμός,
> ἀλλὰ μύσος τοῦτ᾽ ἔσκεν ἐν ἀνθρώποισι μέγιστον,
> 10 θυμὸν ἀπορραίσαντας ἐέδμεναι ἠέα γυῖα.

> They had no god Ares or Battle-Din,
> nor Zeus the kin nor Kronos nor Poseidon;
> but Kupris the queen [Aphrodite] ....
> ....
> her they worshipped with pious images,
> 5 painted pictures and perfumes of varied odours,
> and sacrifices of unmixed myrrh and fragrant frankincense,
> dashing onto the ground libations of yellow honey
> ....
> [her] altar was not wetted with the unmixed blood of bulls,
> but this was the greatest abomination among men,
> 10 to tear out their life-breath and eat their goodly limbs.

Fragment 129

> ἦν δέ τις ἐν κείνοισιν ἀνὴρ περιώσια εἰδώς,
> ὃς δὴ μήκιστον πραπίδων ἐκτήσατο πλοῦτον.
> παντοίων τε μάλιστα σοφῶν ἐπιήρανος ἔργων·
> ὁππότε γὰρ πάσησιν ὀρέξαιτο πραπίδεσσιν,
> 5 ῥεῖ᾽ ὅ γε τῶν ὄντων πάντων λεύσσεσκεν ἕκαστον,
> καί τε δέκ᾽ ἀνθρώπων καί τ᾽ εἴκοσιν αἰώνεσσιν.

> There was among them a man of exceptional knowledge,
> who indeed obtained the greatest wealth in his thinking organs,
> master of all kinds of particularly wise deeds;
> for whenever he reached out with all his thinking organs

5   he easily saw each of all the things which are
     in ten or twenty human lifetimes.

Fragment 130

ἦσαν δὲ κτίλα πάντα καὶ ἀνθρώποισι προσηνῆ,
θῆρές τ᾽ οἰωνοί τε, φιλοφροσύνη τε δεδήει.

All were tame and gentle to men,
both beasts and birds, and loving thoughts blazed on.

Fragment 134

οὐδὲ γὰρ ἀνδρομέη κεφαλῇ κατὰ γυῖα κέκασται,
οὐ μὲν ἀπὸ νώτοιο δύο κλάδοι ἀίσσουσι,
οὐ πόδες, οὐ θοὰ γοῦν᾽, οὐ μήδεα λαχνήεντα,
ἀλλὰ φρὴν ἱερὴ καὶ ἀθέσφατος ἔπλετο μοῦνον,
φροντίσι κόσμον ἅπαντα καταΐσσουσα θοῇσιν.

For [it / he] is not fitted out in [its / his] limbs with a human
    head,
nor do two branches dart from [its /his] back
nor feet, nor swift knew nor shaggy genitals;
but it / he is only a sacred and ineffable thought organ
darting through the entire cosmos with swift thoughts.

Fragment 137

μορφὴν δ᾽ ἀλλάξαντα πατὴρ φίλον υἱὸν ἀείρας
σφάζει ἐπευχόμενος μέγα νήπιος, οἱ δ᾽ ἀπορεῦνται
λισσόμενον θύοντες· ὁ δ᾽ αὖ νήκουστος ὁμοκλέων
σφάξας ἐν μεγάροισι κακὴν ἀλεγύνατο δαῖτα.
5   ὣς δ᾽ αὔτως πατέρ᾽ υἱὸς ἑλὼν καὶ μητέρα παῖδες
     θυμὸν ἀπορραίσαντε φίλας κατὰ σάρκας ἔδουσιν.

A father lifts up his dear son, who has changed his form,
and prays and slaughters him, in great folly, and they are at a loss
as they sacrifice the suppliant. But he, on the other hand, deaf to
    the rebukes,
sacrificed him in his halls, and prepared himself an evil meal.
5   In the same way, a son seizes his father and the children their
        mother,
     and tearing out their life-breath devour their own dear flesh.

Chapter Six

Fragment 146

εἰς δὲ τέλος μάντεις τε καὶ ὑμνόπολοι καὶ ἰητροί
καὶ πρόμοι ἀνθρώποισιν ἐπιχθονίοισι πέλονται·
ἔνθεν ἀναβλαστοῦσι θεοὶ τιμῇσι φέριστοι.

And finally they become prophets and singers and doctors
and leaders among men who dwell on earth;
thence they sprout up as gods, first in their prerogatives.

7

An Anthropological Fiction[†]

FREUD USED THE WORD "HISTORICAL" on several occasions to characterize what he set out to describe in *Moses and Monotheism*;[1] the word implies that he was referring to events that had actually happened, that were not arbitrarily constructed. He could rely on psychoanalysis to assure him that this was the case. On the other hand, given the material and the vast time frame involved, the author was at liberty to choose among the known historical facts, which lend themselves to interpretation, as the book's outline attests; from start to finish, he offers a carefully balanced account of human history. These two aspects—that which was and that which might have been—are constantly intertwined, in accordance with the requirements of Freud's intellectual agenda, becoming speculative whenever clarification is needed.

The history of the earliest Jews consists essentially of three phases: the Egyptian revelation, followed by a relapse in the wilderness, and then by a revival of the original insights.

The "historical novel" focused on Moses starts from a well-known event in Egyptian history—the sudden change in the cultural and political tradition instituted by the pharaoh Akhenaten when he singled out, in a monotheistic vision, the figure of a unique solar deity called Aton.[2] The presence of the Jews in Egypt, an early focus of attention in the Bible, led to the association of the two peoples.

---

†   Originally published as "Une fiction anthropologique," in: *Savoirs et clinique. Revue de psychanalyse* 15 (2012), pp. 177–193.

1   [TN: Jean Bollack cited material in his own translations from the original German text: *Der Mann Moses und die monotheistische Religion* (The Man Moses and Monotheistic Religion), in *Gesammelte Werke*, vol. 15 (London, 1950 [1939]), 101–246 (*Moses and Monotheism*, trans. J. Strachey, in *Standard English Edition of the Complete Psychological Works of Sigmund Freud*, ed. J. Strachey, vol. 23 [London, 1953–66], 3–137; hereafter *SE*). A manuscript draft dated September 8, 1934, "Der Mann Moses: Ein historischer Roman" (*The Man Moses: A Historical Novel*), can be found in the Freud archives in the Library of Congress, Washington, D.C. Jean Bollack alludes to this title in his essay.]

2   Thanks in part to Assman's important work (1997), we know that the theory of Moses' Egyptian origin goes back to antiquity (confirmed by Manetho, in the third century BCE), and we know that it was taken up again during the modern era, especially in the eighteenth century. Freud must have been aware that he was working within a tradition, but he did not study it as such.

The assertion of monotheism had grown out of the purification of a tradition; it began as an intellectual reform that at the same time brought to fruition a potentiality inherent in religion. It was not a Jewish reform. The subversive mystique, born as it was in pharaonic Egypt, was unable to survive—we know this to be the case—for it was too bold, and it rode roughshod over institutions and customs alike. But the revolutionary message and its justification spread. At first the idea gained ground on its own; it was picked up by a man who was not a king. This man was Moses who, according to Freud, behaved as if he were the pharaoh himself. This proximity to power reminds us of other episodes in the Bible, the story of Joseph, for example. Moses the Egyptian not only shared the king's ideas, he almost shared his sovereign authority ("[t]he doctrine of Moses may have been even harsher than that of his master" [*SE* 23:47]). Moses found a receptive consciousness in a foreign community, that of the Hebrews. Just as the measures taken by the reformist pharaoh were abolished by his successors after his death, so Moses' moral and intellectual (as well as spiritual) demands were abandoned in the long run by the community of the Hebrews; the latter turned against the reformer, who was made to pay with his life for his ideas and his adherence to monotheism.

This radical change provides the recurrent theme governing the evolution of Freud's version of the story; he sometimes characterized it as a "novel" centered on the figure of Moses and competing with the legend of Joseph, which Thomas Mann, in his tetralogy *Joseph and His Brothers* (1933–1943), endowed with striking literary currency; it too is somewhat removed from the Bible. Three of Mann's four volumes—the second, *The Young Joseph* (1933), and the third, *Joseph in Egypt* (1936)—were published during Freud's lifetime. Mann chose to make Akhenaten the pharaoh whom Joseph served as his interpreter of dreams. The reformer found in Joseph the inspired companion of his visionary illuminations, a precursor of Moses.

Monotheism marked a decisive break in the theological sphere. For the Jews, the old gods, who had been created as the result of human weakness and lack of imagination, were definitively put to rest. Right from the start, the single god brought with him a whole system, implying a rule of conduct applicable to the world at large and to life. By eliminating the arbitrary, this god restrained what had been rule by brute force. Freud had his own criteria for truth, borrowed from science. Science was as imperious and monarchical as the rational god. As for the old gods, one could only yield to them, and then, at best, learn from the delusions associated with them. In the "novel," polytheism is reduced to a phase that the Hebrews had to get through and overcome, by following a path of initiation that had literary models.

Liberation did not just happen. It required a preparation that could only have taken place in Egypt, at the heart of the most stable and settled organization that existed at the time. Moses the Egyptian was above all an exceptional figure, a "great man"; the pharaoh Akhenaten, his model, had been such a man before him. It is true that Moses did not benefit from the power accumulated by the exercise of kingship, but the energy that motivated him had already been in force since the origins of society. In prehistory, this energy was concentrated in the figure of the leader of the "horde,"[3] before that individual was killed and before separate groups broke away to flee his violence.

One can obviously associate this revenge of the weak against the powerful with Nietzsche's work, without exaggerating the latter's direct influence on Freud.[4] The framework surrounding the projections of *Totem and Taboo* is openly inscribed within the field of anthropology; rebellion leads to the murder of the father; social control is then established by the heirs. The concentration of power comes first, preceding the dispersal of the horde. It is in this way that, in light of its initial unification, the collective can be considered as an individual and treated as such. Resistance comes second; it is the logical and necessary corollary of socialization. Untrammeled power is deposed before new energy can be mustered and reconstituted in the person of a leader, who will again be an exceptional individual. Every time, at every stage, the opposition voices its rejection, right up to Jesus and his teachings. It always starts with a murder—that is a prototype. In the positive phase, whenever power is re-embodied as a governing force in a "great man," the concentration of energy is naturally liberating, and triumphs over dispersal.

Moses is an Egyptian. After Akhenaten, he appears unexpectedly as a new reformer, almost as powerful as the first one, and he provides a second opportunity for the implementation of reform, as if history were repeating itself in order to incorporate the universal, which transcends all affiliations; transferred to another people, the reform would undergo other vicissitudes and dialectically overcome other kinds of setbacks. In this view, evil is inherent in goodness, as a negation profoundly linked to the very existence of goodness. Is this not a counter-history, created out of what was after all a chance encounter,

---

[3] Freud is referring to his anthropological sources: Charles Darwin, master of the theory of evolution, and J. J. Atkinson (*SE* 23:81, 131; he adds "and especially" the Scottish orientalist W. Robertson-Smith, who wrote about the totem feast (*SE* 23:131).

[4] Nietzsche's influence on Freud's work has been clarified in a thorough and enlightening study by Renate Schlesier (1997). The study of this influence, generally glossed over by the psychoanalyst himself, required a scrupulous examination of Freud's activity from his adolescence on (see especially p. 207).

in the context of a doubling? A destiny that had no hint of teleology was to be imprinted as a new direction in the evolution of humankind; religion was certainly not excluded, but it was transformed. There was one man, the king, then another, Moses, and one people mixed with another. This could have happened only in Egypt.

Once the strong man had been murdered,[5] the posthumous impact of the message was the other pole of the construction, which was based only partially on texts and much more on the psychological experience of a buried memory. The act had left traces and had created a "tradition"—one might speak of a heritage waiting to be transmitted. Freud uses the term "latency." Henceforth the Jews carried the memory of a criminal past; they had to atone for rejecting the revelation of monotheism. Evil—that is, the suppression of a good—was to be a mark of their fate.

Everything changed, however, in other accounts of the sequence of events, when historians believed they had found reliable references to the genealogy that the future tribes of Israel had adopted. It was not in Egypt that the Hebrews, after Moses' murder, lapsed back into their old ways, nor in the Sinai as the book of Exodus tells us, but in a different place, discovered by a famous historian who at the time represented scientific authority—Eduard Meyer, of Berlin University; he is cited for *Die Israeliten und ihre Nachbarstämme* (The Israelites and Their Neighbors, 1906).[6] This third center, after Egypt and Sinai, is Meribat-Kadesh, to the south of Palestine, across from Mount Sinai on the Red Sea. A Sinai-Horeb, a different Sinai from the biblical one, was located on the western borders of Arabia, seat of the volcano-god Yahweh. The cult that the Hebrews devoted to this god, an "uncanny, bloodthirsty demon who went about by night and shunned the light of day,"[7] may have been learned from the Midianites, whose name survives in the biblical account. This was where the god Yahweh, an incarnation diametrically opposed to Aton, suddenly appeared before the Hebrews. Freud is happy to bring up this information because it offers valuable support for his thesis; it allows him to preserve the factual elements and to

---

[5] Freud singled out Eduard Sellin's book, *Mose und seine Bedeutung für die israelitisch-jüdische Religionsgeschichte* (Leipzig, 1922), from among the sources he consulted. In the biblical books of the prophets, Sellin discovered the tradition according to which Moses died a violent death, as the victim of a popular revolt (see *SE* 23:37, 47–48, 89, and 93). The murder did not take place in Egypt, but Freud did not consider that this fact invalidated Sellin's information.

[6] Eduard Meyer's *Geschichte des Altertums* (History of Antiquity), a monumental work and a classic in its time, was first published in the late nineteenth century (the first volume in 1884; several others followed). This history included all aspects of the life of peoples and cultures, especially in the Middle East. Freud could have found the history of Israel as well as that of Egypt in a new edition of volume 2, published posthumously in 1931.

[7] Meyer 1906:38, 58.

re-interpret them in line with the biblical account. It can be read as historical evidence of the depravity of life among the Jewish tribes. One can see here the converse of the purified belief that had characterized the Hebrews' life in Egypt before Moses' murder.

The consequences of migration reached well beyond the social sphere. The itinerary was quite remarkable. If migration had first led the Hebrews into Egypt, a powerful country with an advanced civilization, and if textual memories bound them to a site that was historically well known and richly endowed, the new revelation, a counter-revelation, comes to them as an "anti-Sinai." Moving in the opposite direction, the same "people," left without a guide, could mingle with other peoples on the path of their exodus and be absorbed into one heterogeneous melting pot. They returned to the everyday, primitive practices of the cult. In Kadesh, the Hebrews paid homage to the great god Yahweh whom they found there. They knew that they owed their escape from Egypt to Moses, but they thanked the new god for it. Freud comments: "We shall find later that this solution satisfied another imperatively pressing purpose that will be revealed later" (in the final phase [*SE* 23:41]). This inconsistency was resolved by a compromise; they gave Moses his due by conferring his identity on the Midianite priest.[8] It was a new doubling, a Moses II. The Freudian story is thus enriched by the stage of the return from Egypt. The loss of knowledge was a relapse, a forgetting. This negative and contrary experience would also be overcome, and what had been repressed would be restored. Another such experience had been corrected earlier by Moses' revelation.

The Hebrews of Arabia had a dual origin. They had become mixed with other peoples, but the original tribe, returned from Egypt, still distinguished itself from the other groups: "The former Egyptians were probably fewer in number than the others, but showed themselves culturally the stronger" (*SE* 23:38). The split was finally demonstrated during the revolt against Yahweh, and it then spread in the land of Canaan itself, between Israel and the empire of Judea. What is more, the Levites—who did not form a caste—must have originally been part of Moses' entourage; he was a great lord, after all. They retained their difference, even after mixing with the Hebrews at a later date. They constituted a kind of aristocracy.

At this point Freud stays close to the Book of Exodus. The wandering in the wilderness continued. Yahweh was not the sole god to believe in, as Moses had taught, but his opposite (this is the quasi-blasphemy ventured by the historian). We might wonder about the aspects of the biblical story that could lead us to imagine the lapse, or rather the relapse, into a primitive state.

---

8   The Midianites are mentioned in Genesis 37:28 and 36.

Denial is an essential element. But the evocation of the wonders and miracles, remnants of the ordinary, archaic and unreformed representation of the divine, are equally important. The Jews had adopted the powers of a *baal* (a false god) borrowed from the peoples they had mingled with during the course of this preparatory period.

The experience of Yahweh's divine violence led to a reaction that questioned the divine as an exercise in arbitrary power; it led the Hebrews to distance themselves from that god, who now seemed to be a manifestation of the intolerable. Whatever might take its place would no longer be simply the divine.

The ethnic community of the Jews had twice been dependent on a foreign influence. First, in ancient times, the master, whom they killed, adopted the revolutionary vision of a reformist pharaoh; this earlier foreign origin can be placed in the framework of a decisive emancipation, a positive development; it was rejected at the time of the murder. Later, during the wandering in the wilderness, the Jews who had left Egypt reached Kadesh, where they mingled with the barbarian populations who worshipped violent gods such as Yahweh; these gods were inferior even to the pharaohs' gods, who had restored the traditional order after the reformer's murder. Yahweh was just one among many. The Hebrews accepted a brutal and vindictive deity; they allowed themselves—or were forced—to adopt crude and shocking beliefs. We might assume that this time they lived with evil as the antidote to purification. This second initiation constituted another phase; it was the beginning of a later awakening that restored the triumphant figure of the monotheism they had previously rejected.

The savior reappeared, and prevailed, when Yahweh was eliminated. Latency, the long period of forgetting that Freud considered an important factor, matured in this rebalancing. People had to have experienced evil, mistaken—or "ordinary"—ideas, if the good of reform, settled deep in their hearts, was to awaken and take hold. Here was a counterweight. The Jews took possession of this uncompromising force, a reformed religion, which now bore no trace of the religion they had once abjured. Its denial was thus a necessary phase in the sequence of a freely rewritten epic. It was a new Sinai, and it was in this truly cathartic mood that they reached Canaan, the Promised Land.

The impact of this phase was not limited to freeing a people from debased superstitions; it also transferred to them the logical and moral rigor that monotheism represented. Now liberated from what the Jews had taken to be a religion, a different "theology" could be applied in a different domain. So it was no longer a question of imposing one religion as superior to another. Religion had become universal, as its content had been rediscovered and re-interpreted. It no longer depended on belief, unless it confused belief with the reign of the mind.

From this point on, Freud's research defines in detail the figure of an individual destiny, enriched and held in reserve through latency and its subsequent re-awakening within the confines of memory; this figure plays a primordial role. People go through all the phases of a common experience. The intellectual implantation of a truth took place in the past, if only for a short time, and was followed by a rejection that brought about a long period of alienation and repression. According to Freud, among the Hebrews there were many occasions of "infidelity," triggered by the ordinary practices of daily life and by encounters with entrenched customs that conflicted with their own.

So there is no displacement of Judaic origins; here, too, there is reason to accept the premise of a biblical datum, the difficult occupation of the "Promised Land," the crossing of a threshold. The migrant people had already traced its boundaries on the ground, and later by exceeding the limits of their entitlements; these limits were intellectual, but they could be transferred to the natural world. By this last step, preparing their settlement, the Jews had become "other," that is, they were truly "Jewish." Circumcision had been an Egyptian practice. The old Moses had imposed it on the Hebrews. Under these circumstances, its meaning changed; for the Hebrews it was linked to the high point of the monotheism propagated by Akhenaten. A reminder of this legacy, the rite confirmed the foreigners as chosen people, endowed now with a distinctive and privileged status. The universality of which they were the guardians transcended the geographic reality of Palestine. The outcome, fixed and almost absolute, was based on a historical construction. The questions raised in reality found their answers there. Yes, the Jews were "other"; they could only become so by being more fully "human," thanks to a transference; they learned to translate a religious aspiration into a period of purified expectation that can be considered intellectual, that is, scientific. In the logic of a scientist like Freud, the spiritual belongs to the realm of knowledge. Considered from this angle, the interpretation of Freud's book that privileges universality to the detriment of Judaism does not make much sense.

A sentence in section 6, at the end of Part II, contains a profession of faith, setting the triumph of the true Moses in the text of the Bible itself: "And this is the essential outcome, the momentous substance of the history of the Jewish religion" (*SE* 23:47). In section 7, Freud takes stock of his study, going beyond its historical aspect. He accords the highest rank to knowledge of the power of tradition, and associates it with the influence of great men. The importance accorded to intellectual needs, illustrated by monotheism, comes next, and finally in contrast, the study of the ideas on which religions rely to exercise their power (*SE* 23:52). Is this an allusion to the purpose of the book, which will be emphasized in Part III, written in 1938? The first two parts appeared in Vienna in the review *Imago*; the third, which returns to the same topic, adds comments, and completes the content, was written in London in 1938; the book was published in 1939.

The surpassing of religion evolved in two stages: a product of history, it led to science, which spread without any let-up in the permanent struggle against the most violent—and, one has to fear, the most natural—opposition. Freud died without knowing about concentration camps. He may have foreseen them; some find it useful to entertain the possibility. The Jews escaped from the god Yahweh; they escaped through an intellectual act in which emancipation was inscribed. It was the manifestation of a counter-faith. We cannot stop evil, it pervades our world; but neither can we stop science, which combats and analyzes evil. This counter-faith was not revealed; rather, it was a substitute for a revelation in this rewriting of religious history. It reformed a theology.

The approach to reading texts in the service of history was modernized at the end of the nineteenth century; the new approach was based essentially on distinguishing among textual layers. The subject matter was limited to documents that could be transferred into a historical framework. In the Homeric poems, as in the Bible, it is not the letter of the text itself that mattered; the content was supposed to reflect the history of a people. The process constituted an archaeology of literary creation: it entailed excavating the strata as one might do on a dig at an ancient site, and then fitting them all together.

What was Freud doing on the scientific scene of his day? A reading of his times (a "semi" or "mini" reading)? What was he doing in *Moses and Monotheism*? He shared the desire to use texts to uncover and reconstruct history; they provided supporting evidence and revealed some key indications. There was no room for a hermeneutics of the text itself in his work; there was no author. The text does not speak, does not express itself. It provides elements for a reconstitution. There is no need to focus on the literal meaning, nor indeed on the genesis of narratives and their origin, nor on the chronological redistribution of episodes, which preoccupied the critical sciences of his day (philology, psychoanalysis, history), which were themselves in a historicizing phase. The narrative that has been passed down to us conceals the underlying story, one that is plausible and closer to real life, which we must rediscover. "No historian [*sic*] can regard the Biblical account of Moses and the Exodus as anything other than a pious piece of imaginative fiction [*sic*], which has recast a remote tradition [*sic*] for the benefit of its own tendentious purposes" (*SE* 23:33 and 34). These are two moments in history, one of which has been lost. In opposition to the text, Freud promotes the sober results of contemporary research.

Historical construction replaces textual analysis. It rests on hypotheses that lend themselves to discussion. It is these hypotheses, rather than literary compositions, that are now "interpreted." The biblical document bears witness and the writer expresses himself in the name of a collectivity. History belongs to the people; by way of the Bible it provides the material for a new rational projection, one that psychoanalysis can only accept or confirm, or at least make plausible.

This was the procedure with medieval epics, where it was agreed that they recalled events that had actually taken place, even though we are not familiar with them. We extrapolate them from the literary reorganization that transformed them with each new use. The narrative we read is supposed to reveal tendencies, but with no knowledge of the facts transcribed, we have no way of understanding them (*SE* 23:31). So we cannot be certain about anything in the Bible, whether it be the plagues that struck Egypt, or the crossing of the Sea of Reeds,[9] or the laws laid down on Mount Sinai; all these dazzling episodes (*Prunkstücke*) have to be put aside. The truth lies elsewhere.

A twofold modernity was making its way onto the scene. Philology was accompanied by a certain anthropology and by psychology. The former, external to psychoanalysis, was essentially based on the work of the Cambridge school, represented by Jane Harrison, J. G. Frazer, and others.[10] It was broadly integrated into *Totem and Taboo* (1913), which in turn acted as a reference throughout *Moses and Monotheism*. The other modernist basis is secondary in this book; it consists of proofs derived from clinical exploration. In fact, the anthropological framework allowed Freud to project psychological knowledge, acquired from individuals and their neuroses, onto a universal collective, based on the study of ritual and beliefs. Freud speaks of analogy. In general, he relies on his imagination, and it brings him no more than a probability; he then succeeds in confirming that probability by interpreting the documentation. But imagination comes first.

From the biblical version he conserves above all the Hebrews' sojourn in Egypt, their existence as a foreign ethnic group, more open and free, in the midst of a people: their "foreignness." This narrative option is grounded in a displacement of nomadic people; considered in historical and anthropological terms, the displacement can be attributed to the mobility of migratory humankind. The same people who had come from afar had to leave Egypt again at a

---

[9] [TN: Since the Red Sea was an unlikely place, many commentators translate from the Egyptian, and place it in a reedy area of lakes near the Gulf of Suez.]

[10] For the murder of Moses, Freud cites Frazer 1911–1915, vol. 3, "The Dying God"; see *SE* 23:89.

later stage, after the murder of their leader; on this point the story is still in conformity with the narrative of the Scriptures.

The numerous readings of Freud's work vary according to their authors' interests. The authors are quite often content simply to reject Freud's interpretation—and not just with reference to Judaism. It is important to classify the readings according to these divergent interests. The strictly psychoanalytic—that is, internal—reading often integrates the sphere of Freud's person and that of his opinions into a self-analysis. However, Freud uses the earlier work above all as a methodological reference. The experiences of analysis in fact accompany the research into an unfamiliar domain; they support it without being confused with its practice. There is nothing new in the book that expands knowledge gained elsewhere from clinical study. A second trend focuses instead on the application of anthropological discoveries, an external dimension that Freud had included in his earlier research for *Totem and Taboo*. This approach is far removed from psychological science, but perhaps even farther from Freud's personal situation toward the end of his life. The historical construction is closely linked to that situation. A third orientation places the focus on Judaism; it considers that the Jewish question and the upsurge in anti-Semitism form the real content of the book. Some of these studies emphasize the religious aspect. Others derive more directly, and in my opinion quite rightly, from the situation in Europe during the 1930s.

The relation to psychoanalysis in *Moses and Monotheism* is problematic. The rationale certainly relies on clinical experience, always by means of an analogical relation between the concepts of the masses and the individual, a relation that is hard to master, as Freud himself acknowledges. We might say that the whole construction of the book and the very course of its demonstrations proceed without psychoanalysis, or at least could do so in theory. Freud seems to me to be quite conscious of this "auxiliary" characteristic of his project: he is writing as a historian, from his own point of view as a psychoanalyst of course, but outside his own field; he does not abandon the foundations and knowledge of his field, although he does not increase or renew them. It is true that he refers above all to his most anthropological work, *Totem and Taboo*, which is in some ways the most speculative. In the new work, he is dealing with a timely topic that is separate; it offers no new knowledge, no confirmation in the area of his clinical research. Psychoanalysis is put in parentheses, so to speak. Freud speaks in his own name in a relationship that history has imposed on him, still in keeping with his work but as an addition.

Ilse Grubrich-Simitis, in her 1991 book *Freuds Moses-Studie als Tagtraum* (Freud's Study of Moses as Daydream), tried to understand, within the limits of the practice, why Freud dealt with this topic: "Why publish [it] in spite of its obvious imperfections?"[11] She suggested three reasons: the first concerned the "novelties" that *Moses and Monotheism* nevertheless provided psychoanalysts (but in fact is there anything in Freud's text other than references to psycho-analytic doctrine?);[12] presented as digressions, "in passing," these "novelties" attest rather to some confusion. The second reason is Freud's interest in his own Jewishness, which he declared in 1930: "What is Jewish in my writings? ... probably its very essence."[13] Here we are in the domain of the personal. Grubrich-Simitis takes no account of the political situation at the time. Thirdly, she suggests that the book is basically a self-analysis, similar to the one in *The Interpretation of Dreams*. If this were true, the driving force of critical action disap-pears from Freud's perhaps desperate and certainly militant essay. However, that driving force accounts for the lack of completion. All the arguments in the book are formulated intermittently and repeatedly, revealing even in their haste a strong concern for precision. They touch on Judaism, and particularly on anti-Semitism. Neither self-analysis nor a return to origins can be primordial here; if the reason Freud penned these reflections has to do with the global struggle, it does not reside in the self unless it renders the self a Jew and a liberator.

Grubrich-Simitis discovers (or purports to discover) a traumatic event in Freud's early childhood triggered by several deaths in the family circle that threatened his sense of maternal protection. According to her reading, the child Freud transferred this event onto the financial difficulties his father had expe-rienced (1991:32). Grubrich-Simitis sees this event as the key obtained through analysis; it explains the passage in the essay from ontogeny to phylogeny, which is related to the father.

It is as if, after Freud, the master's work had to be reinserted into the closed field of clinical experimentation, even though he himself had liberated himself from it. However, Nazism was a threat not just to culture and wellbeing, but to human survival, an aspect of Nazism well illuminated by the history of religions. Psychoanalysis, in the minds of more than a few readers, should have nothing to do with politics. But Freud's undertaking was highly political. Similarly, the

[11] Grubrich-Simitis 1991:42. Le Rider asks the same question: "Why so much art and so much deter-mination?" (2000:137).
[12] I take as my examples the essential phases in the reconstitution of Jewish religious history, examined in Part 2. Psychoanalysis has no place here; rather, the principles applied are those used in the investigation of the unknown.
[13] [TN: The full quotation reads: "If the question were put to him: 'Since you have abandoned all these common characteristics of your countrymen, what is there left to you that is Jewish?' he would reply, '"A very great deal, and probably its very essence.' He could not now express that essence in words, but some day, no doubt, it will become accessible to the scientific mind." From Freud's preface to the 1930 Hebrew translation of *Totem and Taboo*, SE 13:xv, cited in Le Rider 1993:231.]

earliest readers of Celan's poetry after World War Two did not appreciate the fact that literature, another protected domain, could have a historical dimension reflecting recent events. Lyricism, too, was supposed to preserve its autonomy lest it be lost. However, the war had changed everything, even for Freud. Whence, late in life, such an unexpected and timely investigation.

One analyst, mulling over the debates triggered by René Girard's discussion of Freud's book in *Violence and the Sacred*,[14] notes that Jacques Lacan "early on declared himself very critical of the Freudian hypothesis of murder in *Totem and Taboo*."[15] Yet Lacan remained within the domain of psychoanalysis, which in some ways Freud did not; he ventured beyond it. Lacan recalls that in his Seminar XVII, he replaced the term "Oedipus complex," which is incompatible with the primordial relationship between mother and child, with the formula "paternal metaphor";[16] it led him to elaborate a whole system around the Sphinx, so that the incest in *Oedipus the King* is not a consequence of murder.[17] This debate is crucial. In fact, both Freud and Lacan confine themselves to the myth and to its profound truth. Lacan read it differently, but he expresses fascination with the Freudian construction.[18] Obviously, if we limit ourselves to the meanings that emerge from Sophocles' play, the debate makes no sense. Oedipus is led to commit his actions by the god who is to annul his forbidden birth.[19] The "father" belongs to Freud, as does his Oedipus, but that is another question.

Jakob Hessing, a professor in Jerusalem, sees Freud as forced by events to return to his Jewish origins (Hessing 2011). In reality, he had never lost sight of them. Letters to his fiancée prove this;[20] he was a witness to the events in question, and he took a position. Hitler did not lead Freud to abandon an earlier dissidence; he just pushed the psychoanalyst to defend himself.

At the end of his scholarly study, Yosef Hayim Yerushalmi, after exploring all the themes in *Moses and Monotheism*, adds a section of questions titled "Monologue with Freud."[21] Yerushalmi believes that psychoanalysis is conflated with Jewishness.[22] The boundaries are erased—but for Freud is this only half true? Science may be Jewish, but it is not reserved to Jews. That would be incompatible

---

[14] Girard 1977.

[15] Bormans 2005.

[16] Lacan 2007:112.

[17] "... made, like the half-saying, from two half-bodies" (Lacan 2007:120).

[18] "It is not for nothing that *Moses and Monotheism* ... is absolutely fascinating" (Lacan 2007:115).

[19] See Bollack 2010 and 1995.

[20] See Bollack 2011, "Die Gemeinsamkeit ist ewig und steht doch immer neu in Frage" ("the community is eternal, yet is called into question time and again"), concerning the publication of vol. 1 of Freud's *Brautbriefe* (Letters to his Fiancée), ed. G. Fichtner, I. Grubrich-Semitis, and A. Hirschmüller (Frankfurt, 2011).

[21] Yerushalmi 1991:81–100.

[22] Major 2000 agrees with him, but he disagrees as to the exclusivity of memory.

with universality. Foreignness, throughout history, must be thought of in these terms: people in this state are not so much set apart as banished, threatened and contested. This is the inevitable outcome of persecution.

It seems to me that one cannot say, as Jacques Le Rider does in his study of *Moses and Monotheism*,[23] that the book teaches "a psychic hygiene for its Jewish readers, bound to lead them ... to deactivate the 'delusion of being the Chosen People.'" The Jews were indeed chosen, as Le Rider emphasizes later on in his essay when he refers to the propaedeutics of the scientific turn of mind. It is not a question of a future "vocation," however, but of the countenance imprinted on the Promised Land thousands of years ago.

Is the aim of interpretation to prevent a real reading? I think we have to "read" Freud's text. It has been read by being written and re-written in inevitable projections. The Jews could not be defended in any other way. In response to racism, we can say that the Jews are not a race; they freed themselves by transforming their religious practice—they are anti-racist because they are enlightened by science, the sole possible outcome of religion. This is the way Freud declared his Jewishness, the way he wanted to be Jewish, neither assimilated nor converted. In practice this position encompasses both science and the Freudian being, in perfect harmony.

At this point we cannot avoid discussion of the moment at which Freud was writing. The Jews rediscovered in Hitlerism the savage state in which they themselves had participated in their distant past, and from which they had managed to break away. It was thus an essential moment in history, thanks to their achievement of a position in absolute contradiction to the exercise of violence posited by Hobbes. The Hebrews must have struggled as they tried to reconcile the influence to which they were subject under the aegis of despotic deities with the memory of a vision that embodied justice through the workings of the mind. This struggle, remarkably powerful because of the adversarial positions involved, led them to move on to a new stage. Two opposing elements combined. A memory was restored, reviving the terms of Moses' ancient revelation, but the experience of having overcome a life of submission triggered an almost autonomous action, a result of that experience and at the same time a reinvention. It no longer had the status of the initial revelation. It was no longer expressed in the discourse for internal consumption that Moses had proffered in Egypt; it was a real entry into history, a delayed entry, one might say. This fact had an impact on Freud, and then on us, and it continues to do so right up to the present day. Hitler embodied a return to a stage that the Jews had left behind.

---

[23] Le Rider 2000; see the section titled "Une analyse de l'antisémitisme," 132–135.

This perspective radically shifts Athens from its central role. According to Freud, Greece skipped monotheism, despite all its philosophy. It never experienced an absolute break in the religious sphere; religion, unlike philosophy, was linked to the life of the people. The Greeks were spared this drama, while the Jews had the privilege of being kept at arm's length and marginalized. Freud believed in "science." He had no trouble including the very essence of psychoanalysis under that rubric. It was very "Jewish"—that is, open, without limits or boundaries. The study of anti-Semitism points to a bifurcation in religious history: massacres and idolatry are condemned. The Jews were persecuted because they abandoned a tradition that survived elsewhere. The split was necessary. Their "religion" was different from another that was more widely practiced. Freud's reminder also contains the elements of a response to the question he poses on the origins and the virulence of anti-Semitism, over and above the attacks launched against psychoanalysis in particular. The Jews, who defined themselves by their knowledge, represent, beyond any religious practice, a "spirituality" (*Geistigkeit*) that can be translated in purely intellectual terms. The war Hitler declared against that spirituality defines precisely the opposite pole, in direct contradiction with his actions. This is the kernel of Freud's book, his thesis, his reason for writing it: though "Egyptian," Moses was no less Jewish, if Jewishness was the name for a universal yearning for knowledge. All people of learning are Jewish.

For Freud, mono- (or heno-) theism is not merely symbolic of a principle of order or organization on a universal scale. The divine was already made manifest in the omnipotence personified by a man, by the mere fact that he was "one." That is why truth belongs to history, which cannot be transcended. The "one" existed in protohistory. He was the one struck down with the father. Once dead, he could be worshipped by the murderers, his descendants. Freud recalls the belief in oneness, the better to distance himself from it, and to emphasize that power was a unified whole reigning on earth before it disappeared and was mistaken for an idol, a protective authority (*SE* 23:83–84). Evolution leads to the return of the god-father who inherits from the murdered and devoured despot the quality of being-one and being all powerful. The monotheism of Akhenaten is directly related to, indeed it ensues from, the primal murder; this monotheism involved the illusory transference of a reality, in this case the incarnation of a sun god, Aton. It needed to be re-translated and brought back to the constitution of humanity within the realm of the living. Unity came first, before divinization.

When monotheism reappeared, it had been freed of the elements that had distorted it; it had become science. A negative experience, the loss of knowledge, had had a positive effect. Remnants of the religion appeared as its inverse, still a religion, but stripped of anything associated with magic or the supernatural.

In concrete terms, the inversion was to be newly concentrated in one place and in one people. The theory of monotheism was based on the experience of the Egyptian empire (it was thus a byproduct of imperialism). God was the reflection of the unlimited power represented by the sovereign. The Jews had not been in this situation; before Moses they had worshipped one of the gods peculiar to small nations. This did not prevent them from considering themselves, as a people, the favorite child. Confronted with the oneness of the Egyptian empire, Freud found monotheism in the Bible; furthermore, the Bible provided him with a "great man," the second one called Moses. The logic of Freud's construction lies in the combination of these two factors.

Freud imagined Judaization as a foreshadowing of himself; he felt it working within him in this ethnic form, inspired by the descriptions of the sacred. The conversion happened once; it can only be imagined through the entelechy of a primal murder, productive in its very negativity, which however masked an identification. Science was Jewish. That is what Freud wrote five years after Hitler seized power, acting against religion. Freud did not neglect to mention the political situation around him. The object of persecution was science, his own perhaps first and foremost, a science considered supreme, in spite of everything, in its liberating aspects. Even Christianity could be linked to protohistory; Christ's Passion was accomplished according to the logic of the initial murder, a logic that lived on. Freud places Christ within the sphere of the Jewish tradition and as a stage in its evolution. Christianity is not Greek, derived from a Platonic purification of ideas, as some others, the Pope, or René Girard, like to think. What Freud is defending is a continuity, with the conversion of Paul, in the framework of universality, a likeness and not a difference. Saul of Tarsus introduced the guilty conscience, the awareness of culpability, which replicates original sin. The murder still cried out for atonement. One of the sons, one of the descendants of those who had killed the father, had allowed himself to be killed as an innocent man. Oriental and Greek mystery religions may have provided the model of the "scapegoat." It should be emphasized that Paul was, according to Freud, "in the most proper sense" (*im eigentlichsten Sinn*; the superlative speaks volumes) "a man of an innately religious disposition; the dark traces of the past lurked in his mind" (*SE* 23:86–87). The son now occupied the father's place in the context of the same history. At the same time, Paul was hostile to the primitive tradition. The new religion did not maintain the intellectual level of Judaism. The transformation brought about by spiritualization (*Geistigkeit*) was impaired, adapted to needs that were inferior but more pressing. The Christians were Jewish and yet they were not.

Hitler's violence had precedents among the descendants of the primitive gods. The adversary was there. Everything that fed the persecution could be situated within the framework of an ancient antithesis between monotheism and the Titanic revolts. Within this context, there was no religion more just than that of the Hebrews, which separated itself from the others by sublimating them. Freud learned to identify and analyze this violence and the nature of the enemy. Hitler was fighting a mindset that challenged him. The Jews, when they separated from other peoples in Judea and afterward, throughout their history, right up to the traditional nineteenth-century Judaism to which Freud was connected through his father, had maintained this role of resistance; in Freud's view, which was not a Zionist one, the Jews were responsible for representing a vision of the world confronted with a naturally violent religious practice; a counter-religion was needed that would identify itself in the strictest sense with science, still a religion but transformed, freed from all the constraints of a religious practice, even a purified one. That, for Freud, was what it meant to be Jewish. Under Hitler, science was proscribed; the mind was proscribed. The struggle against persecution was a struggle against these proscriptions, whether one was the founder of psychoanalysis or not.

In London in 1938, Freud returned to the theory of socialization, which explains how the phenomenon of religion could be elevated to the status of a research topic. He recalls the central role of psychology in his demonstration; psychology is his guide. The bases of psychoanalytical research are used as referents, but more or less marginally. He does not really go back to the history of the Jews brought out of Egypt, but limits himself to the idea of monotheism, and what it meant for the good of humankind. It is in this little stand-alone treatise, "Application,"[24] that he turns at last to an analysis of anti-Semitism and to the stakes of a furious hatred toward Christians and Jews alike. The discourse of anti-Semitism has led to the current Nazi period, singled out by name. Freud recognizes in National Socialism a new offensive against monotheism coming from the *baalim* (the false gods), and going back further in time to a primeval violence.

Significantly, Freud concludes his history of religions with the history of anti-Semitism, itemizing the reasons that continue to drive it. He lists eight of these (*SE* 23:90–92). Murder is not among them. The Jews did not admit that they had killed the father, the archetype of the idol: "You will not *admit* that you murdered God (the primal picture of God, the primal father, and his later reincarnations)" (*SE* 23:90). Christ is included in these reincarnations. Father and son are one. The Christians, for their part, the converted barbarians, did not accept the "paternal" religion of the son; their resentment was turned against

---

[24] *Moses and Monotheism* III, part 1, section D: *SE* 23:80–92.

the Jews, the root and the "source." Hitler (who comes at the end of the list), in "his German National Socialist revolution" (*SE* 23:92), does not differentiate between Judaism and Christianity, thus revealing the close connection between the two religions.

Freud could not avoid being torn by this situation. If he fled from the edge of the abyss, it was not even because psychoanalysis, considered a Jewish practice, was being trampled underfoot. The Nazis could have tolerated it if need be, provided it were entrusted to Aryans. Persecution proved that the science itself was Jewish. Psychoanalysts were condemned along with others, equally fated to defend science and fight against the enemy. Under Hitlerism religion was newly unleashed. The two domains, science and Judaism, were closely linked; the situation proved it, but they were far from being joined in public opinion, despite past experience. In 1933, Einstein was about to leave the United States; he was preparing to return to Germany, but he then turned around for good. Freud, in Vienna, had at first tried to save what he could in the face of adversity; he had counted on some kind of resistance among the Catholics, in light of Christ's Passion. In the end, he too had to surrender to the terrifying evidence.

The historical and fictional construction of *Moses and Monotheism* allows us to analyze Freud's situation at the time of writing. When he conceived of the book, the irrational held sway; it ended up winning over Austria and the Vienna of psychoanalysis, so dear to his heart. Struggling against a devastating oral cancer, the man had to abandon everything, not only Vienna and the symbolic address on the Bergstrasse: in a way it can be said that he abandoned psychoanalysis itself, despite its growing recognition and expansion. He would be driven from his home, forced to flee from an "Egypt," just as the Hebrews were when they left Eretz Mitzrahim. One could no longer, as had been the case in traditional enlightened circles, see the Jewish God as the incarnation of justice, nor could one see the faithful whom this God protected as the people of the Book. Nazism occupied the religious stage with brutes similar to all those the Jews had encountered in the wilderness. The *baalim* had taken over and had once more spread their terror; they were dreadful gods.

The Semitic people had allowed themselves to be convinced by an exceptional individual, but then the age-old ideas gained the upper hand, among them and all around them. It was not a restoration of the royal tradition, as in Egypt. Murder made it different. The Hebrews turned against the "savior" who had appeared before them and enthralled them. They rebelled and denied him, but retained the mark of a heritage. With them monotheism passed into the wider world, whether by a rupture or a denial. The path of denial was more powerful because it was buried in the "unconscious." What for Moses had been an idea became embodied in the flesh of a human race. Moses, the sacrificial victim, thus survived in the body, if not the conscience, of the assassins. The function of the murder is to instill a lasting memory and thus assure the victim's survival through guilt. The murder of Moses calls to mind the protohistorical primal murder of the father. The differences are obvious, although the Egyptian's act is closely linked to the foundational event that is lost in the mists of time. But these are two distinct murders. Moses was not resorting to violence. The common thread exists only in oneness, which was perceived as an intolerable constraint that required denying impulses so as to maintain social order. Certain aspects of collective psychology can be found elsewhere and seem widely shared.[25] Social man, humanized, had existed for a long time. Now we have thinking man, freed from his animal nature.[26]

Freud speaks in the name of a persecuted community, but he is not addressing Jews alone; he is writing as the founder of a threatened science. He wants to make people understand the gravity of the situation. The demonstration conducted in *Moses and Monotheism* demands to be "read." Freud's audacity and his subtlety have often escaped the critics.

We can deduce that the problem of Jewishness and of being Jewish remained a central preoccupation for Freud, notwithstanding the horrific events that have left their mark on the world since the Great War. No doubt he is dealing with a personal problem that he tries to analyze and understand. But we should add that these thoughts cannot be separated from his reflections on genocide. On this issue, it is better to distinguish the question of anti-Semitism from that of affiliation; it is not tied to the individual so much as to the Jewish community, even if that community includes atheists. Was he not called upon, as Freud and as a Jew, to take a public stand and to explain the origins of such a terrifying threat? This is the challenge that *Moses and Monotheism* takes up; this is the appeal to which Freud responds. It is the book of a psychoanalyst, not a book on psychoanalysis. If the author is combating anti-Semitism, it is because he thinks that he has the tools to do so, that he can prove that evil is never episodic or fortuitous, that this is a matter of tremendous importance that concerns humankind and what constitutes its humanity. Is humanity not Jewish, and anti-Semitism inhuman? This is in fact Freud's thesis. He wrote *Moses and Monotheism* to highlight it, with even more determination once he had to leave Austria and

---

[25] Schlesier (1997:200): "Did not Freud see himself forced to pay theoretical tribute to 'the repeated criminal acts' from the murder of the primeval father to the murder of Moses?"

[26] To maintain, as some would have it, that Freud turned against the Jews in their time of persecution, by maliciously depriving them of their identity, is a real aberration. Freud's Moses speaks to the Jews as if they were a foreign community capable of welcoming a message of a universal nature.

become a migrant like the Jews of old, at the very moment when Jews have again become "the Jews" and an object of hatred.

The treatise was neither a testament nor an apologia, but specifically a response, the most substantial of all the counter-attacks that Freud could conceive. It was published in 1939 at the beginning of the hostilities; it had been written and produced in great haste, not only because the author was in ill health and losing his strength, but because time was short: the truth had to be told. The book explained in depth the causes of anti-Semitism in the midst of a global conflict. Did it not propose a remedy to war? Did it not come to the rescue of all humanity? Looked at in this light, there is no way to read the book within the framework of psychoanalysis; Freud had to step firmly outside that domain. It pained him to do so; he knew that it was a gamble, but he took the risk, despite his physical frailty.

Works Cited

Assmann, J. 1997. *Moses the Egyptian: The Memory of Egypt in Western Monotheism.* Cambridge, MA.

Bollack, J. 1995. *La naissance d'Œdipe: traduction et commentaires d'Œdipe roi.* Paris.

———. 2010. *Oedipe roi de Sophocle.* 4 vols. Lille. Orig. pub. 1990.

———. 2011. "Die Gemeinsamkeit ist ewig und steht doch immer neu in Frage." *Süddeutsche Zeiting*, no. 83, 9/10. In English as "The Freudian Romance," in *Signandsight.com, Let's Talk European* (electronic review).

Bormans, C. 2005. "Sacrée violence! Le meurtre du père revisité par Freud, Girard et Lacan." In *Psychologie de la violence*, ed. C. Bormans and G. Massat, 63–78. Paris.

Frazer, James George. 1911-1915. *The Golden Bough: A Study in Magic and Religion.* 12 vols. London.

Girard, R. 1977. *Violence and the Sacred.* Trans. P. Gregory. Baltimore. Orig. pub. 1972.

Grubrich-Simitis, I. 1991. *Freuds Moses—Studie als Tagtraum: ein biographischer Essay.* Weinheim.

Hessing, J. 2011. "Sigmund Freuds Buch über Moses. Ein Sonderfall der deutsch-jüdischen Literatur." *Psyche* 65:239–245.

Lacan, J. 2007. *The Other Side of Psychoanalysis.* Seminar, Book 17. Trans. R. Grigg. New York. Orig. pub. 1991.

Le Rider, J. 1993. *Modernity and Crises of Identity: Culture and Society in Fin-de-Siècle Vienna.* New York.

———. 2000. "Moïse l'Égyptien." In "Sigmund Freud, de *L'Interprétation des rêves* à *L'Homme Moïse*," *Revue germanique internationale* 14:127–150.

Major, R. 2000. "La vérité spectrale de *L'Homme Moïse*," in "Sigmund Freud, de *L'Interprétation des rêves* à *L'Homme Moïse*," *Revue germanique internationale* 14:165–172.

Meyer, E. 1906. *Die Israeliten und ihre Nachbarstämme*. Halle.

Schlesier, R. 1997. "Freud, lecteur de Nietzsche." *L'Inactuel* 7:191–209.

Yerushalmi, Y. H. 1991. *Freud's Moses: Judaism Terminable and Interminable*. New Haven.

8

Reading Drama[†]

DURING AN EARLIER PHASE in my career my great passion was Epicureanism, but over the last twenty years I have devoted most of my scholarly work to the field of Greek tragedy, often in collaboration with Pierre Judet de La Combe. Perhaps I should try to explain how this shift occurred. The path from the pre-Socratic thinkers to the tragedians is not a long one. They inhabited the same world, despite their different aims. In any case, I was familiar with the language and the worldview through which the discourses of the tragedies are formed. Playwrights were not philosophers, but they were well acquainted with books, especially the philosophers' books which informed their own writing, as we can see throughout their work.

My knowledge of Epicurus opened up a pathway to reading the tragedians, with a particular focus on his cautious approach to language and his distrust of rhetoric; he dismissed the rhetoric of others and created a language to suit his own purposes. Epicurus analyzes the discourse of others, as well as his own, and constantly leads us back to the tool of the unspoken, where the discursive situation[1] shows first of all that it is a reply, and that the sentence has thus been remade. A given word is full of meaning because it has been uttered, dispatched, just as in the stichomythia—dramatic dialogue in alternating lines—of the trage-dians, whom Epicurus cites frequently.

Among the pre-Socratic philosophers, philosophy formed and expressed itself without any technical constraints save those it took on of its own accord. Epicurus broke away from the legacy of the grand Athenian systems to discover a lost freedom that was almost archaic and highly utopian. The tragic play-wrights felt a similar desire for intellectual sovereignty that was probably not recognized as such.

[†] Originally published as "Lire le théâtre," in: Jean Bollack, *La Grèce de personne: les mots sous le mythe* (Paris, 1997), pp. 309–311.

[1] [TN; Epicurus is known to us principally from three letters addressed to three different corre-spondents, presumably in response to questions.]

The translation of several plays, which I undertook with Mayotte Bollack,[2] became a different project once the plays were conceived as texts to be performed. Using ancient texts and without resorting to primitivism, the theater offers a rare opportunity to make contact with an audience, to show people what the subject matter entails and what it communicates. When the undertaking succeeds, thanks to the talent of a director who agrees to place his trust in the words, the re-created reality is trans-historical: the very time-lessness of theatrical performance annihilates historical distance. Translation and the philology underpinning it prove their worth through the applause of an audience, and they take on the appearance of a manifesto of non-adaptation. Disorientation can be real, and can become part of our culture, when translation takes on the unknown aspects of a different world and endows them with the right to exist.

The transfer of a decoded meaning into another language makes this reception possible, because the language provides access to the author, who for once is reinstated, and, if we mingle with the crowd of Athenian spectators, we have access to others unlike ourselves as well (although not after the fashion of the grotesque scene in which Wilamowitz imagines himself watching Euripides' last play through Sophocles' eyes).

Convention and stylization are reduced to almost nothing. In the theater, speech is paramount. Translating Empedocles or the *Republic* involves a different set of concerns. In the case of drama, the transfer gives an immediacy to discourse that the tragic poet has already uttered secondarily, since he was making a language speak. The exceptional reliability of the translation of the tragedians stems from the use these authors themselves made of effective speech; it is thus directly linked to the act of realization in performance.

Fortunately, in the unique case of the *Electra* plays, we can observe the metamorphosis of speech in a continuity that is fortuitous, since the bulk of the theatrical production of the time has disappeared. Literary history, whose own history is worth exploring, has been concerned with creating an anteriority, and it has constructed somewhat gratuitously all the situations that could serve to defend a cultural tradition—a tradition that Euripides had, however, undermined; he had to cleave to the truth of the myth at all costs, lest he lose his status as a great poet. He had to be great, even if no one would go so far as to compare him with Sophocles. Neither his greatness, whether reflected or direct,

---

2 [TN: At the time this essay was written, three of the Bollack translations had been staged: Sophocles' *Œdipe roi*, by Alain Milianti (La Salamandre, Lille, and Théâtre de l'Odéon, Paris, 1985); Euripides' *Iphigénie à Aulis*, by Ariane Mnouchkine (Théâtre du Soleil, 1990); and *Andromaque*, by Jacques Lassalle (Athens, Avignon Festival, 1994). Later productions have included *Antigone* (Théâtre de la Bastille), *Hélène* (Printemps de Bourges), and *Les Bacchantes* (Comédie Française).]

intellectual or musical, nor the truth that he had seen fit to substitute for other more banal truths, was recognized; the experts had to turn him into someone else. And in spite of everything, he was not completely successful. Strauss's Wagnerian *Electra* was of a very different caliber from his.

From Wilamowitz on, none of the experts discussed aesthetic preconditions (these went without saying), or the problems that literary hermeneutics might have raised. The blind violence of a heroic struggle was understood without recourse to aesthetic theory; in the case of Sophocles, delving into the complexities of the plot led to problems. Perhaps the latter's Electra owed her absurd, theatrical voice to the scandalous portrayal of heroism. Sophocles saw clearly the reversals brought about by his rival Euripides; he was imbued with them—a careful reading makes this clear—but he never abandoned his own problematizing and inquisitive method. So there could have been something of Euripides in Sophocles' *Electra* even before Euripides had written his own tragedy; and Euripides might have wanted to show what it took to really write like Euripides.

9

An Act of Cultural Restoration[†]
The Status Accorded to the Classical Tragedians by the Decree of Lycurgus

THE MEASURES CONCERNING DRAMA have pride of place among the laws promulgated by Lycurgus, according to the *Lives of the Ten Orators* (included in Plutarch's *Moralia*, 841F): these measures include the institution of competitions for the selection of dramatic actors and public honors awarded the classical tragedians, both by the erection of bronze statues and by the official preservation of their works.

Τὸν δὲ ὡς χαλκᾶς εἰκόνας ἀναθεῖναι τῶν ποιητῶν, Αἰσχύλου Σοφοκλέους Εὐριπίδου, καὶ τὰς τραγῳδίας αὐτῶν ἐν κοινῷ γραψαμένους φυλάττειν, καὶ τὸν τῆς πόλεως γραμματέα παραναγινώσκειν τοῖς ὑποκρινομένοις· οὐκ ἐξεῖναι γὰρ αὐτὰς ὑποκρίνεσθαι.[1]

The second [of the two decrees, on the subject of tragedy] orders that bronze statues be erected in honor of the poets Aeschylus, Sophocles, and Euripides; that their tragedies be copied under the supervision of the community, so that they can be preserved; and that the city scribe read the texts alongside the actors: otherwise it would not be possible to perform them [the tragedies] on stage.

[†] Originally published as "Une action de restauration culturelle. La place accordée aux tragiques par le décret de Lycurgue," in: M.-M. Mactoux and E. Geny, eds., *Mélanges Pierre Lévêque*. Vol. 8, *Religion, anthropologie et société*. Annales littéraires de l'Université de Besançon, vol. 499 (Paris, 1994), pp. 13–24.
[1] This text develops my commentary on Sophocles' *Oedipus the King* (1990), ad 1:139–141.
In the Teubner edition of 1971, Jürgen Mau prints the text with Gregorios N. Bernardakis's addition ⟨παρ'⟩αὐτάς (see below, II, 3).

I. Evidence of Early Corruption of the Tradition: The Contemporaneous Use of the Text

1. The Corruption of the Text

The modern usage of the term "corruption" as applied to the history of the texts of classical tragedies, a usage that can be inferred from the interpretation proposed by Hartmut Erbse and others,[2] dismisses the hypothesis of a parallel literary tradition as presupposed by Ulrich von Wilamowitz-Moellendorff[3] and assigns an almost anecdotal origin to the measure.

1. The archiving does not amount to a new initiative: it merely perpetuates the old method for preserving the texts that poets deposited after the original competitions. The condition of these texts had deteriorated, so they had to be restored to repair the marks of wear and tear.

2. The booksellers' copies were unusable because they had been spoiled by erroneous annotations ("*Lesefehler*"). This claim entails a presupposition that has no basis in the text of the decree.

3. The texts had been defaced by the interpolations of actors as well. The practical distinction between the two traditions—the one more general and destined to be read, the other technical and destined for performance—was not taken into account by Erbse.

4. There remains the mystery of the origin of the unaltered copies that Lycurgus managed to acquire, and the hypothesis that these had been preserved in private holdings (perhaps family enterprises, according to Wilhelm Dindorf[4]). These conclusions were drawn from a text of the Pseudo-Plutarch that had already been corrected; the pre-established understandings, as is so often the case, determined its analysis and reinforced the reading. None of these four points can be drawn from the decree. A pre-Alexandrian philological concern was a matter of conjecture.[5] It is not in itself incompatible with the measure, but the decree

---

[2] In Hunger et al. 1961, 1:217–218.
[3] 1907:124–128.
[4] 1868, praef., VII n2.
[5] Erbse agrees with Turner (1951). Wilamowitz holds that the stage directions contained in the books were addressed primarily to the reader. We know that he believes that the tragedians intended their works to be read as books. According to Erbse, "[w]e do not know if Lycurgus had succeeded in obtaining clean copies from the poet's heirs. We can assume that he did his utmost to find the best version whenever authenticity was in question" (in Hunger 1961, 1:217–218). Maybe. Page (1934:2) cites the decree—with a text modified according to Grysar: οὐκ ἐξεῖναι δ' ἄλλως—detecting in it evidence of a longstanding corruption of the texts of the tragedies, owing

had another purpose (see below, III), a political purpose that was part of a much broader and more ambitious program of restoration.

The initial hypothesis of a transmission already diversified by variants or divergent versions came up against a second hypothesis, based on the exception of a single, more pristine copy that offered a model for the critical work of the Alexandrians. This was the role assigned to the city of Athens' official copy, which Ptolemy III borrowed,[6] and to the editorial reaction it is supposed to have demonstrated, without any assurance of real success, according to Rudolf Pfeiffer (1968).[7] Aristides Colonna proposes that Lycurgus' copy, "dating from around 330 BCE," is one of the "models" the Alexandrians had at their disposal when they created their text; the copy was a stage in the historical process of stabilizing this text.[8]

Thus we find interpolations and evidence of "corrections" at a very early date; such a twofold source of uncertainty justifies skepticism, but it is also evidence of a reaction, prefiguring the work of specialists. We waver between the role of tradition, the pole of a guarantee, on the one hand, and, on the other, the role of corruption, with the consequent need to exercise control.

Depending on the point of view, some scholars emphasize preservation, a public function, because individual owners and private commerce could not be relied on,[9] while others stress restoration and repair,[10] tasks promoted by the constitution of an official, authorized text.[11]

---

to actors' interpolations; Zuntz (1965:251–252) posits that the official text obtained thanks to Lycurgus might have helped the work of Aristophanes of Byzantium, noting that the latter did not have to worry about eliminating erroneous readers' notes or interpolations, but aimed "to preserve what was transmitted" (252).

[6] Galen, *Commentary on Hippocrates' Epidemics* [*II in Hippocr. lib. II Epidem—Corpus Medicorum graecorum V* 10.21 (1936), 79.8 (XVII, 607 Kühn)]. See also Pfeiffer 1968:82.

[7] See also Bernhardy 1856, 2.2:110–111.

[8] Colonna 1975, vol. 1, praef., XLII–XLV.

[9] See, for example, Reynolds and Wilson 1968:5. The authors posit the perpetuation of an original archiving that was in place even before Lycurgus. Copies were made for the actors. They did not find what they needed in private collections, when "the original performance plays were revived from time to time." No distinction is made between the two spheres and the dual tradition in the use of the text.

[10] The decree "provided that an official copy of the plays of all three great tragedians be kept in the public archives and the actors compelled to keep to this text, and the implication must be that [Sophocles'] work too was thought to need protection" (Easterling 1973:244).

[11] "Thanks to the 4th century B.C. politician Lycurgus, authorized texts of Sophocles (and Aeschylus and Euripides) were established" (Buxton 1984:5); these texts attest to the popularity of the three tragedians.

2. The Reconstitution of a Less Corrupted Tradition, to Halt the Deteriorations Ensuing from Stage Performances (Dindorf)

Wilhelm Dindorf (1802–1883) outlined the model in the preface to his *Poetae scenici* of 1869.[12] In his opinion, the first reading copies had been made available to the public by the actors; they were stage versions (*Bühnenexemplare*) and thus derivative sources. To understand the full extent of the corruption, one had to take into account copyists' errors and theatrical interpolations (lines inserted, invented, or moved, and words altered). According to this hypothesis, Lycurgus' decree was promulgated to check this development, but it changed nothing and had meager results. Corruption continued unabated.[13] This constant deterioration underlies the reconstitution of the history of the texts. The actors were bound by stricter controls: earlier abuse of the texts, in performance, is inferred from a text considered as a reaction. The canonical versions were newly reconstituted from proper sources that had not been contaminated by theatrical practices.[14] We know nothing of these sources; still, we might imagine that the poets' descendants themselves perpetuated the tradition and thus that some copies must have been found in family collections, sometimes in the author's hand, but in any case less corrupted, and that these copies might have been used in the work of purification established by Lycurgus. Unaware of the importance of a more general use of the texts outside the domain of the theater, scholars could not see the difference between two traditions, one literary, the other more technical and proper to the theater, which complemented one another.

II. Readings of the Text Since the Renaissance

1. The Scribe Takes the Poet's Place by Reciting the Play to the Actors

It seems that this was how the text was understood, judging by Jacques Amyot's translation (1572): "that they had their tragedies written down to preserve them in the public keeping and the town clerk read them to the actors, because it was not possible to perform them."[15] The last phrase, οὐκ ἐξεῖναι (which Amyot translates as "pour ce qu'il n'estait pas loisible de les jouer"), was taken to refer

---

[12] Dindorf 1868, praef., VII–VIII. Wilamowitz later modified this classical interpretation.

[13] " ... laudabili profecto consilio, sed exiguo, ut videtur, successu" ("by a praiseworthy plan, indeed, but with little success, it seems") (Dindorf 1868, praef., VIII).

[14] Some systematic choices must have been involved. Is it conceivable that copies could have been made of some three hundred tragedies?

[15] " ... que l'on feist escrire leurs tragædies pour les garder en public, et que le greffier de la ville les leust aux joueurs, pour ce qu'il n'estait pas loisible de les jouer" (Amyot 1820 [1559], 4:77).

to the practical necessity of instructing the actors, who needed this help. This opinion was repeated, with a more thoroughly archaeological bent, by Karl August Böttiger (1760–1835). The scribes were teachers, as the poets had been in earlier times; they were scholars who knew the tradition and who were capable of working on the text with the actors, right down to such details as vocal inflections.[16] However, Böttiger thought that the last phrase was corrupted: he translated it not as "it was not possible," but as "it was not permitted," but this was contradicted by the facts. We know that the tragedies were performed in the fourth century BCE.

2. Performances are Eliminated and Replaced by Public Recitations

In his edition of Plutarch's *Moralia*, Henri Estienne (1531–1598), an early French translator of the *Lives of the Ten Orators*, imagines that a competition of public readings of the plays replaced theatrical performances, without any discussion: "*ut recitatis tragoediis ex adverso contra eas liceret: neque eis tamen ius respondendi daretur*" ("it was permitted that the tragedies be recited in the scribes' presence, but the scribes were not granted the right of responding").[17] The Protestant orientalist Samuel Petit de Nîmes (1594–1643), in his *Lois attiques* (Attic Laws) of 1635, took the meaning of the last phrase in its strictest sense, making it an essential element of the measures taken by the decree (without really taking account of the function of the explanatory clause), and thus read into the decree a strong desire for moral, even perhaps aesthetic, purification. As he saw it, Lycurgus would have deemed it better to honor the heritage by eliminating performances altogether and replacing them with a simple public reading, or a recitation by the public scribe who would have been an expert in good diction and in declamation. According to the Pseudo-Plutarch, this is how Lycurgus presented the text of the law: "*eorumque Tragoedias publice asservari, et Lege cavit ne quis eas histrio doceret, sed ut publice ab Urbis Scriba recitarentur*" ("that their tragedies be preserved by the state, and forbade by law that any actor should perform them, but mandated instead that they be performed by the scribe of the city").[18] The historian Ernst Wilhelm Gottlieb Wachsmuth (1784–1866), in his *Hellenische Altertumskunde*,[19] specifies that it was not a question of economy, "not because they lacked the means to stage [the plays], but rather the better to pay homage to the aesthetic superiority of these poets" (whose work had

---

[16] Böttiger 1837:259n2.
[17] Estienne 1572:1547.
[18] See Wesseling 1742:139 §XXXII.
[19] Wachsmuth 1826–1830, 2:743.

apparently been betrayed by the actors). The purity of the message was played off against theatrical performance.

In general, critics did not accept the idea that Lycurgus' decree could have been intended to put an end to the performance of the classics. The last phrase could not be understood in this sense; it had to be a matter of new requirements for accuracy and purity.

3. Performances Are Not Categorically Forbidden, but Recitation Takes the Place of Acting Performed on Stage

It never occurred to Xylander (1532–1576) that the scribe could have rehearsed the plays with the actors; Xylander translates παραναγινώσκειν τοῖς ὑποκρινομένοις as "in place of the actors" (*loco histrionum*),[20] which explains the reading of the explanatory clause as a prohibition.

It was difficult to determine what was involved in the substitution, if it was not a matter of instruction (see above, II.1) and if recitation had not been officially substituted for performance, as the Calvinist Petit believed it had been (see II.2). Scholars were dealing with a more open rivalry between recitation and theatrical performance, and they had to find a concrete referent for it. Johann Jakob Reiske (1716–1774) gives short shrift to the last phrase: the performers were obliged to read because "they" (the scribes or the custodians of the archives; Reiske reads αὐτούς for αὐτάς: *ipsos scribas vel tabularum custodes*) did not allow them to perform.[21] The confusion is obvious. Daniel Albert Wyttenbach (1746–1820) added to Xylander's translation a *suo arbitratu*, "of their own free will" (*histrionum, quibus suo arbitratu eas agere non liceret*, "... actors, who were not allowed to perform them [the tragedies] of their own free will").[22] So that the verb "to perform" might have a derogatory meaning, an element of freedom and abandon was inferred. With παραναγινώσκειν translated as "to read, to recite" rather than as "to read beside, to collate, to compare," these scholars necessarily ended up in the aporia of a competition. The actors took too many liberties; the task should be entrusted to more serious people. At one point, Wyttenbach formulates the hypothesis that "perhaps" a better reading would be καὶ οὐκ ἐξεῖναι παρ' αὐτάς, "it was not permitted [to the actors] to perform beyond [the letter of the text]" (p. 319). The almost ludicrous substitution of scribes for actors was thus avoided, and at the same time the *suo arbitratu* was eliminated, rationally enough: actors would be allowed to act, but they

---

[20] See Reiske's edition (1778, 9:38–39.4), which follows Xylander's translation.

[21] [TN: At stake here is the gender of the Greek third-person pronoun: if the masculine *autous* is used, it refers to the actors, if the feminine *autas* is used, it refers to the tragedies.]

[22] See Wyttenbach's edition of the *Moralia* (1830:4.1.319).

had to adhere strictly to the text. Thus Xylander's translation of the preceding sentence, reproduced in his book, could not be maintained.

4. The Scribe Attends the Performances to Supervise the Production and Prevents the Actors from Taking Liberties with the Text

K. F. Heinrich, in his 1806 commentary on Juvenal,[23] proposed a new function for the scribe; he was no longer the director of the actors, nor an actor who did not act, but rather a supervisory authority, in keeping with his dignity. He was present at every performance, following the play on his official copy to make sure that no one deviated from the text. Heinrich adopted Reiske's correction (see above: αὐτούς).[24] "For (or before) the actors" is taken to mean "observing their diction": *agentibus eas in scena histrionibus, iuxta et altrinsecus exscripto exemplari legeret* ("while the actors were performing them [the plays] on stage, he [the scribe] was reading [the script] behind the scenes, to be emulated as a copy [by the actors]"). Gottfried Hermann (1772–1848) agrees;[25] he adopts Reiske's conjecture αὐτούς, but disagrees with him on the pronoun he applies to the actors: *ne quid histriones suo arbitrio* (see above) *mutarent*; ὑποκρίνεσθαι,[26] that is, to use the text freely, for one's own purposes.[27] It was this supervisory authority that W. W. Goodwin retains in his revised and corrected translation of the *Moralia*[28]: "and that the public clerk [i.e., the scribe] should read these copies as the plays were acted, that nothing might be changed by the players [this clause is Charles Barcraft's addition]; and that otherwise it should be unlawful to act them (p. 38)." The scribe no longer "reads" in the place of the actors. His supervision is conceived as concomitant. The play is performed; the scribe is present, with a valid text; he follows along with this copy, like a director, during the performances, to see where the actors are making mistakes. Presumably the

---

23 Heinrich 1839:19.

24 "Ils lisaient; ils n'avaient pas le droit de jouer" (this was the situation imagined in II.3, above).

25 Hermann 1827, 2:155.

26 [TN: This is the middle form of a verb that means "to play a part, be an actor"; it can also have the sense of "to perform [tragedies/comedies]."]

27 August Boeckh (1785–1867) supports a related interpolation (1808:327–28), which he could have read in Johann Matthias Gesner (1691–1761), in his commentary on Quintilian (1738, ad 10.1.66). The idea is almost absurd: the scribe would sit through the performance of a new play that revived one of the many topics that the classical authors had dealt with, and try to detect the borrowings and plagiarisms. He would be defending the authors' copyright.

28 Goodwin 1878, 5:35–42. The same point can be found in Bétolaud 1870, 3, p. 733: "que le gardien de ces archives suivît la lecture du texte pendant que les comédiens le joueraient: autrement la représentation n'en devait pas être autorisée" ("that the guardian of these archives should follow the written text while the actors performed the play: otherwise the performance should not be authorized").

presence of a supervisor prevented any blunders and provided this guarantee to the audience. Heinrich's understanding of the dative as "for the actors" is still awkward; it implies that the scribe helps the actors by reading alongside them (παρ-) (grammatically, the pre-verb and the complement should be linked). From a public reading that takes the place of a theatrical performance, we have passed to a silent exercise, very far from declamation.

5. Prior Verification of the Quality of the Text by the "Men of the Theater"

Friedrich Gottlieb Welcker (1784–1868) was vehemently opposed to Heinrich.[29] He could not envisage an important person, a high-level functionary, sitting in the theater with the archival copy on his lap. Welcker thought it more natural to reverse the roles: the actors themselves were obliged to ensure the quality of the text they were performing. The text of the decree imposed this prior inspection. The actors went to the scribe, who read to them the reference text. The secretary confirmed with them that the text they were rehearsing was the correct one. It would be a kind of *dokimasia*,[30] before a supervisory authority. Once the text passed the test, it would receive a label documenting official recognition. The dative was no longer problematic; "for the actors" was correct.

The success of this interpretation of the text among the historians of transmission was assured. The original letter of the text was defective; what was needed was some library work, with the help of specialists and archivists, to restore a reliable model. Welcker did not alter the text of the final sentence, thinking that one could imagine adding, "simply," that is "without these precautions."[31] Most recent authors, who have for the most part followed Welcker, have preferred to correct the text, usually by adopting Wyttenbach's conjecture of παρ' αὐτάς (discussed above), which could be combined with the hypothesis of a prior reading for verification.[32] I cite here M. Cuvigny's translation in the Budé edition of the *Moralia* (1981, 12:1): "que le secrétaire de la cité devait lire aux acteurs appelés à interpréter leurs oeuvres" ("that the city clerk had to read to the actors called to interpret their works" [these last words are

---

[29] Welcker 1839–41, 3:907n33.

[30] [TN: An examination to prove oneself a qualified citizen of Athens, able to exercise public rights and duties.]

[31] "... denn es sollte *forthin* nicht freystehen ... sie zu spielen, wie bisher" (for *henceforth* it should not be allowed ... [for the actor] to perform them as in the past" (see n. 31 above).

[32] See O. Korn's dissertation (1863:5–6, followed by O. Jahn and F. W. Ritschl); Sommerbrodt 1864:131–132.

not supported by the text]). Indeed, any deviation from the text was forbidden.[33] Obviously, it is hard to account for the repetition of ὑποκρίνεσθαι, following the logic of Welcker's analysis. In fact, we end up where we started, without having made any real progress on the hermeneutic front. The preliminary analysis, didactic and formative and thus technical, as it had been conceived (see above, II.1), had become more of an informational document, more literary and regulatory. One approach was no more plausible than the other; undoubtedly an important aspect of theater life, linked to the staging of plays, had been lost. The change corresponded perfectly with the shifting of methodological interests. The positivist critical method of the nineteenth century is reflected in the last analysis, which became "canonical," but on the whole, if we look at a transhistorical schema, the *letter* of the text and the need to conform to it won the day among scholars, over the realities of the stage, which were quickly put in the same category as superficiality and improvisation (see solutions 2 through 5). Herein lies the flaw, in the methodical suspicion of cultural productions.

Bernhardy's interpretation[34] stands out from the others by the meaning he gives to παραναγινώσκειν, indicating the textual work, the analysis of the literary tradition (*recognitio*), and its dramatic utilization. This marked a step towards an accurate understanding.[35]

III. The Original Meaning Is Political, Aimed at the Complete Restoration of a National Cultural Past

1. Taking the Technical Copies of Theatrical Texts into Consideration

In the fourth century BCE, among the orators, παραναγινώσκειν ("to compare, collate, read beside") highlights a confrontation, a comparative reading, or the collation of a document with another text. The dictionary[36] shows that the dative is used for the object of comparison, next to καί ("and") or following

---

[33] See also Fowler's translation of the *Moralia* (1936:401): "that the clerk of the State read them to the actors who were to perform their plays for comparison of the texts and that it be unlawful to depart from the authorized text in acting."

[34] Bernhardy 1856; see above n7.

[35] Bernhardy accepted a rather indefensible cut before τοῖς ὑποκρ., leaving τοῖς ⟨δ'⟩ ὑποκρινομένοις οὐκ ἐξεῖναι ⟨παρ'⟩αὐτὰς [with Wyttenbach] ὑποκρίνεσθαι without a complement. The repetition seems odd. Moreover (but the argument is valid against other analyses as well), αὐτάς refers to τραγῳδίας, that is, to the works of the tragedians, and not to the revised copy from the public archives, which is mentioned in the same sentence.

[36] Liddell et al. 1940, s.v. 1.

the preposition παρά.[37] The translation of the sentence, following lexical usage, could thus be "to give a reading of them," or "to read them" against the text used by the actors, if τοῖς ὑποκρινομένοις is taken to be neuter. We get a similar meaning with the masculine, which is more natural, if one sees the "men of the theater" as representing—as they do in the scholia—a tradition, a competence, and consequently a particular reading. The specific knowledge that a theatrical acquaintance with the text implies would be designated by the plural: "to make a comparative reading of the text of the tragedies with the actors" (that is, the text they are reciting).

It would be possible to translate οὐ γὰρ ἐξεῖναι ... by "because henceforth it would not be allowed," as is most often done, but it would be much more natural to say "because it was not possible to perform them" (see Amyot, above, II, 1). The referent of "them" must be the tragedies with the text of the public copy, reproducing the booksellers' versions that circulate in the city. Αὐτάς, whose antecedent is τὰς τραγῳδίας αὐτῶν, refers to the texts of the tragedies that had been given quasi-legal status. The translation of the unemended explanatory clause allows us to better understand the preceding phrase. The negative οὐ followed by the particle γὰρ highlights an objective reason (a prohibition would presumably not be expressed in this way—if one were to understand it as "because it would no longer be permitted"); this translation explains the second section of the decree.

The integration of the theatrical tradition is an indispensable element in the survival or the reactualization of the past. The explanatory clause, with the repetition of the word ὑποκρίνεσθαι ("to perform"), contributes to this enrichment. The tragedies must be performed, and so performed in a different way (otherwise, the situation would be just the opposite, with the prohibition presupposed by Petit [see above II, 2]—which under the circumstances is an absurd hypothesis). They could not be performed based on the reading text alone (οὐ ... γὰρ). Without the integration of technical experience, there could be no show—nor any real restoration of the work.

The corruptions inherent in stage productions are frequently contrasted with the relative purity of a literary edition. The antithesis was emphasized by Wilamowitz in his history of Greek tragic texts.[38] His reading was based on his understanding of Lycurgus' decree, an understanding that was as conventional

---

[37] Isocrates *Panegyricus* 4.120, speaks of "compar[ing] the text of the treaties made under our rule [of Athens] with those which have been published recently" (*Isocrates, Panegyricus and To Nicocles*, ed. and trans. S. Usher [Warminster, 1990], 81). Aeschines, in *Against Ctesiphon* 3.201, invites his adversary to "take the board and read out the laws together with the decree" (*Aeschines*, trans. C. Carey [Austin, TX, 2000], 233).

[38] Wilamowitz 1907:124–128.

then as it is today: the decree aimed to put an end to the corruption of the texts at the hands of the actors, imposing on them by law a text *ne varietur* that they had to respect or risk paying a fine.

The problem shifts. The traditions are distinct. The question had been how Lycurgus had gone about correcting the changes that the actors had made in the texts; restoration of the texts was supposed to be the aim of the measure (*ut eius auxilio* [that, is the official book] *ab histrionium mutationibus temerariis fabulae ... integrae servarentur,* " ... so that by his help, the texts would be preserved intact from the rash changes of the actors" [Korn, 1863, 7]). Pure, uncontaminated sources had to be found (*altera instat quaestio, qua quibus fontibus et auxiliis Lycurgus ad hoc exemplum componendum usus sit,* "another question arises: what sources and aids did Lycurgus use for composing this example," ibid.). What had been taken as a source of corruption was, on the contrary, the necessary complement for performing the plays. The "text," without the theatrical annotations, was not itself made problematic by the decree, which says nothing about interpolations; it does not even mention them (nor rule out presupposing them). The actors fulfill the terms of the measure by virtue of their theatrical expertise, which relied on a particular tradition, both written and oral, that could immortalize a very ancient technical knowledge (dating from the time of Sophocles and Euripides). The experience of the men of the theater allows them to restore the works, or to constitute the patrimony of tragedy in a more technically orthodox manner. It becomes obvious that, in the state in which they were found, the texts that were being read could not be used for performance.

2. Two Complementary Measures: The Elevation of Tragedies to the Rank of Official Texts Integral to the Life of the City, and the Perpetuation of the Material Conditions for Their Performance

The secretary is charged with a task of collation that leads him to compare the text written out by city scribes (ἐν κοινῷ, literally "in common," "in the public domain") on the model of booksellers' copies (books as opposed to scripts) with other texts that give the necessary stage directions, if only to clarify the allocation of lines among speakers. The collation process points to a marked difference between commercial texts meant to be read that circulated broadly in the public domain, and more technical copies that contained a whole set of notations associated with staged and musical performance of the plays.

Starting with this distinction, we can extrapolate four stages, directly or indirectly implied by the decree:

- Before they could be transcribed, the texts had to be obtained; these were not texts used by professionals, but books, such as *Oedipus Rex* or *Medea*, that were intended for reading.

- From these publications, Lycurgus had official copies made that were to include—this being the point of the exercise—the complete works of each of the tragedians.

- In order to make it possible for these official texts to be used in performances in the theater of Dionysos (that is, in order to make the text more faithful to the original), the secretary's task was one of revision. He completed what the scribes had copied from the commercial editions (*Buchausgaben*) by adding the stage directions from the actors' copies (*Bühnenausgaben*), which were, in fact, working scripts, prepared and annotated.

- The enterprise certainly affected the actors, depending on the reading proposed, not just in terms of the establishment of the correct text, but more concretely, because they needed the stage directions to do their work. It now remains to be seen what these working scripts might have contained.[39] Wilamowitz thought that the authors had added certain stage directions [παρεπιγραφαί] gleaned from marginal notes to the books that were circulated to readers right from the first performance.[40] These could have come from the separate theatrical tradition. Lycurgus' measure had the inevitable effect of providing the theater with a solid basis for performance and for the stage setting, which cannot be separated from the original or explicit aim.

What this hypothesis allows us to infer is precisely the existence of dual textual traditions, each of which clearly had a function: one was intended for study and for schools, and more broadly for a public of readers and other users of books, who were interested in either the form or the content of the texts, in the art of oratory, the wisdom of the pronouncements, the stories, or the argumentation; but this tradition did not include what the actors needed to perform the plays on stage.

It may be that the stage texts had been significantly altered, and that that is why the literary copies, which had to be completed, were chosen as the official texts. But one might perhaps more naturally conclude that the body of directions that existed for the staging of a given play was added to a version that did

---

[39] An example of the notations can be found in the fragment of Euripides' *Orestes* (lines 338–344): see Pöhlmann 1960:12.

[40] Wilamowitz 1907:125.

not differ significantly from the other, more widely diffused version, despite the added marginal notes. Corruption, if indeed it existed, is not implied in the decree, nor addressed by it.

3. Evidence of a Political Objective

The transcription of the texts at the city's expense by the local scribes is evidence of a desire to treat productions that we would call cultural, and that history textbooks include as footnotes to political history,[41] as official texts of public life, concerning the public interest of the city. Since scholars have put preservation and the deposit of texts in a public institution front and center, ἐν κοινῷ ("in common") has been regularly associated with φυλάττειν ("to guard, preserve").

This decision consists in treating the work of the three tragedians as one would a political agreement or a law. The official secretariat is assigned the task of setting down a written text as a public act,[42] ἐν κοινῷ γραψαμένους ("having been written for the public domain") and secondly, of ensuring its preservation, not as one would do (and as we still do) with books in a public library, but as one would do with the texts of a treaty that people need to be able to consult.[43]

The texts of past performances of fifth-century Greek tragedies were collected by the city as the true basis of its political existence; the past had a central presence thanks to the texts and their public preservation, even as regular performances updated the past, in the framework of theatrical restorations of a political (or cultural) nature. Lycurgus' decree places the three tragedians on the same level. We know from Quintilian (*Institutio Oratoria* 10.1.66) that Aeschylus' plays had been rewritten in response to public expectations. Aeschylus was a cult figure. Whereas, two centuries earlier, the Pisistratidae had endowed Athens with a cultural, pan-Hellenic expansion through the critical examination of the Homeric poems, a new universal patrimony now served, in a very different political situation, to consolidate the political identity of the city. The collection of the works in one place was an affair of state.

Once purely corrective (paleographic) expectations are abandoned, the decree, instead of being considered a document on the state of preservation of

---

[41] See Amyot 1820 [1559]: "pour les garder en public."

[42] On the exact nature of the function designated by ὁ τῆς πόλεως γραμματεύς (which, apart from this passage, appears only in Thucydides' *History of the Peloponnesian War* 7.10), see Romilly 1953–1972, 4:91 n1.

[43] Mossé (1988–1989:25–36) considers the decree a type of regulation linked to the medium of writing, as in the administration of finances: in keeping with the conventional understanding of texts, she insists on control of their literal accuracy, "which would be inscribed in the practice of administrative management, linked to the work of the leader who restored the life of the city" (31–32).

texts, takes on its full significance as an element of a very deliberate political restoration. The three clauses complement one another. A public consecration through the erection of statues, which elevated the poets to the level of beneficent—even foundational—heroes, shows that the city had rediscovered itself and saw in them a part of its identity. Secondly, the deposit of works by the classical authors in the archives established a collection of texts that could be referred to on a daily basis. This decision had a symbolic meaning. Thirdly and more concretely, the decree served to give life to the works through performances that were as close to the original intent as possible; all the directions—stage, choreographic, and musical—had to be gathered together and included. The three decisions all had the same goal.

Works Cited

Amyot, J., trans. 1820. *Œuvres mêlées de Plutarque*, with notes and comm. by G. Brotier. Vol. 4. Revised ed. Paris. Orig. pub. 1559.

Bernhardy, G. 1856. *Grundriss der griechischen Literatur*. 2 vols. 2nd ed. Halle.

Bétolaud, V. 1870. *Œuvres morales et œuvres diverses de Plutarque*. 5 vols. Paris.

Boeckh, A. 1808. *Graecae tragoediae principum*. Heidelberg.

Bollack, J. 1990. *L'Oedipe Roi de Sophocle: le texte et ses interprétations*. 4 vols. Lille.

Böttiger, K. A. 1837. *Prolusione quid sit docere fabulam*. In *Opuscula et carmina latina*, ed. J. Sillig. Dresden. Orig. pub. 1795.

Buxton, R. G. A. 1984. *Sophocles*. In *Greece and Rome, New Surveys in the Classics 16*. Oxford.

Colonna, A., ed. 1975. *Sophoclis fabulae*. Vol. 1, *Ajax, Electra*. Turin.

Dindorf, W. 1868. *Poetae Scenici Graeci*, 5th ed., corrected. Leipzig. Orig. pub. 1830.

Easterling, P. E. 1973. "The Transmission of the Text." In *Sophocles: Electra*, ed. J. H. Kells, 243–252 (Appendix 3). Cambridge.

Estienne, H. 1572. *Vitae X rhetorum, Roberto Britanno interprete*. Geneva.

Fowler, H. N., ed. and trans. 1936. *Plutarch's Moralia*. Vol. 10. Cambridge, MA.

Gesner, J. M., ed. and comm. 1738. *M. Fabii Quintiliani De Institutione Oratoria*. Göttingen.

Goodwin, W. W. 1878. *Plutarch's Morals*, Vol. 5: *Lycurgus*, trans. C. Barcraft. Boston.

Heinrich, K. F. 1839. *Commentatio I in D. Juvenalis Satiras*. Bonn. Orig. ed. 1806.

Hermann, G. 1827. *De Choro Eumenidum Aeschyli dissertatio II*. In *Opuscula*, vol. 2. Leipzig. Orig. pub. 1816.

Hunger, H., et al. 1961. *Geschichte der Textüberlieferung der antiken und mittelalterlichen Literatur*. Vol. 1, *Antikes und mittelalterliches Buch-und Schriftwesen. Überlieferungsgeschichte der antiken Literatur*. Zurich.

Korn, O. 1863. *De publico Aeschyli Sophoclis Euripidis fabularum exemplari Lycurgo auctore confecto*. Bonn.

Liddell, H. G., R. Scott, and H. S. Jones. 1940. *A Greek-English Lexicon*. 9th ed. Oxford.

Mau, J., ed. 1971. *Plutarchi Moralia*. Vol. 5, fasc. 2.1. Leipzig.

Mossé, C. 1988–1989. "Lycurgue l'Athénien: homme du passé ou précurseur de l'avenir?" *Quaderni di storia* 15:25–36.

Page, D. L. 1934. *Actors' Interpolations in Greek Tragedy*. Oxford.

Pfeiffer, R. 1968. *History of Classical Scholarship from the Beginnings to the End of the Hellenistic Age*. Oxford.

Pöhlmann, E. 1960. *Griechische Musikfragmente, ein Weg zur altgriechischen Musik*. Nurenberg.

Reiske, J. J., ed. 1774–1782. *Plutarchi Chaeronensis, quae supersunt, omnia*. 12 vols. Leipzig.

Reynolds, L. D. and N. G. Wilson. 1968. *Scribes and Scholars: A Guide to the Transmission of Greek and Latin Literature*. Oxford.

Romilly, J. de, ed. 1953–1972. *Thucydide. La guerre du Péloponnèse*. 5 vols. Paris.

Sommerbrodt, J. 1864. "Das Staatsexemplar der Tragödien des Aeschylus, Sophokles, Euripides und die Schauspieler." *Rheinisches Museum* 19:130–134.

Turner, E. G. 1951. *Athenian Books in the Fifth and Fourth Centuries B.C.* London.

Wachsmuth, W. 1826–1830. *Hellenische Altertumskunde*. 4 vols. 2nd ed., 1843–46. Halle.

Welcker, F. G. 1839–1841. *Die griechischen Tragödien mit Rücksicht auf den epischen Cyclus*. 3 vols. Bonn.

Wesseling, P., ed. 1742. *Leges atticae, Sam. Petitus collegit, digessit et libro commentario illustravit*. Leiden.

Wilamowitz-Moellendorff, U. von. 1907. *Einleitung in die griechische Tragödie*. Berlin. First published in 1889 as an introduction to *Euripides, Herakles* I Berlin. Orig. pub. 1889 as intro. to *Euripides, Herakles*, vol. 1. Berlin.

Wyttenbach, D., ed. 1795–1830. *Plutarchi chaeronensis Moralia*. 8 vols. Oxford.

Zuntz, G. 1965. *An Inquiry into the Transmission of the Plays of Euripides*. Cambridge.

10

From Philology to Theater[†]
The Construction of Meaning
in Sophocles' *Antigone*

THE PROBLEM FACING the contemporary translator of a Greek tragedy may be found in its historical dimension. I try to put myself in the playwright's shoes: he wrote at a certain moment in time, he took a position within a certain tradition that prevailed at that time, so as to express a certain meaning. Sophocles introduces a new problematic into his plays. I consider *Antigone* to be a play of debates that probes a political, social, and intellectual aporia.

On the basis of such a formulation, the mere fact that Antigone has been depicted as a heroine or a mythic figure needs to be discussed and reexamined. It is a tradition to which almost all modern interpreters since the eighteenth century have subscribed, and in particular Jacques Lacan in his study of Antigone.[1] When I say "a play of debates," I refer to what is specifically democratic, in the space for discussion that was opened up by the Athenian theater starting in the sixth century BCE, under the rule of the Pisistratidae. And by "democratic," I mean the introduction of the political, in which the artistic production delineates the field of a problematics and gives rise to a topic for debate. One can well imagine members of the audience the day after a performance, wondering what Sophocles had meant.

The plot leads one to reflect not squarely on the family and the state, as Hegel thought, but on two perspectives that arise from conflicting interests: one, that of the king, Creon, is rational, and the other, upheld by Antigone, rests on the dark forces of belief. This is a crucial moment. As I see it, there is an essential point here where we need to understand Sophocles' historically determined position vis-à-vis his own tradition. Thus we cannot, in the case of

---

[†] Originally published as "De la philologie au théâtre. La construction du sens de l'*Antigone* de Sophocle," in: *Études théâtrales* 21, "Tragédie grecque. Défi de la scène contemporaine" (2001), pp. 103–110.
[1] Lacan 1992.

Oedipus the King, and even less in *Antigone*, move directly to the myth and say that it explains the play.

In my book *La naissance d'Oedipe* (The Birth of Oedipus), in the chapter titled "The Son of Man," I analyzed the passages in *Oedipus the King* that had attracted Freud's interest. I referred to the problems that were formulated during his lifetime, and first of all at the moment when he went to secondary school in Vienna; he could have re-read the play later on, for example when he was working on *The Interpretation of Dreams* (just before 1900). I use the example of Freud because he is of direct interest for us; I am situating a particular reading. The understanding of incest or parricide must have taken on a specific meaning in a particular cultural context. This positioning came about at a time when people did not understand how Oedipus could have become guilty.

Let me go back in time. When Sophocles wrote this play, he was not illustrating a myth, as Freud supposed. He was not the spokesman for an ancient truth, as the Romantic representation would have it. He was rather a dramatic author and technician trying to make the best use of a tradition, to draw from it whatever would be valid and theatrically effective.

A brief digression here will allow me to deal with the creation of the corpus of Greek mythology, which is problematic. We have to go back a long way, so my proposition is speculative; but no doubt we must assume that all myths taken together form a system, a system of thematized stories with a certain number of niches—say one hundred ninety—full of mutually corresponding similarities and differences. I believe that the system was set up by a guild, by people who had been delegated by society to do this, and who, because of this mandate, had considerable autonomy.

A very long time, a span of several centuries, separates Sophocles from that earlier pre-epic period when the subject matter was being constituted. Let me emphasize again that a great deal of autonomy was required to rework and transform the tradition. Innovation came as the result of reviving the traditional meaning through transformation, not through reproduction. By adopting this position, I am championing the moment of intellectual actualization, the decisive moment of invention, against the supposed eternity so dear to the humanists. In a way, I am historicizing more forcefully than the historians, since I am asking myself what an individual, an author, by virtue of his own experience and in relation to his own project, was able to do with a cultural tradition that was itself already historical. It is this authorial transformation that we read in every Greek tragedy.

In the case of *Oedipus the King*, we are dealing with a mythical tradition, the history of the Labdacids. One of the major changes I was able to make in the understanding of this particular story was to show how Oedipus was endowed with a form of non-existence, that he was responsible during his lifetime for annulling his own birth. The transgression was not his—he was the product of it. The fault lay with his father, who should not have sired him.

The same is not true for Antigone. In the case of Oedipus, the myth already existed; it could be found in Homer. We find traces of it there, and also in Pindar and other writers. We can reconstruct a prehistory in order to understand the particularities and the elements of a transformational process. In the case of Antigone, as far as we know, there is nothing earlier than Sophocles.

Just as Oedipus is positioned in the story of his father, Laius, and the Labdacids, so Antigone has a place in the story of her father, Oedipus. And that changes everything. She is her father's daughter. As such, she is slated to marry Haemon, the king's son, but in the course of the play she renounces the marriage. This planned union played a major role in the events of the past that provide a basis for the construction of the play. Antigone is also her brothers' sister. The love Antigone bears for Polynices is not exclusive. He is in no way different from Eteocles, except that he has not received the same burial rites; he should be treated the same way as Eteocles. To put it succinctly, both brothers are cursed by their father, both destined to oblivion: they share the curse of Oedipus. This is an essential feature. Antigone accepts the curse on the two sons, in contrast to Creon, who rejects it. This is the kernel of the whole dilemma, in the role played by collective memory.

Creon believes in the power of politics: he must put an end to these family stories, these stories of the Labdacids that drag the city down into the abyss. So he needs to make distinctions in the family ties, to differentiate the good brother from the bad, friends from enemies, supporters from opponents. Antigone stands before him and says no. She has said no even before he has opened his mouth, because she knew what he was going to say. She has anticipated Creon's reaction, just as he anticipated her appearance, even before the events dramatized in the play. Antigone, her father's daughter, refuses to accept the difference created by the military victory; everything else, her disobedience, stems from this choice of a primary solidarity.

The curse that Antigone honors can be explained by the logic of Oedipus, in the meaning that his destiny assumes. Oedipus has done what the gods made him do to punish Laius: he has committed parricide and incest. He has killed twice, in two different ways, by the sword and in the bed, the forbidden engendering that he himself represents. He says so in the dénouement of *Oedipus the King*, which we read too quickly, precisely because our attention is focused on the parricide and the incest as such, apart from their genealogical motives. At the end of the play, Oedipus, in an almost analytical way, engages in retrospection in his great speech reconstituting the past where he reviews his entire life,

131

from the baby exposed on the mountain who was supposed to be killed by his father to the final discovery of his own identity. With this speech he claims, so to speak, the cognitive advantage of his actions. He was forced to commit them. So at least we should allow him that: that he had to do what he did!

Here lies the meaning of his self-mutilation. Why does he not kill himself, or just continue to live like everyone else? He remains in an intermediate state, where as a blind man he is the depository, indeed the owner, of what he has done and what is owed him. So he lives a split existence between his being and his non-being, his otherness in self-exile, the exteriority he imposes on his progeny two by two: first on his daughters, Antigone and Ismene, and then on his sons. His sons do not want to share the curse with him; they want to govern. This is the subject of *Oedipus at Colonus*. Eteocles and Polynices both come to beg their father for his support, either directly or through a mediator. But he curses them both, because they have both betrayed him. Why? Because he lives in a state of non-being that he expected them to share with him. His exteriority is the god-given privilege of a non-being, since he was not supposed to exist.

This history of the Labdacids is both the story of madness and the account of a prodigious philosophical probing. It is totally unlike any other Greek mythological construct. And Antigone? She comes on stage and she does not deny her heritage; she keeps repeating that she makes no distinction between her two brothers. And within this logic, she plays her only card. She knows she can play it because she is deeply aware that she has the opinion of the community on her side, that is to say a shared belief in the Erinyes and in the resurgence of the past. She knows that she cannot act as freely or as "royally" as the king—he is not the tyrant he is said to be. Creon is a strictly complementary and antagonistic character; he acts with her in acting against her. In this interpretation, which for me has come to be self-evident, they are both mad together, as if they were in perfect harmony in their opposition.

Translation goes hand in hand with interpretation. One tries to translate completely, that is, to the fullest extent possible. How can one make the text come to life today? Modern interpreters and Sophocles are at opposite poles. The moment of conception and of writing is at the root of an interpretive tradition; and then there is the situation in which we find ourselves, where we have to communicate to an audience of readers and spectators the long, even tedious, seemingly endless work on meaning. At a certain point, one tries to escape from the infinite, from the masses of challenges and discoveries, and return to the simplicity of an artistic, theatrical, and intellectual expression. In the 1970s, when I decided to invest some time in this demonstration, I had worked on a similar preparatory study of other texts, such as Plato's *Phaedrus*; I wanted to show what was at issue in the sentences and the syntax when they were placed in relation to the whole, and concomitantly what was the meaning of the work as a whole. In the end I chose *Oedipus the King*, probably but not entirely because of the impact it has had thanks to psychoanalysis and Freud. No other work has had a comparable influence in today's world.

After I finished this study, an interesting thing happened. In 1982, together with Mayotte Bollack, I began to translate the play, without yet thinking about its staging. Then it so happened that we were asked if the text could be used for a performance. But when one translates, one makes new discoveries at every turn. The extraordinary thing is that when we started translating, I had already been working on the text for several years; I have always been an avid reader of the tragedians. So I had already formulated an idea of the play, but it was only by translating and reformulating the text that I discovered I had misunderstood the meaning of many passages. I began to rethink the meaning in order to translate it. It is at this point that passing through a degree zero of not-knowing becomes essential. One frees oneself by pondering what a given passage means: it is not the Socratic form of abstention, but something different. One really experiences a radical suspension of knowledge in order to reach understanding.

There was thus a real confluence between the idea we were developing about the scenic effects of our new understanding and the request we had received. But we had already come to know the theater, because our work encountered it in every detail of the analysis. We responded to a request, and came up against other difficulties in the limited time at our disposal.

The Codes for Understanding

The current situation rests on a debate between codes for understanding, that is, between competing hermeneutics. Earlier, in the centuries before the Revolution, there were a number of specific hermeneutics, mostly theological or juridical. The meaning of a verse from the Bible had to be applied to a concrete situation, or a law had to be applied to a new situation. Protocols were developed for the application of texts in several domains. Then, soon after Kant's *Critiques* were published, at the height of German idealism, a philosopher-theologian at Berlin University, Friedrich Schleiermacher, developed a general hermeneutics, which encompassed the orientation that can be called specifically literary. My own practice is derived from this theory.

However, there is another hermeneutics that is currently well-established, thanks in part to the influence of Heidegger's phenomenology; it gained particular notice in France with the translation into French of Hans-Georg Gadamer's *Truth and Method*. All our knowledge is said to rest on the idea of a permanent truth that has grown remote, but that we can recapture, despite the distance, through reading, in dialogue with the text. There are some prerequisites to this representation of things, in which something like a revelation or at least the hint of a revelation seems to appear. The very canon of classical authors retains a theological aspect.

This "philosophical" hermeneutics—and this is the name of that method— is of another order than the approach I use, which I call "critical hermeneutics": for me, analysis does not uncover an accepted truth, but rather what has been made of this truth at a precise moment in the transformational process of history. The difference is considerable, even for constituting the meaning of a sentence, because the rupture of non-knowledge must intervene in a radical way: at first, I do not know what the thing I want to know means.

In the creative process, I make a distinction between, on the one hand, an associative inflow with all that the unconscious brings with it, a necessarily uncontrolled verbal potentiality, and, on the other hand, the reference system that allows these elements to be placed in a certain order, without any intervening intention, in the psychological sense of the term. So there are many potential meanings in the language, at this first level of inflow, as I have just outlined it, but there is not yet any organization. Language is culturally— and thus in many or even infinite ways—determined. One might be tempted to relate language to an inherent system, but from the standpoint that I am defending, meaning is constructed independently, based on these inflows, these linguistic elements that coalesce in a purely associative and largely irrational way. Both elements are important, intervening together but without any consecutive relation. Something like a system builds up, infiltrates the material or is superimposed on it, and shapes it, thanks chiefly to syntax but also to other formal factors. Still other structures lead from indetermination to semantic determination.

Contrasting this kind of critical hermeneutics to the other kind requires an intervention on my part, an act that structures the material of language to drive it toward a meaning. It is this structuring format that I decipher. I have to repeat the act that has constituted meaning, and of course this work is done with and against every existing linguistic tradition, be it literary, philosophical, or conceptual. I am interpreting a singular act, even if it is repetitive. It is an invention, and thus an intervention that makes sense. It is a microstructure like that of the syntax of a sentence, in a unit where all the combined elements eventually enable one to wonder what type of reflection this is and what its significance may be.

Thus I go beyond the truths discussed by the hermeneuticists whom Ricoeur follows, as well as the authors I am re-reading. Given that the prevailing Parisian Heideggerianism is beginning to fade, perhaps a position such as mine may be able to score some points. It is becoming possible once again to acknowledge the existence of a subject that is not constituted in language, but that intervenes in language, that language uses but does not control.

Each time a passage is decoded, a meaning is decided: "This is what it is, and nothing else." Conclusions are only reached on the basis of syntax. Take Sophocles, for example: he is a difficult author, difficult to read—even if we succeed eventually—in the play of negations and hypothetical periodic sentences.[2] It is quite staggering sometimes. One must think long and hard before finding and deciding on the appropriate term. The difficulty is considerable, and it confirms that this very technical work belongs to great art, a brilliant construction. Lacan could hardly have understood this, in his study of *Antigone*, and in his day—within the horizons he grew up with and the people he thought had spoken the truth, such as Hölderlin, Hegel, Goethe, Heidegger, and so on—because none of those thinkers had fully grasped the syntactic nuances either. That is why they focused on words rather than on syntactic structures. Without syntax, I would be unable to do anything at all. I always begin with very elementary questions: What is the subject? What is the complement? These are the points that allow me to define the semantic leaning that links them. Lacan deals rather, if not exclusively, with words: he bores into words, but he does not analyze the relational structures that situate them. In any case he did not have access to those structures; he recognized the Greek words, he could translate a sentence, but he was probably unable to choose between two syntactic structures, and had no inkling of the scope of the disparities in the textual tradition; that was not his purpose, nor was it Heidegger's.

Sometimes Heidegger does not even bother to translate; he speaks of the *logos* and we are supposed to know what he means by that. The word can just as well mean "reason" as "group," "gathering," or "discourse," to name a few possibilities. And Lacan does the same thing with *atē*, a word associated with tragedy: sometimes he simply says *atē* in Greek; yet it is difficult. The word has two very different meanings in tragedy: the fatality or curse of a destiny, but also misfortune and ruin. It refers to disorder, or transgression, and on the other hand to boundaries, the boundary and the transgression of absolute desire, which Lacan privileges without discussing his choice. Now, in the passages from *Antigone* I have in mind, *atē* always means "ruin," "misfortune," "chaos," "collapse": in other words, it is used in the second sense. From the cause of ruin, we pass on to the ruin itself. We have retained the word "misfortune." The stakes in this debate are naturally important. Lacan prefers the idea of boundaries; if he sticks

---

2 [TN: A periodic sentence is a rhetorical device; the main verb is left to the end, producing an effect of suspense.]

to the idea of chaos, it is so he can move on through it toward transgression and the limits associated with it. Lacan's construction is entirely predetermined by the cultural, intellectual, and philosophical history of the nineteenth century. We are closer to Hölderlin's Diotima than to Sophocles. There one would find something equivalent to a heroine. One might start with Diotima to construct the emblem of a character caught between need and desire, but one can hardly do this with Antigone.[3]

Heidegger would not be able to go any further toward the meaning of texts, if he were interested in the construction of sentences. Thought is determined with syntax. One chooses to say one thing and not another. The Greek tragedians had read a great deal, if not everything. They read political treatises or their equivalent, or theological treatises, and alluded to them. We recognize the allusions, and it is obvious that what the tragedians say is different from what the treatises say. Our translation tries to show that the tragedians intervene in language and how they do it, the *non* (no) that is implied in every *énoncé* (utterance). Certain sentences reproduce public debates; they have been adopted and adapted. Precedence is given to the inherent negation, the unexpected form the expression takes. In the first scene alone, the dialogue between Antigone and Ismene changes meaning completely when one reproduces what is left unsaid. In most cases, a meaning has been brushed aside. It is this gap that creates the meaning.[4]

Works Cited

Morel, G. 2000. "Antigone, l'énigme: Lectures d'Antigone." *Carnets de Lille. La section clinique de Lille* 5 (March 2000): 1–19.

Lacan, J. 1992. *The Ethics of Psychoanalysis, 1959–1960.* Seminar, Book 7. Trans. D. Porter. New York. Orig. pub. 1981.

---

[3]   Morel 2000.

[4]   The translations of Greek tragedies by Jean and Mayotte Bollack have been published by Editions de Minuit: Sophocles' *Œdipe roi* (1985), *Antigone* (1999), and *Electre* (2007); and Euripides' *Iphigénie à Aulis* (1990), *Andromaque* (1994), *Hélène* (1997), and *Les Bacchantes* (2005). Interpretations of particular sentences and commentaries on the plays can be found in *Œdipe roi*, 4 vols. (Lille, 2000); *La naissance d'Œdipe* (Paris, 1995); and *La mort d'Antigone* (Paris, 1999).

11

Accursed from Birth[†]

Enigma and Enigmatization

THE PLOT OF *OEDIPUS TYRANNUS* is the story of an unveiling, a "tragic analysis," as Schiller calls it,[1] but the dénouement discloses that the play's story
has a prehistory in the form of a "myth": the myth of the Labdacid family.

Now, the dramatic unfolding contains gaps. Why did Laius first consult
Apollo ("an oracle once came to Laius," 711)?[2] What led to the king's last trip, in
which he seemed to be heading to Delphi ("He left to go to Delphi, as he said, and
never returned," 113–114)? What caused the Sphinx to appear (130)? Why was
Laius condemned (713–714)? And by what stratagem did Oedipus' intelligence
triumph over the monster (35–39, or 1525)?

The riddle of the Sphinx referred to in the drama, the secret to be discovered, has a homology in the textual or dramaturgical enigmatization.

The very phrasing of the riddle (in hexameters according to the historian
Asclepiades of Tragilos,[3] to whom we owe its transmission), seemingly so clear,
masks its enigmatic power: failure to decipher it can, according to the legend,
lead to death. Here is the paradox, in the obscurity created by such simple
material:

> On earth there is a two-footed and four-footed creature,
>   whose voice is one.

[†] Originally published as "Né damné," in: Jean Bollack, *La naissance d'Œdipe: traduction et commentaires d'Œdipe roi* (Paris, 1995), pp. 217–237.

[1] Letter from Schiller to Goethe, 2 October 1797, in Goethe 1994:230: "*Oedipus* is, as it were, a tragic
analysis. Everything is already there, it is only being unfolded." See "Le fils de l'homme," in
Bollack 1995:282–321.

[2] [TN: Translations from *Oedipus Tyrannus* are by H. Lloyd-Jones, in *Sophocles: Ajax; Electra; Oedipus
Tyrannus* (Cambridge, MA, 1994). All further translations of *Oedipus Tyrannus* are from this
volume; line numbers refer to the Greek text.]

[3] [TN: This writer from the fourth century BCE produced an account of Greek mythology based on
fifth-century Attic tragedy. His work, largely lost, is known to us through various scholiasts.]

It is also three-footed. It alone changes its nature
of all the creatures
Who move creeping along the earth, through the sky
or on the sea.
But when it walks relying on the most feet,
That is when the speed in its limbs is most feeble.[4]

A great deal of inherited information constitutes the background for the play, an accompaniment and gloss that the original audience managed to decipher. As for us, despite information provided in particular by other dramatic authors of the day, we shall probably never fill in the gaps created by the passage of time. Sophocles himself did not supply the missing information in other plays, for nothing has been lost; *Oedipus Tyrannus*, unlike Aeschylus' *Seven against Thebes*, is not part of a trilogy. What we do not know entails two elements: the gaps as such, and the reasons for them. Thus ellipsis itself gives rise to answers and leads to meaning.

The Fault That Cannot Be Found

First, the origins of the drama are missing: the story of Laius and his "impiety" is left out. Yet what befalls Oedipus is a direct consequence of that story (he is "the child of unholy parents," 1360). Modern critics, whatever methods they use and whatever conclusions they reach, always focus on the figure of the tragic hero. They retain the gap, ignoring what it hides. Oedipus' error, the one that would account for his misfortune, cannot be found, and in fact his deed was not deliberate (1213). When we look farther back, as we must, toward Oedipus' father and mother, the error is not revealed there either. It is not part of some other myth centered on Laius, nor does it stem from some doctrine of abstinence that might have motivated the proscription. Laius' story is not told in the play; when we reconstruct it, we lack the main point, the reason for the tragedy, or its origin. While Voltaire's *Oedipus* accuses the gods, supplying a cause for the action that Cocteau adopts as well,[5] in Corneille's play (the version that Cocteau was reshaping and correcting), Oedipus suffers anguish though he is not guilty, expiates a sin he has not committed, and accepts responsibility for "the crimes of heaven."[6] We could read this version as a deepening of the

---

[4]   [TN: "The Riddle of the Sphinx" is found at Athenaeus *Deipnosophists* 10.456B; trans. D. Mulroy, *Oedipus Rex* (Madison, WI, 2011), p. 91.]

[5]   "A man at the pinnacle of good fortune discovers one day that he has been tricked by the heartless gods" (J. Cocteau, *Oedipe roi, Roméo et Juliette* [Paris, 1928], 9).

[6]   See Scherer 1987:166–168.

Christian interpretation, if anguish had not already been a motif in Seneca's *Oedipus*, which probably served as Corneille's model.

A Necessary Rupture

The marriage was not supposed to happen, or if it did it was to end badly. About Laius, Jocasta reports that "it would be his fate to die at the hands of the son who should be the child of him and me" (713–714).[7] The couple's sterility is not mentioned (as it is by Euripides in his *Phoenician Women*, 13–14) as a motive for consulting the oracle. The couple was to have a son; that son was to kill his father. When Oedipus asks the oracle about his parents' identity, Apollo's answer conveys the same necessity (788–793). It is too late for Oedipus, as it was for Laius: the time for warning is past. Enigmatization, in this instance, makes the accident that befell Laius the Labdacid a necessity. The transgression had already taken place.

What, then, was the proscription that weighed on the marriage between Laius and Jocasta? Or can the answer be generalized? Is procreation itself wrong? Though tempting, this generalization must be dismissed out of hand: it runs counter to the genre. Tragedy is too genealogical, too concerned with generational conflicts, to be preoccupied with the question of families or engendering in general. The cause of the drama must be sought in the particular history of a lineage. It is the malady of a family; a malady so intimately linked to the family's existence that it is presented as self-evident. A dynasty can be doomed because it has built up strength so great that it can only break apart. Nothing else seems to explain why Laius is accursed.

The Tragic Contradiction

If the race of Cadmus and Harmonia is doomed owing to its very plenitude, and if, in the absence of internal conflicts, violence arises from expansion, then there is no reason to seek Laius' fault, at least in Sophocles' version, except in the fault of being born—not being born in the absolute sense, but being born and procreating in this particular line of descent. It is with Laius that the breaking point is reached, the point where the *genos* has expanded at the expense of another (or several others), exceeding all tolerable limits. In Euripides' version, Laius contravenes the proscription under the influence of wine (*Phoenician Women* 21–22). Aeschylus attributes the child to a natural tendency to stray, to give in to lust (*Seven Against Thebes* 750). In *Oedipus Tyrannus*, the "error" is unexplained.

[7]   [TN: In *Electra, Phoenician Women, Bacchae, Iphigenia at Aulis*, trans. C. E. Luschnig and P. Woodruff (Indianapolis, 2011). Further citations of *Phoenician Women* are from this volume.]

In the house of Atreus, violence takes place within the family, between brothers, between husband and wife, between mother and son. The principle of justice is satisfied in the sequence of crimes that follows the natural succession of generations; the concentration of wealth is counterbalanced, canceled out, as it were, by an irreparable tearing apart. In the house of the Labdacids, in contrast, the family perishes as such. In a way, the generational conflict is indirect: Oedipus loves the father he kills, and he does not know that he is killing him. It took Apollo's hand to guide his (1329).

The tragic element in Greek drama is not manifested in the action of the play, nor is it manifested in pure contradiction.[8] A contradiction is woven over time. The past is illuminated by what it has produced. The hubristic stage of unbridled abundance had been reached before Laius came along, even if it was with Laius that engendering led to disaster. His only alternative was to give it up or give in to it. He was the last in his dynasty, although he did not want to be. Had he not produced a child, his line would have died out without tragedy. But because the powerful lineage that had built itself up could not detach itself from the basis of its power, it was fatally hurtled into self-perpetuation, and hence to ruin.

The Legacy of Transgression

The hypertrophy of the family responsible for the fracture revealed by the god Apollo is confirmed by Oedipus' birth; this birth was Laius' sole transgression. The "sacrilege" lay not in the decision to kill the child but in the birth itself; exposure of the child to the elements was an attempt to neutralize that birth.[9]

The transgression, which was first of all that of the lineage, was concentrated in a single individual, Laius. The overabundance that the *genos* no longer restrained accounts for both the power and the ruin of the accursed son, Oedipus, whose individual story reproduces that of the Cadmeans up to their extinction. Oedipus' success brings the Labdacid family to the pinnacle of Theban glory, and his undoing is also that of his lineage. With Oedipus, the power that has been building up since the beginning turns against itself, taking the shape of brilliant success to achieve its own destruction. Oedipus lives out the hubris and the unbridled thirst for more that led to his birth.

---

[8] On Hegel's conception of the tragic, and on the specific significance of *Antigone* in shaping the model of the dual morality according to which, in the *Phenomenology of Spirit*, the world of love advocated by Antigone opposes Creon's law, see Szondi 2002, esp. 15–22. *Oedipus Tyrannus* remains in the background of Hegel's analysis; it is hard to see what principle might represent Oedipus and what the opposing principle might be.

[9] See Bollack 1995:266.

A Repetitive Structure

Reticence, a formal figure of dramatic economy, thus leads to a self-sufficient explanation of the plot, and to an examination of the play on its own. This analysis of its content leads, in turn, to a more categorical avoidance of any material foreign to the play.[10]

Oedipus' story subsumes all previous history. This principle must be followed to its ultimate consequences: Oedipus' accursed union with Jocasta reproduces Laius' infeasible marriage; his unviable children bear the mark of his own birth. His daughters are born of a father who "killed his father; he had issue of his mother, from whom he himself had sprung, and begot [his offspring] from the source of his own being" (1492–1494). Laius and Jocasta committed one act of incest, and are thus responsible for the next. The homology between the two epochs is pushed so far that Laius' fatal trip to Delphi reproduces the one he had undertaken before his son's birth. Hence the mystery that surrounds it: the repetition subsumes the first event. The first voyage condemned Laius; the second kills him. In fact, Laius sets out for Delphi at the very moment his son is returning from there. Euripides provides an explanation for Laius' trip: he wished "to learn whether the exposed child was still alive" (*Phoenician Women* 36–37[11]). In the prologue to Sophocles' *Oedipus Tyrannus*, on the other hand, the absence of justification for the drama, and by the same token the absence of any details about the circumstances, however useful these might have been for the dramatic logic (114–119), has broader value: the gaps transform Laius' undertaking into an almost organic outcome. To Laius' unformulated question, the oracle responds only by an act—it answers without answering—and thus demonstrates the symbolic character of the divine name of the Oblique (Loxias), the act being the necessary result of a previous act. Laius is going to meet a fate he has made for himself.

The play, in which the catastrophe becomes clear in the course of a single day, produces a homologous past, as it progresses and makes that past comprehensible. Analysis is not only, and not even in the first place, one of the perfect forms of theatrical art (Schiller); it is a necessary expression of the way time turns back on itself within Oedipus' own life. By returning to his past, Oedipus goes back to the very origins of the lineage that has banned him.

---

[10] Cf. Bollack 1995:257.
[11] Trans. D. Kovacs, *Euripides: Helen, Phoenician Women, Orestes* (Cambridge, MA, 2002).

Arbitrary Division of the Subject Matter

As we know, the restoration of the disrupted order does not come about, in this story, through a confrontation between opposing interests (Greeks and Trojans, Agamemnon and Clytemnestra). This difference is echoed in the analytical structure: the significance of the action is revealed when that action has reached its end point; it has to be uncovered, and not because the misfortune one party has experienced through the fault of another leads to a retrospective understanding of the chain of events that prepared the way. The evil that Oedipus is led to commit needs no external adversity for it to be recognized. He inflicts it upon himself, during the course of an existence orchestrated as a "return," from beginning to end, from birth to blindness. He himself is the adversity that befalls Laius, the enemy of his own people to whom Tiresias pointed ("you are unaware of being an enemy to your own [stock]" [415–416]). The lines expressing execration ("the two-pronged curse that comes from your mother and your father with deadly step shall one day drive you from this land; now you have sight, then shall you look on darkness" [417-419]) apply wholly to himself. Before becoming the prototype of a detective story (according to Ernst Bloch and others),[12] the clarification of the mystery that we witness during the play has first been developed by divine governance. Yet Oedipus' opponent is not even Apollo, but rather the order of things, of which the god is the manager and to which Oedipus conforms.

If we fail to view Oedipus' life as a regression and fail to see that Laius' error is not included in the play, we end up misunderstanding the role of the gods: they do not intervene to fix things, but rather manifest their power in an incomprehensible way by toying with Oedipus. The aporia in this interpretation comes from the fact that one of the elements, Oedipus' prehistory, is not taken into account, and the heroic figure is isolated. This aporia has influenced the critics and opened the door to ideological prejudices. Without Laius as a counterpart, the punishment strikes, deprived of the correlated fault, and the hero falls victim to meaningless terror. It is this scandal that becomes significant in the context of a conflict between men and gods: paradoxically, Oedipus commits crimes and becomes guilty without being guilty; he is invested with a mission so that the gods, thanks to his sacrifice, will be able to establish their power. The play turns into a "mystery," a staging of a Greek "passion play."[13]

---

[12] Bloch 1965, esp. 255.
[13] Bollack 1995:291, 303.

Phases of Maturation

Having been born after the gods had cursed the house of Laius, Oedipus was born to abolish his own birth—that is, his lineage. Instead of being the heir in his own household, he is thrust out into the wilderness, his "nurse and mother" (1091), where he experiences a second birth. The three three-month seasons of two shepherds, a Corinthian and a Theban, bear the child in a second gestation towards his fate of exteriority (1136–1140); "[Fortune] is my mother; and the months that are my kin have determined my smallness and my greatness" (1082–1083). A time of unrestrained violence opens up to Oedipus, mirroring the transgression responsible for his birth. The familial overabundance that could not be moderated is deposited in and concentrated on its offspring, feeding a force that turns against it. Oedipus does not know it, but he himself is the violent king of whom the Chorus speaks, without naming him, in the foreboding parable of the Second Stasimon (873–879 and 883–891). He takes on the garb of excess. And even the act of legitimate self-defense, which he performs out of concern for his own life (889), and which leads him to jostle—or strike—someone who is jostling him, is an act of violence. Oedipus draws his strength from the unlimited excess in which he moves.

The evil matures in two stages. The splendor of the Corinthian palace announces the splendor of the Theban conquest. Childhood sows the seed of his "secret sickness" (1396). Oedipus is sheltered in a first phase of artificial plenitude, until the words of a stranger with fateful powers disrupt the intoxication of a feast (779–781). But the time of conquests (Laius' murder, victory over the Sphinx, establishment in Thebes) also shines with incredible excess: it is like a fully extended spring snapping back on itself, like a taut bowstring launching an arrow. This tension is the outcome of the Labdacids' story, in Laius. The early stages of Oedipus' life, in their glorious unfolding up to the day of the tragedy, reproduce the ascension of his lineage. At the fatal crossroads, he kills with the multiple arms of a superhuman hero (122–123; cf. 813).

The Fulfillment

For the Thebans, Oedipus is the "savior." He had come before to save them from death. At the time the play unfolds, a new disaster weighs on them, and they beg him to prevent their destruction once again (first in the supplication [31–45]; then after his public action as king [690–696]). The illusory analogy between the two situations (with the terrible "now again may you waft [the country] to safety!" [696]) brings together the terms of the contradiction in a logic of reparation, a logic that transcends the unexpiated murder.

To triumph over the Sphinx, Oedipus has come to Thebes in place of the king who has not come back. The newcomer bears a heightened power, astonishing on the part of a foreigner. He can hold this power only because he is the successor, the son substituted for the father by a murder. Just as the gods are demanding payment of his debt on earth, Oedipus reaches the end of the action that has fallen to him. He has ceased to play the role of super-Laius that murder had initially attributed to him; he is now simply Oedipus, the agent of ruin, who has inherited nothing but misfortune. His ascent masked what was lacking, but it has led to a fall into the abyss (876–79). The murdered king could not be avenged at the time of the killing (126–131). In this story, the *lex talionis*, the law of retaliation, concerns more than a single individual. The killing of Laius did not suffice to expiate his transgression—was he himself not the victim of an earlier error?—nor did it suffice that his murderer be punished for a crime that he was destined to commit, and that he did not know he was committing at the time of the killing. The aim is much broader. For the "good" to be re-established, a murder has to be carried out *and* the murderer has to turn against himself.

Oedipus' Sphinx

The commentators (both ancient and modern) have offered divergent conjectures about just when the Sphinx appeared: before Laius' trip (as a scholium of Pisandrus suggests)[14] or after? Before or after his murder? The question remains open, for at first glance Sophocles' text spells nothing out.

The struggle with the Sphinx opens the gates of the city to Oedipus. This struggle is associated with the salvation of Thebes. After Laius' death, the Sphinx's action prevented the Thebans from avenging their king's murder; we can deduce that her appearance was connected with that murder. Yet the monster does not act as an Erinys on behalf of the victim, intervening to obtain retribution, as the plague does in the course of the tragedy, because Laius' murder has not been avenged and the earth suffers the stain of an unpunished crime. The presence of the Sphinx points rather to the king's absence, his failure to return, as a residual peril that irrupts when the city's defenses have collapsed. The Sphinx is timeless. Now, the Thebans are bereft without their king, since all power was concentrated in the royal family. Oedipus is the custodian of the power they are missing.

The Sphinx poses more than one enigma: not only the moment but also the place of her appearance, her movements, her very being constitute riddles. Hence the uncertainty—one of the uncertainties—on the part of the critics. Was

---

[14] Ad Euripides *Phoenician Women* 1760.

the enigma the subject of Laius' consultation? Was she an Erinys sprung from Laius' blood? Or the foreshadowing of a monstrous marriage? These uncertainties make the absence of information meaningful in itself.

The origins of the figure of the Sphinx, whether Mesopotamian or Egyptian, do not exhaust her meaning. Whatever her function (probably funereal) in Greece or elsewhere, the myth closely couples the Sphinx with the figure of Oedipus, and not in Sophocles' version alone. She is Oedipus' Sphinx. On archaic or contemporary vases, the representation of these linked figures suffices to recall the whole story. In his *Thebanische Heldenlieder* (Theban Heroic Songs), the Homeric critic Erich Bethe (1891) opined that a man-eating monster was not likely to ask subtle questions: the enigma in the myth was therefore secondary to the physical combat in which Oedipus overcame the Sphinx. In his *Oidipus*, the archaeologist Carl Robert (1915) concurred. The motif of the virgin must not have been in the original myth. A more archaic, less intellectual element was sought. Yet the figurative representations showed that the enigma predated the combat; we can see the enigma in Stuttgart on an amphora from 530–520 BCE, a hundred years prior to *Oedipus Tyrannus*. On more recent representations, we see that the two themes could be combined: Oedipus solves the riddle and kills the Sphinx. More often, the Sphinx throws herself down to her death. For a long time, then, victory has been attributed to knowledge. In order to understand Sophocles, it is important to ask what meaning Oedipus' superior knowledge takes on in the story. The scene of confrontation, the most heroic of all, stands out in the background to the tragedy, as the sign of an election.

In *Oedipus Tyrannus*, the virgin is represented as an animal and a musician (36, 130, 391, 507, 1198–1199). As a bitch, she is hard and wicked; as a bird with wings and talons, she sings. She is sterile and she kills. The virtuosity of her siren-like voice mirrors her polymorphism. Her aspect is elusive, she changes shape, she modulates her song: she is a bard, a rhapsode, an oracle, a master of variation. If composite, heterogeneous elements contribute to her "role" as an "absent" female presence, it is because she stands for flight, she is a hyperbole for becoming.[15] The solution to the "riddle" that she constitutes is the abandonment, the rout of the Thebans deprived of their king, the hiatus produced by Laius' departure and death ("He left to go to Delphi, as he said, and never returned home from his journey," 115–116). Deprived of his protection, the Thebans are no longer able to defend themselves against fate and death. The monster's ravages fall within the logic of the history of the Labdacids, of the excessive expansion of a lineage, doomed by its own proliferation and abundance. And if Oedipus stands up in the absence of power like "a wall keeping

---

[15] On these characteristics, see Bollack 1995:128.

off death" (1201), it is because, in order to succeed in his exploit, he has been invested with sovereignty in the logic of a power that turns back on itself in order to self-destruct. He has the royal power of integration of his late father, but, because he has won it from the outside, that power is not his own. It enables him to say and to show that he has it; he uses it to triumph over the Sphinx. What he is facing is no game, not even a fight, but a kind of ordeal in which a truth comes to light. To tell the ages of life is to tell of mastery over life.

In triumphing, then, Oedipus governs time and its stages, from childhood to old age, from the "cruel fetter of [his] feet" on Mount Cithaeron (1349–1350) to the beggar's staff (456). The "foot," common to all episodes, is a speaking anagram of the unspoken riddle. The famous enigma on which all the Thebans stumbled has the simplicity and self-evidence of statements that everyone can make: the animal that has four, two, then three feet is a man—child, adult, old man. Knowing the answer is not enough, one has to be invested with the power that authorizes its formulation.

Double Parricide

The city is not the prize for Oedipus' victory—as if the city could be anything but the power that won it for him. In the very act of freeing the Thebans from the scourge, Oedipus demonstrated his kingship. "Because of that are you called king, and you received the greatest honours, ruling in mighty Thebes" (1202–1204). And he challenges the seer: "Yes, taunt me in matters in which you shall find me great!" (441).

Similarly, Oedipus did not win his wife in a competition, as he does according to the ritualist schema analyzed by Marie Delcourt (1944:163). The familiar motif is used, but in a way that does not yield its meaning. Oedipus could not become king except by inheriting the wife (and the brother-in-law) of his predecessor, because in this case the nub of the myth lay in the excessive concentration of a single family. The marriage was necessary. The power that the Thebans had to offer the newcomer was located in the exclusive space of the palace and the bed. The succession went from the absent king to his substitute, from husband to husband. Incest was required for civic and political reasons. Jocasta was the designated site of the power that the hero demonstrated; more than simply Oedipus' wife-mother, she was wife and mother to the Labdacids.

To oppose the winged virgin to the mother and then to unite them in a common femininity is to cancel out a more essential commonality: both the Sphinx and the queen symbolize the city, the former in her dislocation, the latter in her plenitude. Incest is thus a consequence and a reproduction of parricide—the retrospective passage in Oedipus' monologue explicitly links them

(1401–1403). Laius left the city to leave room for another, and the person who came to take his place was legitimized as another Laius, a perfect homology. In this political identification, Oedipus kills Laius through a symbolic murder, by substituting himself for his father in the act of procreating, by annulling his paternity. This confusion is a blood crime: "fathers who were brothers, children who were fruit of incest" (1406). These relatives kill one another in festivities worthy of Atreus, just as men kill by sacrificing living brothers in Empedocles' *Purifications*.

These elements do not support interpreting the incestuous union as the satisfaction of a parental desire. Jocasta's fantasy of love turned towards the mother is a sophistic argument in the plot (980–983). The underlying thinking is different. Incestuous procreation spills the blood of the father, while reincarnating him through the act of procreation.

The recurrent formulas rigorously exhaust the analysis of the mutual slaughter, variations on the theme of the primal scene of the tragic banquet, adapted to the situation of the play (424–425, 457–460, 1207–1209, 1214–1215, 1246–1250, 1256–1257, 1360–1361, 1403–1408, 1497–1499). Oedipus' children are condemned by their father's defection: he conceived them "from the source of his own being" (1494). His parents, Laius and Jocasta, are deposed because they have procreated only a father who "equals" them, and his children are stripped of their status as successors, on an "equal" basis with their progenitor from birth (1481). In uniting with Jocasta, Oedipus is the agent of his father's death as he deprives his children of their lives. He is the middle term of a destitution that affects both the past and the future (1498–1499).

Oedipus, the survivor of Mount Cithaeron, is indeed a living dead man. He is reborn from death, like a shaman. Lévi-Strauss, comparing the legend with an Iroquois myth, writes about "the double identity of Oedipus, thought dead and yet alive, condemned child and triumphant hero."[16] The unity may be even more fundamental. By killing his father, Oedipus borrowed the dead man's identity, became his father; when he arrived in Thebes, he acted in the other's place, and by taking on his identity he killed his father once again.

Public and Private Domains

The two domains are often confused, but the pollution that had to be purged, according to the oracle mentioned by Creon at the beginning of the play, does not lie in the incest, nor even in the parricide. The action begins with an investigation into a regicide, and a conclusion is reached at the end of the

---

[16] Lévi-Strauss 1976:22.

Second Episode, after the conversation with Jocasta, when Oedipus recognizes himself—or almost: he awaits confirmation as to the number of attackers—in Laius' murderer: "Alas! now all is crystal clear!" (754; see also 738, when Oedipus recalls the seer's insight and thinks only about the king: it is the man targeted by execration who obsesses him). The plague that has struck Thebes arises from the unavenged death of Laius, the lord of the land. When the god is questioned about the plague, the real question concerns this evil.

In the Second Stasimon, which follows, the theme of violence is addressed in the context of a political reflection on the disorder created by the agency charged with maintaining order.

The stain nevertheless hints at parricide. It is not just through a dramatic artifice that the shepherd connects the two parts of an action that could be separated (839–840 and 1051–1053): the country is struck because the victim had no son to defend him. The lack of descendants is part of the curse. Laius, an infanticide, has to expose his own son, anticipating the parricide: he has killed his own paternal self. When Oedipus commits murder, he echoes his father's action. Thus the execration of the king's assassin is proclaimed in absentia, the accused having been eliminated by his victim.

Laius' murder draws the king of Thebes into a public action that dominates the play until its midpoint, when Jocasta enters: "Will you not go indoors, and you, Creon, to your house ... ?" (638). The Chorus, after Creon's exit, insists further: "Lady, why do you delay to conduct him inside?" (679). But no one goes into the house yet; it is still public action that, for Oedipus, remains in the foreground, with Jocasta, until the end of the scene, when the same invitation leads him to cross a second threshold, as it were: "But let us go into the house" (861).

Once the foreigner has dispelled the illusion of a Corinthian heritage, the regicide designated by the god and by the king's action disappears in a blending of parricide and incest. Only then do Jocasta's revelations to Oedipus, and his to her, and the two oracles, the father's and the son's, acquire their terrifying meaning. The uncertainty that had been maintained as to the author of the political crime, and that had been based on the long-standing ambivalence of the witness's testimony (841–847), allows the action to shift toward another uncertainty, which absorbs the first. If this indication is no longer highlighted, it is because it is no longer of interest. When Oedipus discovers that he is Laius' son (after having been fatherless [1019] and then a child of Fortune [1080]), he is the murderer designated by the god's first oracle, and the shepherd's testimony regarding the crime needs no refutation. The city was searching for the man who had killed its king, but the king had killed himself in the parricide that had to be carried out. In Oedipus' story, the symbolic role of the king overshadows that of the father.

Hatred in Action

The condemnation of Laius is thus accomplished through the act of avenging him. The son, his murderer, will act on his own and bring his race to an end. Two movements, from prehistory to culmination: one that leads to the death of the father at the hands of his other self, unknown to him, and the other in which Oedipus destroys himself, upon discovering that he is not the "other" he thought he was—namely, his father's son. The foreigner (from Thebes or from elsewhere) whom he was pursuing is at once "impure and of the race of Laius" (1383).

In order to accomplish his deed, Oedipus had to transit through another identity, make a detour through otherness. As a child, he experienced exposure in a wilderness, in the absolute outside, far from fields and cities. He was born to exteriority. Taken in, in Corinth, he had a place elsewhere that was not his. Driven away by doubt, he went into exile. He entered Thebes, his homeland, through "three roads" (1399)—a murder, a riddle, and a bed; he was projected into his own world as a foreigner, like a god fallen into a vale of ignorance and oblivion (the meadow of misfortune in Empedocles' *Purifications*, frag. 121 D-K[17]), like Orestes sent by Apollo in Aeschylus' *Agamemnon*, whose arrival Cassandra announced (1282): "he who is now a wandering exile, a stranger to this land [Argos, his homeland] will return ..."[18]

The detective-story plot, in which the judge turns out to be the murderer, takes on significance. Oedipus is his own opponent, the adversary of Laius' son, who he is. It cannot be otherwise: to undo the wrong, he is the substance of a self-targeting hatred. An enemy to his own kin (415–419), he is his own enemy. Hatred puts on the mask of alienation, at first a mask of anger, in the scenes with Tiresias where Oedipus is the artisan of his own undoing as king, and then as citizen, with Creon. His outburst is not a "fault," nor a weakness, a sin, or a mistake;[19] it is the expression of the force that inhabits and drives him. Anger is but the mask of a basic drive.

Violence is nourished from the outside (192–197, 215). Even the blow struck at Oedipus from afar is a shock provoked by Strife: "Who is the god that with a leap longer than the longest has sprung upon your miserable fate?" (1300–1302; cf. 1311). Here again, the vocabulary is Empedoclean, and this helps us understand the representation—though it is by no means a sign of doctrinal influence. Oedipus, in his delirium, armed with a useless sword, performs a staging

---

[17] Bollack 2003.
[18] Trans. W. Goodwin, Aeschylus *Agamemnon* (Boston, 1906).
[19] See Bollack 1995:329–330.

of hatred, acting as the firebrand of revenge, a dissociating power from abroad; his exteriority is external to itself.

The Meaning of the Mutilation

In his self-destruction, Oedipus is remote from himself in the execration, but close to himself in the mutilation; it is the destroyer whom he strikes. Through Oedipus' own central agency, standing at the center, the succession of generations overlaps and breaks down. Mother and father alike have lost their lives because of him. He kills them a second time, in advance, with the monstrous reproduction of his forbidden birth. His sons are his brothers, and they multiply him (425). The act of procreation is condemned both in the progenitors and in the offspring, and Oedipus is the mediator. He is a father like his father and a son like his children.

Thus his self-mutilation is first of all an extension of the parricide. The hands that carry out the act, ripping out along with the eyes the symbols of paternal authority, the father's crown, thus attain the status of children, in the wounding and abasement of the progenitor: "Children, where are you? Come here! Come to these hands that are your brother's, which have done their duty of the eyes of the father who begat you, once so bright" (1480–1483).

Allowing Oedipus to live, this act of self-destruction strengthens his role as a righter of wrongs. By striking himself, he wins the autonomy of a subject. No one else has committed the deed: he himself is the "outside" that has accomplished it. The "daimon" in question, when it bears the name of destruction, is called Apollo. Oedipus responds to the Chorus: "It was Apollo, Apollo, my friends, who accomplished these cruel, cruel sufferings of mine!" (1329–1330); but he does not view himself as the god's victim. Nor does he accuse the god. By designating Apollo, Oedipus does more than merely acknowledge the superiority of the force that overcame him. According to nineteenth-century (and twentieth-century) criticism, he could not be incriminating his own action in this passage, because he was not guilty.[20] For these critics, Apollo was the master who had set Oedipus' destiny, but the god did not embody divine justice, either; it would have been necessary to accept his jurisdiction, to which there was no reason for the hero to submit. The god had made all the decisions, but outside any system of justice.

Nevertheless, it is Apollo who symbolizes, from beginning to end, the restoration of justice, through his successive oracles, even before Oedipus' birth. Mutilation itself is an Apollonian deed, that is, a deed of death, in keeping with

---

[20] See Bollack 1995:248 and 253, 282–283.

one of the "etymologies" of the god's name, which characterizes him as the Destroyer, even though the hand that strikes the blow belongs to Oedipus. This inhuman rebalancing, which restores the players to their places, has a logic that cannot be found within the bounds of an individual life.

The Subject Returns

In the Exodos, as he hurls himself into abjection, Oedipus calls at least—and at most—for an outside. While he returns to his origins, in the play, at the end of a life lived backwards, in a way he reaches a naked exteriority beyond that of violence. This long final section has proved hard to accept; it has been viewed as a sort of "passion," a catharsis, a sentimental drama.

The messenger's tale delivers the hero over to madness: he first goes around in circles (1254), then walks straight on, with purpose and resolve. The god prevents him from killing, but he turns Jocasta's weapon, the brooches from her dress, against himself. In mutilation, Oedipus dies and survives; he lives Jocasta's death: this was not the disaster of an individual, but a disaster that befell man and woman alike (1280–1283). When he staggers back in the night and meets the people of the city after his deranged act, he is elsewhere, very far from the world. We see him fighting against the daimon, who is winning. Oedipus recovers an identity only through communication, thanks to the Chorus. Speech, daughter of Apollo, slips away from the god to speak. But when he recovers his lucidity, Oedipus takes leave of the Thebans and the world, taking ownership of his deed, and then of his past, as he reconstructs the stages of his life. The strength that makes him assume responsibility separates him from the others. The monologue ends with his claim to transcendence. Untouchable, he may yet be touched, because he belongs to a different species: "Come, condescend to touch a man accursed! Do as I say, do not be afraid! For there is no human being who can bear my woes but I" (1413–1415). The exile the hero calls for, in compliance with the anathema, is the path toward the abyss, even if the hero has mastery over it because he is the author of his own exclusion. His daughters, who belong to the palace and have no existence outside it, share in the excommunication of the lineage.

The Dénouement or the Distancing of the Tragedy

The tragedy thus avoids ending in bloodshed. On the contrary: Oedipus' distinctive attribute is his persistence in a hereafter, between life and death.[21] If he

---

[21] See Bollack 1995:101–102.

had killed himself, he would have met his parents in death; he would have been united with them as they looked upon one another (1371-1373). But he could not go on living, either; that is, he could not go on perceiving, perception being one of the definitions of life. So the righter of wrongs closes his eyes upon darkness, gives up the gaze that had looked outward as Apollo's sun does, and enters, living, into the realm of death: "we two ... have perished" (1504-1505). Nor can the tragedy settle for making him one of the living dead, a sort of shaman.[22] Oedipus survives both his life and his death. He will have to have a second death.

Exile is the figure of a non-being that was Oedipus' lot since birth—he was not supposed to be. His passage by way of the mountain doubled him, gave him another self, foreign to him, to carry out the act he was "charged with" accomplishing against his own lineage. The fallen daimon serves as a model. The play features no Pythagorean thesis, for such a thesis would not befit the stage. But philosophy and theatre share the same spatial organization and cosmology, as we see at the end of the Parodos (203-215) and the beginning of the Second Stasimon (865-868). The two exiles match: from Mount Cithaeron to Mount Cithaeron, from birth to grave (1451-1454). Even the splendor Oedipus knew in Corinth and saw again in Thebes is foreign to him (1394-1396). The appearance of beauty is twice shattered by a brutal intervention from the outside, a stroke of fate, or a *coup de théâtre*: during the banquet, there is the insult (779-780); in Thebes, even more than the plague, there is the arrival of the Corinthian, which puts an end to the illusion of Oedipus' foreign citizenship and reveals his true nature.

But the "savior" is not saved. His acts, the ordeals to which he is subjected and of which he is the author, bear their own end. This is why he walks away. The tragedy concludes with his distancing. The tragic event is unveiled in his blind gaze. An outsider, he knows. Not the inverse: it is not that he removes himself because he knows, not that he is purified. Had he been purified, the ending would not be tragic.[23]

---

[22] See above, p. 147.

[23] Blanchot (1993:438n2) makes a distinction between Tiresias' words and Oedipus'. Tiresias leaves the facts obscure, whereas Oedipus' insistence on clarity serves to mask the horror of things. We recognize, orienting this presentation, the pendulum of the Heideggerian Being, swinging back and forth between assertiveness and concealment. In short, Tiresias does not disclose what he knows because the truth relates to Oedipus.

When with "luminous universality" Oedipus makes the answer to the riddle clear, he seems to "keep for himself alone ... the obscure horror that escapes revelation—as though in reserving being Oedipus for himself, he authorized us henceforth to be tranquilly 'men'" (Blanchot 1993:438n2). This interpretation is open to two objections. First, the story is a particular story; it does not involve humanity in general. Second, like the psychoanalysts, Blanchot correlates the Sphinx's appearance and her riddle with Oedipus' parricide. Yet the Sphinx made her appearance in the interregnum following the king's death. If Oedipus speaks clearly, it is because he has

Works Cited

Bethe, E. 1891. *Thebanische Heldenlieder*. Leipzig.

Blanchot, M. 1993. *The Infinite Conversation*. Trans. S. Hanson. Minneapolis, MN. Orig. pub. 1969.

Bloch, E. 1965. "Philosophische Ansicht des Detektivromans." In *Literarische Aufsätze, Gesamtausgabe* 9:242–263. Frankfurt.

Bollack, J. 1995. *La naissance d'Oedipe: traduction et commentaires d'Oedipe roi*. Paris.

———. 2003. *Les Purifications: un projet de paix universelle*. Paris.

Delcourt, M. 1944. *Oedipe ou la légende du conquérant*. Bibliothèque de la Faculté de Lettres de l'Université de Liège, fasc. 104. Liège.

Goethe, J. W. 1994. *Correspondence between Goethe and Schiller*. Trans. L. Dieckmann. New York.

Lévi-Strauss, C. 1976. *Structural Anthropology II*. Trans. C. Jacobson and B. Grundfest Schoepf. New York. Orig. pub. 1973.

Robert, L. 1915. *Oidipus: Geschichte eines poetischen Stoffs in griechischen Altertum*. Berlin.

Scherer, J. 1987. *Dramaturgies d'Œdipe*. Paris.

Szondi, P. 2002. *Essay on the Tragic*. Trans. P. Fleming. Stanford.

---

the power to do so as the legitimate heir. His words concern the life of the city-state, and the men in question are the Thebans being devoured by the Sphinx. Tiresias has the advantage over Oedipus of knowing what bond unites political control with the individual circumstances that make such control possible. His knowledge is situated in a context that sheds light on it.

12

Two Phases of Recognition in Sophocles' *Electra*[†]

Preamble

ELECTRA HATES HER MOTHER, CLYTEMNESTRA, and she does not hesitate to tell her so. Their confrontation will represent the play's major contest (*agōn*), a merciless struggle between the two women, up to the point when the dramatic action sets Orestes' plan in motion and at the same time brings about Electra's downfall. She does not want to be her mother's daughter. David Bouvier (2001) reminds us of the customary lines of descent: the son is considered the father's son, and, symmetrically, the daughter is viewed as the mother's daughter. In Sophocles' play, the roles are reversed. For her part, Electra breaks the ties that naturally bind her to her mother; she parts company with the women and at the same time places Clytemnestra's husband, whom she loathes, in the women's sphere. She assumes masculine characteristics and focuses wholly on her murdered father, rejecting all manifestations of life, remaining fixated on her father's assassination, and moving in a space of non-life, which distances her from her entourage.

As she herself asks, did she not denounce the scandalous murder from the very beginning? Did she not choose to be its witness forever, and the guardian of its memory? The king was indeed the male, and he was killed by his wife. Electra rescued the young son who survived. She thus usurped the role assigned to her brother, the appointed heir, and if she incessantly refers to the action she takes against the murderers, legitimizing it on the grounds that Orestes is absent, it is because she has in fact taken his place. She reminds us of Orestes' absence with a lament: "he is always longing to come, but for all his longing he does not think

† Originally published as "Les deux temps de la reconnaissance dans l'*Electre* de Sophocle," in: *Lexis* 30 (2012), pp. 268–274.

fit to appear."[1] The point is not so much that she wants him to come home. In his absence, the mission of vengeance falls to her, in this situation where the killers run the government. Her hatred is focused on life itself—which prevails in the enemy camp of the murderers—and on the rulers' power. Her fury ill becomes her, for two reasons. She is contravening the social order, however just her feelings may be; this is exactly what her entourage—the women, even her sister—try to make her understand. In her relentless revolt, she departs from the paths mapped out for her sex, and offends the very principle of life by wallowing in the ashes.

From the beginning of the play, she can in no way be seen as Orestes' ally, left alone to await the act of vengeance linked to his return. She is in precisely the opposite situation, right up to the moment when the meeting occurs and the stranger from afar is identified. Before this event, she behaves like a pseudo-Orestes. Her recognition of her brother will first of all mean her defeat—the punishment for usurping a male role. The disguise she has clung to, until the final frenzy and the decision to kill Aegisthus, vanishes once the character whose role she has usurped completes the process of demystification and declares his identity. The drama, having set up a double plot, succeeds in representing these fantasies and their share of madness, as it does in *Antigone*. One is tempted to say that this situation is eminently Shakespearian, but it is indeed the work of Sophocles, and he has not always been given his due.

•••

More than any other, the scene I have selected from Sophocles' *Electra* needs to be situated within the dramatic action. It follows the famous recognition scene (lines 1174–1226), which is indeed very beautiful, but only if we understand that it specifically does *not* deal with a mutual discovery of identity between brother and sister, as an almost natural and naïve reading would have it. In the logic of the plot, one of the partners—namely, Orestes—is in control and stages the recognition scene; in this sense, it is like a play. The brother forces the sister to recognize him; he skillfully brings her to this point, step by step. But the game being played can be clearly analyzed only if we are aware that Electra submits to the questioning unwillingly, that she resists, then eventually gives in and rejoices, as if convinced by an excess of evidence rather than by her intuition. At this tragic moment, when Orestes' presence becomes a physical reality in her consciousness, the character that she has embodied since the beginning—since

---

[1] J. March, ed. and trans., *Sophocles' Electra* (Warminster, 2001), lines 171–172. [TN: All subsequent translations from this play are from this edition.]

the moment after the prologue when Orestes flees upon hearing his sister's lamentations in the house—no longer has any reason to exist.

The prologue revealed the whole plot and its planning, as it had been prescribed at Delphi. The action was hatched in darkness and lies, leaving the stage empty for a while, allowing the appearance of another action, one both legitimate and unfeasible. This is Electra's world, incredibly dark, a woman's world, at first triumphant, then shaken and finally breaking down into madness, when the time for revolt is overtaken by the action in the scene under consideration. The two plot levels then merge. The semantic relationship is complex; the contradiction is finally revealed in the drama and becomes essential to it. The plot that collapses had an element of truth; however, divine law sanctioned by Delphi invalidates it.

When the stranger, whom Electra said she was waiting for but who failed to arrive, is finally there before her, she is no longer the person she was when alone. Her actions have become meaningless. Orestes has only to integrate her into his camp, cajole and reconvert her. It is a metamorphosis that makes a disciplined warrior, an ally, out of a false Erinys.

But if the play is to remain intelligible, it cannot be reduced to this sudden change, unless one examines the impact of the break in more detail and evaluates the potential consequences of the event. The drama opens up a designated space where the two protagonists are really able to talk to each other with the necessary distance, to explain themselves and to understand each other. We leave the temporality of the plot for a "time out." The flights of lyricism have this power: the capacity to create a temporary contemplative opening. The question "what are we doing?" is almost a way of asking "what's the use?" Is it not on this second level, in the analysis of the new situation, that the true recognition occurs, in the form of a choral song in the middle of the episode that is performed by the characters, the actors on stage (*apo skènès*)? We do not have the music of the duo. In her commentary on Euripides' *Helen*, A. M. Dale quite rightly speaks of a "recognition duo"; there is no other instance of this form, alternately lyrical and prosaic, in the works of Sophocles that have come down to us.[2] Here, as in the prologue, we can detect the influence of Euripides. The same form can be found in Euripides' tragedies, in *Helen* (lines 625–697, Menelaus-Helen), in *Iphigenia in Tauris* (lines 827–899, Orestes-Iphigenia), in *Ion* (lines 1437–1509, Creusa-Ion), and in a fragment of *Hypsipyle* (Hypsipyle-Euneus).

In *Iphigenia in Tauris*, the scene is crucial; it functions as a pivot. There is a before and an after. First come misrecognitions and misunderstandings; what

---

[2]   Dale 1967:106. [TN: In the duo, according to Dale, Electra's part was sung and that of Orestes was spoken.]

follows is part of the programming and prepares the dénouement. Richard Kannicht offers a perfect analysis of the structure in his important edition and commentary on *Helen*. The duo is the result of a complex dramatic quest (in *Helen* as in *Iphigenia in Tauris*), and in its internal development it moves from an expression of joy to one of questioning and anxiety;[3] Kannicht believes, no doubt incorrectly, that the excerpt in *Helen* is the model. He does single it out for its particular form and thematics, but he includes it in the more general type of lyric exchange (*amoibaion*), of which he finds eleven examples in the tragedies he studies.[4] His analysis is perhaps too psychological; he deduces that the emotion aroused can be attributed to a sudden realization, emphasized by the music associated with the female role, when in a more technical sense we are dealing with a pre-existent dramatic form, well known to the audience.

The distinction between an autonomous formal structure and the unfolding of the dialogue in this framework is worth further examination. The form defines a particular space, reserved for the theme of recognition; it creates a background of intimacy, and a special proximity. The discussion that develops takes place outside the usual progression and apart from the ordinary on-stage confrontations; it opens up to a moment of awareness. Linked to the rhythm and the musical tonality, it is an expression in itself, even before a quiet and deep debate, appropriate to the situation, develops unexpectedly within this familiar framework.

In *Ion*, the recognition scene between Ion and his mother Creusa is by far the longest. It is not just a matter of reunion; the whole play is turned around and replayed in reverse. Ion has assumed several identities right from the start: first, he has been taken for the son of an unknown father, and, inasmuch as he serves in the temple, he has been taken for the son of the god, master of the sanctuary at Delphi, and for the son of Creusa's husband. He is finally recognized as the son of Apollo, a now repentant lover. The mother, like an oracle, discloses her whole story; she goes back in time to the origin, to Apollo's love affairs. In the end, the young man gains his true identity. Thus, after so many false recognitions, he is of one mind with Creusa, singing for a moment with her—as in a choral song—before the play ends with the usual commentary on the tragic alternation of misfortune and happiness.

The damaged text of *Hypsipyle*, a collection of papyrus fragments discovered in 1906, is the one whose remains, despite certain lacunae and unresolved questions, allow for the most complete reconstitution of a recognition scene. The play was composed during the last years of Euripides' life. The scene in

---

[3] Kannicht 1969:176.
[4] Kannicht 1969:175n6.

question, most of which has been preserved, comes at the end (frag. 64, col. 28, lines 1593–1633; the last lines are incomplete).[5] The two sons of Hypsipyle and Jason, Euneus and Thoas, had left Lemnos in search of their mother, who had been banished from her home. They arrive in Nemea in the Peloponnesus, where Hypsipyle, enslaved by Lycurgus and Eurydice, is charged with the care of their child. An initial face-to-face encounter gives both mother and sons a premonition of the identity they are seeking. But it is only after the boys' victory in a race in the newly created Nemean games, when their names are announced, that mother and sons really recognize each other. Euneus, the older of the two, speaks for his younger brother. The duo between Euneus and Hypsipyle recounts the whole story of the women of Lemnos, who hated men and killed all the males on the island, and the subsequent tale of the sons' own rescue by Jason and their departure on the ship Argo. By means of the intervention of the soothsayer Amphiaraus, who mediates between the mother, her sons, and the ruler of Nemea, the expedition of the *Seven against Thebes* intersects with that of the Golden Fleece, on the Pindaric island of Lemnos, under the shadow cast by the tragedy of Hypsipyle.

The recognition scene in Sophocles' *Electra* is clearly different from those found in this group of Euripides' plays. Its strophic structure is much closer to that of a choral ode, which the duo is intended to replicate or imitate, even though it is broken up. The two voices are radically opposed. The female part overflows with vocal, narcissistic, spontaneous, and irrational outpourings; it is extremely lyrical, with the stressed syllables of its dochmiacs and syncopated iambs (bacchees and cretics), with the exception of the trochees of the epode and the final recapitulation.[6] The controlled and critical role belongs to Orestes, the male partner, and remains within the orbit of the dialogue, using ordinary iambic trimeters (with three exceptions, still in the Euripidean mode, in the antistrophe and the epode, where the young hero fails to stay aloof [lines 1257, 1275, 1280]). It is like a music lesson, where the female singer is corrected, and then begins again and again until she gets it right.

•••

The scene in *Electra* is divided into three parts: the strophe (lines 1232–1252) and the antistrophe (lines 1253–1272) are in dialogue; they are followed by an epode (lines 1273–1287).

---

[5] Jouan and Van Looy 2002:212–215.

[6] [TN: These meters in Greek poetry are conventionally characterized as follows, where u represents an unstressed syllable and – a stressed syllable: dochmiac = ◡ – – ◡ – ; iamb = ◡ –; bacchiac = ◡ – – ; cretic = – ◡ – ; trochee = – ◡. The epode is the third part of a choral ode, sung after the strophe and the antistrophe.]

In the strophe, Electra starts singing a song of celebration. Orestes' miraculous arrival allows her to find herself again and to pull herself together in the posture of an admirer, effusive in the adoration of a savior, as if absolved of all bonds. This is the theme of "he has come" (*emolet'*, line 1234). The emphatic plurals increase the exaggeration; they seize each term and amplify it. Electra makes sure to include herself. She was the objective and the conclusion, the object of desire. The other has found her; he has come to her and has seen her. Is this not the end?[7]

The sober and prosaic Orestes interrupts her; he tries to make her focus on the future and on the danger facing the servant who is in the palace. He places himself outside, as required by the plot; Electra remains wholly in the present of the completed event, her brother's return. Within the confines of the palace, there is no danger, there are only women; she has never feared either Clytemnestra or Aegisthus. She invokes Artemis, with whom she identifies; the goddess draws her power from her roving virginity. The women, on the other hand, those cowardly and lazy creatures, are "this useless load of women who live indoors" (lines 1240–1241). This is a sparring match where Electra recovers her old resources, in the combativeness and resistance that resulted from her experience of her father's murder. In order to bring her back to reality, Orestes turns the argument around: has Electra not had occasion to know the warlike power of these women, and of Clytemnestra in particular?

Horrified, Electra cries out: how could Orestes say such a thing to her? Was evil inflicted on her, or did she not rather provoke it herself, by her refusal to forget the crime that had been committed? A second time, she answers by recalling the role she has played in protecting their father's tomb, a job that she accepted in rebellion against forgetting. Thus the strophe ends with a contradictory vision, which expresses the importance of the conflict. Orestes refuses to accept this point of view. Electra is obsessed by the murder, which justifies her actions; Orestes interprets the unhappy fate of the accuser as a punishment inflicted on her by the masters. She has been the victim of the supremacy of "those women," who were defending their own pleasure. She thought that her stance would allow her to take her brother's place and assume a right. The whole play is summarized here, with its two competing levels. So Orestes can conclude by repeating Electra's words: yes, he agrees regarding the crime, which must

---

[7] Line 1232–1233. Kamerbeek (1974:167) went back to the scholia, finding in the body (*sōmatōn*) the character of Agamemnon (see also Schadewaldt 1994 and others). Kamerbeek followed Jebb (1894), who however admitted the possibility of the periphrasis ("dearest of all men ever born") that had been upheld by Kaibel 1911 (*sōmata gegenènema*). Grammarians have misconstrued or rejected an audacious figure of speech blending the meanings of "birth" and "son," which explains the iteration: "o toi, fils, toi qui nais comme le corps le plus aimé de moi" (cf. "Ah birth— birth of a person to me most beloved," in J. H. Kells, ed. *Sophocles' Electra* [Cambridge, 1973], 199).

never be forgotten, but, as for vengeance, it is better to wait until circumstances indicate the right moment.

In the antistrophe, Electra makes the first move and challenges the argumentation: there is no present, there are no circumstances, there is no opportune moment (*kairos*). For her the crime is such that the need to revisit it takes over every instant of life. Justice requires that they speak of what happened. Once again, the same debate is pursued to the end, in greater depth. The crime did not stop life from going forward. Yes, she has now with great difficulty acquired the freedom to speak of it (line 1256), thanks to the savior who stands before her. He acknowledges her point, but turns around the course of the discussion. This freedom has to be realized; it leads to action: now she should get to work! The past has made her keep on talking; she must turn away from it and await the propitious moment rather than reject it! Here, Electra changes the subject and justifies both her tone and the topic. How can she be silent? If it is no longer the evil that has been done that forces her to speak, it is this very present good that she experiences with Orestes' return. Is it not just as incredible? Does it deserve to remain unspoken? Electra, accepting the unexpected event, wants to speak of the good, just as she had earlier spoken of evil. Again Orestes corrects her; he understands that in the past she had to fulfil a responsibility, as long as he was not there; however, he waited (this is not the *Libation Bearers*) until the god called on him to return (the repetition of the term *molein* ["return"] is pregnant with meaning).[8]

Electra appropriates the response again to feed her insatiable loquacity. Has she not been rewarded, against all expectation, with her brother's arrival? Now he mentions that he comes as a messenger of the gods. She is content with this sign, which assures a happy outcome—a guarantee (the word *daimonion* suggests the intervention of the gods). Orestes considers it necessary to make a distinction between the pleasure she feels at the idea of divine intervention and the fear that she will be overwhelmed by it. At this stage, he has already induced his sister to believe in him and in his action. Their debate is like a poem, constantly interrupted; it evolves and recovers, from one lyrical outburst to the next. A certain balance is almost achieved in the epode. And so Electra gets Orestes to join her in a song that looks forward to their future and seals their union. She still evokes her past, but as a "having been," since she has now embarked on the divine path of Orestes' return. It is here, at this very moment, that the recognition is achieved in unison, and that she abandons the persona of "Electra," the

---

8   Line 1264. The *responsio* (see line 1244 in the strophe) requires a trimeter, but the line is missing. We do not need it for the meaning; (for what the reader can infer, see, for example, Kamerbeek: "In the line which has dropped out after this verse [line 1264], Orestes may have encouraged Electra quietly to put her trust in the gods" [1967:167]).

role she has played throughout the tragedy. She casts it off—one might call it a *catharsis*. She looks back: in her former persona, she risked losing her beloved brother. Orestes firmly supports her desire (line 1279), in a reference to the well-known device of upping the ante. In Book 24 of the *Iliad*, Iris describes to Priam the future behavior of Achilles: "neither will [Achilles] himself kill you but will hold back all the others" (line 185).[9] But with targeted irony, Orestes can integrate this phrase in an act of vengeance that would include his sister: "I would certainly be angry if I saw anyone else [prevent you from seeing me]" (line 1279).

Electra concludes: she gives an account of her history and absorbs the presence of Orestes into her soul and her action. At an earlier stage, at the beginning of the tragedy, she heard the voice, even though she had no hope, and then when she was told of his death in the games, she knew to remain silent and did not cry out at the news. Does this not assure the truth of this other Electra that she has resolved to become? So much for the past. As for the present, it is so radiant and convincing that, even in misfortune, it would give her the strength to resist (lines 1285–1287). It is a declaration of love; she is ready to seal a military pact.

Thus a model exists, very likely conceived by Euripides—the broken form of a hyper-lyrical discourse whose function is to create an intimate and closed-off space, an isolation and seclusion that promotes clear-sighted ecstasy. We have only to compare the excessive use of superlatives in the introduction (we find something similar in *Helen* and *Iphigenia in Tauris*). Two characters communicate with two contradictory voices, impassioned and sober, celebrating the joy of being reunited: brother and sister, mother and son, husband and wife. Beginning with this reminder of a close link, the discourse, strongly differentiated in each case, can follow the desired path, ready to confront all threats and advance toward danger. It is as if the confirmed feeling of close kinship had endowed the discourse with the power to transform itself, in the tragic sense, beyond pleasure, into lucidity.

---

[9] *The Iliad of Homer*, trans. R. Lattimore (Chicago, 1951).

Works Cited

Bouvier, D. 2011. "Comment et pourquoi comparer des tragédies? La relation 'père-fille' dans les tragédies d'Électre." Conference paper, CorHaLi [a biennial conference for Hellenists sponsored by Cornell, Harvard, Lille, and other universities], June 9–11. Lille.

Dale, A. M., ed. 1967. *Euripides' Helen.* Oxford.

Jebb, R. C., ed. 1894. *The Electra of Sophocles.* Cambridge.

Jouan, F. and H. Van Looy, eds. 2002. *Euripide, Tragédies.* Paris.

Kaibel, G., ed. 1911. *Sophocles: Elektra.* Leipzig.

Kamerbeek, J. C., ed. 1974. *The Plays of Sophocles: Commentaries*, Part 5, *The Electra.* Leiden.

Kannicht, R., ed. 1969. *Euripides, Helena.* Vol. 2. Heidelberg.

Schadewaldt, W., and H. Flashar, eds. 1994. *Sophocles, Elektra.* Frankfurt.

13

Reading the Cosmogonies[†]

THERE IS NOT JUST ONE COSMOGONY, there are many, a whole typology of cosmogonies; every philosopher could have his own: a typical form could be taken up again and knowingly modified. It was a major step forward when, instead of constructing a fictitious continuity or evolution, I was able to differentiate, according to the doxography, between closed, unique worlds, like that of Parmenides (Bollack 2006), and worlds open to the limitless, like that of the atomists. The world as we see it or as we make it differs from other worlds by the way its elements are brought together in a circumscribed or self-limited space. When matter flowed in, at the initial instant, it was compact, concentrated by a force of attraction; when a mass broke away, as in Empedocles' cycle, the result was, on the contrary, a primal dissemination that had to be contained.

The processes are radically different, and the phases are linked differently, depending on whether one creates *a nihilo*, as Democritus does, or whether one reconstitutes according to a model and a known outcome. It may be the same game, but it is played according to different rules.

This staging places construction in the foreground. The more a thing shows itself as "made," the more it also conceals itself to the benefit of a hypothesis and of a body of knowledge. What is discovered in the atomists, when they avoid dogmatism, can serve for all schemas without exception.

Thus it becomes clear that we are dealing with explanatory systems or guides for thought, ideologies, we might call them, and this led certain thinkers, such as Heraclitus, and no doubt others before and after him, to give them up completely. This epistemological critique has not prevented Heraclitus' interpreters from attempting to reassemble the elements of his analysis of physical speculations in multiple ways. A world he never thought of has been fabricated for him. Everything has been brought back into positivity. However, the original archaic systems are much less naïve than they are believed to be. They derive

[†] Originally published as "Lire les cosmogonies," in: Jean Bollack, *La Grèce de personne: les mots sous le mythe* (Paris, 1997), pp. 181–182.

from rigorous thought, as for example with Parmenides, for whom the world is developed on the basis of an irreducible antithesis.

The rigor of this thought may appear arbitrary, but not its logic, as it unfolds here. The rivalry among cosmogonies shows well enough that the stakes were high, that the vision was not purely physical, but that each system had to transmit a form of mastery. From this point on, one is led to wonder: what were these "worlds," with which novices and disciples were invited to live in the Schools? The followers of a master had to know how to internalize the precise and particular form of one of these worlds in preference to another, in order to think and express that world. Others, such as Heraclitus, took the opposite approach, rejecting constraints and promises borrowed from religious associations. Matter—the elements as well as their products, from the particles to the stars—was free, available, and open to reshaping; at the same time, matter was becoming enigmatic and totalizing within the underlying logic expressed by the organization of the great bodies of the world; it became a matter to be deciphered, an intellectual exercise.

Work Cited

Bollack, J. 2006. *Parménide. De l'étant au monde*. Paris.

14

Empedocles[†]

A Single Project, Two Theologies

RECENT DISCUSSIONS, in part linked to the publication of the Strasbourg papyrus in 1999,[1] encourage a reconsideration of the relation between Empedocles' two poems, *On Nature*, or *The Origins*, and *The Purifications*.[2] My own position on the issue had not yet been resolved when the papyrus appeared, which is why I published my commentary on the first poem separately. The very existence of an endlessly renewed debate was quite striking in itself. The discussion was going around in circles, just like the arguments about the cosmological cycle. Readings oscillated between two contradictory poles, or poles acknowledged as irreconcilable, whereas the debate led historians to analyze biases that had been implicit since the mid-nineteenth century. Were Empedocles' poems works of science or religion? It seems to me that the problem became much more amenable to solution when the conditions under which Empedocles' work was produced began to be considered more freely within the context of his social and political ambitions. The viewpoint of cultural and religious sociology came to the fore.[3]

I have not been persuaded by the attempt on the part of the editors of the papyrus to introduce a demonology into the cosmological poem, a text that I myself published earlier. The editors believed that they could harmonize new

---

[†] First published in A. L. Pierris, ed., *The Empedoclean Kosmos: Structure, Process, and the Question of Cyclicity*. Proceedings of the Symposium Philosophiae Antiquae Tertium Myconense, July 6th–July 13th, 2003 (Patras, 2005), 45–72. Translated by C. Porter; translation slightly modified here.

[1] Martin and Primavesi 1999.

[2] The commentary on the poem concerning the nature of things was published in four volumes in 1965–1969 as *Les Origines*, with an introduction, an edition of the text and autonomous and open numbering, 1–699 (currently available in Bollack 1992). In *Les Purifications: un projet de paix universelle* (Bollack 2003), I followed the order of the Diels-Kranz edition. [TN: For an English-language edition including both texts, see B. Inwood, *The Poem of Empedocles* (Toronto, 2001), or M. R. Wright, *Empedocles: The Extant Fragments* (London, 1995).]

[3] See the discussion of the two poems in Bollack 2003:14–17: "Nature et religion."

testimonies (fragments, paraphrases, summaries)—although these are not so much explicit as deduced—with the current state of research (as represented by Nicolaas van der Ben [1975] or Catherine Osborne [1987]). They conclude that, at the heart of the "interpenetration" (a term that is incontestable in itself, since we are dealing with a single, coordinated undertaking), "the distance between the theory of physics and the theory of demonology is reduced even further"[4]— a claim that cannot be supported by any means. Nevertheless, I was able to draw, from what I took to be a quotation in the papyrus from fragment 139 of *The Purifications*, evidence of a reference, perhaps a crucial one, made to that poem in *The Origins*.[5] In any case, this hypothesis allowed me to maintain, as a matter of logic, that the political project of the exoteric poem represented a primary aim of the poet's overall program. Instead of positing a relation of analogy between the two poems, we might, as a first step, consider their referential function. The intertextual references are significant as such: the author's viewpoint allows him to include in his current text indications of his attitude toward something he has written elsewhere, in another text with which he assumes his readers will be familiar. We have proof of this in the fact that the quotations always imply an obvious, if sometimes minimal, modification of the utterance in question. There is always an adaptation, a specification, an extension, or even a correction. The writing becomes richer in its verbal substance.

The Purified Myth of the Divine in Living Beings

From the difference between the addresses, so strongly marked in each of the two poems, a coherence of conception and of languages could be discerned. An ambitious cultural project lay behind the difference between the two texts in the choice of subject treated and in the way the subject was presented. We thus see a return to the principle of distinction that guided nineteenth-century editors, from Stein (1852) to Diels (1901). This classification was worth keeping; it appears to be largely accurate. Our task today is to reach a better understanding of the way *The Purifications* is organized and the specific way in which the philosophical speculations expressed in it are used.

Perhaps we should not speak of homology—the problem of the relation between the two poems no doubt has to be posed differently—but rather of a shift from one order to another. By means of a verbal re-composition, as it were, we pass from the construction of a world in the text to an intentionally cultural or political application. The orders are not the same: there is nature on the one

---

[4] Martin and Primavesi 1999:119.
[5] See Bollack 2001; on the question of reference in one poem to the other, see p. 174.

hand, human history on the other. Empedocles' language, entirely reconceived, clearly remains the same for the most part; it has a structure that can be deciphered in harmony at every point with the subject matter that it is deciphering. In the presentation, it is clear, too, that the formation of the world precedes the fall of divinity; the gods exist in their natural habitat before they split apart or divide as necessary, with the break being necessarily the same on both sides, ontologically and theologically.[6] The two poems were very probably intended to shed light on one another precisely in their difference. Even homology could be found.

A different society is being invented, one with different beliefs, in harmony with the study of bodies and their faculties. The members of Empedocles' inner circle were erudite scholars, experienced in drawing truths from texts hallowed by tradition. The first-person plural in the papyrus could also refer to a group studying the constitution of human forms.[7] Its textual practice (writing, reading, exegesis) was not burdened with the eschatological promise that prevailed in the Orphic communities. In *The Purifications*, the traditional subject matter is recast in political terms so that it too is commensurate with human needs in the here and now. Everyday life dominates in all its dimensions—religious, ethical, and political. In the account of the daimons' fall, the world is already in place: it is here, fully formed, ready to encompass the divine and human history that unfolds in it.[8] In this sense, the proper realm of nature, with its geneses, logically precedes polities and societies; however, this perspective is only valid from within. It reproduces the viewpoint of the author and his group of friends, gathered together around the exegesis of a text that is being written and commented upon in the process. But the actions of the group and those of the rhapsodes who gave public recitations of the esoteric works can also be foregrounded. Other people, those who dwell in the cities of this world, are not directly touched by the bold and sometimes enigmatic speculations, whether philosophical or cosmological, in which the group engaged in private. The mythic retranslation of these speculations is complex; logically in second

---

6   The problem of analogy, so well formulated by Laks (2004:7–44), has to be discussed in these terms, it seems to me.

7   The Strasbourg papyrus may offer, in the indirect tradition, a first-person plural in several passages where a participle is read. There is an initial question as to whether a variant is really at stake. The editors of the papyrus had drawn a dogmatic conclusion on this point (seeing the "we" as referring to the presence of the principle of Love). Along with others, Laks (2002) refutes this rather extravagant idea, and sees instead a reference to the generative force. Reconsidering the passages relevant to this question, Trépanier (2003a) concludes that we do not have a true variant here, following Mansfeld and Agra on this point. However, the problem is only displaced. We still need an explanation for the presence of the letter *theta* in this context.

8   As an example, we might take the cycle prescribed for the migrations of the daimons, in frag. 115.9–12 (Bollack 2003:68–69).

place, it comes first in intrinsic worth. The old myth is reinvented, countering all the myths of the cultural tradition; the new myth is supreme, for it deals with man and his potential divinization. God for god; nothing could be more critical.

In *The Origins*, the elements are called "gods" (*daimones*). The traditional names of the deities, such as Zeus or Hera, are attributed to them; these are new gods that have emerged from the One, in a more purely physical theogony following the tradition of Hesiod.[9] However, there are also "gods" on the side of products. Like everything else, these figures are produced by the element-gods; they have their place on the scale where all beings of this world are arrayed. Theirs are the greatest honors. These are not the beings venerated in traditional beliefs. It is hard to attribute a place to them except among the stars, at the confines of the ether, near the new Olympus of the heavenly dome.[10]

There is no reason to imagine gods in flesh and blood; these do not exist, and if we situate ourselves on the scale of beings that have come into existence rather than on the scale of formative principles, we find no better candidates for divinity than the quasi-transcendent concentrations of fire, fire being the privileged element in Empedocles, according to Aristotle.[11] A place for them among the stars was there to be defined and filled. Divine entities were not always already here; they came into being, like all living things, like everything that is, after the sphere was broken.[12] Their superiority is secondary and relative, in terms of ontological speculation, properly speaking; the antagonism between Strife and Love succeeds the One and gives birth to the elements, which give birth in turn to all that is formed, everything that comes to be. In *The Purifications*, in contrast, we do not go so far back. We are dealing with our own world, with everything that has to do with the life of human beings here and now. There is no construction of a god Sphairos who reigns separated from the world. "Necessity" leads to a complete alteration of the existing order, at the risk of a universal massacre. The entrance into becoming, the change of state that follows a rupture and an irruption, has to be viewed as the common accident;[13] it is on this point, in particular, that the two poems come closest to

---

9   *Origines* frag. 101 (= 31B59 D-K) and Bollack 1992, vol. 3, sect. 2:417–418.

10 See *Origines* frag. 328 (= 31B44 D-K), and Bollack 1992, vol. 3, sect. 1:268, with a reference to the meaning of the word in Parmenides.

11 See the discussion in Bollack 1992, 1:82–85, "Le feu des contraires."

12 *Origines* frag. 63.12 (= 31B21 D-K), and frag. 64.8 (= 31B23 D-K.). In my commentary (Bollack 1992, vol. 3, sect. 2:118–119), I recognized the powers of the system with their names of gods, but it now seems more logical to me to see the stars associated with living beings, in the enumeration of the bodies formed; they close the world.

13 It is possible to compare *Origines* frag. 110 (cited by Simplicius), and *Purifications* frag. 115, with the variations (see Bollack 1992, vol. 3, sect. 1:151–152, and Bollack 2003:62–63).

converging in their conception. Here, no doubt, is the principal analogy, offering an orientation to the events reported in the narrative.

In the case of the light shed by the stars, the renunciation of an earlier state can only be conceived spatially in the form of a spark that escapes and falls into the infra-celestial shadows; there are no Hells, no Hades, no darkness in the world but that of the earth.[14] The break that intervenes with the idea of an initial murder cannot be separated from this reversal of a parcel of luminous divinity. If, with the gods, we are in the astral world,[15] the indefinite masculine pronoun in fragment 115, "the one whatsoever," might designate as such a form of incarnation corresponding to an individual or personalized human nature (something that distinguishes a *singular* incarnation); the association of a plural form with the "daimons" would show that the passage, which initially concerned the order of the one living alone, is suddenly and unmistakably extended to include the entire set of human beings. It is not clear how else one might explain the nature of the fall that is represented by the intrusion of the divine into a world that is foreign to it. Transcendence resides in light. It is light that transcends itself. The heavens are of another nature, although they are visible. Here is the paradox of this quasi-immanent beyond that is manifested and revealed in the ether and transmitted to the rest of the world. A difference unfolds within the limits of the world, at its outer edges. According to *The Purifications*, this at once unattainable and visible divinity was communicated one day to men when it let itself go. The rupture hollowed out an opening in which the dispersion and the systole of a return were inscribed.

It is not that the stars furnish in themselves a truer idea of what the gods are. On the contrary, divinity, whose place and nature are illustrated in the narrative, is more abstract than is usually supposed; it can be found, retranslated, in the symbolic form of light. Nor is the god Sphairos of *The Origins* any more real; he has taken on the aspect of the sphere in the logic of a reflection on the composition of bodies. The question raised always remains tied to the

---

[14] See *Purifications* frag. 142 (Bollack 2003:107). Given the state of the text and the absence of context, without leaving the horizon of the poem one can only recognize negatively the spaces designated for their non-existence in Olympus and Hades. There is nothing on which to build an allegorical interpretation. Primavesi (2003) has no reason to combat the very understandable impression, put forward at one time by Ettore Bignone, of a conformity between the fragment and widespread beliefs (see p. 63). It is useless to add "popular." What would we do in that case with Homer or Hesiod? The representations are either challenged by Empedocles or else retranslated and reintegrated into his own system. There is no other way.

[15] If I finally convinced myself that gods of light were at issue, it is because it seemed to me, according to the overall logic of construction, that the possibility of a reference to the gods of the traditional pantheon had to be excluded. Testimonies about the differing nature of the celestial world were not in short supply and the "gods" that figured in *Origins* among produced beings could (or should) have been associated with stars.

question of how best to adapt the representations that have been transmitted by language.

The divine can spread from a single point to unite with all that is living, while retaining its separateness. The "daimons" of *The Purifications* necessarily keep their extra-physical alterity and their astral specificity. We can recognize in them a different—that is, immaterial—ethereal nature, provided that we represent the vanishing point of matter as a concentration of light. The daimons are not associated with any of the body's physiological functions; they constitute doubles of living bodies—noetic replicas, as it were, without flesh or blood.[16] Intelligence alone is involved, or an abstract cognitive faculty; nothing else can lead beings to a form of non-eschatological accomplishment and deliverance. If daimons accompany higher human destinies, they have in the end the extraordinary opportunity to find one another again and to rejoin the circle of the gods of light. The "Olympians," then, are men of the highest rank, among the purified; they ensure the governing of matters according to the laws granted to Olympus, the vault of the heavens. The proper understanding of the imagistic terms—the gods' "table" where they gather, as well as the "hearth" that invests them with a center—has to be allegorical if it reveals the astral reality and detaches itself from the world through purity of thought.[17] Reversing the perspective, we could just as well say of the divine that it is accomplished in a negation of itself by means of a necessary transgression. Divinity can thus "make gods" of men who recognize it and identify with it.

The original murder reproduces—if we think about the constitution of bodies in *The Origins*—the physical and material division in the social order. It is the intrusion of an all-powerful evil, which is potentially propagated to all creatures. There is no remedy other than abstinence, rejection of bloodshed, and purifications, which constitute an end in themselves. In this theodicy, divinity leads beings to itself; it offers them the path of divinization through perfection alone, without any eschatological promise. It is close to being a replica of life itself.

From this point on, there is no place for any other god in this world. There is no god who is concerned with anyone at all, anywhere. The reign of the Olympians is abolished. Cypris[18] has neither flesh nor bones; she is a presence of Love in organisms, a translation of the law that governs the course of the universe. Around city-states there remain divine and immortal men, men who

---

[16] In the presentation of *Purifications*, see the discussion of the problematics defined by Burkert (1962, esp. p. 22 [1972, esp. p. 24]).

[17] See the commentary in Bollack 2003:112–113.

[18] See frag. 128, which I have situated in an episode describing the state of the world before the murder and the irruption of the divine (Bollack 2003:86–87).

have become gods on earth. Divinity is simply a participation in the thought that shines throughout the universe. These god-men have become immortal through knowledge: they have become intellectual or (there is no difference) spiritual beings. If we pursue Empedocles' struggle against anthropomorphism to its logical end, the divine will have no body, or else it will have a capacity that distinguishes it from all other forms of biological life. The Epicureans would oppose Empedocles' views, judging from their own standpoint that his purified theology was mythical in its turn, although it was developed in opposition to all the traditional mythic representations that they themselves will leave in place.[19]

Located beyond the classic mind-body division, this intellectualized vision of the world cannot easily be situated within a history of religious spirituality. In a sense, it is opposed to the very existence of such a spirituality, and thus it remains hard to classify. Its governing principle, that of an order of ascension, was introduced among men in relation to scholarly exercises that were developed in the context of a communitarian way of life. This vision allowed men to enhance their ordinary capacities and to seek ways of struggling effectively against despair and wretchedness. The generous morality of the strong, and the succor it brings, are substituted for established beliefs. The traditional aspiration to salvation, to a higher life in a better world, is now satisfied with the "divine" resources that are offered to man. He succeeds in perfecting himself; he becomes divine here below. Nothing else can be expected. The fall has been legitimized in the teleology of a reparation engendered by the fall itself. No future is open in some other existence, in some form of the world other than the one encompassed by its astral closure. Perfection is reached in a limit crossed during the course of a lifetime.

We might return from here to the other poem and the problem of the cycle according to which living beings come to be, but not in order to reopen the discussion of a double cosmogony or zoogony, under the sign of two antagonistic forces, as has often been done. It is impossible to see what meaning the symmetrical duality might have (I still think that the question need not have been raised; I have dealt with this topic in another context, where I titled the section devoted to this cycle "the false problem").[20] Strife does not lead to the

---

[19] The discussion, well attested in Philodemus, must have been at the heart of Hermarchus' book on Empedocles; see Bollack 2003:120–122. The earliest men saw the gods appear in their dreams in anthropomorphic forms. They supplied them with the prolepses of blessed and imperishable beings (see Book 12 of Epicurus' Περὶ φύσεως). In *Against Empedocles*, Hermarchus contested the transformations carried out by Empedocles, as we learn from Philodemus; see Obbink 1996, col. 19, 546–554; cf. frag. 19 (Longo) of Hermarchus. The debate bears on the adaptation of conventional beliefs to the nature of things.

[20] Bollack 1992, vol. 1:95–122. The heart of the argument consisted in demonstrating that the triumph of Hate, or Strife—complete atomization or parcelization—was immediate, to the point

creation of any differentiated organism; concomitantly, it is fair to say that Love creates nothing without Strife. They collaborate so closely that we do well to see them together, an indissoluble pair of contrary and separate forces.[21]

Interaction is paramount. However, once we have acknowledged the single course of evolution, leading from the rupture of the original sphere to its reconstitution, we confront the question of the future of the world and the infinite repetition of the cycle. The schema potentially invites us to conceive of an unlimited repetition starting from the same basis. The presentation offered in certain testimonies may be marked by Aristotelian theory; the biological model, transferred to the birth of the worlds, would confirm the idea of repetition.[22] The fact remains that we have no indication that the poem included an episode containing the description of a "cosmophthory,"[23] and the general context of *The Purifications*, despite the difference in the nature of the bodies or quasi-bodies implied, could well lead us to accept the existence of this lack.

Either we view the world as a great living thing that dies and reproduces itself, or else we distinguish a phase of atemporality in evolution. In the first case, the reign of the god Sphairos might represent a form of being required for the existence of the world, a world that would eventually be threatened with the loss of the demiurgic power that brought it into being, a world that would be weakened as a function of its distance from its origin. Neikos, the antagonist, might have his hour of destruction once again, before being banished to the outer regions; this is a conceivable stage in evolution, even if the destruction of the whole has already occurred. The alternative is to acknowledge that the god of origins, who allowed himself to be fragmented, has only let his empire go "for a time," the time of a temporality, living the birth of time with the stars, and that he later takes hold of himself once more in his center in order to blend all things together outside of this world-time. The idea of the One would thus find mythic expression in a regularly renewed divinization of matter—a form of eschatological monotheism.

We may also reverse the perspective and remain with the model we already know, one in which the origin has bequeathed to the world that is forming a

---

of coinciding with the spherical origin, in the form of an explosion no less initial than the model that preceded.

[21] Most recently, Trépanier (2003b) has returned to the double formation, attributed to a struggle between two visions in Empedocles' mind, one more refined, the other more common (see esp. pp. 40–41). This conceptual flux is difficult to support.

[22] See the doubts expressed earlier in the section "L'origine et la fin," Bollack 1992, vol. 1:146–152 (esp. 151).

[23] [TN: The French neologism *cosmophthorie* is derived from the Greek adjective *kosmophtoros*, meaning "destroyer of the world." *Cosmophthorie* is thus contrasted with *cosmogonie*, "birth of the world."]

perfection that survives, dispersed and present in the least parcel of matter. Men would experience the divine in every object of knowledge; they would rediscover the primal unity in their intellectual activities. Viewed from this angle, *The Origins* is no less a "religious" poem than *The Purifications*, but it is situated within the framework of the esoteric practice of study. In the poem on physics, the god has bequeathed and delegated his radiance to the six agents of the cosmogony. They are seven altogether, a heptad. Through these intermediaries the supreme god is manifested in the world. The divine genealogy retranslates the traditional theogonic structures and reorganizes them. Through the presence, emphasized in the poem, of a transcendence that appears in phenomena,[24] the relation between the god and the world is analyzed in depth as one of true coexistence rather than simple succession.

Philosophical "Theology" in the Formation of the World

The relation established between *The Origins* and *The Purifications*, converted into a confrontation, leads us to see considerable differences between the two texts.[25] The exercises that bring the lives of certain men closer to divine perfection in *The Purifications* localize the divine in the ordering of the heavens, which become a substitute for all the sanctuaries erected on earth. This astral ordering manifests the majesty of the world; it embodies universal justice. Here we are obliged to recognize the application of a science acquired elsewhere and in another way. The transfer shows that this science is broadly beneficent within the social order. The initiates in Agrigento have acquired it by study, in the exchanges of an intimate circle. They have learned to decompose and then to recompose the elements of nature. They teach the public at large that an absolute divinity exists, a divinity unified at the outset by the "thought" that recognizes itself in it. This divinity is called by the name "divine" alone, as if no other were worthy of sanctification.[26] The designation introduced and its

---

[24] Struck by the role attributed to the epiphany, in an earlier discussion of frag. 63 (= 31B21 D-K), I wrote that the visible bodies, "massive, themselves supply the proof of their divinity" (Bollack 1992, vol. 3, sect. 1:108).

[25] I used the term "homology" in the discussion of the autonomy of the two poems, contesting the various hypotheses of their unity. See Bollack 1999:178; it seems to me that one arrives at sounder interpretations with the play of references by stressing each time the difference and the singularity of the viewpoint.

[26] See frag. 134, with the radical commentary of the Neo-platonic Ammonius, who cites it (Bollack 2003:93–94). Thought is distinguished from corporeality as the sphere is distinguished from the world. The same structure is presented in *Origines* frag. 98 (= 31B29 D-K).

conceptual determination could not be further removed from anthropomorphic representations.

In discussions among the initiates, the physical forces themselves are identified and observed in the objects of study, and in the process they are invested with divinity to such an extent that study itself logically becomes divine in turn. In *The Origins*, strictly speaking, neither practices nor beliefs are at issue. Its reading grid corresponds to a system of references that are harmonized with the divinization of the world. The god is presented at the heart of the investigation. What distinguishes the friendship of the "friends" is not the direct propagation of a doctrine—which would necessarily be political, exoteric, broadly subversive—but the affirmation of a limited finality: science serves the purpose of forming masters, and the masters will transform life. Thus it became possible to transform a different theology, to integrate it into a single, universal science; it was to be an exclusive theology tolerating no higher knowledge, no rival of any sort. The exhaustive explanation of the universe, carried to an extreme by Empedocles in all its aspects, from astronomy to psychology, can be better understood if we take into account the openly competing substitutions that the new quasi-scholastic (scholastically exemplary) gods introduced, substitutions that gave new meanings to the ancient names and to the representations associated with them.

We progress in the study of the relation between the two parts of the enterprise by methodically comparing the two poems' quite distinctive approaches to the subject of the gods. In the reformed belief system presented in *The Purifications*, the divine is manifested in the visible order of the world. This is the "law" that emanates from the stars, "that which makes the law" in the universe (note the neuter *to nomimon*) and which imposes its rules on human society, a law written in the sky.[27] For men, this law would entail a peace agreement that they would establish among themselves if they could succeed in harmonizing their actions with this absolute good, which they see gleaming before them like a book, far from the Olympus of Homer and Hesiod and its power struggles. The form given to the good within the limits of this world is exempt from differences and from the avatars of becoming; it thus deserves the attribute of non-mortality, an attribute that was usually assigned to the anthropomorphic (or theriomorphic) gods. Certain men become non-mortals in the end, abstracting themselves in their luminosity, when they succeed in dematerializing themselves and allow themselves to be penetrated by the quasi-immaterial clarity of mastery over the course of things; this divinity is like a retranslation of the

---

[27] This is one of the two passages cited with *Antigone*, lines 456–457, by Aristotle in *Rhetoric*, for the universal sentiment of the just (frag. 135): a unique law for everything that exists (Bollack 2003:100).

liberating and humanitarian activities they carry out in the life that they lead without other gods, activities that are more energetic and inventive, more just, than others.

Turning toward the communitarian side, toward the protected and privileged practice of the initiates, we find that there is no room for the gods except in natural objects and in quasi-professional analyses of those objects. The book being written will be more closed, more difficult as well, despite its programmatic openness toward the beauty of the research undertaken. When it succeeds, study leads to a particular mastery and to a quasi-divine domination in exercises of thaumaturgy.[28] Candidates for this elevation encounter the system of divinities distributed among the natural objects that they learn to make or refashion. They learn—or deduce or invent, it makes no difference—the constitution of these objects. From their vantage point, the world does not lie before them, as it does in *The Purifications*; they seek to understand how the world is made in order to know what it is. They are participants in an ongoing process, and they learn to identify the demiurgic forces at work. These forces are in matter, which is divinized from within.

The four elements have their basic distinguishing names, for example, "fire" or "water." In addition, they can take on the names given to deities in the traditional belief systems; they are the equivalent of those deities, absorbing the representation of the power that had been attached to the gods.[29] This is in a sense the major substitutive stratum in the divine reading. From the differences among the elements, all else proceeds; their power to create the qualitative differentiations inherent in things is virtually limitless.

The presence of a divisive force such as Strife is inherent in the separation of the components. The complex interactions presupposed by the formation of living bodies cannot be explained without this positive adversity, this division in the face of union, this separateness from unity. These two divine forms also have their own names and their own capacity to integrate the traditional representations of the superhuman and universal powers. Philotes works with everything that Neikos has decomposed and virtually dissociated. The disciple learns to understand and to analyze this other type of interaction, which results from strictly contrary interventions. The union of differentiated elements can only be achieved by relying on work already accomplished by the other force,

---

[28] See *Origines* frags. 12 and 699 (= 31B110 and 31B111 D-K). The first stresses the incomparable powers of science; the second emphasizes the necessity of a separated activity for the ordinary life of men. Contemplative life is presented not as the goal of existence, but as the condition of a more effective active life.

[29] See *Origines* frag. 150 (= 31B6 D-K) and the discussion of the attribution of names to the two pairs Fire-Air and Earth-Water, in Bollack 1992, vol. 2, sect. 1:169–185, "Les noms des dieux."

which would thus be primary, as it were, although the success of an encounter can really be attributed only to Love. Every existing form, whatever it may be, proceeds simultaneously from the one and the other. Harmony results from antagonism. Death is part of life. Life will never be absent either. There is no non-life.

At a third level of the discovery of principles, the reflection is situated closer to the origin. Division is relegated to the circumference. A unique case of stereometry is envisaged, in which only the perfect form, sphericity, exists. This will be Sphairos; the god who is supreme by virtue of his unicity has no name but this, a new name made to order for him. He traverses matter and supplies the object of a particular meditation. An absolute model, revealing ontological difference in his own way, he shows in what form Being can be conceived, maintaining himself in the being of the world. He has the power to reunite and to encompass absolutely, integrating everything, including division, which surrounds him and holds everything together. Even the external boundary is integrated; it is the product of concentration. The force of unification reigns alone; distinction falls. In this abstract meditative and analytic vision, probably the ultimate one in the undertaking rather than the starting point, there are neither four god-elements nor Love-and-Strife, but only the concentration that makes the Being-One. The idea proceeds from a progression. It forms an angle of vision. We are no longer dealing with the destitute theogonies, which are deemed mythical; there are no gods who die in battles of succession between one stage and another. Visions coexist, analyses persist and are superimposed.

The god Sphairos, in his concentration of life, is distinguished negatively, in the contrast of a privation on which the text insists. He is the authentic living entity with his own virtual components, but he is deprived of the members that constitute the bodies of the not yet constituted beings.[30] This distinction brings out a global capability. Sphairos is what he is going to be, and what, held in reserve, is not yet. His form leads to an understanding of this higher principle, separately embodying the principle of fitness and that of homogeneity as a condition of life. Other, and apart from life, he must himself nevertheless be alive, paradoxically, with an isolated power of unification that does not reunite differences in order to hold them together; this god brings together in himself elements that are already identical; we might well say "identically ones." In his roundness he "rejoices in" himself; his unicity is doubled. The god encompasses himself and what surrounds him.[31] Circularity is the condition of this doubling; the limit that the sphere gives itself leads, as if in the second place, to awareness

---

[30] *Origines* frag. 98 (31B29 D-K).

[31] The line, with variations that have been elaborated, seems to have been taken up again in the course of the episode; see *Origines* frag. 92.b2 (= 31B27.2 D-K), and frag. 95 (= 31B28 D-K).

of its roundness. Thought is anchored in the perfection of an enclosure and an empire over the self. Equality can be measured in terms of itself, in its limits. In a complementary fashion, the limitless, rather than extending into space, closes in on itself and unfolds in the absence of any internal limit. The adverb πάμπαν[32] can be read in more than one way: first of all as "completely" (πάμπαν ἀπείρων), but also as "at the heart of a reiterated totality," marking the doubling.

The ontological definition brings the attributes of physical speculation back to a rethought origin and applies them to a divine figure. This abstract figure is animated by a personalized force. It is conceived as being potentially coextensive with the productions of nature, their correlative in the form of a male god, as Zeus is in the city-states. The unifying force, central everywhere in the multitude of living formations, opens up to itself and is defined on the basis of an analysis of life. An extreme degree of attentiveness is expected of the disciple in this highest degree of initiation into the mysteries, a principle embodied and disengaged from embodiments. This principle draws and constructs the sole figure that is appropriate to it. It is in this result and in the reflection that produces it that one has to believe. To recognize the god is to abstract him; it is to see the world in the light of this truth. The ontology of the Eleatic tradition is freely treated by Empedocles as an object of discourse, that is, as a position that is in the first place distinct. It is appropriate to give absolute transcendence the meaning that is in harmony with the system that it clarifies, and that depends on it. The eternal order of things, anchored in the truth of the god, is likewise a matter of interpretation and clarification.

Divinity thus deduced, before being installed, is reserved, properly speaking, to the depths attained by study as a convention among friends in which the circle finds its justification. Nothing will be more accurate than this projection of thought, objectified in the study of the world. The friends are immortalized this way in their initiation: their reflection readjusts the traditions. Their constructed "god" can in no way be supposed to form the object of contemplation in the heaven of the world that is so broadly open to the public to which *The Purifications* is addressed. The difference in the two poems' aims and strategies determines the nature of the theologies, which are always transitory. This difference is enough to discredit in a more general way all the attempts to interpret the fragments of the ethical or religious poem by naively transferring to them data borrowed from the analysis of the constitution of the world.[33]

---

[32] *Origines* frag. 95 (= 30B28.1 D-K).

[33] One of the best examples would be supplied by the identifications proposed to the gods in frag. 115 (see Bollack 2003:62–63). The analysis of Empedocles' ontological principles offered in the present chapter constitutes a complementary study concentrating on the adaptation of the Eleatic ontology in frag. 31 (= 17 D-K), an adaptation completed by the beginning of the papyrus.

The poet's exploit lies in the success of the transpositions, on both sides. The horizon of expectations is completely different between Pausanias, the doctor to whom the esoteric discourse is addressed, and the masses being pulled along by the delegated apostle substituting for priests in the other poem. The more we distinguish between the social and cultural contexts of the two spheres, which are coordinated as center to periphery, the better chance we have of grasping the import of a language that remains essentially prophetic, but in the second degree, by differentiating and separating itself from itself.

Works Cited

Bollack, J., ed. 1992. *Empédocle*. 3 vols. Paris.

———. 2001. "Voir la Haine. Sur les nouveaux fragments d'Empédocle." *Methodos* 1:173–185. Lille.

———. 2003. *Les Purifications: un projet de paix universelle*. Paris.

Burkert, W. 1962. *Weisheit und Wissenschaft: Studien zu Pythagoras, Philolaos und Platon*. Nuremberg. [*Lore and Science in Ancient Pythagoreanism*. Trans. E. L. Minar, Jr. Cambridge, MA., 1972.]

Diels, H. 1901. *Poetarum Philosophorum Fragmenta*. Berlin.

Laks, A. 2002. "Reading the Readings: On the First Person Plurals in the Strasburg Empedocles." In *Presocratic Philosophy: Essays in Honour of Alexander Mourelatos*, ed. V. Caston and D. W. Graham, 127–137. Aldershot.

———. 2004. *Le vide et la haine. Éléments pour une histoire archaïque de la négativité*. Paris.

Martin, A., and O. Primavesi. 1999. *L'Empédocle de Strasbourg (P. Strasb. gr. Inv. 1665-1666). Introduction, édition et commentaire*. Strasbourg.

Obbink, D., ed. 1996. *Philodemus on Piety*, Part 1: *Critical Text with Commentary*. Oxford.

Osborne, C. 1987. "Empedocles Recycled." *Classical Quarterly* 37:24–50.

Primavesi, O. 2003. "Die Häuser von Zeus und Hades: zu Text und Deutung von Empedokles B142D.-Kr." *Cronache Ercolanesi* 33:53–68.

Stein, H. 1852. *Empedoclis Arigentini fragmenta*. Bonn.

Trépanier, S. 2003a. "'We' and Empedocles' Cosmic Lottery: P. Strasb. Gr. Inv. 1655-1666, Ensemble A." *Mnemosyne* 56:385–419.

———. 2003b. "Empedocles on the Ultimate Symmetry of the World." *Oxford Studies in Ancient Philosophy* 24:1–57.

Van der Ben, N. 1975. *The Proem of Empedocles' Peri Physios, toward a New Edition of All the Fragments: Thirty-One Fragments Edited*. Amsterdam.

15

The Parmenidean Cosmology of Parmenides[†]

Cosmology has been treated as a poor relation. Here we shall study it for itself, according to its own logic—which is not exclusive to cosmology—without bringing in the question of the relation it necessarily maintains with the successive interpretations of ἔστι ("is") in fragment 8.[1] The status that has been assigned to cosmology is not unrelated to the stagnation into which the discussion has sunk within a false debate, and which is in large measure responsible for the (more than relative) scorn that the cosmological portion of Parmenides' poem has incurred, by virtue of a disdain that was thought to be attributable to its author, in an objectivization of that critical disdain. Perceptible bodies were viewed as less worthy. Parmenides' suspicion regarding matter inevitably lent support to the suspicions brought to bear on the texts that inform us, as it turns out, about the physical system of the cosmos.

Now, the possibility of a reconstitution is quite high. The solid, detailed, and structured summary preserved in Aetius (28 A 37 D-K) allows us to rediscover and retrace with precision the phases in the constitution of the world, with the ultimate outcome being a complete theoretical elucidation. As the details are fleshed out, the process can be conceptualized. The original fragments on matter cited by Simplicius are clarified in the context of the doxographic fragment from Theophrastus (46 A D-K).[2] The latter is precise enough, and at the same time broad enough, for the elements of which the original fragments are composed to be identified in it and to contribute a complement to the skeletal interpretive framework that, with the help of a general outline, makes it

---

[†] Originally published as "La cosmologie parménidéenne en Parménide," in: R. Brague and J. Courtine, eds., *Herméneutique et ontologie. Hommage à Pierre Aubenque* (Paris, 1990), pp. 19–53. [TN: Jean Bollack incorporated material from this chapter into his book *Parménide, de l'Etant au monde* (Paris, 2006).]
[1] That other study and debate remain open, however. On the subject of sphericity as a decisive stage in the progression, see Bollack and Wismann 1974 on verses 42–49 of fragment 8 (D-K numbering).
[2] [TN: For Theophrastus, see Fortenbaugh and Gutas 2010.]

possible to integrate the specimens of the lost achievement. The testimonies corroborate one another remarkably well.

The Doxa of the Unintelligible

The confusion in the doxographic narratives is set up as authoritative by a consensus among scholars: "It is generally acknowledged that the accounts are full of contradictions and do not offer a coherent doctrine" (Gigon 1945:276).[3] Burkert (1962) draws up a list that can be extended.[4] The detailed interpretation can remain in suspense. One does what one wishes with "open" material. Raven made the clearest pronouncement (in Kirk-Raven 1957:284): "It is fortunate that, since he [Parmenides] neither believed in it himself [the tradition of Diels, Burnet, and so on] nor, apparently, succeeded in influencing others by it [the singularity is turned back against the author], Parmenides' astronomical system [the precondition for the expectation to be satisfied] is of little importance [this is the common opinion; see Guthrie and others]; for it is virtually impossible to reconstruct [reconstruction is not worth attempting; thus by default it supplies proof of its lack of interest; the verdict is 'circular']."

For Karsten (1835:243), Parmenides had not gone into detail; he had settled for a "poetic" sketch (*universi specie adumbrate* ["representing a fictitious universe"]). Zeller (1855:482–483) saw Parmenides as interested "in the research of his day," adhering to the Pythagorean world system without following it in all respects.[5]

In 1901, Diels made a note regarding fragment 12, at the beginning of his critical edition: *nondum prorsus explicatum* ("not yet precisely explained"). In his positivist faith, he believed that time would do the rest.

The lack of coherence of the account in Aetius (A37) does not have the same function for all the authors who have cited it. Either the testimony is rejected altogether as unintelligible, as it is by Guthrie (1965), for whom it justifies agnosticism, or else the verdict of incoherence has to allow for a free reconstruction. Scholars feel authorized to accommodate all the arrangements that the restoration "according to Parmenides" calls for. The analysis of the options will necessarily oscillate between an element of scientific discussion, on the

---

3   See especially Mansfeld 1964:274–280; Guthrie 1965:508–522; Zeller 1881:xxiii–xxiii.
4   Burkert 1962:286n45: "In general, it is regarded as an almost hopeless task [the preliminary is at the origin of the failure] to reconstruct the celestial system of Parmenides" (cited from Burkert 1972:307n40).
5   See below, p. 200. There is a definite relation between the incoherence and the eclecticism of the borrowing. The objective restorations are entangled in the muddled nature of the material.

basis of the premises (and prejudices) that the author is trying to advance, and another more personal element that sets science aside and rules out discussion.

For Guthrie, too, Aetius' incoherence is accompanied by a more basic lack of interest. The material is lost; this is not too serious, because Parmenides had treated the topic of cosmology as if it were a duty, trying to improve what he was reading in Anaximander or in the Pythagoreans;[6] it was only "a deliberate concession to human weakness; his contribution to philosophy lay elsewhere" (p. 61). Thus the author refrains from trying to elucidate the texts, preferring to limit himself, since the material does not properly belong to Parmenides,[7] to approximate correspondences to the Ionian and Pythagorean systems and their reflections in Plato's work. The references offer only potential comparative models.

There is nothing to be drawn "from this garbled and confused summary" (Guthrie 1965:62). Confused: this is how Aetius' narrative strikes many others (Mansfeld 1984, for example), even though he accepts the distinction between cosmogony (according to Reinhardt; see below, Aetius A 37 D-K) and cosmology.[8]

The very lengthy discussion of cosmology by Tarán (1965) is particularly disappointing, although it is instructive if one considers the common preconceptions of critical examination; these preconceptions differ in Tarán's case because their application is pushed to the point of mechanical caricature. At the expense of any signifying construction by a language, a language that would be inherent in the design of an abstract structure, Tarán limits himself to the appearance produced by the sensory experience of the world, supplying a horizon of expectation that Parmenides is presumed to have shared with him.[9] Parmenides is thus not read in order to be discovered, but rather to be confronted with what the reference to "reality" makes it probable that he meant.[10]

The texts, and in particular Theophrastus' summary, are systematically deprecated because they do not meet this expectation. The difficulty of finding in the text itself the physical representation that the text is supposed to be reproducing does not lead to a re-examination of the hypothesis, as the laws of hermeneutics, or more generally of scientific practice, would require; the information is viewed as suspect before it is studied on its own terms. Tarán fits into

---

[6] One can go further back, as Morrison does (1955:6), relying on Homer and Hesiod, and find a double system of hemispheres, above and below the earth, which is at the center, without this center being the "center" of the goddess. Guthrie's irony reinforces the discredit heaped on the topic (Guthrie 1965).

[7] Guthrie 1965:5–6: "... suppose that Parmenides is doing his best": "I can at least help you to understand it better than other people."

[8] See Mansfeld 1964:164; note 1 contradicts the assertion in the text.

[9] See the same guiding principle in Finkelberg 1986; see also below, notes 38, 39, and 42.

[10] See the ring of fire circling the earth, Tarán 1965:234–237; see also below, pp. 186–187.

a tradition represented by Cherniss (1935) or, for Theophrastus, by McDiarmid (1953), in which an older skepticism about sources has been generalized, to the extent that non-comprehension attributed to authors such as Aetius of what is being reported on (and contaminated) is elevated to the rank of criterion. The difference between the anticipated meaning and the content of the doxographic account studied is projected (and objectivized) in the irreducible distance of a primary inadequacy at the level of the source. What is not understood by the interpreter is presumed not to have been understood by the author.[11]

Reinhardt's "cosmogonic" hypothesis (1916) has often been ignored, as if it were being censored, and deemed mystifying. It is thus neither discussed nor refuted. Tarán does mention Reinhardt's hypothesis several times, but as a forbidden path, excluded a priori.[12]

The Impasse of Composite Constructions

To be able to harmonize the entirety of Aetius' text and Parmenides' fragment 12[13] with the description of the world as it had come into being, Diels (1897) introduced a whole series of interpretive and critical operations. He had the solid firmament (1) on the upper level, and the layer of fire, the ether below (2), followed by astronomic "spheres" of a composite nature, that is, blended with night; in each of its wheels there is fire, through which the celestial bodies were designated (3).[14] There was no concern for relative proportions, which were to the benefit of night;[15] in fact, the equivalence or relation between masses was not perceived, despite the undeniable parallelism, as an objective of the construction. One also sees that the "crowns" were used, on the one hand, as layers that could represent the parts of the world and, on the other, as cylindrical rings (on the model of Anaximander's wheels), conceived as the dwelling spaces of the planets or of the Milky Way.

Nothing is situated between these astral rings and the earth. The atmosphere, the sublunar region, is lacking. However, since the earth cannot in reality be enveloped by pure fire, Diels corrected Aetius' text, introducing an "underneath" (ὑφ' ᾧ) so as to be able to situate, under the terrestrial envelope

---

[11] See, for example, McDiarmid 1953. The fictitious Aetius cannot be mistaken for a Theophrastian; he is too visibly contaminated by Stoicism. There is no way to localize the goddess.

[12] See Tarán 1965:235–236.

[13] The texts are reproduced below, with interpretations.

[14] Diels 1912:161, *ad* 18 B 12: "Gestirnkränze, deren Elemente ... vermischt durcheinander liegen" ("Crowns of stars, whose elements are mixed together").

[15] Diels 1912:161, ad 18 B 12: "... Ringe, aus denen hier und da das Feuer herausblitzt ... ." ("Rings, from which the fire flashes out, here and there").

(4), a central fire (5),[16] about which it could easily be said that, in this form, it had virtually no analog in any other doctrine of physics.[17]

This outline formed the point of departure for the cosmological discussion starting in the early twentieth century, thanks to the authority of Diels' publications. The other explanations are variations, infinite in number, sometimes minimal, reduced to a single, immutable principle of adaptation.[18] Fränkel distanced himself to a greater degree from Aetius (who was considered beyond recuperation) by freely sketching a degraded loss of the igneous purity of the border areas (*a*. the pure fire of the ether, below the envelope; *b*. the blended zone, starting with the Milky Way; *c*. the terrestrial region).[19]

Without a real analysis of the problems of the "crowns," Karsten (in 1835, two generations before Diels) had divided the world rationally into three parts. Fire was confined to the upper regions; the rampart itself consisted of fire (see Gigon 1945), in "Olympus" and the sky and the region of fixed bodies; the terrestrial region was at the other extreme; between the two, there was mixed matter in the ether, with the planets and the Milky Way, which made it possible to find the astronomers' spheres again, and to give a meaning to the mysterious "crowns." In Karsten's view, the idea that Parmenides had gone very far in this study of the sky remained doubtful.[20]

The most rudimentary reduction was more bipartite: a ring of fire above, another of night below; between the two,[21] a sphere blended with the goddess.

Given the uncertainties of the critics, Couloubaritsis (1986) chose to superimpose the schemas in cosmic space, basing his decision on a global entanglement (see περιπεπλεγμένας, A 37 ["intricate, complicated"]);[22] he could accept a cosmogonic reading (frags. 11, 12), inserted in a static cosmological analysis, articulated around a point considered to be the origin of movement and leading toward the center.[23] The seat of the *she-daimon* and the theogony that proceeds from it are "mythical"; within the same system, mixed circles, situated below

---

[16] In place of στερεόν περὶ ὅ (Boeckh, but without στερεόν, for περὶ ὅν F, περὶ ὧν P) πάλιν πυρώδης (*scil.* στεφάνη), Diels had put the following in his text: στερεόν, <ὑφ᾽ ᾧ> ...

[17] See Burkert's critique (1962:296, and n. 115; in English, see Burkert 1972:317, and n. 92).

[18] The modifications ended up remodeling the text of A 37. Among the earliest were those of Susemihl 1899 and Döring 1911; see Zeller and Nestle 1920:71, n. o.

[19] "Parmenidesstudien" (1930), in Fränkel 1968:157–197. The outline has frequently been adopted by others. "Parmenidesstudien" can be found rev. and trans. as "Studies in Parmenides," in R. E. Allen and D. J. Furley, eds., *Studies in Presocratic Philosophy*, vol. 2: *The Eleatics and Pluralists*, 1–47. London, 1975.

[20] *Incertum adeo an ipse haec accuratius persecutes sit* ("It is unclear whether he pursued these things very carefully"), Karsten 1835:247.

[21] This was Jaeger's sketch (1947:122), a very hasty one, it must be said, unburdened with "details."

[22] Couloubaritsis 1986:322n83.

[23] Couloubaritsis 1986:313.

the *she-daimon*'s seat, belong to a phenomenal or physical order; the passage from one order to the other is made through the figure of the goddess.[24]

The succession of the spheres (in a free, unjustified order), for which Couloubaritsis juxtaposes (without studying their relationship) A 37 and B 12, even though the texts bear on exactly the same object, is localized in an upper part of the world, exempt from becoming, which would begin in a center, amid the mixed crowns (in this case, one would have to acknowledge with Couloubaritsis that the blend preexisted, in a non-dynamic form, below the periphery). The milieu of all the crowns, in the upper part of the world, and the seat of the goddess, at the center of the mixed crowns (according to A 37 and B 12), were for him two distinct places. All of astronomy (even the fixed bodies of the vault) thus had to be situated below the center of the mixed elements. If one were to extract the elements of the reading (they are there) from this free and "synchronic" construction, one would have a way to reread the texts and to decipher the reference on that basis. The construction belongs to the author alone, apart from any possible debate. Immobility does *not* coexist with movement in one part of the world; the blend is *not* partially immobile, and so forth.

The Problem of the Igneous Zone Surrounding the Earth

When the "rings" are reserved for the journeys of the celestial bodies, in a cosmological interpretation of Aetius' account, we go no further down than the moon. If we insist on a minimum of coherence, we cannot put the terrestrial sphere or the envelope of the fixed bodies on the same plane as the moon,[25] nor can we consider the system to be complete. If we stick to a narrow interpretation of the system, it is interrupted (it has a hole in it, in Diels' account), but even in a broader interpretation it is no less interrupted.[26] Yet another instance of incoherence.

Diels eliminates the problem by correcting the text. Fire is relegated to the inside. Other authors, the majority, end the description at the height of the moon, leaving the intermediate space blank. But even in this case the authors have to eliminate the alternation in order to progress, from the "heavens" to

---

[24] Couloubaritsis 1986:322.

[25] It is a matter of the whole, or a part, *ad libitum*. For Fränkel (1968:183n1), the "crowns" designate *both* the circles of the stars (*Sternbahnen*) *and* the spheric envelopes (*Kugelschalen*). Gigon (1945:279) has a contrary opinion: "They naturally *cannot* be considered as rings," on the same basis as the circuits of the celestial bodies.

[26] See the void between the moon and the earth in Fränkel 1968:185 and Fränkel 1951:413. The moon is for "the world of men," who aspire to evade their nocturnal prison.

the moon, toward an increase in the nocturnal element. Fränkel manages this through a critique of Theophrastus' reading of Parmenides (frag. 12),[27] anticipating the method practiced to the point of caricature by Tarán. In fact, Fränkel eliminates a meaning that is approximately accurate,[28] considering it an error on Theophrastus' part, in favor of an erroneous match with reality, drawn from the fragment.[29] The aporia is eliminated mechanically. A first series of astronomical "spheres" is of pure fire; a second, increasingly clouded and dirty (Fränkel 1951:413), culminates in a point of lunar ambiguity announcing the world of men. "Mixed" takes on a deprecatory connotation.

It is hard to know whether the physical system, as constructed by these scholars, is the source of the theories on the status of the *doxa*, or whether it is the other way around. When, for Untersteiner (1958), the *doxa* is distinguished from the "eon" by the fall into temporality, the instruments for measuring time in the sky become essential; a confirmation of this opinion is found in the astronomical spheres, which are thought (or said) to occupy a new place in Parmenides.[30]

Non-mixing (frag. 9)

The principle of non-sharing is formulated in fragment 9, based on the rigorous autonomy of Day and Night.

The opposition, which forms the basic structure found in everything, stems from the constitutive contrary tensions of the figure of the represented Being. Before they were elements in the narrow sense of the term, Aristotle's fire and earth, the principles of Light and Night were witnesses to the division of Being as it appeared. The first designates the centrifugal impulse, the second the centripetal impulse. The attributes of lightness and heaviness, sparseness and density, express and develop this identification. In fact, the identity of each of these principles excludes the identity of the other. Rigorously equivalent, if one sets aside the non-contradictory and supernumerary attribute of softness (ἤπιον), which gives Light an advantage that is hard to measure, the cosmic

---

[27] The alternation of the rings had been introduced by Theophrastus following an erroneous interpretation of frag. 12.2 s. He had made the role of fire (μετά) autonomous in the circles of darkness (Fränkel 1968:183).

[28] The translation "in alternation, the one formed of ... the other of ..." (Fränkel 1968:183) is not the correct analysis of ἐπαλλήλους.

[29] στεινότεραι is applied to the purest celestial spheres, and μετά is read as an indication of the blending that has already taken place.

[30] Untersteiner 1958:cxciv: "This astral cosmology, which is particularly well developed among the Eleatics—in a much more systematic way than among the other pre-Socratics—has a precise *raison d'être*" (the relation of the celestial bodies among themselves, creatures of time ...).

powers divide up the universe and are present in all the intermediate concrete manifestations of the real.

αὐτὰρ ἐπειδὴ πάντα φάος καὶ νὺξ ὀνόμασται
καὶ τὰ κατὰ σφετέρας δυνάμεις ἐπὶ τοῖσι καὶ τοῖς,
πᾶν πλέον ἐστὶν ὁμοῦ φάεος καὶ νυκτὸς ἀφάντου
ἴσων ἀμφοτέρων, ἐπεὶ οὐδετέρῳ μέτα μηδέν

Since all things have been named light and night and also according to the forces belonging to the one and the other, in the case of such things as well as of such others, everything is full together of light and of night without light, the two being equals, because neither one contains anything of the other.

Since all things have been named light and night and also according to the forces belonging to the one and the other [the group τὰ κατὰ σφετέρας δυνάμεις ("the forces. ...") designates the qualities associated with the principles; it is an attribute of πάντα, on the same basis as φάος and νύξ],[31] *in the case of such things as well as of such others* (the prepositional group is not a complement of ὀνόμασται but it determines δυνάμεις[32]), *everything is full together* [ὁμοῦ does not express simultaneity but rather contiguity[33]] *of light and of night without light, the two being equals, because neither one contains anything of the other.* The causal statement of the final hemistich ἐπεὶ οὐδετέρῳ μέτα μηδέν has been related either to the affirmation that everything is full of light and darkness or else to the equality of the two forces (ἴσων ...). The structure of the four lines and μετεῖναι have led to the adoption of the second solution. Indeed, the assertion in line 3, everything is full, is already shored up by a first causal statement, lines 1 and 2, so that the second assertion is very naturally related to that of equality. This is reason enough to set aside the translation "there is nothing that does

---

[31] See the scholia *ad* 8.59: "... by names in conformity with their powers" (Couloubaritsis does not account for καὶ τὰ κατὰ δυνάμεις, for the difference between light and darkness or for the properties of the two "powers"). A double nomination, global and particular.

[32] To the contrary, Coxon (1986:84) and O'Brien (1987:61), follow Diels-Kranz (and see Karsten 1835, earlier) to link the group ἐπὶ τοις ... with ὀνόμασται (see also Tarán 1965:161, with a different construction of τά: "and these ..."); Mansfeld (1964:148n3, 149) is even more acrobatic, as he connects the prepositional complement to the multitude of the particular ("ihrer jewelligen Einzelstruktur ... gemäss benannt" ["named in accord with its jewel-like single structure"]). Plenitude (πλέον) results from a totalization of the capacities by an extensive power of two principles: δυνάμεις ἐπὶ ... . These are properties of Night and Day; their differences are revealed in the multitude of things.

[33] *Zusammen* (Hölscher 1969:31); cf. Mansfeld 1964:150, 154, referring to the "sign" of frag. 8.5, ὁμοῦ πᾶν, rather than *zugleich* (D-K); *alike*, O'Brien 1967; *à la fois*, Couloubaritsis 1986:162, with Tarán.

not belong to one or the other of the two";[34] moreover, μετεῖναι never expresses belonging to individual entities, but only to a group ("to be among"). When the argument turns back to equality,[35] one can understand either that the void is absent from each component, or that neither of the two forces impinges on the attribution of the other. Yet the expression τι μέτα [equivalent to μέτεστίν] τινι does not mean that one thing is included in another (see Karsten 1835:4: *quoniam neutri inane inesti* ["since the void belongs to neither"]), but that one thing participates in another (τινι μέτεστί means τινι μέτεστι τινος). Schwabl (1953, along with others) understands that neither of the two participates in Non-being (weil keine von beiden am Nichtseienden teil hat ["because no part of them contains the non-existent"]).[36] One does not see why Parmenides would have taken care to deny in advance the assimilation, which will be drawn from Aristotle, of Night to Non-being. On the contrary, he must have based equality on absolute purity and without any mixing of the opposed principles.

"In neither of the two [οὐδετέρῳ] is anything blended [μέτα μηδέν]." "Among" (or "in the midst of," μέτα) has a strong predicative value ("nothing that is μετά").[37] It will be understood, then, in accordance with lines 8.56–59, that neither of the two principles shares in anything—that is, in anything other than itself (Mullach 1857: *quoniam neutri quidquam cum altero commune est* ["since nothing of either

---

34 Thus Fränkel 1968:181, adopted by Kranz ("was unter keinem von beidem steht" ["what pertains to neither of the two"]), as opposed to Diels; then Calogero 1977:52n47; Verdenius 1942:77 ("... that does not belong to either"); Tarán 1965:164; Guthrie 1965:57, and so on. More recently still, Cordero 1984:40 (more concisely, "for outside of it there is nothing"); the translation of the preceding line, "What has its proper powers has been named grace for these or for those," is difficult to analyze. What are the referents?

35 See also Simplicius, *On Aristotle's Physics* 6 *ad* B 9: καὶ ἀρχαὶ ἄμφω (Konstan 2014).

36 See Schwabl 1953:64; for the same analysis, one can cite (among the most recent authors) Mourelatos 1970:85: "since nothingness partakes in neither") (relating the explanation to πλέον); Couloubaritsis ("does not harmonize [=?] with nothingness"), and so on; see also Mansfeld 1964:150–153.

37 The subject of the subordinate clause (μηδέν) names the element of the mix that is excluded, as a rejected possibility. Mansfeld's translation (1964:156), "weil keines von beiden Anteil hat an Nichts" ("because neither of them has to share anything") could (except for the capital letter) be justified, against the hypostasis of nothingness or Non-being ("neither of the two contains a nothingness" [Hölscher 1968:107; "a ..." ?]), which substitutes a judgment of existence (Hölscher: "of reality") for the definition of the *reciprocal* relation of exclusion and purity. O'Brien (1967) makes the task extremely difficult by supposing that the rigorous separation between the two principles implies the (denied) possibility of a matter that is not used. He thus makes οὐδετέρῳ μέτα the subject of the clause "what is not part either of the one or of the other" (οὐδετέρῳ μέτα, without a participle), and he makes μηδέν a judgment of existence ("is nothing"). One cannot say that this sentence contains a double negative (p. 62); for O'Brien, the subject is determined negatively. There is no doubt that the analysis of the noun phrase requires the predicative value of μέτα (grammatically μέτεστιν): nothing is a part ... . See also Owens 1974:391; he takes μέτα to be an adverb: "for neither can there be sharing in any way at all" (see also n. 30).

is common with another"]; see ἑαυτῷ πάντοσε τώυτόν, τῷ δ᾽ἑτέρῳ μὴ τώυτόν ["to itself everywhere the same, to the other not the same"] 8.57–58).

The unblended purity of the principles is maintained in the surprising geometry of their initial cosmic distribution. To interpret the fragments of the cosmology in the broad sense (10–15), we must not give up on Theophrastus' interpretation, which is preserved in Aetius's manual. Placed at the beginning of the chapter titled περὶ τάξεως κόσμου (On the Order of the Cosmos) (2.7.1), this text served as a referential framework for doxographic reflection on the spatial representation of systems. Theophrastus' text can be divided into three parts. A first part summarizes a pre-cosmic or pre-cosmogonic structure; a second refers to the movements that give rise to the elementary differentiation and to the interaction of the principles; a third, finally, describes the arrangements of the parts of the world that has come into being, according to the title of Aetius' chapter, "On the Organization of the Universe." One stage follows from the other and leads to this end. To avoid the confusion that characterizes modern readings and compromises the rare attempts to rediscover the coherence of the whole, we must distinguish three developments in the text that correspond to different moments in the cosmographic construction. The first includes a purely geometric structure that is closely tied to the mutual exclusion of fragment 9.

Aetius (A 37) I: Before the Cosmogonic Movement

Preceding the concrete localization of the parts, at the center, at the periphery, and in the middle, the abstract schema presents in the first place the mode of distribution of the principles prior to any interpenetration:

A. The Initial Distribution (A 37 1 A)

Παρμενίδης στεφάνας εἶναι περιπεπλεγμένας ἑταλλήλους, τὴν μὲν ἐκ τοῦ ἀραιοῦ, τὴν δὲ ἐκ τοῦ πυκνοῦ· μικτὰς δὲ ἄλλας ἐκ φωτὸς καὶ σκότους μεταξὺ τούτων.

Parmenides says that there are concentrically embedded spheres [*stephanai*] packed closely together, in each case one made of a sparse body and the other of a dense body; and others, blended, made of light and night, in the intervals between these.

The localizations τὸ περιέχον ("what surrounds") ... ὑφ᾽ ᾧ ("beneath which) ... and τὸ μεσαίτατον ("the middle") ... περὶ ὅ ("around which") ... prove that we are dealing with spheres embedded concentrically and not rolled up or braided.[38] As for ἐπαλλήλους ("concentrically embedded"), the lexicon teaches us that the adjective does not designate alternation—which is expressed by τὴν μὲν ... τὴν δὲ ("one ... and the other")—but rather close succession, without intervals. The existence of two pairs, one localized in the center and the other at the periphery, is explicitly mentioned. The immediate succession of fire and night at the two extremes shows that the *mixed* circles are situated in the interval maintained between the two pure pairs, the one in the center and the other at the periphery.

Figure 1 Diagram of the distribution of the spheres at the pre-cosmogonic stage.

The order in which the layers succeed one another from the absolute center to the absolute periphery—a dense layer, followed by a sparse layer, then by mixed layers, and finally again a sparse layer, followed by a dense layer that forms the outer limit—obviously does not correlate with the organization of the world that surrounds us[39] and that we see. The earth is not separated from

---

[38] As some have understood. For Finkelberg (1986:312n24), the term "braided" is chosen by the doxographer because it translates the actual mix; it does not apply to the pure spheres.

[39] Finkelberg, in contrast, reads the first part of A 37 in such a way as to establish a correspondence, as has always been done, between the "rings" and real referents in the contemporary world. Thus for him the mixed rings are not inserted between pure pairs: there is no darkness in the heavens, but a mix only below the ether; at the center, fire is localized under the terrestrial crust, following the ancient opinion (see Zeller, Diels, and so on); and see below, p. 108.
After the mention of the solids in Aetius (in the center and at the periphery—my 1b), his reading, in a dissymmetry that is more cosmographic than Parmenidean, arrives at a pair (fire/darkness)

the mixed zones of the atmosphere by a ring of pure fire.[40] If the speculative vigor of the system had been recognized, its self-evident pre-cosmic character would have been apparent; instead, the pieces of an incomplete puzzle have been permuted, always because of the rudimentary state of archaic science and the defective state of the information available.

The first part of Aetius A 37 preserves a symmetrical description that, as such, was not usable for a cosmography. This was the source of the difficulties. The symmetry appeared puerile and inadequate. No one, or almost no one, agreed to consider the schematic structure, and even those who did so retained its consequences only partially at best.

The decisive step proceeds, as is often the case, from an aporia; acceptance of the impasse leads to getting beyond it. If one opposes "mixed" to "pure" in the ordinary understanding and application of the terms, the orders are confused; the initial structure is assimilated to the later movements, which it determines. One is necessarily sent back to a "real" reference in the universe, either present or in the process of becoming, in a cosmogonic past. The problem of deciphering the figuration that is visualized but abstract is displaced, and it leads to endless discussions of attribution without an attributable object; it is de-intellectualized ("reified"). "Mixed" has to be understood with the idiomatic value of "mixed by virtue of the presence of the one and the other," and thus "not mixed."[41] For one pure layer, there would be, in the movement of division, two other antithetical layers of fire and night. On one, half of each; and so on. In this way, through a progression by division, the "mix" (interpenetration) is prepared; the separation remains complete, preserving antagonistic identities.[42] The dynamism of the abstract structure leads to the dynamics of the physical forces.

Theophrastus' use of the word "mix" is not accidental, even if mixing as the rhythm of the partition is analyzed at the heart of the structure itself. It expresses the paradoxical truth of an organization that leads to blending through intensification of the antithesis.

---

in the center, around the core, for which there is no corresponding pair at the periphery, under the rampart (fire/mixed). The dissociation is arbitrary.

[40] See above, 184–187.

[41] Which does not prevent the use of "mixed" for the stage of actual interpenetration (frag. 12.4).

[42] Finkelberg raises questions (understandably) about the difference that would make it possible to distinguish each unit in the series of mixed, contiguous rings (pp. 209–210). There is, as for others (see above), only a single region of the world. The question, which ought to have been maintained, was not compatible with the prejudice in favor of the immediate cosmic reference. Finkelberg's interpretation of 12.1–2 (1986:309–312) cannot be defended; there is no darkness that *follows* the mixed layers; for him, lines 1–2 are divided between *a* fire, *c* (in the center) darkness, *b* (in the third place, μέτα) mixed. He reserves the mixed layers for everything that is intermediary between earth and ether.

If Theophrastus' interpretation is correct by virtue of a deeper coherence than the mere possibility of solving the problems posed by the text, line 2 of fragment 12 does not describe a zone of blending, as it is commonly understood, but rather a closer and closer succession, which can be confirmed, on the one hand, with the help of the opposition with "pure" (ἀκρήτοιο, line 1)—there were layers of pure night before there were the layers of pure fire at the extremities—and, on the other hand, by the arrival at the median line, the place from which the goddess acts (line 3).

By *reading* Theophrastus' text after Diels, with Parmenides' fragment 12, and against Diels' rather violent conclusions,[43] Reinhardt (1916) recognized that the first lines could not be related to the actual contemporary state of the world, but that they reproduced a construction that could not be assimilated to a descriptive system.[44] If he called this construction *cosmogonic*, it was in opposition to the cosmological or astrological explanation that had prevailed. In the second part of his book, he opted for genesis as opposed to system, and he accounted for what had preceded the genesis as the description of a previous or precursor state. In itself, this reading is neither true nor false, but in Reinhardt's eyes it implied continuity and kinship, an implication that has led to (considerable) errors. The response remained determined by the position it was combating.

When the rings are interpreted as a stage in the cosmogony, as prior to a more decisive dynamism in the formation of the world properly speaking (which is assimilated to a *koinè*, extrapolated from the other pre-Socratics and thus explained by them),[45] the arrangement retained remains arbitrary. The arrangement, before it is upset, must have some signification with respect to the duality itself.[46] Meaning requires the arrangement of an alternation, and the pre-cosmogonic use of the *stephanai*.

---

[43] See above, pp. 184–185.

[44] Reinhardt (1916:11) was deciding among three hypotheses, the spheres of this world (1), according to the positivist interpretation offered by Diels or Burnet (1930), an order preceding the one that results from the formation of the world (2), or the symbolic expression of the system of physical laws (3). The third is hard to distinguish from the first; in fact, they merge.

[45] In Hölscher's attempt (1969:109), relying on Empedocles (A 49 = 174 Bollack 1972) for the cosmogonic connection, following Reinhardt, the comparison with the later systems introduces a more structural element, in contrast to the dependencies always taken up again by the "Pythagoreans" or by Anaximander.

[46] See Hölscher 1969:108: "permitting the passage from the pure duality of the contraries to the cosmogony." Distributing the rings of fire around a center, and—toward the periphery—around the rings of darkness, Hölscher has, except for the center, a separation of the two masses, but neither their relative separation nor the rings or spheres take on any meaning here (he reserves them for the divisions that *result from* the cosmogony, and thus in fact for the astronomical spheres as well, as the constructions that are being combated).

If the blend is analyzed as a logical consequence of the doubled identity,[47] the maintenance of identity *in* the blend poses a problem. It is not self-evident. The negation of indistinct plurality takes place in duality. The structure of the rings means that the blend is produced by the negation, dominated and controlled by the autonomous principles (according to 8.55–59).

One cannot go back, before cosmology, to find the arrangement of the original duality, without also going back before the cosmogony. As a consequence, the *pre*-cosmogonic structure has to be—this is a postulate—closely related to the conditions and the beginning of the cosmogonic movements.

Fragment 12, Lines 1–2

Contrary to what Fränkel had maintained, the first part of Theophrastus' testimony is in perfect harmony with the data in Parmenides' fragment 12. A system "as differentiated"[48] as that of Theophrastus *may* be more or less drawn from fragment 12. To be sure, this could not be done without the help of the summary.

The relation of the original fragments to the doxographic texts is different in each case. They can all be read thanks to Aetius; however, fragment 12 presents a part of the very process that is being summarized, whereas 10 and 11, which have a global and programmatic character, presuppose the completion of the system, in the coherence of its parts among themselves, as 14 and 15 do for the moon-sun relation.[49] The decoding is not the same.

Lines 1 and 2 describe the arrangement of the layers of fire and night, which, starting from the center and from the periphery, converge toward a line at the center of the mixed spheres. Lines 3 and 6 situate the goddess who presides over the blending in the most central of the mixed layers.

αἱ γὰρ στεινότεραι πλῆντο[50] πυρὸς ἀκρήτοιο
αἱ δ' ἐπὶ ταῖς νυκτός, μετὰ δὲ φλογὸς ἵεται αἶσα.

---

[47] As Hölscher (1968:25) formulates it in *Anfängliches Fragen*, following Reinhardt (Reinhardt 1916:74ff.; see also Hölscher 1969:198ff).

[48] See Hölscher 1969:107ff. He writes that the text (A 37) becomes *even more* disconcerting if it is confronted with B 12.

[49] O'Brien does not consider A 37 (1967:17 ad 12.1–3). The arrangement that he proposes (247) suffers from this lack. The specificity of fragment 12 does not appear; the announcement of the cosmogony (frag. 11) probably is not linked to an earlier stage (see Bicknell's [1968] hypothesis concerning Parmenides frag. 10; and see below, p. 209. In any case, one cannot conclude from the "works" (of the sun and the moon) that it is a matter of a later "development." The two aspects, the origin and the effects, are definitional, complementary, and general.

[50] Simplicius' manuscripts show πανηντο (πύνηντο). Diels followed Bergk (πλῆντο) (Bergk 1886, 2:66–72). Fränkel preferred the present tense πλῆνται (see O'Brien 1967).

For the narrower ones are filled with fire without blending and the ones that follow are filled with night; further still the portion of flames shoots up.

The feminine forms αἱ ... στεινότεραι and αἱ δ᾽ ἐπὶ ταῖς unquestionably refer to the spherical envelopes, called στεφάναι. The comparative *narrower* can be understood either as referring to the relative dimensions of the rays that separate the circles from the center or to the relative thickness of the layers. In the first case, the notion of "narrower" signifies "closer to the center," and the succession is necessarily organized in a single direction starting from the periphery.[51] The progression is symmetrical: it starts, as A 37 confirms, from the two extreme limits. The second meaning is thus imposed: a thick layer of night is followed, in the direction of the periphery, by thinner fire, while the thick band of night at the periphery is followed, in the direction of the core, by a thinner band.[52] According to Theophrastus, the mixed circles are located in the interval between the two pairs. Scholars agree that the description of these circles is found in line 2, deeming either that, in a unidirectional progression, starting at the periphery, the mixed zone forms a third ring (or a series of rings) situated below the pure fire (after the rampart),[53] or else that, following the *double* progression, starting both from the center and from the periphery, the layers of pure fire and pure night are followed by mixed layers.[54] However, the "mix" in question here is not a simple blend. The plural αἱ δὲ ("the ones that follow"), maintained intentionally in Theophrastus' paraphrase, indicates that the two zones of fire immediately adjacent to the core and the rampart at the periphery are both followed by a new band of night, which is in turn followed by fire.

Rather than understanding μετά as though the flame were shooting up *in the middle of* or *in pursuit of* darkness, or that it had been *released* (μεθίεται),[55] considered as a single mass extending over the entire median zone, it seems more accurate to put the adverb on the same level as ἐπὶ ταῖς, translating it as *after, farther*; the fire comes to place itself, in both directions, *after* the internal

---

[51] But others see the movement as coming from the center.

[52] The word "for" (γάρ, 12.1), abrupt in the quote from Simplicius, may relate to the exclusive distribution. The purity of the external spheres of darkness is symmetrically related to the purity of the internal spheres of fire. The decision to translate στεινότεραι by "nearest" (to the median line of encounter) rather than "narrowest" is understandable (Reinhardt 1916:13), but it is problematic.

[53] See Fränkel 1968:184, according to a principle of progressive decrease in light.

[54] See Zeller-Nestle 1920:701, where the symmetry is preserved (provoking the correction by Diels that has been discussed).

[55] Finally, like everyone else, Cordero 1984 or O'Brien 1967: "with them shoots forth a burst of flame." Blending is presupposed.

layers of night. With this reading, the mixed element would be actualized in the repetition *without any blending* of the two paradigmatic couples, which are doubled toward the interior. The term αἶσα, which says that the *portion* of flames is measured according to the law of distribution, signifies that the two layers of fire are added to the layers of darkness according to the same relation as in the external pairs.

The very reduced difference (which is acknowledged) inside a pair of contraries would not call into question the principle of equipollence, if the lesser surface occupied by fire, as compared to night, is compensated by the higher degree of intensity of one mass that is less inert than the other. The mobility and the relation between fine and dense matter would thus also be prefigured, at the heart of the initial division; difference in equality is its leading principle.

The text of the fragment does not indicate that the doubling of the pairs is pursued in the direction of the median line where the divinity of the blend resides, but the superlative in Theophrastus' summary, *the most median of the mixed elements*, allows us to suppose that the initial structure is reproduced an indefinite number of times (see also the indeterminate expression μικτὰς δ' ἄλλας) ["others mixed"]). Moreover, it is consistent with the logic of the system that in a first stage the two opposing forces occupy the whole without blending together. The term *mixed*, used by Theophrastus to designate the internal non-blended rings, is well explained by the hypothesis that posits a decreasing arrangement in which the interior pair, even while preserving the initial proportion of thicknesses, would consistently occupy the breadth of a single one (presumably the first) of the rings that form the preceding pair. The gradual shrinking of the intact rings prefigures and anticipates the interpenetration of the blending.

B / The Extreme Limits Set by Darkness (A 37 1 B)

καὶ τὸπεριέχον δὲ πάσας τείχους δίκην στερεὸν ὑπάρχειν, ὑφ' ᾧ πυρώδης στεφάνη, καὶ τὸ μεσαίτατον πασῶν στερεόν, περὶ ὃ [see n. 15, above] πάλιν πυρώδης

What envelops them all, like a rampart, is solid, with an igneous ring below; and what is most central of all is solid, with another igneous ring around it.

Solidity is a property of night, as is density. It seems that one can infer from the pre-cosmic structure that the universe was circumscribed in an enclosure of two solid spheres (a full one at the center, a hollow one at the periphery).

The use of the adjective "solid" (στερεόν) is thus distinctive; the consequence would be that this enclosure could be viewed as a stable part, surviving the upsetting of the geometry of crowns[56] and that, symmetrically, at the moment of this effacement the contiguous spheres of fire would be the privileged agents of the dynamism that is established, nourished at a distance starting from the median limit. The solid parts are obviously not assimilable to any of the elementary structures, as they are formed during the genesis, starting from the actual blending. The solid core will no more be the "earth"[57] than the external enclosure, designated by the analogy with a rampart.[58]

C / The Middle (A 37 I C; Frag. 12, 3-6)

The duality is canceled out at this breaking point in the system, where unification is sure to come about in the world between two contrary identities:

Aetius A 37 A I *c*. The middle of the mixed spheres:

τῶν δὲ συμμιγῶν τὴν μεσαιτάτην ἁπάσαις <ἀρχήν> τε καὶ <αἰτίαν> κινήσεως καὶ γενέσεως ὑπάρχειν, ἥντινα καὶ δαίμονα κυβερνῆτιν καὶ κληροῦχον ἐπονομάζει, Δίκην τε καὶ Ἀνάγκην.

The sphere that is found in the absolute center of the mixed bodies is for all the "origin" and the "cause"[59] of the movement of becoming, a sphere that he names "divinity that governs," and "that holds the parts,"[60] as well as Justice and Necessity.[61]

---

56   See Mansfeld 1964:164n1.

57   The assimilation is constant: see Fränkel 1968:184: "der Weltkern (die Erde)" ("the world-core, the Earth"). The distinction is made clearly by Finkelberg (1986:307), but, as he maintains the idea of a fire in the interior of the earth (on the model of Etna or Vesuvius), the core will be solid and yet distinct from the earth (*a b a*). He constructs, in disagreement with frag. 9 and (many) other testimonies, a third space of bodies, which would be what is called the "solid" (see p. 304).

58   Seeking equilibrium in the current situation of the world, where the heavy and the murky are localized in the center, Gigon concludes that all the fire must be located at the periphery. A shell of fire then surrounds the ether and the igneous sky (1945:279). The aporia did not escape him, but the "realistic" and anti-constructionist bias prevented him from re-evaluating his hypothesis. Better to remain with the aporia (even if it were absurd). Later on (280), he imagines a wall (of ice?) separating the divine fire from the empyrean realm of the ether.

59   The text has a gap after ἁπάσαις. Only τε καὶ can be read; Diels completed it with <ἀρχήν>, following Simplicius, *On Aristotle's Physics* (cf. ad B 12): πάσης γενέσεως αἰτίάν, which does not pose a problem for the basic content. One may prefer the *cruces*, as Coxon does.

60   The transmitted term κληροῦχον is ordinarily corrected as κληδοῦχον (Fülleborn 1795, in keeping with the proem, frag. 1.14). The grouping is problematic. If Δίκη and Ἀνάγκη are taken together, as a thing (see τε καὶ), κληροῦχον could be an epithet for this group. According to the other option, the adjective also qualifies δαίμονα, and the two nouns are in apposition.

61   The organization of the divine powers (theology) and anthropology are not included in this study, however linked they may be to the analysis of the cosmic structures.

B 12.3–6:

ἐν δὲ μέσῳ τούτων δαίμων ἥ πάντα κυβερνᾷ·
πάντη γὰρ[62] στυγεροῖο τόκου καὶ μίξιος ἄρχει
πέμπουσ' ἄρσενι θῆλυ μιγῆν[63] τό τ' ἐναντίον αὖτις ἄρσεν θηλυτέρῳ.

In the midst of these [narrower spheres] is located the divinity that governs all things; for everywhere it unleashes frightful engendering and union, leading the female to blend with the male and conversely again the male with the female (12.3–6).

A 37 interprets the eponyms of the anonymous power of blending, which governs (κυβερνῆτις) and which holds the parts, by the names *Dikè* and *Anankè*,[64] which appear in the *doxa*. As for the place this power occupies in the universe, it is incorrect to say, as everyone does, that Simplicius, disagreeing with us, situates it in the center of everything; he only replaces Parmenides' terms ἐν δὲ μέσῳ τούτων by ἐν μέσῳ πάντων (Konstan 2014:34, 15). The error is explained by the fact that neo-Pythagorean speculation on the number and the place of the elements sometimes attributes to Parmenides, as it does to Empedocles, the theory of the central fire.[65] Defended by Zeller for the central localization,[66] the assimilation allowed Diels to shore up the conjectural inversion of the lower rings. In the first evocation of blending, the qualities of male and female represent the opposing forces. The symmetry of the movements, the female going toward the male and the male toward the female, illustrates that they initiate their strict equivalence even in union.

The place where the goddess is found is clearly defined. The localization is unproblematic provided that one understands the succession of rings as a complete symmetrical system traversing the universe without a break (since the genitive τούτων applies to the rings, ἐν μέσῳ necessarily refers to the median point). The structure of the pre-cosmogonic exclusion of circles situated closer and closer together produces blending, by pushing the division to the ultimate explosion, at the point where the circles meet.

Interpreted, the diagram would make it clear that union, in blending, results from division, thanks to the finer and finer demarcation of distinct entities. There would be a "blend" without blending, in the terms of the doxographic

---

[62] Mullach and Fränkel have πάντα; Diels proposes πάντα γάρ ἤ.
[63] Stein's (1867) infinitive μιγῆν, for Simplicius' μιγὲν (equivalent to μίγησαν) would presuppose an asyndeton (ἄρσενι ...).
[64] For *Anankè*, see B 10, 6.
[65] Anatolius, p. 20 (Heiberg 1901) (= 28 A 44): see Burkert 1962:296ff. (Burkert 1972:317ff.).
[66] Nestle 1920:717n1.

text, at the heart of the opposition. The two principles thus enter into the effective blend of the genesis of the world, while keeping their own identities; these identities are transferred and preserved beyond the dividing line. The relation between the initial abstract order and the dynamic phase of the constitution of the cosmic order becomes clear in light of this passage, which ensures the preservation of the inalienable features of each of the opposing principles, which are at once refractory and at the same time by that very token the authors of the blend. The goddess represents this law of duality constrained in the One; she presides over it and is produced by it.

All the other localizations that have been proposed, as products of conventional expectations, cannot be the results of analysis, since blending is presupposed to be present everywhere, before it has taken place.[67] The following hypotheses have been supported arbitrarily:

1. *Of ubiquity.* —If blending had already taken place (at the moment established by the line) and if it were therefore everywhere, one could judge that it was arbitrary to install the goddess of blending here rather than there. Thus Reinhardt and Fränkel—arbitrarily, it is true, for the meaning of the expression—analyzed ἐν μέσῳ as a "between," μεταξύ (not "inside" but in the intervals between the rings). Since the rings were only partially blended, the universal principle[68] was limited to the places where blending prevailed, in the world (see Reinhardt 1916:12; Fränkel 1968:185: "Eine feste Lokalisierung ist mit diesem *inmitten* überhaupt nicht gegeben" ["No fixed location is given with this 'in the middle'"]).[69]

2. *Of the center.* —Simplicius' testimony (Konstan 2014, p. 34, 14–15)—"He represents the goddess installed at the center of everything, the cause of every form of becoming, as the efficient cause, one and common"—has been linked to the core, which for Diels is the central fire,[70]

---

[67] Zeller's reasoning (Zeller-Nestle 1920:717n1d) has its logic, in a non-egalitarian dualist vision, which is not that of Parmenides: if the blending is to the benefit of corruption, Aetius' text cannot have placed the goddess in the center of the *less perfect* spheres.

[68] "Omnipresence," according to Mansfeld (1964:164). Rightly so, but on the basis of a single instance (and an instant), and without limits.

[69] "... everywhere the antagonistic principles are in contact," the goddess is at work. For this opinion, one can cite Verdenius 1942:6 and n. 4; Mansfeld 1964:164. Reinhardt (1916:13) had delimited the equidistant point, but since he recognized a blend actually achieved on both sides, the interpretation—which was in fact correct—was contradicted by Reinhardt himself.

[70] *Aut coronarum omnium* ("either of all the crowns"), according to Theophrastus, A 37 (Fortenbaugh and Gutas 2010), the region of the sun (for purity; for Gigon, it will be the moon, on the side of corruption); or else "the center of the universe," *aut universi* ("or of the universe"), according to Simplicius. The interpretation is an ancient one: see Karsten (1835:251ff.): *Plerique ita*

the Pythagoreans' hearth (Ἑστία; D-K p. 242, *ad* frag. 12), whereas the reference is manifestly to line 3 of the fragment.[71] Guthrie, who like Gigon and others was looking for representations external to the system, assimilates the *daimon* to the Pythagoreans' central fire,[72] here immersed in the chthonic depths, so that the eclecticism (or the "syncretism") of the historian, projected onto the *doxa*, makes of the *daimon* Mother Earth and the dispenser of Justice, all at the same time. The tradition is an ancient one; Parmenides' Pythagoreanism was common in the nineteenth century: "At the center of the universe the demiurgic divinity, generatrix of the gods and of all things, had her seat; one cannot but recognize the central fire, the creator mother god of the world of the Pythagoreans."[73]

What was expected won out over all the testimonies.[74]

3. *On the side of the periphery.* —Berger (1895), in order to take the *middle* into account, chose the sun, among the celestial bodies, as the principle of life (in accordance with the solar cults).[75] For Gigon (1945:280–281), the divinity is transcendent; thus she dwells in the external igneous zone, beyond the rampart. The origin of the concept is situated in Xenophanes' divine sphere, transferred by Parmenides into "the world of general opinion." This would be the true god, repre-

---

intellexerunt ... . Sic Simplicius ("This did many think ... so Simplicius"). (Parmenides used the Pythagorean central fire, but had to substitute the earth for it). Neither Reinhardt (1916:12) nor Fränkel (1968:185) doubted this central localization, attributed to Simplicius. Like Theophrastus (Krische *apud* Zeller-Nestle 1920:717), Simplicius could have been mistaken about the meaning of 12.3. Karsten himself (1835:252), however, had positioned himself on the side of the median line, according to Stobaeus (*paribus intervallis a mundi centro et circuitu distantem*, "distant by equal intervals from the center and circuit of the world"), against Simplicius, on the interpretation that he (Karsten) never renounced. Finkelberg, finally, interprets fragment 12 according to Simplicius' erroneous but accepted meaning, and proposes to correct Aetius in order to achieve consensus (1986:311 and n. 21).

[71] The uncertainty, "going back to Antiquity" (Hölscher 1969:108), stems from this Dielsean interpretation of Simplicius.

[72] "This, to his probably Pythagorean-trained mind, was the *daimon* ..." (Guthrie 1965:64).

[73] Zeller (1881), against Karsten's powerful arguments (1835:252).

[74] See also Tannery, taking the *doxa* to be a Pythagorean doxography that was polemical in character (1930:236); and Tannery 1884:285: the divinity is "at the center of the universe"; Tannery took the crowns to be nested cylinders. The position of Burnet (1930:169–196), who believed that in the *doxa* Parmenides was exposing a doctrine that he had gone beyond and that his disciples must have known, the better to combat it, remains dependent on the *a priori* of that tradition (see, once again, Guthrie, after Cornford, and Raven, and the metamorphoses of Pythagoreanism; Burnet is still following Pythagoras and the oral tradition, although sometimes this position is mitigated by Ionian speculations). Against the Pythagorean assimilation, Anaximander is placed in the forefront by Burkert (1962:261n31; in English, see Burkert 1972: n25).

[75] So did Susemihl 1899; see Nestle in Zeller (1881, p. 718, n. o.); Diels 1912, *ad* frag. 12.

sentative of Being; the goddess in fragment 12, comparable to Aphrodite (frag. 12.4–6; see the authors cited and combated in Zeller-Nestle 1920:171n1) in the lunar region of men, would be a secondary force, originating in the other, delegated "into the blend" (the middle is only one "region" for the true god). The indications pertaining to the union of the sexes at the end of the fragment are used in a restrictive way.

Some scholars accepted that at least for Theophrastus, if not in reality, the goddess was "where night and fire blend."[76] Reduced to this observation, the assertion is almost meaningless.

Reinhardt's position, contradictory only in its impure application, was clearly anticipated by Karsten and others (Reinhardt was situating himself vis-à-vis the scientific authority of his immediate predecessors and did not look further back): *habitare hanc Deam ... paribus intervallis a mundi centro et circuitu distantem, unde ipsa ... moderator* ("The goddess lives ... at equal distances from the center of the universe and at a distance from the circuit ... of which she is herself the ruler") (Reinhardt 1916:252). The research could have been linked to that of Karsten and the others, as was the case nearly a century later, in Nestle's conclusions at the end of his discussion (Zeller-Nestle 1920:718).

Cicero's testimony in *De natura deorum* 1.1.28 (28 A 37) is easily harmonized with Aetius's account if we recognize that the term "crown" is transferred to one of the five parts of the ordered world, the ether below the firmament.[77] This zone may be said to be filled with fire or with light, and may be said to "encircle" (*cingit*) the sky, namely, the median zone that Parmenides calls god. As this zone is indeed the substitute, after the cosmogony, of the point of origin of the blending (according to A 37 and B 12), the assimilation is not illegitimate. The murky light of the Milky Way is the sign of blending. The presentation followed in the doxographic account "on the god" in Cicero, with "crown" in the singular, suggests that a theological transposition has interpreted the ethereal zone two as a halo around the head of "the god." The *daimon* has as its finery this *stephanè* (wreath). The association between the wreath and this beyond-the-sky, which is seen as the god's extension, is not accidental.

---

[76] Hölscher 1969:108. For Deichgräber (1959:66), the goddess comes from *before* the blending (see frag. 12); she is thus *inherent* to the principles, outside of the blend. What was her function there?

[77] When the heavens are associated with the Olympus of the fixed bodies, the igneous zone must be situated beyond the extreme limit, as a materialized transcendence, an empyrean beyond the limit: "Das erste ist ein Feuerring um den Himmel herum [Gigon was thinking about the fixed elements]. Diesen Ring nennt Parmenides Gott" ("The first is a ring of fire around the sky. Parmenides called this ring God" [1945:280]). The ring of fire is "the representative of Being, whereas the earth is the representative of Non-being" (one might add *sic*).

Aetius (A 37) II:
The Cosmogony, the Dynamism of Fire

Since the geometric structure of the rings cannot be identified with a phase of the genesis of the world, the cosmogony is organized around its eradication, in blending. As it propagates itself, blending produces the new delimitations that coincide with the major zones of the universe. Theophrastus, in the second part of his summary, clearly marked the principal events:

καὶ τῆς μὲν γῆς ἀπόκρισιν εἶναι τὸν ἀέρα διὰ τὴν βιαιοτέραν αὐτῆς ἐξατμισθέντα πίλησιν, τοῦ δὲ πυρὸς ἀναπνοὴν τὸν ἥλιον καὶ τὸν γαλαξίαν κύκλον· συμμιγῆ δ' ἐξ ἀμφοῖν εἶναι τὴν σελήνην, τοῦ τ' ἀέρος καὶ τοῦ πυρός.

And the air formed upon leaving the earth, rising in vapor owing to its more violent compression; as for the sun and the Milky Way, they were formed by the breath escaping from the fire. The moon is a blend of the two, both air and fire.

Like the succession of alternating spheres, the cosmogonic movements start both from the center and from the periphery. But a dissymmetry appears at once. The centrifugal movement that starts from the "earth," from the central core, occupied by night, is triggered by the whirlwinds of fire. The centripetal movement develops, starting from the fire that has collected under the solid vault. The reason for this dissymmetry is that, in a first phase of the blending, fire had risen up from everywhere, crossing the barrier set up by the dark rings; concomitantly, night established itself below. The intensification of the blending, indicated by the comparative *more violent compression* (βιαιοτέραν ... πίλησιν), reverses the movements. Under the influence of the rotations of the fire, night rises, in the form of air; the fire spreads and descends to form the sun and the Milky Way. The moon is born following the meeting of the two convergent emanations of air and astral fire.

The upheaval that results from the blending is so total within the enclosure that one cannot infer the orientation of the movements of localization of the two principles within the delimited space.[78] The structure produces the blending. The distribution was at the origin of a potential movement, first paradoxically logical and static, leading to the dynamics of the blending. The physical world grew out of the confrontation of contraries "without blending." Once

---

[78] As Hölscher does, supposing that the rings of fire, around a center, were embedded below the rings of darkness, so that in the cosmogony fire rises upward (1969:108).

the upheaval has taken place, the structure is entirely abolished, which amounts to saying that the powers are acting, in the intermingling, according to their own antithetical attributes. Fire will then, according to its own property (κατὰ ... δυνάμεις, frag. 9.2), be more mobile, more "efficient" in the categories of the Peripatetics.

In deciphering the pre-cosmogonic structure, according to its own logic, one recognizes that the blending produced by the increasingly weak opposition, by virtue of the thinness of the layers, takes place in the middle, at the equidistant point, but that the force is all the greater, since the pure masses were more extensive at the two extremities, so that the parts of the fire, by coming back together, freed themselves and precipitated the decantation of the heavy principle. The ascendant movement asserts itself; it bends to circularity through the roundness of the form at the extreme ends of the initial distribution of the layers. The increased compression of the fire leads at the center to the expulsion of the intermediary "elements" (water and air); it presupposes a violent, swirling action of the fire, of which the orbits of the astral bodies will be the regularized residue.[79] The global form of the structure determines the form of the movement, and thus the circularity of the bodies that it fashions; by the same token, the roundness of the earth is not posited as an initial given but results from a series of processes in keeping with the dynamism imposed by the framework.

The earth is constituted when density, in response to the rising movement, is precipitated toward the center.[80] If we take another doxographic testimony literally, some "air," becoming detached from the fire, was then compressed to the point of giving birth, in a first phase, to the hard bodies of the earth, before the expulsion, at a later stage, of water and vapor[81] (a first form of air, *ante*, then a second, *post*, escaping under the influence of the celestial rotations).

---

[79] See the force, the thermodynamics of the fixed bodies, θερμὸν μένος, frag. 11.3.

[80] In the *doxa* of the *Stromateis*, 5 (*Doxographi*, p. 580 = 28 A 22), λέγει δὲ τὴν γῆν τοῦ πυκνοῦ καππυέντος ἀέρος γεγονέναι, ἀέρος was eliminated by Patin (1889:625), then by Diels, and so on; it was defended by others who saw in air a designation of darkness, without contradicting the origin of the atmospheric air by a later compression, according to A 37 (see the references, including those of Burnet and Gigon, listed in Untersteiner 1958:20ff., ad A 22 *in fine*). It is then necessary, notwithstanding the order of the words (τοῦ πυκνοῦ καταρρυέντος ἀέρος), to translate as "when the dense air was precipitated downward."

[81] The epithet for the earth, ὑδατόριζον (B 15 a), might, in density, be aimed at the aquatic origin of the earth by designating the solidifying mud (and might then be applied from this angle to existing geographic representations, such as the Ocean, which rolls itself up; see Untersteiner's doxography, *ad l*).

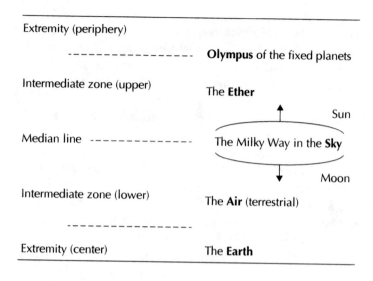

Extremity (periphery)

Olympus of the fixed planets

Intermediate zone (upper)

The Ether

Sun

Median line

The Milky Way in the Sky

Moon

Intermediate zone (lower)

The Air (terrestrial)

Extremity (center)

The Earth

Figure 2 Arrangement of the parts of the world.

If the moon is made of air and if fire (according to A 37) is formed from one of the blends (the cold) from the median zone (A 43), the air in question might not be the air that was separated from the earth (τῆς μὲν γῆς ἀπόκρισιν), but rather the more primitive representative of night, captured in the center, in the Milky Way. Two different blends oppose one another in the sun and the moon (according to A 43).

The Program of Fragment 11

The information supplied by the doxographer is corroborated by the only fragment of the cosmogony, preserved in Simplicius' commentary on Aristotle's *On the Heavens* (*Comm. Arist. Gr.*[82] VII, 559, 22–25):

πῶς γαῖα καὶ ἥλιος ἠδὲ σελήνη
αἰθήρ τε ξυνὸς γάλα τ' οὐράνιον καὶ ὄλυμπος
ἔσχατος ἠδ' ἄστρων θερμὸν μένος ὡρμήθησαν
γίγνεσθαι.

---

[82] *Commentaria in Aristotelem Graeca.*

How the earth, the sun and the moon, with the common ether, with the Milky Way, the outermost Olympus and the burning force of the astral bodies entered into their becoming.

This fragment has been neglected. Mansfeld, for example, does not consider it; Gigon sets it aside.[83] Hölscher makes no comment.[84] Von Stein had declared that the lines were not authentic.[85] Deichgräber (1959) for his part preferred to attribute them to another author; he thought of Empedocles[86] because of certain words found in the fragment.

Beyond the formal testimony of the citation (*they*, that is Parmenides and Melissos, *speak clearly of a birth of perceptible things, Comm. Arist. Gr.* VII, 559, 19), the verbal group ὡρμήθησαν γίγνεσθαι, which adds the inchoative aspect to the duration of becoming (Simplicius presents the citation in these terms: *Parmenides says that he is beginning to speak of perceptible things, Comm. Arist. Gr.* 20–21), proves that in these lines we have the beginning of the stage in which the formation of the parts of the world was described. The program announced was exhaustive. Between the earth at the center and the vault, called *external Olympus* (ὄλυμπος ἔσχατος), with which the fixed stars are closely associated, the sun and moon are situated, forming a pair, then the ether, called common (ξυνός), and the Milky Way, called *Uranian* (οὐράνιον). An account in Aetius (II.20.8 *a* = 28 A 43) establishes, by specifying the indications given in A 37, that the sun and the moon did not emerge directly from the fire that descends and the air that rises, but that they were separated from the Milky Way, the sun from the thinner blend, which is hot, the moon from the denser blend, which is cold. In fact, the Milky Way is not an emanation of the fire, but, as we learn from another account (III.1.4 = 28 A 43 *a*), it is nothing other than the blend formed by the meeting of the two emanations. According to a third account, in the chapter on the order of the celestial bodies (III.15.4 = 28 A 40 *a*), the sun, coming after the other planes, is situated below Venus,[87] just above the Milky Way, which the doxographer calls the igneous zone and Parmenides calls "heaven," οὐρανός (see the epithet οὐράνιον in 11.2). The moon, a relatively cold blend, receives its light from the sun (Aetius II.26.2; II.28.5 = A 42), and turns out to be placed just

---

[83] "Das weniger bedeutende 28 B 11 lassen wir weg" ("we eliminate the less significant 28 B 11" [Gigon 1945:276]). Silence from Verdenius and Mourelatos, and so on.

[84] The fragment is confused with B 10 (1969:106).

[85] See his edition of the *Fragments* (Stein 1867).

[86] Possible confusion on Simplicius' part, p. 64n1. Conversely, Stein, despite the very characteristic style, had attributed frag. 10 to Empedocles, in order to eliminate the problem.

[87] The shepherds' star, identified with the morning star (see also Diogenes Laertes' "Life of Pythagoras," 9.23 = A1; 7.14); see Burkert 1962:285 and n. 43 (Burkert 1972:307 and n. 39). We do not know whether other planets were named; if not, *Hesperus* corresponds to a choice.

below the median zone. This arrangement is in harmony with the function of the ether as revealed by the epithet *common*, which takes its meaning from the power held by the layer of pure fire, separating Olympus from the Milky Way, to cross the median blend and to inundate with light, when the resistance is not too strong, the lower region of the atmosphere (ἀήρ). As the moon receives its brightness from the sun, the terrestrial region is lighted during the day by the common ether.

The traditional interpretation understands as "common" the circular envelopment of the world by the diffuse ether. Untersteiner applies the idea to the duality of day and night; at the outer edges of the sky (namely, the firmament), the ether embraces the (internal) temporality and the atemporality of Being (1958:CXCIIIn98). The communication that is established by the ether in fact connects, *intra muros*, the separate parts of the world. The division is achieved, and is thus surmounted, in the ether.

The communication proceeds in ascending order, but without a simple succession. The elements regroup. After the earth (5), come the astral bodies that concern it directly (2 and 4). They are situated symmetrically on one side and the other, above and below the *heavens* with the Milky Way (3). The ether of the upper zone (2) is "common" because it connects Olympus to the atmosphere; its light crosses the sky below to penetrate all the way into the lower zone of the moon. The sun (in the ether, 2) and the moon (4) surround the median zone (3), The Milky Way (3) and Olympus at the extreme point (ἔσχατος) (1) surround the ether in turn; it is thus named in relation, mediated by the sun and the moon, with the earth; then situated between the astral zones below and above.[88] The enclosure of the whole is marked by the extreme limits at the beginning and the end (the earth and Olympus, 1 and 5).

The fixed astral bodies are distinguished as an entity of the vault, Olympus. Heat is not exclusive to the sun that heats the earth. The other astral bodies, originating from the same principle, have the same property, which escapes us. It is not transmitted to us. Whereas the sun and the moon, originating from the median blend, attest by their difference to the opposition of thin-hot and dense-cold, the astral bodies of the vault, originating at the outer limits of pure fire, are hot (hence their distinctive epithet, "burning force" (θερμὸν μένος), in relation to the localization at the extremities: "outermost" (ἔσχατος).

---

[88] The common representation of the interpreters groups the ether, the Milky Way, Olympus, and the fixed astral bodies according to the realistic preliminaries chosen, in an indistinct unity (see above). Couloubaritsis ingenuously takes Olympus to be Zeus' mountain, and thus supposes that the earth, with this summit, could reach the astral bodies (why not?), and go beyond, "even, perhaps, [beyond] the Milky Way" (1986:315). Is this serious?

Aetius (A 37) III:
Beyond Cosmogony, the Division of the World

The third and properly cosmogonic part of Theophrastus' summary confirms the analysis of the cosmogonic process.

περιστάντος δ᾽ ἀνωτάτω πάντων τοῦ αἰθέρος ὑπ᾽ αὐτῷ τὸ πυρῶδες ὑποταγῆναι τοῦθ᾽ ὅπερ κεκλήκαμεν οὐρανόν, ὑφ᾽ ᾧ ἤδη τὰ περίγεια.

As the ether extends in circular fashion in the highest region of all, the igneous zone, the very zone we have called the Heavens, is placed below the ether, and below the Heavens, in turn, the terrestrial region is placed.[89]

It is essential not to confuse the ether, the region of pure fire, with the solid nocturnal envelope, the zone of fixed bodies, which Parmenides calls *Olympus*.[90] It is no less essential to recognize that Theophrastus astutely emphasizes, precisely because the thing is astonishing, that the intermediate zone of the Milky Way, included *between* the ether and the περίγεια ("the terrestrial region") is given the name *Heavens* (οὐρανός), following the Parmenidean use of the word that is found in fragment 11 (οὐράνιον). One must not be led astray by the term "igneous" (πυρῶδες); it designates the Milky Way. In fact, the blend is characterized this way because of the stars that shine there, entities that must not be confused with the fixed bodies (see Aetius II.15.4 = A 40 *a*): τοὺς ἐν τῷ πυρώδει ἀστέρας, ὅπερ Οὐρανὸν καλεῖ ("the stars in the fiery region, which he calls heaven"); the mood is characterized as igneous like the sun (II.25.3 = A 41), its blend is cold, and its light is borrowed (see fragments 14 and 15). If a final proof were necessary, we have the passage in Cicero's *De natura deorum*, in which a ring of light—that is, ether—encircles the heavens.[91] When one fails to identify the heavens with the blended zone of the Milky Way, one does not understand why it is called god, and described as the origin of births, in conformity with lines 3–6 of fragment 12 (the masculine *deus* for δαίμων is explained by the syntactic agreement: *caelum, quem appelat deum* ("heaven, which he calls god"); the absence of identity is expressly asserted: *in quo neque figuram divinam*

---

[89] The sentence has served to justify the three zones, in certain presentations (see Karsten 1835, above); the rest was read from the perspective of the end.

[90] The designation might be common to Parmenides (and Empedocles) and to the Pythagoreans (see Burkert 1962:227n35 [Burkert 1972:244n31]): "an *acusma*" [TN: a saying attributed, in the Pythagorean community, to Pythagoras himself]; moreover, Burkert resolutely limits the Pythagoreanism of Parmenides in favor of a dependence on Anaximander (see 1962:261n31 [Burkert 1972:282n25]: Anaximander—Parmenides—Empedocles).

[91] See above, pp. 201, 205–206.

... *suspicari potest* ("in which no divine form ... can be supposed"): the divinity is nameless.[92]

All that men see of the sky, taken as the reunion of the astral signs, is perceived in relation to the assembly of the milky trail in the center, and, as it were, through that trail. Thus Parmenides distinguished the igneous zone "which we have called [κεκλήκαμεν] the Heavens," from the reference points that are above the planets in the ether and the fixed bodies in the firmament (called "Olympus").

Fragment 10. —The lines of fragment 10 sketch in the cosmology, the current state of the world; they expose the internal tripartition that is reproduced by Theophrastus:

—the upper region of ether with Hesperus for the planets, up to the sun:

εἴσῃ δ' αἰθερίαν τε φύσιν τά τ' ἐν αἰθέρι πάντα
σήματα καὶ καθαρᾶς εὐαγέος ἠελίοιο
λαμπάδος ἔργ' ἀίδηλα καὶ ὁππόθεν ἐξέγενοντο

you shall know the birth of the ether, all the signs that are in the ether, and the always clear works of the pure torch of the very brilliant sun, as also the place from which they emerged to be born;

—the lower region of terrestrial air with the moon:

ἔργα τε κύκλωπος πεύσῃ περίφοιτα σελήνης
καὶ φύσιν,

you shall also learn the vagabond works of the round eye of the moon as well as its birth;

finally, the intermediate region of the galactic blend called the sky:

εἰδήσεις δὲ καὶ οὐρανὸν ἀμφὶς ἔχοντα
ἔνθεν [μὲν γὰρ] ἔφυ γε καὶ ὥς μιν ἄγους᾿ ἐπέδησεν Ἀνάγκη
πείρατ᾿ ἔχειν ἄτρων.

you shall know the skies, which maintain apart, on both sides, the place from which it is born, and how, leading it, Necessity stopped it to hold the limits of the astral bodies.

---

[92] When the heavens are confused with Olympus, that is, the external vault, which is almost always the case, one is obliged to accept a zone of fire that surrounds the universe from the outside. As a way out of this impasse, this transworldly empyrean has been assimilated to Being (see above, p. 200).

It suffices to give ἀμφὶς ἔχειν the (epic) meaning of *to separate on both sides* in order to be constrained once again to give up identifying the sky with the external limit of the world (περιέχον). Interposed between the ethereal region and the vaporous region, the Milky Way is the place where the divinity who governs acts. It is she who, under the name of Necessity (see A 37), leads the expansion of the blend, on both sides of the median line, and stops the course of the astral bodies, preventing the sun from penetrating into the atmosphere and the moon from rising into the ether.

While the arrangement of the proem of fragment 11 corresponds to a very erudite entanglement, from which one cannot directly infer an ordering, that of fragment 10—which, on the contrary, corresponds to an ordering (2 4 3: extreme terms, middle)[93]—serves as testimony rather than as proof, although the triad (ether-sun, then moon, and the sky *between* the two), is a configuration attested elsewhere in Aetius.[94] The lines presuppose not only something that follows, regarding the center of the universe, but also a preceding part, which is missing, on the bodies of the periphery. Fragment 10 is constructed differently from fragment 11; it does not serve a dual purpose. The affinities of composition with the end of the proem (frag. 1), and also the affinities of structure (see μαθήσεαι, 1.31; εἴση, εἰδήσεις 10.1 and 5), suggest that the lines come from the part of the proem that came immediately after 1.32.[95] The cosmology would thus be anticipated in the announcement of the content by the *daimon*. Archaic thought is said to know a thing by knowing its origin, its *physis* (the primitive is an aspect of primitivism).[96] The "origin" marks rather the supremacy of the interpretation over the things themselves; the prior elucidation of their formation makes it possible to say what they truly are, or what one has to acknowledge that they are in order for them to be understood.

Instead of recognizing in the participle ἀμφὶς ἔχοντα a reminder of the encompassing function of what was taken for an envelope surrounding the world ("the all-embracing sky"),[97] Untersteiner, who saw the time of the astral

---

93 Gigon (1945:274ff.), without concerning himself with the agreement of the testimonies among themselves, identified in turn the fixed bodies (ether), followed by the sun and the moon (= Anaximenes), then a return to the sky (the vault) for the role attributed to Anankè.

94 Besides A 37, see II.20.8 *a* = A 43, corroborated by II.5.4 = A 40 *a* on the order of the astral bodies.

95 The hypothesis, formulated by Bicknell (1968:631), was perhaps more than simply "conceivable" (O'Brien 1967:247n33); it has in its favor the formal elements and the advantage of distinguishing between fragments 10 and 11.

96 See Verdenius 1942:51. The cosmology is given in the form of a cosmogony, by means of a more primitive "narrative exposition." The explanation of phenomena (Verdenius cites Cornford; see his n. 2) is opposed to the process of genesis, with reference to the different temporal aspects, used in frag. 12.1–2, whereas this genetic process is on the contrary fundamentally interpretive.

97 Cf. Fränkel 1951:412, "the whole sky"; Hölscher 1969:29, "the sky surrounding the rings"; and so on. Most recently, see Cordero's translations (1984:41) or O'Brien's (1967:63): "of the heavens

bodies separated at the outer limits of the atemporality of the ἐόν ("being"), proposed the translation "che da una parte e dell'altra [ἀμφίς] allontana" ("separates on both sides"), following the Homeric usage of the figure (1958:cxcii and n94); the function of division fell back on what was, for him, conflated in a unity, οὐρανός—ὄλυμπος—αἰθήρ (Ouranos—Olympos—Aither). He would have had to tell himself that all that could or should be *distinct*. But the separation, provided that it is transferred to the median zone of the sky, offers a homology that can be maintained.

Anankè is at the outer limits of the world because it is situated in the heavens, as is written in fragment 10 (line 5), and because the heavens are naturally associated with Olympus;[98] yet the texts distinguish between the two: Aetius (A 37, but also A 40 *a*, 43 *a*) situates the heavens after the igneous zone of the ether with the planets, which is below Olympus (the vault); Parmenides himself, in fragment 11, clearly dissociates the Milky Way from the sky (γάλα τ' οὐράνιον), between moon and sun, and from Olympus at the outer limits with the fixed bodies. The commentators have thus found in Necessity a force that encloses[99] and holds together, starting from an extreme limit. The logic of the system, which the common expectation must experience as a paradox, would have it on the contrary that it holds together starting from a median limit, by means of a separation so perfectly "right" and balanced that it has its principle in the point of encounter. Necessity thus lies in the equipollence produced by the duality of the distinct principles.

The system of astral bodies is governed and regulated from the center of the world. The difference in viewpoints is fully apparent in the translation of the ἀμφὶς ἔχοντα of fragment 10, which, in the logic of the general distribution determining the median separation of the celestial zone, must be understood as "setting aside" toward the upper and lower regions, whereas the common representation leads to the repeated reuse of a translation "encircling all around," which is in contradiction with the structure of opposition.

Parmenides' cosmology has incited far fewer studies than the ontology on which it is based. For a long time, it was not attributed to him. What makes the interpretation of the physical system so arduous is not that there are gaps in our information, however real these may be, but the force of abstraction in the representation of the world, which is just as strong as the force of speculation in

---

that encircle them on all sides" ("them" = "the works of the moon"?) or Couloubaritsis's: "the heavens that hold them all around."

[98] Let me refer, a bit randomly, given that the opinion is so widely shared, to Tannery (1930:282) and Untersteiner (1958:cxcii, with the references cited, n. 92): "The οὐρανός, which is explained as ὄλυμπος ἔσχατος ..."; Coxon (1986:229); and so on.

[99] "Necessity" reduced to the obligation to introduce the rampart of a limit against nothingness; see Fränkel 1951:467.

the definition of what is. Rigor makes the reconstruction easier, allowing us to rely on the implacable logic of the whole.

Originating in the contrary tensions that traverse the figure of visualized Being, the opposition between the elementary powers is reaffirmed at the various stages of the perceptible revelation. The initial, geometric diagram of concentric circles makes comprehensible the description of the cosmogonic process leading to the rise of fire and the descent of the dense element. The blend resulting from the median encounter produces new separations. The cosmology makes visible the primordial antagonism in the regions of the universe, the ether lodged under the nocturnal vault, the atmosphere surrounding the terrestrial globe, and in the middle the divine region, called the sky or the Heavens, of the differentiated blends and of separation. The gentle (ἤπιον) light of perceptible knowledge, where Aristotle saw an equivalence of Being, is spread over the ordered totality of phenomena, over fire and what is not fire, and ends up harmonizing with knowledge because it is regulated according to the figuration of Being.

Works Cited

Berger, E. H. 1895. "Die Zonenlehre des Parmenides." *Berichte der Königlich-Sächsischen Gesellschaft der Wissenschaften* 47:57–108.

Bergk, T. 1884–1886. *Kleine philologische Schriften von Theodor Bergk.* Ed. R. Peppmüller. Halle.

Bicknell, P. J. 1968. "Parmenides, Fragment 10." *Hermes* 96:629–631.

Boeckh, A. 1966. *Encyklopädie und Methodologie der philologischen Wissenschaften.* Ed. E. Bratuschek. Darmstadt. Orig. pub. 1886.

Bollack, J. 1992. *Empédocle.* 3 vols. Paris.

Bollack, J., and H. Wismann. 1974. "Le moment théorique." *Revue des Sciences humaines* 39:203–212.

Burkert, W. 1972. *Lore and Science in Ancient Pythagoreanism.* Trans. E. L. Minar, Jr. Cambridge, MA. Orig. pub. *Weisheit und Wissenschaft: Studien zu Pythagoras, Philolaos und Platon.* Nuremberg, 1962.

Burnet, J. 1930. *Early Greek Philosophy.* 4th ed. London.

Calogero, G. 1977. *Studi sull'eleatismo.* 2nd ed. Florence. Orig. pub. 1932.

Cherniss, H. 1935. *Aristotle's Criticism of Presocratic Philosophy.* Baltimore.

Cordero, N.-L. 1984. *Les deux chemins de Parménide.* Paris.

Cornford, F. M. 1952. *Principium sapientiae: The Origins of Greek Philosophical Thought.* Cambridge, UK.

Couloubaritsis, L. 1986. *Mythe et philosophie chez Parménide.* Brussels.

Coxon, A. H. 1986. *The Fragments of Parmenides: A Critical Text with Introduction, and Translation, and the Ancient Testimonia and a Commentary.* Assen.

Deichgräber, K. 1959. *Parmenides' Auffahrt zur Göttin des Rechts: Untersuchungen zum Prooimion seines Lehrgedichts.* Wiesbaden.

Diels, H. 1897. *Parmenides Lehrgedicht.* Berlin.

———. 1901. *Poetarum Philosophorum Fragmenta.* Berlin.

———. 1912. *Die Fragmente der Vorsokratiker.* 3rd ed. Berlin.

D-K = Diels, H. 1951–52. *Die Fragmente der Vorsokratiker,* 6th ed. by W. Kranz. Berlin. Repr. of the 5th ed, 1934–1937, with *Nachträge.*

Döring, A. 1911. "Zu Parmenides und zum Eleaten." *Zeitschrift für Philosophie und philosophischen Kritik* 144.

Finkelberg, A. 1986. "The Cosmology of Parmenides." *American Journal of Philology* 107:303–317.

Fortenbaugh, W. W., and D. Gutas, eds. 2010. *Theophrastus: His Psychological, Doxographical, and Scientific Writings.* New Brunswick, NJ.

Fränkel, H. 1951. *Dichtung und Philosophie des frühen Griechentums.* New York. [*Early Greek Poetry and Philosophy: A History of Greek Epic, Lyric, and Prose to the Middle of the Fifth Century.* Trans. M. Hadas and J. Willis. Oxford, 1975.]

———. 1968. *Wege und Formen frühgriechischen Denkens: literarische und philosophiegeschichtliche Studien,* 3rd ed. Munich. Orig. pub. 1955.

Fülleborn, G. G. 1795. *Fragmente des Parmenides.* Züllichau.

Gigon, O. 1945. *Der Ursprung der griechischen Philosophie. Von Hesiod bis Parmenides.* Basel.

Guthrie, W. K. G. 1965. *A History of Greek Philosophy.* Vol. 2. Cambridge.

Heiberg, J. L., ed. 1901. *Anatolius sur les dix premiers nombres.* Macon.

Hicks, R.D., trans. 1925. *Lives of Eminent Philosophers,* by Diogenes Laertes. Rev. ed. Loeb Classical Library. Cambridge, MA.

Hölscher, U. 1968. *Anfängliches Fragen.* Göttingen.

———. 1969. *Parmenides. Vom Wesen des Seienden.* Frankfurt.

Jaeger, W. 1947. *The Theology of the Early Greek Philosophers.* Oxford.

Karsten, S. 1835. *Parmenides.* Amsterdam.

Kirk, G. E. and J. E. Raven. 1957. *The Pre-Socratic Philosophers: A Critical History with a Selection of Texts.* Cambridge.

Konstan, D., trans. 2014. *Simplicius On Aristotle's Physics 6.* London. Orig. pub. 1989.

Mansfeld, J. 1964. *Die Offenbarung des Parmenides und die menschliche Welt.* Assen.

McDiarmid, J. B. 1953. "Theophrastus on the Presocratic Causes." *Harvard Studies in Classical Philology* 61 (1953):85–156.

Morrison, M. S. 1955. "Parmenides and Er." *Journal of Hellenic Studies* 75:59–68.

Mourelatos, A. P. D. 1970. *The Route of Parmenides: A Study of Word, Image, and Argument in the Fragments.* New Haven.

Mullach, F. G. A. 1845. "Parmenidis carminis. Reliquiae A." In *Aristotelis De Milisso, Xenophane et Gorgia Disputationes, Cum Eleaticorum Philosophorum Fragmentis et Ocelli Lcani, Quie Fertur, De Universi Natura Libello*, 111–121. Berlin.

O'Brien, D. 1987. "Le poème de Parménide." In *Études sur Parménide*, ed. P. Aubenque, vol. 1. Paris.

Owens, J. 1974. "The Physical World of Parmenides." In *Essays in Honour of Anton Charles Pegis*, ed. J. R. O'Donnell, 378–395. Toronto.

Patin, A. 1899. "Parmenides im Kampfe gegen Heraklit." *Neue Jahrbücher für das klassische Altertum, Geschichte und deutsche Literatur und für Pädagogik*, supplement to vol. 25, 652–654. Leipzig.

Reinhardt, K. 1916. *Parmenides und die Geschichte der griechischen Philosophie*. Frankfurt.

Schwabl, H. 1953. "Sein und Doxa bei Parmenides." *Wiener Studien* 66:50–75.

Susemihl, F. 1899. "Zum zweiten Theile des Parmenides." *Philologus* 58.

Tannery, P. 1884. "La physique de Parménide." *Revue philosophique* 18:264–292.

———. 1930. *Pour l'histoire de la science hellène: de Thalès à Empédocle*. 2nd ed. Paris. Orig. pub. 1887.

Tarán, L. 1965. *Parmenides: A Text with Translation, Commentary, and Critical Essays*. Princeton.

Untersteiner, M. 1958. *Parmenides: Testimonianze e frammenti*. Florence.

Verdenius. 1942. *Parmenides: Some Comments on His Poem*. Groningen.

Von Stein, H. L. W. 1867. "Die Fragmente des Parmenides." *Symbola philologorum Bonnensium in honorem Friderici Ritschelli collecta*, 763–806. Leipzig.

Zeller, E. 1881. *Die philosophie der Griechen in ihrer geschichtlichen entwicklung*, 4th ed. Orig. pub. 1855. Leipzig. [*A History of Greek Philosophy: From the Earliest Period to the Time of Socrates, with a General Introduction*, trans. S. F. Alleyne, 2 vols. (London, 1881).]

———. 1967. *La filosofia dei greci nel suo sviluppo storico. Eleati*. Ed. G. Reale, trans. R. Mondolfo. Florence. Orig. pub. 1855.

Zeller, E., and W. Nestle. 1920. *Die Philosophie der Griechen in ihrer geschichtlichen Entwicklung*, 6th ed. Darmstadt.

16

Expressing Differences[†]

IF HERMENEUTICS IS CRITICAL, it must be historical; its task is to reconstitute a project in its own time. Precision remains forever inscribed in the letter of the text. Distinctive expression has the power to endure. This is the property of written works, and also oral works, works "written" orally before writing, and composed as if they were going to be engraved. This is to say that the critic composes in turn, when the art of deciphering is virtually prescribed for him, produced by the object itself that develops in the world he is reconstituting.

The irreducible complexity and uniqueness of a work are diminished, or even annulled, when the text, by virtue of its content, is situated within the continuity of an interest or a problematics. External time is doubtless constructed with no less legitimacy, but it entails great simplifications. Explanatory schemas, superimposed one upon another, lead to reductions. Thus Antigone is the family, Creon the State, Heraclitus the river. Comprehension will be all the more definitively obstructed to the extent that the emblem does not mislead by its falsity: there is some truth in it, but the compact mass of opinion makes it impossible to go further, and does not allow itself to be called back into question, as it should be.

Heraclitus said almost nothing of what he has been made to say from Plato on: nothing about fire or flow. But culture and its memory draw strength from this, and play with simplification. Effacing by substitution is still the most powerful form of forgetting.

[†] Originally published as "Dire les différences," in: Jean Bollack, *La Grèce de personne: les mots sous le mythe* (Paris, 1997), p. 263.

The Heraclitean *Logos*[†]

HISTORIANS OF GREEK thought have tended to begin by trying to read Heraclitus as a systematic thinker; they have tried to decipher a world-system in his work comparable to those of other archaic thinkers, and they have sought to reveal its place in a general cosmology. The repeated failure of these attempts at reconstruction finally convinced me that Heraclitus did not have his own system, and that the unity of his approach did not lie in any positive content but rather in his critical analysis of cosmological theories, nourished by assertions that were current in the learned circles of his day.

By projecting each fragment from Heraclitus onto the specific horizon of its transmission and of its metamorphoses, we gradually manage to clarify the reflexive structure of the aphorisms, by distinguishing, among all the established uses of the language, the tension created by language itself, the tension inherent in words, in the *logos* as word in its relation to a thing. This distinction, made explicit in the texts, between a reflective use of the logic of discourse and a non-reflective use of language, implies abstraction; it emanates from the content, but at the same time it leads to a return to the content in order to apply to it the laws of abstraction in a complementary fashion. The fragments are concerned alternately with one process or the other, with the analysis of the inherent contradiction in discourse or with the reconfiguration of discourses by means of this internal reference.

This was the focal point of the commentaries I published with Heinz Wismann in 1972.[1] The present essay reconsiders the underlying premises of that work, in the light of certain works published in the interim.[2] Some

---

[†] Originally published as "Réflexions sur les interprétations du logos héraclitéen," in: Jean Bollack, *La Grèce de personne: les mots sous le mythe* (Paris, 1997), pp. 288–308.

[1] J. Bollack and H. Wismann 1995 (hereafter B-W).

[2] Roussos 1971, which included titles published up to 1970, has been completed by two collective works: De Martino, Rossetti, and Rosati 1986 (alphabetical catalog of titles, with *Complementi 1621-1969* for the earlier periods) and Paquet, Roussel, and LaFrance 1988 (see "Études particulières" IV: "Héraclite" [pp. 444–555, nos. 1775-2436] for brief summaries of the content). The

syntactic analyses (and syntax predominates) might well be discussed further; the commentaries on several fragments could be clarified. But the arguments we proposed then still hold true, on the whole, and need only to be reaffirmed.

Our break with the interpretative tradition, in its ancient but especially its modern form, remains unchanged. In the tradition, the *logos* is usually charged with doctrinal content; it is presented as the site or receptacle of a "truth." In the modern hermeneutic experience, it shifts away from this role and uses abstraction as the instrument for analyzing what is presented as truth.

If Heraclitus' thought does not focus on the presence of Being but on the universe of meaning (generally speaking, on everything that seems to be endowed with meaning or that is likely to be subjected to analysis by the law inherent in the *logos*), then the elimination of distance and the return to hypostasis, from Schleiermacher's critique up to the present—if we confine ourselves to the modern period of scientific approaches to the texts—have to be understood as an *a priori* move, manifesting the structure of a prejudice, and should thus be linked to the critics' own motives.[3]

The definition of the word *logos* has been central to the construction of a functional system that the critics see as founded on what the *logos* is thought to express other than itself, that into which it has been assimilated. Hence their approach to the initial aphorism, in fragment 1,[4] which is not presented as an independent unit and is a "fragment" only in relation to the collection:

> Now, men always live far from understanding the discourse [*logou*], which is this one, before they have listened to it, as after they have listened to it the first time. For everything lives according to this discourse, so that one sees them apparently ignorant of what they practice, their words and their actions, such as those that I myself develop thoroughly, dividing each one according to its nature and

---

number of titles listed in De Martino, Rossetti, and Rosati is higher than all the publications recorded by Roussos since 1499: "A truly surprising result" (7). It remains to be seen how to generate discussion on the conditions of communication among the authors.

[3] Barnes 1979, Chap. 4 ("The Natural Philosophy of Heraclitus"), does not discuss the general thesis of our book [B-W] and thus takes no account of its interpretation of the Fragments. He cites the title in his bibliography (349), setting it in a different sphere of scientific interest from his own (no doubt in another cultural tradition): "Idiosyncratically French accounts may be read in ... "; a list of names follows. Would the author be able to say what he means by "French"? B-W was published in France.

[4] [TN: The Greek texts of the numbered Fragments, followed by Kathleen Freeman's English translations (Cambridge, MA, 1962), are reproduced at the end this chapter, pp. 243–245. The translations incorporated into the text are based on Jean Bollack's French translations, which differ significantly at many points from Freeman's.]

showing how it is made. Other men are unaware of what they do when they are awake and of all they forget during their sleep.

Since discourse (*logos*) indeed occupies the central position, as the sole reference of the passage, it sufficed to erase the difference between the word and what, according to the Heraclitean corpus, it expressed, that is, the difference between the *logos* and the utterances to which the structure deduced from it is applied. Thus the logos was seen as a term of pure substitution, the sign of an objective message.

Based on the attributes of war in Fragment 53 ("War is both king of all and father of all"), which were thought to be identical to those of the *logos*,[5] critics believed they could infer the true nature of the referent, of which the term *logos* was just an equivalent, presenting things in a didactic order.[6] The thesis is absurd, but instructive, first because of its excess (or its radical nature), and then because appearance, a very obvious similarity, reveals the shift to application. But this principle of pure contradiction can be found nowhere else apart from discourse.

---

[5] "Der Streit ist der Vater und Herr aller Dinge, das allgemeine Recht und die Ordnung der Welt" ("Strife is the father and the master of all things, the universal law and ordering of the world"): Zeller-Nestle 1920:655, based on frags. 53 and 80; see Zeller 1961, 1:101–105. This is a common position, taken to the extreme by Gigon (1935:116): "Es ist überall, allgemein gültig, allgemein wahr" ("it is universally established, it is universally true") (against Hesiod *Works and Days* 276–279); "Die allgemeine Krieg ist recht" ("universal war is just"). A divinization of war, which is also a known fact: "Wir stehen ... auf dem Boden historischer ionischer Wirklichkeit" ("we stand ... on the ground of the historical reality of the Ionians") (119). Gigon goes as far as to write: "Der Kriegertod als solcher entspricht eben allein dem Logos, der 'Krieg' heisst im Gegensatz zum 'Strohtod' der bequemen allzuvielen" ("only the warrior's death can respond to the truth of the *logos*, called 'war,' to distinguish it from the 'death on the straw' of the lazy masses [according to frag. 24]") (120). Again (but less violently), in Gigon 1945:210: "Die Wirklichkeit, mit der wir rechnen müssen, ist der Krieg" ("the reality we have to deal with is war"). A universal principle or an empirical truth? Kirk adds to the discussion (1954:248): "All spheres of life." And likewise, Conche (1986:440), on frag. 80: "[La guerre] est coextensive à toute la nature ... et, dès lors qu'elle est le grand phénomène naturel, elle est normale et fatale" ("[War] is coextensive with all of nature ... and once it is the great natural phenomenon, it is normal and inevitable"). Kahn (1979:209) limits the significance of frag. 53 to "the destiny of mankind." (Conche, on the other hand, takes πάντων as a neuter ["of all things"]; however, it is masculine; see B-W:185).

[6] The *logos* is the representative in speech of the truth of War (Gigon 1935:18; war accounts for the style of Heraclitus' work). The *logos* is just an abbreviation for the book, that is, "the eternal truth." A radical position: "eine Lehre, ein System steht am Anfang" ("a doctrine, a system, is there at the beginning") (5). "Krieg ... ist für Heraklit evident, die evidente Wahrheit von Frag, 1. Was er zeigen will, ist die Entwicklung des Gegensatzes in der Welt" ("For Heraclitus, war ... is the obvious truth of fragment 1. What he wants to show is the development of the opposites in the universe") (p. 25); see also 60–61: "Der Logos ... ist ... eine Abkürzung für die ewige heraklitische Wahrheit" ("*logos* is an abbreviation for the eternal truth of Heraclitus"), that is, "die Paradoxie des Kosmos," the paradoxical identity of fire and the universe, and so on.

This is an extreme position; it is limited to the cosmic dynamic of opposites, drawing from it a principle that controls and explains physical and cosmological evolution,[7] whereas the reduction to this principle, favored over the Platonic flow of Schleiermacher and Hegel,[8] had allowed us to see in the *logos* not the exposition of opposites but the law of opposites, with its tension.[9]

Starting out from the word, with its possible orientations, scholars sometimes clung to what Heraclitus said with regard to the subject, and to the reasoning that articulates his discourse;[10] sometimes, regarding the content, they preferred meanings that referred to an objective organization, understood as "moderation," as "relationship" or "reason."[11]

In any case, it was an objective truth that was to be revealed and could quite easily be fitted in with the translation of "discourse," if it is in language that this truth can be expressed, as it appears throughout Heraclitus; and, as Heraclitus is alleged to have said, it appeared even before his time. In the nineteenth century, the *logos* was understood as the "language of nature," as "nature's revelation of an intelligible discourse."[12] According to Heidegger, language speaks Being and spoke Heraclitus before Heraclitus.[13] Being speaks in the language that reveals

---

[7] See Kirk and Raven 1957:195: "The total balance in the cosmos can only be maintained ... if there is unending 'strife' between opposites," and also: "The *logos* or proportion remains the same—again it is the measure and regularity of change, this time of large-scale cosmological change, that is stressed" (201); cf. Kirk 1954:402–403: the distinctive aspect of the *logos* that is fire is by nature kinetic; it ensures the regulation of cosmic movements.

[8] Along these lines, Zeller's introduction, which is more inductive, culminates in a spectacular presentation where everything is swept along by movement (see Zeller-Nestle 1920:806: "everything *becomes* and *is* not, caught in the movement of the life of nature"). It is the flux of Cratylus and Plato, and the antithetical Becoming of Heraclitus—Being of Parmenides (see Hegel's introduction to *Phenomenology of Spirit* [1977: §12]). One denies the principle that the other conserves.

[9] It is the reason for *heimarmenè* [TN: the personification of fate or destiny] to be considered as the global law, which cannot be directly identified with the physical process it encompasses. See Schäfer 1902, summarizing the definitions of P. Schuster, M. Heinze, and others.

[10] Barnes (1982:59, ad frag. 1) is firm in his choice of "account:" "The noun *logos* picks up, in an ordinary and metaphysically unexciting way, the verb *legein*; it is wasted labor to seek Heraclitus' secret in the sense of *logos*." He stresses the "clear exposition of the right view" of West (1971:318n7), whose *Early Greek Philosophy and the Orient* places him in opposition to Guthrie, Hölscher, and Marcovich (see esp. West 1971:124–129). This is what Burnet wrote more than one hundred years ago (1930:133n1): "The *logos* is primarily the discourse of Herakleitos himself." But Barnes (p. 59) is obliged to relate the "account" to the law of nature: "everything happens [objectively] in accordance with the account," which explains how phenomena occur (objective) and what is "the essential nature of each thing."

[11] Kirk (1954:39) proposed "formula of things" as an approximation of *logos*, where the idea of measure that he considers essential for the organization of things and the world is "implicit."

[12] In opposition to the translation of *logos* with "reason" in the Hegelian tradition, cf. Schuster (1872:19): "the revelation that nature offers us in a language that we can understand"; he opts for "discourse" (20).

[13] See Heidegger (1979:292): "[*Logos*] ist die ursprüngliche, Ursprung verleihende, im Ursprung einbehaltende Versammlung als das Wesen des Seins selbst" ("the *logos* ... by which Heraclitus

meaning. For F. J. Brecht, a proponent of this line of thinking, man is led by the *logos* to his own truth, torn away from his alienation.[14]

This shift entailed a move from "listening," in the strict sense of the word, to "hearing," that is, knowing how to understand discourse; discourse had thus become a fable of truth, rather than an account or an analysis.

If the more immediate question is that of universal reason, the *law* that controls becoming, it is more difficult to account for texts like fragment 1, where one had to acknowledge that reference was made to discourse, as it is spoken, produced, and pronounced. The two aspects had to be reconciled. In fact, they could not be made to agree with either option. So certain scholars resorted to the expedient, or the compromise, of explaining the aporia as the result of the deficiency of a thought that was still archaic and unable to distinguish between the two aspects.[15]

In the fragments, words are often used with the meanings that were conventional in Heraclitus' time, as for instance the word "reputation" (frag. 39). Elsewhere we find "speech" and "discourse," as such, distinguished by Heraclitus, each isolated in its own function and structure. We remain within the logic of discourse, moving on to the composite formed by the act of saying and what is said, and to the relational value of the "reason" inherent in the relation between contradictory terms. This is neither worldly reason nor the reason of argument in discourse. The internal relationship is projected onto existing utterances. It is thus reproduced, in the restructuring of specific discourses, according to measures and ratios; this "reason" provides an explanatory principle suitable for governing languages, because it is drawn from language.

The crucial problem, which gave rise to the debate over criticism and its aporias, is confined to the rare passages that are directly concerned with the nature of discourse. Secondary uses, where the inferred principle is transferred to meanings and imprints on them a structure that has been rectified and clarified by means of language, have, in the history of criticism, served to organize a system of positive assertions, which was then arbitrarily established as a content, occupying the position of the *logos*, whose analysis had provided the means to bring these assertions into question.

---

names Being itself, the One that unites all that is; the logos is the original structure, that imparts the origin, that upholds in the origin, as the constitutive characteristic of Being").

[14] Through the word of Being, man is torn away from daily distractions, brought back to himself, to the *logos* within him: Brecht 1949:37–45. These are the tones of a homily, so frequent in books on Heraclitus, up to and including Conche.

[15] This is true for Marcovich (1978), who often resorts to this principle to explain or excuse incoherence (see *ad* frag. 1, for the non-distinction in archaic thought between the subjective aspect, discourse, and what it expresses, the truth); but the same is true of Kahn. It is a way of objectivizing the unresolved contradictions of interpretation, as is done with the principle of ambiguity.

Heraclitus speaks of a reference provided by language; he never tires of talking about situations that show how the people around him miss the point of analysis and fail to grasp the structure of the language that they use and that impinges on their behavior. This presumably very violent struggle, committed to a pure reflexivity that refuses to accept any form at all of a prior external foundation, is something quite simple, yet of capital importance.

This bias is evident right from the first words of the prologue that constitutes fragment 1, an opening that is "parodic" in the broad sense of the word; in a kind of repeat performance, Heraclitus adopts the form of prologues that had preceded his.[16] The content is first of all "this one," concerning the very situation of the discourse: to show what its status is, what a program is, and what use is made of the genre of the *arkhē*, the beginning. It is the opposite of an immediate discourse "about everything," or "of everything," as is evidenced by the use, so eloquent in its limitative precision and singularity, of the demonstrative, tearing the *logos* away from any other reference, from any use that would not be self-referential.

Aristotle cites this beginning in a famous passage of his *Rhetoric*,[17] to show how difficult it is to regroup the words in Heraclitus' book, because their autonomy, and thus the freedom of construction, is so great. In the first sentence, "Now, men always live far from understanding the discourse [*logou*] which is here explained," one can punctuate by separating a second part of the sentence after "always": "this Logos, which *is* always [or: is always true],[18] men are [or: become] incapable of understanding it." It is a distancing from the eternal truth. The adverb "always" goes with "which is."[19] Or else one makes the

---

[16] The reuse of certain elements of discourse that have been analyzed is often seen as a component of the battle In favor of a new doctrine: "eine offene Parodie der Prädikation des Zeus" ("an obvious parody of the celebration of Zeus"); "die bewusste Verdrängung des Zeus durch das eigene erkannte Weltprinzip" ("a conscious displacement of Zeus, by means of the universal principle he discovered") (Gigon 1935:119, ad frag. 53). The new science is opposed to popular beliefs. However, the language of science offers the same analyzable matter as the others; it reveals its contradictory structure for the same reasons as do rites. When Heraclitus was linked to the Ionians for his physics, the repetitions were interpreted as proof of his links and the mark of an affiliation.

[17] Aristotle's text is reproduced among the testimonies (Diels and Kranz 1951 [hereafter D-K]), 22 A 4 = *Rhetoric* 3.5, 1407b 11–18. I do not deal here with Diels' addition, line 13 (which Kassel 1976 does not retain). Within the narrow context, Heraclitus' case and, by way of an enlightening example, "the beginning of his book," illustrate the difficulty of the reading in the absence of a clear-cut division. A feature of the *obscuritas*: we do not know before analyzing the passage what the words in the sentence go with. In Heraclitus, this is a problem (*ergon*).

[18] Sometimes scholars opt for "which always exists" (past, present, future); sometimes, with the stress on the verb "to be," meaning "to be true," they opt for "which is always true" (cf. Kirk 1954:35; Zeller 1961:21, and so on).

[19] This is what we might call the dominant opinion: see Zeller 1961:21: "Il participio ἐόντος, che l'interpretazione tradizionale unisce con ἀεί (esistente sempre, ossia: eterno)" ("the participle

break *before* "always," by taking the demonstrative as the predicate: "this Logos, [which] is as here explained."[20]

The first of these interpretations may seem more natural, and Aristotle considered it to be so, adding that the text as it is formulated does not oblige us to be confined to this "evidence," which the ontological reading he refers to suggests.[21] He does not say: it is this or it is that, but: it is not necessarily this.[22]

Aristotle's comment takes interpretative practices into account. He says nothing of an essential ambiguity; he does not leave the question open, but rather exposes the difficulty. Starting from an already established "natural" reading, Aristotle is interested in the manner of its enunciation, which does not seem clear to him. His account is concerned with an interpretation that

---

ἐόντος, which the traditional interpretation links to ἀεί [existing always, or: eternal]"), citing Burnet, Snell 1924, and Gigon; or Kirk 1954:34: "modern scholars have for the most part concurred with the view of Hippolytus and Amelius that ἀεί qualifies ἐόντος" (Zeller, Diels, Capelle, Gigon, Verdenius). Later on, see, among others, Kahn 1979:97: "Although this account (*logos*) holds 'forever'," it is true that ἀεί is translated a second time with ἀξύνετοι: "men ever fail to comprehend" (see Gigon's proposition of a double construction [1935:2ff.], picked up by Kranz; cf. E. Kurtz 1971:85, contested by Verdenius [Kirk 1954:34n1]); we must make a choice, and not only according to Aristotle, who was well aware of the stakes of meaning.

20 The choice often adheres to formal criteria (ἀεί should go with ἀξύνετοι). The predicative meaning of the demonstrative does not lead to the acceptance of its real semantic significance. It is applied to the content of the book, which the pronoun presents in its specificity: being what it is ("'which is *as I describe it*'" [Kirk 1954:36]). The doctrine is assumed to be known through an earlier oral teaching (cf. Kirk), or it will become known in the following part of the work: "Doch für die Rede—den Logos, der dies [Folgende] ist" ("But for the discourse—the Logos which is the following") (Hölscher 1985:14). To this more qualitative meaning, other scholars have preferred a stronger deictic function, and in support of this stance assumed that what Aristotle and Sextus (22A 16, §132) present as the beginning was, in fact, preceded by something else, without necessarily making the pronoun a predicate (the problem of translation arises with the epithet [τοῦδε]; see, for example, Kurtz 1971:83ff.: "although this discourse may be ..."—namely, what will follow; likewise, Barnes 1982:59: "'Heraclitus of Ephesus says thus': what he says (*logos*) is this."

21 Diels (cf. 22A 4 D-K) with Vettori's correction of δεῖ στίξαι for Bekker's διαστίξαι (with the manuscripts) prints <δεῖ> διαστίξαι (Gaisford, Roemer, etc.). Kassel (1971:145) believes that διαστίξαι is superfluous. The brevity of the expression seemed excessive (see Diels in his apparatus, before Kassel). Manuscript A gives us προτέρῳ; the presence of the awkward infinitive could lead us to consider the lesson: it would not be said that we cannot see what to link the word ἀεί with, but that one of the approved divisions is uncertain: "for attaching the word 'always' to what precedes (that is, ἐόντος) is not obvious" (τὸ ἀεὶ πρὸς προτέρῳ διαστίξαι).

22 In other words: ἄδηλον does not indicate an uncertainty from the start, as it does three lines earlier. The phrase here, after the quotation, comments on an interpretation considered evident, and ends up saying that it does not emerge obviously from the letter of the text. It merely offers a choice between two possibilities, and this confirms the general observation of the writing style. One cannot infer from the text that Heraclitus did not give an opinion. Aristotle affirms that the syntactical relationship does not appear immediately.

is situated and dated.[23] So he does not consider the possibility of making "this one" the attribute of "which is,"[24] as one must if it is a question of isolating the discourse as such. The construction of the demonstrative is still corroborated by the iteration of the same phrase, later on in the same fragment 1: "which is this one." The meaning surely excludes the other construction, which is considered by the supporters of a tradition whose legitimacy had been called into question by Heraclitus' use of the verb "to be" as a copula, a significant choice; the pronoun *toud[e]* ("this one") indicates the discourse, *logos*, already determined by the article in its raw state as discourse. His use of the pronoun in this context helps to define the *logos* in its specificity.

The aporia lies right there, and it basically concerns the comprehension of the text: when one chooses, either directly or by way of a revelatory discourse, to understand the term *logos* as meaning "law," the "law" that governs the course of the future, the anthropological break that characterizes life encompasses a before and an after, or at least a time opposed to an anteriority, the very moment of listening.

If it is "discourse," as it is structured in light of its "object," then the opposition is clear. The contradiction can only be elucidated for those who are prepared to separate themselves from the community of men, not necessarily through arrogance or disdain, but by the methodical necessity of making distinctions. The thing—that is, the practice of symbolic systems—is always there. *Homo loquens*. People live with it, next to it, without discerning the meaning that its use holds and that exempts them from introducing any other. Any other reference would be ritual, ritualized, subject to the same analysis, reducible to the status of practices: a poem or a tribune, a tribunal or a religious procession.

If it is "law," we have to admit that it was formulated before Heraclitus, in the form in which now, it is thought, he reveals it in his book, so that men could have *previously* been unaware of it or unwilling to accept it. The message, one might say, is not at all subjective: "The art is to listen well, not to me but to reason, to know how to listen to all-things-that-are-one" (Fragment 50).[25]

---

[23] I cannot agree with Kirk (1954:34): "Aristotle himself suggested no answer to the problem." The interpretation of Hippolytus and Amelius (*apud* Eusebium) is well known to Aristotle; he discusses it.

[24] Nor can one attach ἀεί to the verbal group ἀξύνετοι γίνονται in relation to καὶ πρόσθεν ἤ ... καὶ ... in the next section (cf. Kranz in the apparatus of D-K).

[25] Law *and* discourse (Gigon 1935:6ff.), if we wish to avoid the absurd (or again, Babut 1976:496: "the very voice of the *logos*," and n. 110: "indissolubly the word [*parole*] ... and the supreme Principle"). Resorting to the "principle" offers one of the answers, when the problem is raised, which is not always the case. But does the text not suppose a real listening (ἀκοῦσαι), that is, to *speech*? The aporia offers one of the many signs that persuade us to give *logos* the sense of "discourse," apart from the content.

Scholars have often accepted the idea that the voice of an objective law had been heard before, favored by earlier Heraclituses, in a line of prophets of truth, without having been heard by anyone among men, before Heraclitus had repeated it.[26] This is surprising, and no doubt a false logic.

Without doing violence to the text, we begin to assume that men lived without hearing or listening to what Heraclitus focuses on in his discourse, as he listens and analyzes the current discourses around him. This is the only proper subject for critical reflection, to examine and then question the legitimacy of the examination; but instead of postulating this type of thought—however eloquent the distance between fragments, constructed by the reader, may be—one could, in an even more restrictive way, posit the subject as the only possible reference of what is said about it, by exploiting the aporia, which, since Aristotle and even before him, offers the most reliable heuristic method.

On this condition, we can accept the following: we can understand as an intelligible outcome that a thinker might come and say to you, to the Greeks, and then to the West, even to the whole planet, that what he says will not be "heard"—one should say "listened to"—*before* being heard, because Heraclitus, by invoking this unique object and by defining it thus, constructs an absolute, paradoxical situation, the borderline case of the paradox where the practitioner is invited to turn his reflection away from practice, not toward a theory, which would be just a new (theoretical) practice, with its own technicalities, of course, but rather to draw from it the opposite law, lying beneath what he does, simultaneously within reach (*zuhanden*) and at a distance.

Any other discourse is secondary, that is, a substitute; the latter negates another and clarifies it with an imitation. Heraclitus enters the world of existing forms, not to make use of it according to its form, but in a different way, according to the law of language, which is the single necessary—not arbitrary—condition.

But in general the not-listening, understood as not-hearing or incomprehension, is linked to the oracular form of Heraclitus' discourse (is it not "a natural one on the part of an author who has chosen the language of enigma and equivocation"?[27]) Since the discourse had already failed to be heard before Heraclitus had written it, it is not this discourse but the truth, an objective correspondence called "meaning" that alone, it is thought, deserves to be called

---

[26] Comparison is sometimes made with fragment 72; the "strangeness" of men is found in the sentence (*Fremdheit*, often with a Heideggerian tint). See also Kurtz 1971:87ff. But do they listen as strangers (and superficial minds) to the word of the Being that they do not hear?

[27] According to Kahn (1979:98), "once they have heard," it is too obscure and too difficult for the public; but "*even before*" remains disconcerting. Whence the passage from actualization in speech (which is the single meaning for Barnes, but he does not discuss the problem; one wonders why) to the content of the discourse, and to the hypostasized unity. The aporia remains intact as long as Heraclitus is supposed to have called eternal a truth that is new and his alone.

eternal, like the fire, which for that reason is compared to the *logos*, accommodating this elevated primitivism through the idea of a rationalization of more primitive beliefs. Depending on the critic's perspective, the author may be ahead of his time; from other perspectives, he may be archaic. A historical objectivization is created that ratifies the false logic of the exegesis.

Non-perception, in this particular component of the sentence (and only here), changes the scene; we move from the inner voice through which, unbeknownst to human subjects themselves, the truth of the universe is expressed, to the enigmatic revelation of a philosopher, determined to disguise it—but why disguise it, since it lives in everyone? For the pleasure of misleading?

However, this eternity could be problematized, and restored to a meaning. It has been seen as an attribute of the world, as if eternity had been one of Heraclitus' concerns, which was not the case. If the truth is general, conceived as a revelation that has come down through the ages, one might add that it is foreign and inaccessible to the common man, in the past as in the future, before and after Heraclitus, who was acquainted with the notion, but for nothing—or for no one.

The two moments in time are not really symmetrical in this representation. The intervention of the person, and his speech, are an indispensable element, as we have seen. The moment, and thus the "after," cannot be reduced to a new utterance of a common truth, proclaimed in ancient times and then later unknown. To understand the reason for the role attributed to the "self" (*moi*), the content must justify the difference between that person and other men. It must be possible to define the separation at the heart of the relation between the person and what he is listening to. What men, separate from Heraclitus' person, could have listened to, and have always not listened to (in the literal sense), was language, which makes them, not being, but men, in an eternal world, one might say; and in another world, as well. The ceaseless becoming, on which the attribute is based, is not an affirmation—a *doxa*—on the part of Heraclitus; it could only become one, as it did for Plato, if it were confronted with the contrary statement, in a discursive organization where opinions are classified—that is, placed in relation, by reference to a system of thought or a world system, whatever it might be.

There is nothing like this in Heraclitus. If we wonder about the meaning in fragment 1 of a phrase like "whereas all things come into being in accordance with ..." (*ginomenōn kata*), we are virtually obliged to include the distance introduced by the reference, which distinguishes from the structure of the *logos* the decision to apply that structure, as the only available parameter, to all constructions and etiological claims.[28] This is where the "always" comes in: "in any case, in the face of the natural phenomena that we see occurring, it will always be this non-speculative principle that prevails," and it must always have prevailed, ever since thinkers started to explain and order, not to state the truth, which has no place here, since it is only a matter of making a statement, but to come as near to the truth and as perfectly as possible, using the key provided by the fact of talking about it. The agreement (*kata*) refers to an explicative principle that makes it possible to grasp the shift from listening to the *logos* to practical inexperience, in the domain of the word and of deeds. So what is at issue is no longer simply discourse as such: in a broad sense, it indicates all the situations where people come together in the exchange of given discourses and in rituals: when these occur according to the same mode of language, discourse applies to their study and analysis.[29]

There is rivalry and predominance, in this sense self-assurance, claimed by a man who expresses a distance that can justly be considered absolute, since this distance refuses to follow customary discourses or to construct others. The fragments are split up according to categories. No assertion is situated outside the norm imposed by the reference drawn from the discourse: the reference does not express the world, but the world can be expressed according to the reference.

According to the fragments, "they," men, are agents, or interpreters, subject matter, or rivals in the analysis. There is a perceptible parody, perhaps even a sneer: "they" analyze, and yet they have no idea what they are doing, which is "what I am doing there, and they say they are doing, but do not do."[30] The individual self (*moi*) is in its place in that place where Heraclitus situates himself, in

---

[28] The demonstrative, in its richest sense (see above) is repeated, κατὰ τὸν λόγον τόνδε, to be isolated and separated from any utterance that might fix its meaning. Obviously the phrase γίγνεσθαι κατά, as what follows, with κατὰ φύσιν, shifts the claim of a unitary speculative explanation that interpreters extend to Heraclitus, with the same words, as they are used by the authors of systems. The point of reference appears to be even more different.

[29] It is the whole of human activities: καὶ ἐπέων καὶ ἔργων; see Reinhardt 1959:218; Kurtz 1971:90, and so on.

[30] The relation between τοιουτέων and ὁκοίων reveals the identity of the practices and experience, expressions of a language that has not been analyzed because it is applied. It is erased with the contrast (which is a break): "Whereas I, for my part ..." (Marcovich 1978:6 and 9: "perhaps an Ionian idiomatic expression"). When it is formally maintained, the difference is related to the truth, sought for unconsciously but unknown (see the translation of κατὰ φύσιν: "according to its true nature" [Reinhardt 1959:218]); the opposition is then introduced in the participle πειρώμενοι, Hölscher 1985:14 "ob sie gleich ihre Erfahrungen machen ..." ["if they immediately have the experiences ..."]), as well as in Kirk 1954:33 ("'even when they experience ...'").

a practice where listening allows him, having chosen this course, to do better than the others. The words imitate one another; imitation eliminates them.

"[This is the order of things] that I myself develop thoroughly, dividing each one according to its nature and showing how it is made" (frag.1). The sentence is in no way oracular. The syntax does not innovate here; the style *re-produces*, as happens elsewhere; it delineates the domain of cosmologies" (*peri phuseōs*) with the words of practitioners, and chooses the most sober and unadorned words—*to set forth, to divide, to show*—always with the basic idea of a guiding structure. "Nature" (*phusis*) is not the "all," not the "Universe"; but as it is for doctors, it is the constitution of a particular being, a constitution that can be analyzed according to what it is, according to its nature.

Why would Zeus be presented by the formula "the name Zeus," if it were a question of his ritual empire, or of another, which the rite allegorizes?

"One, art. It does not allow, and allows, the name of Zeus to be spoken alone" (frag. 32).

At the outset, it might seem plausible that the choice of the term "name" has the function of detaching from the god the word that refers to him under his specific identity, and that the act analyzed by the antithetical figure concerns the fact of "being said," according to the words of the fragments, thus related to the "name of Zeus" (*Zēnos*, the genitive of Zeus), distinguished from "Zeus" in the nominative.

The god's name is etymologized in the formula: it speaks of "life" (*Zēnos*, from *zēn*, "to live") as an essence of the thing to which it refers.[31] The word, in this free and interpretative use, detached from simple denotation, reveals the contradictory structure of language. If it means "life" by superimposition, independently of the word "Zeus," it would move to its opposite by applying what it names to itself. At the other extreme, on the side of the designated object, it will mean death—the god is his own thunderbolt.

"The name of *Zēnos*," if one groups the two words together, wavers between the instrumental use of the designation ("unwilling [for the name of Zeus] to be spoken alone") and the interpretation of the designated thing by the word "life."[32] If "life" is used separately, it is cut off from the thing and can only be

---

[31] Interpreters of Heraclitus do this when they see in Zeus a figure of "fire-life" (see Guthrie 1962, 1:463), and many others; the etymology is contested by Marcovich (1978), who takes Ζηνός to mean Διός.

[32] The "name" uncouples the appellation from the god through "life" (Ζηνός). It is a restriction (μοῦνον), which, as such, is contradicted by the usual designation of Zeus, who is the righter of wrongs. Kraus's analysis (1987:32ff.) makes the name of Zeus, according to a theological interpretation, the principle of the coincidence of opposites (life and death); but the "name" is just one of the poles. The understandings intersect: "to be named alone"—does this refer to one of the poles (life as opposed to death), or to the two together (life and death)?

applied to it by passing over to the opposite pole. In this case the etymology leads to a contradiction because it is partial. There is no homonymy, as there is for the bow, that might reveal the contradictory structure.[33]

The statement, understood as an analysis of the process of naming, in its dual function, no longer has the predicative significance of revealing the fundamental ambivalence of any hypostasized power. In support of this conclusion, we have the linguistic operation designated by the words "name" and "to be spoken," and also the formula used to present it: "One, knowledge," if we consider that semantically "knowledge" (*sophon*), which is "skill," is not about an apophthegmatic content[34] but about mastering something through analysis. Without this transfer to the means of expression, what would "knowledge" and the uniqueness of the limitation to this single process be ("one")? What uniqueness is there other than the single reference?[35] "One, art"—the meaning of "one" is restrictive, exclusive: "it is always that process"; there is no other.

"One" (masculine) will not be the totality "one" (feminine), but a restriction—the exclusivity of a technique or a competence (*sophiē*). "What real knowledge is [*to sophon* is determined], is that thing exclusively." The formula recurs in the attested fragments (it was probably more widely used in the complete

---

[33] [TN: Bollack is referring here to Heraclitus' fragment 48 on the bow: "the bow is called life, but its work is death." This is a pun, where the word at issue is *bios*, which, depending on the accent, can mean either bow or life.]

[34] It is not easy for the apostles of transcendence to justify use of the term that means "knowledge" or even "competence" in the language, for this knowledge that is divine in nature, outside the world or the "all"; nor is it even easy, if the aspect is neglected, to justify resorting to the word "wisdom" (*das Weise, sagesse*); the meaning is doubtless anachronistic. Does "wisdom" (for humankind) consist in being aware that a "wisdom" exists beyond human reach, according to the proposed interpretations of fragment 50? See below, note 46.

[35] In the order of ontological hypostases, some scholars have constructed, in defiance of syntactical possibilities, in my view, ἕν as the subject of the clause, and μοῦνον as a determination of the apposition τὸ σοφόν: see D-K or Marcovich 1978:445: "one (being), the only (truly) wise, is ... ," all the categories are combined; Kahn (1979:267) ties μοῦνον to ἕν in his translation: "The wise is one alone, unwilling ... ," but weakens the impact of his choice by resorting to ambiguity (268); Hölscher 1985:16: "Eines ist das Weise: allein (pro aduerbio) es will nicht ..." is not easy to understand, compared to "es will nicht allein—und will doch ... ," (Hölscher 1968:132ff.; see n10: "μοῦνον concerning λέγεσθαι, required by the meaning as well as the rhythm of the sentence"; and Hölscher 1968:n47. μοῦνον necessarily leads us to consider the "name" in its apodeictic capacity. If the One (and the Wise One) refers to a metaphysical principle, the contradiction must take note of an arbitrary passage from one order to another: philosophy (a transcendent metaphysical principle) against religious belief (Zeus), according to Diels 1901:10, or Marcovich 1978:446; similarly, Kirk 1954:392-393: "unrivalled wisdom" versus "traditional religion" (cf. D-K); the *logos*, as the unity of opposites (life and death) versus Zeus = life, according to Guthrie 1962:463; the cosmic principle is life, but it is more than that: "life and death are two sides of the same coin," according to Kahn 1979:271 (more or less like Guthrie).

book), always referring to the same principle of analysis.[36] It is yet another set linguistic expression; the formula pre-existed, or else it parodies another one; the language is re-used to make its structure apparent. What is said is what constitutes knowledge. There is no reason not to assume this, while making it clear that the predication of a speculative assertion—an "all is one" or even "all things, one," re-introduced into Heraclitus' work by one of the doxographic traditions[37]—has not been distorted, in the written phrase, so that the speech act can substitute for it. The statements systematically examine this speech act as being the one thing of which one can say, in analyzing it, that there is nothing else by way of knowledge. The speech act refers neither to this One, which would be a Zeus, nor to any unity, but to the uniqueness of a particular structure, inherent in language, which actuates all thoughts as the discourses that they are, without being understood as such.

When language is analyzed in its structure, there can be no relation to a content. Such a relation is, however, what authors assume when, in choosing the meaning of "discourse," they make it external to the whole; they go on to express the truth of this external whole outside the nature of things in a kind of transcendence, as the law that governs the nature of things or, in other words, as the "unity of opposites" or the "all-one."

The *logos* cannot be pressed beyond the contradictory structure that constitutes it in its enunciatory power, being chosen as the unique reference, which introduces no opinion constituted in language, neither "subjective" nor "objective," no positive assertion. All the analyses of Heraclitus in the surviving fragments (and the same was obviously the case for those that have not survived) delve into the practices, either to identify the structure of the *logos* that did not appear to those who used it, or to project this structure onto explicative systems, somewhat haphazardly, stripping them of their arbitrary, imaginary, or speculative content, and linking them to this single, logically scrutinized reference.

If the formula of the "all-one" is to be found in Heraclitus' work, it is not as a *doxa*, a succinct resume of his own doctrine—he has none—but as the repetition of an utterance, of an earlier *doxa*, for the purpose of examination, of

---

[36] Apart from fragment 32, see the use of the same formula applied to the analysis of an opinion on physics, fragment 41, and the definition of knowledge, indicated by the neuter σοφόν, as absolutely separate from the learned discourses (λόγους) in fragment 108, also with this variant without ἕν (σοφόν ἐστιν), the application to analysis of the constituent discourses.

[37] The analysis cannot be condensed; it remains specific. Doxography, whatever its origin, is disarmed when faced with Heraclitus, who cannot be summarized or translated, in contrast to other pre-Socratic systems of thought, which can be re-constituted with great precision by the doxographers.

spectroscopic analysis, under the fires of the *logos*. It is quite true that the assertion was upheld in the past; it condenses, better than any other, the prerequisites of an Ionian physics with which Heraclitus has been doxographically associated since Aristotle.

The "I" is not an assertion of superiority based on a widely held truth, on the professorial model, or on an elective revelation, along prophetic or shamanistic lines; it can be defined only in relation to discourse, to what is said, true or false, about truth or election.

So the listening in question is not directed toward the perception of a message, whatever it may be, but toward what this message communicates through its expression. There is no other knowledge but listening to the mode in which the various forms of knowledge are expressed.

The step taken by listening to the word leads to acceptance of another transcendence, another position of exteriority. One does not enter the system of established references, according to the field of social activity, in order to make use of it; one leaves it in order to analyze its functioning, by going back to the structure of the utterances and by studying what is being expressed in what is said. The "I" defines very precisely the limits of this exclusionary option, which one might legitimately call methodical. It situates itself beyond communion, attracted by the magnetic pole of a singularization that has never been refuted.

The "I" creates a problem in the traditional reading and in the framework of the convictions imported by many scholars. If it is the "I" who is speaking, in the name of the new doctrine that we imagine he is introducing and that he is "publishing" in fragment 1 just as we read it, we may wonder why he presents it as being incomprehensible to everyone, because it is so personal to him. This is the first aporia, which involves communication and the closure of the subject. But then, as fragment 50 signals (these are the same words): "as you are listening, not to me (I don't count) but to the ... *logos*," the authority reserved for the speaker is abandoned in favor of the "objective" truth that is always known (by whom?) but never understood, or else that exists, even though unknown, pre-existing like an eternal origin, like the world, awaiting Heraclitus' revelation. The contradiction is blatant. *I am the only one who speaks the truth of all.*

The terms of the aporia, rather than being swamped in the incoherence of an inspired prophetic discourse or in the loftiness of melancholy and despair, can be pinned down as such by the observer. In order to put aside our prejudices, as we always should, we must force ourselves to stay within the system of thought, so that we can distinguish between two agencies, that of the "I" and that of the *logos*. The most natural hypothesis is that the "I" who speaks—and this happens rarely—is not the same as the *logos*, but refers to the structure of the *logos*: the "I" does not make the *logos* appear, but applies it by re-considering the systems of organized thought. As a result, the opposition becomes clearer at the heart of the distinction, right from the prologue: such that, depending on the role I choose, I decompose and re-decompose the material without losing the single non-speculative referent that the utterance offers. The dual operation is immediate or applied, which makes it easy to understand fragment 50: the contemplated (and expected) feat is in this case more arduous than in others, for it relies on immediate listening, without recourse to the science mastered by Heraclitus, the competence. The transfer is indicated thus: "By listening to the language in its nature and structure [with the article, as at the beginning, fragments 1 and 2], and not to me."

The remainder of the sentence is usually (indeed, practically always) translated and understood as if it said: "It is wise to agree that all things are one."[38] A formula that sums up the truth: "The all is one." An agreement that, incapable of being applied, according to the presuppositions, to a formerly accepted doctrine, is related to the *logos* itself, and finds in these paired terms its highest expression; this explains the choice of the word "wisdom" (*sophon esti*), to designate the recognition of a supreme principle.[39] It is the *logos* that speaks through Heraclitus, its servant, and who here gives it voice in the place of his own. It speaks in the soul of every man.[40]

The shift from the "I" to the *logos* is read as a dispossessing of self in favor of an invitation addressed to a "you." If it is universal, the *logos* will be dialogical: it will speak to another. At the same time, it is clear that in fragment 1, this other is not listening. An expression of wisdom tossed into the breeze.

---

[38] See Gigon (1935:44): "Das ἕν πάντα εἶναι ist der Kern der Heraklitischen Kosmologie in seiner abstraktesten Form" ("The ἕν πάντα εἶναι is the nub of Heraclitean cosmology in its most abstract form"); the One is just a special case, an "abstraction" of the theory of opposites: "The unity of opposites and the community of the *logos* provide the initial clues for interpreting this extraordinary claim ... The rest of our commentary will be an exegesis of this proposition" (Kahn 1979:131).

[39] A transition to the metaphysical plane for Hölscher (1985:20): unity transcends plurality, as god does (Hölscher, following Reinhardt, believes that through a reversal of the succession of the two thinkers, the concept of unity was prefigured for Heraclitus in Parmenides' Being); the formula expresses the content of the *logos*; and Babut 1987, in accordance with Conche, concludes (*ad* frag.108, Conche 1986:329) that: "the unique god ... is transcendental [to the other gods], as well as to men." Elsewhere (Hölscher 1985:28), the unique transcendental Wisdom is that of "nature" (as opposed to man) etc.

[40] For the antithesis of the "I" (who speaks) the word itself, Kahn (1979:130) substitutes: I-you others (as well as me), listening "to the discourse within your soul," which contradicts the interpretation of fragment 1, even if there one gives λόγος an objective meaning (98): how can anyone perceive in his soul what no one else has ever perceived? The message has not been put forward: he is addressing those who have not yet heard it. Universality remained to be revealed. We go round in circles.

As for textual criticism, the interpreter notes that the verb "to be" is introduced by a correction: the Hippolytus manuscript has "to know" (*eidenei*); the content "all-one" is considered an essential, or central, assertion; grammatically it depends (via the infinitive clause) on the verb that this probable correction introduces.[41]

As for the history of the language, we ought to think that the word *sophon* is not the correct term for the supreme degree of initiation into knowledge of the *logos*; it does not encompass speculative knowledge so much as competence. This knowledge is closer to the technical virtuosity of an artist or a soothsayer than of a philosophical or moral wisdom. Prior expectations lead to neglect of the linguistic data.

The word *logos* is reiterated in the verb "to say together" (*homologein*, "to say in harmony," to make the *logos* agree). The achievement, resulting from unmediated listening, presupposing an absolute exteriority, here concerns a formula, "one-all" (*hen panta*), on the principle of the Milesian speculation about the *arkhē*; we can acknowledge that it is not repeated to indicate a content known to all those to whom the book was addressed—a book whose interpreters have gone so far as to make it Heraclitus' *credo*—but rather to demonstrate the difficulty of justifying its terms within the structure of the *logos*: to know how to "say together" (*homologein*) within the inherent and constitutive contradiction.

Heraclitus does not reject any system. To do so would mean putting something else in its place. The reuse of the formula shows that the examination is more critical, that he is wondering about the meaning of what is said, or about the means of justifying its use. The repeated axiom will not be rejected, it will be re-said, bearing new content that transforms the meaning in opposition to its authors and users. What do the words *say*?

The four fragments (50, 32, 41, and 108) in which the nature of art, of the *sophon*, can be identified and localized, so to speak,[42] apply the term to this

---

[41] εἶναι: Miller, in the Hippolytus edition (1851; "universally accepted" according to Kirk and Marcovich, who cite, however, several references to defenses of the text of Parisinus: Bernays, Gomperz, and others) The understanding of εἰδέναι does not, in fact, depend necessarily on the construction of the sentence; I refer here to the defense of the transmitted text in B-W:175–177.

[42] Recurrence (see n. 36) obviously does not provide clues for the classification of the aphorisms in the book (contra Hölscher 1985:16). I should note in passing that the observations I develop here express my disapproval of the attempts at reconstruction according to the contents or the progression of the work (Marcovich, Kahn, Conche, or Hölscher, following Bywater, Schuster, and others; many authors have accepted the principle, giving up attempts at application; see Gigon 1935:11, or Guthrie 1962:427). Diels (1901:viii) was more correct in admitting that the aphorisms did not have the coherence of a system. He underestimated the development and the work of reflection; the principle he upheld was good, with the distance he nevertheless gave to the observation. The groups closed ranks, and obscurity is linked to this closure.

external listening, this traversal of discourses—until discourse can be perceived as such. Fragment 108 establishes a strict differentiation:

> Of all those whose discourses I have heard, none arrives at the point where it distinguishes that which, separated from all others, makes art.

Thus "art" (or knowledge) can only come from discourses (in the plural) on a topic, before which the "I" of the fragments—through which the separate subject constructed by Heraclitus speaks—arises as a "listener" (*ēkousa*).[43] The content of knowledge that speech organizes carries it away and distances it from the distancing on which the Archimedean point of listening is constituted, when it produces this art outside the topic, separate from all the topics touched on in discourse. Speaking does not provide access to this point. All aphorisms have as a presupposition this basic mechanism of a distance beyond speech, which determines the choice of words on the basis of absence and negation.

The point of view of exteriority is made autonomous in the recurring formula "one, art [of knowing]" which, each time it appears, presents the result of an absolute listening, the contradiction revealed by the "name of Zeus" (frag. 32), or by the formula of universal government, applied to cosmic principles (frag. 41).[44] The application, that is, the justification, is especially difficult in the case of "all-one," where the speculative nature may, or should, at first glance, seem too obvious. Getting past it will be quite a feat. The difficulties in translation encounter a serious problem with the logical or philosophical core, when

---

[43] See B-W: 305-307, for fragment 108. Of all the fragments, this is the one where interpreters have found transcendence to be most clearly enunciated, with σοφόν and πάντων κεχωρισμένον (understanding of one is deduced from the other), and where it is the least clear, if the least makes any sense, with separation applying to language as such, in all types of discourse. In the usual interpretation, Heraclitus claims to go beyond the intuition of the divine of which men may have had an idea before him (in the ambiguity raised in principle by Kahn 1979:115, his principle would be *at the same time*, with πάντων masculine, unknown to men, and separated from all things, in the neuter). The conditions of understanding are more concerned with the gender of ὁκόσων, which should be discussed first ("none of the discourses, οὐδείς, whatever their object"); we should return to the construction that links οὐδείς to ὁκόσων , and make it masculine.

[44] See B-W:154-156. Kahn (1979:321n204) believes we should eliminate the form ὁτέη for linguistic reasons; he refers to Bechtel 1924, 3:171. Diels (1901:11) had mentioned a "conscious archaism," with reference to Parmenides' form: Bechtel notes that there is no trace of a feminine -*tea* ("I have some difficulties"). Kahn's conclusion (1979) that there is simply no such thing as a feminine stem for τις (= Latin *quis*) might not apply to this secondary formation, fitting Attic ἥτις and Attic ὅτου, next to οὔτινος. Diels (1897:90, *ad* 28 B 8, 46) had proposed τεος as an analogical formation that would justify οὔ τεον (= οὔ τι). Bechtel (1924:169) accepts this as a possible invention of the poet (because of the antithesis οὔτεον-τὸ ἐόν) on τέου, τέῳ. Since one has ἥτις next to ὅστις, Heraclitus may have used an Ionian form, by analogy with the oblique forms (τέο or τέῳ), ὅτεος, ὁτέη (with the first element undeclinable). Nothing permits us to eliminate the form, even if it justifies the meaning in the context. (See the commentary in B-W:155, 2, 4.)

one hears: "*It is wise to agree* [for certain people: within the community of the enlightened[45]—there must be one, after all] *that all is one*" (and not that "the one is all"[46]); wisdom is considered the supreme degree of knowledge of the *logos*,[47] extended to the universal, where the organization of the world appears in the truth of a fundamental unity, discovered by Heraclitus. Even recently, it was possible for one scholar to write: "[T]his is the earliest extant statement of systematic monism, and probably the first such statement ever made in Greece."[48] This surprising opinion has, in fact, almost unanimous support in the scholarly field.

This proposition has been made the fundamental one, from which all the rest can supposedly be derived. However, its relation to the law of opposites, which the experts moreover still keep at the center, presents a problem, unless one asserts, as some have, that the equation of the "all" and the "one" prove that cosmology "is just a particular case of the law."[49] In fact, it is the unity of the framework that we see expressed, a framework in which the alternating phases of a cosmic cycle can follow their course, the site of a cosmology. Mutation of all, then mutation of the one,[50] according to the doxographical disposition of fragment 10.[51] One would have expected that it would be more a question of plurality. Thus these scholars imagine the movements of a pluralized totality towards unity, and vice versa, the exchange of fire for all things according to fragment 90:[52]

> At the cost of fire everything is exchanged, fire at the cost of all things together, as one exchanges goods for gold and gold for goods.

---

[45] If the consensus is based on the quite uneven penetration by the Spirit, the members of this community end up having the pleasure of saying what the *logos* says "in them" (Kurtz 1971:106n97). The thought is familiar. To avoid the idea of general consent (the listeners' agreement among themselves, e.g., Conche 1986:27—in manifest contradiction to frag. 108, however), the agreement has often been limited to just listening to the *logos* (D-K; Kirk 1954:68; Kahn 1979:131; Hölscher 1985:17, and so on).

[46] Marcovich (1978:116) finds it useful to make clear that ἕν is the predicate.

[47] See above, note 34. τὸ σοφόν denotes "the highest degree of knowledge" (Kurtz 1971:108); thus the formula stands out from all the others, explaining the order of the universe.

[48] See Kahn's discussion (1979:131: he discusses a "monism," distinguished from the assimilation of fire into air proposed by Anaximenes, according to Aristotle's *Metaphysics* 1.3, and that one might, following this point of view, qualify as Milesian. It would be another path leading to the key to its meaning.

[49] See Gigon 1935:44.

[50] Gigon 1935:43.

[51] [TN: Freeman's translation of fragment 10: "Joints: whole and not whole, connected-separate, consonant-dissonant."]

[52] See Kahn 1979:285.

"From all its components a unity emerges, and from this unity all things emerge," writes Kahn.[53] What has become of all the opposites and the tension that has been made the driving force,[54] along with the Ionian Muses and Plato's *Sophist*?[55]

Of course, opposites do not constitute the body of doctrine, as some would have it; they are a construction derived from the inherent contradictory structure of the *logos*, but even supposing that we might agree hypothetically on a reading that is, in fact, falsely literal—that is, non-reflexive—of the paired terms day-night, fire-earth, and so on, the "all-one" or the "one-all" are irreconcilable.

What has been made the central dogma is a pure aporia of interpretation, which from a scientific and logical standpoint should have led to a new challenge to the hypothesis. These fundamental reading processes did not take place because the readers would have had to deal with the principal questioning formulated by the text. But it is this difficulty that we must tackle—first of all the hermeneutic difficulty and then the objective problem. Heraclitus formulates the problem that the tradition of speculative language poses. "Knowing how to do it" means using other reflections, no less interpretative, of established formulas, as in fragment 41:

> To govern all things [torn away and unique] through all things [taken as a whole]

Similarly, fragment 90 distinguishes the totality of things that restore fire from the exchange of fire for all things, isolating and characterizing itself [the exchange of fire] as a total negation. In both cases, the doxographical interpretation has reinstalled the object in place of the reflection that the aphorism probes, by questioning the way of saying what one says by way of the reference to what makes it possible to say it.[56]

With regard to fragment 30, one wonders what poetic or philosophical work deals with a god who has created the world:

---

[53] See the paraphrase he proposes for frag. 10 (Kahn 1979:286).

[54] 242D–E (= 22A10 D-K).

[55] The significance of Plato's doxographical evidence is strongly undermined by Kahn (1979:316, n. 156); the unity of opposites can be illustrated by Plato without this reference to the cycle: "Heraclitus does not *need* this periodic pattern." So what differentiates Heraclitus from Empedocles? We should point out that: 1. the passage in the *Sophist* is an ordering of the fragments under discussion; 2. there is no periodicity to be found in Heraclitus; 3. the aphorisms connected with cosmology examine the Milesians' system.

[56] See Barnes (1982:61), who argues from fragments 30 and 90 that Heraclitus constructed with the prime stuff of fire a "monism" that represented "a physical science of a standard Milesian type." That would be true if this tradition had not been attributed to Heraclitus *too*, as it was to Anaximenes. If it is not, then fire no longer has the function of a universal substratum; see B-W:154–156, 264–267.

The world, the same for all, no one, neither god nor man has created it, but it always was, is, and will be ever-living fire, kindled in measure and quenched in measure.

No such reference can be found.[57] One can get around the problem by taking the phrase as a "polar" expression—"neither god nor man"—meaning "no one."[58] But why say "no one," why "the uncreated"? The facts of the problem can be reversed. One can say that neither god nor man is a being that can be considered from this angle, as a creator of worlds ["One does not see which god ..."]. Gods do some things, but they do not create. They operate within. The statement is a negation, and by excluding any possible causality, divine or human, one might say what is said about the eternity of the world; we must choose this path in order to take up and transfer, as has been done, the famous formula that characterizes divination in the *Iliad*.[59] The life of the world is before us, the "always" can also be added to it, the "ever-living" fire. The diversity of imaginable concretions of igneous energy must make us adopt—or prefer—this hypothesis as the site of elementary tensions. The famous opposites would intervene here, once the nature of the substratum is established. We might use the term "blaze"; we might say "extinction" for the fire; and we might say "for one portion" when speaking of the proportion, according to the rules of discourse, that the survival of the world confirms and whose survival presupposes existence. Is there anything oracular, or prophetic, about that?

In this same fragment 30, the structure of the world (*kosmos*) does not distinguish the world before our eyes—from what would we distinguish it?[60]—but presents it as a subject of the current discourse, which clarifies its structure, in order to produce a fixed reduction: it is "the same for all." Whatever the

---

[57] Cf. Kurtz 1971:200; why does he raise the problem of the creator?

[58] Reinhardt 1959:176n.1, based on Wilamowitz 1895, *ad* line 1106; Gigon (1935:55), who however eliminates the problem of creation (κόσμον ἐποίησε = διεκόσμησε); Kirk 1954:311, and so on. Kahn dismisses the stylistic expedient, which he relates to the perfection of the order that we have seen expressed in κόσμον: the *natural* world, neither god nor man has made it; it made itself. "Thus the cosmological idea begins to emerge ..." (1979:134; see also 135).

[59] *Iliad* 1.70.

[60] Clement of Alexandria, who alone gives the fragment in its entirety, omits the demonstrative (*Stromata*, V, 9, 59, 5); it is there in Simplicius and in Plutarch, where τὸν αὐτὸν ἁπάντων is missing, often eliminated by critics, as what follows after ἐποίησεν (summarized with ἀλλ᾽ ἦν ἀεί in Simplicius); see B-W:131. The demonstrative, if it were included, would not say: "such as it is before our eyes" (Kurtz 1971:200; and see Kirk 1954:314: "the addition of τόνδε is important, since it obviously limits the κόσμος to that which we experience") nor the constitution or the state in which it is found (Reinhardt 1959:175ff; cf. Hölscher 1985:18: "Diese Welt [wie sie ist] ..." ["This world (as it is)"]); it would be rather "such as I say it is" (in line with the structure of the discourse).The determination by τὸν αὐτὸν seems to exclude one of the two citations and leads us to opt for Clement's coherent version.

constructions may be, they can be applied to what is said here, what is identical to all the schemas (and not shared by all men).[61] Whatever the model, we shall always be taken back to this irreducible analysis of all the possible cosmological hypotheses. What can one *say*?

The freedom to reorder the words, their isolation, with the new regroupings it allows, and the fragmentary use of idioms, according to language and outside of language, to lead toward that freedom, have not been read as marks of mastery and of control in line with the laws of *obscuritas*, not as signs of an intentional enigmatization, but rather as evidence of an uncontrollable inspiration.[62] The revelation itself is revealed through the irrational mode of the vivid utterance. One could thus stop at the linguistic or semantic aporia, accepting it with its ambiguity, with its mysterious contradictions, which ring "true," but whose falsity (or devices) can be adopted for all uses, according to the preconditions set (or followed) by each individual.[63]

There is a wide gap between the contradictory structure that the aphorisms extract from a matrix, that they *show*, and the ambivalences that prophetic expectations assume. "Heraclitus, after all, is a *prophētēs* [a spokesman] of [that is: for] the *logos*."[64]

---

[61] By ἁπάντων we understand men living in this world or everything that populates the world (cf. D-K), to accentuate the concept of unity: what all beings have in common; the reason for this world unity, in the context, does not appear (it is easy to understand why that part of the sentence has often been rejected). We should understand it as: τὸν αὐτὸν ἁπάντων τῶν κόσμων. In any case, it is still the same structure (cf. B-W: 132).

[62] Whatever Hölscher has to say (1985:1), in keeping with Kahn, the *thought* is not more obscure than the *style*, as it is understood. Heraclitus does not abandon logic, he does not resort to enigma to make the unutterable comprehensible ("his listeners cannot follow a plain tale," Kahn 1979: 270). The paradoxes are precise and significant. "Obscurity" concerns a freedom of composition, and the difference in the language compared to set-piece parlance. It serves as a guide, avoiding confusion. Clarity lies at the end.

[63] Barnes (1982:58, 80–81) rejects the characterization of Heraclitus as oracular and enigmatic, but he accepts the metaphysics of flux, of opposites, and of unity (60), which fits in with science ("he offered a philosophy of science which exhibits an admirable articulation," 81). Rejecting the "enigma," which is perhaps oracular in the writing process, he rejects the deciphering of the fragments that support abstraction and a logical transposition that is not established by the reading of the text. Obscurity, left in place, then becomes really obscure; it is perceived as incoherence, indicating a relative primitivism ("his account of the world is fundamentally inconsistent," 80). This "enlightened" arrogance masks the weaknesses of the critical approach. The thought is historically determined; it is thus "archaic," obviously; but it has the coherence that the author gave it, and it requires analysis before it is judged, and then compared to Spinoza and other philosophers. Otherwise, we are groping in the dark.

[64] "Heraclitus is *after all* a 'spokesman' for the *logos*," (Kahn 1979:130): it is the *logos* that speaks, and Heraclitus at the same time, in its place, "an attempt to make this larger discourse audible to a few, at least." Since the aporia is not formulated as a hermeneutic impasse, or is not accepted, we are obliged to accept the compromise.

If Heraclitus "demythifies" (without the anachronistic meaning "freeing of opinions" being attached to this word), and if one limits oneself to linking the word to the systematic analysis of the existing discourses, all the interpretative discourses that take what he says back to the philosophical or archeological "mystery"—a mystery that in fact he deconstructs profoundly by an analysis of the underlying assertions—assume the function of mystification (re-mystifying what has been de-mystified).

The idea of a solitary prophet who remains misunderstood when he has spoken, knowing that he speaks for no one, is an arbitrary extrapolation from what Heraclitus says about listening, the correlative of speaking, that can be understood only logically from speech as such.

We find descriptions in the fragments that are familiar in Greek thought and tradition. Obviously the author does not confine himself to them, and his own thought is in no way anticipated. It is the matter that he analyzes, that he does not invent or modify; he examines it to confirm his analysis of language— as if language could and should receive a maximal expansion, language as a symbolic system that expresses itself beyond just its verbal associations—and to apply to it equally systematically the structure resulting from the analysis.

The two points of view necessarily converge. The more one discovers by listening and by testing the extent of the principle's validity, the more the application, by turning around the assertions of etiological systems, can take it into account and dismantle the artificiality of those systems. The transition, "in the final analysis," is imperceptible.

Nothing, not even—or especially not—thought, can be compared to the *logos*, which only provides the schema or the model from which (and by reference to which) the phenomenon can be analyzed, or rather, constructed in order to be illuminated and clarified. Analysis of discourse provides the matrix for analytical discourses.[65]

Philological (and philosophical) truths are challenged as they are formulated; they seem unacceptable. If everything is just language, and does not convey anything else, while conveying everything, nothing refers to any Being or to any substance. No truer Being appears (or is revealed) through language.

Heraclitus has no doctrine of opposites. One never comes to understand a fragment as a stage in a demonstration. Besides, the fragments have a strict autonomy; like lyric poems, they are closed in on themselves and perfectly decipherable, in their limited context, if the aphorisms are not cut out.

---

[65] If the *logos* has the same structure as the law that rules Becoming, as is often asserted, it is because the analysis of assertions about the laws is made through the structure of the discourse. The two levels hang together thanks to this radical distinction (saying, and what is said).

This is always just an explicative hypothesis, renewed again and again, which only circumscribes the framework in which a single fundamental structure is applied. The word "fire" gets to the heart of the matter by boring into the abyss of darkness; it says "night." This is a one-way, irreversible relationship; reversion is the result of a symmetrical operation. So one cannot claim, as some do, that Heraclitus proposes opposites as the basis of his system. Strictly speaking, he has no system, nor any "opposites." The clash results everywhere from a contradictory linkage.

No other author has ever given rise to more divergent discourses. One scholar speaks of his "religious sense," emphasizing the "worthlessness of human knowledge in comparison with divine,"[66] when there is never any question regarding beliefs or gods, of anything but human practice. In light of this profession of humility, the initiate's pride masks the truth that he reserves for "those who have no ears."[67] The "oracular style,"[68] which has been compared to prophetic inspiration, would translate both the loftiness of the person who knows he is chosen—chosen for speech, displaying a justified disdain for the "common man" (even though the *logos* is said to be "common")—and the mark of passion, both a chosen protective screen and a sign of election, a necessity imposed on reason for communicating itself through this irrational form. Within the limits of this framework, all interpretation, absolutely all, can come, and has come to stay.

There has been a misunderstanding of the meaning of the *obscuritas* that concerns the use of elements of language, the gap that another usage inscribes, in relation to conventional forms. There is comparable confusion in the interpretation of the lyrical parts of tragedy, where the unexpected, the most rigorously thought out, is supposed to translate unrestrained ecstasy. Obscurity in Heraclitus, based on a great autonomy in the elements of the discourse, whether he makes or quotes or remakes them, obliges us to listen to the language, to define what is being said and how it can be said. In a necessary re-composition of the subject, it traces a path *toward*, including the perception of a unique

---

[66] Guthrie (1962:413) discovers yet another side of Heraclitus, his religiosity; see also 1962:414: "Many things in the fragments suggest the religious rather than the philosophic teacher." Babut (1976:496): "Le porte-parole ou l'instrument privilégié d'une révélation qui s'apparente à la parole d'un dieu" ("The spokesperson or the privileged instrument of a revelation that is like the word of a god").

[67] "He that hath ears to hear, let him hear": Guthrie (1962:413) attributes this idea to Heraclitus, citing Clement (*Stromata* 5.14.718), "who actually compares Fragment 34 with this saying of Jesus" (Guthrie 1962:n. 2).

[68] Guthrie 1982:414; Hölscher 1985:1, and others.

referential structure and a return movement—*anō, katō* ("up," "down")—toward its projection, or its re-injection into the figures of established language.

Imposing the principle of self-reflection as a prerequisite for every assertion, Heraclitus' approach marks a rupture; it is not so easy to measure its impact or assess its significance. It is squarely situated in a speculative tradition, however radical the re-examination of positions may be. A global view, considering the speculative rise of the Ionians initiated by Thales and his force (of which we do not have a perfect representation), suggests that the movement was on its way to realization, and that reflection, appearing at this pivotal moment, found the means to reach its ultimate goal. Heraclitus does not give up on reconsidering totalization. In a way, the reversal, through the definition of art as knowledge of knowledge, creates the possibility of a reflexive speculation in which, whenever the dry is opposed to the wet, what is foregrounded is the unique possibility of producing the relationship.

This is a general rule: it is only when literality is established that the question of meaning, that is, the meaning of this meaning, of the philosophical significance, can be posited.

Heraclitus did not invent truth; he extracts it from the lack of understanding in which it has been held "until the present day."

Works Cited

Babut, D. 1976. "Héraclite critique des poètes et des savants." *L'Antiquité classique* 45, 2:464–496.

———. 1987. "Une nouvelle édition d'Héraclite." *Revue philosophique* 177, 2:201–213.

Barnes, J. 1982. *The Pre-Socratic Philosophers*. I. *Thales to Zeno*. 2nd. ed., rev. London. Orig. pub. 1979.

Bechtel, F. 1924. *Die griechischen Dialekte*. 3 vols. Berlin.

Bollack, J., and H. Wismann. 1995. *Héraclite ou la séparation*. 2nd ed. with new preface. Paris. Orig. pub. 1972.

Brecht, F. J. 1949. *Heraclit. Ein Versuch über den Ursprung der Philosophie*. 2nd ed. Wuppertal.

Burnet, J. 1930. *Early Greek Philosophy*. 4th ed. London. Orig. pub. 1892.

Conche, M. 1986. *Héraclite: Fragments*. Paris.

De Martino, F., L. Rossetti, and P. Rosati. 1986. *Eraclito, Bibliografia, 1970–1984*. Perugia.

Diels, H. 1897. *Parmenides*. Berlin.

———. 1901. *Herakleitos von Ephesos*. Berlin.

Diels, H., and W. Kranz, eds. 1951. *Die Fragmente der Vorsokratiker*, 6th ed. Berlin.

Gigon, O. 1935. *Untersuchungen zu Heraklit.* Leipzig.

———. 1945. *Der Ursprung der griechischen Philosophie, von Hesiod bis Parmenides.* Basel.

Guthrie, W. K. C. 1962. *A History of Greek Philosophy.* 6 vols. Cambridge.

Hegel, G. W. F. 1977. *Phenomenology of Spirit.* Trans. A. V. Miller. Oxford. Orig. pub. 1807.

Heidegger, M. 1979. *Heraklit. Gesamtausgabe II (Vorlesungen, 1923–1944),* vol. 55. Frankfurt.

Hölscher, U. 1968. *Anfängliches Fragen.* Göttingen.

———. 1985. "Heraklit zwischen Tradition und 'Aufklärung.'" *Antike und Abendland* 31:1–24.

Kahn, C. 1979. *The Art and Thought of Heraclitus.* Cambridge.

Kassel, R. 1971. *Der Text der aristotelischen Rhetorik. Prolegomena zu einer kritischen Ausgabe.* Berlin.

———, ed. 1976. *Aristotelis Ars Rhetorica.* Berlin.

Kirk, G. S. 1954. *Heraclitus: The Cosmic Fragments.* Cambridge.

Kirk, G. S., and J. E. Raven. 1957. *The Pre-Socratic Philosophers: A Critical History with a Selection of Texts.* Cambridge.

Kraus, M. 1987. *Name und Sache. Ein Problem im frühgriechischen Denken.* Amsterdam.

Kurtz, E. 1971. *Interpretationen zu den Logos-Fragmenten Heraklits.* Hildesheim.

Marcovich, M. 1978. *Heraclitus.* Florence. Orig. pub. 1967.

Miller, E., ed. 1851. *Origenes philosophoumena sive omnium haeresium refutatio.* Oxford.

Paquet, L., M. Roussel, and Y. LaFrance. 1988. *Les présocratiques. Bibliographie analytique (1879–1980).* Montreal.

Reinhardt, K. 1959. *Parmenides und die Geschichte der griechischen Philosophie.* Frankfurt. Orig. pub. 1916.

Roussos, E. N. 1971. *Heraklit-Bibliographie.* Darmstadt.

Schäfer, G. 1902. *Die Philosophie des Heraklit von Ephesos und die modern Heraklitforschung.* Leipzig.

Schuster, P. 1872. *Heraklit von Ephesus.* Leipzig.

West, M. L. 1971. *Early Greek Philosophy and the Orient.* Oxford.

Wilamowitz-Moellendorff, U. von. 1895. *Euripides, Herakles* I. 2nd ed. Berlin.

Zeller, E. 1961. *La Filosofia dei Greci.* Ed. and trans. R. Mondolfo. 4 vols. Florence.

Zeller, E., and W. Nestle. 1920. *Die Philosophie der Griechen in ihrer geschichtlichen Entwicklung,* 6th ed. Darmstadt. Orig. pub. 1855. In English as *A History of Greek Philosophy: From the Earliest Period to the Time of Socrates, with a General Introduction,* trans. S. F. Alleyne, London, 1881.

Fragments

[TN: The English translations are from *Ancilla to the Pre-Socratic Philosophers*, by Kathleen Freeman (Cambridge, MA: 1962), "Hêracleitus of Ephesus," 24–34. The traditional interpretations reflected in these translations were often modified by Jean Bollack.]

Fragment 1

τοῦ δὲ λόγου τοῦδ' ἐόντος ἀεὶ ἀξύνετοι γίνονται ἄνθρωποι καὶ πρόσθεν ἢ ἀκοῦσαι καὶ ἀκούσαντες τὸ πρῶτον· γινομένων γὰρ πάντων κατὰ τὸν λόγον τόνδε ἀπείροισιν ἐοίκασι, πειρώμενοι καὶ ἐπέων καὶ ἔργων τοιούτων ὁκοίων ἐγὼ διηγεῦμαι κατὰ φύσιν διαιρέων ἕκαστον καὶ φράζων ὅκως ἔχει· τοὺς δὲ ἄλλους ἀνθρώπους λανθάνει ὁκόσα ἐγερθέντες ποιοῦσιν ὅκωσπερ ὁκόσα εὕδοντες ἐπιλανθάνονται.

The *Logos* (*the intelligible Law of the universe*) is as here explained; but men are always incapable of understanding it, both before they hear it, and when they have heard it for the first time. For though all things come into being in accordance with this Law, men seem as if they had never met with it, when they meet with words (*theories*) and actions (*processes*) such as I expound, separating each thing according to its nature and explaining how it is made. As for the rest of humankind, they are unaware of what they are doing after they wake, just as they forget what they did while asleep.

Fragment 2

διὸ δεῖ ἕπεσθαι τῷ <ξυνῷ>· τοῦ λόγου δ' ἐόντος ξυνοῦ ζώουσιν οἱ πολλοὶ ὡς ἰδίαν ἔχοντες φρόνησιν.

Therefore one must follow (the universal Law, namely) that which is common (*to all*). But although the Law is universal, the majority live as if they had understanding peculiar to themselves.

Fragment 30

κόσμον τόνδε [τὸν αὐτὸν ἁπάντων] οὔτε τις θεῶν οὔτε ἀνθρώπων ἐποίησεν, ἀλλ' ἦν ἀεὶ καὶ ἔστιν καὶ ἔσται· πῦρ ἀείζωον, ἁπτόμενον μέτρα καὶ ἀποσβεννύμενον μέτρα.

This ordered universe (*cosmos*), which is the same for all, was not created by any one of the gods or of humankind, but it was ever and is and shall be ever-living Fire, kindled in measure and quenched in measure.

Fragment 32

ἓν τὸ σοφὸν μοῦνον λέγεσθαι οὐκ ἐθέλει καὶ ἐθέλει Ζηνὸς ὄνομα.

That which alone is wise is one; it is willing and unwilling to be called by the name of Zeus.

Fragment 41

ἓν τὸ σοφόν· ἐπίστασθαι γνώμην, ὅκη κυβερνᾶται πάντα διὰ πάντων.

That which is wise is one: to understand the purpose which steers all things through all things.

Fragment 50

οὐκ ἐμοῦ ἀλλὰ τοῦ λόγου ἀκούσαντας ὁμολογεῖν σοφόν ἐστιν ἓν πάντα εἶναι.

When you have listened, not to me but to the Law (*Logos*), it is wise to agree that all things are one.

Fragment 53

πόλεμος πάντων μὲν πατήρ ἐστι, πάντων δὲ βασιλεύς, καὶ τοὺς μὲν θεοὺς ἔδειξε τοὺς δὲ ἀνθρώπους, τοὺς μὲν δούλους ἐποίησε τοὺς δὲ ἐλευθέρους.

War is both king of all and father of all, and it has revealed some as gods, others as men; some it has made slaves, others free.

Fragment 90

πυρός τε ἀνταμοιβὴ τὰ πάντα καὶ πῦρ ἀπάντων ὅκωσπερ χρυσοῦ χρήματα καὶ χρημάτων χρυσός.

There is an exchange: all things for Fire and Fire for all things, like goods for gold and gold for goods.

Fragment 108

ὁκόσων λόγους ἤκουσα οὐδεὶς ἀφικνεῖται ἐς τοῦτο ὥστε γινώσκειν ὅ τι σοφόν ἐστι, πάντων κεχωρισμένον.

Of all those whose discourse I have heard, none arrives at the realization that that which is wise is set apart from all things.

18

Reading A Reference[†]

FREUD WAS PREOCCUPIED BY THE ROLE he had had to attribute—or so he thought—to the death principle, a role for which Empedocles' cosmogony provided a distant model. I later reconstituted that cosmology in very different terms, which were not understood in the same way in Freud's day.[1] Freud was undoubtedly led astray by a dualism that does not reproduce the original form of the system. It was easy to establish an analogy between the object he sought and the information he found; he was probably inspired by a representation that was not as far removed from his own as is commonly believed. I dealt systematically with the problems of Freud's reading of *Oedipus Tyrannus* in "Le fils de l'homme,"[2] following a day of discussions organized by Barbara Cassin at the Sorbonne, with psychoanalysts among the participants. Freud seeks to characterize the effect that the memory of the myth, transmitted by the inspired intuition of the poet, conveys deep within the spectator's soul, as it meets the latent zones of dreams. The spectator's pleasure is the sign that he is resuscitating in his unconscious the virtually timeless recollection of a primal murder and a primal incestuous desire, close to one of the "age-old dreams" of humanity in its youth.

There remains the problem of understanding how such an elaborate and complex literary work could, on its own, resist being transferred into the order of myth. Depending on whether one follows Freudian logic or the logic that ensues from close textual analysis, the mythical story and its interpretation by Sophocles—and, with these, the signification of the murder and the incest—are situated at two different levels of reflection. During numerous sessions with groups of psychoanalysts since 1984, I have added to this example that of *Antigone*, which was central for Lacan. The use of a cultural tradition illustrates

---

[†] Originally published as "Lire une référence," in: Jean Bollack, *La Grèce de personne: les mots sous le mythe* (Paris, 1997), pp. 106–106.

[1] The most recent manuals keep on lazily reproducing the traditional understanding—which I consider outdated—without even discussing it.

[2] This study, devoted to Freud's analyses of the myth, was reprinted in Bollack 1995.

less a case of conflict than a case of competing hermeneutics, if the term can be applied to psychoanalysis (it is used in that context for the "reading" of non-manifest fragments of dreams). We can try to engage in straightforward debates about competencies in order to discover under what conditions the one may become fruitful for the other.

Work Cited

Bollack, J. 1995. "Le fils de l'homme." In *La naissance d'Oedipe*, 282–321. Paris.

19

The Scientistic Model†
Freud and Empedocles

Preliminary Remark

A DICHOTOMY IS INTRODUCED into the analysis of any object of study. The phenomenon studied is situated along a line of evolution. Given the goal of assigning meaning, this dichotomy produces a division between anticipation (or "intuition") and primitivism, between "going beyond" and "falling short." In fact, it is only a matter of separating those aspects of the object that have been assimilated to subsequent knowledge by critical work—and falsely valorized, since modernity legitimizes the object—considering the value that the institution attributes to them. But this leaves a remainder, which cannot have been assimilated and valorized. Operating from the standpoint of an outcome that transcends the work, as if the work were, or could have been, conceived in view of an unknown endpoint, brings about a qualitative dissociation. Historicization globalizes from the outset. In historicizing, one renounces the option of proceeding to reconstitute a scientifically provisional totality. Historically, such totalities have been conceived and constructed in relation to other totalities, each equally self-contained and no less provisional, each entering into competition with the others at the moment of genesis, and, in the same way, each will itself be disintegrated and replaced in turn. The very "project" of historicization, anchored in a particular form, will be abandoned in that form. The moment of stoppage and concentration, marked by the work or the system that one is deciphering, constitutes its own temporality; we have to yield to the rhythm of that temporality if we want to grasp the "sense" of the work or the system, that is, the sense that the elements take on in the structure as a whole, emitting their own language and determining the nature of the utterance. It is this structure as a whole that makes sense, starting from its center; in a second

†   Originally published as "Le modèle scientiste, Empédocle et Freud," in: Jean Bollack, *La Grèce de personne: les mots sous le mythe* (Paris, 1997), pp. 105–106.

phase, the structure can be questioned as to its signification—or its import—*in itself*, apart from the conditions of its deciphering, with respect to other prior or subsequent thoughts, and with respect to ourselves.

Reading of "Analysis Terminable and Interminable" ("Die endliche und die unendliche Analyse"), Section VI, on Empedocles[1]

The Empedoclean doctrine of Love and Strife is at the center of what Freud calls "our interest" (*unser Interesse*), based on the "psychoanalytic theory of the instincts" (*SE* 23:245). The assimilation is so tempting, he notes, that one could almost speak of identity, if there were not the cosmic, non-scientific imagination on the one hand, and a scientific limitation on the other, validity in psychoanalysis being restricted to the biological domain ("the Greek philosopher's theory is a cosmic phantasy while ours is content to claim biological validity" [*SE* 23:245]; "während unsere [Phantasie] sich mit dem Anspruch auf biologische Geltung bescheidet" [*GW* 16:90]).

However, this difference is immediately abolished, or at least reduced, on the basis of a theory of universal animation, a pan-psychism that strongly influenced positivist or scientistic descriptions of pre-Socratic thought at the beginning of the century, before the rehabilitation of a more ontological position by phenomenology and the later reintroduction of a more logical point of view. Even Wilhelm Capelle, the compiler whose text Freud followed,[2] made this assumption here, based on the attribution of the name "daimons" (*daimones*) to the forces at issue; no one really raised any questions about what type of transposition or transference Empedocles had in mind. The primitivist phenomenon effaces a border and erases distances, and produces a backlash in favor of a scientific approach. On this point, Freud refers directly to Capelle, who is anxious to limit the effect of the demonic personalization of the two forces and opts for a new opposition in which he stresses their status as "natural forces," devoid of intelligence, according to Aristotle's critique, and thus devoid of teleological import; furthermore, equally under the influence of the Aristotelian critique,

---

[1]   [TN: Citations from Freud in English are from the *Standard Edition of the Complete Psychological Works of Sigmund Freud*, trans. and ed. James Strachey, 24 vols. (London: Hogarth, 1953–66), hereafter *SE*; citations in German are from Freud, *Gesammelte Werke*, 1968–1978 (hereafter *GW*).]

[2]   Wilhelm Capelle, a well-informed academic, published his popularizing work devoted to pre-Socratic thought, *Die Vorsokratiker; die Fragmente und Quellenberichte*, in a widely-distributed collection, *Die Vorsokratiker* (1935), just before Freud made use of it (there were new editions in 1938, 1940, and again after the war). This seems to have been the only book Freud had in front of him as he wrote the pages on Empedocles.

he considers their function "mechanical," sees them in deterministic terms, and deems their causality fortuitous.

Freud's presentation is closely tied to this summary. On the one hand, he turns Capelle's words to his own purposes with the adjective *triebhaft* (instinctual), which Capelle uses in a *physical* sense (the de-divinized sense of physics) to characterize these powers, which he represents as mere "forces." Freud's attention had been caught by this phrase, which he cites: "natural forces operating like instincts" (*SE* 23:246; "triebhaft wirkende Naturkräfte" [*GW* 16:91]); on the other hand, slightly transforming the source, he retains the role of chance in a description that he classifies among "modern ideas," in particular evolutionism, with the role it attributes to chance and with a history he tinges with Darwinism: the development of living beings in stages, or even the survival of the fittest, which he found formulated in Capelle[3]; however, Theodor Gomperz had already indicated, in his *Griechische Denker: Eine Geschichte der antiken Philosophie* (1896–1909),[4] that this progression through stages translated the profundity of the naturalist's intuitions.

In this assimilation to later or even contemporary doctrines, the fact that evolution was in no sense open was not taken into account. Evolution was inscribed within a fixed framework: its point of departure and also its endpoint were known in advance, so that the stages along the way, with the cosmic events that served as milestones, drew their signification from a premise. Furthermore, both Freud and Capelle, like almost all critics of the time, acknowledged double, competing versions of evolution, one under the sign of strife—a version that was not only gratuitous (and perhaps unfeasible, or unthinkable) in itself, but in even more pronounced contradiction (given the reversibility at work) with the evolutionism that was being discovered or otherwise extrapolated.

In the context of "Analysis Terminable and Interminable," Freud is still more interested in the definition of the two forces, one of which tends to bring the constitutive particles together into "a single unity," while the other seeks to undo these compositions by freeing the primal components.

With the antagonists distinguished in this way, the adversarial positions are set up as a confrontation between equal principles, with no qualitative differences; a catastrophe taken to be essential is capable of imprinting on future developments a structure comparable to that of demiurgic power—a becoming by way of a de-becoming? In this formal dualism, Freud reproduces the opinion (predominant at the time, and not yet abandoned even today) that there are

---

3   See Capelle 1935:187, 215.
4   In English as *Greek Thinkers: A History of Ancient Philosophy* (London, 1901–1912). The first volume of this well-known book was initially published in 1895. Gomperz was a professor of philosophy and philology at the University of Vienna; his wife was among Freud's patients.

two parallel evolutions (one pointing to the triumph of Love, the other to the triumph of Strife). The defective logic of this system does not manage to hold his attention (had it done so, he would have been struck by it): it is the very duality of these separate instincts that he seeks to impose or to make credible: "I am well aware that the dualistic theory according to which an instinct of death or of destruction or aggression claims equal rights (*gleichberechtigt*) as a partner with Eros as manifested in the libido, has found little sympathy and has not really been accepted even among psychoanalysts" (*SE* 23:244). It is to combat this deficiency (and this reticence) that he invokes the authority of Empedocles.

Freud does not hesitate to situate himself under the protection of this guarantee. To be sure, the theory of the double instinct is his own (it is the one he is developing in this essay). However, considering the full extent of his readings (especially in the earlier years), there is no reason to rule out the possibility that he is already professing Empedocles' opinion—or that of Empedoclean criticism—by virtue of a phenomenon of cryptomnesia, even before he has acquired additional credibility for his thesis—or his hypothesis—in the face of his collaborators' doubts, through testimony invoked in support of the defense. He was perhaps drawing on elements of Empedoclean language to testify in favor of Empedocles. Nothing was to stop Freud, nothing could have stopped him, in this context; nothing could have prevented him from proceeding to an assimilation (if the idea in question was perhaps, even probably, generically the same). *Philia*, Love, was one of our two "primal instincts"; *Neikos*, Strife (or Hatred) was the other. Didn't they have the same functions—on the one hand, Love, that of combining the matter present (*das Vorhandene*) in sets of ever-increasing size, like an expanding, unifying dynamism; and, on the other hand, Strife, that of annihilating the formations produced by the action of the antagonistic principle?

As Freud sees it, what differentiates Empedocles' thought from his own is related, in turn, to temporal evolution. The ideas are no longer the same. First, there is the disappearance of the cosmic dimension ("the restriction to the biophysical field, which is imposed on us" [*SE* 23:246]), which would presuppose—so that the difference between the domains can be maintained in these terms—that the cosmos is only an extension, a separable entity, as it were; but matter, the component particles, have also changed in nature; in order not to confuse the inanimate realm with life, as Empedocles did, one cannot continue to consider the "elements"; thus "we no longer think of the mingling and separation of particles of substance, but of the soldering together and defusion [*Entmischung*] of instinctual components" (*SE* 23:246).[5]

---

[5]   If Freud was able to see (or believe) that his own principles had been mythically anticipated in Greek thought, after Freud some have been tempted to see the fragments from Empedocles' work with the help of concepts used in psychoanalysis, in search of common intuitions, as

Furthermore, along the line of actualization, he adds that Strife (or Quarrel) has been demythified in yet another way; it has been endowed with a biological substratum, and the instinct of destruction has been conflated with the death instinct; now, that instinct (which is introduced in a dialectical relation with its opposite) is simply the impulse that pushes the living to rejoin the inanimate— as if the latter formed the inseparable counterpart of the vital impulse.

Destruction was thus reattached to the "biosphere" as a negation of life, accompanying the vital instinct. And at the same time Empedocles, the author of the *Katharmoi* (*The Purifications*), was purified and whitewashed, stripped of all his compromising functions as mystic and magician, sectarian, missionary in the service of a politics and of a religion, all this for the greater profit of science, whose domain had only to be circumscribed. By getting rid of certain speculative thrusts that were no longer in fashion, Freud had in Empedocles, against the detractors of duality, the sought-after scientific authority, archaic but modernizable—and metamorphosed, "reincarnated"—to borrow the terms of metempsychosis, which had been eliminated from the discourse.

Freud stressed the facets of Empedocles' personality, presenting the figure as an exceptional being, Faustian and somewhat disturbing, someone who manifested in his person contradictory and irreconcilable "incarnations": using our modern categories, we would call him a researcher, a thinker, but also a prophet and a magician, a politician, a doctor initiated into the arcana of nature (all these elements are drawn from the stories, more symbolic than anecdotal, found in Diogenes Laertius' famous biography, a text that, before Hölderlin, had more strongly marked the figure of Empedocles than the fragments of the lost work). Here again, Freud was following a tradition of modern interpretation (the absence of unity is stressed in an article by Diels, but no less so by Gomperz or Capelle): in order to come to terms with regressions in progressivism, modern thinkers had constructed a complex character, a virtually proteiform nature, without questioning either the possible significance of the will to displace, socially and culturally, a discourse and the effects of a body of knowledge, or the means that might be connected with the realization of that ambition and might supply indices to it. However, rather than showing himself to be troubled, Freud fell back strategically on historical distance to excuse, or at least to explain, the richness of some aspects of the work by temptations that

---

Sarah Kofman does in her interesting study, "Freud and Empedocles" (Kofman 1991). Instead of exploring the difference that matters, Kofman treats the speculative construction globally (without taking particular bodies of knowledge, such as embryology, into consideration) as "mythical," and she transposes the "psychobiological" truth as such: "Investigations by a specialist in one particular field are doomed to failure and can only help to keep mankind in a state of metaphysical illusion" ("Judith," Kofman 1991:56).

had been forbidden after Empedocles' time: for "the realm of science was not yet divided into so many provinces" (*SE* 23:245). Everything that Empedocles had also been—in addition to being a doctor and a biologist—he would not have chosen to be in Freud's day.

In fact, by firmly linking the death impulse to life, Freud has in a sense drawn closer to Empedocles, for whom Strife was inseparable from the creative movements of life (it is the condition of their partial existence—and the reign of absolute Strife existed only among nineteenth-century commentators). However, as if that definition or that approach to a definition still remained too close to an undemonstrable postulate (it still "convinces"), he adds at the end that he will not deny that an instinct said to be "analogous," namely, an instinct of destruction unconnected with life, pushing toward its own end, could have existed independently of "life": one cannot "assert that an instinct of this sort only came into existence with the emergence of life" (*SE* 23:246–47). Knowing that, by the limitation that is in harmony with his own ends, he has appropriated the testimony available to him, he goes back to his Greek authority to restore to him, integrally, his intuition (he thinks he is returning; in fact, he is moving further away). Freud's procedure is rather remarkable. Should he not have left to Empedocles what was his due, if Empedocles was not Empedocles (a claim Freud actually made) but rather "truth," a "kernel of truth" (*ein Wahrheitskern*), that future discoveries could enrich and clarify and that it was thus all the more important to conserve intact, in its original form, like a thought to be rethought?

When he comes back to this same point in Chapter II of the posthumous "Outline of Psychoanalysis," by reminding the reader of the resistance he knows he will have to overcome among the analysts, the interaction of the fundamental instincts (the role of collaboration and struggle in the interplay of the antagonists, the "concurrent and mutually opposing action of the two basic instincts" (*SE* 23:149 [*das Mit- und Gegeneinanderwirken*]) is related to the more general laws of attraction and repellence that govern the inorganic world just as much as the organic. This last sentence opens the way not to a better understanding of Empedocles by the analysis of the distortions that have been imposed upon him—that is, fallacious expectations (this was not his concern)—but rather to a better comprehension of the thing itself. Empedocles shows the duality, he figures it impressively in the intuition of "love" and "strife," an intuition that maintains its force whatever it may have been, designating a stronghold within which we shall indeed end up finding out exactly what to think of these two instincts.

Problems of a Non-critical Attitude in the Face of Cultural Values

The doxography is adopted and integrated as such. This is because, while the work, which is being constructed, in which all creativity is being invested, forms the system of reference, all the rest, everything external, is either interpreted (in the light of the system) as a matter, or set into relation with elements internal to the doctrine, but not analyzed in its own "truth."

1. First, one cannot do otherwise ("materially"); one could at least, in principle, introduce a doubt.

2. This attitude can be explained if the main scientific interest lies at the heart of an expansive activity apt to supply an understanding of things, of a virtually universal nature; it is then displaced onto a terrain that is taken for what it is and as it is—for what one thinks it is. There is an element of conformity, imposed, as it were, which is also found in other, similar positions—an absence of critique, the price of critique.

3. One could doubtless go further and detect (through Freud's recognition of the established or public values of art or history) the will to maintain elsewhere, in another domain, the monopoly on emancipation and demystification, perhaps even to institute, or to accept, a competing academic legitimacy, or some other—a moral legitimacy— that leaves in place the mechanisms that regulate social interplay, because these latter intervene, as such, in the field that gives priority, as one of the factors—and as a determining factor—to biological struggles.

Works Cited

Capelle, W. 1935. *Die Vorsokratiker*. Leipzig.

Freud, S. 1968-1978. *Gesammelte Werke, chronologisch geordnet*. 18 vols. Frankfurt.

Gomperz, T. 1896-1909. *Griechische Denker: Eine Geschichte der antiken Philosophie*. 3 vols. Leipzig.

Kofman, S. 1991. "Freud and Empedocles." In *Freud and Fiction*, trans. Sarah Wykes, 21–52. Boston. Orig. pub. 1973.

Benjamin Reading Kafka†

Kafka Then and Now

KAFKA'S UNIQUE WORK—unique in more than one sense—never brings to light anything but its own making, in progress; its status is not that of the already "made," however carefully composed it may seem (even though the texts were often written in great haste). The strongest linguistic concentration tolerates the maintenance of a certain distance, as controlled as possible, and astoundingly free.

More and more, we see this work today for what it is: a work thought out in literary terms, on the basis of readings—that is to say, fully situated in language, by language, and in language.

Kafka has not been—and could not have been—read in this framework until recently, however.[1] Today, readers are accepting the stories in their complexity and their strained polarity, while re-examining their difficulty, which is deliberate, more studied than had been thought: bolder, more critical, more experimental.

It is to *us*, with the new distance we possess, that the possibility of appreciating the original distance is offered, after a very long time during which the texts began to emerge and came to be perceived as texts, then came to be understood and finally rediscovered; it has become possible to *read* them anew. It has taken about a hundred years to produce a prodigiously instructive history of the work.[2]

[†] Originally published as "Benjamin devant Kafka," in: H. Wismann, P. Lavelle, eds., *Walter Benjamin, le critique européen* (Lille, 2010), pp. 213–277.

[1] To measure the changes that have occurred, I am taking the sentences, chosen from the most varied domains, on which the Frankfurt newspaper *Frankfurter Allgemeine Zeitung* invited readers to comment during the summer of 2007 (Kafka 2009).

[2] In the foreword to her collection of essays on Benjamin, Sigrid Weigel (2013) uses the formula "neither theological nor secular"; she prefers the term "postbiblical" (xxii). Detaching Benjamin from theology, she does not situate him, any more than Hans Blumenberg does, within the process of secularization that Blumenberg defined and critiqued (Blumenberg 1983; see Weigel 2013:xxiii). In the interpretations cited by Benjamin, Weigel thinks she can recognize

This reading-rereading frees itself from every purpose it has served, from everything that people have thought they could link it to and call, *ad nauseam,* Kafkaesque. The writer, relentlessly persistent in his nocturnal quest for writing, will continue to defend his exercises, more conquering than extravagant, against all odds, against distortions. He is no stranger to metamorphoses; he remains their master. Did he not put them at the core of his writing, in the thousand and one conquests of a singular imaginary? In Kafka, broadenings of the horizon remain tied to the most meticulous precision; expression and reflection converge in the minuscule. The explorations exhaust themselves as they unwind; often, they peter out; if they end up in failure, it is because that is where they led.

Kafka expressed himself about everything around him. His wit, his acuity are attested; his persona is known to us. We have his notebooks, often already organized, his private diaries, all the notes he took, the abundance of letters he wrote. We have accounts by his friends. The testimony does not really touch on the writing; the world that was being built at his table was located elsewhere. There is no contradiction, obviously, between the two spheres, whether they are in communication between themselves or not, but one does not pass from one to the other ingenuously. One sphere is constructed in the vicinity; it could not have been built anywhere but there, in Prague, before, during, and after the war. The other sphere lies elsewhere: in the world of literature, precisely.

Kafka's narratives belong to a profoundly scriptural universe; they all seek to please before they seek to convince. They are exploits. Their success is all the more striking in that themes of failure are not only taken into account in them but constitute, almost to the point of excess, a kind of counterpoint to an unshakeable base. The style and even the echoes that the descriptions bring to life are anchored there; this is the secret of the transformations that particularize them. The pleasure one takes in reading them is of a strange nature; it is jarring, but it remains nonetheless literary and perfectly free.

In 1931, under the title "Von den Gleichnissen" (On Parables), Max Brod published a conversation on parables.[3] The debate bears on profit. The author of the parables has transformed himself into a parable. Yes, we have profited, but the profit is not here; it lies elsewhere, the interlocutor says with dismay. He is corrected: No, it is here that we profit, in everyday reality, given that there, in the counter-part, logic would have it that everything is lost, by virtue of having become the object of pure reflection. This correlation is found everywhere; it brings us necessarily from being to non-being.

---

theologoumena [TN: theological statements of opinion as opposed to doctrinal pronouncements] encompassed in a secularization from which Benjamin distances himself.

[3]   Kafka 1971:457.

Benjamin's Kafka

Walter Benjamin's essay on Kafka dates from 1934.[4] It was one of the most important and the most carefully studied that the critic ever wrote; it is situated closer to Kafka's time than to ours, and thus further from him than it should have been, so effectively does distancing do its work, before it is diminished. Kafka's work made an impression on its earliest readers, as it does on readers even today, by dint of its difference and its singularity, but especially by its sheer force; its literary quality has sustained it and ensured a presence for it. The power of the writing imposed its effect of presence or even self-evidence before the text's meaning and scope could come into view. It was not a matter of the "meaning" of Kafka's writings.

At the time Benjamin was writing, there were the seven books, short and precious, that had appeared in Kafka's lifetime, before 1924. In these volumes a good number of the densest, most polished and best known of his writings appear. It is a first period, probably the most representative, despite being quite slim; it is pertinent in its own right, despite the inevitable reticence on the part of the author, prodigious without affectation, more concerned with his creations than with their dissemination. The writer's qualities were received as a contribution to expressionism, so disconcerting were they; then they were gradually discovered in their true originality and their uniqueness.[5] All of Kafka—the real one—was there. In a second phase, there followed the surprising mass of what was published after his death by his friend, Max Brod, the executor of his will, who, since their student years together, had more or less anticipated the task that awaited him. He was like the evangelist; he introduced the three novels: the oldest, *Amerika*, written between September 1912 and January 1913, came out in 1927, after *The Trial* (1925) and after *The Castle* (1926), which had been written last, in 1922. The volumes of previously unavailable texts show that the unpublished work, the whole literary estate, was animated (from 1907 on) by almost ceaseless creativity—a virtually limitless momentum, essentially oscillating, stopping sometimes but never losing its way. The continuous work of writing was found in the intervals: the suspensions were lodged in a feverish movement of accomplishment.

---

[4] "Franz Kafka: On the Tenth Anniversary of His Death" (Benjamin 1999d [1934]). For the original German, see Benjamin 1978, 2, pt. 2:409–438, and notes, 2, pt. 3:1153–1276. Schweppenhäuser 1981 is a very useful pocket edition that includes Benjamin's essays and notes on Kafka along with excerpts from his correspondence with G. Scholem, T. W. Adorno, and W. Kraft on the subject of Kafka. [TN: In our translation of Jean Bollack's article, we follow the author's practice of frequently referring to Benjamin's piece on Kafka as the Essay.]

[5] Volume 1 in Brod's 1935 edition brought together everything that Kafka had published in his lifetime under the title *Erzählungen*.

Later, there was to be a third period, in which reflection, always renewed, on the resources and demands of writing would become still more widely available, in large part after Benjamin's death. The focus now was on the self and its vicissitudes, as well as on the worlds that surround and bind us. This was yet another overture; in its aftermath, other stories mingled with the rich personal diaries. Then came the series of letters, with their accounts of encounters and long engagements, begun again and again with numerous partners: love and what opposed it, life and non-life. Benjamin, in 1931, had set out, as best he could, to mark the importance of the complements and the supplements that had just appeared.[6] He surely had an intimation of the scope of all the rest, with which he was yet unfamiliar.

Six years earlier, on July 21, 1925, describing his readings, Benjamin told Gershom Scholem that he had requested some of Kafka's posthumous texts for the purpose of reviewing them, adding that the short story "Before the Law" now struck him, as it had ten years earlier (the collection in which the text appeared had been published in 1919!), as "one of the most beautiful in the German language."[7] Later, he wrote to Scholem that he should have purchased everything (he hadn't received the books he sought to review). He didn't have either *The Castle* or *Amerika*, "to say nothing of the rare, out-of-print *Meditation* [*Betrachtung*]"; this 1913 volume was the only one published during Kafka's lifetime that Benjamin lacked.[8] Ten years earlier, taken literally, it would have been "The Judgment" (1913). Or "Metamorphosis" (1915)? Did Benjamin become attached, a posteriori but explicitly, to the early Kafka?

The Outline of the Essay

He did not read him. But did anyone read? He read in his own way, as others read in theirs. He knew Kafka; the acquaintance was perhaps more recent than he indicated. He had penetrated into the work as if, owing to the disconcerting singularity he somehow perceived there, he had to retranslate it. Kafka's greatness could be grasped by Benjamin in an irrational framework; that way, it

---

[6] In a radio program in 1931 about the volume of stories that had just appeared (Benjamin 1978, 2, pt. 2:676–683: notes, 1978, 2, pt. 3:1155–1177, 1458–1460; cf. Kafka 1970). The text includes a whole series of elements that were taken up again in the 1934 essay.

[7] Benjamin 2012:279. In a note appended to this letter, Scholem remarked that "this is the first indication of WB's interest in Kafka, which WB maintained until the end" (280). According to U. Steiner (2010:132), this was one of the earliest traces in Benjamin's work of a reading of Kafka, after the appearance of the collection *Ein Landarzt* (*A Country Doctor*) in 1919.

[8] Benjamin 2012:336 (letter to Scholem, May 28, 1928). Among the novels, he had read *The Trial*: "As a ministering angel, I have Kafka at my bedside. I am reading *The Trial*" (Benjamin 1995–2000, 3:303, letter of Nov. 18, 1927). In the May 1928 letter to Scholem, Benjamin mentioned that Kafka was to be part of a book project that would bring together several essays.

became interpretable, and could be situated. This global vision did not allow Benjamin to recognize the power of a gaze on the things of this world, on opinions and beliefs. The world's unpredictability and absurdity struck him as too profound to be attributable to art, to be constructed by and to emanate from an artist, a mind, or an individual.

Kafka's work was called to communicate a message on the history of humankind; it was a remote origin that Benjamin was charged with unveiling in his place, in his capacity as a socially engaged literary figure. Not only did this entail not reading the text in its original form, it entailed reading what was thought to be there. In Kafka's case, Benjamin should have been interested in an individual author and an original creation, but his theoretical approach linked Kafka to a collective experience. The essayist constructed a framework that allowed him to situate what he retained from his reading, on a vast background supplied by the work. He had to project onto a past his own construct, a discourse considered inspiring and instructive, if not missionary in its import; it was a message that had come from an unknown and unknowable source. The text was transferred into a religious structure and was then reread through that framework, with the transformations required by the operation. It was endowed with a social context that corresponded to the discourse and gave it its meaning. This discourse was half projected into a history, enlarged to a mythical anthropology, and half constructed, closer to a theological or philosophical theory.

This is how the discourse spoke to him, to him and his readers; this is how it became expressive. One held onto what it had to say, what one was to draw from it. Once projected onto this new terrain, the author under scrutiny no longer retained the liberty he had taken, faced with a tradition he knew well, in order to express himself as he had done before. For the essayist, in contrast, the reorganization of the subject matter was the way the work, interpreted and newly situated, was adapted to the political situation and became intelligible and meaningful. Although the Essay outlined stages in an evolution, it is probably not possible to find in it an actual philosophy of history. Continuity is lacking. The evolution toward a classless society provides the context that made it possible to categorize the flashes of messianism uncovered in Kafka. The more welcoming and eclectic speculation of anthropology had opened up to the politically opposed paths traced by such authors as Ludwig Klages, of the "cosmic" and conservative revolution.

Some claim that Benjamin read Kafka as a philologist; he was indeed attentive to detail.[9] Did he succeed in putting his readers off the scent? In reality,

---

[9] Mariani-Zini 2004: "Benjamin reads Kafka like a philologist coming to grips with an unknown language ... every detail is an indicator and not a sign, and comprehension is not given at the outset" (13). See also Jennings 1988: "The essay's thematic concerns ... are dictated by close

he was not intent on deciphering Kafka according to his own logic, which was surprising and precise; he believed he understood Kafka as he interpreted him, more "naturally"; he naturalized him. Starting in his early years, so thoroughly researched by Marino Pulliero,[10] Benjamin found himself in a context in which philology (the dominant discipline in the nineteenth century) and its claims to restitution were less appreciated than before. The response to this decline did not consist in examining the prerequisites to the type of reading practiced; instead, a recasting of the work's content was substituted for the work itself. Proceeding on this path, Benjamin would ultimately deem Kafka's writings in part incomprehensible. This was because he could not understand them, reading the way he read. He scrutinized the work—which was familiar to him and which impressed him—according to the principles of a foreign schema, set up from a distance. Stéphane Mosès saw this clearly, although he did not limit himself to the written text either. He mortgaged it—in a different way, to be sure—by introducing formal figures of composition that he borrowed from the formalist theories of literary writing; to that end, he identified limited entities in these structures that could guide the reader.[11]

Not in connection with Kafka, but in the discussion of the subject, connected and no less primordial, constituted by his essays on Baudelaire,[12] Benjamin commented on the place of philology (he refers explicitly to the practice of interpreting ancient authors), singling out the magical element that surrounds it and that philological interpretation is called upon to exorcise.[13] The text does not escape from the hold of this magic, but communicates its charm, tying it to the astonishment that is a pre-eminent *object* of this type of knowledge. The remedy then lies in the historical perspective, which repositions the object as a monad, as an enlivening agency. The mythic rigidity of pure textual facticity will thus be surmounted and extended into a connection with our own historical experience. One sees clearly that Benjamin does not grasp the ability of

---

reading of a broad spectrum of Kafka's texts ..." (200). I wonder if he really followed this path. Mosès limits himself, on the contrary, to ambivalence: "Benjamin's hermeneutics ... leads to a type of critique in which are mingled, almost indissociably, elements of *interpretation* and elements of *projection*" (2006:94). Manifestly, rather the second. [TN: Unless otherwise indicated, the translations provided here and throughout this chapter are from the French text cited by Bollack.]

10 Pulliero 2005.

11 Mosès 2006:94; he speaks of *configurations* applying to Benjamin's thought in connection with the interview with Brecht on "The Next Village" (see Wismann and Lavelle 2010:45-48), as much as to the "logic proper to the text studied." The logic proper to the text was purportedly found in the figure of its composition. Does one also find "the thought" there?

12 See Benjamin 2006b.

13 See Benjamin 2012:585–592 (letter to Adorno, December 9, 1938), where Benjamin defends his way of proceeding.

the text to situate itself by means of a perspective that is constructed in it. He isolates a language effect that, however refined it may be, needs to be related to a wider constellation.

One must consider the sometimes deviant paths that he follows in the Essay, which he views as its own genre. The flow of a free demonstration comes to shed light with a new lens, broader and more "metaphysical." The raw material is borrowed from the author. For Benjamin, what is at stake is not a text that one would have to read in order to understand it, but rather matter containing a sacred message with multiple meanings, modeled on the Bible and on contemporary practices. The treatment moves away from its object. Updating that makes use of revised Marxist categories doubtless plays an essential role; the reader's gaze necessarily has to adjust to it. The term "parable," which Kafka himself questioned,[14] and which is frequently used to designate his narratives, might not be adequate either if one privileges the path of a symbolic interpretation, available and transferable. The "parable" as commonly understood is notably lacking in Kafka's compositions. His narrations are constructed. Kafka tells stories in a new way; their aesthetic form is specific to him. The exploration, in each instance particular and unexpected, is entirely determined.

The Essay, prepared and thought through over a long period of time, followed its own rules and thus took liberties. Benjamin went to Kafka,[15] then he came back with his plunder; he had started out with his own ideas, if not his own system. His ideas *could not* have had an equivalent in the object, which would have resisted them. As an experienced reader, Benjamin took Kafka's originality into account in spite of everything. Certain specificities were undeniable, but Benjamin integrated even these features into the preconceptions of his own vision; this vision was charged with welcoming them, not shedding light on them.[16] The Essay, as such, develops by following a demonstrative line; it does not lend itself to an exercise of elucidation, and it cannot be reduced to a summary of what is gleaned from a reading. It has its own logic. A genuine reading would have been troubling for Benjamin. It is thus appropriate to study the Essay as an autonomous product, according to the rules of its genre, and to discover its rhythm, which results from a particular composition. It does not

[14] See above, p. 258.
[15] See the notes: "Schemata, Dispositionen und Aufzeichnungen" (Benjamin 1978, 2, pt. 3:1205–1248).
[16] One justification of the procedure, among others, appears in the defense, against Adorno, of the idea of traces with regard to Baudelaire. This idea has its empirical place in "Le flâneur," and it can be corroborated by a contextuality proper to Edgar Allan Poe. [TN: Baudelaire translated many of Poe's poems for publication.] The reuse of the subject dealt with is anticipated for another section, where it will receive a dazzling clarification (Benjamin 2012:585–592, letter to Adorno, December 9, 1938).

lead to Kafka, and Kafka does not lead to it. To be sure, this is troubling for us. What views are we to adopt? To what are we to relate this text?

The author studied would be invited, rather, to introduce himself a posteriori, in the Essay, and to take on meaning in that context. Something has appeared in the writer's writings, and has attracted the attention of the critic; this element comes to occupy a place assigned to it by the interpreter.[17] We must recall that Benjamin treated Kafka's work as a whole, speaking in the mode of the usual approaches, which were most often religious; they were, in fact, applications—and Benjamin's, in spite of everything, was no different. His voice would have been his own only if it had been allowed to develop in the enclosure created in each instance by the narrative. However, Benjamin distances himself from such transpositions, in which the work channels reflection in and of itself, with its own means; for him the work is charged with translating a historical state of human society. It neither reflects nor problematizes further; it serves to attest or confirm a hypothesis of a general nature. At bottom, Benjamin passes from one terrain to the other without warning the reader and without explaining what Kafka furnished for the elaboration of the theory or, conversely, what the theory supplied to the writer's reading. Problematization, always particular and begun anew in Kafka, is scrapped. For Benjamin, it is a matter of revealing, through Kafka, the existence of a timeless experience of humankind, a truth that no one in the world could deny. In this way, universality becomes a reality; at the same time, in contrast, it de-intellectualizes very powerfully, through Benjamin's failure to consider the reflective and interrogative import of the contexts exploited.

The Composition of the Essay

The Essay is divided into four parts. The first, "Potemkin," is organized around an old story identified by Benjamin that prefigures Kafka. It presents characters at first broken down and shackled, later all-powerful, in the enclosed courtyard of a building. Via this presentation, the reader enters into a detailed accounting of the stories. The creatures are the accusing fathers; they wallow in filth and hide behind their stooges and acolytes. The laws, kept secret, go back to the time of a prehistoric world, which the young women, in their complicity, bring back to life. Family and administrations are merged. Only the onlookers are

---

[17] In Bouretz 2010, in a chapter devoted to Benjamin ("Walter Benjamin [1892–1940]: The Angel of History and the Experience of the Century," 165–233), see the section dedicated to the Essay, "Revelation in Kafka's World" (172–179): "Kafka remained for Benjamin the figure par excellence of the failure: by his refusal to answer the questions he raised ..." (178). Always failure, as if this had not been introduced by Kafka as an element of his compositions.

freed from them; this is the world of the assistants, who have not been able to break their ties, but who do have hope. With them, it is easier to return to a past that is restructured into ages of the world, the time before myth and the time after; they regain access to music, singing.

The second section, "A Childhood Photograph," also takes its impetus from a vision, the photographer's workshop. Dreams are embodied there; they lead to America and to the other (the "third") novel—which comes last only in the order of reading. This is the world of the theater, the runway of an unfettered chase, the discovery of the Chinese supremacy of gesture. Nothing is described any longer, no group; everything is in action. Kafka's stories, in their form, are to be read according to their own code, which is gestural; this is how their strangeness is explained (on this point, Benjamin is very close to interpreters such as Kraft or Brod). With theatricality, a boundary is crossed: the idea unifies the entire section. Then Benjamin pulls away: the attempt to grasp the form becomes complicated; it blossoms like a poem, which it is not, nor is it a parable. The doctrine to which it might refer does not appear. Benjamin attempts to put the problem of social organization at the center (this suits his purposes), and we are thus brought back to China (where we remain; as with Bertolt Brecht, the milieu is Chinese). The critic takes a stance, opting for enigma. The parable remains indecipherable. Kafka has done his utmost to prevent exegesis. We are still at the theater, playing out our existence, our leave-taking, our departure. In the last scene we are back at the village at the foot of the castle. We now know, thanks to the Talmud, that we are dealing with the body (is this not, however, an exegesis?).

The third section, "The Little Hunchback," begins again with a story (by Hamsun) that we approach expansively. The venue is still Brecht's China. But the decisive step concerns the interpretation that had been excluded previously; this is the doxographical moment when theology prevails. Benjamin argues and refutes. It is as if he had to make a clean slate of beliefs, to rediscover the forces of the prehistoric world that survive, secularized. Guilt reflects the state of the world, and messianic judgment (deliverance) is the object of constant deferral. Kafka has withdrawn rationally, leaving the parable with its murky appearance. Criticism then intervenes. Kafka, in gestures, has limited himself to the timeless, to the ages of the world. The primary promiscuity is forgotten, but it remains present. The theme imposes itself, with the return of swamps and the stories of women from the first section. Doesn't *The Trial* dissolve into oblivion? The doxography opens onto the god of the Jews, who remembers. Animals forget, but they rummage in their feelings and find anguish there, the sign of a lost hope. The strange figures have an ancestral model; it is an originary image, the little hunchback, in Odradek and everywhere, a master of "disfigured life";

the hunchback leads to the swamps and to all the buried knowledge. Kafka is reconnected with the broadest possible trans-ethnic experience.

The fourth section, "Sancho Panza," starts once again with a parable-story, in the spirit of Kafka's Hasidic world. Such is Benjamin's view, as he connects it with the story of life's brevity.[18] These stories have to do with time and bring us back once again to the strange beings—madmen, or students—who live out oblivion or await deliverance. He brings together situations in which extreme agitation is juxtaposed with the void of Lao-Tse. The actors from Oklahoma have been freed; the students are not free. Perhaps fragments of Kafka's existence unwittingly recall this world of gestures, the way modern man remains alienated while watching movies or listening to recordings. The experience of modernity and its negativity allows us to feel the breath of the prehistoric world, which has come all the way here, marked by the return of Bucephalus accompanying the death of the conqueror, traversing history and finding himself again in the story being told. Kraft wanted to see in this the advent of justice after the myth. Benjamin disagreed. Alexander's horse remains faithful to his mystical origin; he simply does not exercise his right. With study, one reconnects with the authority of the writing. Benjamin finally takes this step, including the tradition. We are on the threshold of justice. But tradition does not keep its promises; there remain only the books in which Sancho Panza has Don Quixote do what he, Benjamin, reads in them.

•••

Kafka did not answer the questions he had been asked; and no one asked him the questions to which the stories would have responded, the ones that the stories inspired in the first place. It is a vicious circle. The exegesis of the narrations has been hugely diversified,[19] but it has not often come close to the meaning, which was freely developed there. Benjamin cannot rid himself of the idea that Kafka, in what he describes, was referring to something other than what one supposes, something that must have been a truth close to those that directed his own historical speculations. In the end, it is theological in nature, even if it is aligned with the history of the world—looking back, in the construction

---

18   See below, p. 293.
19   See below, pp. 277–281, for the Essay; as for Kafka, there is already a brief doxographic summary in the Essay itself (Benjamin 1999d:806). Benjamin distinguished two tendencies, one natural (H. Kaiser), the other supernatural, and more often chosen (H. J. Schoeps, B. Rang, Groethuysen, W. Haas, without forgetting Brod); both tendencies miss the truth, which can be deduced from the "motifs" and which leads to the collective experience of the prehistoric. Kafka "could only describe what presented itself to him, coming from who knows where" (Benjamin 1978, 2, pt. 2:425).

of a mythical origin, as well as looking ahead, toward a utopia or a messianic deliverance. Not that he failed to situate theology, from his own standpoint; in his essay on language, for example, he wrote: "the highest mental being, as it appears in religion, rests solely on man and on the language in him."[20] For the origin, one is dealing with an inaccessible tradition, which one can replace as one sees fit. This tradition will be fragmented and more or less amorphous—and will always be something, better than nothing. It is as though the era were waiting for the space to be occupied. Benjamin asserts insistently that Kafka is aiming at a future. In fact, Kafka does not "aim" at anything of the sort. It would be more accurate to say that he does not aim, that he raises questions, instead, about what one aims at and why.

Another feature of the Essay concerns the writer. Kafka ought to be treated as a subject, with his own perspectives; for Benjamin, it is a question of a higher necessity, to which the writer is "subjected." The reference to the tale ("Märchen") in the Essay, and to popular wisdom, helps reinforce a search for authenticity. A truth deposited in the tradition comes to confirm the hypothesis advanced by historical or anthropological speculation. Benjamin notes, furthermore, that Kafka and Proust had in common the *ego* that governs their writings, an ego so transparent that everyone can assimilate it or leave it behind at will.[21] He does not see the freedom that the writing creates for itself; reflexive, it is situated outside of psychology, revealing no system and referring to psychology only while at the same time abolishing it.

Scholem's Messianism and Benjamin's

In the exchange of letters between Benjamin and Scholem, the discussion of Kafka goes back quite far, although not to the very beginning of their friendship.[22] It coincides with the first breakthrough of Kafka's work, still marginal nevertheless, in intellectual and literary consciousness in Germany.[23] Benjamin

[20] "On Language as Such and on the Language of Man" (Benjamin 1996d:67).

[21] See "Brod und Kafka" in the preliminary notes (Benjamin 1978, 2, pt. 3:1221: "There is something that Kafka and Proust have in common, and who knows whether that something is found anywhere else. It has to do with the use they make of the 'ego.'")

[22] Their friendship began in July 1915; see Scholem 1975:193. As already indicated, the first mention of Kafka in Benjamin's correspondence occurs in a letter to Gershom Scholem dated July 21, 1925 (Benjamin 2012:279–280).

[23] J. Unseld (1994) describes the situation in 1922, when Kafka was writing *The Castle*: "The German literary industry had in his experience remained closed to him; in order to break out of the anonymity that he had suffered, greater efforts would have to be expended. Kafka therefore chose a path via his closest friends" (231). In contrast, U. Steiner, along with H. Binder, recalls that in certain circles his fame was exceptional (Steiner 2010:132). The divergent appreciations depend on the critic's point of view.

constituted for himself something like a prehistory of reception, a mythical past, pushing it back in time beyond the point of plausibility—a form proper to an era of sacralization. The fact remains that the two friends shared a discovery; it left them with a very powerful impression, and they tried to integrate it, each into his own world. They were each "interpellated," no doubt separately, from the start. Interest in Kafka grew markedly after the publication of the novels. It was in the area of this common interest, around Judaism, and of their divergences, against a background of undeniable dissension, at once disguised and evaded, that the preparation of the Essay took shape, before 1934. There was an enigma to decipher. Intuition guided the two friends, united in the common search for a mediation that would orient their critique. From our standpoint, they were mistaken not to focus on the writing; presumably they were unable to do so.

But what did Scholem think? He was the first to take a stand. The stakes were considerable; the thing had to be said. In Jerusalem, he composed a poem (Benjamin too, in his correspondence, occasionally used that form[24]) addressed to God, in the finest German, fourteen stanzas, quatrains composed in the grandiloquence of a no doubt restrained faith; a Romantic tradition was transferred into the post-war Judeo-German world.[25] One might say that he was trying, a century after the fact, to oppose Heine, who had been excluded from Judea. The profession of faith is intended to be absolute. Yes, there is revelation first; yes, there is the Last Judgment at the end, and the law that prepares us for it (whether he, Scholem, a historian who is a Zionist or a Zionist who is a historian, has personally followed the law or not). Benjamin connects the data provided; he transfers them while retaining the framework.

The conflict was set off by Asja Lacis, the friend Benjamin met in Capri, and it was powerfully rekindled by Bertolt Brecht's presence at her side. Benjamin was staying with him in Skovsbostrand, Denmark, during the summer of 1934, as he was to do in later years.[26] On this occasion, he was confronted with the essential, the prerequisites, which concerned a Jewish author; Scholem insisted on reminding them (without discussion or nuance) that this author was a "Zionist" like himself and like Brod. (The latter's work is still viewed today as the business of the Israeli state, as is shown by the problems encountered on the matter of the autograph manuscripts bequeathed to the descendants of Brod's secretary.) Kafka, an attentive observer of his entourage in Prague, was of course nothing of the sort, despite his interest in the movement and in the problems that had

---

[24] See his letter to Scholem, April 8, 1939 (Benjamin 2012:600–603).

[25] The poem attached to Scholem's letter of July 9, 1934 (Benjamin 2012:445–447) is discussed by Benjamin on July 20 (448–451).

[26] He returned there in 1936 and 1938.

given rise to it, whatever may have been said about him.[27] He was neither that nor anything else, or else he was everything all together; nor was he a denier of any outcome whatsoever. Rather, everything remained dependent on a reflective dialectic that expressed itself in its own structures. The transformation that takes place in his stories develops the logic appropriate to the narrative in each case; the facts are put to the test, analyzed in a construction.

Kafka was not an assimilated Jew, unlike others in the milieu in which he lived in Prague. His friends, close or distant, were for the most part Jews. He consistently followed the ups and downs produced by their internal divergences and their social difficulties, which increased after the fall of the Austro-Hungarian monarchy.[28] One would thus have to say that he wrote his work as a Jew, analyzing his own experience. In no case can one say that the work was conceived by him as testimony in favor of Judaism or of some religious tradition. His words presuppose all possible belongings. He claims none; on the contrary, he excludes them.

Written far from religious conflicts and commitments, the chapter Bernard Lahire devotes to the cultural situation of the period integrates Kafka into the German-speaking milieu, without neglecting the very virulent ancient and recent anti-Semitism on the Czech side as well as on the German side.[29] The excerpts from the letters addressed to Milena, who was not Jewish, reveal complete lucidity about the precarious status of an "Occidental Jew" and Kafka's interest in the minorities that surround him, each group with its own language: the increasingly numerous Czechs, the Jews of Eastern Europe, and the prevalence of Yiddish mean that Hebrew itself and Zionism can be situated in a single vast sphere of distancings, which ultimately accentuates the contradiction of his own status as a Jew.

When Kafka's unpublished writings were presented on the radio in 1931, Benjamin consulted his friend Scholem. In Jerusalem, the latter had gone ahead and made his own position clear. He made a breakthrough that shed light on an entire state of mind and a prejudice. Kafka's place was not within the continuity of German literature; he belonged to Judaism (Scholem did not anticipate

---

[27] On Judaism in the intellectual milieu in Prague, see Pulliero 2005:151–175. In the early part of the century, this was "a form of ideological reappropriation of a lost identity, following upon assimilation" (the formula is borrowed from Giulio Baioni [1984:3]). Kafka witnessed the debates in which "Occidentals" were opposed to "Zionist trends"; see Pulliero 2005:238 and 275–277 (notes), where Kafka's reservations about Martin Buber are expressed. Kafka did not belong to any of the circles, but he followed the debates closely.

[28] In *Franz Kafka: Éléments pour une théorie de la création littéraire*, B. Lahire cites reflections from Kafka's diaries that call into question the existence of God (2010:126). This too is "noted" and thus situated in a sphere that is all the more essential, in that it remains structurally reflexive.

[29] See Lahire 2010:109–134, "Prague 1880–1924."

the writer's universal success). He had to be reconnected to the Bible, to Job, and to the theme of the possibility of God's judgment (*Gottesurteil*): "I consider that that is the sole object of Kafka's production"[30]). He spoke out aggressively against Benjamin and against Brecht before him. Kafka's language, his prose, becomes clear only in the canonical light of the Last Judgment. "The world is expressed [in Kafka] in a language in which no redemption can be anticipated."[31] The Jewish reader is opposing the Christian theologians.

Scholem connected his Zionism to the Jewish mysticism he was studying, and this allowed him to distance himself from other tendencies. He was working to validate his position, which, accredited by a religious anchoring, allowed him to play the whole game of cultural relations on an international level, as a theologian. Thus he attended meetings organized by C. G. Jung in Ascona, Switzerland. He was his own minister of Jewish affairs. One can understand, then, that he wrote the following to Benjamin: "I assume that you will dedicate the first volume of your collected critical reflections to the memory of [Friedrich] Gundolf" (a Jewish Germanist, a disciple of Stefan George, who had just died).[32] A former sycophant of George's movement, he had been excluded from the circle—and thus perhaps even restored to his origins. He was in any case closer to Scholem's ideas, and he was not a Marxist.

Facing a flat rejection, in an intense exchange of letters in 1934, Benjamin negotiated. He designated the stanzas in Scholem's poem to which he could subscribe. At bottom, he gave in, but with the aim of constructing his own response on that basis. Within the framework adopted, he sought a vision compatible with Marxism. This world would be founded on a form of semi-secular belief that one ought not to be able to reject, and in which he could include Kafka. Thus the vision remained largely theological. Benjamin's position was dual: he situated himself within his own domain, when he took his distance from the usual or "official" forms of theology, where Brod could be found, before Scholem, and before Robert Weltsche, the editor of the German-language Zionist magazine that was still published in Nazi Germany. But he was just as careful to distance himself from an aesthetic or artistic reading; such a reading would have had less import for the Marxists. He had to use force (and artifice) to preserve the framework of what he was fighting; he noted that his

---

[30] Cf. Scholem's letter to Benjamin of August 1, 1931, reproduced with ample commentary in Scholem 1981:169–174.

[31] The famous theological declaration, as radical as possible, in Scholem's August 1931 letter to Benjamin is also important for the description of the status of Zionism. Kafka is invoked in order to contradict the promise made to Christians, a promise that for Scholem included the Marxist utopia.

[32] Scholem 1981:170 (the same letter). On March 7, Benjamin had written to Max Rychner that he had "little to do ... with the monuments erected by a Gundolf or a Bertram" (Benjamin 2012:371).

essay had "its own broad—although admittedly shrouded—theological side."[33] He gave up the traditional religious framework, which was always both present and absent, but he acknowledged that the author he was discussing was not free either to invent or to compromise. His lot was to reproduce a deformed state of human consciousness, which was expressed in a world "of images."[34] Thus the literary or poetic character of Kafka's narratives is shattered. The stories are marked by the pursuit of and search for an absent doctrine, which they flee and never articulate—hence the reduction to hope or anguish. Uwe Steiner thinks that Brod's "grace" has been transferred to that absence of salvation. Expiation has no function other than a return to guilt, which is only manifested by flight into forgetting.[35] We witness, moreover, a veritable suppression of the creative agency, of the subject behind the creation. Benjamin anchors this claim in a para-aesthetic postulate, more philosophical or cultural than religious: these are religious texts (as is acknowledged), but without religion; they demand, in this case, through their form and their extreme primitivism, to be attributed to an original state of society.

On this basis, an agreement was reached between Jerusalem and Paris, despite positions that were, in fact, irreconcilable; after all, they were Jews, both of them—or all three of them: the author of the Essay, the interlocutor, historian of the Jewish religion and guardian of the tradition, and the object of their interrogation, who had expressed himself with great lucidity. They were living under Hitler, Year Two. Where could they publish, and how? Scholem, the intransigent friend, had Zionist relations, which were necessary, under the current regime, in the Jewish milieu. Benjamin yielded. He adapted a second time; the negotiations were more concrete. The Essay would appear, but only in excerpts,[36] in the journal published by Robert Weltsch, who was from Prague, as was Kafka's friend Felix Weltsch.[37] But publication was also controlled by

---

[33] Letter to Scholem, July 20, 1934 (Benjamin 2012:448).

[34] In the same letter, he opposes suspense in Kafka to the theological responses. From his own reading, Benjamin retains the scenic and gestural elements, which refer to the structure of a state of the world in which questions are set aside (*weggehoben*).

[35] The violence Benjamin exercises on his object, preferring the theological interpretation of Willy Haas, then that of Scholem, even as he readapts them, remains implicit in Steiner's presentation (2010:133).

[36] "Franz Kafka: Eine Würdigung," *Jüdische Rundschau* 39, nos. 102/103 and 104 (December 1934), including the sections "Potemkin" and "Das bucklichte Männlein" ("The Little Hunchback"); cf. Tiedemann 1965:170.

[37] The Jewish encyclopedia (*Jüdisches Lexikon*, Herltz and Kirschner 1927) informs us that Robert "supported a new orientation of Zionism (defended by Martin Buber in *A Land and Two Peoples* [Buber 1983]) taking into account the Arab demands in Palestine. The project of a binational state has been violently contested but has also exercised great influence." Robert Weltsch published *Rundschau* starting in 1919.

agents of the Nazi party, which imposed its orders. The *Jüdische Rundschau* was still tolerated, as long as this organ addressed a Jewish public exclusively, and not Germany. Thus Benjamin "Judaized" his text by adding some ten allusions— not too many!—without renouncing universalization. References and developments were dispersed throughout the texture of the Essay for the readers of the journal and the Nazi censors. The paradox of convergence is only apparent. One was under orders to be Jewish, in order to be excluded.

Benjamin adapted his language to this contemporary reality, ten years after Kafka's death. He was also humoring Max Brod, at the time. Scholem defended Brod from his own standpoint, approving, against his detractors, the publication of Kafka's posthumous works. They must not be destroyed; they indeed belong to "literature," but must be treated as religious documentation. Benjamin can thus defend them, as the motivation is sacred. Brod expressed himself in similar terms. By insisting on Kafka's "demoniacal" nature in his biography, Brod could be said to have distinguished himself from Kafka's other friends during the writer's lifetime.[38] His perception of his classmate was singular, in Prague; his devotion was by no means common. Long before the edition of the posthumous works, which represented by far the bulk of Kafka's production, there had indeed been a question, on the part of the friend, of "recognition" in the most rigorous sense. The perception and the adherence were not simply positive; they were absolute. Others viewed this difference as alienation.

That moment, in Prague, took on historical value; its exceptional character was thought to be linked to a religious affiliation. Yet this affiliation is hard to defend. Was it in harmony with the great fresco of matriarchal promiscuity that Benjamin was constructing? It was going to form the background for the Essay and make it possible to transfer the current social expectation onto the ancient history of the human race. Only disparate elements were being considered in Kafka; they were integrated by Benjamin into a whole. These elements remained disconcerting for later interpreters, and even for recent ones. The two orientations, religion and history, are not always mutually exclusive. The examples are chosen from among hundreds, given the considerable influence that has been exerted by the Essay. Everything is mixed together, through the necessity of the "schema" that is adopted each time, whatever it may be. Every stop

---

[38] In the preparatory notes (*GS* II, 3:1220), Benjamin speculates that "perhaps Kafka looked at Brod and his deep Jewish philosophemes the way Sancho Panza looked at Don Quixote." See Scholem's letter to Kraft on this subject (February 27, 1929): "Authoritative Kafka experts (such as Hugo Bergmann) also assure me that Brod's description of Kafka in his last book hits the mark, all the way down to the demonic details. It must be true, given the fact that Kafka's friends had until the end a deep and abiding mistrust of Brod" (Scholem 2002:168). Scholem chose his side.

is articulated, either on the object of a revelation or else on language and the virtues of Benjamin's discourse, but always under an arbitrary constraint.

Kafka's Absence from the History of Criticism

Hannah Arendt summarizes or virtually anticipates the critical treatment of the relation between Kafka and Benjamin by erasing all differences. The theme of failure is central for her, too; she establishes an identity between them. In her reflections on Benjamin, she writes that he had not needed to read Kafka in order to think the way Kafka did. The last sentence of his essay "Goethe's Elective Affinities" could have been formulated by Kafka.[39] She devotes her attention to lucidity and experience, focusing much less on art.[40]

Numerous studies have been devoted to that essay. Sigrid Weigel, in her contribution to the *Benjamin-Handbuch*, includes a list.[41] The viewpoints and interests diverge, but no study has concentrated on the reading and its deficiencies. It is as though the question did not arise, as though the author's work indeed corresponded to what the critics discuss. The almost exclusive focus has thus remained on Benjamin and his relation to the work, and the critics have by and large remained in Benjamin's world, with the evolution that it had undergone. This viewpoint is illustrated perfectly in a well-documented article by Hans Mayer, who establishes the chronology with supreme confidence and knows how to clear up the story of what he calls the intellectual "constellations" in which Benjamin gradually found himself.[42] This is to leave the text behind, to the benefit of a viewpoint borrowed from a history of ideas, a *Geistesgeschichte*—a history that is ideally represented by the interests and readings of a universal author. What Benjamin had projected in the form of a system could also be undone in such a way as to isolate particular aspects, such as the

---

[39] "Only for the sake of the hopeless ones have we been given hope" (Benjamin 1996c:356; see Arendt 1968:170.)

[40] Arendt 1968, 183–187.

[41] "Zu Franz Kafka," in Küpper 2006:543–557. (I have retained here, somewhat at random, Jennings, Mayer, Palmer, and Weidner.) The article Weigel wrote for the *Handbuch* was included as a chapter in her monograph on Benjamin (2013:130–163) under the title "Jewish Thinking in a World Without God: Benjamin's Reading of Kafka as a Critique of Christian and Jewish Theologoumena" (I refer here to the latter edition).

[42] Mayer 1988:185–209. The article is dedicated to Gershom Scholem.

"tradition,"[43] or the "image,"[44] or the Benjaminian "aura."[45] The author Benjamin represents literary theory as such; he embodies it, and this is the source of his success. There is thus no obstacle to establishing various connections with the new problematics. Derridean deconstruction might find a distant prefiguration there.[46] Benjamin was an essence, a whole, a particular and astonishing object. Wolfgang Matz, in his review of Jean-Michel Palmier's unfinished biography of Benjamin,[47] situates the book by stating that it "follows the history of the life and the work in chronological order."[48] This is essential: "By this decision alone, Palmier avoids seeing Benjamin solely from the perspective of his theoretical interest. The staggering parallelism of the metaphysician and the critic, of the autobiography and the political writings, leads to doing justice to all these aspects in a historical rather than a systematic presentation"[49] (this leaves the floor to Scholem, Theodor Adorno, Max Horkheimer, Brecht, Ernst Bloch, or Hannah Arendt). For my part, I have been led to include this approach, in order to highlight the distances and the divergences.

Bruno Tackels' recent monograph on Benjamin[50] cannot deal with the matter in the end, because the author construes Kafka's "frightening logic" as a positive doctrine. Benjamin is congratulated for having been able to identify this logic and place it at the center of his reading: the son is accused "of the simple fact of having ... been a witness to the world of the fathers, which was collapsing" (according to Tackels' reading of "The Judgment"). Tackels follows the speculative construction of the Essay and makes no effort to figure out how to read and decipher Kafka. The content of the work will be that of Benjamin's interpretation, according to the "reading matrix" developed with regard to

---

43 Alter 1991; the text consists of lectures given at Hebrew Union College in Cincinnati in 1990); Weidner 2000:234–249. (See p. 246: "Kafka is the author of a modernity that is not a loss of values, but marks the crisis in a form of tradition, oscillating between extinction and transformation." We are far from a reading, here.)

44 See Weigel 2013, especially Chap. 6, in particular the section titled "From the Midst of the Image World" (140–144), and the foreword: "with images [poetic language] concerns the survival of the cultic, sacred, and magical meanings" (xxiv). This is Benjamin's Kafka.

45 See Jennings 1988. Kafka is, with Baudelaire, the only writer whose aura is shown "*in the process of its decay*"; the greatness of his work lies in its antitheses between the mystical tradition and the shock of its destruction, according to Jennings (207–208).

46 One can cite Deuring 1994 and Palmer 1999. Kafka's texts are not simply self-referential. They refer to a previous glance at what is buried in the depths; according to Palmer, this "applies to the work of Benjamin and Derrida. It is no doubt true for Kafka's works as well, but not in as certain a fashion" (1999:48).

47 Palmier 2006. The author died in 1998.

48 Matz 2010, a review of the 2009 German translation.

49 Matz 2010.

50 Tackels 2009; see the appendix devoted to the Essay, 727–737.

Oklahoma in *Amerika*. The distinctive feature of the theatre, which one discovers here, is that actions can be dissolved in a world of gestures.[51]

The Matriarchy

The Essay, as in a musical composition, distributes the movements of a dominant motif with a play of repetitions that creates a unifying agency. Thematically, the prehistoric world holds everything together; it becomes better known, however, or better identified, toward the end, where the accent falls more strongly on human sexuality, which Benjamin associated above all with scenes from novels. He resituates these in a non-hierarchical social organization, legitimized by the association with Johann Jakob Bachofen, and the resonances, more political than religious, that reference to Bachofen elicited at the time. The latter's work on matriarchy, extensive excerpts of which had been published with an introduction by Alfred Bäumler in 1926, had considerable success in diverse if not conflicting milieus. For a Marxist, Bachofen offered the model of a classless society. In 1926, Benjamin received Carl Albrecht Bernoulli's massive tome on Bachofen;[52] he told Scholem that the book had reached him as in a fairy tale (*märchenhafter Weise*). He convinced himself that "a confrontation with Bachofen and Klages [was] perhaps unavoidable," even though at bottom he had to recognize that "this can be strictly conducted only from the perspective of Jewish theology"—which the advocates of promiscuity in Munich must have feared, or rather abhorred.[53] They did not suspect that redemption could have such a past, in disorder and denial. The subject was in the air. In April 1933, Adorno, for his part, was preparing a study on Bachofen and Klages. The two names were associated, and the study was intended to broaden the horizon of mythic thought, which Adorno had circumscribed in his recent book on Kierkegaard. In the end, Adorno did not complete the new project.[54]

A year later, Benjamin had the occasion to renew his interest in Bachofen's work in the context of a presentation of the Basel historian's work, which was intended for the *Nouvelle Revue Française* but ultimately remained unpublished.[55] He wrote to Scholem from Denmark on July 20, 1934: "I believe I wrote you

---

[51] Tackels 2009:730.

[52] Bernoulli 1924.

[53] Benjamin 2102:288 (letter to Scholem, January 14, 1926). Benjamin wrote as though he were in the situation of his addressee (who had been in Jerusalem for three years by then). He added that the "European" Institute of the University of Jerusalem should procure a copy of Bernoulli's book.

[54] See Adorno 2007:305, 307.

[55] See "Johann Jakob Bachofen," Benjamin 2002. According to a note by Scholem, the article was rejected (Benjamin and Scholem 1980, no. 55 [July 19, 1934]:151–153).

that I began working on an essay on Bachofen ... . This means that for the first time I shall get to read him myself; up to now I have always relied on Bernoulli and Klages."[56] Scholem reacted vigorously to the way Bachofen was used in the Essay.[57] His insistence is striking. He invokes anthropology and law against theology. In *Walter Benjamin: The Story of a Friendship*, Scholem deduced the young Benjamin's interest in myth: "Benjamin must have been more familiar around this time [1916] with the writings of Johann Jakob Bachofen and also must have read the works of the ethnologist Karl Theodor Preuss"[58]; Benjamin was trying "to formulate the laws governing the world of pre-mythical spectral phenomena." He distinguished between two historical ages of the spectral and the demonic that preceded the age of revelation, or messianism.[59] Here we have an "origin" of Benjamin's speculation. In his work, the phase of a pre-mythical world, in the process of formation, can be related to the category of ambiguity, imposed by fate, illustrated in the essay on Goethe's *Elective Affinities*, and in "Fate and Character."[60]

The themes alternate and overlap. One might suppose that with "the Oklahoma theater," an excerpt from the novel *Amerika: The Missing Person*, and with his focus on theatricality as such and especially on gestures, to which he attributes a central function in his evocation of this past, Benjamin would come closer and closer to a study of Kafka's highly idiosyncratic "style." This is not at all the case: these elements are again interpreted as ritual expressions, making it possible to go back to that "prehistoric world" or "before-world" (*Vorwelt*); they are related to that constraining and, as it were, archaeologically "natural" background. The reading pulls away from the writer's models; it rises up from the depths, rediscovered and excavated from the basement of Kafka's imaginary. The procedure could be described as appropriation. Kafka was unable to prevent readers from speaking about things he was not speaking about.

Adorno opposed the use Benjamin made of this theory, first in his critique of the Essay,[61] then in his discussion, written in the United States, of Benjamin's presentation of *Passages* at the Institute for Social Research in New York (which had migrated from Frankfurt), and then elsewhere;[62] Adorno denounced a

---

[56] Benjamin 2012:450; also 452 (late July 1934?) and 479 (February 19, 1935).The *Nouvelle Revue Française* passed the text on to the publishing house Mercure de France, where Benjamin imagined it buried in a pile (Benjamin 2012:481, May 20, 1935).

[57] Benjamin and Scholem 1989:126–127 (letter of July 17, 1934).

[58] See Scholem 1981:1.

[59] Scholem 1981:61.

[60] See Steiner 2010:135; for "Fate and Character," see Benjamin 1996b:201–206.

[61] Adorno and Benjamin 1999:66–73.

[62] Adorno and Benjamin 1999:104–114, letter of August 2-4, 1935: "the basic epistemological character of Kafka is to be identified, particularly in Odradek, as a commodity that has survived to no

"mythologizing and archaizing tendency" in Benjamin's draft, recalling the reactionary political positions of thinkers like Ludwig Klages in Munich or Carl Gustav Jung in Zurich.[63] A methodical reflection on this subject has not seen the light of day; at least, Benjamin did not write or develop one. Later on, in 1937, when he was writing his study of Baudelaire's poetry, he seems to have made Adorno's objections his own.[64]

Divine Virtuality

What makes Kafka speak, for Benjamin, is what he himself, Benjamin, speaks about. The reflective and analytic power of the original projections ought to have radically proscribed the procedure in his case. Every experimental dimension remains intimately tied to an act of invention. At the point where the narrative is the darkest and most tortured, the reader will still be looking for a way out. The stage is set; it bursts forth and *causes itself to be seen,* to be contemplated, as it were, in its necessary arbitrariness. The constraints are unexpected, unbelievable; they are always of a self-evident necessity because the reader remains within the singularity that is being constructed. It is not that Kafka's universe is not profoundly literary. But Benjamin freely and deliberately integrates all the literary or cultural associations possible, whether his public is familiar with them, ignorant of them, or in the process of learning them (the list of evocations is impressive). He not only totalizes the cases that he can usefully gather, in relation to his own project, but he also universalizes the object of his study, with all his brilliance as an essayist, through a multitude of associations and allusions, which are, in fact, charged with bringing outside confirmation to the interpretations imposed on the text. The Essay is not limited to one particular perspective. Benjamin drafts an aphorism-sentence that is intended to situate "Kafka's work": "the magnetic field between Thora and Tao." It is universal (*west-östlich*); the synthesis belongs to the horizon of expectations of the reader, toward whom the critic is opening up an at once familiar and disorienting path.

---

purpose" (108). On June 19, 1938, Benjamin mentions his new activities on the subject of Kafka and on Brod's biography; he has "returned with great interest" to Adorno's letter of December 17, 1934 in connection with his own notes on Kafka, "which take a different point of departure from my earlier essay" (260); on February 23, 1939, he discusses the comic and terrifying "type" in Balzac that was realized in Kafka's work (310–311).

63 Letter of August 2–4, 1935 (Adorno and Benjamin 1999:110). "The disenchantment of the dialectical image [by the Golden Age] leads directly to purely mystical thinking, and, then Klages appears as a danger, just as Jung did before": Adorno and Benjamin 1999:107; the two had been juxtaposed earlier in relation to collective consciousness).

64 Benjamin to Scholem (Benjamin 2012:540): "it is my desire to safeguard certain [methodological] foundations of *Paris Arcades* by waging an onslaught on the doctrines of Jung, especially those concerning archaic images and the collective unconscious." He was in full retreat.

In a 1921 article, Max Brod reported on a conversation he had had with Kafka on the decline of the contemporary world.[65] "'We are nihilistic thoughts,' Kafka said, 'suicidal thoughts, that come into God's head.'" This was a theme. Brod, the interlocutor, evoked the maleficent demiurge of gnosis. "No," said Kafka, "I believe we are not such a radical relapse of God's, only one of his bad moods. He had a bad day." Brod responded "Then there is hope outside this manifestation of the world that we know." Kafka replied, smiling: "Oh, plenty of hope—for God—no end of hope—only not for us." He must have been thinking of the virtualities of the *plérōma*, the void, as if it were close at hand. Kafka's friend Brod viewed this brief dialogue as an exceptional and characteristic piece (he cites it again as such in his *Biography*).[66]

Kafka in no way evokes the ambiguous creatures of the Essay. Benjamin did not invoke the hope that would be denied us in God's pure surroundings, endowed with virtualities entirely different from our own (Brod was specific: outside of the state of "this world, whose form we know"). He recognized in that "other world" a stage in the evolution of this one; but if it is different from ours, it is because the other world is that of the "assistants," who have left the family and the father's authority and are the repository of hope. The connection is not apposite.[67] Benjamin found in it an allusion to the primitive promiscuity that obsessed him. Still, one cannot see that prehistoric world according to Kafka as a divine presence in our own world. Benjamin does not do so, even if he does misinterpret the reference in the brief exchange recalled here. He transfers the speculative confrontation between God and the world to a hypothetical substratum (in the literal sense) in history.

In the chapter of her book on Benjamin titled "L'oubli et le souvenir" (Forgetting and Remembering),[68] Patricia Lavelle follows a thread that she sees as a key element in the entire construction of the Essay: memory succeeds in establishing a tension between the present and an allegorical break in the past. She then situates Benjamin's reading of Kafka within this opposition. The oblivion in which certain creatures live in Kafka's tales and novels, as read by Benjamin, is based on a social experience proper to the contemporary period, which itself calls for the analysis of a veritable alienation; moreover, this first step cannot be understood correctly unless one sees it as including the survival of a primitive state that arose in the course of human history prior to the era of rational judgment. In Lavelle's interpretation, that state was perpetuated in

---

[65] Brod 1921:1213; cited in the Essay, Benjamin 1999d:798.

[66] Brod 1960:75.

[67] "These words provide a bridge to those extremely strange figures in Kafka, the only ones who have escaped from the family circle and for whom there may be hope" (Benjamin 1999d:798).

[68] Lavelle 2008:244-261.

another form, subservient to the established powers, and it encompassed the moments of a messianic revolt. Benjamin could have read Kafka in the light of this evolution. The stratifications belong to a projection proper to Benjamin, adapted to his Marxist positions. He first anchors them in a look toward the past, treated as the locus of a primitive state of nature. The counterpart of salvation is reserved for the future, deferred to the end of time, and concomitant with a withdrawal. This was a foundation that could be seen as a consolidation of the strangeness of Kafka's singular work and an objectivization of his instructions. But Benjamin also turns away from this construct, reaffirming a dialectical structure that Adorno deemed inadequate.

There is no need to leave the world and its evolution behind. Benjamin situated this evolution in the context of a dialectical and "scientific" anthropological quest that was to substitute for a philosophy of history. Lavelle, returning to the dialogue with Brod, which Benjamin cites in the essay, limits herself to theological speculation, which one finds in Kafka but not in Benjamin. She juxtaposes other texts—for example, "Imagination," a fragment written around 1920–1921,[69] *Berlin Childhood*,[70] or "On the Mimetic Faculty"[71]—from which she retains a gnostic perspective, and she interprets the prehistoric world as an extra-worldly stage. She associates "female supremacy" with a state that avoids the "self-negation" of God in the world of the fall,[72] "the feminine element of the spirit." This association is problematic. The primitive matriarchy of humans cannot be conflated with the reign of "Sophia," which is described by Hans Jonas, a historian of the Gnostic doctrines, as a stage extrapolated by antithesis to the demiurgic act reserved for the masculine element at the heart of a divine cleavage.[73] These are separate matters: if the one, the theological theme, is evoked in Kafka's brief dialogue, the other, which predominates in the Essay, is anthropological in nature, however great the speculative component may be. At the end of the dialogue cited, Benjamin retains the note of hope: "These words provide a bridge to those extremely strange figures in Kafka ... for whom there may be hope," outside the family.

Hope, for Benjamin, had been transmitted thanks to these ambiguous, nebulous creatures that stand out against a background; he identifies them with their contemporary descendants, acolytes, or assistants, who play significant roles in Kafka's novels.[74] For them, hope exists. Beyond the dialectic as it is

---

[69] Benjamin 1996a:280–282.

[70] Benjamin 2006.

[71] Benjamin 1999c.

[72] Lavelle 2008:249.

[73] Jonas 2001.

[74] See the central announcement in the early pages of the Essay: "These assistants belong to a group of figures which recurs throughout Kafka's work" (Benjamin 1999d:798). Everything will

sketched in the exchange between Kafka and Brod, with these beings Benjamin reintroduces a utopia—no doubt more Marxist in character—that recalls the indeterminate and salutary production of an immemorial past. The contemporary messengers, survivors or others nostalgic for lost worlds, bear in themselves the contradiction of another time, a more indecisive age that they take on. The author explains: "To speak of any order or hierarchy is impossible here. Even the world of myth of which we think in this context is incomparably younger than Kafka's world [that of the intra-worldly "prehistoric world"], which has been promised redemption by the myth."[75] The transition toward the later world of rational organizations prefigures the disappearance of these hybrid beings, these oppositional existences. The archaic world of strange creatures, privileged or ungraspable, can be restored. Thus Kafka must have carried nostalgia for the bygone creatures in his heart of hearts. He is not presumed to have sought to describe how non-doing remained inherent in doing. The duality, however regenerative it may have been, was transferred onto the objectivity of a speculative intuition. The reference to the enigmatic creatures bears upon an anterior, primary, historical, and pre-historical non-distinction.

There are two approaches—as if the creatures aspired to transmission and it were denied them: "What may be discerned, more tenderly subdued, in the activities of these messengers is the law that reigns, in an oppressive and gloomy way, over this whole group of beings. None has a firm place in the world, or firm, inalienable outlines. There is not one that is not either rising or falling,"[76] and so on. This flight of lyricism is worthy of an epic; it inspires Benjamin's narrative and demonstrative inventions.

In the collection of notes and aphorisms titled "He" ("Er"), Kafka says that he wondered one day what wish he could formulate on the subject of his own life.[77] He was implicitly referring—a singular occurrence—to his existence as a writer. Benjamin makes such a reference in the Essay as well.[78] The description (often studied) is fundamental and, in a sense, unsurpassable. It was a matter of formulating a vow that could be maintained all one's life, in life's ups and downs (*Fallen und Steigen*). During one's own lifetime, one had to be in a position

---

be taken up again near the end, according to a musical principle of composition. In the end, with hindsight, "they have not yet been completely released from the womb of nature," since "it is for them and their kind, the unfinished and the hapless, that there is hope" (798–799), transferred from an entirely different "prehistoric world."

[75] Benjamin 1999d:799.

[76] Benjamin 1999d:799.

[77] Kafka 1970:153–161. The selection of major tales collected by Martin Walser was published as *Beim Bau der chinesischen Mauer* in the *Bibliothek Suhrkamp* in 1970; it was initially supposed to be titled *Er*.

[78] Benjamin 1999d:808. See also the reference to "Nachweise" in Benjamin 1978, 2, pt. 3:1275.

to recognize one's existence as a void, a dream, a suspension. Kafka explains: it is not as if one were declaring that the fabrication of an object were nothing, or that, once abolished, the object would be a void. No, the two orders coexist, and govern one another. Benjamin rediscovers the archaic gestures that, as he sees it, illustrate the inability of the student-scribes to listen to a dictation and follow its rhythm. They have to approach the master before they write, for every sentence. This is not exactly the case, or, if it is, it is only in a derivative manner. Others have been better readers of Kafka.[79]

Kafka's "Testament" demanded that his writings be destroyed; this was interpreted by Benjamin as evidence of inadequacy.[80] In this light, the essential feature of Kafka's epic story would consist in constant deferral, as in *The Thousand and One Nights*, based on an incomprehensibility that makes the text nebulous. This is the explanation ("the gesture that he did not understand") of the retreat that Benjamin found again in the terms of Kafka's will, demanding the destruction of his writings. Benjamin saw this gesture as an expression of the writer's dissatisfaction: Kafka had not succeeded and had to recognize that he himself belonged to the human category he had described, condemned to failure. This is perhaps the key statement in the entire essay: "He did fail in his grandiose attempt to convert poetry into teachings, to turn it into a parable and restore to it that stability and unpretentiousness which, in the face of reason, seemed to him the only appropriate thing for it."[81] If his critics were right—if he meant failure to be paramount, and the interpretation to remain open—he would have had to have had a theoretical ambition. This was to attribute to Kafka an ambition that he did not have. Perhaps Kafka went further by including negativity, introducing it systematically in his writings as a counterpoint that is necessarily associated with existence.

In 1928, in a newspaper article countering an attack, Benjamin defended Brod's decision to publish Kafka's works, invoking the friendship between the two poets. He began with the idea that the interdiction could be explained by the unfinished state of the works, without the intention of keeping the content secret. Kafka must have said to himself: "I have had once again to relegate what is done to the benefit of what has not been done," but he must have known as well that his friend would save the work and take responsibility for the decision

---

[79] Paul Celan, "Sprich auch du" ("Speak—You Too"), Celan 2000 [hereafter *GW*] 1:135. Paul Celan, "Sprich—/ Doch schneide das Nein nicht vom Ja" ("Speak— / But don't split off No from Yes" [Celan 2001:77]). It is the meaning and the shadow of non-being. See also the poem "Stille!" ("Silence!"), in *Mohn und Gedächtnis* (Poppy and Memory), *GW* 1:75.

[80] See Benjamin 1999d:804.

[81] Benjamin 1999d:808.

in his stead.[82] The secret was theological and buried in the work, "which on the outside looks unostentatious, simple and sober." He was already pointing to the core—his own "interpretation."

The Double Separation of Ulysses and the Sirens

If, in Kafka's "Silence of the Sirens,"[83] the sirens do not sing, it is because they are showing Ulysses that they have understood his resolution and the stratagem he has invented so as to hear them. They evade him by choosing a different direction; his countering move is neither unknown nor forbidden to them. Ulysses has attuned himself to the music he wills to hear, in the intimacy of his distant vantage point. Thus he is unable to perceive the absence of the singers; he is as if imprisoned by his own power. The means he has adopted for listening, while they are not singing, seduce the women in return. The weapon of their silence glides over him. As Ulysses is persuaded of the effectiveness of his precautions, however puerile they may be, he believes he is hearing the Sirens sing. His conviction wins the day, it prepares the reversal: the seduction against which he is protecting himself disappears. The sirens no longer seduce; they are fascinated in their turn by the effect of their seduction, their reflection in Ulysses' eyes. Even as he protects himself from them, to the extent of making them disappear, he makes them live. It is at this point that their meeting takes place, at the core of a tension, in an antithesis. They do not sing; as for him, he *believes* he hears them. The conclusion is poignant: "If the Sirens had possessed consciousness, they would have been annihilated at that moment. But they remained as they had been; all that had happened was that Ulysses had escaped them."[84] Absence triumphs twice, once on each side.

Kafka exhausts the analysis of the possible interpretations of his story. A codicil is attached to the draft, mentioning that, according to another interpretation, a more subtle or more radical one, the crafty Ulysses might not have locked himself into this illusory stratagem. He knew perfectly well that the sirens were not singing, but he set about uselessly, in the void, producing a fiction. He equipped himself with a defense that under normal circumstances would have been effective. The story is then paralleled by a second interpretation, resting

---

[82] "Kavaliersmoral," Benjamin 1978, 4, pt.1:466–498. In a letter to Robert Weltsch, Benjamin invokes this intervention in favor of Brod, necessarily singling out his own reading of the work (Benjamin 2012:442).

[83] Franz Kafka, "The Silence of the Sirens" (1931), in Kafka 1971:430–432. This short story was included in the 1931 collection, *Beim Bau der Chinesischen Mauer* (*The Great Wall of China*, 1970), where Benjamin read it. Later (in 1953), Benjamin had to refer to the second posthumous collection, *Wedding Preparations in the Country, and Other Stories* (*Hochzeitsvorbereitungen*; see Kafka 1979).

[84] Kafka 1971:432.

on the first, at a higher degree of consciousness. Absence is made even more present.[85] The real and the unreal are face to face.

In the logic of his own construction, Benjamin interprets the story as a triumph over the powers of the myth. For him, the Sirens defend themselves with their silence, but Ulysses was able, marvelously, to escape his destiny by playing the game of fiction, the supreme ruse.[86] This is because the philosopher remains faithful to his own speculative schema, applied to evolution in the history of humankind. He classifies and pigeonholes. Ulysses plays the role of an agent of history; he resists the myth, which is embodied as such, as a state of the consciousness of humanity, represented by those exemplary singers, the seductresses. Through the angle of music, Benjamin manages to slice history in two. The Sirens are the myth, which Ulysses transcends; but music goes back further, bringing support inherited from a mediating world represented by the tribe of assistants—so Kafka-like.[87] He has no concern either for the construction of the narrative or for its logic. However, more than elsewhere, he is attentive to Kafka's words, his well-wrought expressions. The triumph over the Sirens finds an objective correlate in history in the symbolic surpassing that Benjamin extrapolates from the story. For him, it represents the advent of another age, characterized by the form of the *tale*. Ulysses' strategy was able to break down the violence of the mythic powers. Now freedom of invention was available to the intellect in the story told by Homer, before Kafka. Homer does not reproduce a "myth," and the episode of the Sirens does not contribute any change; he is composing a story. The myth as such shines in the distance, as it were, under the rewritten story. If one were to follow Benjamin, one would conclude that Kafka before him, as a historian, transformed the world of the *Odyssey* and made the hero of the epic a transitory and intermediate figure, representative of a new age of humanity—the third age, post-mythical. This is an extrapolation. In place of a reading or an interpretation, a desire proper to the genre of the essay asserts itself, a desire for a historical projection.

---

85   In a chapter titled "Ulysse chez Kafka," Mosès (2006) studied this text along with others on the basis of formal analyses and codified schemas of literary composition (he refers frequently to Bakhtin). Form is substituted for an exploration of the content. Mosès proceeds at the expense of a study of the writing and the freedom of invention that asserts itself in that writing, beyond predictable limits. The specific organization of the text is discovered much more in the reflection imposed on the reader and in the decoding provoked by the degree of enigmatization.

86   See Benjamin 1999d.

87   Benjamin 1999d.

The Reception of the Essay (1934)

The framework of the elements saved from early oblivion allowed Benjamin, and readers sensitive to his virtuosity, to understand the strangeness of Kafka's plots and their unsettling outcomes. If Kafka's entire work is taken as a unified whole, and if one sees it as the expression of a universal experience situated in a particular stage of history, it offers the advantage of being applicable, like Freud's work, to the destiny of the human soul. Kafka is transformed: he becomes the hero of the forgetting of a memory, and of a memory of forgetting, a witness to what survives. The power of a recollection is embodied in him, unknown to him. He examines his knowledge and, like an oracle, he reveals the way things were in the most remote past, just as Freud does—a past that still controls us, as it does in *Totem and Taboo*. The analogies are striking, and they probably arise from similar expectations. The most fantastic and least comparable world, the vast realm of unpredictable inventions, all these are taken together as a path apt to bring to light humanity's primitive or archaic past, a past treated as an experience of origination. Kafka made it possible to gain access to this world; he somehow brought it back to life from the depths of his own unconscious. The horizon of psychoanalysis remains just as present as it does in Benjamin's analysis of Proust.[88] The life discovered by involuntary memory relegated Proust to a place in the Marxist framework of a collective project; this life was limited to the psychic adventures of the individual, which remained happenstance. Benjamin's Kafka, equipped with a dual function, through primitive experience and ulterior recollection, lent himself better to social expansion.

Witnessing supplied the principal angle through which Benjamin linked Kafka with burning contemporary political realities on every side. He had been living in exile in Paris for more than a year. "Ten Years after Death": the title of the Essay can or must be read this way, in the second degree, as an adaptation to circumstances. Benjamin's reading of Kafka was thus legitimized, even for a Marxist; it was no longer naïve. The outline of the Essay was drawn up from this perspective. The reconstruction was that of a state of consciousness attributed to Kafka and presumed present in the highly diverse content of his novels and stories. The distancing that would be demanded by the reading of his fictional works, which were literary and eminently precise—indeed, they were brought to life by their unequalled precision—and the discovery of a meaning that was achieved by the study of their composition, could not then be taken

---

[88] From Freud's treatise *Beyond the Pleasure Principle* (1920), Benjamin drew the concepts with which collective memory in the experience of men of modernity could be mastered, a memory that is not based on conscious impressions; see Steiner 2010:163. See also Kahn 1998:73, who cites I. Wohlfarth on the extension to the social division of labor.

into consideration. The revelation achieved by strangeness, always specific, is, paradoxically, more universal: it even achieves freer expression as a result of the strangeness. Yet it never appears in this light in the preparatory reading for the Essay, for it was predetermined by expectations. Most of Kafka's reading notes (which can be found in his complete works)[89] are situated in another order, which is already that of the transference through which the distancing of another speculative and autonomous projection, *sui generis*, is legitimized.

It is thus Benjamin whom we read in the logic that belongs to his own competence. We observe the way the essayist proceeds via detours in the use of the "pre-text," balancing the developments of his demonstrative project and the multitude of references to Kafka's work and associations with other skillfully intertwined authors. The Essay does not deal with Kafka. An interpretation is embodied in it; Benjamin takes hold of the author, *in absentia redivivus*. The choice is hard to uphold, and has had to be defended against other views, against Adorno's reading, for example, which was more distant in one sense, or against Brecht's, closer in another sense.[90]

Contemporary Reactions

1. Adorno

We find a significant reaction to the appearance of the various unpublished writings in a comment by Siegfried Kracauer: "I must write about the volume of writings, which is naturally very important, even though it is sometimes unintelligible and unfortunately of a monotony that is in the long run tiresome. This has to do no doubt with the lack of sensuality."[91] The volume is important, it must be discussed, but readers were neither ready for it nor prepared to read and enter that world. Adorno's "Aufzeichnungen zu Kafka" ("Notes on Kafka") appeared more than twenty years later, in 1953.[92] In a more critical part of his observations, Kracauer noted, rightly, it seems, that the references to political and social conditions do not suffice to define Kafka's relation to the realities of his epoch. This relation was, in fact, vast and omnipresent, almost unfathomable,

---

[89] See the copious annotations reproducing Benjamin's excerpts in Benjamin 1978, 2, pt. 3:1153–1276, especially 1188–1264.

[90] See Adorno's letter of August 2–4, 1935 (Adorno and Benjamin 1999:104–114). Adorno was "keen, ardently keen" to read the Essay: "We have all surely owed a redeeming word to Kafka," he wrote to Benjamin on December 5, 1934 (Adorno and Benjamin 2008:62).

[91] Letter to Adorno, July 29, 1931, in Adorno and Kracauer 2008:289.

[92] See Adorno 1967. Adorno suggested that he had been working on this text for some ten years (letter to Benjamin, December 17, 1934, in Adorno and Benjamin 1999:66); see the remarks by Kracauer, who deemed the essay one of the best things Adorno had written (469–470). In his essay, Adorno stresses the importance of taking Kafka literally (Adorno 1967:247).

given the degree to which the elements were interwoven, transferred, and yet refashioned and rethought.

In the letter Benjamin was expecting, which he received in December 1934,[93] Adorno, who had access to the full text of the Essay,[94] begins by congratulating the author. After some dithyrambic praise, he proceeds in a second phase to question systematically all the positions Benjamin has defended. He lectures the author on the dialectical method he should have followed. He challenges the dominant thesis in particular, the idea that a prehistoric world survived in Kafka's work. One might say that he gets his praise out of the way in order to be freer and more equitable in a critical section; it seems fairer still to accept the duality fully, as such. Adorno certainly recognizes Benjamin's art, power, and virtuosity, reinforced by the composition and the theoretical project of the Essay, but he considers that the argumentation often fails to stay on track. He essentially challenges its basis, what he calls the inversion of theology, its ciphered nature. Benjamin in effect distances himself from both natural and supernatural interpretations. He, Adorno, would say that Benjamin is a great essayist, but that the dialectical foundation on which he himself relies is not sturdy enough in his friend's case. Is this foundation compatible with messianism?

The strange figure of Odradek in "The Cares of a Family Man"[95] offers a good illustration of the divergence. Benjamin makes Odradek a creature from the prehistoric world, crushed by a feeling of guilt and seeking to avoid judgment in a desperate flight. The extravagant mechanism of its structure—"the most singular bastard which the prehistoric world has begotten with guilt"—would reproduce "the form which things assume in oblivion."[96] It is as though he were holding a coat of arms or an emblem of that world of oblivion that he is trying to reconstitute. Setting out to describe the object as if it were not a product of Kafka's invention, Benjamin takes hold of the figure and readapts it, deformed (*entstellt*) as an image of the family man's "care," and also as the folkloric "Little Hunchback" who would be "housed" in that world.[97] Odradek represents the bygone era of history that Kafka brings back to life. The "intermediary" world that came out of the prehistoric world cannot be explored. Everything is

---

[93] See Adorno and Benjamin 1999:66–73 (Adorno to Benjamin, December 17, 1934).

[94] Adorno and Benjamin 1999:59–60 (Benjamin to Adorno, November 30, 1934).The beginning of the letter has not survived, but the sending of the full manuscript was mentioned there (Adorno and Benjamin 1999:59–60).

[95] Kafka 1971:427–429. First published as "Die Sorge des Hausvaters" in *Ein Landarzt* (*A Country Doctor*) in 1919, it was republished by Brod in *Die Erzählungen* (1935).

[96] Benjamin 1999d:810–811. Two essential pages of the Essay are devoted to these creatures, witnesses to a world of oblivion and contemporaries of guilt.

[97] A whole series of figures is linked to this archetype (*Urbild*) of deformity. He is a "man who bows his head far down on his chest" (Benjamin 1999d:811).

blended together there. Benjamin refers broadly to Franz Rosenzweig's *The Star of Redemption* for the ancestor cult, but that work is set in China. The deaths of primitive people lead him into the subterranean world of animals. But not with total forgetfulness: a reference to Ludwig Tieck allows him to bring along "a strange guilt." Reflection is installed in animals. Well-known stories lead him to Odradek.

In "The Little Hunchback," folklore has invested a song with the same symbolic meaning: the hunchback inhabits "distorted life" and awaits deliverance by the Messiah, anticipating a full restoration on all fronts. Here Kafka has been left behind: "In his depths, Kafka touches ground which neither 'mythical divination' nor 'existential theology' [that of Benjamin's day] supplied him with. It is the ground of folk tradition, German as well as Jewish."[98] There is truly nothing individual. Everything is mobilized against this. Kafka's attention was able to embrace every creature. Is this nature or the supernatural? For Adorno, here again, dialectics claims its due: closer to the story that Kafka invents and writes, Adorno views "care" as the danger weighing on the household. Heidegger is overturned: a "cipher," a "figure" of hope has appeared, implying the suppression of the domestic economy, a transcendence that sustains organic nature in an opposition that turns upon the presence of death.[99] The exegesis is more dialectical: it is guided by reflection and it relies on a different narrative rigor; it retains its strength, even if Kafka's story fails to correspond to it.

In the chapter he devotes to Benjamin,[100] Pierre Bouretz deals with the Essay in passages in which the discussion of the divergences between Benjamin and Scholem provides the essential framework. Bouretz does not fail to notice that Benjamin's interpretation of the Odradek figure is very reductive. Indeed, the absence of a common reading of the stories by the two friends, Benjamin and Scholem, is striking. They do not engage in discussion, but talk past each other; they oppose one another. They *could* not recognize, at that time, that narrative distance was all the more methodical in that it remained inherent in the thing described and in the writing. The projection of a dualist schema—original sin, then oblivion—with its obscure deformations (according to Bouretz's summary) did not allow Benjamin to arrive at a reading.[101] The procedure that Benjamin thought he could apply to Kafka's work can be compared to the mimetic faculty

---

[98] Benjamin 1999d:812.

[99] Adorno and Benjamin 1999:66–72 (letter of December 17, 1934). Heidegger was the reference: "truly a case of Heidegger put right side up" (69).

[100] Bouretz 2010:165–223.

[101] In Bouretz 2010, see the sections titled "The Little Hunchback," "Revelation in Kafka's World" (following Scholem), and "Tradition in the Shadow of the Castle" (168–185). Roughly half the chapter is devoted to the essay on Kafka. Scholem, for his part, thought that to understand the Kabbalah, one had to read Kafka's work (Scholem 1981:125). According to Bouretz, man in

that he detected later on in Baudelaire's *Flowers of Evil*, when he found support in a collective remembering that offered the poet a way to conceive of historical temporality.

It is clear that Adorno's critique does not aim to grasp the meaning of the work, either; it corrects an exegesis. Adorno inserts himself between Kafka and Benjamin; he, too, fails to "read" Kafka. Rather than seeing the strangeness of the singular figure as the symbol of an objective state of society, he explores the virtues of his interpretive method, making this strangeness the negative symbol of the society that is reflected in the domestic and familial economy. For my part, limiting myself to the words and the writing, I would link the "care" inscribed in the title of the story with the creature's bizarre body, concretized in its phantasmatic appearance. The absence of any meaning is most perfectly described there. The creature is neither a fright nor a threat, but an intermittent presence that remains ungraspable. The tendency of the artifice to position itself stably, which it is granted in spite of everything, makes it a projection. Its very fabrication becomes an animated process that is able to show itself sparingly in the form of a specter, an occasional and undying vis-à-vis. The text unfolds; it explains itself from within, according to its own logic.

2. Kraft

Werner Kraft,[102] more rational than Benjamin, and recognized by the latter as someone who knew Kafka well,[103] found that the Essay, spoiled by its mysticism, fell into esotericism and lacked clarity. He distinguished Kafka from the workings of the Essay, which precluded all intervention in depth. According to Kraft, Benjamin limited himself to a level of meaning that was superficial or, as it were, phenomenological, reserving interpretation for himself.[104] The observation was entirely pertinent, even though the discovery of meaning required the acceptance of the literary form, from which the reflection cannot be separated. Benjamin responded that one could legitimately find the form problematic: "I wanted to have a free hand; I did not want to finish."[105] The moment had not come. Benjamin's motives were no doubt contestable, but they are instructive: "every interpretation that ... proceeds from the assumption of a

---

Kafka, as conceived by Benjamin, would be "in the presence of an unfathomable mystery"; even Odradek ultimately "offers us nothing but the image of failure" (Bouretz 2010:176).

[102] Kraft lived in Paris as an émigré from October 1933 to July 1934. Benjamin met him there, before Kraft went back to Jerusalem.

[103] The relevant texts have been collected in Kraft 1968.

[104] See Kraft's letter of September 16, 1934, reproduced in the notes to the Essay (Benjamin 1978, 2, pt. 3:1167).

[105] Benjamin 1978, 2, pt. 3:1167. See also Benjamin 2012:462.

body of mystical writing realized by [Kafka], instead of just proceeding from the author's own feeling, his rectitude, and the reasons for the inevitable failure, would miss the historical nexus of the entire work."[106] Benjamin justifies himself by evoking another, more legitimate mystical exegesis, which he did not supply but which would have to be conceived in the same framework; he did not do this because he remained too close to Kafka. He responds to Brecht's objection, which Kraft shared, that the Essay employed a phenomenological approach, by suggesting that this was not the project expected, based on historical materialism. The description is rather convoluted. The reading to which Benjamin says he adhered too closely is imaginary; furthermore, he refers to an interpretation that has not yet been carried out and that would disturb minds like Scholem's even more than his own interpretation.

3. Brecht

Benjamin noted the content of his conversations with Brecht about Kafka on three occasions during the summer of 1934, on July 5, August 6, and August 31. He had Brecht read the text and waited for a critique. The second conversation brings out the divergences clearly. For Brecht, the Essay read like a personal, non-objective journal—the aesthetic or literary requirement was as determined for him as the state of society. As for Kafka, he was a Jewish boy (*ein Judenjunge*) in a complacent, unconscious, or corrupt milieu in Prague. But from another standpoint, Kafka was a great writer. The form of the parable is "serviceable" (*brauchbar*; Brecht returns to this central term: what traditions to integrate?), apart from any construction ("the danger of a Jewish fascism" exists—is he thinking of the Zionists or the believers among Kafka's "advisors"?). On this terrain, Kafka's genius is undeniable: he is no longer the Jew, his stories perpetuate the best Chinese (and Brechtian) tradition; thus he sees Lao-Tse address him as a disciple. In addition (thinking of *The Trial*), Brecht recognized that Kafka grasped the alienation of the inhabitants of large cities, connecting history and a critical "modernity" (despite his milieu in Prague). On this point, Benjamin followed him, making use of that "real" antithesis in the face of the mythical matriarchy. Brecht operated in a highly radical fashion, against Scholem and against Benjamin.

Brecht had a hard time accepting Kafka. Benjamin knew this; in 1931, he wrote: "I have been surprised, during some conversations over these last weeks [when he went back to the Kafka dossier] at Brecht's extremely positive attitude

---

[106] Benjamin 2012:463.

toward Kafka's work."[107] One must not lose sight of the fact that he is addressing Scholem; the latter had just explained his own position to him. Benjamin recalled the existence of a powerful antagonist who had something to say. Brecht was not unfamiliar with the work, whereas he did not read Proust, nor did he read Valéry. He did not reject Kafka, admiring his calm, the power in his descriptive distance, and his "images." Yet he saw the writer as a dreamer. His esoteric thinking (deemed incomprehensible) bypassed the economic reality by which, for a Marxist such as himself, consciousness was driven.

In his conversations with Benjamin, Brecht recognized Kafka as the author of parables (a form he saw as homologous with Chinese wisdom) and as a visionary—two focal points that Benjamin would make his own in the long letter he wrote to Scholem on June 12, 1938. Mystical experience and modernity are two foci of an ellipsis, he wrote, distant from one another. The first is above all representative of tradition, the other of the anonymous figure, the contemporary city-dweller.[108] The two poles of the antithesis are not entirely distinct, however. Brecht, even as he accepted the antique form of the parable, reproached Kafka the writer, whom he admired, for not having been able to make the form transparent; this is to say that he did not see its autonomous, contrasted, contradictory, or paradoxical orientation. Kafka was a visionary; Brecht's interpretation, inspired by the fear of an ant-hill society, clings to this point: he feels the alienation produced by communitarian life and concern for its organization, but that obsession would have alienated Kafka himself and prevented him from analyzing the reality around him. In short, it would have kept him from seeing the world as it is. In Brecht's eyes, the "precision" of the stories could be nothing but the privilege of an imprecise mind, the wandering of a dreamer. The unbelievable exactitude was dialectically ungrounded, a product of the imaginary. That in no way prevented Brecht from making a strong case for Kafka's inventiveness and his style.

"The Next Village,"[109] a short text and yet a micro-totality, has been linked by Stéphane Mosès to the interpretations offered by Benjamin and Brecht. Mosès limits himself, here as elsewhere, to one of Kafka's compositional devices, in this instance "embedding" (he distinguishes four speaking voices). Once again, the formal analysis called for (borrowed chiefly from Bakhtin) falls short[110]; it compromises the search for invention, which goes hand in hand with reflection upon—and analysis of—the idiomatic narrative logic. In the memory of an

---

[107] Benjamin 1995–2000, 4:56, letter of October 3, 1931: "Brechts überaus positive Stellung zu Kafka's Werk."

[108] See the analysis below, pp. 290–295.

[109] Kafka 1971:404 (originally published in *Ein Landarzt* in 1919).

[110] See Mosès 2006:71–101, "Brecht et Benjamin interprètent Kafka."

elderly man, life closes in. To give an idea of his experience, he goes to the other pole, to his youth, where life is concentrated in its fullness and is thus reduced to nothing. Kafka gives the floor to no other speaker; only the grandfather speaks, and he does so from his own perspective, which makes him evoke time that is slipping away. Deprived of the time he is living through, the young man risks falling short of his goals, even the one closest at hand. The insufficiency is pushed to an absolute degree in the extension to an opposite pole. The seemingly most natural enterprise is doomed to failure. The experience of conscious loss is intensified by the inclusion of inexperience or unconsciousness; reflection takes hold, from a distance, of the most natural spontaneity.

Benjamin competes with Brecht in interpreting this story. Brecht relates it to the Eleatic paradox of the race between Achilles and the tortoise. In this view, the story illustrates the power of memory recapturing at lightning speed all the life that has been lived.[111] If the race is divided up and we consider the infinitely small segments of which it is composed, the rider does not achieve his goal, but someone else will have succeeded. Brecht includes a human collectivity to come. The two situations contrasted in the story, linked to age, are thus neglected. The cause is no longer connected with reasoning, which extends to all of life and includes youth in the grandfather's old age. According to Benjamin's reading,[112] life in the memory of the elderly is transformed into writing that they can only read backwards, in the present instant. Benjamin retains a deformity, and he sees in it an infirmity and a lack of wisdom. Old people succumb to time; they can only decipher the writing in reverse. Thus they "meet themselves" and can understand the book "in the flight from the present." They rely on a tradition, and their reading can, from this perspective, be related to the episode from the Essay in which the students do not sleep.[113] The letter is dead; it does not lead to meaning. Writing becomes a circuit on which things are upside down and where life is transformed.[114] In truth, one can see something else in the tension that structures this story. Life is condensed in memory to the point of rising up against itself and preventing its own most natural deployment. The explanatory principle leads the end of life to produce its own negation and to impose on life the complementary truth of a non-life.

Kafka's great rival, the other protagonist, Baudelaire, turns out to be in an analogous situation as far as the text is concerned. We have to wonder how far

---

[111] In the Essay, Benjamin recognizes the messianism that is expressed in a final straightening out of our temporal experience (1999d:812–813).

[112] "Gespräche mit Brecht," in Benjamin 1981:153–155.

[113] See Benjamin 1999d:813.

[114] A set of preparatory notes and excerpts for these pages of the Essay can be found in Benjamin 1978, 2, pt. 3:1242 –1245.

Benjamin, translator and exegete, went in his reading of *Les Fleurs du Mal* (*The Flowers of Evil*). The poems attest to a contemporary state of society and the city, not to a remote origin of humankind; nevertheless, here too, as in myth, the socially and historically speculative approach does not lead straight to the originality of the writing. Benjamin's interpretation consists essentially in relating the content to its allegorical expression.

Later Commentary: The Final Projects

With the only partial publication of 1934, however, Benjamin had not reached the end of his study. He would have liked to rewrite the Essay. He carefully collected the reactions of critics, which were communicated to him through letters.[115] Might he have thought about an aesthetics that could have included a place for the literary phenomenon? The question tormented him. Kafka's work was undeniably powerful, and yet so strange, so singularly original. Nevertheless, Benjamin does not go back to the author in his particularity; he does not define what the work, speculative in its own way, encompasses intellectually. The material Benjamin is dealing with, the philosophy of history, precludes such a definition. He proceeded, in 1934, as though Kafka had retranslated Bachofen's ideas in his prose. The approach was aberrant; it had allowed him to project an even more aberrant model onto the object that led him off course.

The Essay had not satisfied everyone, not even its author. The problem it raised[116] continued to preoccupy Benjamin.[117] It might supply the material for a book. The letter he later wrote to this end, the one addressed to Scholem on June 12, 1938, sketched out the lineaments of a project; it could be presented to Salman Schocken, the editor, who might find it persuasive.[118] We have to read this project, such as we have it, by situating it in its contemporary and existential, almost alimentary, perspective. It is divided into three parts: a ferocious

---

[115] See Benjamin's own reflections (starting in September 1934), Benjamin 1978, 2, pt. 3:1248–1256, and his preparatory notes for a revision, 1256–1264.

[116] See, for example, a letter to Carl Linfert from late December, 1934, indicating that both the published version of his essay and the larger manuscript were "fragmentary" (Benjamin 1995–2000, 4:557).

[117] He had reached a crossroads (see his letter to Scholem, September 15, 1934 [Benjamin 2012:454–456]). If he accepts the "'absolute concreteness' of the word of revelation," in agreement with his partner ("a truth which definitely applies to Kafka"—which is not the case), he must also gain access to the "perspective that for the first time makes the historical aspect of his failure obvious" (455).

[118] The first of the two letters written the same day, June 12, 1938 (Benjamin 2012:560–566), was drafted in such a way as to be shown to Schocken (at Scholem's request); the content is announced at the outset: an analysis of Brod's biography of Kafka, which had just been published, is completed by reflections of a more general nature; see Brod 1960.

diatribe against Brod, the author of the biography, is followed by another look at the historical and philosophical themes that structure the work, and it ends with a critical assessment of the position occupied by Kafka. This was to be Benjamin's last response to the question.

The polemic against Brod has several aspects. Benjamin sees the weaknesses and inadequacies of the man who was Kafka's friend and the editor of his works. Benjamin evokes and deems impossible a disposition (*Haltung*) on Brod's part toward his object.[119] The two terms—friendship, editing—were incompatible. Brod thought he was dealing with the figure of a "saint" of whom he was the apostle. This is not very far from a certain truth, however tendentious; the relationship of Brod and Kafka was unique. Their perfect friendship is indeed the principal reason for the survival of the work, and even in part for its very existence. Benjamin did not understand what could have brought the two men together. Their relationship remained, for him, an enigma without a solution. Brod could not have had anything in common with the Kafka that Benjamin imagined. The latter saw Brod as a Jew ignorant of the kabbalistic initiations that Scholem had deciphered. These initiations were, in fact, for him a sort of "opening." Was the invective directed at the conversation between Scholem and Schocken? Benjamin's polemic reads as a settling of scores, a duly administered exercise in denigration. Scholem briefly approves, but with reservations; at the same time, he ups the ante, speaking of a "dirty trick." Benjamin "almost deserved the garland," for his skillful dealing of a death blow.[120] The terms used show, however, that Schocken was not fooled. Neither Scholem nor Benjamin ever spoke that way. They had, at another level, always taken Brod into account and recognized their debt. Then they were able, without a real change of heart, to think that he overstepped the role of heir and witness that had fallen to him.[121] It was now necessary to kill the enemy, the rival vis-à-vis Schocken, the editor. But the root of the opposition also had to do with the religious beliefs of Schocken himself, whatever Scholem may have said.[122] Moreover, if the June 1938 missive was ultimately aimed at Schocken, it was really necessary to warn the currently most influential Jewish publisher (as Weltsch, the Prague publisher, had had to be convinced in 1934) that the planned book would not have a religious or hagiographic orientation, neither in its Judaism nor in orthodox Zionism. Brod

---

[119] Benjamin 1995-2000, 6:107.

[120] On Brod, see Scholem's letter of November 6-8, 1938 (Benjamin and Adorno 1989:237). In the letter, Scholem summarizes other encounters that took place during his stay in New York (235–236). He did not deem it possible or opportune to transmit Benjamin's letter (236). Moreover, the divergences between the two friends remained unchanged (236–237).

[121] The roles played in the masquerade are not easy to disentangle. Did Scholem approve against his will, on this occasion alone?

[122] Scholem's letter of November 6-8, 1938 (Benjamin and Adorno 1989:237).

had no resemblance to the fictional character that Benjamin sought to introduce among Jews. This was written *ex negativo*.

Kafka, on this account, is disfigured. Benjamin, more Brechtian than ever, places him within the mystic tradition, which is ultimately crucial for Benjamin himself, and within the historical experience of modern alienation, provoked by the degradations of urban life and technology. The "crazy" and "grandiose" aspect is that the vision of this impossible present was communicated to him by the tradition itself (it is no longer a question of the "prehistoric world," set aside, perhaps owing to Adorno's critique).[123] The move to update is decisive. He cites a page in which Arthur Stanley Eddington, a physicist, exposes the consternation of scientists in the face of their discoveries; the text reads like Kafka.[124] He does not forget the war and the exterminations, very near at hand. In a new dialectics, he makes Kafka a solitary individual, apart from the world, who has no recourse but to turn toward the past, toward a shining, lost world, as a "complement" or a counterpart to the period in which he is living: "The experience that corresponds to that of Kafka as a private individual will probably first become accessible to the masses at such time as they are about to be annihilated."[125] Marxism reveals the catastrophe. Benjamin, a visionary in his turn, points to the extermination camps to come, but he presents them as intended for the victims of a repressed collectivity. The place of the Prague writer's work must be purely complementary, as is Klee's work, on the margins of reality. Nothing in it is reincarnated in behaviors or survives in consciousness, as is the case in the 1934 Essay. The times have grown darker. There remain flight and the introduction of an illusory complement—a pure antithesis, fictional and artificial, the product of art.

In the critical part of the June 12 letter, Benjamin lets himself be drawn toward a new form of dialectic, even more pessimistic. The tradition in which Kafka found refuge is sick; it no longer contains any wisdom capable of helping humanity; there is no longer any solid truth. He has to say it: "a negative characterization probably is altogether more fruitful than a positive one."[126] The content is adapted to the catastrophic political situation. Thus the problem of the incomprehensibility of Kafka's texts, underlined by Brecht, is easily resolved. Kafka clung to tradition, but without retaining any truth or dogma. He chose *hagada*, gloss, rather than *halakha*, law. The parables had to be maintained and legitimized without the help of any reference or foundation. Is he not in the

---

[123] See Benjamin's letter of June 12, 1938 (Benjamin 2012:564–566).
[124] Benjamin 2012:563–564. Was this passage intended for Schocken?
[125] Benjamin 2012:564; this is harsh and terrible.
[126] Benjamin 2012:565. The sentence is in parentheses; it does not explain a qualifying judgment, but supports a judgment that situates the work on the side of failure and negativity.

process of staging a trial that concerns himself? Benjamin retains two residues from the old, two productions of decomposition, rumor, and Don Quixote-style madness. These seem to him to be adapted to the course taken by history. It is in this altered form that he now identifies the strangeness of Kafka's stories.[127]

The indignation and scorn provoked in Benjamin by Brod's biography continue to fester. Benjamin returns to them again the following year in a letter to Scholem: "I think I am on the track of the truth when I say: Kafka as Laurel felt the onerous obligation to seek out his Hardy."[128] Here again, nothing is in harmony with the strategic positions taken earlier in favor of Brod. Benjamin holds the bow, Scholem applauds from a distance; they amuse themselves by shooting down an absent target. After all, doesn't humor carry the day in Kafka? Does he himself not represent the comic vein, which was not unknown in the Jewish tradition? "I think the key to Kafka's work is likely to fall into the hands of the person who *is able to extract the comic aspects from Jewish theology.* Has there been such a man? Or would you be man enough to be that man?"[129] We are in the grotesque; the relationship between the letter-writers can henceforth be likened to a farce worthy of Aristophanes.

Kafka did not consider all his efforts fruitless. Benjamin presumed that he did; he thought he had found proof of this in the terms of his will.[130] The opinion is widespread today: "Kafka remained for Benjamin the figure par excellence of the failure," Bouretz writes, retranslating this observation: it was a "way of evading the exegesis of his own parables."[131] He analyzed the writing while including failure in the enterprise, whatever it may have been. However, failures are elements in the stories on the same basis as successes. The difficulty of reading is transferred to the difficulty that the author could have experienced; it can be attributed, we are told, to a pathological state. One ought to say instead

---

[127] "... in the case of Kafka, we can no longer speak of wisdom. Only the products of its decay remain. There are two: One is the rumor about the true things (a sort of theology passed along by whispers ...); the other product of this diathesis is folly [*Torheit*] ... Folly lies at the heart of Kafka's favorites—from Don Quixote, via the assistants, to animals" (Benjamin 2012:565).

[128] Letter of February 4, 1939 (Benjamin 2012:592–595); his proposition now would be to say: "Kafka as Laurel felt the onerous obligation to seek out his Hardy—and that was Brod" (595).

[129] Benjamin 2012:595; the italics are the author's. The theology is necessary, and so is the buffoonery that is inherent in Kafka and that mocks theology. The writer is addressing his friend Scholem; the irony is acerbic. Benjamin couldn't have known about a passage in Kafka's diaries that would have delighted him: "The great days of the court jesters are probably gone never to return ... I at least have thoroughly delighted in the institution, even if it should now be lost to mankind" (Kafka 1929:170, letter of July 29, 1917).

[130] Letter to Scholem, June 12, 1938: "He was obviously unwilling to bear responsibility to posterity for a work whose greatness he was well aware of" (Benjamin 2012:561). Another parenthesis—on the side of failure.

[131] Bouretz 2010:278 (and even earlier, 176–177)—again in relation to the demand that the work be destroyed).

that Kafka included failure in the action in an exemplary fashion. The invention and the composition of his stories impose this observation, which does not authorize us to say that he did not devote himself essentially to it. However, he did not write, either, in order to put failure at the center of human existence. This would be a religious point of view, inspired by the fall; he simply incorporated failure for its truth, as a necessary counterpoint to his writing and his thought, far from any preconceived system, even from any experience at all. What has to be considered and examined in depth everywhere, in reading him, is of the order of correlation.

•••

Benjamin expected a great deal from the completion of his book project.[132] It would have freed him from his dependence on Horkheimer and the Institute for Social Research. He said he was ready to go to Palestine to write the book, if necessary. But Salman Schocken had never been really interested either in Brod's work or in those of an adversary such as Benjamin; Scholem had not convinced him, which was something Scholem could not tell his friend. Scholem wrote in his memoirs that from a man like Schocken he would have expected genuine comprehension for a mind like Benjamin's. In the end, Scholem must have observed that Schocken, quite to the contrary, "made fun of [Benjamin's] writings and gave me a lecture in which he declined to support Benjamin, concluding that Benjamin was something like a bogeyman of my own invention."[133] We do not know, either, how he had presented the project, with which he was not fully pleased himself. Benjamin was far from being engaged in the same cause; for

---

[132] He regularly came back to the Schocken affair in his correspondence with Scholem, which was much less intense in this later period; see his letter of February 20, 1939 (Benjamin and Scholem 1989:244). (In a letter dated March 2, 1939, Scholem assured him that he had done everything possible "within the bounds of advisable tactical considerations" [Benjamin and Scholem 1989:246]; see also Scholem's letter of March 14, 1939 [Benjamin and Scholem 1989:248–249]. Benjamin added that he was ready to accept any other project). More recently, Tackels (2009:543–548) has devoted several pages to a fierce critique of Brod's sanctification of his idol and of the religious simplification of the mystery in the novels, without situating his remarks in the context of the expectation of a decision on Schocken's part. The attack on the enthroned rival is nevertheless inseparable from this expectation. He is right to evoke the displeasure aroused at the same time by the meeting and the alliance between Scholem and Adorno in New York; the sociologist must not have been informed about the Judaizing project that was intended to free Benjamin from a dependency that weighed on him—he was fully engrossed in his work on Baudelaire.

[133] Scholem 1981:217; we understand that it was a matter of real antipathy, even aversion. A void, precisely where Benjamin was building a way out for himself. Disappointment followed (218–220). Scholem played at being the protector; he could do this only by reducing his solidarity by half (211, 214–215 If he had approved of the attack on Brod, it was because this attack was part of the strategy that was supposed to convince Schocken.

Scholem, Zionism came first by a long stretch. Hannah Stern (that is, Arendt), to whom Benjamin described the situation, no doubt had the last word, which Benjamin communicated to his friend: she "was of the mitigating opinion that Schocken thinks more of Brod alone, in the depths of his soul, than of you and me put together."[134] Thus everything was false and to a great extent dissimulated.

Scholem apparently did not want to hear anything about a failure, which offended his faith. In his letter of November 6–8, 1938, he played the fool, as he well knew how to do (I once saw him make the gesture with his hand and his finger): "I would really like to know what you mean by that." He could not understand (either he was playing the fool or else he really was a fool if he didn't understand ...) what disconcerted Benjamin, nor could he see that the latter was caught in the vise of a contradiction: "you really seem to understand [Kafka's] failure as something unexpected or bewildering ... , whereas the simple truth [is] that the failure was the object of endeavors that, if they were to succeed, would be bound to fail" (this is virtually to observe, with irony, a "correlation"). This amounts to calling into question the very idea of failure, as Benjamin construed it.[135] For him, on the contrary, this was the main if not the only interest that supported the project, which was marked at that point, in 1938, by a negativity that reflected the political situation. His feelings got the upper hand in the face of the events he saw taking place and the anticipation of the troubles to come. History was winning out over religion.

Celan's Response

Paul Celan read Benjamin's 1935 collection of essays (*Schriften*) very closely and his text on Kafka, in particular. The publication of his "annotations" in *La Bibliothèque Philosophique / Die philosophische Bibliothek*[136] makes it possible to spot the passages that caught his attention. They seem sometimes visibly to form the motive or the subject matter of poems, with points of agreement and, more often, of contradiction. His reading is dated 1959,[137] but it is clear that Celan went back to it later and, in particular, at the time of the May 1968 demonstrations, when he was living in the Latin Quarter, on the rue Tournefort near the École Normale. He saw himself in Kafka, and indeed for Celan Kafka was a unique model.

---

[134] Letter to Scholem, January 11, 1940 (Benjamin 2012:624).

[135] Benjamin and Scholem 1989:236; the passage is interesting.

[136] Celan 2004:268–303, comprehensive catalogue of his reading notes.

[137] Date indicated at the end of the essay: December 11, 1959. The poet may have referred later on to this first reading.

I came across Celan's reading of the Essay, as part of his creative work as a poet, under quite special circumstances. We had participated together in the earliest demonstrations at the beginning of May 1968. Then there was the aftermath. Certain correspondences between these critical poems and my own research emanate from a reflection that I undertook separately, at a time when Benjamin's image was evolving: his prestige was growing, even as he was changing sides. Derrida's Benjamin is no longer the same as Szondi's. Celan's reactions and his clarifications avoid all identification with any particular tendency. They underline the differences between his highly personal approach to Benjamin and that of other readers.

The Benjaminean series is closely linked with the Essay, and is not merged with the strong presence of Kafka in the work, for which one could first of all cite "In Prag" ("In Prague," *GW*, 2:63) and "Von der Orchis her," which follows ("Starting from the Orchis," *GW*, 2:64), and "Frankfurt, September" (*GW*, 2:114).[138]

In the collections published during Celan's lifetime or in the posthumous work,[139] one can identify five places where positions defended by Benjamin in his Kafka essay are discussed. The reactions on the occasion of a reading (already older, and preparatory) shed light on the poetic responses that he is drafting. They refer to one or more passages in the Essay; all were noted between May and July 1968. They are, in the chronological order in which they were written:

1. "Wallslogan," in *Snowpart* ("Mauerspruch," *GW*, 2:371), May 26.

2. "24, rue Tournefort," in the posthumous poems collected in *Gedichte aus dem Nachlass* (Celan 2003 [hereafter *GN*]:223), June 6.

3. "From the moorfloor," in *Snowpart* ("Aus dem Moorboden," *GW*, 2:239), July 19.

4. "Now grows" ("Jetzt wächst," *GN*:203), July 26.

5. "Venality" ("Bestechlichkeit," *GN*:228), July 29.

The very day when Celan composed (among others) the poem "From the moorfloor" (July 19), he wrote a very harsh diatribe against Benjamin, "Port Bou—Deutsch?" ("Port Bou—German?" *GN*:187), on which I have published a

---

[138] One could add "Ars Poetica 62," *GW* 6:87; "Sprüchlein-Deutsch" ("A little saying- German"), *GW* 7:183; and the important poem "Vom Anblick der Anselm" ("From beholding the blackbirds"), *GW* 2:94. On the theme of Kafka in Celan, we have Liska's 2006 study. [TN: several of the poems mentioned are available in English translation: "In Prague," Celan 2005:103–104; "Frankfurt, September," Celan 2005:110; "From beholding the blackbirds," Celan 2014:95.]

[139] Benjamin 1997; Wiedemann 2003, with annotations by B. Badiou and B. Wiedemann; see also *GW* 7.

comment.[140] My reading has often been found shocking, judged "subjective." I was thought to have lent Celan hostile sentiments that he had not had. This is not the case. It suffices to understand the words. Celan's attack is virulent; it is, however, neither absolute nor radical. Celan recognized Benjamin's importance perfectly well, despite their divergences. This double gaze can be compared to the one he turned on Adorno; he, too, had often disappointed Celan. The poems targeted one of the aspects of the man. They responded to the vision that he could have had about the author, given his own positions. It is Celan, the archer, who is "subjective." He sets up his target.

Several years earlier, in 1960, in Celan's Büchner Prize speech in Darmstadt, Benjamin had been honored precisely with a citation from the essay that paid tribute to the name of Kafka. In a passage in *Der Meridian* (*The Meridian*),[141] "attention" is, in fact, in question (the word is found in one of the poems); it results from a concentration of the mind, at a distance from the world of images. Benjamin, at the end of the section of his Essay titled "The Little Hunchback," had written: "Even if Kafka did not pray—and this we do not know—he still possessed in the highest degree what Malebranche called 'the natural prayer of the soul': attentiveness."[142] He attributed this reflection to the wisdom of peoples, residing in a ground (*Grund*) that does not go back only to mythic apprehension or existential theology—in this case, one has to go farther back, to the origins. These show that such popular sentiment is common to all people, valid for the Germans, of whom he has just cited a traditional saying, and for the Jews as well.[143] Benjamin's citation is spurred by a sentence from Malebranche, through a characteristic literary detour. All that has been said by another is retained, whether it is accepted or rejected. One may think that the indication added, in *The Meridian*, "according to Walter Benjamin's Kafka essay," was intended to show that the idea of a "natural piety" was inspired in him by Kafka; this is confirmed in the versions of the speech in which Celan had specified: "I quote [the sentence by Malebranche] from the article originally published

---

[140] See Bollack 2001:93–101, "Walter Benjamin en 1968." Schöttker (2008) acknowledges that the poem "Port Bou—deutsch?" ("Port Bou—German?") has to be read as a response to the 1930 review of Max Kommerell's *Der Dichter als Führer in der deutsche Klassik* (Berlin, 1928); he invokes Hannah Arendt, too, on this subject. But whatever he may say, the poem can (or must) be read without this reference.

[141] Here is the form of the repetition in the speech: "'Attention'—allow me to refer to Walter Benjamin's essay on Kafka, in which something Malebranche said is cited—'Attention is the natural prayer of the soul'" (*GW* 3:198).

[142] Benjamin 1999d:812.

[143] "It is the ground of folk tradition, German as well as Jewish" (Benjamin 1999d:812), just before the sentence to which *The Meridian* refers.

in the *Jüdische Rundschau*."[144] The place of publication was the equivalent of an agreement, denouncing self-abandonment and assimilation, at the same time as the idea of an indistinct ground of common saintliness (the date of the reading, December 11, 1959, preceded by very little the period in which Celan was preparing his Darmstadt speech; the invitation reached him on March 14, 1960).

Israel Chalfen, in his biographical account of Celan's youth, notes, on the basis of several interviews he conducted with witnesses, that "Kafka, once discovered [around 1937; Celan was seventeen years old], was to hold him in a spell all his life."[145] According to his friend Ruth Lackner, Kafka had become his daily reading matter in his mature years. He was perhaps the author with whom Celan was the most closely intimate. Celan's mother, fleeing from the Russian troops during the 1914–1918 war, had spent three years in Bohemia. Reference is made to this stay in the poem "Es ist alles anders" ("Everything's different").

> what is it called, your country
> behind the mountain, behind the year?
> I know what it's called.
> Like the winter's tale, it is called,
> it's called like the summer's tale,
> your mother's three yearland, that's what it was,
> what it is,
> it wanders off everywhere, like language,
> throw it away, throw it away,
> then you'll have it again, like that other thing,
> the pebble from
> the Moravian hollow
> which your thought carried to Prague,
> on to the grave on to the graves, into life.[146]

Here we have the kernel of an imaginary genealogy, created out of whole cloth, at once poetic and Jewish. His mother had gone there before she had her child (born in 1920), who would be a poet. She was impregnated by the country; she bore a living being, whom she did not know. Thus in a letter written in 1962 to Klaus Wagenbach (who knew the work of the Prague writer well), at the time he was composing the poem, Celan could present himself in this lineage: "for me as a Kafkaian, waiting to be brought into the world as such" ("für mich

---

[144] "Attentiveness is the natural prayer of the soul." See nos. 32/74 (p. 63) and 50 (p. 68) in Celan 1999. (In all, one finds six states of this unity.)

[145] Chalfen 1991:77.

[146] *GW* 1:284–286); cited from Celan 1988:219.

nachzugebärender Ka[f]kanier"[147]). In the poem "Frankfurt, September," a dying Kafka meets Freud, who is also dying—in a similar way[148]; Kafka sets himself apart, strenuously distancing himself from psychology: "for the last time." Such was Celan's rejection of Benjamin.

Celan returned to these Bohemian origins in a letter to Franz Wurm on April 29, 1968, in the context of the Prague Spring[149]: "I am myself 'Bohemianized,' as you know quite well; this goes back to my mother's three-year stint in Bohemia ... : it isn't called 'lupine' but rather 'wolfsbean' [German "Wolfsbohne" instead of "Lupine"] ... , then again on one side (see 'In Prague') (and on another side, and on yet another)." He is referring to a poem that his interlocutor could not have known: the poem "Wolfsbohne" appeared in the posthumous collection. There we find, in lines 14–20, the following: "... Which / flower, mother, hurt you there [in Ukraine] / with its name? / You, mother, who said *Wolfsbean*, not: / Lupine."[150]

●●●

Wallslogan

> Disfigured—an angel, anew, stops dead—
> a face comes to itself,
>
> the astral—
> weapon with
> the memoryshaft:
> attentively, it greets
> its
> thinking lions.[151]

Celan had initially added to the title the specification "for Paris." This was not an additional motto that would have to be reconstituted by readers (how could they manage to do so?). Celan noted and retained certain of these inscriptions, for example, in his correspondence with Wurm.[152] The date May 26, 1968, estab-

---

[147] This term is a transformation of "Kakanier," based on "K.K.," "königlich-kaiserlich." Excerpts from the letter are cited in Wiedemann 2003: "It all started for me in Lubenz and Aussig, on the banks of the Elba, where my mother had taken refuge during the war of 1914" (712).

[148] See Bollack 2005b.

[149] Celan 1995, no. 104:142–143.

[150] Celan 2001:381; for the complete German text, see GW 7:306–309.

[151] Celan 2014:357; for the German text, see "Mauerspruch," GW 2:371.

[152] The face has lost its structure (it is "disfigured," *entstellt*) and has simultaneously found support for its negativity. J.-P. Lefebvre translates *Mauerspruch* as "Dazibao" (Celan 2007:52). [TN:

lishes the epilogue of the days of revolt, the end of a period of freedom. The city of the Commune has met Versailles. It is forced to learn once again to work with its opponent. Inebriation meets its total inversion. Everything has two faces. The reader is to retain from this that the motto concerns the event of the month of May, its glory and its decline, and the reader discovers that the word "face" or "visage" (*Gesicht*), applies here to vision, which has prevailed during this period, and not to the face alone; the values are merged. The face recovers its meaning and its mission; it recognizes itself in its disfigurement and the fatal exhaustion of a liberating illusion.

The words of the interpolation are a reduction of the last lines of Benjamin's essay on Karl Kraus, which preceded the Kafka essay in the edition of the *Schriften* that Celan was reading.[153] The poem is associated, not without irony, with a story from the Talmud recalled by Benjamin, in which countless angels, recreated by God at every moment, sing and then depart. In the essay on Kafka, their ephemeral existence was supposed to evoke their infinite flexibility and the diversity of Kraus's interventions. In Paris, at the present time, the angel has been making himself heard on the pavement, in the marches and in meeting rooms before disappearing. The angel encounters his own face in its disfigurement.

The duality comes from Bohemia; it is taught in the city of Paris by an event that is taking place at the same time elsewhere. The poet's attention is directed toward the city of Prague, toward the markedly more cruel threat that weighs on the city in revolt. The city will become aware of this when it is crushed. Russian tanks will strike in the summer. The lions of the Prague emblem will recall the threat; they appear in the correspondence with Franz Wurm[154]; the Czechs have forgotten neither the failures nor the sufferings of their history. With "thinking," there is once again an appeal to memory, which is re-marked by the consideration of historical objects. The poet, with the weapon of his

---

"Dazibao" is a Chinese word referring to an inscription on a wall; cf. "What the Wall Says," Celan 2006:7.] Must one not preserve the wall? It is a counter-word, come from afar; the mortuary experience in a sense contains and surpasses everything that one has been able to read on the walls.

[153] Benjamin 1999d:433–457. It is essential to have opened the book and observed what is found on the facing page. The first stanza cannot be understood without being juxtaposed to the last sentence of the essay on Karl Kraus, which precedes the Kafka piece: "Like a creature springs from the child and the cannibal, his conqueror stands before him: not a new man—a monster, a new angel" (Benjamin 1999d:457). What follows is underlined: "Perhaps one of those who, according to the Talmud, are at each moment created anew in countless throngs, and who, once they have raised their voices before God, cease and pass into nothingness. Lamenting, chastising, or rejoicing? No matter—on this evanescent voice the ephemeral work of Kraus is modeled. Angelus—that is the messenger in the old engravings" (Benjamin 1999d; cf. Celan 2004:294, no. 349).

[154] See Wurm's letter, no. 106 (Celan 1995:145) where he mentions the lion with two tails.

astral art,[155] "salutes" from afar the place of his Jewish origins[156]; he rejoins a Jewish Bohemia in the Latin Quarter.

From Benjamin, Celan moved on to all the slogans translating the revolts and expectations that had been disappointed by the May event. The truths they find, when they have expressed themselves, are as numberless as the angels; having expressed themselves, they cancel themselves out. They had to speak, in multiple adages; they had to be spoken and contradicted, distorted by repression. The relation to the angels of Klee's *Angelus Novus* tradition takes on its full meaning in the constant repetition of an erasure.

The poem redefines in every circumstance a power that confirms it. What does poetry do in the face of all these denegations? It moves in the most radical duality, aspiring to astral light without leaving the world of destruction. Its "arm" (one is tempted to hear, too, the French *âme* [soul] in the translation of "Waffe") is like a shotgun, aimed at its target, its barrel charged with a munition of memory. This is what makes it indestructible: no wound is forgotten. The gaze resting on the multitude of mottos allows the poet to reassure himself. Recalling the role granted to attention in *The Meridian*,[157] he salutes history in its cruelty, in Prague and in the Jewish past, both present in solidarity in the memory of the "lions."

•••

24 Rue Tournefort

> You and your
> kitchensink German—yes, sink—
> yes, before—ossuaries.
>
> Say: Löwig. Say: *Shiviti.*
>
> The black cloth
> they lowered before you,
> when your breath
> swelled scarward,

---

[155] Lefebvre is surely right not to relate the weapon to the measures of governmental repression (or even to a nuclear missile), but to the militant power, rising toward the stars, of poetry put to the test (Celan 2007:130).

[156] As for the syntax, it seems to me that it would be best not to see in "the weapon" an apposition to "face," but to make it a second proposition, which is extended in the result of the action (beyond the colon).

[157] Celan 1999:9, section 35d.

brothers too, you stones,
image the wordshut behind
side glances.[158]

The number 24, the street number, was added after the fact. A possible interpretation of this addition might be based on the poem "Zwölf Jahre" ("Twelve years"), from *Die Niemandsrose* (*GW*, 1:220). These are not twelve additional years since 1949, but Celan may have measured a second dozen differently. The years, more troubled, marked by accidents, could express in that way a different temporality, a duration of another weight.

The first two stanzas are addressed to the familiar "you," to the hand that is writing; they admonish it. What is the poet doing, after all, but laundering the language of the torturers in order to lead it up to the charnel house and amend it in that way? One takes blackness and whitens it. This amounts to casting a sarcastic gaze on one's own writing. Now there is a more direct and more autonomous way to proceed, by coming back to one's personal origins, rather than moving through the victims and those piled-up corpses. It will be less combative, but it will avoid a detour; monstrosity sticks to the words. The return to the self, dated June 6, is connected with the earlier poem in *Schneepart* (*Snowpart*) written on May 26, which includes the emblem of Prague. This is also the lion of Judah. In a desperately violent poem in *Fadensonnen* (*Threadsuns*), Celan had addressed the lion that he was, asking him to sing the song of men, the Jews, "the humansong /of tooth and soul," of the two "hardnesses" (the response and the victims).[159] The symbols merge and reinforce one another; this amounts to declaring that other traditions are available to the poet, going back to Kafka, and before him the Prague cemetery, no less Jewish and German-speaking. He can recover a purer identity, less altered by the struggle against the adversary. The lion that emblematizes Prague and the Jews leads to verse 8 of Psalm 16: "I have set the Lord always before me." The word *chiviti*, bearing the rejection of false gods in its trajectory, had become a principle of Jewish law,[160] which Celan transfers. Thus the "I" is freed in the gap, by separating itself from an indefinite task of redressing; it teaches the "you" to speak once again: "say first something true, something Jewish, not something in re-Judaized German,

---

[158] "24 rue Tournefort," *GN*:203; cited from Celan 2014:601.

[159] See "Gezinkt der Zufall" (*GW* 2:115; in English as "Chance, marked," in Celan 2014:113). [TN: *gezinkt* translates more literally as "toothed" or "pronged."]

[160] Arnau Pons wonders whether Celan is also referring to the twentieth-century Jewish thinker, Rabbi Abraham Yoshua Heschel; he used to say that every person is a "shiviti."

and behind it, you find the ancient profession of faith, Jewishness in Hebrew, '*chiviti*' directly ahead."

In her commentary, Barbara Wiedemann informs the reader that this June 6th is the birthday of Celan's son Eric (Celan 2003). They could have celebrated his bar mitzvah. One wonders whether the analysis of the poem's language is likely to serve the transference that she imagines, assuming that Celan could even have thought of it. The reference to the Psalms that she introduces would, according to this rather incredible logic, be related to the reading of the section from the *Books of Moses* that was reserved for this Sabbath, as was the case every week. It would have been recited in part by the boy in the synagogue; the Hebrew word cited (*shiviti*) being reproduced on an "image" adorning the pulpit of the reciter (one would see Eric standing next to the *hazan*, the cantor). To construct a religious staging for a synagogue, Wiedemann had access to the notes Celan had taken in a notebook, on the occasion of an exhibit at the Petit Palais, "Israel through the Ages," which he apparently visited on May 25, 1968 (the date inscribed on the catalogue). Here one reads that "*shiviti* is the first word of the Psalm. It means 'I put before,' 'I see,' 'I imagine.'"[161] One could see three objects designated under the name *Shiviti*. Clearly, external information of this sort can lead to error and misuse; it becomes a practical obstacle to a "reading" worthy of the name. Only a deciphering can call forth and legitimize references of this nature; without this, the references remain gratuitous and mute. They ask to be situated.

The "they" in line 6 of the poem does not refer to anything actually mentioned. It refers to the "others," the adversaries, who are all the more daunting for the "you," whose eyes are fixed on the "scar," in that he meets them along his road, traced by memory. The black flag (which could also be harmonized with the content of the Psalm cited) obscures the darkness of the event. The "Reds," and among them the Stalinists, all Jews, are the ones who are, with their words, in the end strangely in harmony with the assassins' slogans. (This is perhaps also the blackness of anarchy, recuperated, distorted.)

What kills are the images. We understand the fourth stanza, which is addressed from this angle directly to the words, to the "stones" with which the poems are made: the plural "you" (*vous*) is addressed to them. We thus return to the meaning embodied in the syntactic rhythm; we realize that the "brothers" target the pseudo-allies, the authors of evil, traitors to the cause, which the stones are obliged to recognize in their own camp ("also": the declared enemies are not the only ones). They become aware of what is happening around them, of the so-called good side. These are the "friends"; they have been drawn in by

---

[161] See Celan 1997:490, and the excerpts included with the posthumous poems, 490–491.

false solidarities, and have left behind the straight and narrow path (*shiviti*). These lamentations are corroborated in letters that were written on the same days.

•••

From the Moorfloor

> From the moorfloor to
> climb into the sans-image,
> a hemo
> in the gun barrel hope,
> the aim, like impatience, of age,
> in it.
> Village air, rue Tournefort.[162]

•••

Celan read in Benjamin's essay on Kafka: "No other writer has obeyed the commandment 'Thou shalt not make unto thee a graven image' so faithfully."[163] He found there something like the definition of his language and its liberating and ultra-superlative power.[164] Vertical polarity defines the utopia that is being constructed in the essay. It is now anchored in an entirely different story. It is not the swamp of matriarchal promiscuity that Benjamin read in *The Castle*. Celan counters him with the vision of a different sexuality, which would be upright, male, and determined. The gun barrel has the shape of the masculine member. It is charged with representing sex, which is not lost in oblivion; in becoming erect, it remembers. The political hope turns out to be transferred into the non-forgetting of the acts of violence. Blood has flowed; it brings the poet his ammunition; "hemo" is the essential ingredient in hemoglobin.[165]

---

[162] *GW* 2:389; cited from Celan 2014:373.

[163] Benjamin 1999d:808.

[164] A first study of this poem appeared in German (Bollack 2005a); see esp. 1186–1194, where Celan's reading of Benjamin's essay on Kafka is much in evidence. [TN: The French text is not included in Bollack 2005b:262.]

[165] The poem stimulated a reflection on poetry and its historicity in a documented study by W. Hamacher (2000). The discussion of the options is difficult in the context of this study. I have chosen to limit myself to the position Celan took in relation to history and a literary past. Hamacher proposes to open himself to the text in its virtualities. He deciphers a potential future for history, which constitutes for him the true content of the poem: the latter, as such, "detaches itself from itself" (language speaks in its lack and its absence, not the poet who writes). From this perspective, it is important for the interpreter to recognize "the unfinished, that which is open and possible" (this is the orientation defined from the beginning of the study, p. 173). Benjamin's "prehistoric world" will be past history (the war, 1968, and so on) from which the

The blood of massacres orients the undertaking toward a future. The localization that is accomplished in the text makes the surpassing visible. It takes place at the center of the gaze, turned toward the past. Suffering is transformed into a "target"; it is unique by virtue of a transmutation, which will have liberated messianism from any theological charge. Born of the experiences of history and of their non-forgetting, it is conceived as the negation of Benjamin's visions. The German term "mündig" (formed from "Mund," mouth), rests on a very free semantic transposition. The mouth "speaks"; the verb "münden" (to flow into), evoking the mouth of a river, moreover, translates a result (it contains the evocation of an "opening into," an estuary); the no less idiomatic use of the verb "mündigen," two pages earlier in the same collection,[166] presupposes a value close to "preparing to release."[167] The semantic creations are neologisms, perhaps; they are extensions, which do not have much to do with "the majority" (*Mündigkeit*), itself consigned, according to the dictionaries, to the place of an idiomatic lexicon.[168] The context makes it possible to grasp the reforms introduced into the language. The fact that death, the outpouring of "blood," affirms its presence in the orbit of sexuality and offers something like an outcome is not at all surprising. It is a constant in Celan's love poetry, from the earliest collections on.

Celan forcefully underlines a sentence from Benjamin's essay in which there is a reference to the "air of the village": "'In Kafka,' said Soma Morgenstern, 'there is the air of a village, as with all great founders of religions.'"[169] Kafka's short text,

---

text separates itself, no longer situating itself in relation to that history; it projects a future that may not come about. The author of the study reads the lines one by one, pushing a possible fixation onto a higher "open" fabulation, which one can no longer rigorously separate from an expressive intent. The term will be the blank space on the page, the stopping of a language that would delimit instead of pulling back. Thus the central term "hemo" will be in itself a polyvalent complex made up of possible words ("and in addition a word in which each word is broken"). In multiplying, meaning de-valorizes all the information that is gathered.

166 See "Aus der Vergängnis" (*GW* 2:387), line 4. A whole lexical field (revealed in the Index) is implied, concerned with the general work of re-semanticization around a word.

167 [TN: Joris has "emancipates" (Celan 2005:371).]

168 Isn't the translation by *majeure* ("major") in *Partie de neige* (*Snowpart*)—the German-French bilingual edition translated and annotated by J.-P. Lefebvre (Celan 2007:73)—contradicted by the note to line 5, p. 142? For "mündigt" in "Aus der Vergängnis" ("Out of future-past fate"), Lefebvre retains "y munit de parole l'antan" (p. 70), then comments with "*émancipe*, closer to *majeure*." One ought to choose advisedly. [TN: Joris has "come of age."]

169 Benjamin 1999d:806; and Wiedemann's commentary in Celan 2003; Celan 2004:296, n379. Adorno drew a portrait of Morgenstern, whom he knew in Vienna, in the group around Alban Berg. He thought that he could be Kracauer's disciple: "he is nice, subtle, intelligent ... ; he is thirty-two years old; his mother tongue is Polish, or else Yiddish; everything that relates to the forms proper to the West is problematic for him; the literary manners that are now its danger are due to that search for a formation that has not been given him and that his little Talmudic head meets at an angle. Experiential data is by no means lacking to him, it is his reality in the human

"The Next Village," leads Benjamin, perhaps too quickly (and superficially),[170] to bring in Lao-Tse, associating a good—the attraction of proximity—with the advice not to move. Celan, however, distinguishes between the two authors: no, Kafka was an author of parables, he did not found a religion. Benjamin retained only the village, thus passing to *The Castle* and from there to the legend of a princess relegated to a village, which according to the Talmud symbolizes the body. Benjamin thus returns, via this detour, to Kafka's world and his theme. In his village in *The Castle*, K. represents the contemporary man who risks seeing his body get away from him. Alienation has returned (along with insects). It is that air, that village that spreads in Kafka, in "A Country Doctor," as well as in *The Castle*. "The air is permeated with all the abortive and overripe elements that form such a putrid mixture."[171] Celan retains the context of what he reads, including the consonances. He reads: "This is the air that Kafka had to breathe throughout his life." Whatever the interpretation supplied by the essay may be, it is the same Prague air that comes to "turn powerfully" (*tourner fort*), with the lions. In the word *Dorfluft*, "village air," there is the sexuality of *The Castle* and the presence of repression. These are not mutually exclusive. The swamps are there; we hear *Torf* (peat) in *Dorf*, the village. Power is anchored in the return and the reversals: by turning, "one comes back there."

Now Your Weight Grows

> Made heavy by all the lightnesses
>
> now you unmask
> the imitation, which is
> nameless.
>
> now you send the syllable-
> stabbing steam hammers
> under the spur
> of the one who
> leaps over
> the treacherous wood in the hedgerows,

---

realm (a barbaric reality, and yet belonging to a tender, fragile being); this is his best feature" (Adorno and Kracauer 2008:87–88).

[170] See above, pp. 290–291.

[171] Benjamin 1999d:806.

now

you write.[172]

Benjamin conceives of Kafka in the framework of the "ages of the world" (*Weltalter*), opposing them to Lukacs's temporal ages: "On many occasions ... Kafka's figures clap their hands. Once, the casual remark is made that these hands are 'really steam hammers.'"[173]

Celan's reworking circumscribes the last word, which is introduced in Kafka's story "Up in the Gallery."[174] Its structure contrasts two panels: the alternating applause of a circus audience gives rhythm to the delirium that is aroused by the skill of the horsewoman on the track. Benjamin comments: the slightest gesture in Kafka shifts eons (*Weltalter*). This is not in the story. The ecstasy is at its peak. A complementary tableau, evoking a well-ordered artistic production, will follow for contrast. Benjamin insists: "once, it is said that hands evoke ages of the world."[175] In Kafka's context, it is not even the gesture that counts, but the exasperation.

As he often does, Celan preserves the surroundings, read or cited. Here he goes back to the story, with the magnification of the applause, but also with the horse on the track, with its leaps. The ecstasy is transferred to the poet. The familiar "you" struggles and gets carried away; he affirms himself against falsity, against mockery and diversions, sustained by all the traces of violence that the hammer impresses on the cavalcade. One might see that he is again taking Kafka's side, that he is defending the author against a distortion that he is undergoing.

Art is redefined, as in the poem "Bei Wein und Verlorenheit,"[176] which serves as a reference. It catches up with his imitators in a hurry. Mockery is hunted down: the adverb *nämlich* lies in the orbit of the "name." The word *Namen* has to be analyzed semantically anew, as is the case with *heimlich*. This is semblance, deprived of real "names" (the words that say the truth are called "names"). The troupe of these specters, false Celanian, prowls around the poet. He does not manage to get rid of them, but he knows how to catch them, with Kafka's help. Again we find the cavalcade and the obstacles. This time the poet manages to attach the proper, powerful syllables of ecstasy to the spurs of the rider who mounts the machine-animal and controls it. The word is situated in the orbit of war machines (see above, "Wallslogan") and of a poem like

---

[172] "Jetzt wächst dein Gewicht," Celan 2003:516.

[173] Benjamin 1999d:795; Celan 2004:294; the word *Dampfhammer* ("steam hammer") is underlined by Celan.

[174] Published in *Ein Landarzt*, 1919; see Kafka 1988:401–402.

[175] Benjamin 1999d:000.

[176] *GW* 1:213; in English as "Over Wine and Lostness," Celan 1988:155.

"Sperrtonnensprache."[177] The betrayal is thus denounced, "de-sliced" (torn away from ecstasy), annulled. The remaking is victorious. One "writes" in one's own time—the "now" as constitutive as the *hic*—and in abundance, even if it is against the shades of counter-fashioning.

•••

Venality

> this is not a hope,
> norms, also called prehistoric world,
> get stuck in the sand on the near side
> of liberty.
>
> Transmitted is
> the secret beginning
> in its opening.
>
> Did the coin fall at your place?
> In mine,
> the neighboring village mounted
> on my horse
> where the pebble was supposed
> to be put down,
> the mountain suckled its tree
> raising it in the conversation.[178]

In the last collections, where the poems, annotated and composed, are presented as a poetic "journal," Celan takes a position in two directions, sometimes tending toward Kafka's side, sometimes rather against Benjamin. The most direct attack concerning the Essay can perhaps be read in "Venality" ("Bestechlichkeit"), one of the poems dated July 27, 1968, in which sentences that Benjamin had drawn from Kafka's *Trial* are turned around: "A boundless corruptibility is not their worst feature, for their essence is such that their venality is the only hope held out to the human spirit facing them."[179] The "norms" go back just as much to the

---

[177] *GW* 2:314; in English as "Roadblockbuoy," Joris 2014 :303. See Wögerbauer 2010:285–292, "Une Iliade sous le pavé."

[178] "Bestechlichkeit," *GN*:228 and 492.

[179] Benjamin 1999d:796. ("An ihnen [Gerichtskanzleien] ist eine grenzenlose Korrumpierbarkeit nicht das Schlechteste. Denn ihr Kern ist von solcher Beschaffenheit, daß ihre Bestechlichkeit die einzige Hoffnung ist, die die Menschlichkeit in ihrem Angesicht hegen kann" [Benjamin 1978, 2, pt. 2:412]; see also Celan 2004:294, including the first sentence).

description provided of the prehistoric world: "Laws and definite norms remain unwritten in the prehistoric world."[180] The qualification "also called preworld" (*auch Vorwelt genannt*) adds a good dose of sarcasm.

In the second stanza, Celan resolutely corrects Benjamin: no, what he himself, in his ego, is attached to is a "self," a belonging, a form of dependence on the self that makes it possible to advance into the opening and to expose oneself bravely to dangers. It is to designate an inalienable core of one's person. The other, the poet, who writes, is beside him, with his machine. The penny (*Groschen*) could fall into the slot and make the usual mechanism of creation turn. The "I" explains and distinguishes itself; it intervenes to explain itself by a self-doubling. The poem, which is being written by the other, is in reality fabricated in a little office reserved for the ego. The classic situation of a gathering in the next village of "A Country Doctor" is reversed. The hostile population has mounted the doctor's horse. How could the mother's stone, perpetuating her memory, have then been brought to Prague, as was indicated in the poem "Everything is different" (in *The No One's Rose*), where the force of this transfer was evoked. The stone was something German, nothing else. It came from the low country, from the basin that stretches into Moravia; transformed in memory, it was transferred (see above p. 399, lines 49–52 of this poem). No, it is no longer true, according to this detour, rethought in the light of the attachment of the self, confining oneself in the truth of the person. The mountain has been left behind in line 40; now it bars the road to poetry, which is always going about burying and evading (*bergen*) to nourish the tree of death that is rising up, contrasting the tombs of Prague, in line 52 of the poem cited, with "life"; death plays against another death.

The "I" is eclipsed. His solitary project of carrying the stone cannot be realized. The adversaries have gotten together on his horse; he is surrounded; the mountain, which buries, weans the other from death (one can also hear silence, *Stille*, in *stillt*, "to suckle"), makes it quiet. One no longer has a "subject" to deal with, but rather an encounter that opens onto an identifying reflection. There is a good chance that one can (or must) reunite the mountain and the conversation in order to find, once again, the problems raised in relation to Adorno, the absent party in "Gespräch im Gebirg" ("Conversation in the Mountains"),[181] at a distance from the songs. The charges are distinguished.

The vertical line that can be discerned in Kafka's emblem, regularly reiterated: "fall and climb" (*fallen und steigen*), transcends the dissociation between the "you" and the "I"; here it separates the studies from the instances of poetic

---

[180] Benjamin 1999d:797 ("Gesetze und umschriebene Normen bleiben in der Vorwelt unge-schriebene Gesetze" [Benjamin 1978, 2, pt. 2:412], a passage heavily marked by the reader).

[181] Celan 2001:397–400 ("*Gespräch im Gebirg*" [1959], *GW* 3:169–173).

creation. The "I" recalls for itself the role that is imparted to it by the tradition to which it knows it is attached, and it seems to exhaust itself in seeking to elevate its own personal experience to this level of "conversation." This thought suffices to compromise the triumphant accents in "Everything's different" (see line 46), during the trip in the mother's country, "like the language" ("wie die Sprache").

I thank Arnau Pons, Tim Trzaskalik, Heinz Wismann, and Werner Wögerbauer for their readings and re-readings.

Works Cited

Adorno, T. W. 1967. "Notes on Kafka." In *Prisms*, trans. S. and S. Weber, 243–271. Cambridge, MA. Orig. pub. 1953.

———. 1994– . *Briefe und Briefwechsel*. Frankfurt.

———. 2007. *Briefwechsel 1923-1966*, vol. 7. Frankfurt.

Adorno, T. W., and W. Benjamin. 1999. *Complete Correspondence, 1928-1940*. Ed. H. Lonitz, trans. N. Walker. Cambridge, MA. Orig. pub. 1994.

Alter, R. 1991. *Necessary Angels. Tradition and Modernity in Kafka, Benjamin, and Scholem*. Cambridge, MA.

Arendt, H. 1968. *Men in Dark Times*. New York.

Baioni, G. 1984. *Kafka, letteratura e ebraismo*. Turin.

Benjamin, W. 1934. "Franz Kafka: Eine Würdigung." *Jüdische Rundschau* 39, nos. 102/103 and 104 (December).

———. 1955. *Schriften*. Ed. T. W. Adorno and G. Adorno. 2 vols. Frankfurt.

———. 1966. *Briefe*. Ed. G. Scholem and T. W. Adorno. 2 vols. Frankfurt.

———. 1978. *Gesammelte Schriften*. Ed. R. Tiedemann and H. Schweppenhäuser. 5 vols. Frankfurt.

———. 1981. *Benjamin über Kafka: Texte, Briefzeugnisse, Aufzeichnungen*, ed. H. Schweppenhäuser. Frankfurt.

———. 1987. *Briefe an Siegfried Kracauer*. Ed. T. W. Adorno. Marbach am Neckar.

———. 1995–2000. *Gesammelte Briefe*. Ed. C. Gödde and H. Lonitz. 6 vols. Frankfurt.

———. 1996a. "Imagination." *Selected Writings 1, 1913-1926*, ed. M. Bullock and M. W. Jennings, 280–282. Cambridge, MA. Orig. pub. 1920–1921.

———. 1996b. "Fate and Character." *Selected Writings 1, 1913-1926*, ed. M. Bullock and M. W. Jennings, 201–206. Cambridge, MA. Orig. pub. 1921.

———. 1996c. "Goethe's Elective Affinities." *Selected Writings 1, 1913-1926*, ed. M. Bullock and M. W. Jennings, 297–360. Cambridge, MA. Orig. pub. 1924–25.

———. 1996d. "On Language as Such and on the Language of Man." *Selected Writings 1, 1913-1926,* ed. M. Bullock and M. W. Jennings, 62–74. Cambridge, MA.

———. 1999a. "Karl Kraus." *Selected Writings 2, 1927-1934,* ed. M. W. Jennings, H. Eiland, and G. Smith, trans. R. Livingstone et al., 433–458. Cambridge, MA. Orig. pub. 1931.

———. 1999b. "Franz Kafka: Beim Bau der chinesischen Mauer." *Selected Writings 2, 1927-1934,* ed. M. W. Jennings, H. Eiland, and G. Smith, trans. R. Livingstone et al., 494–500. Cambridge, MA. Orig. pub. 1931.

———. 1999c. "On the Mimetic Faculty." *Selected Writings 2, 1927-1934,* ed. M. W. Jennings, H. Eiland, and G. Smith, trans. R. Livingstone et al., 720–722. Cambridge, MA. Orig. pub. 1933.

———. 1999d. "Franz Kafka: On the Tenth Anniversary of His Death." *Selected Writings 2, 1927-1934,* ed. M. W. Jennings, H. Eiland, and G. Smith, trans. R. Livingstone et al., 794–818. Cambridge, MA. Orig. pub. 1934.

———. 2002. "Johann Jakob Bachofen." *Selected Writings 3, 1935-1938,* ed. H. Eiland and M. W. Jennings, trans. E. Jephcott, H. Eiland, et al., 11–24. Cambridge, MA.

———. 2006a. *Berlin Childhood around 1900.* Trans. H. Eiland. Cambridge, MA. Orig. pub. 1950.

———. 2006b. *The Writer of Modern Life: Essays on Charles Baudelaire.* Ed. Michael W. Jennings. Cambridge, MA.

———. 2012. *The Correspondence of Walter Benjamin, 1910-1940.* Ed. G. Scholem and T. W. Adorno, trans. M. R. Jacobson and E. M. Jacobson. Cambridge, MA. Orig. pub. 1978.

Benjamin, W., and G. Scholem. 1980. *Briefwechsel 1933-1940.* Ed. G. Scholem. Frankfurt.

———. 1989. *The Correspondence of Walter Benjamin and Gershom Scholem, 1932-1940.* New York.

Bernoulli, C. A. 1924. *Johann Jakob Bachofen und das Natursymbol: ein Würdigungsversuch.* Basel.

Blumenberg, H. 1983. *The Legitimacy of the Modern Age.* Trans. R. M. Wallace. Cambridge, MA. Orig. pub. 1966.

Bollack, J. 2001. *Poésie contre poésie: Celan et la littérature.* Paris.

———. 2005a. "Wie Celan Freud gelesen hat." Trans. W. Wögerbauer. *Psyche—Zeitschrift für Psychanalyse* 59, no. 12:1154–1194.

———. 2005b. "Celan lit Freud." In "Transferts littéraires," *Savoir et clinique* 6:13–35.

Bouretz, P. 2010. *Witnesses for the Future: Philosophy and Messianism.* Trans. M. B. Smith. Baltimore. Orig. pub. 2003.

Brod, M. 1921. "Der Dichter Franz Kafka." *Die Neue Rundschau* 11:1213.

———. 1960. *Franz Kafka, a Biography.* Trans. G. H. Roberts and R. Winston. New York. Orig. pub. 1947.

Buber, M. 2005. *A Land of Two Peoples: Martin Buber on Jews and Arabs.* New York. Orig. pub. 1983.

Celan, P. 1986. *Paul Celan, Poèmes.* Trans. A. du Bouchet. Bilingual edition. Paris.

———. 1986. *Paul Celan, Collected Prose.* Trans. R. Waldrop. Manchester, U.K.

———. 1989. *Poems of Paul Celan.* Trans. M. Hamburger. New York.

———. 1995. *Paul Celan, Franz Wurm: Briefwechsel.* Ed. B. Wiedemann with F. Wurm. Frankfurt. Orig. pub. 1965.

———. 1997. *Die Gedichte aus dem Nachlaß.* Ed. B. Badiou, J.-C. Rambach, and B. Wiedemann. Frankfurt. [*GN*]

———. 1999. *Der Meridian. Endfassung—Entwürfe—Materialen.* Ed. B. Böschenstein and H. Schmull. Frankfurt.

———. 2000a. *Gesammelte Werke.* Ed. B. Allemann et al. 7 vols. Frankfurt. [*GW*]

———. 2000b. *Threadsuns.* Bilingual ed., trans. P. Joris. Los Angeles. Orig. pub. 1968 (*Fadensonnen*).

———. 2001. *Selected Poems and Prose of Paul Celan.* Ed. and trans. J. Felstiner. New York.

———. 2003. *Die Gedichte: kommentierte Gesamtausgabe in einem Band.* Ed. B. Wiedemann. Frankfurt.

———. 2004. *La Bibliothèque philosophique.* Ed. A. Richter, P. Alac, and B. Badiou. Paris.

———. 2005. *Paul Celan: Selections.* Ed. and trans. P. Joris. Berkeley.

———. 2006. *Snow Part = Schneepart.* Trans. Ian Fairley. Riverdale-on-Hudson, NY. Orig. pub. 1971.

———. 2007. *Partie de neige.* Ed. and trans. J.-P. Lefebvre. Paris. Orig. pub. 1971 (*Schneepart*).

———. 2011. *The Meridian: Final Version—Drafts—Materials.* Ed. B. Böschenstein and H. Schmull, trans. P. Joris. Stanford, CA. Orig. pub. 1961 (*Der Meridian*).

———. 2014. *Breathturn into Timestead: The Collected Later Poetry.* Bilingual ed., trans. P. Joris. Los Angeles. Orig. pub. 1967 (*Atemwende*) and 1976 (*Zeitgehöft*).

Chalfen, I. 1991. *Paul Celan: A Biography of His Youth.* Trans. M. Bleyleben, intro. J. Felstiner. New York. Orig. pub. 1979.

Deuring, D. 1994. *"Vergiss das Beste nicht": Walter Benjamins Kafka-Essay.* Würzburg.

Freud, S. 1955. *Beyond the Pleasure Principle. In The Standard Edition of the Complete Psychological Worlds of Sigmund Freud,* ed. J. Strachey, vol. 18, 1–64. London. Orig. pub. 1920.

Hamacher, W. 2000. "Häm. Ein Gedicht Celans mit Motiven Benjamins." In *Jüdisches Denken in einer Welt ohne Gott: Festschrift für Stéphane Mosès*, ed. J. Mattern, G. Motzkin, and S. Sandbank, 173–197. Berlin.

Herlitz, G., and B. Kirschner, eds. 1927. *Jüdisches Lexikon*. 4 vols. Berlin.

Jennings, M. 1988. "'Eine gewaltige Erschütterung des Tradierten': Walter Benjamin's Political Recuperation of Franz Kafka." In *Fictions of Culture: Essays in Honor of Walter H. Sokel*, ed. S. Taubeneck, 199–214. New York.

Jonas, H. 2001. *Gnostic Religion: The Message of the Alien God & the Beginnings of Christianity*. Boston. Orig. pub. 1978.

Kafka, F. 1935. *Erzählungen*. Ed. M. Brod. Frankfurt.

———. 1947– . *Gesammelte Schriften*. Ed. M. Brod. 8 vols. New York.

———. 1949. *The Diaries of Franz Kafka, 1914–1923*. Ed. M. Brod, trans. J. Kresh, vol. 2. New York.

———. 1970. *The Great Wall of China: Stories and Reflections*. Trans. W. Muir and E. Muir. New York. Orig. pub. 1931.

———. 1979. *Wedding Preparations in the Country, and Other Stories*. Trans. from the German. Harmondsworth.

———. 1980a. *Beschreibung eines Kampfes. Novellen. Skizzen. Aphorismen aus dem Nachlass*. Ed. M. Brod. Frankfurt. Orig. pub. 1936.

———. 1988. *The Complete Stories*. Ed. N. Glazer, trans. from the German. New York. Orig. pub. 1971.

———. 2000. *Oeuvres*. Trans. M. de Gandillac, rev. P. Rusch. 3 vols. Paris.

———. 2009. *Kafkas Sätze*. Ed. H. Spiegel. Frankfurt.

Kahn, R. 1998. *Images, passages: Marcel Proust et Walter Benjamin*. Paris.

Kommerell, M. 1928. *Der Dichter als Führer in der deutsche Klassik*. Berlin.

Kraft, W. 1968. *Franz Kafka, Durchdringung und Geheimnis*. Frankfurt.

Küpper, T., et al. 2006. *Benjamin-Handbuch: Leben—Werk—Wirkung*. Stuttgart.

Lahire, B. 2010. *Éléments pour une théorie de la création littéraire*. Paris.

Lavelle, P. 2008. *Religion et histoire: sur le concept d'expérience chez Walter Benjamin*. Paris.

Liska, V. 2006. "Ein Meridian wider die Zeit. Von Celan zu Kafka." In *Franz Kafka und die Weltliteratur*, ed. M. Engel and D. Lamping, 210–233. Göttingen.

Mariani-Zini, F. 2004. *Parabole in scacco: Benjamin = Kafka*. Ferrara.

Matz, W. 2010. "Halbe Arbeit einer Entmythologisierung." *Frankfurter Allgemeine Zeitung* (Feb. 2).

Mayer, H. 1988. "Walter Benjamin and Franz Kafka: Report on a Constellation." In *On Walter Benjamin. Critical Essays and Reflections*, ed. G. Smith, 185–209. Cambridge, MA.

Mosès, S. 2006. *Exégèse d'une légende: lecture de Kafka*. Paris.

Palmer, G. 1999. "Geheimnisse eines bereitwilligen Kellners: Abraham bei Derrida, Benjamin und Kafka." *Zeitschrift für Religions und Geistesgeschichte* 51:49–63.

Palmier, J.-M. 2006. *Walter Benjamin: le chiffonnier, l'ange et le petit bossu: esthétique et politique chez Walter Benjamin.* Ed. F. Perrier. Paris.

Pulliero, M. 2005. *Walter Benjamin: le désir d'authenticité.* Paris.

Scholem, G. 1981. *Walter Benjamin: The Story of a Friendship.* Trans. H. Zohn. Philadelphia. Orig. pub. 1975.

———. 1986. *Briefe an Werner Kraft.* Ed. W. Kraft. Frankfurt.

———. 2002. *A Life in Letters, 1914–1982.* Ed. and trans. A. D. Skinner. Cambridge, MA.

Schöttker, D. 2008. "Celan, Adorno, Arendt deuten die Schoah." *Merkur* 66, no. 710 (July):579–587.

Schweppenhäuser, H., ed. 1981. *Benjamin über Kafka. Texte, Briefzeugnisse, Aufzeichnungen.* Frankfurt.

Steiner, U. 2010. *Walter Benjamin: An Introduction to His Work and Thought.* Trans. M. Winkler. Chicago.

Tackels, B. 2009. *Walter Benjamin, une vie dans les textes: essai biographique.* Arles.

Tiedemann, R. 1965. *Studien zur Philosophie Walter Benjamins.* Frankfurt.

Unseld, J. 1994. *Franz Kafka: A Writer's Life.* Trans. P. F. Dvorak. Riverside, CA. Orig. pub. 1982.

Weidner, D. 2000. "Jüdisches Gedächtnis, mystische Tradition und moderne Literatur: Walter Benjamin und Gershom Scholem deuten Kafka." *Weimarer Beiträge* 46:234–249.

Weigel, S. 2013. *Walter Benjamin: Images, the Creaturely, and the Holy.* Trans. C. T. Smith. Stanford. Orig. pub. 2008.

Wismann, H., and P. Lavelle, eds. 2010. *Walter Benjamin, le critique européen.* Villeneuve d'Ascq.

Wögerbauer, W. 2010. "Une Iliade sous le pavé." In *La philosophie au présent. Pour Jean Bollack*, ed. C. König and D. Thouard, 285–292. Lille.

21

Reading the Codes[†]

THE HERMENEUTICS OF TEXTS decodes what has always been coded, in some sense; this is the rule, and it is the underlying principle of univocity, which integrates ambivalence and polysemy. Its practice has not seemed to me to be limited to a particular literature. I have needed to know the language of the literature in question, along with relevant aspects of its history and social circumstances. One lives in a given country, one reads its authors differently than one would if they were transmitted in their original forms. One can even be on a familiar basis with the authors; one can be present at the genesis of a poem. But one also lives with other literatures, foreign literatures, translated or not, and why not ancient ones as well?

I have approached the great classical texts as I have approached those that were close to me, even while strictly observing the principle of distancing. It has been a new apprenticeship of difference, but at the same time I have benefited from greater freedom in the face of aesthetic problems. I have been led to recognize the unity of a global literary phenomenon, the existence of a field that is historical and trans-historical without being eternal, in which every sentence has always been taken up again or has awaited its repetition. We must turn the pages of this "book," about which Celan speaks as Mallarmé had spoken, with the cognitive means of the critic, a creator in his own way, even if it is not the way of the poet.

After a period of distancing from Saint-John Perse, I discovered in 1987 the then-unrecognized extent to which his work was Nietzschean. I then tried to grasp his procedures of execution in the linguistic material, as the signs of a liberation embedded in a subtle and contradictory dialectics. It was probably no accident that several of the letters on which I most relied (to Gabriel Frizeau, March 1907, March 23, 1908, and February 27, 1909) turned out finally to lack manuscript versions, as others do too, perhaps. This coincidence no doubt shows

[†]   Originally published as "Lire les codes," in: Jean Bollack, *La Grèce de personne: les mots sous le mythe* (Paris, 1997), pp. 221–222.

that, for certain aspects of his aesthetic, Saint-John Perse settled his opinions in a later phase of his life, in a way rather close to my own. Is not the *vita* understood and reinterpreted the truer one? For the poet André Frénaud, in the case of certain poems it was a matter of pushing the work of decoding to the point where it brings to light the momentum of the reflection inherent to writing. On these grounds, the two poets bore witness to a fragmented cosmology that characterizes modernity.

A Sonnet, A Poetics—Mallarmé[†]
"Le Vierge, Le Vivace ..."

A poem by Mallarmé, the second of the tetrad titled "Plusieurs sonnets" in the 1899 Deman edition, "Le vierge, le vivace et le bel aujourd'hui" (Mallarmé 1998:36[1]) has generated abundant commentary; it has been understood in contradictory ways. It could serve as a model, and lead to a re-examination of the conditions under which a meaning is established and then gains legitimacy, if it is discussed according to the rules of literary hermeneutics. The interpretive process pleads in favor of a univocal meaning; we see confirmation of this in all literatures. The semantic construction that is elaborated merges with the work

---

[†] Originally published as "Un sonnet, une poétique—Mallarmé: 'Le vierge, le vivace...'," in: D. Weisner and P. Labarthe, eds., *Mémoire et oubli dans le lyrisme européen: Hommage à John E. Jackson* (Paris, 2008), pp. 581–594.

[1] [TN: Here is the sonnet in Barbara Johnson's translation (1985:371):

The virgin, vivacious, and lovely today—
Will it rend with a blow of its dizzying wing
This hard lake, forgotten yet haunted beneath
By the transparent glacier of unreleased flights!

A bygone day's swan now remembers it is he
Who, magnificent yet in despair struggles free
For not having sung of the regions of life
When the ennui of winter's sterility gleamed.

All his neck will shake off this white agony space
Has inflicted upon the white bird who denied it,
But not the ground's horror, his plumage inside it.

A phantom assigned by his gloss to this place,
Immobile he stands, in the cold dream of scorn
That surrounds, in his profitless exile, the Swan.

N.B. Translations interpolated in the text may diverge slightly from Johnson's translation, in order to bring out additional dimensions of the phrasing.]

in the making. The interpreter comes to occupy the place of the author. The demonstration has almost necessarily as a corollary the search for the reasons that have led to the rejection of this initial fixation of meaning. The sonnet is a poem about poetry, even about the particular poem that is in the process of being written.

If the semantic system exists, and if it imposes itself by its logic and its coherence, the contrary hypothesis of a free, even deliberately arbitrary, scaffolding, is eliminated *ipso facto.* These are two distinct viewpoints. To the extent that the denial of a poem's meaning, sacrificed to a free or personal reading, depends on conditions that antedate the reading, these conditions do not concern the particular manner and structure of the text. The constitution of meaning is doubtless at the heart of artistic creation, and it presupposes that the production of the text is controlled and autonomous, disengaged from the real. It seems indeed that this condition of disengagement, which does not count for Mallarmé any more than it does for many others, is primordial: it is intimately linked to the exercise of the art, to the very reason for the production of the object. One must either accept the principle it entails or else reject it. If one holds to the principle, it is appropriate to go back and look in technical terms at the process of composition *ad se*, and, in a second phase, to measure its autonomy, which is always historical and relative—*ad nos.*

It is hard to follow the thread to the point of making a vision of the whole appear by identifying the progress of a thought that is shaping and discovering itself in the linking of words. One is led to note, moreover, the multiple and often contradictory approaches that are often based on a different conception of the text. The hypotheses underlying these approaches have to do only partially with the initial reading, which is carried out by the author and which results from his work of writing. One would have to be able to discuss the deviations; yet the commentators seem to let themselves be guided by the text and at the same time seem to leave it behind, without really seeking the coherence of the whole. Thus the interpretations are divided up according to various points of view. An overall expectation spells out the pros and cons of each approach, but often the idea behind a given approach misses the unity of composition inscribed in the textual material.

I am not pointing a finger at any commentator in particular; I am seeking rather to pin down the principles of an explanatory practice. I am prepared to except, in part or in full, the studies (and there are surely some with which I am not familiar) to which the critiques formulated do not apply. The stakes are not negligible. Are the questions put to the text the right ones? Does the logic being reconstructed exist? Why is doubt so often one's response to the most fruitful hypotheses? The present hermeneutic situation calls for a confrontation of readings. I have chosen to reproduce this confrontation in part, recalling paren-thetically, in the course of my analysis, a certain number of propositions made by the critics. The textual material remains the same; however, the principles followed bring about remarkable differences. Juxtaposing these readings makes their differences self-evident.

> Stanza 1:
> Le vierge, le vivace et le bel aujourd'hui
> Va-t-il nous déchirer avec un coup d'aile ivre
> Ce lac dur oublié que hante sous le givre
> Le transparent glacier des vols qui n'ont pas fui!

The type of poetry Mallarmé has adopted here implies an *intention*. This inten-tion is entirely deposited in an irreducible movement toward abstraction. This aim brings the poet all the more overtly into competition with philosophy, in that we are not dealing with a form of philosophical poetry. It suffices to consider the rigor in the poetic redefinition of the notions and their connections within the framework of a system. The syntax is not disjointed; it is not subject to the arbitrariness of untrammeled violence (legitimized in Finas 1961:32). The *aujourd'hui* ("today") placed at the threshold of the composition can be posited as a precise temporal entity. The context leads us to see represented in the poem something like an order of things, the dynamism of life or the reality of nature, life in its constancy and its perpetuation, opposed to art. The *aujourd'hui* does not mark a particular moment in lived experience. It stretches infinitely to the point of reigning uninterrupted, without past or future.

For Jean-Pierre Richard, in the section of *L'univers imaginaire de Mallarmé* titled "La métamorphose manquée" where this sonnet is discussed (1961:251–256), this *aujourd'hui*, far from designating the temptation of immediate experi-ence, evokes on the contrary, as it does for others, the plenitude of a Dionysian eruption, an accomplishment promised but put off by the sterility of winter. There is no question, then, of a division of domains or of antagonism: "this erup-tion had only been dreamed; it has not yet come about; ... a counter-dynamism of retention has in fact arisen in opposition" (253). The present in this reading is the ideal; the past, which comes up further on, in the second stanza, then intervenes to disturb the present: the poet no longer manages to "bring out any present, or rather any eternity. Today, if it were to happen, would manifest an eternal being ..." (253). This is exactly the opposite, it seems, of what ought to be said. Eternity lies in the art, and ecstasy in the writing. In reality, one does not exit from time; the poet enters into a different temporality, countering the present, in which the intellect rather than nature is triumphant. The hindrance of "retention" mutates into a highly positive element.

Along these same lines, Yves-Alain Favre comments: "the first line suggests dynamism and momentum, confidence and hope" (1998:518n1). The form of the utterance *va-t-il nous déchirer ... ?* ("will it rend [for us] ... ?") refers to the deceptive and seductive return of the same living ideal, sacrificed to immobility; in Favre's reading, the question designates a "hope of liberation" that is also disappointed. The break is conceived as unhappy and negative; it interrupts the initial momentum. It would be more accurate to acknowledge that what is at stake, on the contrary, is the condition under which poetry comes into being, by removing itself from the grip of life. The threat is circumvented by the exclamation (the implied answer is "no"). The objection may still be raised that intoxication would no longer be attributed to the essence of an irrepressible upsurge; the exaltation would translate only a mad illusion, a "desperate spurt" before the engulfment and paralysis of the ice (518n2).

The series of three adjectives recalls a poetic form established by Shakespeare's sonnets (see Sonnet 105: "Fair, kind and true," discussed by Peter Szondi [1978]). The relation among the three words (positioned between the article and the noun) becomes clear in the face of the idea that brings them together, that of the imperious power of becoming. The origin remains unaltered; it is not confused with a source from which everything springs; unbroken, it supplies a necessary base for deployment. The duality leads to the aesthetic quality of the productions that emanate from it. This is not to deny that virginity is in itself the opposite of the fecundity of raw life, but the seal is broken. The two words *vierge* (virgin) and *vivace* (vivacious) form an antithetical couple. Negativity is already at work; it is denied, instead of being maintained, surmounted in this synthesis in which nature lends itself to a first aesthetic emotion. From the very analysis of the proliferation, an element emerges to which a liberating transgression holds exclusively.

Aujourd'hui is self-evident; it contributes an essential element, something other than a psychological experience; the word lends itself to becoming the starting point for reflection; it is the basis for a debate, even an entire dialectics. The secondary, abstract transpositions of linguistic transcendence remain threatened in their very conversion by the power of reality. The primary reality remains present and constitutes a formidable partner. A spontaneous plenitude is still observed, even when it has been excluded by the writing. The surpassing relies on the world, at this initial stage, the world as it is, and as it delights. Tension is exercised within the limits of a precarious correlation; the first impression constantly threatens to take over again. Thus the exclamation translates an anxiety (*va-t-il nous déchirer ...?*); it signals toward a competing end point, toward beauty, which demands to be transferred. The artist is concerned with the threat exercised by the living. The power with which he arms himself is

induced by death; this power draws its resources, against the devastating proliferation, from the presence of non-being. The reign of negation is always endan-
gered by the unleashing of the forces it denies.

It is poetry that is exiling itself. The *nous* ("we") of line 2 is unambiguous:
it is an ethical dative that calls for attribution.[2] It could apply to the readers, to
everyone (see Bénichou 1998:323, "une émotion sympathique" [an empathetic
emotion]); however, one must specify that, in this case, it clearly seems that
poets are the ones who compose another world with their art, even if we recognize that they do so for the benefit of men, as Mallarmé affirms on occasion,
when he situates his art "in the spirit of the times" (Bénichou 1998:25–29). The
empire of poets is constructed with death. The confrontation is inevitable. Evil
reaffirms itself ceaselessly in the context of the antagonism that opposes it to
life. Negation comes afterward: a beautiful thing that comes after the beautiful,
after perception.

And yet the new reign is able to maintain itself; it consolidates itself in the
opposition, for self-protection. The closed, congealed haven of the frozen lake
designates this site: the world of verbal creation. The lake is not "forgotten" in
some lost place; it is its forgetting, remote as it is from every place in this world;
the object designated by the past participle *oublié* ("forgotten") is charged with
symbolic value. The separation has been produced with the help of the antithetical structure that is taking shape. The implied passive can be understood
to refer to the quality of being forgotten itself, equivalent to *fait d'ennui* ("made
of boredom"). This is "l'oubli fermé par le cadre" ("the forgetting closed in by
the frame") in "Ses purs ongles ..." ("Her pure nails ..."), the sonnet that appears
on the facing page (Mallarmé 1985:69). Reflection on the grammatical resources
of the language accompanies the literary creation, and the two are inseparable.
Language is exploring itself.

The autonomy of the reign is affirmed. The hardening, in order to welcome,
is doubled; it has its own progeny. One sees that the abstract domain, marking
out its boundaries, is divided (in lines 3 and 4). The stop produces a break; the
movement is fixed, immobilized (see below, line 13). Language lives on this
paradox; one negation takes shape, another asserts itself within the first and is
reaffirmed in the antithesis. One sees the very surges of poetic invention being
constituted and annulled; they find their form through alteration, through the
determination of a difference. Flight indicates a departure, or at least the vague
desire for a loss far away; the negation (*n'ont pas*) succeeds in producing this

---

[2] [TN: An ethical dative, sometimes called a dative of interest, refers to someone affected by
an action but not directly involved. Omitted in many translations, the *nous* of stanza 1, line
2, is included in others; cf. "will it tear from us with a wing's wild blow the lost hard lake ..."
(Mallarmé 2006:67).]

movement by a stop. Negation blocks, it retains against nature. The glacier is stratified in its transparency, emerging from a succession of luminous concentrations. Forms accumulate; they become clarified, superimposed, aspirated, coordinated, and condensed by the light of the poem.

The distinction between the two orders in stanza 1, the transfer into the universe of words, leading to a break with the phenomena of nature, has not been recognized, despite the emphasis placed on the "reflective" and the model of Mallarmé's "Hérodiade," as is well demonstrated by Richard's analysis of the text. Reflection has not been applied to the objective transition in which the freeing of art is brought about. To the aesthetic passage into language, from one world to another, all in all metaphysical, commentators have preferred the chronicle of a personal experience and the psychology of failure. The impotence that was discovered finally had to be valorized as a negative but indispensable stage; what Richard called the necessity of a metamorphosis was due to a psychic interiority. The terms then take on a diametrically opposed function.

Thus the *aujourd'hui* is not immediacy, never entirely surmounted; it will be indifferently the surging forth of art, promising successes, then drying up. The poem is called upon to supply the interpretation of this malady. The schema is therapeutic; the illness is placed in the foreground, it ends up with a self-accusation. Is not the poetic subject guilty? He is responsible. One option, of religious origin, is enriched by a moral notation, extrapolated from the text, to the point of the poorly deciphered apotheosis of the second tercet. Subjective impotence is substituted for the quite objective negation, situated in art. Pathology is introduced into an essential negativity, whereas the drying-up itself is productive.

With the methodical withdrawal into immobility called for by the poet, aesthetic composition becomes the virtually absolute condition for liberation. There is no other transcendence, except in art. When commentators place the emphasis, on the contrary, on the description of a fatal breakdown, the lake and the freezing take on completely different meanings. Rather than evoking the enclosed space of a welcoming and a deliverance through the negation of natural movement, these have been seen as an isolation cell and become the symbol of a hindrance, an impediment. Their morbid vision has deported the reading into inappropriate zones. The resistance to the world of appearances and the defense of an autonomous space have been missed; instead, one sees painful introspection, a psychic form of descent into hell. Pathology has been substituted for the analysis of the conditions of poetic production, rich with all the symbolic and substitutive tendencies that are discovered here.

Bertrand Marchal's presentation in the Pléiade edition (1998, 1:1186) is grounded from the start in three preliminary assumptions. The swan "is a prisoner of the ice." This is not stated in the text (Marchal does not indicate otherwise). Then the ice is identified with impotence and sterility—unnecessarily. Finally, this mental state is extended to the poem as a whole with *agonie* ("death throes," line 9), *horreur* ("horror," line 11), and *mépris:* ("scorn," line 13), terms that are grouped together without any consideration of the proximate or remote context. The words respond to one another from a distance, but in a more constructed fashion. The compositional framework is more constraining, more specific: the *sol* ("ground," line 11) is not ice; it is determined differently in the context.

Marchal does say that, in stanza 1, the swan can be read only in counter-relief (see also Bénichou 1998:322): it cannot be read at all, not even in counter-relief (see above). How can one then conclude that the bird is caught in the ice, a prisoner of the lake? Marchal understands that it is already present in the *aujourd'hui*, by virtue of the wing-stroke, in the direction of success; then he finds it again in the break that he too takes as an expression of sterility, "in the logic of the double metaphor," the "today" and the fatal lake.

The swan, as an emblem of poetry, cannot simply be integrated into the antagonism of stanza 1. It is announced indirectly by the flight—by one of the figures preferred in the writing of the virtual, prolepsis. The dynamism proper to becoming can be manifested poetically, with a rival "wing-stroke"; the effects are situated in the orbit of the most familiar poetry, the poetry least affected by the transposition. The feelings and the pathos aroused by the immediacy do not allow for the methodical transfers that Mallarmé prefers. At the other pole, in the separate verbal enclosure symbolized by the rigidity of the lake, the same "wings" translate the force of the retention. The negation evokes their mode of existence, a reinvention, the symbolic retranslation of experience, proceeding from the non-reproduction of the real. They "have *not* fled." This is to say that they have flown without fleeing. It is neither a lack nor a failure nor a matter of impotence, but rather a manifestation of happiness, the fortunate fixedness that has come out of the void.

The religious critique may not be expressed directly, where poetic creation is involved—this is true also for the sonnet cited above ("Ses purs ongles ..."), which was originally subtitled a "sonnet that is an allegory of itself" (according to Marchal, who may be mistaken).[3] The recognition of the void sets aside the false divinizations and the poetic or poeticizing language that has remained attached to the real, in the first place in the dominant tradition of Romanticism. This void forms, more directly, the relay for a new symbolization; it creates the liberating suspense in which resemanticization is organized (for the conflict between religion and poetry, I refer to my study of "Toast funèbre" [Bollack 2006]).

---

[3] Mallarmé 1998, 1:37–38 and 1189–1192; see also 1:131.

Stanza 2:
Un cygne d'autrefois se souvient que c'est lui
Magnifique mais qui sans espoir se délivre
Pour n'avoir pas chanté la région où vivre
Quand du stérile hiver a resplendi l'ennui.

The swan appears in counterpoint. It has not been directly at issue up to now, except implicitly through the aviary gestures that situate the poetic momentum. The adventure is initiated here by a narrative. What came before set forth the framework, the preliminaries. The opposition is introduced with the emergence of the bird; its deliverance is accomplished in a strongly marked distancing. The theme is reversed with the triumph of winter, every threat set aside. No overflowing of the perceptible in proliferation. The swan guarantees purity, a withdrawal accomplished. As the choice of the passage to liberated language has been made, the swan is the master of the kingdom, the author of the surpassing, the conqueror of a truer world. The transition has enthroned immobility. The liberating aim of the words has been turned back with the swan; this aim escapes the destructive succession of natural creations.

The *lui* ("he") can thus be reclaimed; the awakening reminds the bird of his power and his status. He belongs to another order, which stems entirely from the sphere of art. The distancing is due to the story that is introduced by the song, if not by the writing. The swan does not free himself directly from language, which is still attached to nature. The operation is accomplished within language itself; by this means, the swan detaches itself from itself. The emphasis on the pronoun through assonance and rhyme (the *u-i* has been abundantly discussed, most often apart from questions of semantic coherence) does not open up access to the spiritual sphere of a consciousness or an interiority, but it distinguishes the order of the achievement; the surpassing of the outside is doubled on the inside. Separation from the living does not suffice in itself; it is motivated by a desire for freedom. The end remains a driver, required in the conquest of a domain where a wholly literary frankness submits to its own laws.

The stabilization of language depends on the mastery of the past. This process establishes another time for itself, a time that must have been. The vision that results from the transfer rests on memory; it goes back on itself. One could still call it philosophical. The reflection emanates yet again from a study of the processes of poetic composition. Anteriority proves to be inherent to the act of writing. Poetry recollects; time is its time. Time is the primary privilege of the bird.

The swan is riveted to time gone by. The act of returning to the past eludes the grip of the present; art rests on this act. Thus it is also the act that has constituted the art. Without the act, there would be nothing that could be remembered. The act—the swan—challenges history for this power.

Thus a new temporality arises, in the face of the uninterrupted dynamism of becoming evoked in stanza 1; it has been created by a primordial act of the intellectual rather than the natural order. At the origin there was the invention of an object to be fixed in place, which was neither a production nor its reproduction; more simply, the thing was situated. The swan liberates itself, the act belongs properly to it; its exit is more radical than the surpassing granted to other creatures. It can rise higher, aspire freely to a destiny. The future is invented symmetrically; anteriority has a counterpart, at the other pole. Thus art structures itself in temporality; the future brings together the elements of its consecration. The surpassings take place in alternation.

The poem's interpreters have above all let themselves be led to detect in this second stanza something like a lament, where the poet would be bent on evoking the painful experience of sterility (line 8) and despair (line 6). They are (very largely) mistaken in conferring a negative value on a whole series of words that, in fact, take on a positive function, and are consonant with the elementary dissociation of levels of language. Psychology wins out over an analysis of the poem's making. Negativity is presented as an essential counterpart and the initial condition of the poem.

It is known, moreover, that the swan, in an ancient tradition, is the symbol of the creative act or of the subject that is expressed in such an act. In line 5, interpreters acknowledge that the evocation of the bird refers to the person of Mallarmé, whereas it is difficult not to relate the indefinite *un* ("a") to some poet or other from the past. The completive *que c'est lui* ("that it is he") does not develop a complement (*autrefois* ["formerly"]) that would be in opposition to *aujourd'hui* in line 1. The action of memory is taken as such, as the constitutive instance; it has to do with the privileged destiny of the poet, who according to this reading is always of another time, and always of his own. The poet remembers his own time. From this fixed viewpoint, the anteriority available to him is, as it were, absolute and essential. It is well represented by the poem by Baudelaire that bears the name of the bird as its title, "Le cygne" ("The Swan"). It would thus indeed be that original capacity that makes it possible to discover both writing and its autonomy. If the swan "frees itself," it is not from the ice; on the contrary, it is the ice itself, that of the lake, that provides the swan with its power, bringing together the extremes of the contradiction inherent to immobility. Thus it is not the pathological state of despair that is associated with glory and splendor, but on the contrary a renunciation that avoids the expectations of the public, which are loftily abandoned at the moment of the break. The *lui* suffices unto itself. The poet frees himself, distinguishes himself as such, by his own faculties.

The second pair of lines develops the oxymoron. It vigorously reconnects art with the act of necessary acceptance of aridity. A position is taken here in favor of a poetic art that redefines itself and excludes other linguistic attitudes. The *pas chanté* ("not having sung") is presented, from this perspective, as a title to glory. The negations in the two stanzas are obviously in dialogue: it is the same *pas*, the same advantage drawn from the void, the assertion of a non-participation in the poetic tradition based on emotion. Winter leads to two opposite reactions: either flight toward *la région où vivre* ("the region in which to live"), in poetry itself, whatever it may be, or the refusal of this choice and the exploration of destitution. Boredom is not the scourge, precisely because it is on the side of non-life and of death, and because this domain represents the preliminary, indispensable stage of every recomposition, it is the product as well as the condition of sterility. Boredom cannot, in the context of this reflection on the first conditions of expression, be the object of lamentation or remorse. It is before this bifurcation that the various readings have gone wrong. How can one not recognize that light is concentrated, collected in a depth that is made of absence? Boredom "has shined"; its radiance determines an aim inherent to writing. This aim will be defined in the two tercets.

> Stanza 3:
> Tout son col secouera cette blanche agonie
> Par l'espace infligée à l'oiseau qui le nie,
> Mais non l'horreur du sol où le plumage est pris.

The bird is cut in two; it is divided between its neck, held up straight, and its plumage, trapped in the earth. Elevation, separated from natural movement, transcends itself. The primary division is reproduced in the conquered realm, changing its nature. There are now two fastenings, one downward and the other upward. The one is left behind; it allows the other to propagate itself. Space opens up, flight unfolds there, exploring all the possibilities of ascension. The upward thrust claims the entire network of movements, all the entanglements possible; it is vanquished by the unique power of a distant resistance. It takes advantage of the irresistible support of the double fastening, in which anchoring and elevation come together. The opening disavows itself, welcoming also its negation. Thus speech triumphs through its gravity over space; it imposes its law on space.

The future is traced forcefully by the distinctive grammatical mark in the verb *secouera* ("will shake off"). The new surpassing as such responds to the present tense of the earlier one, that of the rupture, by coming to announce a beyond, the sketch of an eschatology and the promise of an enlarging of the letter. The end point is yet another death, no longer opposed to life, but emerging from the already achieved passage into the spheres of the funereal. The qualities correspond, term for term. The bird pays its ransom to movement, which it has denatured, as it were, through its fictional power. It is still winter, but the swan extracts from winter its unaltered luminosity. Its neck straightens, and is assimilated to the ether, while another part of the bird—its plumage, the very instrument of flight—is as if buried and rejected. Purification, too, plays on the mode of the absolute.

There is no need to return to the lake and attribute to it once again the function of a prison by assimilating it to the earth. Instead, the lake would be a tomb, but a liberating tomb. The bird has freed itself by entering into this counterfeit space, a counter-space. We are indeed dealing, in a cosmic projection of the terrestrial universe, with an earth on which men would walk. The swan is now abandoned in an ultimate division, absorbed by light, a pale copy of the soul and of what it was.

> Stanza 4:
> Fantôme qu'à ce lieu son pur éclat assigne,
> Il s'immobilise au songe froid de mépris
> Que vêt parmi l'exil inutile le Cygne.

The apotheosis is outlined; it is developed as a stunning masquerade in the conceit of the sonnet. At its culminating point, the fixation of the words, called to structure space, has allowed an emblem to rise into the heights. The bird has not positioned this sign or the writing that the sign transfers and retraces. The constellation that bears the name Cygnus, the Swan, is already there, installed in the sky, like the other stellar figures, preceding poetic elocution. The bird, or what remains of it—namely, that into which it has been reduced and purified— has rejoined the constellation, stripped of all substance. The "phantom" is the sketch, released not from the shadows, but from an empyrean region, a figure for light adapted to its final destination.

Clarity is the sole movement that can harmonize with this new and ultimate cosmic domination. Immobility is animated in this concentration; it does not come to occupy a place, but is a form of "shade." The "ghost/phantom" is united with the "shade" that is the "dream"; the one and the other are only configurations. The features of a pure intelligibility are recovered, to the detriment of all the creatures that could take on consistency according to the laws of natural or even scriptural development. The stellar bird shines; it is augmented by an increase in which it would shine more purely still, by a quasi-immaterial substance. Space, in this cathartic process, has become an exteriority from which life is banished and whose productions are transmuted.

The second tercet has raised the problem of the meaning of the constellation, and thus of the capital letter. Does the swan join, in the heavens, the constellation of the same name? The reference to Ronsard's sonnet is unmistakable: "My feather [pen] flies to the heavens to be some sign."[4] Homonymy unites the words; it can be heard throughout the poem. Marchal (1985, 1:1187) sets aside the myth, however: "Mallarmé has not dissolved the myths to make new ones"; this is true. It is no less true that we are dealing with a constellation of words ("the poem offers itself to be read as a swan of words" [ibid.]). The problem is not resolved for all that. First, the constellation does not suffice to include a myth, despite the mythic name; it does not stop being "stellar," which means that it represents a different form of permanence, more luminous, inherent to this world. Thus in the end the figure cannot replace the missing title and sum up the whole. The very doubling indicates that something else is at stake.

The eternal swan transcends all incarnations. The poem identifies itself here with the poet who is creating it. The heavens are thus defined twice, first in their own place of light, by the *exil inutile* ("profitless exile," line 14), and then twice set in phonic relation with *stérile* ("sterile," line 8). The end point that is established for the ascension, traversing the beyond, has as its matter pure exteriority. Uselessness qualifies the unreality of the artifice, unburdened of any mission or message. The poem is only written; it operates in its own domain, drawing its freedom from its composition alone.

The constellation symbolizes well the principle of art; it adapts to a magnetic encounter and changes form. The dream is as denuded as the phantom that it welcomes; a circumstance blends them. The subject is without consistency; it finds in the dream envelope an object that is in conformity with it, opening at the same time onto the unreal. It is still winter, and set against this background of refusal, there is the paradoxically driving essence nourished by the rejections and the exclusions (there is nothing moral about the *mépris* ["scorn"]). Summing up the interpretations, Favre (1985:520–521) contrasts a faction he finds on the side of the void and failure leading to nonexistence (always the frozen lake) in Émilie Noulet (1972), Georges Poulet (1959), and Léon Cellier (1975), with another camp for which impotence would be redeemed and mastered, as it

---

[4] In the second stanza of "Il faut laisser maisons et vergers et jardins ...":

> C'est fait, j'ay devidé le cours de mes destins.
> J'ay vescu, j'ay rendu mon nom assez insigne,
> Ma plume vole au ciel pour estre quelque signe
> Loin des appas mondains qui trompent les plus fins.

Also cited in Marchal 1998:1187.

were.[5] In each case these are isolated elements, separate from a real "reading" according to the words and their connections. As for Favre, he does not choose, having nothing to choose. Does the swan fail to reach the goal or does it repudiate the goal? The abandonment itself deserves analysis.

On the one hand, Mallarmé's lines are considered by definition beautiful and powerful. This is because the music takes priority, as in Verlaine's poetry. Here is where we see the side of art. The matter, from this angle, is safe, even if there is nothing to understand: if Mallarmé proceeded in such a way that the interpretation is obscure (and this emerges from the disagreement among the critics, which Favre presents as a compelling conclusion), it is because he wanted us to enjoy the image in itself (and no longer the music). The anti-intellectual bias of this critique is clearly formulated. Immediate perceptions are substituted for meaning, which nevertheless prevails in poetry; sound and image are equally subordinated to meaning.

First of all, according to Favre, there is no "intellectual play," as there is in Valéry, whom Favre sets up as the representative of the intellect. He would have classified the present study in that category, since it denies the supremacy of the music ("many critics have been mistaken about this"). The symbolism would be first of all that of absence. Where this absence is constitutive of poetic language, it is erected as a barrier, not against a use of language, but against meaning as such. The methodical polysemy (of Lucette Finas) that is promoted by the dogmatic renunciations of post-structuralist criticism derives from a "non-sense" that itself derives from a *non liquet*, "it is not clear."[6]

Works Cited

Bénichou, P. 1998. *Selon Mallarmé*. Paris.

Bollack, J. 2006. "Die Dichtung und die Religion. Zu Mallarmes Toast funèbre." *Zeitschrift für Aesthetik und Allgemeine Kunstwissenschaft* 51, 1:103–114.

Cellier, L. 1975. "Discours inaugural." In *Colloque Mallarmé: Glasgow, novembre 1975: en honneur de Austin Gil*, ed. C. P. Barbier, 11–17. Paris.

Favre, Y.-A. 1985. Notes to "Le vierge, le vivace ... ." In *Œuvres de Mallarmé*, 517–521. Paris.

Finas, L. 2002. *Mallarmé, le col, la coupe*. Paris.

Johnson, B. 1985. "*Les Fleurs du mal armé*: Some Reflections on Intertextuality." In *Lyric Poetry: Beyond New Criticism*, ed. C. Hošek and P. Parker, 264–280. Ithaca, NY.

---

[5]   See Richard 1961:256: "a failure as conceived and transmuted into a sort of victory."

[6]   [TN: In a legal context, *non liquet* refers to a situation in which there is no natural law.]

Mallarmé, S. 1985. *Oeuvres de Mallarmé.* Ed. Y.-A. Favre. Paris.

———. 1998. *Oeuvres complètes.* Ed. B. Marchal. 2 vols. Paris.

———. 2006. *Collected Poems and Other Verse.* Trans. E. H. and A. M. Blackmore. Oxford.

Marchal, B. 1998. "Introduction" to Stéphane Mallarmé, *Oeuvres complètes*, Vol. 1. Paris.

Noulet, É. 1972. *Vingt poèmes de Stéphane Mallarmé.* Geneva.

Poulet, G. 1959. *The Interior Distance.* Trans. E. Coleman. Baltimore. Orig. pub. 1952.

Richard, J.-P. 1961. *L'univers imaginaire de Mallarmé.* Paris.

Szondi, P. 2003. "The Poetry of Constancy: Paul Celan's Translation of Shakespeare's Sonnet 105." Trans. H. Mendelsohn. In *Celan Studies*, ed. J. Bollack, trans. S. Bernofsky with H. Mendelsohn, 1–26. Stanford. Orig. pub. 1978.

23

Between Hölderlin and Celan[†]

A Thunderbolt

THE OCCASION was the meeting of the Hölderlin Society in Tübingen on May 22, 1986, on the topic "Hölderlin, the View from France."[1] André du Bouchet, in the notes and reflections associated with the talk he gave on that occasion, referred at the start to another talk on Hölderlin he had given sixteen years earlier, in Celan's presence, a short time before the latter's death. It was in Stuttgart in 1970, at a bicentennial commemoration of Hölderlin's birth. The text of that talk had been published immediately in the review *L'Éphémère* (du Bouchet 1970). We were all moved when we heard what du Bouchet had to say in the second talk about what had happened at the first one. Celan had made some remarks that, "until that day," wrote du Bouchet, "he had preferred to keep secret." A thunderbolt had struck du Bouchet. He would never have expected to hear his friend, whom he so much admired, declare out of the blue: "There is something rotten in Hölderlin's poetry."

Du Bouchet conveyed his surprise to us in a striking reappraisal of the matter: "Yes, [something rotten] in [Hölderlin's] work, which among all others appeals to purity as an absolute." In the face of this incredible situation, du Bouchet was driven to re-imagine and reconfirm his own testimony: "I repeat, and word for word, the distressing sentence, at the time incomprehensible, yet uttered quite calmly." Celan dispelled any misunderstanding. Du Bouchet

[†] Originally published as "Entre Hölderlin et Celan," in: *Europe: revue littéraire mensuelle* 986–987 (2011), pp. 193–207.

[1] The topic was proposed by Bernard Böschenstein. The text of the lecture appeared in the Society's yearbook (du Bouchet 1988). It includes a general outline by Böschenstein in German: "Hölderlin in Frankreich. Seine Gegenwart in Dichtung und Übersetzung" ("Hölderlin in France. His presence in poetry and in the translation of his work") (304–320); then comes the German translation of du Bouchet's presentation (321–342), followed by the French text (343–359). This latter text was published the following year (1989) as "Tübingen, le 22 mai 1986" by Mercure de France, together with "Désaccordée comme par de la neige."

reports the incident in a slightly grandiose fashion, and his writing reflects his horror. He would have preferred not to have had such an experience, provoked by just a few words. He was shattered.

However, Celan was not telling him anything new; it was exactly what he had written in the very poem in which he evoked quite precisely the site of the insane man's home on the banks of the river Neckar. It was the poem "Tübingen, Jänner" ("Tübingen, January"), which du Bouchet was about to translate without realizing what it was saying, despite its enigmatic but clear and easily decipherable form.[2] The enigma is not the mystery, which it condemns; it is a means for

---

[2] [TN: Here is the German text, followed by an English translation:

Tübingen/Jänner

Zur Blindheit über-
Redete Augen.
Ihre—"ein
Rätsel ist Rein-
entsprungenes"—, ihre
Erinnerung an
Schwimmenden Hölderlintürme, möwen—
Umschwirrt.

Besuche ertrunkener Schreiner bei
diesen
tauchenden Worten:

Käme,
käme ein Mensch,
käme ein Mensch zur Welt, heute, mit
dem Lichtbart der
Patriarchen: er dürfte,
Spräch er von dieser
Zeit, er
dürfte
nur lallen und lallen,
immer-, immer-
zuzu.

("Pallaksch. Pallaksch")

The quotation in lines 3–5 is from Hölderlin's poem "Der Rhein." The last line represents a word Hölderlin used frequently during his periods of insanity; according to Jallet (2006:192), the word could be a dialectal form of Yiddish, meaning "perhaps," that the poet may have heard in the Jewish communities in the Rhineland.

Tübingen/January

Eyes talked into
Blindness.
Their – "an enigma is
the purely
originated"—, their

---

achieving clarity.[3] Du Bouchet was all the less able to grasp the pronouncement because the poem, as he understood it on its face, brought together two widely separated names, Hölderlin and Celan. A little later on, du Bouchet harks back to his confusion and his struggle with the text: "I cannot get the intonation quite right." Did Celan "at that moment really understand what he was saying?" Du Bouchet's hesitation notwithstanding, that moment was the perfect time for Celan to make this trenchant declaration. It took the form of a judgment that applied not only to the Swabian poet (treated ironically, for example, in the second stanza of the posthumously published "Ars poetica 62" [Celan 1997:87]: "I taught Hyperion the language that matters to us, professionals of the hymn"), but also to the recent use made of the Germanized work in Hitler's Reich, which Celan had detected in his youth.[4] For Heidegger, an interpreter of Hölderlin, and for those around him, in France and elsewhere, it was a powerful reference.

I took some of the courses taught by Jean Wahl during the years preceding du Bouchet's return from America in August 1948, and du Bouchet took the same courses later on. Wahl's courses were more open and appealing than others, as he did not address himself exclusively to a university audience; there was a lot of discussion of "metaphysical poetry." Later, there were lectures at the Collège de Philosophie in St. Germain-des-Prés, which were just as popular. Heidegger

---

memory of
Hölderlin's towers afloat, circled
by whirring gulls.

Visits of drowning joiners to
These
Submerging words:

Should,
should a man,
should a man come into the world, today, with
the shining beard of the
patriarchs: he could
if he spoke of this
time, he
could
only babble and babble
over, over
againagain.

("Pallaksh. Pallaksh.")

Michael Hamburger's translation (Celan 1988:177); Du Bouchet's French translation can be found in Celan 1986:28.]

[3]   See Bollack's preface to Wismann and König, 2011:13–19.
[4]   [TN: Hölderlin's work was appropriated by the Nazi regime. The centenary of his death was celebrated in Tübingen in 1943 in the presence of a group of Nazi dignitaries (Jallet 2006:174). The Hölderlin Society was founded at that time under Goebbels' aegis (Jallet 2006:176).]

was very much on the scene, despite the reservations he aroused. The intellectual climate makes one suppose that the setting adopted by the poet was not so much endured as chosen.

Celan loathed this world. Clearly, he had studied it closely when the occasion required, but he did not glorify it; on the contrary. Hölderlin did not figure among the writers with whom he was really associated—the canon is not very broad. Hölderlin was too "hymnic," too Greek and too Germanic; he was invoked at an inauspicious time, against the times. Du Bouchet had only to recognize Celan's allusion to the Wannsee conference, where in early 1942 the Nazis decided on the extermination of the Jews, as a reference in the word "January" ("Jänner") in the poem's title. Basically, du Bouchet's account of his astonishment re-opens the whole field in which the truth had already found its means of expression.

Soon after the discovery of Hölderlin's "Friedensfeier" ("Celebration of Peace"), I translated it at Bernard Böschenstein's behest; it was published by the Bibliothèque Bodmerienne in Geneva.[5] Du Bouchet sent me the large-format edition of *Hölderlin, Poème* published by Jean Hugues in 1961 (without engravings). We had just become acquainted: "Thank you, dear Sir, for your translation," he wrote, "faithful in every respect, and so clear, that it would have dissuaded me from undertaking my own, if I had known about it in time. Yours truly." It marked the beginning of our reading each other's work. André was not always very sure of the German. At that time, I had neither the knowledge nor the judgment that has guided me since then.

On September 12, 1964, he wrote to me: "Dear friend, may I turn to you once more? I have been asked to attach to this translation of "Friedensfeier," which you have gone over so carefully [this had been done in the meantime], the first version of it, which in fact constitutes a different poem: "Versöhnender der du nimmergeglaubt" ("Conciliator, you that no longer believed in")—I did my best to do it this summer—but I am unable to verify the French translation, and I came up against *fragen, wer es gewesen* ("ask who it was"[6]), as you can see. Would you have time to take a look at it?" Hölderlin's *Poèmes* published by Mercure de France date from that year (1986).

5   See Hölderlin 1955–1956. [TN: A holograph of the poem was discovered in 1954.]
6   [TN: Hölderlin 1980:428–429.]

Contemporary History in the Waters of Tübingen

I have published a study of Celan and Hölderlin, in which I analyzed as best I could the Heideggerian approach that generally prevailed in France at that time.[7] Jean Beaufret's books and the French translation of Beda Allemann's *Hölderlin und Heidegger*[8] all exerted a definite influence. I was obliged to point out the preconceptions—for example, those of Philippe Lacoue-Labarthe[9] (which he rectified later). The present discussion of du Bouchet's translation derives from these analyses, but does not depend on them; it has a different slant.

In du Bouchet's translation, the word "Jänner" ("January") could be misunderstood and thus fail to orient the reading. We know, however, that du Bouchet was familiar with Celan's talk, "The Meridian," published in French at the beginning of the first issue of *L'Éphémère* in 1966. Near the end of that text, we find a reminder of the journey that the writer Lenz had made in the Vosges mountains in the eighteenth century on the very date mentioned earlier in the speech, January 20.[10] Celan refers to it in "The Meridian" when he recalls his missed meeting with Adorno in the Engadine valley (more mountains), and inscribes it within the frame of his own experience. Du Bouchet translates: "Je m'étais, l'une et l'autre fois, à partir d'un autre '20 janvier,' le mien, sur tel pas transcrit. / Une rencontre m'a mis en présence de ... moi-même" ("In both instances, I'd begun writing from a '20th of January,' from my '20th of January.' It was ... myself I encountered" [Celan 2001:412]).[11] How did du Bouchet understand the mention

---

7   "De la dissolution du langage poétique. 'Tübingen, janvier' de Paul Celan," in Bollack 2001:105–138.

8   Allemann 1959. In Zurich, the Germanist Beda Allemann was a disciple of Emil Staiger, a professor and critic who was greatly influenced (to put it mildly) by Heidegger. Allemann was the editor of Celan's posthumous work; he remained true to Heidegger's line of thinking. One might call it orthodoxy; for the followers, it was not only necessary, but experienced as an initiation or a liberation, establishing a way of being and a habitus.

9   See Lacoue-Labarthe 1999.

10   "He: the true Lenz, Büchner's, Büchner's figure, the person we perceived on the story's first page, the Lenz who 'went walking in the mountains on the 20th of January,' he—not the artist and one concerned with the questions of art, but he as an I" (Celan 2001:407); and, in the preparatory notes: "we are still writing, even today, January 20—that January 20—this January 20, to which a certain number of things have since been added, in writing" (Celan 1999:30). [TN: The reference is to Georg Büchner's unfinished novella *Lenz*, written in 1836 and published after his death in 1837. Lenz was a poet who suffered from schizophrenia. See Michael Hamburger's translation (West Newbury, MA, 1969).]

11   Celan 2001:412. ("Ich hatte mich, das eine wie das andere Mal, von einem '20.Jänner,' von meinem '20. Jänner,' hergeschrieben. Ich bin ... mir selbst begegnet" [Celan 1999:11]). In Büchner's work it is not a premonition; the date becomes significant and reveals its import to the reader. In "Shibboleth: for Paul Celan" (1994:3–72), Jacques Derrida develops a long construct around the date in itself, in such a way that he empties the reference of its precise application.

of the date, here, and the upsurge of an identity, which was to be that of the poetic subject? The importance of this "origin" had been clear for forty-five years. I could cite, almost at random, a paperback of the poems with commentary by Jean-Michel Maulpoix, containing a section titled "January 20" (Celan 2009:42–44). Still, we have to wonder about du Bouchet's silence. Did he not perceive the clue, or did he repress it and brush it aside? The political commitment to which the clue attests exclusively and unilaterally was not compatible with his conception of writing and its internal data. Hölderlin, he thought, had the power to blur differences. So he performs an act of assimilation; it alters the smallest detail. With *Je m'étais ... sur tel pas transcrit*, emphasizing the literary rather than the political dimension, one perhaps loses the idea of a (Jewish) affiliation; a great tradition, claimed by the Jewish writer, is eliminated by a linguistic coup.

The meaning inscribed in the words may hide from the light, but it can still be uncovered. Not the poetry but the discourse surrounding it has carried it into another world. The quotation from Hölderlin recovers this transferred meaning: *ce qui est pur jaillissement* (the "purely originated") is an enigma, according to du Bouchet's translation; "pure" is, for Celan, "without stain" and without compromise. The eyes have their memory, which corrects—their own memory (this is repeated). "Hölderlin's towers" are in the water, given over to a conscious re-reading of the event. The seagulls do not add a merely descriptive element: the word "gull" (*mouette*) has more to say; it is a signifier.

"Visits of drowning joiners" in stanza 2: in this context, should one not say that they are all "drowned"? All the witnesses are dead, and by the same token their reception has lost its meaning, if we understand the prophetic speech (uttered in stanza 3). The prophecy from beyond the grave is formulated by the camps' victims. For a "man" (the German word *Mensch* doubtless has a Yiddish intonation) considering "this time" (*heute*, "today"), there would no longer be any language at all. A Talmudist, a prisoner of his ancestral customs, was there, in this delirium, the Hölderlin of madness. He would have spoken the truth by shaping the unspeakable.

If we want to translate the opening of "Tübingen, January," we have to take into account the sense that the word "eye" assumes in Celan's poetry. It has an idiomatic meaning: it represents an agency that follows and observes the writing, controlling the enigma and the process of re-semanticization. Du Bouchet translates it as *pupilles*, rather than *yeux* ("eyes"). Might his own blindness be a factor here? It is here, after all, that the false is obliged to tell the truth, by betraying itself. To recognize this betrayal, it is important to distinguish between ordinary discourse, "talking" (*Rede*, stanza 1), and poetic language, "speaking" (*Sprache*, stanza 3). The false subject does not lend itself very well to the principles to which du Bouchet adheres. His translation neutralizes and ignores the verdict that strikes what is called "persuasion," as when it was imposed in the intense celebration of Hölderlin beginning around 1900. It left in place all the wrong ideas that perpetuated repression.

We hear Celan talking to his friend, the French translator of his poems. Those people in Germany have laid claim to an impenetrable origin, ancient and modern; they have texts they can refer to. But these are *talmi* (counterfeit), these unequivocally initiatory but spurious compositions. What we must fight against now was already a "fake." That is how we should read the whole poem, written by Celan in 1961 and included in *Die Niemandsrose* (*The No One's Rose*) in1963. The "drowned joiners" are numerous; a whole crowd of them got together in Hölderlin's tower. The joiner Zimmer, the host responsible for his poet lodger, had a clear vision of this delirium. It was a madness that spoke the truth. The ancestral tradition, guarantor of humanization, if one needed to claim it in opposition to Hölderlin's devotees, should not be sought in Greece, nor in Christianity. But the other, Jewish tradition, which "speaks," no longer exists. It is dead in today's world, in "this time" (it is not *telle époque* ["such a time"], as du Bouchet would have it). If we were to make this past speak, it would be merely a babbling, in keeping with the words uttered by the madman.

The poem closes (twice) on a repeated fragment, shreds of language. Du Bouchet comes back to this conclusion and comments on it without considering its history. He cannot manage to find a place in his reflection for the existence of a dead tradition, nor can he accommodate the placement of a madman's word. He wonders: "the word *Pallaksch* ... is it Hölderlin's word or Celan's, when the latter appropriates it in his own poem?"[12] One can see the immense distance Celan has created, though not for du Bouchet in particular. In a historical projection he shows what separates us forever from all the traditional legitimizations, be they Jewish and Talmudic. Now only a critical gaze survives. In desperation he denounces and dismantles repressive systems. Du Bouchet, however, makes this babbling a "word ... that has not been translated, a murmured word ... it too lies at the origin of the poem (like the word 'coarse')."[13] A substratum of language. This word, "out of tune within the Hölderlin poem [he is referring to "Tübingen, Jänner"] is nevertheless a word," or a "way into the poem." What lies "outside," access to the common reality of history, cannot (or: could not) keep its place in the work; thus the translator goes around in circles. Later on, he will return to the poem and to his conception of the way language shifts ("the clear word ... becomes temporarily opaque again").

---

[12] Du Bouchet 1989:69.
[13] "Krudes," in the poem "Todtnauberg," where "the coarse" is called "monstrous"; see below, p. 343.

In the meantime, I recalled (quite fortuitously) that Gilles Jallet had written a paper on Celan's comment on Hölderlin's poetry—the comment that du Bouchet had reported to the Hölderlin Society (du Bouchet 1989)—and that Jallet had related Celan's comment to his own grasp of the poem du Bouchet was translating.[14] Jallet is aware that Celan's language expresses a radical critique of poetic discourse and its veneration. Hölderlin did not take history into consideration—no more and no less than du Bouchet. Nor could the French poet measure the critical and almost transcendental distance that poetry, when it freed itself, could open up before its deployment.

In Hölderlin's hymn "Der Rhein" ("The Rhine"), at the beginning of the fourth stanza, the line *Ein Räthsel ist Reinentsprungenes* ("A mystery are those of pure origin") refers to the tension created by an origin that is no longer Greek, but linked to the water,[15] to the river if it truly manifests the power of that origin, and to the reality of the song that celebrates it. Jallet recognizes that it is not this meaning, the meaning of the phrase in the hymn, which is expressed in the quotation from the poem, but an interpretation; it retains the presence of the water and extends it to the point of "almost total dissolution" (which he finds in the second stanza of Celan's poem). However, the context connects the words to *Augen* ("eyes"), to their transformation into poetry. With enigmatization, they present to language the "freedom" of a readjustment. Memory is consolidated here, in a place where in the end the deadly towers float (still "swimming" [*schwimmende*], as the eye implies the poetic idiom). Memory is surrounded by seagulls, birds of death. One can hear in the word *Möwe* ("gull") an assonance (*Löwe*, "lion"), and if we think of the French (as Celan often does), we have the word *mouette*, which can be related to mutism through the apophony *muet* ("mute"). It is in any case a question of destruction (Jallet himself sees the flotsam); there is no shortage of reference to the killers.

It is not enough to say that the plural ("joiners") is confused with "Hölderlin's visitors," who existed and were known to him and to us (Jallet 2006:189). The reverse is more accurate. The protectors of a longstanding demand in poetry will be the visitors to the disaster; they are all dead ("drowned in poetry"); they rush to hear the message. Celan had already told his friend du Bouchet, without addressing him directly, what he needed to know.

Jallet is right to insist on the demonstrative adjectives, correcting du Bouchet. The visitors, in their funereal domain, are drawn by *"these ... words"* (*diesen ... Worten*); in the second stanza, they announce the intractable statement of the third, which concerns *"this time"* (*spräch er von dieser Zeit*). But this is

---

[14] Jallet 2006:173–193.
[15] Hölderlin 1966; cited from Hölderlin 1980:410. [TN: In German there is a play on the homonyms "Rhein" ("Rhine") and "rein" ("pure").]

not syllabic babble, which would be the only appropriate language. We have to include an intermediary position: if the "just" of the Talmud, perpetuating the tradition of the fathers of the Torah, were concerned with defining what had occurred, their knowledge would be unproductive; they would end up with an iteration that closes up into an unintelligible and incommunicable language. This is what the poet in his madness must have known. We have to conclude that the wisdom of the *tzaddiks* (righteous men) is obsolete, that a tradition is dead. One can no longer create a poem without knowing that, and without speaking of its loss, as Celan did. It is not only the Greeks and Hölderlin who are mute; one can no longer lay claim to the Jewish tradition either. Celan does not do that; he contradicts and corrupts a poetic tradition to protect himself from corruption.

Henri Meschonnic, with his customary violence, attacked André du Bouchet's translations in a diatribe published in early January 1972 in *Les Cahiers du chemin*, which was edited by Pascal Quignard ("On appelle cela traduire Celan"—"They call that translating Celan").[16] André informed me of his indignation in the autumn of 1971: "My dear Jean, 'for your archives,' these thoughtless and insulting pages, which I would hope—for Quignard's sake—will not be published. I was determined to tell him so, and in these terms ... ." Quignard did not listen to him. I recall that I dissociated myself from the polemicist and told him why. I reproached him for not railing against his mentors and colleagues, who were weaker. Now, on a quite different plane, I want to point out the insuperable gap between the two kinds of writing.

Language Triumphs over Meaning

In the poem "Todtnauberg," "The Mountain of Death,"[17] which captures the essential features of a visit to Heidegger in his cottage (*Hütte*) in the Black Forest, Celan focuses in particular on the guest book (it is not "a book" but "the book," in which everything that matters to the visitor is inscribed); these are lines 6 to 16 of the third stanza:

> The line
> —whose name did the book
> Register before mine?—,
> the line inscribed

16 Meschonnic 1973:367–405.
17 See "Le Mont de la mort: le sens d'une rencontre entre Celan et Heidegger, un commentaire du poème 'Todtnauberg,'" in Bollack 1997:349–376. Du Bouchet had probably not read it in Michel Surya's review *Lignes* (Bollack 1996)—his *Pourquoi si calmes* was published the same year—but rather in my 1997 book.

in that book about
a hope, today,
of a thinking man's
coming
word
in the heart[18]

The poet makes a request of the philosopher. He reveals his expectation that the latter account for his Nazi past. The "thinker" is Heidegger. In the interpretation required by the Celanian idiom, "thinking" presupposes memory; it remains bound to history, to the truth of political events.

With *relevés* ("recorded"), the reader does not immediately understand, as he should, that these are the names already written in the guest book (earlier visitors, dignitaries of the Nazi intelligence community), the book open before the "thinker." Du Bouchet does not really sustain the reference to the Nazi past; for him, the thinking refers to what the philosopher (not the reader) will remember from the entries (*de qui méditera*). His thought remains anchored in the perspective of a future that is always open, or never closed. However, the expectation concerns the present moment, and even more so the poem—the moment of this poem ("today"), the *hic* of the fountain and the *nunc* ("today") of the visitor.[19] The philosopher ensures the broadest possible philosophical justification—immutable, existential, ontological—of what is to come. But the supplicant will be more demanding. It is *this* hour that counts, what it brings and what will be given to it. Celan has come for that purpose: so that his host, if he *thinks*, should think not of death in the abstract (*Sein zum Tod*, "Being-towards-death"), but of the victims murdered in the camps. The "word," for a thinker, would be to agree to this and to reserve a place in his philosophical system for

---

[18] [TN: English translation from Celan 1988:293.] Here is du Bouchet's translation of the lines from "Todtnauberg":

> la ligne dans le livre
> —quels sont les noms
> accueillis avant le mien?—
> la ligne écrite
> dans le livre
> touchant l'espoir
> dans le coeur, aujourd'hui,
> d'un mot
> à venir
> (à venir incessamment)
> de la part d'un penseur

[19] [TN: Reference in earlier lines in the poem to the "fountain," a well from which Celan drank (Celan 1988:293).]

the extermination, as the poet does in his poetical work. The poet's insistence is not relegated to an infinite opening; it relates to an immediate realization.

Du Bouchet's reading of the text is instructive (1989:81–88). The appeal becomes a lesson. "Meditation" ennobles. The poet is presumed to have come so as to understand the other, his partner, when in fact he is issuing an order. Thus the conflict is erased, and with it, the reason for the visit that the poet, unwillingly, had decided to make. The philosopher will not bend. During the drive after lunch he is careful not to do anything but recall his own vision of history, and that confirms all Celan's misgivings.[20]

No doubt du Bouchet could not see that in his translation he only half-filled in the gulf or the abyss that the philosopher opened up. The "monstrous" appears. Du Bouchet is Heideggerizing. The driver (a student who is present during the conversation) hears what is said; Celan attributes to him the role of witness, an objective "third party" (stanza 7). What is said is remembered; *lui-même à son écoute* ("he himself listening") does not convey that. It should be *entendre dire* ("hearing [what is] said"). The translation, as is so often the case, is too refined; it misses a simpler rendering that would maintain the precision. Questing too deeply into language makes the meaning disappear. The driver hears what is said; he is charged with preserving memory and with transmitting it to the future.

In his talk in Tübingen in 1986, du Bouchet returned to this passage in the poem. He made a serious error: "thus, along the way [a telling expression of his approach], in the poem titled 'Todtnauberg,' where, more than in the book, or books [implying the presence of a great number of books, where there is in fact only one, the one in which successive guests have left traces], belonging to the philosopher Paul Celan wished to visit one day, there emerges, I believe, what might be the origin of a poem." Theory regains the upper hand. Du Bouchet ought to have identified the reason for the "wish." Is he thinking about the "way"? About the unexpected benefit of a meeting? The truth of a "way of thinking," which Celan knew well and had always opposed, emerged clearly during a meeting. Borrowing du Bouchet's terms, we could say that it took place "along the way," that is, that it had been planned, then staged by the poet, who knew perfectly well what he was taking on. He knew that he would not be heard (du Bouchet, too much of a Heideggerian and a phenomenologist, could not see this), but that the wound of discord would first of all be exposed, and then would remain open. In both situations—du Bouchet faced with Hölderlin, Heidegger faced with the Nazi past—Celan speaks in the name of a tribunal. Du Bouchet

---

[20] See below, Chap. 27, "The Mountain of Death."

had just written, paraphrasing Heraclitus:[21] "what one wishes for is not always desirable." (Did Celan's desire go astray in this wish?) The return to this crucial stanza in Celan's poem, which du Bouchet appropriates, is in line with the localization of nothing, of an "origin" (*Ursprung*) outside a particular language (*langue*) lodged in language (*langage*). This non-being is obvious in the layout of du Bouchet's printed page, in all the blank spaces that separate and disconnect. He is twice confronted with the cruelty of fascist speech. Celan relates this nothingness to the incomprehensible babble of insanity, the *Pallaksch* that expresses Hölderlin's denial. However, in the situation of the drive in the Black Forest, so carefully circumscribed, the philosopher, in the car that "carries him away," gets "carried away" in turn by exposing his hand, as anticipated. He confirmed and sealed his old commitments to Hitler. In du Bouchet's 1986 talk, the political dimension that guided Celan is completely overlooked.

One might go further, moving away from the meaning of the texts but approaching instead du Bouchet's conception of the language of poetry. What could be better than all these books, a whole library (we understand the importance of the plural that he introduces), and the whole culture, a receptacle of all the chance currents of history? The line break certainly raises this question. They left the cottage, getting back to a less absolute "outside." The "along the way" expresses the whole truth. The visit was nothing but a whim on Celan's part, a place where "he wanted to go one day," on impulse or out of envy. Du Bouchet's reading becomes clear. What Celan hears the other person say in the car would be remarks about the pine trees, about the great moments revealed by a truer nature, between fire and water. Du Bouchet situates the "appearances" against a background of absence. He provides a reading independent of words that rehabilitates Heidegger, leads back to himself and at the same time to his own aesthetics.

•••

André du Bouchet often sent my wife and me signed copies of his publications. He regularly informed me of his interest in mine. These are beautiful letters. I cannot remember all that I sent him—probably several of my interpretations of Celan. He read them with inevitably contradictory feelings, opening himself to them, questioning them and defending himself; in 1992, when he sent us *Axiales*, he wrote: "in true agreement, disagreement and friendship"; in 1994, for *Carnet*, he wrote: "the thick layers of time sometimes crossed / with my friendly regards"; this was a step in a precise direction. Then, going much further in 1996

---

[21]   See frag. 110 in Bollack and Wismann 1995:308–309.

(*Pourquoi si calmes*): "in admiration of his exegesis and the incessant advance of meaning / their friend." It is in this book that we find the reflection "Autour du mot la neige est réunie" ("Snow is gathered around the word"), a return to Celan's language that I probably helped to bring about.

Du Bouchet was surely shaken by my discussion of "The Mountain of Death." He wrote to me on April 17, 1997:

Dear Jean,

This generous and courageous book reached me in Paris; a few health problems have kept me here. Reading your book has thrown some light on my own difficulties with syntax. By the way, as you say so well, reading the poem, which is already so familiar, as if one had never read it before, places limits on decoding at the same time, if—once more— one can be led to read it in the dimension that again escapes us. I see myself there, thrown back on my own difficulties with reading and syntax, however indefensible they may be, and which I usually do not experience as difficulties. But the conversation you keep opening will always be both profitable and enlightening for me.

To you and Mayotte, my regards and admiration, from your old friend, André.

The repetition of the word "syntax" may seem surprising. It is the tool of clarification. According to du Bouchet, the poet "usually" cares nothing about it. In the end the argumentation remains dogmatic. My own reading renews and changes the data, but it is as if the newness is proof above all of the resources of language, transcending still more, in the composed work, all the obsessions, and as if the process would otherwise have to be challenged.

One evening when Celan was accompanying me (here again I know where: we were walking along the quays on the way home from a talk at the Goethe Institute on the Avenue d'Iéna in Paris), he said—just like that, without any context—that the vocabulary of du Bouchet, whose work he was translating or had translated (*Vakante Glut / Dans la chaleur vacante* was published in 1968), was limited. He was unquestionably implying that du Bouchet should have moved beyond the restrictions or the asceticism he had imposed upon himself. A different outside demanded words other than those devoured by the empty spaces on the page. Du Bouchet was to be found in his empty spaces; Celan discovered in these same spaces a whole literary tradition, an expressive force that was not, after all, unique to du Bouchet.

At the closing session of the colloquium dedicated to Celan's work at the Maison des Écrivains in 1995, du Bouchet came to read his translation of "The Meridian." He knew that other translations had been produced in the interim, and he had not revised his text. He read it very deliberately, like a document written by him and in his language. He delivered it just as it was, like something that had been important in his life at one time. In this gesture, as elsewhere, there was both obstinacy and a natural honesty.

For du Bouchet, poetry formed a truth, much as the heritage of past thinkers concerns philosophers. He included certain authors and excluded others. Celan proceeded in the same way, to some extent, but the split was not cultural: it was based on a conscious decision; it was more radical. In short, there was no poetry but his own. Different from others', his was both personal and definable; it had its own criteria. The rejections were not implicit, nor were the (less common) alliances. It was thus a constitutively positive relationship to a whole literary tradition that led du Bouchet almost spontaneously to include Celan, out of admiration and friendship but also necessity, in the circle he set up for himself. These choices are cultural, or perhaps aesthetic. Celan isolates himself, he separates himself more than he seeks himself, otherwise he would be less subversive. The "person" he speaks about in his reflections precedes any entry into language—whether, if one adopts du Bouchet's point of view, it be that of a Baudelaire or a Reverdy (Mallarmé, overly autonomous, is obviously exempt). Du Bouchet allows himself to be guided by his philosophical concepts, almost by a system. Nothingness will no longer be the same; it is, as it were, embodied.

A Definitive Clarification

In 1996, in "Autour du mot la neige est revenue," with the repetition of the word *neige* so characteristic of Celan's language, du Bouchet returned to the discussion and to a difference of which he became more clearly aware at that moment (1996:11–16).[22] Thus the two points of view can be contrasted. He argues, spells out his own position, transforms, and challenges. From reference to history and events, to which as a poet he declares he cannot submit, he passes resolutely to an ambition to orient and transcend language, and to a kind of metaphysics. His demonstration focuses on words associated with "terrible" (and "terror"). Of the thirty-six units, small blocks that divide the page according to the style of poetic composition, these two words recur in some form nine times: once on page 12, then five times on page 13, twice on page 14, and once more on

---

[22] [TN: The collection *Pourquoi si calmes* included "Autour du mot la neige est revenue" ("Around the word snow has come back"), an essay in which du Bouchet (1996:92) focused on Celan's work.]

page 15. If one were referring to the reality of war, suppressions, and annihilation, one would shake off much firmer and more radical wellsprings of poetic work. Du Bouchet depends on a prior authority to which nothingness (and consequently all forms of absence and destruction) remains attached above all else. Du Bouchet takes a strong stand; he is defending a fundamental cause, and so, without losing his customary style, he composes, better than an *ars poetica*, an authentic well-formed plea in favor of his art before an adversary. One can sense his fury.

The position of the adversary is constructed with words drawn from Celan's poems, which du Bouchet listens to again in his own way, reinterprets, and transposes. The references take little or no notice of their original context; to this extent, they remain indeterminate in an absence of meaning.

From the start, a certain transcendence is introduced by way of a borrowing from Celan's "L'entretien dans la montagne" ("Conversation in the Mountains");[23] these are the two colors of "nature" ("green" and "white"). What characterizes a language, in Celan's text, to which the two Jews who are talking have no access,[24] is presented by du Bouchet as the language of an external space ("which, outside, is the language of the glacier" [du Bouchet 1996, p. 11, line 8[25]]). It is not the other, nor is it a tradition to be adapted, but a language outside the human realm, a language that is at the same time and by analogy the approach to a "self" (11,10). The conclusion is formulated starting on the first page—there is no place for any "name" (the "name" in Celan tells the truth). Du Bouchet, in the tension of the "meantime" that he conjectures (12, 1), knows for himself, and as for himself, that "the elements" involved are "not solely those of his language" (12, 9). Transcendence claims its due. With the disappearance of time, we approach another kind of "terrible," reconfigured as a meta-presence (12, 6–10). Du Bouchet refers to another term—*Schreibzähnen* ("writing-teeth")—in Celan's collection *Schneepart* (*Snow Part*):

> To speak with the blind alleys
> of the opposite,
> of its
> expatriated
> meaning—:
> to chew

---

23 "Gespräch im Gebirg," Celan 1983, 3:169–173; in English, cited below from Celan 2001:397–400.

24 [TN: "Jew Gross" and "Jew Klein" are the two speakers in the "Conversation in the Mountains," representing Adorno and Celan in a planned meeting in the Engadine valley that did not take place (see above, Chapter 25.)

25 Further citations from this text are given in abbreviated form, with the line number following the page number.

> this bread, with
> writing-teeth.[26]

Languages are obviously situated within the limits of the human, almost super-human, mission. One needs "teeth." Du Bouchet re-translates; he escapes the impasse and finds the "bite ... of the elementary." The displacement allows him to reconsolidate the powers of the outside as action taking place inside, close to language. The terrible is removed and installed elsewhere; it has infinitely more sovereignty than history: "Not a word can be placed on it" (12, 17). From this one has to deduce that "to the terrible, which is the subject of Paul Celan's poetry, it [that poetry] will not have returned, strictly speaking" (13, 1–2). The last words drive in the nail; they describe in positive terms the system as du Bouchet conceives it. The misunderstanding is not, cannot be, specified; there is a basic incompatibility between two poetic pursuits that will never see eye to eye. These remarks are merely details. Another's word—an opinion—is transformed into a retort, a blunt rejection. Celan's "terrible" basically repudiates the real terror that nourishes poetry, in du Bouchet's view. Thus du Bouchet tries to explicate the most intimate experiences produced by writing (see the progression in the description or successive definitions of negativity [13, 2–6]). Moving forward in the exploration of the "unknown elementary components" (13, 18), he considers that he has taken *a step outside the human* (in italics in the text, 13, 20–21). Does he think he has encountered Celan's strangeness, when Celan has alienated himself in order to break free from discourse-obstacles? The "step" for du Bouchet reveals an internal and integrated antecedence, an absolute anteriority in speech. He communicates an experiment he purports to have carried out on language.

The "outside" opens onto closer cohabitations; provisionally, one can "share oneself" with that outside (14, 2). In this first section, which is more audacious and speculative, du Bouchet refers to two poems in the collection *Atemwende* (*Breathturn*): on the one hand, he mentions—from the end of the first part of the collection—a very carefully composed poem, "Weggebeizt" ("Eroded"), which does not interest him; on the other hand, he goes on to consider "Singbarer Rest" ("Singable Remnant").[27] From these poems he retains two expressions, two ideas, that of a residue (or "survival") and that of hospitality, found in the context of the glacial structures, revealing the complex relations stemming from the interventions of the external pole.[28]

---

[26] "Mit den Sackgassen sprechen," Celan 1983, 2:31, 36; in English, "To speak with the blind alleys," Celan 2014:342–345.

[27] Celan 1983, 2:31, 36; Celan 2014:18–19, 20–21.

[28] See du Bouchet 1996: 14, line 6 to the end.

A logic follows its course. How can a great poet not be affected by a system whose power another poet has felt? Should the system not be re-integrated at all costs, instead of being assimilated, when it is a question of poetry itself, of its practice?

Works Cited

Allemann, B. 1959. *Hölderlin et Heidegger: recherche sur la relation entre poésie et pensée.* Trans. F. Fédier. Paris. Orig. pub. 1954.

Bollack, J. 1996. "Le Mont de la mort. Le sens d'une rencontre entre Celan et Heidegger, un commentaire du poème 'Todtnauberg.'" *Lignes* 29:157–188. Repr. in J. Bollack, *La Grèce de personne* (Paris, 1997), 349–376.

———. 2001. *Poésie contre poésie, Celan et la littérature.* Paris.

Bollack, J., and H. Wismann. 1995. *Héraclite ou la séparation.* Paris. Orig. pub. 1972.

Böschenstein, B. 1988. "Hölderlin in Frankreich. Seine Gegenwart in Dichtung und Übersetzung." *Hölderlin-Jahrbuch* 26 (1988–1989):304–320.

Celan, P. 1968. "Tübingen/Jänner." Trans. A. du Bouchet. *L'Éphémère* 7:22–23.

———. 1978. *Poèmes de Paul Celan.* Trans. A. du Bouchet. Paris.

———. 1983. *Gesammelte Werke.* Ed. B. Allemann et al. 7 vols. Frankfurt.

———. 1986. *Paul Celan, Poèmes.* Trans. A. du Bouchet. Bilingual edition. Paris.

———. 1989. *Poems of Paul Celan.* Trans. M. Hamburger. New York.

———. 1995. *Paul Celan, Franz Wurm: Briefwechsel.* Ed. B. Wiedemann with F. Wurm. Frankfurt. Orig. pub. 1965.

———. 1997. *Die Gedichte aus dem Nachlass.* Ed. B. Badiou, J.-C. Rambach, and B. Wiedemann. Frankfurt.

———. 1999. *Der Meridian: Endfassung-Entwürfe-Materialien.* Ed. B. Böschenstein and H. Schmull. Frankfurt.

———. 2001. *Selected Poems and Prose of Paul Celan.* Ed. and trans. J. Felstiner. New York.

———. 2004. *Strette. Poèmes + Le Méridien and L'entretien dans la montagne.* Trans. A. du Bouchet. Paris. Orig. pub. 1971.

———. 2009. *Choix de poèmes.* Ed. J.-M. Maulpoix. Paris.

———. 2014. *Breathturn into Timestead.* Trans. P. Joris. New York.

Derrida, J. 1994. "Shibboleth: for Paul Celan." Trans. Joshua Wilner. In *Word Traces: Readings of Paul Celan,* ed. A. Fioretos, 3–72. Baltimore, MD. Orig. pub. 1986.

Du Bouchet, A. 1970. "Hölderlin aujourd'hui." *L'Éphémère* 14 (Summer):158–170.

———. 1988. "Tübingen, le 22 mai 1986." *Hölderlin-Jahrbuch* 26 (1988–1989):343–359.

————. 1989. *Désaccordée comme par de la neige* et *Tübingen, le 22 mai 1986*. Paris. Orig. pub. 1988.

————. 1996. *Pourquoi si calmes*. Saint-Clément de Rivière.

Hölderlin, J. C. F. 1955-1956. "Friedensfeier." Trans. J. Bollack. *Hölderlin-Jahrbuch* 9:226–231.

————. 1980. *Poems and Fragments*. Trans. M. Hamburger. New York. Orig. pub. 1966.

Jallet, G. 2006. "'Dans la langue, le pourri': André du Bouchet et Paul Celan." In *Le crâne de Schiller: langue incomparable de la tête de mort*. Paris.

Lacoue-Labarthe, P. 1999. *Poetry as Experience*. Trans. A. Tarnowski. Stanford. Orig. pub. 1986.

Martinez, V. N. d. *Aux sources du dehors: poésie, pensée, perception dans l'oeuvre d'André du Bouchet*. Unpublished dissertation.

Meschonnic, H. 1973. *Pour la poétique II: épistémologie de l'écriture poétique dans la traduction*. Paris.

24

Grasping Hermeneutics[†]

PETER SZONDI was a very important influence, in my personal and intellectual life first of all, but equally in the history of my work, thanks to the discussions we carried on for more than twelve years about literatures—of which he was a marvelous connoisseur and judge—and about the theory of interpretation. His dense and demonstrative essays have surely transformed literary studies, and they have even more effectively rehabilitated the status and the rights of reflection in this area. After his death, I was asked to edit, with the help of some of his students, a major posthumous work that was published starting in 1971 by Suhrkamp (Frankfurt); the work included his truly innovative *Einführung in die literarische Hermeneutik* (*Introduction to Literary Hermeneutics*). The pages that follow constitute the afterword to the French edition (Paris, 1989).[1]

The course of the same name marked a turning point in Szondi's positions. He had combated the idea that works have an internal autonomy based on a system of established values that can be rendered explicit, although the system itself had not been questioned; consequently, he had emphasized the stages of social and historical mediation. Then, during the 1960s, he came to take the construction of the works increasingly into consideration, by including forms of poetic expression through the aesthetic character of textuality. This new orientation led him to take an interest in the birth of a non-theological hermeneutics, proper to literature, starting in the eighteenth century. Countering Gadamer, he showed what an immense liberation had come to light at the point when, pulling away from general hermeneutics, another more specific gaze, anticipating Mallarmé, had striven to shed light on the technical problems of verbal creation and composition.

[†] Originally published as "Dire les herméneutiques," in: Jean Bollack, *La Grèce de personne: les mots sous le mythe* (Paris, 1997), pp. 115–116.
[1] See below, Chap. 25.

25

A Future in the Past[†]
Peter Szondi's Material Hermeneutics

PETER SZONDI'S REDEFINITION of the science of literature challenged the influence that the analysis of Heidegger's structure of *Dasein* had exerted in Germany, in university circles, both during and after World War II.[1] Szondi takes aim at the model constituted by Heidegger's commentaries on the poems of Hölderlin, Trakl, and Rilke. What actually underlay Szondi's struggle in favor of a critical philology was his rejection of an approach based on a theological premise. Even in France, where some thinkers are fascinated by the deceptive allure of going beyond traditional scholarship, such an approach appears to be dominant.

Although the model for the new ways of reading had been borrowed from the philosophy of existence, it was well suited to the stylistic traditions and age-old practices of exegesis. Hans Georg Gadamer included and legitimized them in his theory of hermeneutics.[2] He found "philology" too unrepresentative of positivist science to be incorporated in his theory of hermeneutics or to contribute to the business of "regenerating" knowledge. He aimed to separate the theory of historical understanding from the method of the so-called historico-philologists. The success of this new codification depended on the justification of current practices in literary discourse, but also on positions assumed in the cultural and political arena.

[†] Originally published as "Un futur dans le passé. L'herméneutique matérielle de Peter Szondi," in: Jean Bollack, *La Grèce de personne: les mots sous le mythe* (Paris, 1997), pp. 117–127.

[1] Works dealing with the response of German scholars to Heidegger's philosophy in the two decades following World War II are presented and explained in relation to their origin in Duroche 1967. The author conducts an analysis of the theoretical prerequisites for reading such authors as Emil Staiger, Max Bense, Theophil Spörri, and especially Johannes Pfeiffer, and helps to explain the reaction that arose in the sixties.

[2] Gadamer 1982:251. Historical research echoes quite magically the self-generated display of tradition—the "thing" that is also called "dogma," both in texts and in language.

The role played by the "inexplicable" or by implicit structures survives today in almost identical form in other types of discourse. Although these do not assign the permanence to the values of "tradition" that Gadamer did, they have the same function as Gadamer's discourse: they work to erase the boundaries and blunt the edge of a criticism that differentiates between its objects.

All the critics maintained the radical distinction that had been introduced between "thought" as a noble term, and what was reduced, by the very process of distinction, to a positivist science of literature, even though scholars like Gadamer expressed reservations about the violence perpetrated on texts, or about the obsessive interrogation of language as it was pressured into revealing its contents. The distinction remained in force even after the anti-positivist reaction that Szondi had encountered in his youth, in immanent or empathetic exegeses, had been abandoned in favor of the auscultation of language; and in the shifting of signs, it continued to reveal the intermittent structure of Being, just as existentialist philosophy was doing. The explication of poetic texts, enhanced and ennobled by the prestige of their reference to sacred texts, with their eclipses and their proximity, had the advantage of being strengthened by a theory. At the same time, the ontological leap, through a kind of hyperbaton[3] or exaggeration, concealed a regression, which brought interpretation, falling short of analysis, to a rhetoric conceived as a collection of figures, what we might call a trans-substantiated rhetoric.

Now that positivist science had been irreparably devalued, reduced to the common rank of historical fact, an alternative conservative legitimacy had to be found. Neither theoreticians nor interpreters were ready to give up the premise of the continuity and unity of Greek and German cultures. Whenever a claim was made for science, it was treated with scorn, as being out of reach and illusory; it was compromised even before being examined and compared to a collection of facts that could exclude it from the field of hermeneutics. Science was considered contingent and trivialized. What remained, auscultation of the text, was not subject to any analysis; indeed, it referred to the psychological expectations that structure it,[4] owing to the hermeneutic circle.

Consequently, Szondi's critique of the deficiencies of philological criticism came with a turn to "hermeneutics," construed as a "science" on the basis of a redefinition of its specificity (literary, historical, or juridical) and determined

---

[3]   [TN: A departure from the expected word order.]

[4]   See Szondi 1995:16, for his critique of Chladenius' work: "It is also empirical, which means it is specific enough not to ignore individual problems for the sake of concentrating on an act of understanding." [TN: Johann Martin Chladenius (1710–1759), a German philosopher, theologian, and historian, was considered one of the founders of hermeneutics. He declared reading to be a science, not an art. Szondi dedicated four chapters to him in his *Introduction*.]

by the nature of the object (see below, p. 358). With hindsight, we can better understand the implications of what seems like a closing-off, because Szondi intends not only (*intra muros*) to analyze the errors caused by excessive application of the positivist methods of the natural sciences to philological knowledge,[5] he is also concerned (outside this sphere) with the pretentious contestation, still alive today, of any critical approach in the field of writing, and with the way this attitude is legitimated by the assumption of total knowledge, an all the more dangerous assumption because it embraces and authorizes ignorance. Heidegger's arbitrary transfers between languages, applied to the reinterpretation of texts, had changed the rules. The claim to immediate existential knowledge, based on trans- and a-historical categories, eliminated anything in textual analysis that could not meet philosophical expectations, creating an unexceptional methodology inherent to the discipline. Critical justification of these approaches had fallen out of favor. Hence the twofold movement imposed on what was a real advance. In the face of such contempt, one had both to distance oneself from the rejection of critical re-examination within scientific production and to demystify the theme of external immediacy that phenomenology provided. This dual orientation is a fundamental characteristic of Szondi's approach—the critical *catharsis* in action—and of the battle he waged against a form of usurpation. The domain of textual criticism should be expanded; rules would ensue from that expansion.

Szondi was Emil Staiger's student in Zurich, where he was introduced to more than just philology: he focused primarily on the analysis of "style" in relation to the differences between genres, which, according to Staiger, emanate from ontological categories,[6] and, more generally, on the theoretical reflection that accompanies interpretation in a process of mutual fortification. It is here, on this single issue, that their positions converged; otherwise, their points of view were diametrically opposed. Very early on, Szondi viewed grandiloquence as a disturbing figure in the decoding of Being, and he rejected it; he took refuge in reading other scholars, particularly Lukács. Thus he fell indirectly, through Staiger, under Heidegger's influence, but quickly rejected it, offended by a pretention that bore the outward signs of depth and lived off the prestige of literature writ large.

The hermeneutics of the phenomenological schools under the influence of Wilhelm Dilthey holds that the field of historical consciousness controlled by the subject is limited. Consciousness is transcended by the appeal of the "dogmatic" power of tradition, rather than of the work itself. An interpreter cannot escape

---

[5] See the conclusion of Szondi 1986:3–22, "On Textual Understanding."
[6] See Staiger 1991.

it without hampering the artistic or poetic experience. It is tradition that, in principle, prevails over its objectivization in a "science of literature."[7] Since the Romantic era, the front lines of literary criticism have been redrawn, and are still in flux. Interpreters remain the slaves of tradition. They can understand a text only if they allow themselves to be imbued by the voice, which stems not from the literary work, nor even from the author, but which nevertheless makes itself understood through the act of writing and listening, always the same and yet multiple. Empathy, doggedly rejected by Szondi, has a theoretical justification. It is not merely a matter of participation; if the literary work produces the elements that allow it to be understood, it is because these elements are inherent to a deep, general, and common structure. "Grasp what grabs us"; the paradox became the watchword of this doctrine for reading.[8] The vicious circle is not only accepted, it is set up as an end in itself. Understanding binds the reader, "grabs" him, just as, in Lacan's theory, the imagination is in thrall to language. It is from this constraint, which obstructs the path to knowledge, that historical understanding and aesthetic analysis can emerge. Knowledge is pre-structured; its determinations direct and control both writing and interpretation. Order does not originate in the text; rather, it has multiple origins, whether unconscious or informed by layers of preconceptions. The common thread among different points of view is the search for an authority that could possess and at the same time dispossess the reader.

If descriptive hermeneutics methodically disparages the author's reflection on his own work, and if such reflection is by definition suspect, it is because artistic production escapes the producer, who is continually outpaced by the inherent dynamism, anonymous and collective, of a power flowing through him that he can control only at the cost of becoming a mere "artist," a master of artifice and fake authenticity. The more fettered the author, the more independent the interpreter. He can discover, re-invent, or even invent the meaning of a work that has not been subjected to the oversight of a consciousness. Indeed, science—as long as it sticks to its method and to its will to objectivize—is thought to misunderstand the nature of its own knowledge, which transcends the analytical power of exegesis, just as creation transcends the impulse of a subject-creator.

---

[7] Gadamer (1982:469) uses the term "dogmatic" to refer to content untouched by historical objectivism. See also Gadamer 1974, col. 1069: the validity claimed by art should always be called "dogmatic."

[8] Gadamer's adaptation (1974) of a quotation from Staiger (1953:11): "was uns der unmittelbare Eindruck aufschliesst, ist der Gegenstand literarischer Forschung; dass wir begreifen, was uns ergreift, das ist das eigentliche Ziel aller Literaturwissenschaft" ("our immediate impression on reading a text is precisely the object of literary research; that we should grasp what grabs us, that is the real aim of the science of literature").

Instead of reflecting on the difference between the historical situations of author and reader and including this difference in the interpretive process, first acknowledging and then evaluating it, Gadamer uses it against History. The rationalistic gap advanced by the Enlightenment theorist Chladenius between the text or the author, on the one hand, and the meaning of the text on the other,[9] is exploited in favor of a move toward a profound distortion, which testifies against History and in favor of a productive "historicity." Gadamer praises Chladenius, "who does not yet see understanding in terms of history."[10] If we agree with Gadamer that "the real meaning of a text ... is always partly determined also by the historical situation of the interpreter," the radical discrepancy between the points of view appears in his conclusion: "and hence [*und damit*] by the totality of the objective course of History [*das Ganze des objektiven Geschichtsganges*]."[11] The "course of history" occupies the position that Szondi assigns to the interpreter. The same credo is applied to the creator-subject and the interpreted subject, invested with the same dogmatic content: "An author does not need to know the real meaning of what he has written."[12] The gap is the sign of a genuine, "authentic" production, leading not to the author, but to what becomes, and what comes in the place of history, that is, the process (*Geschehen*).[13]

So, to cite a particularly apt example, the myths of antiquity are reduced to "mythical beliefs" and confused with religious and even pedagogical traditions; at least the interpreters' conventional wisdom has always taken this to be the case. Gadamer is merely codifying a practice that goes against the text. Tragedy, if defined as a "demonstration of myth," derives its meaning or its message from that demonstration.[14] Euripides strips myth of its truth, reducing it to the reality of contemporary events. Why does he write of the gods if he does not believe in them? Is it a dramatic effect sought by a man of the theater, or a demonstration of the absurd by a critical thinker? Art is a profession, a questioning of values. In true hermeneutic tradition, meaning is handed down as a legacy; it animates and determines invention. Euripides is nothing but an inspired scriptwriter, a

[9]   Literary hermeneutics is special, in that it is doubly separated, both from the imitation of nature and from an object that is assumed to be assigned to it in advance.

[10]   Gadamer 1982:263.

[11]   Gadamer 1982:263. The "remainder," not included in the original totality, is "contingent" on both the author and his public. "Not occasionally only, but always, the meaning of a text goes beyond its author. That is why understanding is not merely a productive, but always a reproductive attitude as well" (264).

[12]   Gadamer 1982:263.

[13]   Gadamer 1982:265 ("a genuine productivity of process" [*einer echten Produktivität des Geschehens*]).

[14]   The formula is borrowed from an article by the philologist Uvo Hölscher titled "Wie soll ich noch tanzen?" ("Why should I honor the gods in the dance?"; Hölscher 1975, from line 896, spoken by the Chorus, in Sophocles' *Oedipus the King*).

wandering minstrel. If the poet is defined by what he transmits, he is not worthy of this title. In the plays of Aeschylus, who is closer to the origins of our culture, the character embodying the Chorus stepped outside his role to become the mouthpiece, not of the poet, but of the myth, of "the divine causality behind the tragedy." According to Gadamer, "what happens in tragedy is changed"—by the voice of myth—"because understanding is always a genuine event" ("weil Verstehen immer ein echtes *Geschehen ist*").[15] What remains is neither authentic nor productive.

Gadamer refrains from adapting hermeneutics to the specific features of the text he is analyzing and from problematizing the relation between texts and existential exegesis, the hermeneutics of the artifact that literary analysis is required to take up. After banishing criticism from the temple and relegating it to its secondary and preparatory function, he makes a double detour via theology and law to come back to the tabernacle of art. The validity of meaning—salvation in the Bible or the Roman legal code—is united through a "historicity" in which the origin persists. The application to the new situation,[16] its actualization and relation to the present, becomes part of the continuity linking history to its mythical foundation, and shapes the prerequisites for understanding ("fore-meanings" is Heidegger's term).[17]

Szondi was totally opposed to Gadamer's approach, partly because of his own reserved temperament, but also with regard to method, where he subjects the criticism of literary understanding to the specificity of its objects. Tradition entails ruptures. Their presence can be detected only through their shifts. On the one hand, history can be grasped in the dialectical movement produced by the work, with its formal structure, and the external conditions of its production; on the other hand, it can be grasped in the distance experienced by the interpreter, since the latter can only overcome this separation in history by scrutinizing the initial gap through a critical reflection on his own distanciation. The interpreter includes the analysis of his own determinations in the act of comprehension. Thus one break in viewpoint can capture another. The critic situates himself by situating the author, who had situated himself before him.

[15] Gadamer 1982:361.

[16] For an incorrect usage of the concept of "application," see Gadamer 1982:278. Theology and law provide the "true model." (We can see here the stakes involved in the claim for a specific hermeneutics.) Also 302: "Understanding ... involves application," that is how it attains the "character of an event." The philologist weaves "the great tapestry of tradition which supports us."

[17] Gadamer 1982:236–238, following Heidegger 1941, §63, 310–316. The reader "must be, from the start, sensitive to the text's quality of newness." And then turning away from difference: "The important thing is to be aware of one's own bias, so that [*und damit*] the text may present itself in all its newness, and thus be able to assert its own truth [*seine sachliche Wahrheit*] against one's own fore-meanings" (238, also 260–266).

Subjective prejudices are obstacles set up between the interpreter and the object of study, risking further distancing and distortion; they are viewed neither as positive elements, within the range of a productive "application," nor as a contribution to general understanding, independent of the work. The postulate of a trans-subjective element, "beyond races and cultures," leads to a misunderstanding of the specificity of historical mediations, and for Szondi such mediations can be placed among the prejudices and biases that Gadamer believes he can single out.[18] Similarity might mask differences; the hermeneutic experience might posit other universals, not recognized as such, whose description would have been precluded by the hypothesis. The results obtained by Szondi's method clearly demonstrate that the prerequisites of a common perception and the repetition of the original conditions establish a fictitious permanence and identity. The reader is both complicitous and deceived.

For Szondi, history embraces real life experience, but above all its tragic truth; it challenges its own celebration, be it vitalist or organicist. Indeed, history is revealed in failure and exclusion, in the distance taken and the distance sustained. Its excesses are inherent to movement since, being inscribed in its negation, they are anticipated by it. Ideology doubtless has its source in the negation of this negation, more definite and more absolute than the hypostases derived from Presence or Absence. One failure is not the same as another. Each one is unique, a single signifier. Movement is not unique; neither is swallowing up. Movement neither adds nor subtracts anything, but it does destroy. The work is the moment of an unremarkable resistance; it derives its meaning from that moment because the moment is not followed by any other that concerns the work: the instant in question is just "that instant, there," for want of a "being-there." This threat is what ensures the work's unique identity.

The *Introduction to Literary Hermeneutics* links the multiplicity of dogmas or normative rules that philosophical hermeneutics had taken on at the time of its pre-philosophical origins.[19] Szondi analyzes this hermeneutics as a total impasse. Art, which is not art but a call to art, affects the work as it does the commentator—giving rise to an artificial mediation, theological in essence, and to a communion. This *a priori* arouses such a strong aversion in Szondi that he fears he might find counterparts in the systems of Marxist inspiration or orientation that he has espoused, and especially in Adorno's work; thus he carries out yet another cathartic selection, which allows him to carefully separate the principle of mediation, in all its forms, however refined the principle may be,

18 See Gadamer 1974, col. 1070.
19 See Szondi 1995:2–3.

from etiological constructions. Speculations run the risk of merging together because of their violent nature, and in spite of their conflicting propensities.[20]

Szondi never invokes History. We are subjected to it in specific situations. And the very utopia that inspires him in the works of Benjamin or Adorno appears in his books more as a commonly used concept than as a principle. He speaks of historical philosophy only as a reference. If his reticence attests to a scruple, it also derives from a method: History, like other etiological systems, implies an arbitrary bond.

Clearly the method implies the permanence of cognitive elements in a changing world. Differences produced by historical evolution, which has been popularized in texts, do not bring about a radical epistemological break. The analysis of differences clearly defines a conceptual outline in the object. If the continuity of the conditions of understanding is accepted as a given, discussion no longer introduces responses that block critical analysis, and it no longer prevents the interpreter from making free use of his cognitive tools. With regard to literary hermeneutics—that is, "material" hermeneutics—Szondi chose to adhere to this pragmatic stance.

In his opposition to the philology of immanence, Szondi used the criterion of social mediation; the work was no longer considered the depository of traditional values. His demonstration remained incomplete because he deliberately limited his purview to the specific genealogy found in variable systems of interdependencies. Since he did not address directly either the social sciences or a science of society, he was able to avoid a direct approach to the problem of totality, at the heart of which dialectical movements occur, and from which they derive their meaning. Theories are documents designed for the historical understanding of the period in which they were conceived, reproducing their determinations as well as their interpretive opinions. Depending on the topic, Szondi confined himself to pointing out the text's opposition to a prejudicial reading.

Duality creates historical hermeneutics. First of all, in the object, there exists another, always earlier moment, which is not the moment of the work, but the other moment that the work breaks away from, present in absentia,

---

[20] A theory, by virtue of its weak points or its ambiguities, can be used, at least in part, by a rival family, through a continuous process of assimilation. So certain Heideggerians have been able to lay claim to Adorno's thought. Szondi has not been spared these misunderstandings. To enhance one's reading, one risks tempering differences cumulatively, in order to respond to the plurality of viewpoints (see, for example, Nägele 1985:56). Relativism is reintroduced in a roundabout way. Szondi had chosen his alliances, moderating each one by the others, as is usually the case, and as shown here. His reticence as a critical theoretician, in the face of excessive and audacious theoretical speculations, protected him from other misrepresentations. The attitude or position triumphed over dogma.

various; the moment of the work still takes place within it when it authorizes, through its own temporality, the coexistence of contradictory positions, and the internal dialectic of the genetic method, which Szondi notes in his *Introduction* as one of Schleiermacher's important contributions.[21] Finally, the duality of viewpoints caused by another temporal difference, changing the meanings from reader to reader, means that hermeneutics is principally the art of establishing a distance; and it can only eliminate the relativism of differences and indifference by analyzing both instances, that is, the complex time of the subject and the complex time of the object. Nothing could be more contrary to the Gadamerian "fusion of horizons"[22] through identity, which Ast is assigned to defend in the *Introduction*, erasing the intractable element of the particular.[23] Szondi overcomes historicism by a full and methodical acceptance of the consequences of historical hermeneutics.

Was Szondi actually engaged in a battle on two fronts against ontological historicity and the complementary ideological bias of Marxist reductionism?[24] The stakes were unequal. The steps taken in reaction to nineteenth-century historicism had arisen to compensate for the "crisis of meaning," the result of relativism and the implicit but often unacknowledged loss of "values." In practice, these steps blocked all the amendments that dialectical theories brought to positivist reification. The positivist method, the subject of the essay on textual understanding,[25] is not the only one in question; the defense of the legitimacy of the idea of a historical point of view, amended by Marxist theoreticians among others, is also in play. When Szondi discusses the vicissitudes of meaning and the philological consciousness of temporality before the historicist era,[26] and when he sheds light on the need for semantic changes, he defines the difficulty of all historical understanding. The factor of time, encompassed in the distance of the critical act, must be examined in relation to the history of meaning. The object, however, should not be confused with this history, if the point of view of the knowing subject is to remain intact. The relation maintained by the work

---

[21]   Szondi 1995:114.
[22]   *Horizontverschmelzung*. The use of the concept of "immersion" (*Versenkung*) in history, traces of which can be seen in the work, refers to a contrary theory.
[23]   To transport oneself into the horizons of the past is to attain "a higher universality that overcomes not only our own particularity, but also that of the other" (Gadamer 1982:272). See the homologous position attributed to Friedrich Ast, in Szondi 1995:101–103.
[24]   Nägele 1985:54–56.
[25]   The essay "Über philologischer Erkenntnis," which has been republished several times, has become a classic in the theory of literary methodology; the *Introduction* complements and extends it (see Szondi 1978, 1:263–286, and n5). In English, as "On Textual Understanding," in Szondi 1986:3–22.
[26]   See Szondi 1995:49–50.

with its users in the tradition can be problematized without resorting to the theory of productivity, as Hans Robert Jauss does.[27]

We should go back some thirty years and look at Szondi's critical work in the context of the time of his writing. There we can better understand his particular aims, without losing any of his current presence *ad nos*. Knowledge of the moment when he was elaborating his ideas is not a restrictive move. Historical determination offers the safest criterion in the battle he waged in favor of an analytics of reading. He saw no difference between the two institutional orders—academic and literary—in critical activity. The chapters of the *Introduction* are part of a course and were published as such after his death in 1971.[28] Each lesson, however demonstrative, becomes autonomous and tends towards the genre of the essay, at once scientific and literary, which Szondi illustrated in masterly fashion. He imposed on the essay the distance of a reflection on the legitimacy of the moment of approach, as a necessary complement to each description.

The debate is not over. Just recently, Hans Ulrich Gumbrecht related the criticisms currently being formulated in Germany against the poststructuralist positions of Jacques Derrida and Paul de Man to the survival of a specifically German ideal of "science," renewing Heidegger's attack on science (*Wissenschaft*) in a different form.[29]

Szondi's thought is always focused on the redefinition of philological practice; in his view, practice is impure because it is methodologically weak, and is impervious to the open analysis of research. The definition of the literary object in its aesthetic determination—historically mediated, prior to the study, in the *Introduction*, of categories of literary judgment—derives its meaning within the limits of a critical but also very academic struggle for the rights of criticism, even as the author also denounces the biases of anti-academicism. Szondi situated himself squarely in the tradition of the dialecticians, right from his earliest research; that tradition was represented for him by the books of Benjamin, Lukács, and Adorno.[30] Marxist positions and the principle of social

---

[27] For Jauss (1970:185-186), the "fusion of horizons," with an explicit reference to Gadamer's theory, takes on the appearance of "an active process of understanding" in the form of an overt tension between question and answer.

[28] For this course, see the first part of Szondi 1974-1975:5, and the comments added on pp. 2-3. Szondi never taught anything that he would not have published.

[29] Gumbrecht 1988.

[30] Adorno was very important to Szondi in his personal life; Benjamin's work was the model of an exceptional relationship to literature (and to the book), and both he and Lukács exemplified the form of the essay. A study of their importance in the development of Szondi's method should be based on the differing use he made of each of the three bodies of work. See, for example, the critical defense of Lukács, namely of his theoretical premises, against his own position, in

mediation were made clear in a context of aesthetic reflection. It was with these authors that Szondi learned to decode the movements inherent in the invention of aesthetic forms. If one is to avoid constructing an ineffectual schema, it is important to recognize the relation's meaningful and accepted link. One must take the references for what the author intended them to be.

The core of the debate bears on the function of the work and of the task. A re-examination of the tools should allow critics to project their aim into the field of that specific and unfeigned "science" that is contested and contestable because of its excessive assimilations, and to acknowledge the precision that it gains. It is preferable not to tamper with the philological tool kit, since it might then have the after-effect of promoting the displacement of hermeneutics toward the "philosophical" position, leaving no space for the critical approach. The position Szondi chose condemns an alliance between a theory and a practice. The one is just as poor in philosophy as the other is poor in philology, if they both avoid the scrutiny of the interpreter's historical insights.

On this point Szondi differed from such theoreticians of understanding as Dilthey. Material hermeneutics is devoted to the materiality of the text: language and form. The work is inscribed within a gap; it emphasizes its difference. The philologist re-evaluates the appropriateness of the aesthetic criteria deployed in order to understand the viewing angle and to know what he is talking about. The choice of the term "literary" instead of "philological," which one might prefer when designating this secular hermeneutics, is the result of a refusal, since the philology of the ancients had not been obliged until then to submit its judgment either to a prior definition of the object or to the analysis of the critic's position. It is clear that the ambition arising from modern philologies is of a resolutely and tactically modernist nature.

This *Introduction* belongs to a "genre" and to a moment,[31] and to a place, as well—the Berlin of 1967, where student protests and widespread contestations

---

Szondi's course, published as "Die Theorie des bürgerlichen Trauerspiels im 18. Jahrhundert" (Szondi 1974–1975, 1:31).

[31] Despite his undeniable precautions, Michael Hays' presentation of Szondi's method (and of his work as a whole) ends up erasing the sharpest distinctions, which he has, in fact, mapped out for himself ("situating oneself in relation to one's own critical discourse, as well as in relation to the textual object" [Hays 1986:ix]). Hays fails to distinguish the hermeneutics analyzed and practiced by Szondi from that of Heidegger or Derrida, which goes by the same name. Thus he ends up writing that Szondi abandons the "hermeneutic method" (when has he practiced it?) or uses it against the hermeneutic tradition (which one?). The origin of the error lies in not dissociating Szondi from deconstruction (xxi), and failing to situate deconstruction in the tradition from which it stems, a tradition that Szondi contested. Thus one needs to find what is hidden in his discourse, "what is unspoken," so that dialectics can be displaced into the sphere of language and the unconscious, towards its true object legitimated by the post-modernists. "While the polysemic nature of language inscribes the difference between subject and object, signifier

prevented Szondi from continuing the course up to Dilthey and the current era, as he had planned.[32] The distance that separates us from them situates them in their own "historicity." It is up to the reader to be an interpreter, following the very principles the *Introduction* defends, by comparing the meaning of these thoughts on the history of literary understanding to the statements that inspired them, and to the meaning that they have at this time and in this place.

Works Cited

Cusatelli, G. 1979. "Intorno a Szondi, dopo Szondi." Foreword to P. Szondi, *Introduzione all'ermeneutica letteraria*. Parma.

Duroche, L. L. 1967. *Aspects of Criticism: Literary Study in Present-Day Germany*. The Hague.

Gadamer, H.-G. 1974. "Hermeneutik." In *Historisches Wörterbuch der Philosophie*, vol. 3. Darmstadt.

———. 1982. *Truth and Method*, trans. from the German. London. Orig. pub. 1965.

Gumbrecht, H. U. 1988. "'Über allen Wipfeln [sic] ist Ruh.' Literaturwissenschaft jenseits der Literatur." *Frankfurter Allgemeine Zeitung*, no. 166, July 20.

Hays, M. 1986. "Foreword. Tracing a Critical Path: Peter Szondi and the Humanistic Tradition." In *On Textual Understanding and Other Essays*, ed. P. Szondi, vii–xxi. Minneapolis.

Heidegger, M. 1941. *Sein und Zeit*. 5th ed. Halle. Orig. pub. 1927. In English as *Being and Time*, trans. J. Macquarrie and E. Robinson, New York, 1962.

Hölscher, U. 1975. "Wie soll ich noch tanzen?" In *Sprachen der Lyrik: Festschrift für Hugo Friedrich zum 70. Geburtstag*, 376–393. Frankfurt.

Jauss, H. R. 1970. *Literaturgeschichte als Provokation*. Frankfurt.

Nägele, R. 1983. "Text, History and the Critical Subject: Notes on Peter Szondi's Theory and Praxis of Hermeneutics." *boundary 2*, vol. 11, no. 3, *The Criticism of Peter Szondi* (Spring):29–42.

Staiger, E. 1953. *Die Zeit als Einbildungskraft des Dichters*. Zurich. Orig. pub. 1939.

---

and signified, idea and event in the text, a dialectical understanding of this difference allows nonetheless for a *critical* evaluation of these relationships; for knowledge is derived not from an assumed sublation of difference, but from an effort to allow the poles of difference to comment on each other" (xix). One cannot serve two masters. An even more tendentious presentation can be found in Cusatelli 1979.

[32] The circumstances are regrettable. We should not misjudge the situation. However much pain he experienced, Szondi knew, as did Adorno, that the protesters' favorite targets were the most open minds; on the whole, he shared with the students a good number of the reasons for their rebellion. He was certainly not defending his own status. It is true that in the end he felt like a foreigner in his own place. But did he even have a place?

————. 1991. *Basic Concepts of Poetics*. Trans. J. C. Hudson and L. T. Frank. University Park, PA. Orig. pub. 1946.

Szondi, P. 1972. *Lektüren und Lektionen*. Frankfurt.

————. 1974–1975. *Studienausgabe der Vorlesungen*. Ed. Jean Bollack. Frankfurt.

————. 1978. *Schriften*. Frankfurt.

————. 1986. *Peter Szondi, On Textual Understanding and Other Essays*. Trans. H. Mendelsohn. Minneapolis. Orig. pub. 1978.

————. 1995. *Introduction to Literary Hermeneutics*. Trans. M. Woodamsee. Cambridge, U.K. In French as *Introduction à l'herméneutique littéraire*, trans. M. Bollack, with an afterword by J. Bollack, Paris, 1989.

26

Reading the Signifier[†]

M Y ESSAY ON THE FREEDOM OF SIGNIFIERS in Plato's *Cratylus*[1] was written as an extension of work on that dialogue that I had pursued with a group of researchers from the University of Tübingen who were defenders of Plato's unwritten doctrine. At a colloquium focused on the theory of language, I had presented an overall interpretation, which has remained unpublished; one section had to do with discussions about the way the network of signifiers is structured in the dialogue. The orientation that Plato's text imposes on "etymology," on the figure of the phonological reinterpretation of words among the Ancients, the use of puns to express truths, enabled me to demonstrate that analyses of a superimposed meaning can create the illusion that a truth is deposited in the sonic underpinnings of language. By shifting to the conceptual order, Plato's dialectics condemns the enterprise to collapse. Nevertheless, the fact remains that an entirely different reading of the world is constructed here, in the mode of a fictional narrative, showing that enigmatization can be pursued indefinitely from one element of language to another, and that it can suppress the appearance of arbitrariness in designations.

Familiarity with that particular exercise of decoding, which evokes the magic of a mysterious mathematics, has certainly been of use to me in my lengthy search for the meaning taken on by the idiomatic words in Paul Celan's poems, a project begun systematically some fifteen years ago. From the start, I had followed a procedure that borrowed Mallarmé's means of verbal restoration. The effort to make this procedure explicit occupied a central place in all my work.

I discovered little by little that I was indeed working with a network of truth that was introduced into the common language like a different language,

---

[†]   Originally published as "Lire le signifiant," in: Jean Bollack, *La Grèce de personne: les mots sous le mythe* (Paris, 1997), pp. 337–339.

[1]   [TN: Bollack 1997:341–348.]

a personal secondary idiom. The first language was not relegated, but rather clarified and contradicted, by rereading as an act tied to creation.

With "Eden encore,"[2] the first essay I wrote on Paul Celan, I presented and defended the position of Peter Szondi, who around 1970 had profoundly shocked his colleagues, Hans-Georg Gadamer first and foremost, by proposing an interpretation of a poem written by Celan in Berlin, almost in Szondi's presence. Szondi had been reproached for basing his reading on factual references with which he was familiar. "Biographism," in fact, transformed the hermeticists' customary horizon of expectation. It was not the horizon that one knew in advance; specifically, it was constitutive of a network of particular or personal references that remained to be found, and it no longer belonged to the shared content of a culture or to an age-old experience. It had to be reconstituted. Gadamer asked, in effect, "What must one know in order to understand?" Szondi's reply: one must know how to restore the aim or the grid through which one is decoding, how to restore the circumstances along with the critical eye that has captured them.

I sought to show in addition that the text ceases to be hermetic when one approaches it with the knowledge of the "Celanian" that is procured by familiarity with his poems. Hermeneutics then succeeds in identifying the particular by relying on the stable references of a vocabulary, and on the initially enigmatic data that come from a personal encounter with the world.

"Le mont de la mort"[3] comes into play in this lengthy debate. Celan wrote the poem after visiting Heidegger in 1967 at his home in the Black Forest. Readers had sought to locate an act of homage in this text. One had to read it, here again, in order to be able to identify the precise circumstances and decipher the texture of a linguistic restoration that gave those circumstances their meaning. This meant paralleling hermeneutics with a historian's work; the two approaches merged to restore the unicity of a testimony. The poet made the philosopher speak; his own words position speech on the horizon of its actual referents.

Works Cited

Bollack, J. 1947. "L'en-deçà infini: l'aporie du *Cratyle*." In *La Grèce de personne*, 341–348. Paris.

———. 1985. "Eden encore." In *L'Acte critique: un colloque sur l'oeuvre de Peter Szondi, Paris, 21-23 juin 1979*, ed. M. Bollack, 267–290. Lille.

---

[2] Bollack 1985:267–290.
[3] [TN: See below, Chap. 27.]

27

The Mountain of Death[†]
The Meaning of Celan's
Meeting with Heidegger

Todtnauberg

Arnica, Augentrost, der
Trunk aus dem Brunnen mit dem
Sternwürfel drauf,

in der
Hütte

die in das Buch
—wessen Namen nahms auf
vor dem meinen?—,
die in dies Buch
geschriebene Zeile von
einer Hoffnung, heute,
auf eines Denkenden
kommendes
Wort
im Herzen,

Waldwasen, uneingeebnet,
Orchis und Orchis, einzeln,

Krudes, später, im Fahren,
deutlich,

[†] Originally published as "Le mont de la mort: le sens d'une rencontre entre Celan et Heidegger," in: Jean Bollack, *La Grèce de personne: les mots sous le mythe* (Paris, 1997), pp. 349–376.

der uns fährt, der Mensch,
der's mit anhört,

die halb-
beschrittenen Knüppel-
Pfade im Hochmoor,

Feuchtes,
viel.[1]

---

[1] Celan 2000, *Gesammelte Werke* (hereafter *GW*) 2:255. The English translation below is by Michael Hamburger (Celan 1989:292–293):

> Todtnauberg
> Arnica, eyebright, the
> draft from the well with the
> starred die above it
>
> in the
> hut,
>
> the line
> —whose name did the book
> register before mine?—,
> the line inscribed
> in that book about
> a hope, today,
> of a thinking man's
> coming
> word
> in the heart
>
> woodland sward, unlevelled,
> orchid and orchid, single,
>
> coarse stuff, later, clear
> in passing,
>
> he who drives us, the man,
> who listens in,
>
> the half-
> trodden wretched
> tracks through the high moors,
>
> dampness,
> much.

The Poem

The name "Todtnauberg," the place in the Black Forest that gives the poem its title, needs to be broken down into its component syllables. Such an analysis can give us *Toten-Au*, the "meadow of the dead"; and the "mountain," *Berg*, can be linked to the verb *bergen*, which here refers more to the act of sheltering and preserving than to that of merely hiding. Our reading also suggests that the first syllable, *Todt-*, can be linked to the Nazi *Todt* organization, which was probably responsible for the death of Celan's parents,[2] and that the syllable *–au* recalls the presence of the extermination camp of Auschwitz.

Nouns speak volumes if we can understand what they say, and if, from words, we make "names." The place, named in the title, heralds the opening that will be brought about through language. The mountain (*-berg*) guards, it generates and hides, protects and preserves the "meadow of the dead," the site of a descent into hell (*Todtnau, Totenau*), the place of an inescapable destiny, that of a modern katabasis, a plunge into the underworld. It is into this infernal place that the owner of the cottage will be led by his visitor, who will unlock the secret of the swamps. The visitor has the necessary credentials for taking him there. All is ready, right up to the ferryman, the guide and witness appointed to take them there together. That was the purpose of the ride in a car.

The Entry

> Arnica, eyebright, the
> draft from the well with the
> starred die above it
>
> in the
> hut,

The first verse might be considered a prologue to the lyrical adventure. We are indeed talking about a little epic: a stranger arrives at a lonely chalet, like Odysseus at the house of Eumaeus; a subsequent journey leads to the underworld. Just as in a Homeric poem, the essentials of the narrative event are announced beforehand. First comes the historical past, with the star of the yellow flower designating the stain of Jewishness. Next to this reference, another flower name symbolizes the language of poetry, the language that has become capable of

---

[2] Named for its founder Fritz Todt (1891–1942), who was then the Reich's Minister of Armaments, the "Organisation Todt" was responsible in particular for the civil engineering works of strategic importance in the countries occupied by the Germans; see also Chalfen 1991:151.

recounting these events. The word *Augentrost* (*solacium oculorum*)[3] can, in fact, be analyzed: the eyes, representatives of the senses, have imprinted in the verbal matter a response to the experience of disappearance. It is a gift of eyes. Consolation is not offered to them, as it is by the healing plant; it is the eyes that are able to broadcast this comfort. With these instruments of abstract vision, one has the means to draw up water from the depths of the well. The draft drunk from the well defines the flow of a dark matter; in the throw of the dice, it gets properly organized in an orderly way, oriented by the star. The die is stellar, a starwort. The depths of the abyss have as their counterpoint this pinnacle of a vertical line that they themselves thrust up to the heights. Language is found in this place, deciphered and read.

The mountain has revealed its secret to the visitor, emitting its signs from the very first words. The flowers are the messengers of the chthonian depths: first, on the side of history, the yellow star, the visitor's history, the history of the Jews; and then, on the side of death, the euphrasy (eyebright), beneficial for the eye, where poetry is revitalized in the light of a new gaze. It can say what this history has been. The mark of a color, the yellow flower, has as its counterweight the benefits the word implies. The eye clears, far from the inherited hymns and in their embrace, the senses, which have been adjusted to the stain of infamy. The balm of another light, rising from the funereal meadows, *Totenau*, turns into "eyebright" (*Augentrost*). Language seizes the topography, it remakes the site, recovers it, shows that it covers and uncovers it, leaving it covered also in its initial opacity.

The problem of biographism, of reference, anecdotal at first—reality encountered, left in place, then interpreted, turned into its meaning—finds its aesthetic solution in the double movement of a reconstitution and a moving beyond that intersect and overlap. Heidegger's country is the terror of the Black Forest. His celebration of this pan-Germanic nature before students in 1933 blackens pseudo-poetry forever. Now a poet has come to introduce the philosopher to his own forest and, more than that, to impose on him the truth of a place by remaking it *de profundis*. What is perceptible vanishes before the truth of words. The "die" will be the figure decorating the well, but it will also have become the star that guides the poet continually, from one poem to the next, shaping biographical chance, its throw of the dice, a new adaptation. One will

3   The French translator François Turner (cited in Bollack 1997:351–355) translates *Augentrost* as *luminet*, a word that connotes light (*lumen, lumière*). Bertrand Badiou's more literal rendering of the common German botanical name, *délice des yeux* ("delight for the eyes") illustrates a general problem in translation. The work of reconstructing meaning—in many cases quite subtle work, which the distance between two levels of precision requires of the reader—does not survive. [TN: The English common name for the plant, "eyebright," is another illustration of the problem; as with Badiou's choice, the sense of solace is lost.]

be in a familiar region. The fountain is the right one, the one in the poem ... "the fountain murmurs."[4] The first flower was the right one too, auspicious, familiar: *Arnika*, the yellow flower, recalls the persecutions and perpetuates the presence of the victims, perpetuates the calamity, lest the dead be forgotten.

The water that flows and that we drink is made of words. The poem draws on another source. The gesture can be interpreted; it lends itself to interpretation: "What you see me doing has its own meaning, which perhaps escapes you; however, what I come to ask, by agreeing to drink from this fountain, your fountain, is clear. The expected reply will no doubt be denied me. One can fear so. But let there be no mistake: I shall already have obtained it, during this visit. I shall have turned the denial to my advantage." Interpreters have been mistaken or have been unwilling to read it this way; they have not wanted to make this visit such a funereal occasion, the response to a denial of murder.

As in the other poems, the relation of the linguistic organization to the external reality to which it refers, a reality less reproduced than reconstituted, is problematic. The well near Heidegger's cottage exists, and the figure carved in the wood above the fountain is that of a star etched in a cube. No precision in the evocation of objects impedes the complete reworking. The second scene takes place in the house: we are in the cottage, the "hut" (*Hütte*). The prepositional phrase has a particularly expressive force in a purely substantive setting, throughout the eight stanzas of the candelabra.[5] The stress of the repeated two-syllable line: *in der / Hütte* ("in the / hut"), envelops the whole prologue in its own ambience, and means that Celan, with the language—his language—that he has introduced into this place, has taken over the interior of the home. He has a magic lever that allows him to bring up vast distances. The powers named in the prologue are all ensconced in this place, in the nocturnal domain of the cottage.

> the line
> —whose name did the book
> register before mine?—,
> the line inscribed
> in that book about
> a hope, today,
> of a thinking man's
> coming
> word
> in the heart

---

[4] "... rauscht der Brunnen" (*GW* 1:237) ("... splashes the fountain" [Celan 1989:183]).

[5] [TN: The candelabra refers implicitly to the menorah, with its eight branches for eight candles plus the central *shamas*, which lights all the others.]

The inner sphere of the dwelling can, for this reason, be represented by a book. And first of all it is a book as such, as a place and as an object where what is written is received, as one speaks of the Bible, as Mallarmé speaks of his impossible project.[6] But in a second stage, which becomes clear in the parenthesis, the book turns into another book, a very distinctive one that is opened only in this poem. In reality, as conveyed anecdotally, it is an album in which Celan has written his name. The sentence inscribed in it is known.[7] Celan makes a distinction between the lines he has written and those of other houseguests: in other circumstances he would not have agreed to leave his signature next to theirs. In this place, its presence was important and significant; it defined an intellectual and political horizon.

Where are we now? In the philosopher's cottage, which was called a *Hütte*,[8] or in another place, in a utopian thatched cottage ("peace to the cottages") to which Celan is referring, following Büchner?[9] The passage by way of utopia surely leads to the "hope" the poet harbors, inscribed in the book, before the imposition of the dead, the hope for a future shaped by devotion to the memory of the victims. The book will not be an object in which visitors inscribe their names, but will have been transformed by the line the poet has traced in it. He has the power to transform it, such as it is, despite all it contains—"*that* book": the very book that must open onto its own integrated past and onto a future of freedom that will be based on that memory. What has the poet been doing all along, if not reconverting German by Judaizing it? No matter that the other, the thinker, did not say what was expected of him; the thing will have been said for him and as an expectation. The future is formulated and inscribed forever in a "thought" that cannot be subtracted from memory (*Gedenken*), if it aspires to be "thought" (*Denken*) and "word" (*Wort*), at the request of a "heart."[10] The speech of horror looms; it is brought to the brink of this advent that expectation bears.

6   [TN: Mallarmé dreamed of producing a Book that would encompass all literature, even all reality.]
7   The inscription has been reprinted with the poem in the work of Bernd Martin (1989:143–144). [TN: "In the book in the cottage, with a view of the well star, with the hope of a word to come in the heart. July 25, 1967, Paul Celan."]
8   Nevertheless, it appears that one should not translate it as *hutte* in French.
9   [TN: Georg Büchner's radical pamphlet "Friede den Hütten, Krieg den Palästen" ("Peace to the cottages! War on the palaces!") was published in July 1834 in *Der Hessische Landbote*, calling on the peasants to revolt against the ruling classes.]
10   Translators (*passim*) have not linked "in the heart" to "hope," as both the meaning and the syntax require: *von einer Hoffnung... im Herzen* form, despite the separation, a single unitary expression, opening up to the object of an expectation (*auf*). Bad syntactic analysis is not, however, limited to translators; it is also evident in Germany, for example in Otto Pöggeler (1986:264–265), who discusses the two possibilities of syntactic construction, and invokes as the principal argument in favor of his solution the place that in the theological tradition belongs to the "word in the heart." According to him, Heidegger transferred this expression to his own philosophy, and

The poetic text to be analyzed is clearly written, without equivocation or ambiguity, without any possible means of escape. Hope, at the moment of writing ("today"), lives on thanks to an expectation. In the course of a journey that has already been mapped out, thought becomes what it should never have refused to be. Like the book, the guide driving the car doubles as a witness, in a role that the context assigns him. Driver when it is time for a drive, he becomes the involuntary guide on an infernal journey. The punning on *Namen / nahms* ("names" / "registered") does not stress the reality of the signatures, but refers to the transfer of the world of those inscribed in the book, the brigades of the persecutors, into the register of the Last Judgment that is now being compiled. The names must appear before Celan's, because the poet, through the meaning given to the inscription of his name, provides a counterweight. An act of real resistance is connected to a person. The name: "mine" (next to what others?) implies an incriminating neighborhood. The question addressed to the book also designates the very place of poetry, a habitual and constant place, a component of liberation. The cohabitation is experienced as something always imposed—impossible but imposed.

The lines that follow (stanza 3, lines 8–10) reproduce, with some significant differences, the sentence in the book, which was written a week later. It is evasive and revelatory. At first glance, a superficial reader would read it as a friendly compliment to his host. This is how it has often been interpreted. But this kind of reading takes no account of the meaning of the words. In fact, the relation between the two levels of language is comparable to the relation that might exist between the sculptured cube with the star and the function it assumes in its context. Thus, the term "thinking man" (*Denkenden*) might make one think of Heidegger the thinker; however, in his work Celan uses it only in reference to recollection and commemoration; in the same way, the word "heart" (*Herz*) is commonly conceived as an organ of memory, and this semantic orientation determines the meaning of the other words. Hope, if one stays close to the moment as reconstituted, relies on a distancing from all that the names in the album represent; it remains attached to the present day; in turn, the present boils down to what the book has become in this text: a book that writes, and re-writes.

Finally, the epithet "coming" (*kommendes*) concerns less the speech of the future than a declaration that will be actualized, will "happen," and will go to its addressee. The expectation formulated by Celan will not come to pass, but it is no less important for the understanding of the whole to consider the fact that

---

Celan followed him out of respect. But Celan wrote in his own language and with his own words. Besides, the over-determination of *Wort* at the end seems implausible, in comparison with the loop that the reader naturally establishes between "hope" and "heart."

it has been expressed. This is the way the poet retains the fault: the philosopher will not say what the poet may have come to ask him to say, that he suggests he say, but the poet already knows that the philosopher will not comply. In response to this absence, the second part of the text confirms the reasons that keep him from doing so. Speech is actualized in an open acknowledgement, revealing the continuity of an attachment to the past.

> woodland sward, unlevelled,
> orchid and orchid, single,
>
> coarse stuff, later, clear
> in passing,
>
> he who drives us, the man,
> who listens in,
>
> the half-
> trodden wretched
> tracks through the high moors,
>
> dampness,
> much.

The next episode takes place outdoors, outside the cottage. The drive through the Black Forest follows a precise scenario planned in advance. Gerhard Neumann, a young assistant to Gerhart Baumann, a professor of German literature in Freiburg,[11] was driving the two men in his car. The route was organized in such a way that it was already part of the not-yet-written poem. Perception adopts this selective form.

The five stations of the excursion construct a descent into Hell. The first visit is to the torture sites, and their victims' graves, in the middle of the Black Forest. The confession wrenched from the thinker comes after the visitors turn back. They go first to the realm of the dead. They need a witness to hear the confession of the unthinkable, the thing that the poet succeeds in making the thinker say. After the judgment of the underworld, they return to the surface of the earth, and the confession is made as an offering to the victims of the extermination camps. All that remains is to display the ritual scene of mourning in the shedding of tears.

The initiatory rite of saturation under pressure (stanzas 5 and 6) entails a movement of departure and a fit of anger, like a whirlwind, perhaps. The

---

[11] He later became a professor of German literature in Munich.

circles open onto the abyss. The stage is surrounded by two other more horizontal visions, along similarly stagnant lines. The opening (stanza 4) prepares for the journey. The summoned victims are there: the soul of each one of the dead blooms by itself, individually, with its own little candelabra. Each one has its own power of resistance, a virile force concentrated in the tubers of the *orchis* ("the boys' plant," *Knabenkraut*), in the form of testicles. A legion rises up, uncountable; each blossom has its genitals. Domination seems irrepressible. So the journey will take place, and it has some chance of succeeding.

The content of the text would justify the hypothesis of a transposition of the title of Thomas Mann's novel *The Magic Mountain* into Celan's title, at least through the word "mountain" (-*berg*): it could well be a subverted form of a *Zauberberg*, of the dark site of an "unveiling," for the workings of black magic—as black as the Forest so praised by Heidegger. We know people who never went back there.

The Tribunal of the Dead

A great many camps were set up in marshy regions. The meadows (*Wasen*) were not only wetlands, but also cemeteries where some elevated sections can be seen, so many tombs surviving in memory, one beside the other.[12] Each one is marked by the shape of an orchid candelabra. The flowers are fires that burn. Nature is transformed into intelligence, forced to remember.

An alert reader, led by memory or chance, will discover at the same time, on the horizon of an unsuspected intertextuality, the very audible if not explicit negation of a classic leveling out of cemeteries, which can be read as a terrible prefiguration, a parable of the future destruction of cemeteries. In Goethe's *Elective Affinities*, Charlotte decides to replace the uneven ground of the graves in the churchyard with a bed of clover, and thus suppresses the differentiations that the raised earth, borders, and stones create between the dead. The episode of the argument in the first chapter of the second part of Goethe's novel comes to mind here. In a way, the discussion allows Celan to take sides against the position preferred by the architect who acts as arbiter in the novel, and perhaps by Goethe himself. "Unleveled" in the place of "leveled" introduces an oppositional "-un," a "not": it is not what Charlotte wants and imposes (against the wishes of the neighbor and her lawyer: "the space thus vacated had been levelled."[13] The historical vision drawn from reality, rewritten with natural turf (*Wasen*), says the opposite. The erasure of a violent unification in anonymity will

---

12 The sense of a mortuary is attested in Grimm and Grimm 1922, vol. 13, col. 2282.
13 Goethe 1994:118 ("Der übrige Raum war geebnet" [Goethe 1982, 6:361]).

not take place ("no, it is not that kind of leveling, *un-ein-ge-eb-net*" [each syllable is stressed in turn]).

The remembered dialogue is reconstituted, taking on the aspect of a tragic revolt. Celan rereads the words, his own notes, in his Goethe. He discovers them in the mouth of the young scholar, a well-read jurist, defending the cemetery: first of all, the term "no one," which we know from "The Meridian" and which allowed Celan to re-interpret in a similar way a "himself" (*er selbst*) from Nietzsche's *Birth of Tragedy*, and then, too, the "presence" (*Gegenwart*) of the dead. That presence is transferred into the order of language. In Goethe, the survivors gather together "as if around a boundary stone" (the German is very eloquent: "wie um einem Markstein"); they keep the enemies away from this rallying sign. If we needed a proof of the legitimacy (or necessity) of the connection, it is provided by the importance attributed to the enclosure that is distinguished, and repeated, in the first version of the poem, by the adjective *ungesäumt* (without a border).[14] Celan's reader passes spontaneously from the sense of "incessant" to that of "without a border."[15] Reading the *Affinities* where the word is used in conversation by the architect (*ungesäumt vergleiche*,[16] a comparison of equality and non-distinction) offers the possibility of fitting it in with the core of the nihilistic erasure in the philosopher's speech. In any case, Goethe is presented as a forefather of this depersonalization. One can imagine the interest and the irony of the interlocutor, who knew how to "make people speak," faced with the Goethean professions of faith from the Freiburg Germanist.[17]

When we read the two lines of stanza 4 while relying on the materials available, we encounter, first, something humid, a sign of verbal abundance, pre-structured in the tear (see Celan's poem "Flower"[18]), and, in a more material sense, in the orchid, in the male plant, the testicular flower, a figure of the

---

[14] Goethe 1982:363. See the presentation of the variants below, p. 389. Moreover, in *Elective Affinities* the word *Augentrost* is applied to Ottilie, providing further confirmation: *Dadurch ward sie den Männern ... ein wahrer Augentrost* (Goethe 1982:283: "she thus became to the men ... what we can properly call a solace to the eye" [Goethe 1994:41]).

[15] [TN: See Turner's French translation, based on the first version of the poem:

> une attente, aujourd'hui,
> de qui méditera (à
> venir, in-
> cessament venir)
> un mot
> du cœur]

[16] Goethe 1982:36. [TN: In one English translation, "levelled without delay" (Goethe 1994:120).]

[17] See Baumann 1986:102.

[18] "Blume," *GW* 1:164.

revolt that lives on in each of the deceased. In death every man is for himself, and fights, even in his annihilation, for himself alone, beyond the beliefs and conventions that caused his death.

By burrowing under the graves, we discover the root of these beliefs. Proclamations led to murder. While conversing with the philosopher in the car, Celan, after this visit to the dead, goes back to the very *origin*. The journey leads to the depths of the abyss. The word "late" (*spät*), in Celan's language, situates a word—one that lies on the horizon of a truth—close to the departed souls and death.[19] The violence of the words proffered "later" (*später*), so close to a bloody and abyssal aptness, indicates the shocking subject of the conversation during which Heidegger had been led by the poet to speak "in plain language" about the murders, because his words were as precise as his interlocutor could have wished.

I think that the word "clearly" (*deutlich*) must also be analyzed. It does not mean only "distinctly," for the German word used here includes the characteristics of exegesis (*deuten*, ""to interpret"). The suffix -*lich* could take on a sinister meaning here as elsewhere,[20] and might remind us of the German word for corpse (*Leiche*).[21] The detours surrounded this object. The path of the philosophical discourse is interpreted, and so it is "revealed."

In the meadows, amidst the ponds, the poet initiates his hosts, and leads them from earthly spirituality to the tonalities of belated truths (see the expression "seven roses *later*" in the poem "Kristall"[22]), knowing how to draw from the depths the distinct accents of cruelty, as the infernal journey gains speed. The transmission has worked. The signs were clear, and the host was unable to ignore them; he could not have remained indifferent to the evidence offered all around him. The third person, the driver, "the man," vested with supreme authority by his presence among the graves, bears witness in an almost juridical and constraining way. The guide listens to what he must have heard during the journey of initiation. He is the guarantor, through the magical power of a ritual, of what the other, the interviewee, should he be questioned one day, will never be able to deny without committing perjury.

The oft-celebrated encounter with "poetry" (*Dichtung*) has this power and these inevitable effects, like the waters of the Styx in mythology.[23] Nothing

---

[19] Cf. "Später Pfeil, der von der Seele schnellte" ("Late arrow that the soul released") in the poem "Unter ein Bild" ("Under a Picture"), *GW* 1:155.

[20] I am thinking for example of *bläulich* ("bluish") in the poem "Einiges Handähnliche" ("Hand-like"), *GW* 1:236.

[21] Cf. *König- / liche,* ("Re- / gal one") in the poem "Chymisch" ("Alchemical"), *GW* 1:227–228.

[22] "Kristall" ("Crystal") *GW*, 1:52.

[23] Revealing the perjury of the gods. See the episode in Hesiod's *Theogony*, lines 775–806; see Bollack 1958.

more will ever protect Heidegger, if he does not admit that he has spoken these words before a witness. According to the express terms of the poem, he remains doomed, delivered up to one who has initiated speech. The ordeal takes place in front of the guide, a man in the land of inhumanity. On this journey, the driver represents a community of survivors for whom the message of the confession is intended. The witness listens to what is said (*anhört*) "with" (*mit*: "with," "at the same time as") the others. The word *mit* has particular weight. It is responsible for recording the monstrous speech.

The Descent

If this text were describing concrete facts, "the person who is driving us" would be that person, the car's driver, the guide whose identity we know. Obviously, we cannot settle for this. The real point of departure has been maintained and, transferred into another domain, opens up in the dimension of speech. As journeys go, this one quickly takes them far from the plateaus of the Forest. The occupant of the cottage has been drawn by his guest into the kingdom of darkness. Both are escorted in their descent or voyage ("journey in Hades," Hades*fahrt*, or "journey into the Underworld," Unterwelts*fahrt*, and so on) and in their exploration by a being who *has a man's name*. Neither priest nor God nor poet, but a man, a figure of ordinary humanity, showing the way among the victims of inhumanity.

The transitive use of *fährt* ("drives," "leads") does not describe the actual situation of the car driven by Gerhard Neumann, but rather the journey, according to the terms of poetic transposition. The difference between *Fahrer* (driver) and *der uns fährt* (who drives us), following *im Fahren* (in passing) in the preceding verse, is important. Stress is placed on the load that is being transported (compare the noun *die Fuhre*, "cart load"), the cargo carried off by a coachman or a wondrous boatman. Celan explained to André du Bouchet that "to convey" (*voiturer*) would be an equivalent;[24] the meaning and the orientation of this information become clear. The conveyer is responsible for carrying far away, right to the point where it is borne, the burden produced by the conversation between the two passengers. At the same time, he maintains contact with the other shore: he is a man. His role is to remain human in the domain of the inhuman. The pronoun "we" is detached in this adventure, producing a "him" and a "me" who are just as irreconcilably separated as the orchids (*einzeln*, "separate"). Celan speaks from his side: he hears what his interlocutor says to

---

[24] According to a note at the end of the collection of poems translated by du Bouchet (Celan 1978): "The translation of 'Todtnauberg' was based on the first version of the poem, dated Frankfurt am Main, August 1, 1967."

him, from the side where he is sitting and where he has chosen to be (Celan did the same thing with Martin Buber in 1960, when we visited him together in a Paris hotel, and again with Nelly Sachs, the same year).[25] The same process is repeated three times. One speaks bluntly, to induce and record the response. This needed to be said, by Heidegger.

The first time it happens (*im Fahren*), the internal dynamics of Celan's language—internal, as in intertextuality—promotes the great migratory movements, of the stars or the birds. One witnesses a departure, in the order of verbal imagination, the impulse of an unbridled acceleration.[26] Nothing offers resistance, everything comes to light, emerges from the dark in this flight. It is the contrary of what has usually been written. Hans-Georg Gadamer, in particular, cannot imagine that the overly brutal words of the master were aimed at an inadmissible self-evidence: at stake must have been a depth that Celan began to understand only later, "once he got home."[27]

Now, the magician was Celan; he worked on assignment, his own. He set himself the project, and with a magician's artistry he produced the confirmation he was expecting.

Return to the Visions of Memory

Now the mountain's peat bogs take the place of the wooded meadows. This is where the killing took place. In the circular composition of the second part of the poem (stanzas 4 to 8), the poet, following the infernal discussion, recovers his own language; the "paths" (*Pfade*) are the passages that open up in his own poems. They lead to the paths of cudgels; here, the prisoners were beaten with those clubs. We remain within the framework of the constitution of the idiom. The words bear traces of the blows.

Once down on this lower level, one stops at a point that leads not to the world of the dead, but further back, to the sites of suffering and torture, to the swamps where the camps had been set up. The clubs one walks on to avoid sinking in the mud recall the brutality of the treatment the prisoners endured. One steps on their suffering, "half-treading," so as to leave the weight of that suffering there, like a flag at half-mast (*auf Halbmast*). To do this is to abandon time, to leave it to the truth of tears (stanza 8).

---

[25] See "Histoire d'une lutte, Celan et Nelly Sachs," Bollack 2000:45–56.

[26] The word *Fahren* indeed has this value and this ecstatic tonality, as in "Flimmerbaum" ("Glimmering Tree"): "Offen / lagst du mir vor / der fahrenden Seele" (*GW* 1:234), or in "Kolon" ("Colony"): "für / wieviel Vonsammengeschiedenes / rüstest du's wieder zur Fahrt" (*GW* 1:265).

[27] Gadamer 1983:138–144, esp. p. 143.

They are now four (Gerhart Baumann had rejoined the group). They walked a short distance on a log trail with marshy ground on either side. Celan did not have the right shoes for the swampy terrain. They gave up on their walk.[28] However, they had really been there. The concrete details coincide precisely with the event, just as it happened and just as it was read, poetically; that is, newly arranged for reading. The event assumes its meaning; it is transferred with precision into the appropriate semantic universe.

The eternal question of biographism, raised by Gadamer and other hermeneuticists, along the lines of phenomenological presuppositions, keeps on coming up, countering Peter Szondi's interpretation of the poem "Du liegst" ("You lie") in the early 1970s.[29] We know that the walk along the log trails across the marsh was interrupted by the rain. "Half- / trodden" can thus be explained, but we have no need of this knowledge (inessential knowledge, "backstage chatter," for Otto Pöggeler, although no less Heideggerian for all that).[30] However the transposition, if it has a factual basis, presupposes another fact, one inherent in language, but no less historical; the initial, constitutive reference is already biographical. In principle, there is no difference between the Eden guest-house in Berlin in the poem "You lie" and the repetition of a passage from Meister Eckhart in "You be like you" ("Du sei wie du" [*GW* 2:327])[31] or here, in the interruption of a hike. A primary meaning, if it is factual, takes on a meaning that is primary in a different way; this is the case for "half" ("half- / trodden"), which is elevated to the status of a rallying sign and a signification newly given but not yet acknowledged. It is the serious play of enigma.

Precision is recognized by interpreters as long as it contributes to the inventory of reality, but not when it allows one to grasp a reference created by reflection in poetry. The interpreters prefer to move on to the "symbolic," which is universally known: the marsh is water; one might say that in Celan's work, it is poetically "the water of life."[32] There can be no divergence between expectation and reading. The horizons "merge." The problem of the relation of

---

[28] Baumann 1986:70.

[29] See Bollack 1985, and above, Chapter 26, p. 368.

[30] Pöggeler 1980:255 ("Hintergrundwissen" ["Background Knowledge"]).

[31] See Bollack 1996. [TN: Meister Eckhart was a medieval German theologian; Celan cites him, referring to Isaiah (Celan 2000:419).]

[32] This is also the role attributed to the waters of the Neckar River in "Tübingen, Jänner" ("Tübingen, January"), analyzed in a study of this poem, which is another key element in Heideggerian interpretations in France and in Germany (see above, Chapter 23); similarly vitalist representation guides Sieghild Bogumil's interpretation (1988). The author casually dispenses with the constraints of verbal logic to move to a properly metaphysical conception of water, the symbol of an undifferentiated origin that makes it possible to resolve all contradictions. The indistinct is not distinguishable, thus neither are history and nature. The choice of unlimited opening allows one—almost obliges one—to recognize Celan's commitment on the side of memory and to rather

purely descriptive elements with their textual interpretation is always posed in the same way. The walk may have been interrupted on account of the rain. But the "half" makes it clear that the steps have been conveyed towards the shadows, just as "high" marks a point on an ascending line: the more distant the depths to which the journey has led, the more powerful the force of a new representation of what happened. The swamp rises upwards. Thus tears make the words grow, as in the poem "Flower" ("Blume"); they are boundless. Their mass is contained in the compact element of moisture. The water of the meadows and of the marshes has been transferred into this neutral expression *Feuchtes* ("dampness").

The Dossier[33]

I note here with some emotion the content of the dossier of photocopies about this poem that Gisèle Celan was kind enough to put together for me in 1981, and then to complete, after a conversation on the improper appropriations of the text that I had discovered. This took place as I was starting work on Paul Celan (cover letters from Gisèle Celan from January 14 and 23, 1981):

1. Several versions of the manuscript (together with the preparatory pages of the critical edition, sent to me at that time by Rolf Bücher and Stefan Reichert).[34]

2. Gisèle Celan's correspondence with Heidegger's son Hermann, on the topic of the sentence in the guestbook, the request dated November 8 (or 10), and the reply of December 10, 1980.

3. A list made by Paul Celan of fourteen people to whom he had given a copy of the separate edition of this poem, published in Vaduz (Brunidor) in 1968, with some responses (Kostas Axelos, Heidegger).

4. Letters from Gerhard Neumann (October 17, 1967, and January 16, 1968) and from Robert Altmann (February 5, 1968). Altmann is the editor of the non-commercial publication in Vaduz of 50 copies

---

slyly abolish the consequences in a contrary ontological structure. Something is said and not said.

33 [TN: In this section Jean Bollack interrupted his reading in order to set forth the new material that he had been able to consult before publishing his own interpretation of the poem some fifteen years after Celan's visit to Heidegger.]

34 See Celan 1997, the volume *Lichtzwang* (*Lightduress*) in the critical edition of Bonn, which contains variants of the poem.

(from Altmann, in addition, a reply to Beda Allemann, published April 17, 1977 in a journal of the Principality of Liechtenstein).[35]

5. The French translations by Jean Daive, in *Études germaniques* 25.3 (1970):243–249, and in *Terriers* (1979):9ff., by André du Bouchet, *Poèmes de Paul Celan*, 1978 (later published in *Poèmes*, 1986:28ff.); see also Marc B. de Launay, below.

6. Several studies that appeared later in French, from the Heidegerrian vantage point: Philippe Lacoue-Labarthe, *Misère de la littérature* (Paris, 1978), 67–69; a booklet: "Todtnauberg, by way of Truinas" (the name of the place where du Bouchet had a house); *Les Fleurs*, by Jean-Michel Reynard, published by Thierry Bouchard (Losne, 1982), 11–14, with the German text and du Bouchet's translation; Hans-Georg Gadamer, "Le rayonnement de Heidegger," with the poem translated by Marc B. de Launay, in the *Cahier de l'Herne* devoted to Heidegger (no. 45 [1983]:138–144).

An Aporia Pointing toward Its Solution

I did well to wait some fifteen years before publishing my own interpretation. It was not that I had failed to see immediately that I needed to interpret the elements of the background and to capture their intellectual significance, and I certainly knew how to go about it. But before the late 1980s, I had been convinced that Celan, as he more or less allowed us to believe or state, expected Heidegger to express an opinion. To better understand the situation, I needed to penetrate to the core of an analysis of the constitution and the power of language. The text that follows, revised in 1991, was presented in Gerald Stieg's seminar at the Austrian Institute in Paris, on January 8, 1992.

Celan had come to see me before his departure for Freiburg. He told me that he was going to meet Heidegger when he did a reading there. He thought that I would be disappointed or astonished, given all the conversations we had had about Heidegger during the preceding months and weeks. "He will be obliged [or: "I will oblige him"?] to speak to me." I told Celan that Heidegger would do no such thing. I was thinking of an explanation of his behavior during the Nazi period, such as others had tried to obtain from him. Celan must have shared my skepticism, but he did not reveal his stratagem to me. I had no idea of the way he had chosen to make Heidegger speak. On his return from Germany, Celan very quickly came to report that he had, in fact, seen Heidegger, and that indeed he (Celan) had "done nothing," meaning: nothing I might imagine; Celan did not

---

[35] *Liechtensteinisches Volksblatt*; also published in Lacoue-Labarthe 1999:108–110.

tell me that he had done something else. It took some time for me to understand what had happened, despite the precedents that I knew about. One should take the magic of art literally. Making the spoken word speak brings with it a terrible power. I knew that he had had no intention of going there to pay homage to Heidegger.[36]

The Circumstances of the Meeting

Gerhart Baumann describes all the elements of the strategy in his account of the visit. One has to have understood Celan's poem to recognize the game that was played, in part without the knowledge of the protagonist or the witnesses involved. One can infer nothing, neither from the poem nor from the half-unconscious account, which unveils and masks. When, in Paris in the spring of 1988, Celan gave Baumann a copy of the Vaduz edition, he had added: "Please read it soon. You'll be surprised."[37] He knew it would not be read for a while. Baumann was not ready to understand.

The narrator Baumann reduces the content to a dialogue that could have developed but that did not occur, between two geniuses whose contradictions, and particularly those of the Freiburg professor, should be respected. Such contradictions belonged to them and testified to their greatness. The event has no effect on this dialectic of the mind. When it is well thought out, philosophical nihilism embraces the history of Nazism and situates it as a necessary, inevitable event. Moreover, one can plead that it is hard to understand today what it must have been like at the time when German professors made their regrettable decisions and the Jews were dismissed from their academic chairs. We judge from a distance. "Are we right to do so, for all that?"[38] History itself, which unveils, is stripped of its reason. That is a bit much.

The account mentions all the explicit and public manifestations of the distance that Celan intended to keep. He did not want his photograph taken with Heidegger: "His reluctance was insurmountable";[39] "He found it hard to

---

[36] Renate Böschenstein-Schäfer reminded me (October 10, 1994) that she first met Celan soon after this visit. She remembered that she had expressed her surprise when she saw how merciless he was in general about people's behavior during Nazism. Celan, in response to her astonishment and even indignation, added: "I simply wanted to see how he would respond [*Ich wollte ja nur sehen, wie er so redet*]—in fact, I wrote a poem on the subject; I'll send it to you" (and he did). This was naturally not a sentence that toned down the importance of his visit: quite the opposite, appearances notwithstanding: the response was in perfect harmony with his strategy.

[37] Baumann 1986:73: "Lesen Sie bitte bald, Sie werden überrascht sein!"

[38] Baumann 1986:76: "... liegt darin immer ein Verdienst?"

[39] Baumann 1986:69: "Die Vorbehalter, die er gegenüber Heidegger erhob, blieben unüberwindlich."

meet a man whose past he could not forget."[40] And even less so because he had not been acquainted with that past beforehand. Celan also resented that he had once placed his trust in Heidegger, reading him without any background knowledge. The relation between Heidegger's work and his past had only dawned on him later. Baumann cannot understand him. A reproach, perhaps an ill-founded one, makes Baumann see in Celan "suspicion" and "rancor."[41] He chose his side. History could not have this weight.

At the same time, Celan accepted the philosopher's compliments and engaged in conversation with him on the subjects they had in common, on the landscape, on the flora and fauna of the Black Forest.[42] Indeed, he needed to express a certain freedom and trust, the appearance of conviviality, for his project to succeed. And afterwards, everything had been said. Celan felt free. He had liberated himself. But at the same time, as if to situate his decision, he immediately expressed remorse for it. He was crossing a divide and made it known. He might have had some doubts about the outcome of his action. There is a perfect logic in the contradiction of the two successive gestures of saying yes while meaning no, and then a definitive no. He expressed the fundamental duality of his task.

Should one not explore the psychology of the victims? For a while the philosopher's presence had dissipated Celan's reserve: the poet had surrendered to an obvious power, in Baumann's view; this reserve would then reassert itself, regain the upper hand. Baumann could not explain the fleeting moments of good humor other than by feeling their effect, even though he himself revealed its limits. The poet, he believed, had been thrust back in time to his old ordeals, being no longer confronted with the hardness of granite. "How many times has Celan trodden the painful path from *Death Fugue* to *Todtnauberg*," he writes in black and white, "without attaining his goal?"[43] Namely, the extermination camps in their Germanic grandeur and depth. Wandering and failure were the lot of the Jewish poet; they had nothing to do with the Germans, who had been chosen for another destiny. This is the conviction to which Celan, in fact, succumbed.

The poet expressed his desire to see the marshes close to the cottage. His companions suggested the Horbach area. On the way they could stop by the

---

[40] Baumann 1986:68 : "Es falle ihm schwer, mit einem Manne zusammenzukommen, dessen Vergangenheit er nicht vergessen könne."

[41] Baumann 1986:79: "Argwohn und Vorbehalte."

[42] Baumann 1986:71–72.

[43] Baumann 1986:79: "Den schmerzlichen Weg von der 'Todesfuge' zu 'Todtnauberg'—wie oft wohl hat ihn Celan zurückgelegt, ohne ein Ziel zu erreichen?" We have very few such explicit comments on the way Celan's work was really read in Germany. The Iron Curtain came down and cut off access to all opinions.

legendary house at Todtnauberg. We know that Celan settled on this itinerary ahead of time. He knew where he was going and where he was going to take Heidegger; nothing was unexpected. Baumann was not present during the discussion in the cottage. He rejoined the group later in the morning, for the visit to the marshes: he had come in his own car, which explains why he did not hear the second, more decisive conversation between Celan and Heidegger, in the car Neumann was driving. However, thanks to him, we have the story of the interrupted walk on the log trail.[44]

The script was programmed. Germanic mists and grey skies accompany it, as if by magic.[45] Celan had achieved his ends. He was visibly satisfied with the way things had worked out. His success was such that it dispelled his usual melancholy. Baumann was struck by Celan's serenity when he met up with the two men in the town of Sankt Blasien, in the valley of the Black Forest, halfway through the trip. The visit to Heidegger's house had already taken place.[46] He was surprised, as was Marie Luise Kaschnitz in Frankfurt, where Celan wrote the poem a few days later. She did not recognize him; he seemed so reinvigorated.[47] She also did not know why—never imagining that it was because his action had succeeded, by making the event conform to its profound truth.

The Witness

In the first of the letters he sent to Celan more than two months after the meeting, Gerhard Neumann recalls, in a rather conventional way, the conversations that took place in his presence in the car (letter of October 17, 1967). In the meantime, Celan had spoken with him on the telephone. He apparently mentioned the poem he had written, and thus indirectly the role he had made Neumann play in the infernal scenario; it was a distinction the meaning of which the young Neumann could not have understood. He responds emphatically: "I will never forget this conversation; without doubt something like it can occur only once in several decades." But he adds a more precise reference to the events of the past, even though it remains particularly vague—or perhaps confused: "I did some soul searching, in view of the fact that I was able to be present during this conversation; believe me, I try to continue this search, in my own mind." He must have been acting by way of a transference, interposing

[44] Baumann 1986:70.
[45] Baumann 1986:70, "Lichtarmes Grau und langgeschwänzte Wolkenschwaden."
[46] Baumann 1986:70, "Von Celan war alle Schwere gewichen."
[47] Baumann 1986:72. Another person found him in despair (see Lacoue-Labarthe 1999:94). Celan sometimes revealed the true darkness of the depths, sometimes focused on the poetic and political achievement, depending on the occasion or the interlocutor.

himself, as if Celan had asked him to take responsibility for the accusation himself. Later, when he receives the Vaduz book with the poem, his reaction is in some ways even more uneasy: "I was bowled over (literally), and I realize that the appeal formulated in the poem is also addressed to me [*which is not the case, not in that way*]; I have reasons to fear that I am not equal to the appeal [*which was the case*]. I beg your indulgence; please continue to think kindly of me." He seems to be asking permission to withdraw, and to escape the consequences of an affair in which he had no desire to be involved.[48]

In his memoir,[49] Baumann reports that during a meeting with Celan that took place on May 24, 1970, shortly before his death, the poet regretted that he had not received Neumann's article on the "absolute metaphor."[50] His curiosity must have been aroused. We can understand how Celan, later in the evening, flew into a towering rage when he found out about it. He learned that the metaphorical decomposition in his poetry did not succeed in capturing the real. The author was thinking about such a depraved reality that it evaded the possibility of any meaningful apprehension. The verbal explosion translated the decomposition of the world. Neumann thought this was an example, in one of its various manifestations, of the doctrine of technological degradation that figured so frequently in Heidegger's work, and he thought he could base his argument on that premise. It featured prominently in a whole section of the interpretations he put forward of Celan's work. Relations between Celan and Neumann were thus irreparably damaged. The lack of comprehension revealed a lack of solidarity. "The man" in the poem was not a man; he was not the incarnation of the non-human. Baumann, in recounting the incident, sides implicitly with his young assistant: in his study, he had put his finger on the unintelligible character of an art to which the poor poet remained attached. The decomposition that he re-translated was the expression of his absurd destiny. This is still another trend in the history of the reception accorded to Celan's work. He had tried to utter the unutterable with more or less success. His illness bears witness to a transgression. The mystery cannot be denied.

---

[48] He had been present during the whole scene, representing "man" as such (*der Mensch*). The word thus assumes a strong qualitative value, unsurpassable in a way. For Sieghild Bogumil (1988:51), it refers to the anonymous recipient, on the horizon of an open meaning. For Celan, what was at stake was a demand that, he thought, the person present and targeted could not evade.

[49] Baumann 1986:85–86.

[50] Neumann 1970.

Variants

If, in one of the variants, Celan reverted to "stone" (*Steinwürfel*) instead of "star" (*Sternwürfel*), the passage to the order of poetry should be marked more globally and clearly (for this purpose, see for example the poem "Erratic" (*Erratisch*).[51] The star is an element of the system; the star that guides the traveller, and the mark of infamy. The "stone" of the poems translates the transfer into words. With *Sten*, which he had written without the *r*, the choice remained to be made.

The process led, through the integration of the crime, to the advent of a word for the future, and was made explicit in the first version by the addition of a parenthesis:

> kommendes (un-
> gesäumt kommendes)
> Wort[52]

The *hic et nunc* of a word standing in for the weakness of another was accentuated. Again, the variant supports an interpretation that needs to have been made in order to appreciate it, and that one makes without it. One follows the path of a meaning.

The adverb *ungesäumt* ("without delay") certainly does not mean (as Baumann would have it[53]) that a statement on Heidegger's part had seemed to Celan, at a certain point, to be probable or imminent. Superimposed on "incessant" one can hear: without an edge, without a border, openly (based on *Saum*, "hem," and not on *säumen*, "to delay, hesitate"). He knew what he was going to do and obtain. What he was considering was endless and unfettered.[54]

The Sentence Inscribed in the Book
and Its Recomposition in the Poem

We can read the sentence Celan actually wrote in the guest book at Heidegger's house on July 25, 1967. He refers to it a week later, in the poem he dates from Frankfurt, on August 1:

---

51 "Der Stein, / schläfennah einst, tut sich hier auf," "Erratisch" (*GW* 1:235).
52 [TN: "A coming, / (un- / delayed coming)" (Felstiner 2001:315).]
53 Baumann 1986:75, 77, 78.
54 See Turner's translation in note 15, above. The syntax raises some problems: the heart is the site of expectation on the part of the recipient—and the variant *ungesäumt* must be understood as an involuntary confession *that will brook no delay* and will have no border. [TN: see Felstiner 2001:15: "for a thinker's / (un- / delayed coming) / word / in the heart."]

"In the book in the cottage, with a view of the well star, with the hope of a word to come in the heart. July 25, 1967, Paul Celan."[55]

The poetic writing is transferred into the sphere of economic poverty, repression, and insurrection. For him, "the cottage guest book" is just that (*Friede den Hütten* ["peace to the cottages"]).[56] The sentence is inscribed in the book; it is his first impulse (*ins*), before the invocation to the supports of art (*mit*). The gaze then moves outside towards the vertical, which rises from the shadows of the well and looms up to its other pole stemming from the night. This is already the site of the conversation that will follow, and the glow of the star under which it will be placed. The poet makes sure that this prerequisite is present, the actual object, which is there and which serves the transposition.

Memory takes care of the rest. The heart remembers. It has the strength for it. Hope rests on it; it cannot cut itself off from continuity. The word rises, it springs up at the horizon of its language, "in the hope of the heart"; it has the virtue of opening up to what is to come (*ein kommendes Wort*). If one confines oneself to this logic, it cannot be the case of awaiting a declaration, or of some kind of justification on the part of the host. Rather it anticipates the confession that will be wrung out of the host. The survival of the past, of the initial act, evokes an implicit contradiction, by the mere fact of being uttered. The confession-confirmation will serve as a lever for the production of a terrible denial. Nothing is merely described. Everything is transferred. The descriptions involve a passage to the interior of language, preventing the negation of the values that are associated with it at this site. The cottage and its well are spoken again like the book, the heart that remembers.

In the poem, the phases are apportioned, distinct: first the well, outside, then the indoor space of the cottage, which is organized around the book, to the extent of being confused with it, and with the line of writing traced in this book. The inscription written in it now gives way, with the narrative distance of the poem, to the gesture of a presentation and a doubling. The book, still his, is written from one poem to another, from one note to another; but it is enriched once more, in enemy territory, with the names and the language of the adversary, on the tracks of an incursion, always already programmed. To slip under the skin of the beast; the book will be that book, with all the names of the Nazis.

---

[55] "Ins Hüttenbuch, mit dem Blick auf den Brunnenstern, mit einer Hoffnung auf ein Kommendes Wort im Herzen. Am 25. Juli 1967 / Paul Celan." The text is reproduced from Hermann Heidegger's letter of December 10, 1980, to Gisèle Celan.

[56] See the end of the poem "In One" ("In eins"), in *The No One's Rose* (*Die Niemandsrose*, GW 1:270). The quotation from Büchner, indicated as such, makes up the entire fourth stanza.

The repetition of the sentence from the guest book—a form of auto-inter-pretive intertextuality—introduces the present tense of a recollection. It is the present of this day, "today," highlighted. This day (*heute*), the story of the encounter will be inscribed; it has been extended to the murderers in the book, in the land of death, so much so that the "philosopher" of the Black Forest has begun, against his will, to think about the memory he rejects. The more he rejects, the less he renounces, and the more his thought is led to draw from itself the power to turn against itself. The "philosopher" in the counter-language has become an other. Nihilism has changed into memory of the annihilation. The future will open up if it is the depositary of that history.

Readings

Beda Allemann methodically ruled out any political or factual references. He saw in the word "hope" an eschatological expectation, the arrival of the poet of the future that Kleist evokes in a letter to his sister Ulrike on October 5, 1803.[57] Doctrinal positivity triumphed. The publisher Robert Altmann reintroduced the political dimension, but he failed to see that the hope for an explanation still expressed a reaction that was too positive, respectful, and almost beseech-ing.[58] He believed that the sadness of the marshes revealed the doubt Celan still harbored.[59] The meeting of two great minds, between two equally "absolute" (!) languages, should continue to remain at the center of the poem, for the sake of literature. Otherwise, what meaning did the thing have, in such beautiful attire? Would the example of the bottle cast into the ocean, dear to so many readers and interpreters, not be the in-depth decoding, still to come?[60] The fact that, whenever he could, Celan personally distributed copies without trusting the book to the mail system, reserved the meaning to an open future. Each recipient would do as he liked with it.

My friend Kostas Axelos, whose thought was greatly influenced by Heidegger (he was one of the recipients of the Vaduz edition), was at the Austrian Institute in 1992 when the interpretation proposed here was presented. He admitted to me that it was extremely coherent, but he still wondered if others just as coherent might exist. The future is open. One should maintain the possibility in principle. In this case, the construction would not have the same necessity or,

---

57 Allemann 1977.
58 *Liechtensteinisches Volksblatt*; see above, n. 35.
59 Lacoue-Labarthe maintains a similar position (1999:38).
60 [TN: A reference to Celan's speech at the award ceremony for the Bremen literary prize in 1958. "A poem ... can be a message in a bottle, sent out in the—not always greatly hopeful—belief that somewhere and sometime it could wash up on land, on heartland perhaps" (Celan 2001:396).]

more precisely, it would be merely one "construction" that was stronger than another. Herein lies the problem. Reading opens up; it is in search of a meaning that can always be made more precise and profound, but not exchanged for another, unless it is an erroneous one. Otherwise, this would just be a game; it is conceivable that some play it.

Heidegger, as is clear from his own letter (dated January 30, 1968), either understood nothing, or did not want to understand anything: "My own wishes? That at the appointed time you would hear the language in which the poetry to be written would be addressed to you."[61] One can see a certain lack of sensitivity here, but also (if there is any difference) some impertinence, a retort to the sentence in the guest book. Celan had got his revenge in advance. In his lecture in Athens the same year (1967),[62] Heidegger quotes a sentence from Nietzsche: "Man is an animal which has not yet been certified."[63] He concludes that man's existence is not assured. Celan, in their conversation, made him speak the inhuman, before a representative of the human species.

Philippe Lacoue-Labarthe asserts that, for Celan, the dialogue with Heidegger, "at least in reference to the essence of poetry" (*das Wesen der Dichtung*), was decisive, and that that was why the meeting "had assumed ... such importance."[64] But when, in Celan's work, has "poetry" been, even in its shortest syllables, separated from the persecution of the Jews? His relentless pursuit of erasing the opposition, the gulf continually being retraced between the two worlds, is as infinite as the chasm.

Certain readers speak of the poet's expectation as if it were a condition of the inevitable experience of failure. They cannot deny the existence of an appeal, and one cannot find a direct expression of the homage one would like to see, without the detour of an unfulfilled wish. So they read in it a confession "that tears apart the horizon of the world."[65] One can understand the sorrow

---

[61] "Und meine Wünsche? Daß sie zur gegebenen Stunde die Sprache hören, in der sich Ihnen das zu Dichtende zusagt" (first published in an article by Stephan Krass in the *Neue Zürcher Zeitung*, Jan. 3-4, 1998).

[62] Heidegger 1983:11–22; see p. 17.

[63] "... daß der Mensch das noch nicht festgestellte Thier ist" (Nietzsche 1980, 5:81).

[64] 1999:109. It ought to be possible to agree on what is "decisive." From essence (*Wesen*) one moves on to the meadow (*Wasen*), to *Waldwasen*—to the forest dampness, which speaks of what the invocation of the spirits of the Baden forest has led to. Likewise, Andrea Zanzotto (1992) assumes that the conversation was about poetry. Perhaps, on the contrary, Celan avoided this subject—especially if his interlocutor had clammed up, "almost on the verge of autism," as Zanzotto believes (1992). Celan's text refuses to speak of his personal "torture," and even more so of "uncertainty." His determination was absolute.

[65] This sentence comes from Baumann ("Ein Bekenntnis, welche einen Welthorizon aufreisst" [1986:74]). The general appreciation of the poem on this page offers a specimen of just how vague and hollow a Germanist's dithyramb can be.

of the Jew—the word "Jew" is scarcely uttered; it is avoided, or replaced by "foreigner" or "someone from far away." The Jew cannot understand that the German philosopher was determined to remain loyal to his origin and to his fatherland,[66] to bear the weight of his past commitment all by himself, without having to account for himself to anyone,[67] and to protect the logic of his work, which could not be called into question on account of his personal conduct. In light of this mission, the Jews did not count for much. Heidegger had not acted in his own name, but on an official mission, for a higher and thus trans-historical reason.[68] The question Celan posed *could* not find an answer. Perhaps he had a vague suspicion of this himself. The question concerns neither the past nor the future; it is focused on an opening; by its very essence, it cannot be answered.[69] Heidegger's silence bears witness to an essentially higher experience embodied in German thought. It is a truth of another order. We have to admit that the celebrated encounter did not take place. Because of a fundamental divergence, which determines the status of history and memory, interpretations will remain condemned to operate in a vacuum. In this confrontation, Celan bears witness to his own weakness.

Peace of the Soul

Everything can be euphemized and toned down. Ill fortune dogs Celan, who however tones down nothing. He writes poetry; consequently, one does not expect to find in him something so unpoetic. Christoph Schwerin may well mention the disappointment felt by the poet during the visit, but to no avail.[70] He too euphemizes from beginning to end. The word "Jew" is not uttered here either.

---

[66] "Forever attached to the landscape of his country of origin" (*mit der Landschaft seines Herkommens bleibend verknüpft* [Baumann 1986:75]). One has to know what the word "landscape" (and even more so *Landschaft*) implies in the eyes of conservative historians.

[67] "Ohne darüber ein wort zu verlieren" ("Without saying a word about it" [Baumann 1986:75]).

[68] Baumann 1986:74. The *credo* is rooted there, in the mission that excuses everything. Altmann's more naïve indulgence is not far removed from it. I learned of the supplement to Baumann's book of recollections, *Erinnerungen*, published in paperback (1992) only after finishing this article in 1996, thanks to Stephen Krass's radio program in May 1997. Baumann corrects his description, but his interpretation of Celan's silence remains, in my opinion, inadequate and perhaps even inappropriate. It bears witness to a considerable distance. In this supplement, I also discovered Heidegger's postscript, his "last word" written in verse, titled "Preface" ("Vorwort")—perhaps for his own benefit, to situate his thought on a higher plane and to cover Celan's text. These lines themselves deserve critical commentary.

[69] "... eine Frage, die ins Offene weist" (Baumann 1986:74).

[70] Schwerin 1981:73–81; see p. 80.

We are bathed here in the light of reconciliation. Of the two flowers seen on arrival, one is for bodily health, the other for healing the soul. It is the "soothing" that the sick poet hoped to find; he went there seeking it. The roles are reversed. The cottage is Mecca: he wanted to "reconcile himself with his own past." He found in the water of the fountain this other "thou," whom he addresses so often. It is the terrible testimony of a necessary reading, dialogical and internalized. Remorse leads to forgiveness, forgiveness to salvation; but the attempt failed.

The poet was thought to have come with good intentions, to make peace. It was fruitless. In the car, Heidegger is relaxed, talking cheerfully. He obliterates an earlier, more serious conversation that had taken place in the cottage (*the poem, however, does not mention this*). In the second part of the journey, Celan notes some impressions of the Black Forest, making use of an antidote to overcome his disgust in the face of such nonchalance. These impressions will remain fixed and will serve as a refuge, by virtue of their consoling function. The poet's good will has been abused. He had come to make peace.

This is perhaps the right moment to point out that Heidegger, according to his son, was unaware that Celan was Jewish. This seems hardly credible, but possible nonetheless, and it provides real evidence of insensitivity, of non-recognition and a denial of identity: "According to my mother's account, it was only after [Celan's] death that my father learned that your friend was Jewish, and of the fate he had suffered in his family" (*... welches Familienschicksal er erlitten hatte*, in his letter to Gisèle Celan, cited above).

The School of Hardness

The idea of reconciliation was quite alien to Celan's mentality. At least the project preserves a moment, and in the offense he felt one can see the passage of the shadow of a failure, without elevating it, as Baumann does, to the level of an inevitable necessity. So many others have rehabilitated the man and the pilgrimage.

According to Otto Pöggeler—and to Lacoue-Labarthe, as well—Celan merely developed or explicated Heidegger's assertions. Thus Pöggeler hypothesizes, through a projection that is easy to analyze but incomprehensible in itself, that the trails made of logs—which are actually cudgels—mark the path laid out by the philosopher. Celan follows him. Heidegger taught him how to walk on these paths, to seek danger and to hold fast. In 1980, the doctrine is very much alive: to "seek out" danger, but how? "Where danger lies, therein lies the remedy" ("Wo aber Gefahr ist, wächst das Rettende auch": this Hölderlin reads like Ernst Jünger). I quote: "it is to this end, to prepare this resistance, that Heidegger's thought had chosen its path." It is true that the meeting was interrupted halfway through. Here the reason given is that the poet did not have the strength to endure the philosopher's language, which was too raw and too coarse for his sorrow. In the same way, Pöggeler hears Heidegger give a powerful lesson in existential philosophy: "During the walk, which is at the same time (etymologically) a shared experience [*one can hardly believe one's eyes*], a well-known coarseness takes shape"; the pupil hears the master.[71] "The life-giving water," after all, brings to mind the swamps, and the tonality of the word *Moor* has "a deadly and menacing" feel to it.[72] This would be the same danger to which Heidegger had taught us to expose ourselves fearlessly.

Everything must be swathed in the desired atmosphere; everything must fit back into the German order. The flowers are part of the philosopher's retreat. They exist in the meadows. If the orchids are separated, it is because botanical observation is precise (why would it not be?). If we hear shocking words in the philosopher's mouth, it is the usual coarseness of his writings—which Celan, during the conversation in the car, "must have experienced," as had many others among his readers and interlocutors. Nothing is allowed to take on a different meaning. Nothing remains to be found. We know everything "hermeneutically": the plants and the thoughts of the time and of all times.

The cube-star above the fountain "unites the opposites," Pöggeler reminds us. Depth is controlled. It does not occur to him that the figure guiding Celan in his poems might recall the star of David or the yellow star the Jews were obliged to wear; no, in this place, they did not exist; these heights had no desire for them. It was true nearby, where the Jews lived. The idea that the yellow flower evokes this reality, or that the cube might be something else, has no place here. The word *Würfel* refers, of course, to a cube where we find Mallarmé's die that is thrown and that indicates a number.

In a 1988 article titled "The Walk in the Marshes,"[73] Pöggeler returned to this presentation of things. He now wrote more clearly; it was after the explication of the text that I presented at the seminar-colloquium that he had organized at Bochum, July 2, 1985: "Heidegger had not the least idea of the thoughts that preoccupied Celan when they were sinking into the marshes." He does not say (and does not see) what those thoughts were, but he admits the existence of a ditch: "The word must at the same time [*at the same time as something else*] have referred to 1933." I had said that the clearing, which for Heidegger was the

---

[71] "Im Fahren, das zugleich ein gemeinsames Erfahren ist, wird 'Krudes' (wie es aus Heideggers Veröffentlichungen bekannt ist) deutlich" (Pöggeler 1980:224–225).

[72] "… in dunkler und tödlicher Bedrohung" (Pöggeler 1980:235).

[73] "Der Gang ins Moor. Celans Begegnung mit Heidegger" (Pöggeler 1988).

figure of the non-harboring[74] of Being, was for Celan, in the word *Waldwasen*, the site of torture containing human remains.

In this article, Pöggeler made partial and unfortunately partisan use of some elements that I had gathered in opposition to his interpretation. They could have been integrated; "nothing obstructs," according to the end of the poem "You lie."[75] Presumably, in his eyes, one acknowledges the emendations made by other scholars by referring to them and incorporating their ideas. This form of "eternity" has no scruples about accepting still another truth, better adapted.

Water was life; but it can just as well be the sign of catastrophes, provided that one encompasses them all in a great cataclysm, in the image of universal nature. Rain brings additional moisture from the sky. "The region and the peat bogs need it; but too much water reminds us of the deluge, even the sulfurous showers of Sodom and the 'yellow tide,'" so Pöggeler insisted on making clear to us in a seminar he gave in 1984.[76] Thus all is (sub)merged, life in death, and death in cosmic threats.

Works Cited

Allemann, B. 1977. "Heidegger und die Poesie." *Neue Zürcher Zeitung*, April 15.

Baumann, G. 1986. *Erinnerungen an Paul Celan*. Frankfurt. Expanded edition with epilogue, 1992.

Bogumil. S. 1988. "Totnauberg." *Celan-Jahrbuch* 2:37–51.

Bollack, J. 1958. "Styx et serments." *Revue des études grecques* 71:1–35.

———. 1966. "La pointe en hébreu." *Dédale* 3-4:533–555.

———. 1985. "Eden, encore." In *L'Acte critique: un colloque sur l'oeuvre de Peter Szondi, Paris, 21-23 juin 1979*, ed. M. Bollack, 267–290. Lille.

———. 1997. *La Grèce de personne*. Paris.

Celan, P. 1978. *Poèmes de Paul Celan*. Trans. A. du Bouchet. Paris.

———. 1989. *The Poems of Paul Celan*. Trans. M. Hamburger. New York.

———. 1997. *Lichtzwang: historische kritische Ausgabe*. Frankfurt.

———. 2000. *Gesammelte Werke*. 7 vols. Frankfurt.

———. 2001. *Selected Poems and Prose of Paul Celan*. Trans. J. Felstiner. New York.

---

[74] [TN: In the French term *non-recèlement*, the noun *recèlement* is based on the verb *receler*, meaning to receive, harbor, or conceal stolen goods.]

[75] "Du liegst" (*GW* 2:334).

[76] The expression "yellow tide" (*Gelbflut*) is taken from a poem in *Atemwende* (*Breathturn*) "Ruh aus in deinen Wunden" ("Rest in your wounds" [*GW* 2:103]). Elsewhere, (*Spur des Worts* [Pöggeler 1986:235]), Pöggeler quite rightly relates it to the yellow star that Jews wore during the Nazi regime. I should add the yellow of betrayal, which for Celan represented the non-recognition of the events that took place.

Chalfen, I. 1991. *Paul Celan, a Biography of his Youth.* Trans. M. Bleyleben, intro. J. Felstiner. New York. Orig. pub. 1983.

Gadamer, H.-G. 1983. "Le Rayonnement de Heidegger." In *Martin Heidegger,* ed. M. Haar, 138–144. Paris.

Goethe, J. W. von. 1982. *Goethes Werke.* Ed. E. Trunz. Munich.

———. 1994. *Elective Affinities.* Trans. D. Constantine. Oxford. Orig. pub. 1809.

Grimm, J., and W. Grimm. 1922. *Dictionary of the German Language.* Leipzig.

Heidegger, M. 1983. "Die Herkunft der Kunst und die Bestimmung des Denkens." In *Distanz und Nähe. Reflexionen und Analysen zur Kunst der Gegenwart,* ed. P. Jaeger and R. Lüthe, 11–22. Würzburg.

Lacoue-Labarthe, P. 1999. *Poetry as Experience.* Trans. A. Tarnowski. Stanford. Orig. pub. 1986.

Martin, B., ed. 1989. *Martin Heidegger und das 'Dritte Reich': ein Kompendium.* Darmstadt.

Neumann, G. 1970. "Die 'absolute' Metapher. Ein Abgrenzungsversuch am Beispiel Stephane Mallarmés und Paul Celans." *Poetica* 3:188–225.

Nietzsche, F. 1980. *Jenseits von Gut und Böse.* In *Sämtliche Werke: kritische Studienausgaben.* Ed. G. Colli and M. Montinari. 15 vols. Munich.

Pöggeler, O. 1980. "Kontroverses zur Ästhetik Paul Celans (1920-1970)." *Zeitschrift für Ästhetik und Allgemeine Kunstwissenschaft* 25.2 (1980):202–243.

———. 1986. *Spur des Worts. Zur Lyrik Paul Celans.* Freiburg.

———. 1988. "Der Gang ins Moor. Celans Begegnung mit Heidegger." *Literatur und Kunst,* supplement, *Neue Zürcher Zeitung,* December 2.

Schwerin, C. 1981. "Bittere Brunnen des Herzens. Erinnerungen an Paul Celan." *Der Monat* 279 (April-June) :73–81.

Zanzotto, A. 1992. "Écrire dans la langue de l'ennemi." *Le Monde des livres,* July 13.

Index

CPSIA information can be obtained
at www.ICGtesting.com
Printed in the USA
FFOW01n0946210418
46322491-47898FF